Management
of Organizational
Behavior

PRENTICE HALL BUSINESS PUBLISHING
MANAGEMENT TITLES FOR 2001

Bowin/Harvey: Human Resource Management: An Experiential Approach 2/e
Caproni: The Practical Coach: Management Skills for Everyday Life 1/e
Carrell/Heavrin: Labor Relations and Collective Bargaining 6/e
Coulter: Strategic Management in Action 2/e
Coutler: Entrepreneurship in Action 1/e
Daniels/Radebaugh: International Business 9/e
David: Strategic Management: Concepts and Cases 8/e
David: Concepts in Strategic Management 8/e
David: Cases in Strategic Management 8/e
Dessler: Management: Leading People and Organizations in the 21st Century 2/e
DiBella: Learning Practices: Assessment and Action for Organizational Improvement (OD Series)
Ghemawat: Strategy and the Business Landscape: Core Concepts 1/e
Gomez-Mejia/Balkin/Cardy: Managing Human Resources 3/e
Greer: Strategic Human Resource Management 2/e
Harvey/Brown: Experiential Approach to Organization Development 6/e
Hersey/Blanchard/Johnson: Management of Organizational Behavior: Leading Human Resources 8/e
Howell/Costley: Understanding Behaviors for Effective Leadership 1/e
Hunger/Wheelen: Essentials of Strategic Management 2/e
Hunsaker: Training in Managerial Skills 1/e
Jones: Organizational Theory 3/e
Mische: Strategic Renewal: Becoming a High-Performance Organization 1/e
Martocchio: Strategic Compensation 2/e
Narayanan: Managing Technology and Innovation for Competitive Advantage 1/e
Osland/Kolb/Rubin: The Organizational Behavior Reader 7/e
Osland/Kolb/Rubin: Organizational Behavior: An Experiential Approach 7/e
Robbins: Organizational Behavior 9/e
Robbins/DeCenzo: Fundamentals of Management 3/e
Sanyal: International Management 1/e
Sloane/Witney: Labor Relations 10/e
Thompson: The Mind and Heart of the Negotiator 2/e
Tompkins: Cases in Management and Organizational Behavior Vol. I 1/e
Wexley/Latham: Developing and Training Human Resources in Organizations 3/e

Other Books of Interest

Dessler: Human Resources Management 8/e
Dessler: Essentials of Human Resource Management 1/e
Mondy/Noe/Premeux: Human Resource Management 7/e
Henderson: Compensation Management in a Knowledge-Based World 8/e
Blanchard/Thacker: Effective Training: Systems, Strategies and Practices 1/e
Feldacker: Labor Guide to Labor Law 4/e
Sovereign: Personnel Law 4/e

Management of Organizational Behavior

Leading Human Resources
EIGHTH EDITION

Paul Hersey

Center for Leadership Studies
Escondido, California

Kenneth H. Blanchard

The Ken Blanchard Companies, Inc.
Escondido, California

Dewey E. Johnson

Sid Craig School of Business
California State University, Fresno
Fresno, California

Prentice
Hall

Upper Saddle River, NJ 07458

Library of Congress Cataloging-in-Publication Data

Hersey, Paul.
　　Management of organizational behavior : leading human resources / Paul Hersey,
　Kenneth H. Blanchard, Dewey E. Johnson.— 8th ed
　　　　p.　cm.
　　Includes bibliographical references and index.
　　ISBN 0-13-017598-6
　　1. Organizational behavior.　2. Management.　3. Leadership.　I. Blanchard, Kenneth H.
　II. Johnson, Dewey E.　III. Title.
　　HD58.7.H47 2000
　　658.3—dc21
　　　　　　　　　　　　　　　　　　　　　　　　　　　　　　　　　　　　　　　00-032701

VP/Editorial Director: James C. Boyd
Executive Editor: David Shafer
Editorial Assistant: Kimberly Marsden
Assistant Editor: Michele Foresta
Executive Marketing Manager: Michael Campbell
Permissions Coordinator: Suzanne Grappi
Media Project Manager: Michele Faranda
Director of Production: Michael Weinstein
Manager, Production: Gail Steier de Acevedo
Production Coordinator: Kelly Warsak
Manufacturing Buyer: Natacha St. Hill Moore
Associate Director, Manufacturing: Vincent Scelta
Cover Designer: Karen Salzbach
Full Service Composition: BookMasters, Inc.

To

RALPH E. HERSEY, SR., a retired telephone pioneer with over 50 patents for Bell Laboratories, whose work made direct dialing a reality. In looking back over his 39 years of work with the telephone industry, he once commented that of all his contributions, the most rewarding aspect to him personally was that he became known as a *developer of people.*

and

the REAR ADMIRAL THEODORE BLANCHARD, USNR, former naval officer who was decorated with two Silver Stars, the Bronze Star, the Presidential Citation, and a Navy Unit Commendation for his courageous and competent World War II leadership in the Pacific. People who worked for him over the years always described him as an inspirational, dedicated, and caring leader who always fought for his people and the "underdog," whether in peace or war.

and

DEWEY EMANUAEL JOHNSON, entrepreneur, small business owner, farmer, and community leader. He was known for his selfless dedication to others. He could always be counted on to give personal leadership and financial support to business and civic organizations.

BRIEF CONTENTS

CONTENTS

Contents

Contents

Contents

Contents

Contents

PREFACE

More than 30 years ago, we introduced our first edition with the following statements, which we still believe:

> For a long time, management theory has been characterized by a search for universals—a preoccupation with discovering essential elements of all organizations. The discovering of common elements is necessary, but they do not really provide practitioners with "principles" that can be applied with universal success.
>
> In the past decade, there has appeared a relative maturity in this field as it begins to focus on "patterned variations"—situational differences. We assume that there are common elements in all organizations, but we also assume differences among them and in particular the managing of their human resources. As the inventory of empirical studies expands, making comparisons and contrasts possible, management theory will continue to emerge. Common elements will be isolated and important variables brought to light.
>
> We believe that management theory is important to all categories of organizations—business, government, military, medicine, education, "voluntary" organizations such as the church, and even the home. We thus have drawn our illustrations and cases from a variety of these organizations and incorporated concepts from many disciplines. Our purpose is to identify a framework which may be helpful in integrating independent approaches from these various disciplines to the understanding of human behavior and management theory. The focus of this book is on behavior within organizations and not between organizations. Our belief is that an organization is a unique living organism whose basic component is the individual, and this individual is our fundamental unit of study. Thus, our concentration is on the interaction of people, motivation, and leadership.
>
> Though this book is an outgrowth of the insights of many earlier writers, we hope it will make some contribution to management theory.

The response to our first seven editions has been very gratifying and encouraging. Individuals and organizations, not only in the United States but throughout the world as well, have made use of the behavioral science concepts, tools, and techniques to improve performance. Our goal of writing a readable book that would make the behavioral sciences come alive for operating managers, parents, teachers, and students alike appears to have been accomplished through this broad-based acceptance.

In writing this eighth edition, as in the previous editions, we have assumed the serious responsibility of preparing you for the real world through a quality research-based approach to the behavioral sciences. You will note a change in the subtitle to "Leading Human Resources" to reflect that this is a leadership book. This change was made to emphasize our purpose to equip you for the real world, not the fantasy world—a real world where each of us has to understand the challenges of leading human organizations in a highly competitive environment. This is why our primary emphasis is on practical applied behavioral science concepts, tools, and techniques.

What's New in the Eighth Edition?

All of the continuing developments in our thinking and the varied research and consulting activities of our respective organizations are reflected in this edition. In addition to a thorough updating and revision of each chapter, you will find a number of major changes to the following chapters:

Chapter 1, "Management: An Applied Behavioral Science Approach," has been extensively revised to reflect the dramatic trends affecting leading and managing in the twenty-first century.

Chapter 7, "Diagnosing the Environment," includes a new section on leading the generations, a discussion of the changing needs and roles of Generation Y to Generation G.

Chapter 8, "Situational Leadership," incorporates a revised and expanded Situational Leadership model.

Chapter 13, "Effective Communication," has been updated with the assistance of communications professor Tom Weise and now includes the transactional model of communication.

Chapter 14, "Leading Effective Teams," now places more emphasis on the increasing importance of teams in modern organizations.

Chapter 15, "Implementing Situational Leadership, Managing People to Perform," includes a new section on the 360-Degree Performance Evaluation.

Chapter 17, "Planning and Implementing Change," has been shortened, focused, and now includes the familiar Beckhard and Harris change model.

Chapter 18, "Leadership to Achieve Quality," includes the latest developments in the Baldrige Award criteria.

Chapter 19, "Leadership Strategies for Organizational Transformation," has been extensively revised by its author, international consultant, Gustav Pansegrouw.

Chapter 20, "The Organizational Cone," contains the latest thinking of its author, international consultant, Bo Gyllenpalm.

We trust that this eighth edition will make an important contribution to your personal and professional leadership growth and development.

Acknowledgments

We owe much to colleagues and associates, without whose guidance, encouragement, and inspiration the first edition of this book—much less the eighth—would never have been written. In particular, we are indebted to Harry Evarts, Ted Hellebrandt, Norman Martin, Don McCarty, Bob Melendes, Walter Pauk, Warren Ramshaw, and Franklin Williams.

We wish to make special mention of Chris Argyris, William J. Reddin, and Edgar A. Schein. Their contributions to the field of applied behavioral science have been most valuable to us in the course of preparing this book, and we hereby express our appreciation to them.

We also want to express our gratitude and appreciation for the tremendous contributions of Ron Campbell, President, Center for Leadership Studies, to the preparation of this book and for his thoughtful review of the manuscript.

Our thanks and appreciation also go to the following colleagues:

- Tom Weise, Professor of Communication, College of the Sequoias, Visalia, California, for major contributions to Chapter 13, "Effective Communications."

- Gustav Pansegrouw, President, Center for Leadership and Organization Studies, Johannesburg, South Africa, for writing and revising Chapter 19, "Leadership Strategies for Organizational Transformation."

- Bo Gyllenpalm, Founder and President, Situational Management Services, AB, Stockholm, Sweden, for writing and revising Chapter 20, "The Organizational Cone."

The comments and suggestions provided by students, managers, teachers, researchers, consultants, and reviewers have been particularly important to us as we have prepared this revision. Special assistance has been provided by Elizabeth Cordero, Shjorayne Slaughter, Doug Grannis, Richard I. Lester, Sam Sit, and Lai-Yung Lai.

Reviewers for Prentice Hall—Barbara Daley, University of Wisconsin-Milwaukee; Charles Galloway, University of North Florida; Roger Ditzenberg, University of North Texas; and Richard I. Lester, Air University (AETC)—provided insightful suggestions and comments.

Our appreciation once again goes to David Shafer of Prentice Hall for his dedication to the development, design, and production of this eighth edition.

Finally, special thanks are due to Suzanne, Margie, and Joan, our wives, for their continued patience, support, and interest in the progress of our work.

Paul Hersey
Kenneth H. Blanchard
Dewey E. Johnson

ABOUT THE AUTHORS

Paul Hersey

PAUL HERSEY, ED.D., is chairman of the board and Professor of Organizational Behavior and Management, California American University, Graduate School of Applied Behavioral Sciences. Paul is also founder and chairman of the board of the Center for Leadership Studies, Inc.

Paul has helped develop well over 10,000,000 managers and salespeople from more than 1,000 businesses and other organizations. He has made presentations in over 125 countries and is an internationally known behavioral scientist and highly successful entrepreneur. He has been recognized by the Academy of Management and *Training and Development* magazine as one of the world's outstanding authorities on training and development in leadership, management, and selling.

Paul has authored or coauthored more than 50 books, monographs, and articles, including three Prentice Hall books: *Management of Organizational Behavior: Utilizing Human Resources* (with Ken Blanchard), *Organizational Change Through Effective Leadership* (with Ken Blanchard and Robert Guest), and *Selling: A Behavioral Science Approach*. He has also coauthored *The Family Game: A Situational Approach to Effective Parenting* (with Ken Blanchard). His recent books include *The Situational Leader, Situational Selling: An Approach to Increasing Sales Effectiveness,* and *Situational Parenting* (with Ron Campbell).

Kenneth H. Blanchard

KENNETH H. BLANCHARD, PH.D., is the chief spiritual officer of The Ken Blanchard Companies, a full-service global management training and consulting company that he and his wife, Dr. Marjorie Blanchard, founded in 1979 in San Diego, California. Ken is also a visiting lecturer at his alma mater, Cornell University, where he is a trustee emeritus on the board of trustees. He teaches a master of science in the Executive Leadership Degree Program, jointly sponsored by the University of San Diego and The Ken Blanchard Companies. Ken is also cofounder of The Center for FaithWalk Leadership. The Center advocates and promotes Jesus Christ and His teachings as a model for leadership.

Ken's best-selling book *The One Minute Manager*®, coauthored with Spencer Johnson, has sold more than 10 million copies worldwide, is still on best-seller lists, and has been translated into more than 25 languages. Among his many other books are *The Power of Ethical Management* with Norman Vincent Peale and *Managing by Values*, coauthored with Michael O'Connor. *Raving Fans*® and *Gung Ho!*™, coauthored with Sheldon Bowles, continue to be on best-seller charts. Ken's latest book, *Big Bucks! Leadership by the Book*, coauthored with Bill Hybels and Phil Hodges, contains the teachings upon which The Center for FaithWalk Leadership was founded.

Dewey E. Johnson

DEWEY E. JOHNSON, PH.D., is Professor of Management at the Sid Craig School of Business, California State University, Fresno.

Elected to more than a dozen offices in national and regional professional associations, Dewey is a cofounder and former chair of the Management Education and Development Division, Academy of Management; past National President and Fellow, Small Business Institute Director's Association; and recipient of the 1995 Provost's Outstanding Professor Award for Service from his university.

Prior to entering the academic community, Dewey served with the U.S. Air Force as a pilot, commander, and staff officer, retiring with the rank of colonel. He was awarded the Legion of Merit with one oak leaf cluster and many other decorations.

Dewey has published many articles and has been a presenter at more than 170 domestic and international conferences in the areas of leadership, small business, and performance management. He has specialized in consulting for small businesses and is currently Professor of Management and Director, Small Business Institute, at his university. Dewey teaches at the undergraduate and graduate levels and is a professor in California State University, Fresno's Joint Doctorate Program in Educational Leadership with the University of California.

Management
of Organizational
Behavior

Management: An Applied Behavioral Sciences Approach

Every country's legacy has many examples of courageous men and women who have made what they believed in happen under extremely challenging conditions. These men and women saw the need for action, believed in what they were doing, inspired others and, in spite of incredible odds, changed the world. This is the essence of leadership. These men and women sought leadership roles and accepted the responsibilities that were part of those roles. Doing so is a leader's duty: to take what you believe in, something that flows out of your core values, and make it happen. ✧

Effective performance rarely happens by accident. Effective performance is the result of predictable, planned actions that can be learned and applied by almost anyone in any organization anywhere. This is the good news. The even better news is that many forward-looking managers throughout the world are now using these planned actions. They are effectively using new management methods and techniques—and you can, too. Our purpose in writing this book is to provide you with an essential framework that will help you to excel in this age of leadership and management.

The leadership and management of organizations have never been more challenging, and this is a tremendously exciting period for understanding and practicing both. Now, as perhaps never before, there is a growing awareness that the success of our organizations depends directly on effectively leading human resources. The applied behavioral sciences provide a basis for such effective use. As we consider the challenging problems in the management of organizations—business, government, not-for-profit, school, military, or family—we realize that the real test of our abilities as

1

leaders and managers is how effectively we can establish and maintain human organizations for the purpose of achieving results.

What are effective managers doing that sets them apart? What is it that makes some managers succeed and others fail? It is a way of looking at where they want to go and how they are going to get there. It means having an idea, a framework, a mental plan, and the skills to execute their ideas. Managers must know where they are going if they are to achieve their purposes. What then is management's essential purpose?

THE PURPOSE OF MANAGEMENT

The fundamental purpose of management is to create value as perceived by the follower(s). We endorse the view of Peter Drucker, the principal contributor to contemporary management, that for managers to be successful, they must achieve the results valued by the people who have a stake in their organization's accomplishments. Managers must meet the needs and aspirations of followers. Therefore, when we define management as the influencing of people and other scarce resources, this means influencing toward meaningful purposes, toward results.

Professor Dave Ulrich, University of Michigan, and consultants, Jack Zenger and Norman Smallwood, confirm that results matter in their *Results-Based Leadership.* "Leaders who are not getting results aren't truly leading. Or, more specifically, leaders who aren't getting *desired* results aren't truly leading. . . . Leaders must learn to understand and focus on desired results."[1]

Successful organizations are deeply aware of their sense of purpose. Just as a search for meaning is a principal human motivation, it is also a principal characteristic of dynamic, growing organizations. These organizations have declared their responsibilities toward customers, society, environment, owners, and employees: all of the key stakeholders that affect their performance.

Capabilities of Effective Organizations

What are the performance capabilities of effective organizations? Effective organizations focus on quality and customer satisfaction; respond quickly to environmental changes; innovate; develop and implement appropriate strategies; have a global mindset; are willing to "network" with strategic partners; cope with changes in management; and are committed to continuous learning.[2] That is a long list of demanding challenges, but managers must meet these challenges.

MANAGING IN A RAPIDLY CHANGING WORLD

We are in the midst of political, economic, social, and technological revolutions that are sweeping our globe. Domestic and international events swirl

Chapter 1   Management: An Applied Behavioral Sciences Approach

around us as ne[...] [...]ything we
have seen before [...]

Inspired lea[...] [...]es that are
sweeping the w[...] [...]courage to
turn their aspira[...] [...]verywhere
in our global so[...] [...]s are making a positive co[...] [...]at the vast
majority of these [...]

What Is Caus[...]

Megawaves of c[...] [...]way managers and their o[...] [...]sper in the
twenty-first cent[...] [...]ape as they
crash ashore, so[...] [...]mic megawaves are destro[...] [...]Organiza-
tions that have r[...] [...]are disappearing through mergers,
acquisitions, or bankruptcy. Those that have changed their management methods are benefiting with increased profits, delighted employees and customers,
and operating efficiencies from the energy contributed by these megawaves.

What Are Some of These Megawaves of Change?

The Pace of Change Is Continuing to Accelerate

Rosabeth Moss Kanter, a professor at Harvard Business School, foresaw this
new world: "The major challenge management faces today is living in a
world of turbulence and uncertainty where new competitors arrive on the
scene daily and competitive conditions change. We can no longer count on a
stable world that is unchanging and unvarying and manage accordingly."[3]

Power Is Shifting from Sellers to Buyers

Michael Hammer, coauthor with James Champy of the influential book,
Reengineering the Corporation, describes this shift:

> ... powerful modern customers—whether consumers or corpora-
> tions—want one thing: *more*. They want more products for less money,
> more quality and service, more flexibility and convenience, and more
> innovation. The guilty party in the morality play that is modern busi-
> ness is not the rapacious capitalist or the manipulative manager; it
> is you and I, every consumer who looks carefully at price and quality,
> who shops around, who abandons yesterday's product for today's bet-
> ter one. It is the powerful customer who has forced radical changes on
> the reluctant managers of organizations in every industry.[4]

Technology Is Making Your Competition One Click Away

Not only is power shifting from sellers to buyers, but Internet technology is giving buyers the ability to search for the best quality, service, terms, flexibility,
and innovation. It is giving them the convenience of searching with just one
click. If you are not pleased with one firm's products or services, another's Web
site is just a click away.

Technology is also giving organizations the systems and tools to be relentless cost cutters. Traditional layers of management are being stripped away because the Internet is reducing the need for brokers and distributors. People now have the tools to gain immediate access to anyone, anywhere in the world. The geographic distance between leader and follower is increasing. The pace of change is frenetic. The need for employees to be self-directed is increasing. The rate of knowledge obsolescence is accelerating. The ability to cope with all of this is in jeopardy. Andrew S. Grove, cofounder of Intel, has captured the urgency of these changes.

> You have no choice but to operate in a world shaped by globalization and the information revolution. There are two options: Adapt or die. The new environment dictates two rules: First, everything happens faster; second, anything that can be done will be done, if not by you, then by someone else, somewhere. Let there be no misunderstanding. These changes lead to a less kind, less gentle, and less predictable workplace.[5]

Unlimited Substitution Is Posing New Leadership and Management Challenges

David M. Noer, Center for Creative Leadership, anticipates a world in constant transformation. "Tomorrow's leaders will be the freelancers, contractors and analysts for hire. Mobility and flexibility will be the watchwords for 2000 and beyond."[6] The traditional workplace where most people spent their careers working from 9 to 5 is vanishing. Fewer than one-third of current employees follow this schedule. Think of a comparison with a typical college football team composed of specialists who, with unlimited substitution, shuttle in and out of the game, performing specialized tasks. Everyone has a specialized role. For example, there are short-yardage fullbacks, place kickers and punters, goal line defenders, and quarterbacks who perform best in running or passing situations. There are very few "two-way" team members playing both ways—defense and offense.

Similarly, today's typical employee may work part-time or change jobs frequently, although not always by choice. Downsizing, mergers, accompanying a spouse to a new location, and/or telecommuting can affect the employee.

What happens when football players shuttle in and out of the game? Players miss assignments, which result in penalties or broken plays. They do not know the playbook. The same is true of employees who move to different assignments in different organizational units, new employees, employees who have been telecommuting, or have been/are on distant projects. Unlimited substitution places severe stress on a manager or coach's ability to get everyone on the same page.

The Domain of Leadership and Management Has Become Worldwide

Market economies are developing everywhere. There is no local niche where an organization can hide, content and secure. Change stimulated by aggressive, capable competitors is occurring daily on an international playing field. Michael Porter, also of Harvard University and author of three widely quoted books on strategic management, expressed this idea of change in an international dimension:

> Real . . . leaders believe in change. They possess an insight into how to alter competition, and do not accept constraints in carrying it out. Leaders energize their organizations to meet competitive challenges, to serve demanding needs, and above all, to keep progressing. . . . Leaders also think in international terms, not only in measuring their true competitive advantage, but in setting strategy to enhance and extend it.[7]

Rosebeth Moss Kanter has combined the power of buyers and globalization into the powerful concept of "limitless shopping."

> "Shopping" is what globalization is all about. It is not about whether any one company does business internationally; it is about a fundamental shift as customers, particularly organizational customers, want to go shopping—to exercise choices, to have the best of the world's goods and services available wherever they are in the world.[8]

The Knowledge Age Is Here

In the past, control of information was a primary source of a manager's power. It is no longer. The information sharing vital to organizational success made possible by modern information technology has eroded the manager's power. Therefore, managers must develop new ways of influencing their organizations. The major impact of increased technology, discussed earlier, is that it makes previous knowledge, skill, and experience much less relevant. As the poet James Russell Lowell stated, "Time makes ancient good uncouth." The pace of change makes existing knowledge, skill, and experience obsolete . . . much less relevant. This is a very significant concept and signals a fundamental change in how leaders are developed. Until recently, what you knew, what you could do, and how you could do it were extremely important in a relatively static, unchanging world. When your environment is not changing, your knowledge, skill, and experience is easily transferred to new situations. However, when situations require new knowledge and skill, experience is not as relevant as before.

The ability to *acquire* knowledge, skill, and experience is becoming much more critical. This does not mean that ability as an essential factor is irrelevant, but that it is taking on a new dimension: the ability to acquire *facilitating* knowledge, skill, and experience. It is the ability to learn, not existing ability, that will become increasingly important. This is why the emphasis in *Management of Organizational Behavior* is on your personal leadership development.

Technology as it affects the dissemination of information is also affecting self-assurance. As technology provides the tools and globalization the requirement, individuals must become more self-sufficient. Self-sufficiency requires high levels of confidence, commitment, and motivation, because the person's leader is becoming less physically able to provide proximate leadership. Distance leadership is becoming the norm. Telecommuting, e-commerce applications, the Internet, and worldwide operations are increasing.

A New World Order Is Emerging

Over the past few years, tremendous economic, social, and political changes have occurred that have shifted the international competitive arena from human warfare to human welfare, from munitions to market economies. For example, EU (European Union), GATT (General Agreement on Tariffs and Trade), and NAFTA (North American Free Trade Agreement) are just a few of the trade arrangements that are becoming more powerful than military alliances.

THE IMPACT OF THESE TRENDS

The most effective leaders will be people who use their energies to accomplish desired results. Leadership will focus on action and implementation. Leadership, change, implementation, and results: These are the operative words for the new world order. They will become, as never before, core influences on an organization's environment, thus profoundly affecting the leadership of effective organizations. It is clear that exploding technology in such areas as communication will accelerate the pace of life as well as give individuals the freedom to be self-directed leaders. It is also clear that effects of globalization will intensify personal and organizational demands by subjecting everyone to the rigors of global competition.

This means that effective leaders must be able to diagnose, adapt, and communicate—all major themes of this book—to meet the needs of a rapidly changing and challenging world, a world in which inflexibility will not work. Leaders, even more than before, must become aware of each situation and be able to use the leadership style appropriate to that situation. Our approach, Situational Leadership®, has helped people worldwide for more than 3 decades to use the behavioral sciences to lead effectively.

ORGANIZATIONS AS SOURCES OF COMPETITIVE ADVANTAGE

The sources of a competitive advantage have changed through social and technological development at various international levels. According to Ed Lawler of the University of Southern California, the sources have progressed from control of natural resources, through economic and financial expertise, to improved marketing ability, to control of technology, and to the improved use of human resources.[9] It is the organizations—that is, their ability to marshal their skills in employing all of their resources—that are going to give them a competitive advantage. Vincent Omachonu and Joel Ross, authorities on quality management, support Lawler's conclusion.

> Historically, productivity improvement has focused on technology and capital equipment to reduce the input of labor cost. Improved

output was generally thought to be subject to obtaining more production by applying industrial engineering techniques such as methods analysis, work flow, etc. Both of these approaches are still
appropriate, *but the current trend is toward better use of the potential
available through human resources [emphasis added].*[10]

THE CHALLENGES OF LEADING AN ORGANIZATION

This book is about special skills that we need to meet those challenges. It presents fundamental behavioral science concepts and theories and simple-to-
use behavioral science techniques.

Some concepts in the behavioral sciences give you some good ideas to think
about, but they do not always tell you how or when to put those ideas into practice in the management of human organizations. We have all seen people who
just show up in leadership and management situations. But success requires
much more than just showing up. We believe that it requires the knowledge and
application of tested behavioral science concepts, plus the "timing" skills to get
things done. This book will help you not only to acquire the knowledge but also
to develop the skills necessary to be a high-performing leader.

Leading, influencing the behavior of others, is not a single event. Leadership and management are full-time responsibilities that must be practiced
every hour of every day. Each minute must be spent wisely. Of course, doing
so is not easy. Leadership and management, because they involve the complexities of people, almost defy description and understanding. We have all
known courageous men and women who have provided the vision and energy to make things happen in very difficult situations. But even after
decades of research, we are still unable to identify with certainty the specific
causal factors that determine leadership and management success at a specific time and place. This is because real-life situations are never static. They
are constantly changing, with many factors or variables interacting at the
same time. Consequently, the behavioral sciences, unlike the physical sciences, deal in probabilities. Our purpose then is to help increase the odds in
your favor, not to suggest rules. In the behavioral sciences, there are no rules.

What has long been needed is an approach to leadership and management that is both conceptually sound and practical in application. We have
found—through our research and writing, our conversations with thousands
of managers throughout the world, our consulting and seminars—that most
people want an easy-to-grasp approach that is broad enough in scope to permit its application to different organizations and situations. Such an approach
would promote a common understanding and language that would make it
possible for managers to work together and act upon the problems they experience in managing their human resources. In developing these ideas
and skills, we wanted to build upon the considerable legacy of the behavioral

sciences by using a common language so managers could easily master the key ideas and skills. Situational Leadership provides such a common language to help solve performance problems. It provides a valuable language that can be used on the job, in the home, and in every leadership situation. It provides a common language we can use to diagnose leadership problems, to adapt behavior to solve those problems, and to communicate solutions.

It is human nature to react to problems in an emotional way. Situational Leadership provides a model for talking about performance problems in a rational way that focuses on the key issues involved. We also wanted to present an approach that is intuitively valid and that is based on empirical evidence. The acceptance that Situational Leadership has received for more than 30 years has indicated to us that this approach is easily understood, accepted, and implemented at all levels of organizations. It is a fundamental approach to the management of organizational behavior.

In summary, despite changes in concepts of organization, successful leadership is fundamentally determined by leader-follower interaction in the pursuit of goal accomplishment, readiness assessment, leadership intervention, appraisal of the results of this intervention, and effective follow-up . . . all essential elements of Situational Leadership.

A LOOK BACK

The transformation of American society has been breathtaking. We have progressed from a basically agrarian society to a dynamic industrial society, with a higher level of education and standard of living than was ever thought possible. In addition, our scientific and technical advancement staggers the imagination.[11]

This progress has not been without its seamy side. At a time when we should be rejoicing in a golden age of plenty, we find ourselves embroiled in conflict—conflict between nations, conflict between races, conflict between management and workers, even conflict between neighbors. These problems that we face cannot be solved by scientific and technical skills alone; they will require social skills. Many of our most critical problems are not in the world of things, but in the world of people. Our greatest failure as human beings has been the inability to secure cooperation and understanding with others. Shortly after World War II, Elton Mayo recognized this problem when he reflected that "the consequences for society of the unbalance between the development of technical and of social skills have been disastrous."[12]

MANAGEMENT DEFINED

Any review of the literature will quickly show that there are almost as many definitions of management as there are writers in the field. A common thread that appears in these definitions is that the manager is required to accomplish organizational goals or objectives. We shall define *management* as the process of working with and through individuals and groups and other resources (such as equipment, capital, and technology) to accomplish organizational goals.

This definition, it should be noted, does not specify business or industrial organizations. Management, as defined, applies to organizations whether they are businesses, educational institutions, hospitals, political or military organizations, or even families. To be successful, these organizations require their management personnel to have interpersonal skills. The achievement of organizational objectives through leadership is management. Thus, everyone is a manager in at least certain activities.

LEADERSHIP DEFINED

In essence, leadership is a broader concept than management. Management is a special kind of leadership in which the achievement of organizational goals is paramount. The important distinction between the two, therefore, lies in the term *organizational goals*. Our definition of leadership is that leadership occurs whenever one person attempts to influence the behavior of an individual or group, regardless of the reason. It may be for one's own goals or for the goals of others, and these goals may or may not be congruent with organizational goals.

Distinctions Between Management and Leadership

Warren Bennis, a highly regarded leadership scholar, differentiated the extremes of management and leadership in a number of provocative ways:

> Leaders conquer the context—the volatile, turbulent, ambiguous surroundings that sometimes seem to conspire against us and will surely suffocate us if we let them—while managers surrender to it. The manager administrates; the leader innovates. The manager is a copy; the leader is an original. The manager maintains; the leader develops. The manager focuses on systems and structure; the leader focuses on people. The manager relies on control; the leader inspires trust. The manager has a short-range view; the leader has a long-range perspective. The manager asks how and when; the leader asks what and why. The manager has an eye on the bottom line; the leader has his eye on the horizon. The manager imitates; the leader originates. The manager accepts the status quo; the leader challenges it. . . . Managers do things right; leaders do the right things.[13]

Are Management and Leadership Really Necessary?

Perhaps the concerns felt by people are such that leadership and management cannot effect change or solve problems. Let's look at one study, in which 500 respondents in a variety of organizations were asked to rank their concerns. The results are listed in Table 1-1.

Every concern is the result of ineffective leadership and management, and can be corrected by enlightened leadership and management. This brings us to a central theme of this book. The effective management of human organizations comes down to the one-on-one or one-on-a-group influence process. Performance starts with this essential building block.

RHI Management Resources, a division of Robert Half International, Inc., initiated a national survey of executives with the United States' 1,000 largest companies. The executives were asked, "Which of the following management skills do you believe to be the most valuable?" The results are shown in Table 1-2.

> Cecil Gregg, executive director of RHI Management Resources, observed, "Today's growth economy has businesses moving rapidly to keep up with expansion efforts . . . amid this environment, leadership skills are critical.[14]

Peter Drucker, one of the most influential and respected observers of management, confirms our view:

> The center of a modern society is the managed institution. The managed institution is society's way of getting things done these days. In addition, management is the specific tool, the specific function, and the specific instrument to make institutions capable of producing results.
>
> The institution, in short, does not simply exist within and react to society. It exists to produce results on and in society.[15]

Table 1-1 Top Ten Leadership and Management Concerns

CONCERN	RANK
Ineffective communication	9.0
Crisis management for most situations	8.0
Lack of feedback on performance	7.0
No or inappropriate goal setting	6.2
Not enough training	5.7
Lack of opportunity for advancement	5.6
Rewards not related to performance	4.9
Unreasonable workloads	3.9
Boss will not let me do my job	3.2
Lack of challenging work	1.8

Source: Contributed by Richard I. Lester, Ph.D., Educational Adviser, Ira C. Eaker College for Professional Development, Maxwell AFB, AL, January 1995.
Note: 10 = most important; 1 = least important.

Chapter 1   Management: An Applied Behavioral Sciences Approach

Table 1-2 Valuable Management Skills

Leadership abilities	47%
Communication/interpersonal skills	35%
Team-oriented approach	9%
Organizational/time management	5%
Decisiveness	4%
	100%

Source: RHI Management Resources, Menlo Park, CA, 1998.

Are Leaders Born or Made?

Whether leadership can be learned is an issue that has perplexed researchers for decades and one that has important implications for the readers of this book. If leaders are *born,* why spend time reading and developing your skills? Your leadership success or failure has already been determined. If leaders are *made,* then everyone can become a leader, and there is hope for us all. As Jay Conger suggests, "These perspectives are quite different, and their implications for the training and development of leaders are profoundly different. If leadership ability is genetically determined, training could hardly play a role in its development. But if leadership is learned through experience, training might well be used to develop new skills and to help synthesize past experiences into useful insights."[16]

Our position, and that of almost all other leadership researchers as well, is that leaders are both born and made, particularly within the broad context of leadership that we have adopted. In chapter 4, we will discuss some of the traits that may contribute to and facilitate leader effectiveness, such as intelligence, physical energy, and social potential.[17] But formal and informal experience also play a critical role; in particular, "Work experience, hardship, opportunity, education, role models, and mentors all go together to craft a leader."[18] We believe that learning and practicing the leadership skills presented in this book will enhance every potential leader's effectiveness.

THREE COMPETENCIES OF LEADERSHIP

Leading or influencing requires three general skills, or competencies: (1) *diagnosing*—understanding the situation you are trying to influence; (2) *adapting*—altering your behavior and the other resources you have available to meet the contingencies of the situation; and (3) *communicating*—interacting with others in a way that people can easily understand and accept. We will discuss each of these competencies in greater detail in subsequent chapters, but for now here is a brief summary of each.

- *Diagnosing is a cognitive—or cerebral—competency.* It is understanding what the situation is now and knowing what you can reasonably expect to make it in the future. The discrepancy between the two is the problem to be solved. This discrepancy is what the other competencies are aimed at resolving.
- *Adapting is a behavioral competency.* It involves adapting your behaviors and other resources in a way that helps close the gap between the current situation and what you want to achieve.
- *Communicating is a process competency.* Even if you are able to understand the situation, even if you are able to adapt behavior and resources to meet the situation, you need to communicate effectively. If you cannot communicate in a way that people can understand and accept, you will be unlikely to meet your goal.[19]

MANAGEMENT PROCESS

Many authors consider the managerial functions of *planning, organizing, motivating,* and *controlling* to be central to any discussion of management. These functions, which constitute the management process (a step-by-step way of doing something) are relevant regardless of the type of organization or level of management being discussed. As Harold Koontz and Cyril O'Donnell said: "Acting in their managerial capacity, presidents, department heads, foremen, supervisors, college deans, bishops, and heads of governmental agencies all do the same thing. As managers they are all engaged, in part, in getting things done with and through people. As a manager, each must, at one time or another, carry out all the duties characteristic of managers."[20] In today's world, even a well-run household uses these managerial functions.

Planning involves setting goals and objectives for the organization and developing "work maps" showing how those goals and objectives are to be accomplished. Once plans have been made, *organizing* becomes meaningful. This step involves bringing together resources—people, capital, and equipment—in the most effective way to accomplish the goals. Organizing, therefore, involves an integration of resources.

Along with planning and organizing, *motivating* plays a large part in determining the level of performance of employees, which, in turn, influences how effectively the organizational goals will be met. Motivating is sometimes included as part of *directing,* along with communicating and leading.

In his research on motivation, William James of Harvard found that hourly employees could maintain their jobs (that is, not be fired) by working at approximately 20 to 30 percent of their ability. His study also showed that highly motivated employees work at close to 80 to 90 percent of their ability.[21] Both the minimum level at which employees might work and yet keep their jobs and the level at which they could be expected to perform with proper motivation are illustrated in Figure 1-1.

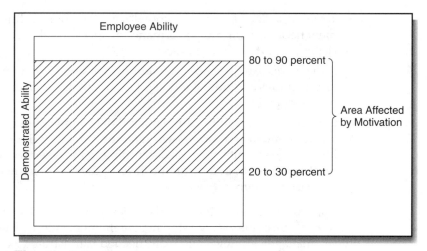

Figure 1-1
The Potential Influence of Motivation on Performance

This illustration shows us that if motivation is low, employees' performance will suffer as much as if their ability were low. For this reason, motivating is an extremely important function of management.

Another function of management is *controlling*. This involves feedback of results and follow-up to compare accomplishments with plans and to make appropriate adjustments where outcomes have deviated from expectations.

Although these management functions are stated separately, and as presented seem to have a specific sequence, one must remember that they are interrelated, as illustrated in Figure 1-2. At any one time, however, one or more functions may be of primary importance.

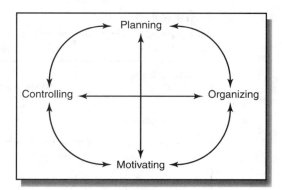

Figure 1-2
Interrelated
Management
Functions

SKILLS OF A MANAGER

There is general agreement that at least three areas of skill are necessary for the process of management: technical, human, and conceptual.

- *Technical skill.* Ability to use knowledge, methods, techniques, and equipment necessary for the performance of specific tasks; acquired from experience, education, and training.
- *Human skill.* Ability and judgment in working with and through people. This includes an understanding of motivation and an application of effective leadership.
- *Conceptual skill.* Ability to understand the complexities of the overall organization and where one's own operation fits into the organization. This knowledge permits one to act according to the objectives of the total organization rather than only on the basis of the goals and needs of one's own immediate group.[22]

The appropriate mix of these skills varies as an individual advances in management from supervisory to top management positions. The relationship between management level and skills needed is illustrated in Figure 1-3.

Proportionately less technical skill tends to be needed as one advances from lower to higher levels in the organization, but more conceptual skill is necessary. Supervisors at lower levels need considerable technical skill because they are often required to train and develop technicians and other employees in their sections. At the other extreme, executives in a business organization do not need to know how to perform all the specific tasks at the operational level. However, they should be able to see how all these functions are interrelated in accomplishing the goals of the total organization. This ability is particularly important because the executives' focus at the higher organizational levels is increasingly more external and global.

The amount of technical and conceptual skills needed at these different levels of management varies; the area of human skill appears to be crucial at all levels.

Figure 1-3
Management Skills Necessary at Various Levels of an Organization

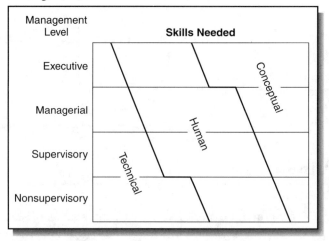

Chapter 1   Management: An Applied Behavioral Sciences Approach

ORGANIZATIONS AS SOCIAL SYSTEMS

Although the emphasis in this book will be on human skills development, we must recognize that the organizations in which most managers operate are social systems comprising many interrelated subsystems, only one of which is a human/social subsystem. The others could include an administrative/ structural subsystem, an informational/decision-making subsystem, and an economic/technological subsystem.[23]

The focus of the administrative/structural subsystem is on authority, structure, and responsibility within the organization: "who does what for whom" and "who tells whom to do what, how, when, where, and why." The informational/decision-making subsystem emphasizes key decisions and their informational needs to keep the system operating. The main concern of the economic/technological subsystem is the work to be done and the cost effectiveness of that work within the specific goals of the organization.

Although the focus of the human/social subsystem is on the motivation and needs of the members of the organization and on the leadership provided or required (the major emphasis of this book), it should be emphasized that within a systems approach there is a clear understanding that changes in one subsystem affect changes in other parts of the total system. As illustrated in Figure 1-4, if the total system is healthy and functioning well, each of its parts or subsystems is effectively interacting with the others. Therefore, an organization over a sustained period of time cannot overemphasize the importance of one subsystem at the expense of the others. At the same time, the internal management of the organization cannot ignore the needs and pressures from the external environment.

INGREDIENTS FOR EFFECTIVE HUMAN SKILLS

If one accepts the fact that human skill development is important, one may ask what kind of expertise managers and leaders must have in order to influence the behavior of other people. We feel that managers need three levels of expertise. They must understand past and current behavior, be able to predict behavior, and learn to direct, change, and control behavior.

Understanding Behavior

First, managers need to understand why people behave as they do. To get things done through other people, you have to know why they engage in certain characteristic behaviors.

What motivates people? What produces the patterns of behavior that are characteristic of individuals or groups? Motivation and its causes are the

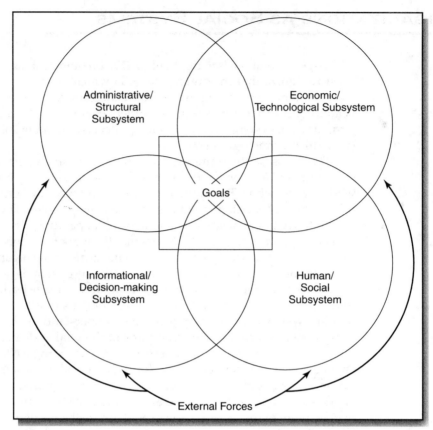

Figure 1-4
The Interrelated Subsystems of an Organization

areas on which most of the literature in the behavioral sciences focuses. In both popular and scholarly books and periodicals, there are literally hundreds of different classifications that are useful in communicating the patterns of behavior that describe individuals and groups interacting with other people. We can say a person is energetic or distracted or is a task leader or a team leader, and so on. All these are useful classifications for communicating to others why an individual or group is behaving in certain ways.

Predicting Behavior

Understanding past behavior is important in itself for developing effective human skills, and it also provides a framework for the next level of expertise—predicting behavior. Understanding why people did what they did yesterday enables a supervisor to predict how they are likely to behave tomorrow, next week, and next month under similar as well as changing environmental conditions.

Directing, Changing, and Controlling Behavior

The next level of expertise that an effective manager or leader needs is the ability to direct, change, and control behavior. (You must also accept the responsibility for influencing the behavior of others in accomplishing tasks and reaching goals.)

Note that the first two skills are passive; understanding and predicting do not require actions involving other people. The key to obtaining results is developing the skills needed to direct, change, and control the efforts of people in the accomplishment of organizational goals. That's where the manager translates thoughts and intentions into end results.

Controlling People

People who hear the word *control* often ask, "Does that mean that we have to manipulate others?" Words that suggest control and manipulation sometimes have a negative connotation to many people. When you accept the role of leader, however, you accept along with it the responsibility of having an impact on the behavior of other people—influencing the behavior of others toward achieving results. That's true whether you're at work striving to gain the commitment of your people, or at home attempting to assist your children in developing their basic values.

It's also important to remember that words are simply packages of ideas and, as such, are often misinterpreted. If *manipulation* means taking unfair advantage, being deceitful, and influencing others for self-interest, then it has a negative connotation. On the other hand, if manipulation means using influence and strategies skillfully and managing people fairly for mutually rewarding and productive purposes, it's an appropriate and necessary means for goal accomplishment.

If you are still concerned about words such as *control* or *manipulation*, think instead of *training* or *facilitating*. Whatever words you choose, your overall effectiveness depends upon understanding, predicting, and influencing the behavior of other people.

A Hammer Won't Always Do the Job

For every job, there is an appropriate tool. Hammers are great for pounding nails. You could also use a hammer to cut a two-by-four, but it would leave a lot of rough edges. For that particular job, there is a better tool. To build effectively, you need a variety of tools and the knowledge of how to use them.

The same is true for leadership and management. It is unrealistic to think that a single tool is all that's needed to manage effectively. If all you have is a hammer, then all you will see are nails. Many people fall into the trap of relying on the latest fad to solve all their management problems. They seem to develop an unrealistic assumption of what this new idea will do for them. Many useful management tools have been developed over the years. But you should know what to expect from them and, just as important, what not to expect. You need to understand and be able to use different tools when leading and managing people.[24]

Learning to Apply Behavioral Science Theory

Learning to apply behavioral science theory is much like learning anything; for example, you learn to hit a baseball by stepping up to the plate and attempting to hit—by practice, by doing what you are attempting to learn. There is no way you are going to learn to hit a baseball by merely reading books (even those by people considered to be experts in the field) or by watching (in person or on slow-motion film) great hitters. All those methods will do is give you conceptual knowledge of how to hit a baseball.

Psychologists define learning as a change in behavior—being able to do something different from what you were able to do before. So, in watching others and reading about them, we can perhaps change our knowledge or change our attitude. If we actually want to learn something, we have to "try on," or practice, that which we want to learn to make part of our relevant behavior.

Another thing to keep in mind in terms of learning is how you feel about learning something new. How did you feel the first time you ever tried to hit a baseball? If you were like most people, you felt anxious, nervous, and uncomfortable. This is the way most of us feel any time we attempt to do something new—something significantly different from the things we are already comfortable doing.

It's the same with learning to use behavioral science. Much of what you read in this book may have an impact on your knowledge and attitudes, but this book becomes relevant only if you are willing to "try on" some new behaviors. If you are, we think you should recognize that the first time you try on a new pattern of behavior in terms of attempting to implement behavioral science theory, you are going to feel ill at ease. We have to go through a period of "unfreezing" if we want to learn.

Another caution is to be patient—give the new behavior time to work. If you are up at bat attempting to hit a baseball for the first time, what is the probability that you will get a base hit from the first ball the pitcher delivers? The probability is low. It is not any different in learning behavioral science theory. The first time you attempt to behave differently on the basis of a new theory, you probably will be less effective than you would have been had you used your old style of behavior (although in the long run the new style may have a higher probability of success). Practitioners who go through a training experience in which they learn new knowledge and attitudes often find when trying on the new behavior for the first time, that it does not work. As a result, they begin to respond negatively to the whole training experience, saying such things as, "How can we accept these things?" "They are not usable." "They do not work in the real world." It is this kind of attitude that has hindered managers from attempting to make behavioral science theory an integral part of managing more effectively. All of us have to recognize that, just like hitting a baseball, applying behavioral science theory takes practice. The first few times up, the probability of success is quite low. But the more we practice, the more we attempt to get relevant feedback, the more the probability of success will increase.

APPLIED BEHAVIORAL SCIENCES

If managers are able to understand, predict, direct, change, and control behavior, they are essentially operating as behavioral scientists.

What Is a Behavioral Scientist?

One way to define a behavioral scientist is to say that a behavioral scientist attempts to bring together, from a variety of disciplines, those concepts, theories, and research that may be useful to people in making decisions about the behavior of individuals and groups. A behavioral scientist integrates concepts and theories and the results of empirical studies from the areas of cultural anthropology, economics, political science, psychology, sociology, and social psychology. At the same time, a behavioral scientist borrows from other areas such as engineering, physics, quantitative analysis, and statistics. For example, force field analysis (developed by Kurt Lewin), which we discuss in chapter 17, is modeled upon one of the fundamental principles of physics. Perhaps the best way to look at behavioral science is to say that practitioners attempt to make use of all those areas or disciplines that can aid in better understanding, predicting, and having an impact on the behavior of individuals and groups.

The emphasis in this book is on the applied behavioral sciences: those concepts from the behavioral sciences that can have an impact on making leaders more effective—whether they be executives, supervisors, teachers, or parents. The hope is to apply behavioral science concepts in such a way as to move these concepts from being strictly theoretical and descriptive to being more applied and prescriptive. It should be remembered, though, that applied behavioral science is not an exact science such as physics, chemistry, and biology. There are no universal truths when it comes to management. People are difficult to predict. All that the behavioral sciences can give you are ways to increase your behavioral batting average. In other words, the behavioral sciences are probability sciences; there aren't any principles of management, only books titled *Principles of Management.*

THE DESIGN OF THIS BOOK

In the chapters that follow, we will improve your understanding of how to use the field of applied behavioral science. As we noted in *Organizational Change Through Effective Leadership,* with Robert H. Guest,

> By sharing the insights of those who have studied organizational change and linking their observations, however briefly, to an evolving situation, we hope that managers out on the firing line might

come to realize that there are available, in the organizational behavior literature, concepts and frameworks that might help them to do a better job. We believe that these behavioral science contributions might assist managers, in a variety of institutional settings, to sharpen their diagnostic skills and to develop appropriate change strategies. They might, in short, go beyond the intuitive, beyond seat-of-the-pants experience, to sense better the probabilities that one course of action will work and another will not.[25]

The plan of this book is a straightforward, developmental approach. Chapters 2 and 3 on motivation are designed to provide information to help you to understand and to predict the how and why people behave as they do. Chapters 4 through 12 trace the development of modern leadership theory and introduce Situational Leadership. After chapter 13, "Effective Communication," chapters 14 through 16 apply Situational Leadership. The last part of the book begins with chapter 17, "Planning and Implementing Change," and continues with three chapters that emphasize leadership in three important dimensions: "Leadership to Achieve Quality" (chapter 18), "Leadership Strategies for Organizational Transformation" (chapter 19), and "The Organizational Cone" (chapter 20). The book concludes with chapter 21, "Synthesizing Management Theory: Integrating Situational Leadership with the Classics."

What happens after chapter 21 is up to you. You are the author of your own leadership and management behavior. We think you will find your journey through this book interesting, informative, and, most importantly, of practical value.

ENDNOTES

1. Dave Ulrich, Jack Zenger, and Norman Smallwood, *Results-Based Leadership* (Boston: Harvard Business School Press, 1999), p. 27.

2. Ed Lawler III, *The Ultimate Advantage: Creating the High Involvement Organization* (San Francisco: Jossey-Bass, Inc., Publishers, 1992), pp. 10–24.

3. Rosabeth Moss Kanter, *The Planning Forum Network,* 2, no. 1 (July 1990), p. 1. See also Rahul Jacob, "The Struggle to Create an Organization for the 21st Century," *Fortune,* April 1995, p. 90.

4. Michael Hammer, "Is Work Bad for You?", *The Atlantic Monthly,* August 1999, pp. 89/87–93.

5. Andrew S. Grove, "A High Tech CEO Updates His Views on Managing and Careers," *Fortune,* September 18, 1995.

6. Quoted in Rifkin, Glenn, "Leadership: Can It Be Learned?" *Forbes ASAP,* April 8, 1996.

7. Michael Porter, "New Strategies for Competitive Advantage," *Planning Review,* May/June 1990, p. 14.

8. "Strategies for Success in the New Global Economy, An Interview with Rosebeth Moss Kanter," *Strategy & Leadership,* November/December, 1997, pp. 20–26.

9. Ed Lawler III, *The Ultimate Advantage: Creating the High Involvement Organization* (San Francisco: Jossey-Bass Inc., Publishers, 1992), pp. 3–24.

10. Joel E. Ross, *Total Quality Management,* 3rd. ed. (Delray Beach, FL: St. Lucie Press, 1999), p. 335.

11. Glen D. Hoffherr and Robert P. Reid, "Achieving a Highly Effective Organization," *Quality Digest,* August 1995, pp. 27–30.

12. Elton Mayo, *The Social Problems of an Industrial Civilization* (Boston: Harvard Business School, 1945), p. 23.

13. Warren Bennis, quoted in Cherie Carter-Scott, "The Differences between Leadership and Management," *Manage,* November 1994, p. 12. Also see Tom Payner, "Go Forth and Manage Wisely," *Supervision Magazine,* August 1994, and Bernard M. Bass and Ralph M. Stogdill, Bass and Stogdill's *Handbook of Leadership* (New York: The Free Press, 1990).

14. Cecil Gregg, RHI Management Resources, Menlo Park, CA, 1998.

15. Peter F. Drucker, "Management's New Paradigms," *Forbes,* October 5, 1998, p. 176.

16. Jay A. Conger, *Learning to Lead* (San Francisco: Jossey-Bass, Inc., Publishers, 1992), p. 15.

17. *Ibid.,* p. 21.

18. *Ibid.,* p. 29.

19. Paul Hersey, *Situational Selling* (Escondido, CA: Center for Leadership Studies, 1985), p. 8.

20. Harold Koontz and Cyril O'Donnell, *Principles of Management,* 5th ed. (New York: McGraw-Hill, 1972), p. 20.

21. William James, *The Principles of Psychology,* 1 (London: Macmillan and Co., Ltd., 1890).

22. These descriptions were adapted from a classification developed by Robert L. Katz, "Skills of an Effective Administrator," *Harvard Business Review,* January-February 1955, pp. 33–42. See also Robert S. Dreyer, "Do Good Bosses Make Lousy Leaders?" *Supervision,* March 1995, pp. 19–20.

23. Paul Hersey and Douglas Scott identify these components of an internal social system in "A Systems Approach to Educational Organizations: Do We Manage or Administer?" *OCLEA* (a publication of the Ontario Council for Leadership in Educational Administration, Toronto, Canada), September 1974, pp. 3–5. Much of the material for that article was adapted from lectures given by Boris Yavitz, Dean, School of Business Administration, Columbia University.

24. Adapted from Hersey, *The Situational Leader,* pp. 20–22.

25. Robert H. Guest, Paul Hersey, and Kenneth H. Blanchard, *Organizational Change Through Effective Leadership* (Upper Saddle River, NJ: Prentice Hall, 1986), p. 222. See also Kevin John Philips, "Six Keys to Basic Success," *Supervision,* May 1994, pp. 11–13.

Chapter 2

Motivation and Behavior

The study of motivation and behavior is a search for answers to questions about human nature. Recognizing the importance of the human element in organizations, we attempt in this chapter to develop a theoretical framework that will help managers understand human behavior—not only to understand the "whys" of past behavior, but to some extent to predict, to change, and even to control future behavior. ✧

THEORIES OF BEHAVIOR

Let's begin our search for the "whys" of behavior with psychologist Kurt Lewin's fundamental equation of human behavior:[1]

$$B = f(P \Leftrightarrow S)$$

where B represents individual behavior, f means "a function of" or "is caused by," P is the person, and S is the situation. Lewin's equation then suggests that B is a function of something both *inside* the Person and *outside* the person in the Situation.[2] This "something" inside the person is motives or needs that are reflected in individual attitudes—the way individuals feel about things—and represented by personality—an individual's tendency to act.[3] P and S are not independent, but rather are interdependent. Persons are influenced by the Situations in which they find themselves, and Situations are influenced by Persons. These are important ideas in the context of "situational," or "contingency," leadership, in which the appropriate leader behavior is determined by the situation. We will revisit this significant point later.

Goal-Oriented Behavior

Behavior is basically goal oriented. In other words, our behavior is generally motivated by a desire to attain some specific result. The goal is not always consciously known by the individual. All of us may wonder at times, "Why did I do that?" The reason for our action is not always apparent to the conscious mind. The drives that motivate distinctive individual behavioral patterns ("personality") are to a considerable degree subconscious and, therefore, are not easily accessible for examination and evaluation.

Sigmund Freud was one of the first to recognize the importance of subconscious motivation. He believed that people are not always aware of everything they want; hence, much of their behavior is affected by subconscious motives or needs. In fact, Freud's research convinced him that an analogy could be drawn between the motivation of most people and the structure of an iceberg. In Freud's view, a significant segment of human motivation appears below the surface of the conscious mind, as indicated in Figure 2-1. Therefore, one usually is aware of only a small portion of one's motivation.[4] Some individuals may make no effort to gain self-insight. But even with professional help—for example, psychotherapy—understanding oneself may be a difficult process, yielding varying degrees of success.

The basic unit of behavior is an *activity*. In fact, all behavior is a series of activities. As human beings, we are always doing something: walking, talking, eating, sleeping, working, and the like. In many instances, we are doing more than one activity at a time, such as talking with someone as we walk or drive to work. At any given moment, we may decide to change from one activity or combination of activities to another. This aspect of human nature raises some important questions. Why do people engage in one activity and not another? Why do they change activities? How can we as managers understand, predict, and even control what activity or activities a person may engage in at a given moment? To predict behavior, managers must know which motives or needs of people evoke a certain action at a particular time.

The Causal Sequence

Norman R. F. Maier, the noted industrial psychologist from the University of Michigan, put the elements previously discussed—the situation, person, behavior(s), and activities—together in his classic causal sequence model:

$$S \leftrightarrow O \rightarrow B \rightarrow A$$

S represents the *Situation*, or *Stimulus*; *O* the person, or *Organism*; *B* the *Behavior*; and *A* the *Activity* or *Accomplishment*. In Maier's words:

> In order to explain behavior, one must include a description of the *S* [Situation] as well as of the *O* [Organism]. The interaction between them must precede the behavior which results from the interaction. The product of this interaction in psychology is called perception. [The resultant] behavior (*B*) causes changes which alter the

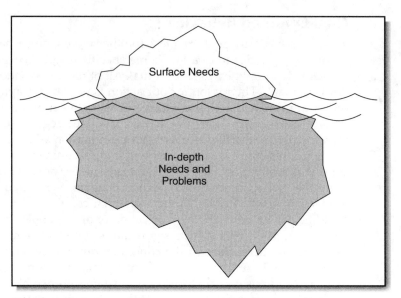

Figure 2-1
Freud's Iceberg Analogy

relationship between the organism (*O*) and its world. The change produced by behavior is an accomplishment (*A*). This accomplishment may be desirable or undesirable. In either case it may alter the stimulus-situation. . . . Thus the behavior of one person may influence that person's world and it may also influence other people.[5]

Motives

People differ not only in their ability to do, but also in their will to do, or motivation. The motivation of people depends on the strength of their motives. Motives are sometimes defined as needs, wants, drives, or impulses within the individual. Motives are directed toward goals, which may be conscious or subconscious.

Viktor Frankl, a German psychologist, asserted in his book, *Man's Search for Meaning*, that, "The striving to find a meaning in one's life is the primary motivational force in man."[6] This was the same theme Tom Peters and Robert Waterman used in their best-selling book, *In Search of Excellence*, particularly in chapter 3, "Man Waiting for Motivation." They observed that, "The dominating need of human beings is to find meaning, . . . to control one's destiny, . . . to be an expert in the promotion and protection of values."[7]

Motives are the "whys" of behavior. They arouse and maintain activity and determine the general direction of the behavior of an individual. In essence, motives or needs are the mainsprings of action. In our discussions we shall use these two terms—*motives* and *needs*—interchangeably. In this context, the term *need* should not be associated with urgency or any pressing desire for something. It simply means something within an individual that prompts that person to action.

Goals

Goals are outside an individual; they are sometimes referred to as "hoped for" rewards toward which motives are directed. These goals are often called *incentives* by psychologists. However, we prefer not to use that term because many people in our society tend to equate incentives with tangible financial rewards, such as increased pay, although most of us would agree that there are many intangible rewards, such as praise or power, that are just as important in evoking behavior. Managers who are successful in motivating employees are often providing an environment in which appropriate goals (incentives) are available for need satisfaction.

Motive Strength

We have said that motives, or needs, are the reasons underlying behavior. All individuals have many hundreds of needs. All of these needs compete. What, then, determines which of these motives a person will attempt to satisfy through activity? The need with the greatest strength at a particular moment leads to activity, as illustrated in Figure 2-2. In Figure 2-2, motive B has the highest motive strength, and therefore it is the need that determines behavior.

Changes in Motive Strength

A motive tends to decrease in strength if it is either satisfied or blocked from satisfaction. Satisfied or blocked needs normally do not motivate individuals to further action.

Figure 2-2
The Strongest Motive Determines Behavior (Motive B in this Illustration)

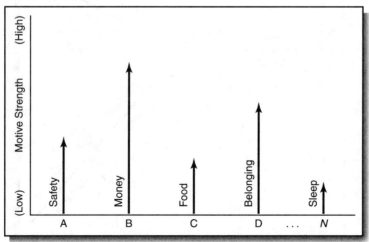

Need Satisfaction

When a need is satisfied, according to Abraham Maslow, it is no longer a motivator of behavior.[8] High-strength needs that are satisfied are sometimes referred to as "satisficed"—that is, the need has been satisfied to the extent that some competing need is now more potent. If a high-strength need is thirst, drinking tends to lower the strength of this need, and other needs may now become more potent.

Blocking Need Satisfaction

The satisfaction of a need may be blocked. Although a reduction in need strength sometimes follows, it does not always occur initially. Instead, there may be a tendency for the person to engage in coping behavior. This is an attempt to overcome the obstacle by trial-and-error problem solving. The person may try a variety of behaviors to find one that will accomplish the goal or will reduce tension created by blockage, as illustrated in Figure 2-3.

Initially, this coping behavior may be quite rational. Perhaps the person may even make several attempts in direction 1 before going to direction 2, and make several attempts in direction 2 before moving in direction 3, where some degree of perceived success and goal attainment is finally achieved.

If people continue to strive for something without success, they may substitute goals that can satisfy the need. For example, if Mary has a strong desire to be a CPA but continually receives average grades in accounting, she may be willing eventually to settle for another career in business.

Figure 2-3
Coping Behavior When Blockage Occurs in Attempting
to Accomplish a Particular Goal

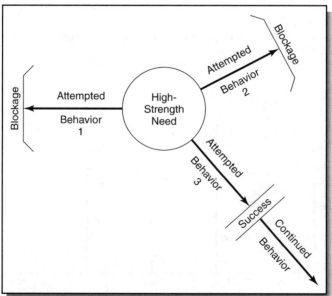

Chapter 2   Motivation and Behavior

Cognitive Dissonance

Blocked motives and continually unsuccessful rational coping behavior may lead to forms of irrational coping behavior. Leon Festinger analyzed this phenomenon.[9] His theory of cognitive dissonance deals primarily with the relationships that exist between perceptions people have about themselves and their environment. When individual perceptions have nothing to do with each other, they are considered irrelevant to each other. If one supports the other, they are said to be in a consonant relationship. Dissonance is created when two perceptions that are relevant to each other are in conflict. This situation creates tension, which is psychologically uncomfortable and causes the individual to try to modify one of the incompatible perceptions so as to reduce the tension or dissonance. In a sense, that person engages in coping behavior to regain a condition of consonance or equilibrium. For example, Festinger did research that showed that "heavy smokers are less likely to believe that there is a relationship between smoking and lung cancer than non-smokers."[10] In other words, if they cannot give up smoking, they can at least remain skeptical about research that reports harmful effects. The same phenomenon is at work when a person goes out fishing all day, doesn't catch anything, and remarks about the beautiful weather.

Frustration

The blocking or thwarting of goal attainment is referred to as frustration. This phenomenon is defined in terms of the condition of the individual, rather than in terms of the external environment. A person may be frustrated by an imaginary barrier and may fail to be frustrated by a real barrier.

As previously discussed, rational coping behavior can lead to alternative goal setting or decreasing need strength. Irrational behavior may occur in several forms when blockage to goal accomplishment continues and frustration develops. Frustration may increase to the extent that the individual engages in aggressive behavior.

Aggression can lead to destructive behavior such as hostility and striking out. Freud was one of the first to demonstrate that hostility or rage can be exhibited by an individual in a variety of ways.[11] If possible, individuals will direct their hostility against the object or the person that they feel is the cause of frustration. Angry workers may try to hurt their boss through gossip and other malicious behavior. Often, however, people cannot attack the cause of their frustration directly, and they may look for a scapegoat as a target for their hostility. Scapegoats may be other workers, family members, or innocent pets.

As Norman R. F. Maier said, aggression is only one way in which frustration can be shown.[12] Other forms of frustrated behavior—such as rationalization, regression, fixation, and resignation—may develop if pressures continue or increase.

Rationalization simply means making excuses. For example, an individual might blame someone else for an inability to accomplish a given goal: "It was my boss's fault that I didn't get a raise." Or the person may downgrade the desirability of that particular goal: "I didn't want to do that anyway."

Regression is essentially not acting one's age. "Frustrated people tend to give up constructive attempts at solving their problems and regress to more primitive and childish behavior."[13] A person who cannot start the car and proceeds to kick it is demonstrating regressive behavior; so too is a manager who throws a temper tantrum when annoyed and frustrated. Roger G. Barker, Tamara Dembo, and Kurt Lewin showed experimentally that when children are exposed to mild frustration, their play may resemble that of a child two or more years younger.[14]

Fixation occurs when a person continues to exhibit the same behavior pattern over and over again, even though experience has shown that it can accomplish nothing. Thus, "frustration can freeze old and habitual responses and prevent the use of new and more effectual ones."[15] Maier showed that, although habits are normally broken when they bring no satisfaction or lead to punishment, a fixation actually becomes stronger under those circumstances.[16] In fact, he argued that it is possible to change a habit into a fixation by too much punishment. This phenomenon is seen in children who blindly continue to behave in an objectionable manner after being severely punished. Thus, Maier concluded that punishment can have two effects on behavior: It may either eliminate the undesirable behavior or lead to fixation and other symptoms of frustration as well. It follows that punishment may be a dangerous management tool, because its effects are difficult to predict. According to James A. C. Brown, common symptoms of fixation in industry are "the inability to accept change, the blind and stubborn refusal to accept new facts when experience has shown the old ones to be untenable, and the type of behavior exemplified by the manager who continues to increase penalties" even when doing so is only making conditions worse.[17]

Resignation or apathy occurs after prolonged frustration, when people lose hope of accomplishing their goal(s) in a particular situation and withdraw from reality and the source of their frustration. This phenomenon is characteristic of people in boring, routine jobs, where often they resign themselves to the fact that there is little hope for improvement within their environments.

A manager should remember that aggression, rationalization, regression, fixation, and resignation are all symptoms of frustration and may be indications that problems exist.

Increasing Motive Strength

Behavior may change if an existing need increases in strength to the extent that it is now the high-strength motive. The strength of some needs tends to appear in a cyclical pattern. For example, the need for food tends to recur regardless of how well it has been satisfied at a given moment. One can increase or delay the speed of this cyclical pattern by affecting the environment. For example, a person's need for food may not be high-strength unless the immediate environment is changed such that the senses are exposed to the sight and the aroma of tempting food.

People have a variety of needs at any given time. They may be hungry, thirsty, and tired, but the need with the highest strength will determine what they do.[18] All of these needs tend to be cyclical over time.

CATEGORIES OF ACTIVITIES

Activities resulting from high-strength needs can generally be classified into two categories—*goal-directed activity* and *goal activity*. These concepts are important to practitioners because of their differing influence on need strength, which can be useful in understanding human behavior.

Goal-directed activity, in essence, is motivated behavior directed at reaching a goal. If one's strongest need at a given moment is hunger, various activities such as looking for a place to eat, buying food, or preparing food would be considered goal-directed activities. On the other hand, goal activity is engaging in the goal itself. In the case of hunger, food is the goal and eating, therefore, is the goal activity.

An important distinction between these two classes of activities is their effect on the strength of the need. In goal-directed activity, the strength of the need tends to increase as one engages in the activity until the goal is reached or frustration sets in. As discussed earlier, frustration develops when one is continually blocked from reaching a goal. If the frustration becomes intense enough, the strength of the need may decrease until it is no longer potent enough to affect behavior—a person gives up.

The strength of the need tends to increase as one engages in goal-directed activity; however, once goal activity begins, the strength of the need tends to decrease as one engages in it. For example, as one eats more and more, the strength of the need for food declines for that particular time. At the point when another need becomes more potent than the present need, behavior changes.

On Thanksgiving Day, for example, as food is being prepared all morning (goal-directed activity), the need for food increases to the point of almost not being able to wait until the meal is on the table. As we begin to eat (goal activity), the strength of this need diminishes to the point where other needs become more important. As we leave the table, our need for food seems to be well satisfied. Our activity changes to that of watching football. This need for passive recreation has now become most potent, and we find ourselves in front of the television set. But gradually this need decreases, too. After several games, even though the competition is fierce, the need for passive recreation may also decline to the extent that other needs become more important—perhaps the need for fresh air and a walk or, better still, another piece of pumpkin pie. Several hours before, we had sworn not to eat for a week, but now that pie looks very good. So once again hunger is the strongest need. Thus, it should be remembered that we never completely satiate a need. We satisfy it for only a period of time.

MOTIVES, GOALS, AND ACTIVITIES

The relationship among motives, goals, and activities can be shown in a simplified fashion, as illustrated in Figure 2-4. The strongest motive produces behavior that is either goal-directed or goal activity. Because not all goals are

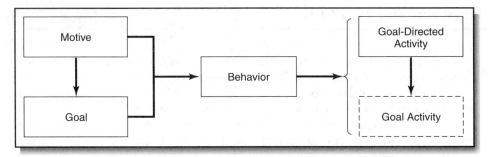

Figure 2-4
Relationship among Motives, Goals, and Activities

attainable, individuals do not always reach goal activity, regardless of the strength of the motive. Thus, goal activity is indicated by a dashed line. An example of use of a tangible goal to influence behavior is illustrated in Figure 2-5.

Food is a broad goal, and the type of food that will satisfy the hunger motive will vary from situation to situation. The same is true for any broad goal. If individuals are starving, they may eat anything; at other times, they may realign their goals, and only a steak will satisfy their hunger.

A similar illustration could be given for an intangible goal. If individuals have a need for recognition—a need to be viewed as contributing, productive people—praise is one incentive that will help satisfy that need. In a work situation, if their need for recognition is strong enough, praise from their manager or supervisor may be an effective incentive in influencing people to continue to do good work.

In analyzing these two examples, remember that if you want to influence another person's behavior, you must first understand what motives or needs are most important to that person at that time. A goal, to be effective, must be appropriate to the need structure of the person involved.

A question that may be considered at this point is whether it is better to engage in goal-directed activity or in goal activity. Actually, staying at either level exclusively creates problems. If one stays at goal-directed activity too

Figure 2-5
Use of a Tangible Goal

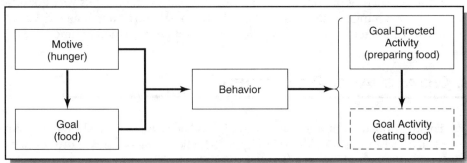

long, frustration will occur to the extent that the person may give up or may display other patterns of irrational behavior. On the other hand, if one engages exclusively in goal activity and the goal is not challenging, a lack of interest and apathy will develop, with motivation again tending to decrease. A more appropriate and effective pattern might be a continuous cycling between goal-directed activity and goal activity, as shown in Figure 2-6.

A goal that is appropriate for a 6-year-old may not be a meaningful goal for the same child at age 7. Once the child becomes proficient in attaining a particular goal, it becomes appropriate for the parent to provide an opportunity for the child to evaluate and set new goals. In the same light, what is an appropriate goal for a new employee may not be meaningful for an employee who has been with a corporation 6 months or a year. There also may be distinctions between employees who have been with an organization for only a few years and those who have been with it for longer periods of time.

This cycling process between goal-directed activity and goal activity is a continuous challenge for the parent or the manager. As employees increase in their ability to accomplish goals, it is appropriate that the manager reevaluate and provide an environment that allows continual realignment of goals and an opportunity for growth and development. The learning and developing process is not a phenomenon that should be confined to only one stage of a person's life. In this process, the role of managers is not always that of setting goals for their workers. Instead, effectiveness may be increased by providing an environment in which coworkers can participate in setting their own goals. Research indicates that commitment increases when people are involved in their own goal setting. If individuals are involved, they will tend to engage in much more goal-directed activity before they become frustrated and give up. On the other hand, if their manager sets the goals for them, they are likely to give up more easily because they perceive these goals as their manager's and not as their own.

Goals should be set high enough so that a person has to stretch to reach them, but low enough so that they can be attained. Thus, goals must be realistic before a person will make a real effort to achieve them. As J. Sterling-Livingston so aptly stated:

> [Followers] will not be motivated to reach high levels of productivity unless they consider the boss' high expectations realistic and achievable. If they are encouraged to strive for unattainable goals,

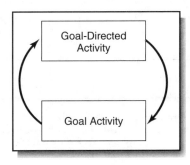

Figure 2-6
Cycling Function
of Goal-Directed
Activity and
Goal Activity

they eventually give up trying and settle for results that are lower than they are capable of achieving. The experience of a large electrical manufacturing company demonstrates this; the company discovered that production actually declined if production quotas were set too high, because the workers simply stopped trying to meet them. In other words, the practice of "dangling the carrot just beyond the donkey's reach," endorsed by many managers, is not a good motivational device.[19]

David C. McClelland and John W. Atkinson demonstrated in their research that the degree of motivation and effort rises until the probability of success reaches 50 percent; then it begins to fall even though the probability of success continues to increase.[20] This relationship can be depicted in the form of a bell-shaped curve, as illustrated in Figure 2-7. As the figure suggests, people are not highly motivated if a goal is seen as almost impossible or virtually certain to achieve.

Another problem with goals is that often final goals are set and the person is judged only in terms of success in relation to those goals. For example, suppose a team has an established completion date for its work on a new marketing plan, a project that is scheduled to take 4 months. After the first month, the project is only 5 percent completed. Ordinarily, the vice president for marketing would become upset and start "micromanaging" the team, that is, watching and criticizing their every move. If this behavior continued, there

Figure 2-7
The Relationship of Motivation to Probability of Success

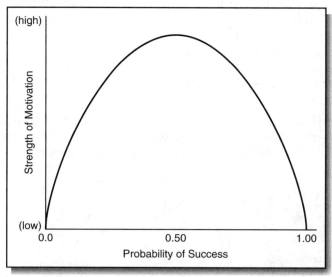

would be a high probability that the team would stop trying. Progress on the marketing plan, instead of accelerating, may get worse. An alternative for the marketing vice president is to set interim goals—realistic goals that move toward the final goal. This moderate change in the marketing plan would allow positive reinforcement to be used, rather than reprimand.

EXPECTANCY THEORY

We have already discussed the strength of needs. What additional factors affect the strength of needs? Victor Vroom suggested an approach in his expectancy theory of motivation that attempts to answer that question.[21] Furthermore, his theory is consistent with our previous assertion that felt needs cause human behavior.

In simplified form, felt needs cause behavior, and this motivated behavior in a work setting is increased if a person perceives a positive relationship between effort and performance. Motivated behavior is further increased if there is a positive relationship between good performance and outcomes or rewards, particularly if the outcomes or rewards are valued. Thus, there are three relationships that enhance motivated behavior, as shown in Figure 2-8: a positive relationship between effort and performance, a positive relationship between good performance and rewards, and the delivery or achievement of valued outcomes or rewards, intrinsic, extrinsic, or both.

Figure 2-8
An Expectancy Model for Motivation

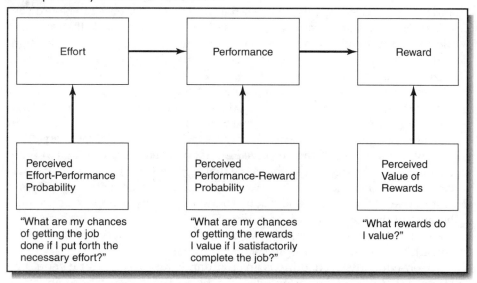

Source: From *Organizational Behavior Foundations, Realities, and Challenges,* 1st edition, by Nelson/Zwick © 1994. Reprinted with permission of South-Western College Publishing, a division of Thomson Learning. Fax 800 730-2215.

Let's look at an example. A new manager perceives that a 60-hour work-week is vital to good job performance. Further, the manager also perceives that good job performance will probably result in an early promotion that carries with it a badly needed 10-percent raise. If this sequence of events happens, both the manager's willingness to work hard and confidence in the behavior pattern will be reinforced. "Success breeds success!" However, should one or more steps in the sequence be proved wrong—for example, performance does not improve, promotion is denied, or pay raise falls short of expectations—motivation, willingness, and confidence will decline.

This linkage between effort and performance and between performance and valued outcomes is important not only to our understanding of motivation but also to our understanding of a number of leadership theories, especially the path-goal theory discussed in chapter 5.[22]

AVAILABILITY

Another important factor that affects need strength is availability. Although expectancy and availability are related, expectancy tends to affect motives, or needs, and availability tends to affect the perception of goals.

Expectancy is the perceived probability of satisfying a particular need of an individual on the basis of experience. Although *expectancy* is the technical term used by psychologists, it refers directly to the sum of the past experience. Experience can be either actual or vicarious. Vicarious experience comes from sources the person considers legitimate, such as parents, peer groups, teachers, and books or periodicals. To illustrate the effect that experience can have on behavior, let us look at an example. Suppose a boy's father is a basketball star, and the boy wants to follow in his footsteps. Initially, his expectancy may be high, and, therefore, the strength of the need is high. If he is cut from the eighth-grade team, the boy might continue to try. A single failure usually is not enough to discourage a person (in fact, it sometimes results in increased activity) and will not significantly affect his expectancy. But if he continues to get cut from a team year after year, eventually this motive will weaken or decrease in priority. In fact, after enough unsuccessful experiences, he may give up completely.

Availability reflects the perceived limitations of the environment. It is determined by how accessible the goals that can satisfy a given need are perceived by an individual to be. For example, if the electricity goes off in a storm, one cannot watch television. That goal activity is no longer possible because of the limitations of the environment. One may have a high desire to watch television, but a person who cannot satisfy that desire will settle for something else, such as sleeping.

Consequently, availability is an environmental variable. Yet it should be stressed that it is not important whether the goals to satisfy a need are really available. It is the perception of availability, or the interpretation of reality, that affects one's actual behavior. In other words, reality is what a person perceives.

An example of how perception can affect behavior was dramatically illustrated in an experiment with a fish. A pike was placed in an aquarium with many minnows swimming around it. After the fish became accustomed to the plentiful supply of food, a sheet of glass was placed between the pike and the minnows. When the pike became hungry, it tried to reach the minnows, but it continually hit its head on the glass. At first, the strength of the need for food increased, and the pike tried harder than ever to get the minnows. But finally its repeated failure of goal attainment resulted in enough frustration that the fish no longer attempted to eat the minnows. In fact, when the glass partition was finally removed, the minnows again swam all around the pike, but no further goal-directed activity took place. Eventually, the pike died of starvation while in the midst of plenty of food. In both cases, the fish operated according to the way it perceived reality and not on the basis of reality itself.

An expanded diagram of a motivating situation including expectancy and availability is presented in Figure 2-9. Motives, needs within an individual, are directed toward goals that are aspirations in the environment. These are interpreted by the individual as being available or unavailable. This interpretation affects expectancy. If expectancy is high, motive strength will increase. The pattern tends to be cyclical, moving in the direction of the solid arrows. But to some extent these are interacting variables indicated by the dashed arrows. For example, experience may affect the way we perceive availability. The presence of goals in the environment may affect the given strength of motives, and so forth.

Figure 2-9
Expanded Diagram of a Motivating Situation

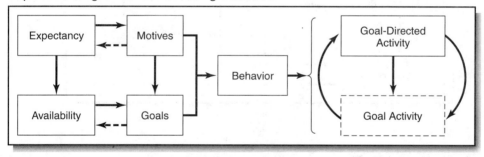

PERSONALITY DEVELOPMENT

As individuals mature, they develop habit patterns, or conditioned responses, to various stimuli. The sum of these habit patterns, as perceived by others, determines their personality.

$$habit\ a + habit\ b + habit\ c + \ldots + habit\ n = personality$$

As individuals begin to behave in a similar fashion under similar conditions, this behavior is what others learn to recognize as them—as their personality. They expect and can even predict certain kinds of behavior from these people.

Changing Personality

Many psychologists contend that basic personality structures are developed quite early in life. In fact, some claim that few personality changes can be made after ages 7 or 8. Using a model similar to the one in Figure 2-9, we can begin to understand why it tends to become more difficult to make changes in personality as people grow older. Note that in the model in Figure 2-10 we are using *sum of past experience* in place of the term *expectancy* used in the earlier model. These terms can be used interchangeably.

When an individual behaves in a motivating situation, that behavior becomes a new input to that person's inventory of experience, as the feedback loop in Figure 2-10 indicates. The earlier in life that this input occurs, the greater its potential effect on future behavior. The reason is that, early in life, this behavior represents a larger portion of the total past experience of a young person than the same behavior input will later in life. In addition, the longer behavior is reinforced, the more patterned it becomes and the more difficult it is to change.

Figure 2-10
Feedback Model

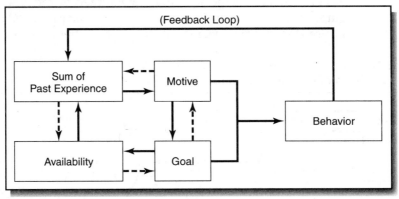

HIERARCHY OF NEEDS

We have argued that the behavior of individuals at a particular moment is usually determined by their strongest need. It would seem significant, therefore, for managers to have some understanding about the needs that are commonly most important to people. A classic framework that helps explain the strength of certain needs was developed by Abraham Maslow.[23] According to Maslow, human needs arrange themselves into a hierarchy, as illustrated in Figure 2-11.

The physiological needs are shown at the top of the hierarchy because they tend to have the highest strength until they are somewhat satisfied. These are the basic human needs to sustain life itself—food, clothing, and

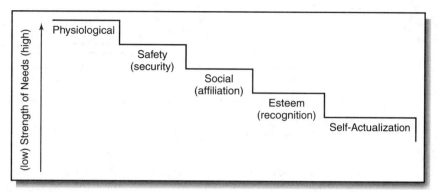

Figure 2-11
Maslow's Hierarchy of Needs

shelter. Until these basic needs are satisfied to the degree needed for the sufficient operation of the body, the majority of a person's activity will probably be at this level, and the other needs will provide little motivation.

But what happens to a person's motivation when these basic needs begin to be fulfilled? Instead of physiological needs, other levels of needs become important, and these motivate and dominate the behavior of the individual. And when these needs are somewhat satiated, other needs emerge, and so on down the hierarchy.

Once physiological needs become gratified, the safety, or security, needs become predominant, as illustrated in Figure 2-12. These needs are essentially the need to be free of the fear of physical danger and deprivation of the basic physiological needs. In other words, this is a need for self-preservation. In addition to the here and now, there is a concern for the future. Will people be able to maintain their property or job so they can provide food and shelter tomorrow and the next day? If an individual's safety or security is in danger, other things seem unimportant.

Once physiological and safety needs are fairly well satisfied, social, or affiliation, needs will emerge as dominant, as illustrated in Figure 2-13. Because people are social beings, they have a need to belong to and be accepted by various groups. When social needs become dominant, a person will strive for meaningful relations with others.

Figure 2-12
Safety Needs Dominant in the Need Structure

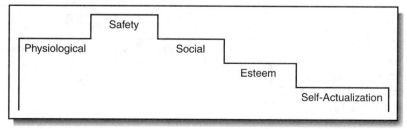

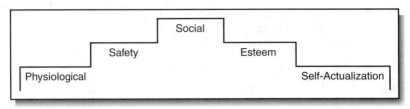

Figure 2-13
Social Needs Dominant in the Need Structure

After individuals begin to satisfy their need to belong, they generally want to be more than just a member of their group. They then feel the need for esteem—both self-esteem and recognition from others, as seen in Figure 2-14. Most people have a need for a high evaluation of themselves that is firmly based in reality—recognition and respect from others. Satisfaction of these esteem needs produces feelings of self-confidence, prestige, power, and control. People begin to feel that they are useful and have some effect on their environment. There are other occasions, though, when persons are unable to satisfy their need for esteem through constructive behavior. When this need is dominant, an individual may resort to disruptive or immature behavior to satisfy the desire for attention—a child may throw a temper tantrum, employees may engage in work restriction or arguments with their coworkers or manager. Thus, recognition is not always obtained through mature or adaptive behavior. It is sometimes garnered by disruptive and irresponsible actions. In fact, some of the social problems we have today may have their roots in the frustration of esteem needs.

Once esteem needs begin to be adequately satisfied, the self-actualization needs become more prepotent, as shown in Figure 2-15. Self-actualization is the need to maximize one's potential, whatever it may be. A musician must play music, a poet must write, a general must win battles, a professor must teach. As Maslow expressed it, "What a man can be, he must be." Thus, self-actualization is the desire to become what one is capable of becoming. Individuals satisfy this need in different ways. In one person, it may be expressed in the desire to be an ideal mother; in another, it may be expressed in managing an organization; in another, it may be expressed athletically; in still another, by playing the piano.

Figure 2-14
Esteem Needs Dominant in the Need Structure

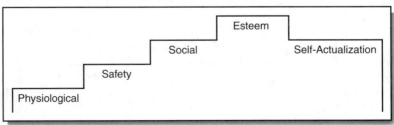

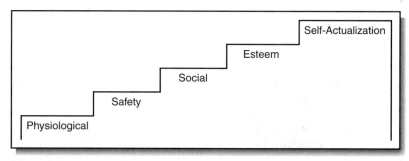

Figure 2-15
Self-Actualization Needs Dominant in the Need Structure

In combat, a soldier may rush a machine-gun nest in an attempt to destroy it, knowing full well that chances for survival are low. This courageous act is not done for affiliation or recognition, but rather for what the soldier thinks is important. In this case, you may consider the soldier to have self-actualized—to have maximized the potential of what is important at this time.

The way self-actualization is expressed can change over the life cycle. For example, a self-actualized athlete may eventually look for other areas in which to maximize potential as physical attributes change over time or as horizons broaden. In addition, the hierarchy does not necessarily follow the pattern described by Maslow. It was not his intent to say that this hierarchy applies universally. Maslow felt this was a typical pattern that operates most of the time. He realized, however, that there were numerous exceptions to this general tendency. For example, the Indian leader, Mahatma Gandhi, frequently sacrificed his physiological and safety needs for the satisfaction of other needs when India was striving for independence from Great Britain. In his historic fasts, Gandhi went weeks without nourishment to protest governmental injustices. He was operating at the self-actualization level while some of his other needs went unsatisfied.

In discussing the preponderance of one category of need over another, we have been careful to use such phrases as "if one level of needs has been somewhat gratified, then other needs emerge as dominant." We do not want to give the impression that one level of needs has to be completely satisfied before the next level emerges as the most important. In reality, most people in our society tend to be partially satisfied and partially unsatisfied at each level, with greater satisfaction tending to occur at the physiological and safety levels than at the social, esteem, and self-actualization levels. But even people in an emerging society, where much of the behavior engaged in tends to be directed toward satisfying physiological and safety needs, still operate to some extent at the other levels. Therefore, Maslow's hierarchy of needs is not intended to be an all-or-nothing framework, but rather one that may be useful in predicting behavior on the basis of a high or a low probability.

Figure 2-16 attempts to portray need structure in an emerging nation. In contrast, Figure 2-17 shows the need structure in a developed society. Many people in our society today might be characterized by very strong social or

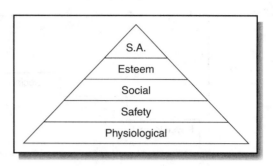

Figure 2-16
Need Structure
When Physiological
and Safety Are High-
Strength Needs

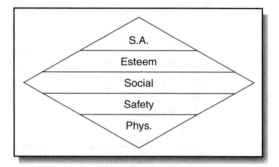

Figure 2-17
Need Structure
When Social Needs
Are High-Strength
and Self-
Actualization and
Physiological Needs
Are Much Less
Important

affiliation needs, relatively strong esteem and safety needs, with self-actualization and physiological needs much less important. Some people, however, can be characterized as having satisfied to a large extent the physiological, safety, and social needs, and their behavior tends to be dominated by esteem and self-actualizing activities, as shown in Figure 2-18. This structure will tend to become more characteristic if standards of living and levels of education continue to rise.

These are intended only as examples. For different individuals, varying configurations may be appropriate. In reality, they would fluctuate tremendously from one individual or group to another.

Clare W. Graves developed a theory that seems to be compatible with Maslow's hierarchy of needs. Graves contended that human beings exist at different "levels of existence." "At any given level, an individual exhibits the behavior and values characteristic of people at that level; a person who is cen-

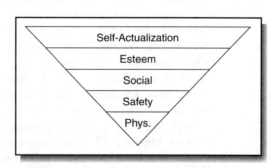

Figure 2-18
Need Structure
When Esteem and
Self-Sctualization
Needs Are High-
Strength Needs

tralized at a lower level cannot even understand people who are at a higher level." According to Graves, "Most people have been confined to lower [subsistence] levels of existence where they were motivated by needs shared with other animals. Now, Western man appears ready to move up to a higher level of existence, a distinctly human level. When this happens there will likely be a dramatic transformation of human institutions."[24]

ALDERFER'S ERG THEORY

A revised and realigned version of Maslow's hierarchy of needs, ERG theory, was developed by Clayton Alderfer of Yale University.[25] Alderfer suggested that there are three core needs: *Existence*, *Relatedness*, and *Growth*. Alderfer's existence grouping generally corresponds to Maslow's basic physiological and safety needs; relatedness corresponds to social needs; and growth corresponds to esteem and self-actualization. Table 2-1 illustrates these relationships.

What does Alderfer's ERG theory add to our understanding of needs? Stephen Robbins suggests it is a more valid description of the need hierarchy than is Maslow's theory for two principal reasons:

1. Maslow's step-by-step hierarchy assumes that only one of the five categories of needs will be predominant at a given time. ERG theory allows for more than one need—for example, safety and social—to be operating more or less equally at one time.
2. Maslow's theory asserted that a person will remain at a need level until it is adequately satisfied. ERG theory suggests that a person frustrated or blocked at a need level will regress to a lower level.[26]

Table 2-1 Comparison of Maslow's and Alderfer's Categories of Needs

MASLOW	ALDERFER
Self-Actualization/Esteem	Growth
Social	Relatedness
Safety/Physiological	Existence

MOTIVATIONAL RESEARCH

Having discussed Maslow's and Alderfer's hierarchies of needs, we can now examine what researchers say about some of our motives and the incentives that tend to satisfy them.

Physiological Needs

The satisfaction of physiological needs (shelter, food, clothing) is usually associated in our society with money. It is obvious that most people are not interested in dollars as such, but only as a means to be used to satisfy other motives. Thus, it is what money can buy, not money itself, that satisfies one's physiological needs. But to suggest that money is useful only in satisfying physiological needs would be shortsighted, because money can play a role in the satisfaction of needs at every level. Extensive studies of the impact of money have found that money is so complicated an incentive that it is entangled with all kinds of needs besides physiological ones, and its importance is difficult to ascertain. It is clear that the ability of a given amount of money to satisfy seems to diminish as one moves from physiological and safety needs to other needs on the hierarchy. In many cases, money can buy the satisfaction of physiological and safety needs and even social needs if, for example, it provides entry into a desired group, such as a country club. But as one becomes concerned about esteem, recognition, and eventually self-actualization, money becomes a less appropriate tool and is, therefore, less effective. The more individuals become involved with esteem and self-actualization needs, the more they will have to earn their satisfaction directly, and thus the less important money will be in satisfying their needs.

Safety Needs

We mentioned earlier that motives are not always apparent to the individual. Although some motives appear above the surface, many are largely subconscious and are not obvious or easy to identify. According to Saul W. Gellerman, safety, or security, needs appear in both forms.[27]

The conscious security needs are quite evident and very common among most people. We all have a desire to remain free from the hazards of life—accidents, wars, diseases, and economic instability. Therefore, individuals and organizations are interested in providing some assurance that those catastrophes will be avoided if possible. Gellerman suggested that many organizations tend to overemphasize the security motive by providing elaborate programs of fringe benefits, such as health, accident, and life insurance and retirement plans. Such emphasis on security may make people more docile and predictable, but it does not necessarily make them more productive. In fact, if creativity or initiative is necessary in their jobs, an overemphasis on security can thwart desired behavior.

Although concern for security can affect major decisions, such as remaining in or leaving an organization, Gellerman indicated it is not likely to be an individual's dominant motive. Conscious security needs usually play a background role, often inhibiting or restraining impulses rather than initiating outward behavior. For example, if a particular course of action, such as disregarding a rule or expressing an unpopular position, might endanger one's job, then security considerations motivate a person not to take that course of action. Organizations can influence security needs either positively—through pension plans, insurance programs, and the like—or negatively, by arousing fears of being fired or laid off, demoted, or passed over. In both cases, the effect can be to make behavior too cautious and conservative.

Peter F. Drucker suggested that one's attitude toward security is important to consider in choosing a job.[28] He raised some interesting questions: Do you belong in a job calling primarily for faithfulness in the performance of routine work and promising security? Do you find real satisfaction in the precision, order, and system of a clearly defined job? Do you prefer knowing what your work is today and what it is going to be tomorrow, that your job is secure, and what your relationship is to the people above, below, and next to you? Or do you belong in a job that is less predictable, that offers a challenge to imagination and ingenuity—with the attendant penalty for failure? Do you tend to grow impatient with anything that looks like a "routine" job? The answers to these questions are not always easy, even though we all understand ourselves to some degree. But the answers are involved with how important the security motive is for a particular individual.

A strong subconscious orientation toward security is often developed early in childhood. Gellerman discussed several ways in which it can be implanted. A common way is through identification with security-minded parents who are willing to accept whatever fate comes along. This mindset often develops in depressed economic areas where the prospects for improvement are poor.[29] The world seems uncertain and uncontrollable to people raised in a security-minded home. As a result, such people may not feel they are competent enough to be able to influence their environment.

The security-minded people we have been describing are often very likable and pleasant to have around. They are not competitive and, therefore, do not put people on the defensive. Others tend to expect little of them and thus are seldom critical of their work. Such people often are able to obtain a secure, nonthreatening position in an organization.

Subconscious security motives may also develop in children through interaction with overprotective parents. Such parents are constantly trying to shield their children from heartache, disappointment, or failure. The supportive attitude of these parents in many instances permits their children to have their own way. Conflict is avoided at all costs. As a result, these children are given a distorted picture of reality and gain little insight into what they can expect of other people and what others will expect of them. In some cases, they become unrealistic in their optimism about life; that is, they have a false sense of security. Even in the face of disaster, when they should feel threatened, they seem to believe that all is well until it is too late.

When such people leave home after high school to seek their way in the world, they quickly wake up to reality. Often they find themselves ill-equipped to handle the hardships of life because they have not been permitted the opportunity to develop the capacity to handle frustration, tension, and anxiety. As a result, even a minor setback may throw them for a loop. Drucker suggested that getting fired from their first job might be the best thing that could happen to such young people, that, perhaps, getting fired from the first job is the least painful and least damaging way to learn how to take a setback, and that is a lesson well worth learning. If people learn how to recover from seeming disaster when they are young, they will be better equipped to handle worse problems as they get older.

Many people regard the need for security as a weakness or fault. A strong security need is frowned upon, for some reason, as if it were less respectable than other motives. This attitude seems unjust, especially because nearly everyone has some conscious and subconscious security motives. Life is never so simple or clear-cut that one does not maintain some concern for security. In addition, many segments of our society often cater to these needs to the exclusion of such important needs as affiliation and self-actualization. We have already mentioned how industry concentrates on security needs by providing elaborate fringe benefits. Unions have a similar effect with their emphasis on seniority, and the government does much the same thing with welfare and other similar support programs.

Social Needs

After the physiological and safety needs have become somewhat satisfied, the social, or affiliation, needs may become predominant. Because people are social animals, most individuals like to interact and be with others in situations where they feel they belong and are accepted. Although this is a common need, it tends to be stronger for some people than for others and stronger in certain situations than in others. Even such a commonplace social need as belongingness is, upon examination, quite complex.

In working toward a better understanding of our need to belong, Stanley Schachter of the University of Minnesota made a significant contribution.[30] His efforts were directed, in particular, toward studying the desire to socialize as an end in itself—that is, when people interact simply because they enjoy it. In some of these situations, no apparent reward such as money or protection was gained from this affiliation.

Schachter found that it is not always simply good fellowship that motivates affiliation. In many instances, people seek affiliation because they desire to have their beliefs confirmed. People who have similar beliefs tend to seek each other out, especially if a strongly held belief has been shattered. In this case, they tend to assemble and try to reach some common understanding about what happened and what they should believe (even if it is the same as before). In this instance, the need for affiliation is prompted by a desire to make one's life seem a little more under control. When a person is alone, the world may seem "out of whack," but finding an environment in which others hold the same beliefs somehow makes order out of chaos. This attitude hints at some of the problems inherent in any change.

In pursuing this question further, Schachter found that when people are excited, confused, or unhappy, they do not seek out just anyone—they tend to want to be with others "in the same boat."

Misery does not love just any company; it loves other miserable company. These conclusions suggest that the strong informal work groups that Elton Mayo found developing in the factory system might have been a reaction to the boredom, insignificance, and lack of competence that the workers felt.[31]

As a result, workers congregated because of mutual feelings of being beaten by the system.

Observations of loners and rate-busters (people who exceed group-defined production goals) in similar factory situations made it apparent that there is not some universal need for affiliation as an end in itself. But these exceptions to the affiliation tendency were special types of people. They tended not to join informal work groups because they felt either suspicious or contemptuous of them or else secure and competent enough to fend for themselves.

Management is often suspicious of informal groups that develop at work because of the potential power these groups have to lower productivity. Schachter found that such work-restricting groups were sometimes formed as a reaction to the insignificance and impotence that workers tend to feel when they have no control over their working environment. Such environments develop when the work is routine, tedious, and oversimplified. This situation is made worse when, at the same time, the workers are closely supervised and controlled but have no clear channels of communication with management.

In this type of environment, workers who cannot tolerate this lack of control over their environment depend on the informal group for support of unfulfilled needs such as affiliation or achievement. Work restriction follows not from an inherent dislike for management but as a means to preserve the identification of individuals within the group and the group itself. Rate-busters are not tolerated because they weaken the group and its power with management, and to weaken the group destroys the only dignity, security, and significance the workers feel they have.

Lowering productivity is not always the result of informal work groups. In fact, informal groups can be a tremendous asset to management if their internal organization is understood and fully utilized. The productivity of a work group seems to depend on how the group members see their own goals in relation to the goals of the organization. For example, if they perceive their own goals as being in conflict with the goals of the organization, then productivity will tend to be low. However, if these workers see their own goals as being the same as the goals of the organization or as being satisfied as a direct result of accomplishing organizational goals, then productivity will tend to be high. Work restriction is therefore not a necessary aspect of informal work groups.

Esteem Needs

The need for esteem or recognition appears in a number of forms. In this section we shall discuss two motives related to esteem—prestige and power.

Prestige

The prestige motive is evident in our society today. People with a concern for prestige want to "keep up with the Joneses"; in fact, given the choice, they would like to stay ahead of the Joneses. Vance Packard and David Riesman probably had the greatest impact in exposing prestige motivation.[32] Packard wrote about the status seekers and their motives; Riesman unveiled "other-directed" individuals who were part of "the lonely crowd."

What exactly is prestige? Gellerman described it as "a sort of unwritten definition of the kinds of conduct that other people are expected to show in one's presence; what degree of respect or disrespect, formality or informality, reserve or frankness."[33] Prestige seems to have an effect on how comfortably or conveniently one can expect to get along in life.

Prestige is something intangible bestowed upon an individual by society. In fact, at birth children inherit the status of their parents. In some cases, this is enough to carry them through life on "a prestige-covered wave."

People seek prestige throughout their lives in various ways. Many tend to seek only the material symbols of status, while others strive for personal achievement or self-actualization, which might command prestige in itself. Regardless of the way it is expressed, there seems to be a widespread need for people to have their importance clarified and, in fact, set at a level that each feels is deserved. As discussed earlier, people normally want to have a high evaluation of themselves that is firmly based in reality as manifested by the recognition and respect accorded them by others.

Power

The resource that enables a person to induce compliance from others or to influence them is power. It is a person's influence potential. There tend to be two kinds of power—position and personal. Individuals who are able to induce compliance from others because of their position in the organization have position power; individuals who derive their influence from their personality and behavior have personal power. Some people are endowed with both position and personal power. Others seem to have no power at all.

Alfred Adler, a one-time colleague of Freud, became very interested in the power motive.[34] By power, Adler essentially meant the ability to manipulate or control the activities of others to suit one's own purposes. He found that this ability starts in infancy when babies realize that if they cry they influence their parents' behavior. Children's position as babies gives them considerable power over their parents.

According to Adler, this manipulative ability is inherently pleasurable. Children, for example, often have a hard time adjusting to the continuing reduction in their position power. In fact, they might spend a significant amount of time as adults trying to recapture the power they had as children. Adler did not feel, however, that children seek power for its own sake as often as they do out of necessity. Power, for children, is often a life-and-death matter because they are helpless and need to count on their parents' availability. Parents are a child's lifeline. Thus, power acquires an importance to children that they somehow never lose, even though they are later able to fend for themselves.

After childhood, the power motive again becomes very potent in individuals who feel somehow inadequate in winning the respect and recognition of others. These people go out of their way to seek attention to overcome

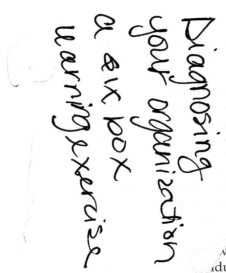
Diagnosing your organization a six box learning exercise

s often felt but not recognized. In this connection, Adler
ting and now well-known concepts in his discussion—
d compensation.

nferiority complex has underlying fears of inadequacy,
have some basis in reality. In some cases, individuals
eriority complex by exerting extreme efforts to achieve
(they feel) inadequacy would deny. In many cases, ex-
e an overcompensation for something not clearly per-
Once accurately perceived, the frame of reference can
ty and can result in more realistic behavior.

er interesting thing. If children do not encounter too
mature, their need for power gradually transforms it-
fect their social relationships. They want to be able to
without fear or suspicion in an open and trusting atmo-
iduals often move from the task aspect of power, wanting
to structure and manipulate their environment and the people in it, to a concern for relationships, developing trust and respect for others. This transformation is often delayed with individuals who have had tension-filled
childhoods and have not learned to trust. In these cases, the power motive
would not only persist but might even become stronger. Thus, Adler, like
Freud, felt that the personality of an individual is developed early in life and
is often a result of the kind of experiences the child had with adults. We will
discuss power in much greater detail in chapter 9.

Self-Actualization Needs

Of all the needs discussed by Maslow, the one that social and behavioral scientists know least about is self-actualization. Perhaps because people satisfy
this need in different ways, self-actualization is a difficult need to pin down
and identify. Although little research has been done on the concept of self-
actualization, extensive research has been done on two motives that we feel
are related to it—competence and achievement.

Competence

According to Robert W. White, one of the mainsprings of action in a human
being is a desire for competence.[35] Competence implies control over environmental factors—both physical and social. People with this motive do not wish
to wait passively for things to happen; they want to be able to manipulate
their environment and make things happen.

The competence motive can be identified in young children as they move
from the early stage of wanting to touch and handle everything in reach to
the later stage of wanting not only to touch but to take things apart and put
them back together again. Children begin to learn their way around their
world. They become aware of what they can and cannot do, not in terms of
what they are allowed to do but in terms of what they are able to do. During
these early years, children develop a feeling of competence.

This feeling of competence is closely related to the concept of expectancy discussed earlier. Whether children have a strong or weak sense of competence depends on their successes and failures in the past. If their successes overshadow their failures, then their feeling of competence will tend to be high. They will have a positive outlook toward life, seeing almost every new situation as an interesting challenge that they can overcome. If, however, their failures carry the day, their outlook will be more negative, and their expectancy for satisfying various needs may become low. Because expectancy tends to influence motives, people with low feelings of competence will not often be motivated to seek new challenges or take risks. These people would rather let their environment control them than attempt to change it.

According to White, the competence motive reveals itself in adults as a desire for job mastery and professional growth. The job is one arena in which people can match their ability and skills against their environment in a contest that is challenging, but not overwhelming. In jobs where such a contest is possible, the competence motive in an individual can be expressed freely, and significant personal rewards can be gained. But in routine, closely supervised jobs, this contest is often impossible. Such situations make the worker dependent on the system and, therefore, completely frustrate people with high competence needs.

Achievement

Over the years, behavioral scientists have observed that some people have an intense need to achieve; others, perhaps the majority, do not seem to be as concerned about achievement. This phenomenon has fascinated David C. McClelland. For more than 40 years, he and his associates at Harvard University have been studying this urge to achieve.[36]

McClelland's research led him to believe that the need for achievement is a distinct human motive that can be distinguished from other needs. More important, he believes that the achievement motive can be isolated and assessed in any group.

McClelland illustrated some of these characteristics of people with a high need for achievement in describing a laboratory experiment. Participants were asked to throw rings over a peg from any distance they chose. Most people tended to throw at random—now close, now far away; but individuals with a high need for achievement seemed to measure carefully where they were most likely to get a sense of mastery—not too close to make the task ridiculously easy or too far away to make it impossible. They set moderately difficult, but potentially achievable goals. In biology, this approach is known as the overload principle. In weight lifting, for example, strength cannot be increased by tasks that can be performed easily or that will injure the organism. Strength can be increased by lifting weights that are difficult enough to stretch the muscles but not enough to cause injury.

The high need for achievement surfaces only when people believe they can influence the outcome. Achievement-motivated people are not gamblers. They prefer to work on a problem rather than leave the outcome to chance.

In the case of managers, setting moderately difficult but potentially achievable goals may be translated into an attitude toward risks. Many people tend to be extreme in their attitude toward risks, either favoring wild speculative gambling or minimizing their exposure to losses. Gamblers seem to choose the big risk because the outcome is beyond their power and, therefore, they can easily rationalize away their personal responsibility if they lose. The conservative individual chooses tiny risks where the gain is small but secure, perhaps because there is little danger of anything going wrong for which that person might be blamed. Achievement-motivated people take the middle ground, preferring a moderate degree of risk because they feel their efforts and abilities will probably influence the outcome. In business, this aggressive realism is the mark of the successful entrepreneur.

Another characteristic of achievement-motivated people is that they seem to be more concerned with personal achievement than with the rewards of success. They do not reject rewards, but the rewards are not as essential as the accomplishment itself. They get a bigger kick out of winning or solving a difficult problem than they get from any money or praise they receive. Money, to achievement-motivated people, is valuable primarily as a measurement of their performance. It provides them with a means of assessing their progress and comparing their achievements with those of other people. They normally do not seek money for status or economic security.

A desire by people with a high need for achievement to seek situations in which they get concrete feedback on how well they are doing is closely related to this concern for personal accomplishment. Consequently, achievement-motivated people are often found in sales jobs or as owners and managers of their own businesses. In addition to concrete feedback, the nature of the feedback is important to achievement-motivated people. They respond favorably to information about their work. They are not interested in comments about their personal characteristics, such as how cooperative or helpful they are. Affiliation-motivated people might want social or attitudinal feedback. Achievement-motivated people might want task-relevant feedback.

Achievement-motivated people behave as they do, according to McClelland, because they habitually spend time thinking about doing things better. In fact, he has found that whenever people start to think in achievement terms, things start to happen. College students with a high need for achievement will generally get better grades than equally bright students with weaker achievement needs. Achievement-motivated people tend to get more raises and are promoted faster because they are constantly trying to think of better ways of doing things. Companies with many such people grow faster and are more profitable.

Neal Gilbert and Charles Whiting warn that if professionals, for example, are not afforded the opportunity to self-actualize (increase their competence and achievement) in their organization, "their only recourse [will be] to leave the organization."[37] Employees who are not empowered will look elsewhere to empower themselves, perhaps placing their considerable talent in the hands of a competitor. This is a formidable threat in knowledge-based organizations where the departure of two or three key individuals may mean the death knell of the company.

McClelland even extended his analysis to countries; he found that the presence of a large percentage of achievement-motivated individuals is related to the national economic growth. Achievement-motivated people are most likely to be developed in families in which parents expect their children to start showing some independence between the ages of 6 and 8, making choices and doing things without help, such as knowing the way around the neighborhood and taking care of themselves around the house. Other parents tend either to expect this independence too early, before children are ready, or never to expect it, thereby smothering the development of the personality of their children. One extreme seems to foster passive, defeatist attitudes as children feel unwanted at home and incompetent away from home. They are just not ready for that kind of independence so early. The other extreme yields either overprotected or overdisciplined children. These children become very dependent on their parents and find it difficult to break away and make their own decisions.

Given all we know about the need for achievement, can this motive be taught and developed in people? McClelland is convinced that it can. In fact, he has developed training programs for businesspeople that are designed to increase their achievement motivation. He is also in the process of developing similar programs for other segments of the population.

Achievement-motivated people can be the backbone of most organizations, but what can we say about their potential as managers? As we know, people with a high need for achievement get ahead because as individuals they are producers—they get things done. But when they are promoted—when their success depends not only on their own work but on the activities of others—they may be less effective. Because they are highly task oriented and work to their capacity, they tend to expect others to do the same. As a result, they sometimes lack the human skills and patience necessary for effectively managing people who are competent but have a higher need for affiliation than they do. In this situation, their overemphasis on producing frustrates these people and prevents them from maximizing their own potential. Thus, although achievement-motivated people are needed in organizations, they do not always make the best managers unless they develop their human skills. As was pointed out in chapter 1, being a good producer is not sufficient to make an effective manager.

Money Motive

As stated earlier, money is a very complicated motive that is entangled in such a way with all kinds of needs besides physiological needs that its importance is often difficult to ascertain. For example, in some cases, money can provide individuals with certain material things, such as fancy sports cars, from which they gain a feeling of affiliation (join a sports car club), recognition (status symbol), and even self-actualization (become outstanding sports car drivers). Consequently, we delayed our discussion of the money motive until other basic concepts were clarified.

From extensive research on incentive pay schemes, William F. Whyte found that money, the old reliable motivational tool, is not as almighty as it is supposed to be, particularly for production workers.[38] For each of these workers, another key factor, as Mayo discovered, is their work group. Using the ratio of high-producing rate-busters to low-producing restrictors as an index, Whyte estimated that only about 10 percent of the production workers in the United States ignore group pressure and produce as much as possible in response to an incentive plan. It seems that, even though workers are interested in advancing their own financial position, there are many other considerations—such as the opinions of their fellow workers, their comfort and enjoyment on the job, and their long-range security—that prevent them from making a direct, automatic, positive response to an incentive plan.

According to Gellerman, the most subtle and most important characteristic of money is its power as a symbol. Its most obvious symbolic power is its market value. It is what money can buy, not money itself, that gives it value. But money's symbolic power is not limited to its market value. Because money has no intrinsic meaning of its own, it can symbolize almost any need an individual wants it to represent. In other words, money can mean whatever people want it to mean.[39]

Stephen Bushardt, Robert Toso, and M. E. Schnake suggested that: "While money is one of the most powerful motivational tools, its use must be tailored to each employee's values."[40] One approach to this "tailoring" is through the use of expectancy theory discussed earlier in this chapter. These authors suggest that for money to motivate, three considerations must be met. One, the employee must have a high "net" preference for money. This concept of "net" is important because frequently long hours are part of higher pay. The positive motivating effects of more pay must be greater than the negative effects of undesirable hours. Second, there needs to be a direct relationship between money and performance that the employee can perceive. If performance increases, then pay should increase and vice versa. Third, there needs to be a direct relationship between effort and performance. If effort increases, performance should increase.

There are many problems with implementing such a system, including the difficulties of assessing employee perceptions, measuring performance, establishing a pay system tied to performance, and so forth. Both the costs and the benefits in this approach need to be determined, but overall it has a sound motivational base.

Some Recent Thoughts about Money

Today's financial burdens are causing a dramatic change in people's attitudes toward work as compared to 1960 when Herzberg did his research. In a study by William M. Mercer Inc. and Yankelvich Partners Inc. of "Why I Do This Job," financial reasons are the single most important reason (40%) of why people work.[41] The remaining 60% is composed of other reasons: coworkers (15%), job satisfaction (15%), benefits (13%), and other (17%). One might argue successfully that benefits such as health care and retirement should be included in financial reasons. If this argument is followed, then financial reasons are increased (53%).

Another factor is the growth of incentive programs, such as gainsharing, that tie productivity improvements to pay. The number of employees in pay-for-performance programs doubled from 1990 to 1995.[42] Employees are also becoming more aware of their company's performance through management's sharing of financial data, their investments in employee stock ownership plans (ESOPs) and pension funds, and the growth of company stock purchase plans.

There is another aspect to "regular" pay and incentive pay. We have observed that employees may look at their regular check as "show-up" pay, while bonus or incentive pay is "real money." Why? One explanation is that our usual living expenses are related to our normal paycheck. Any extra money has not been allocated, so it is available to be spent on nice-to-have desires. There is a motivational message here. If you want to increase money's power as a motivator, implement an incentive plan. The extra money will be a powerful motivator because it will be spent on high-value "extra" items.[43]

What Do Workers Want from Their Jobs?

It is important to remember that people have many needs, all of which are continually competing for their behavior. No one person has exactly the same mixture or strength of needs as another. There are some people who are driven mainly by money, others who are concerned primarily with security, and so on. Although we must recognize individual differences, this does not mean that, as managers, we cannot make some predictions about which motives seem to be currently more prominent among our employees than others. According to Maslow, these are prepotent motives—those that are still not satisfied. An important question for managers to ask is: What do workers really want from their jobs? The answer, as we will see in the following paragraphs, will vary. First, let's go back to research reported in 1949.

What Do Workers Want?—1949

For decades, research has been conducted among employees in U.S. industry in an attempt to answer the question, What do workers want? In one such study, supervisors were asked to try to put themselves in a worker's shoes by ranking in order of importance a series of items that workers may want from their jobs.[44] It was emphasized that in ranking the items the supervisors should not think in terms of what they want but what they think a worker wants. In addition to the supervisors, the workers themselves were asked to rank these same items in terms of what they wanted most from their jobs. The results are given in Table 2-2.

As is evident from the results, the supervisors in this study generally ranked good wages, job security, promotion, and good working conditions as the things workers want most from their jobs. On the other hand, workers felt that what they wanted most was full appreciation for work done, feeling "in"

Table 2-2 What Do Workers Want from Their Jobs?

	SUPERVISORS	WORKERS
Good working conditions	4	9
Feeling "in" on things	10	2
Tactful disciplining	7	10
Full appreciation for work done	8	1
Management loyalty to workers	6	8
Good wages	1	5
Promotion and growth with company	3	7
Sympathetic understanding of personal problems	9	3
Job security	2	4
Interesting work	5	6

Note: 1 = most important; 10 = least important.

on things, and sympathetic understanding of personal problems—all incentives that seem to be related to affiliation and recognition motives. Only job security was among the top four concerns of both workers and supervisors, but the former ranked it fourth, whereas the latter ranked it second. The other top three things that workers indicated they wanted most from their jobs were rated by their supervisors as least important. This study suggested very little sensitivity by supervisors as to what things were really most important to workers. Supervisors seemed to think that incentives directed at satisfying physiological and safety motives were most important to their workers. These supervisors, undoubtedly, acted as if these were their workers' true motives. Therefore, they probably used the old reliable incentives—money, fringe benefits, and security—to motivate workers.

We have replicated this study periodically over the last several decades as part of management training programs and have found similar results in the perceptions of managers. The only real changes seem to be that workers, until the late 1980s, were increasing in their desire for "promotion and growth with the company" and "interesting work." With the economic decline of the 1980s and early 1990s, "good wages" and "job security" once again became high-strength needs for workers. It is important that managers know the tremendous discrepancies that seemed to exist in the past between what they thought workers wanted from their jobs and what workers said they actually wanted. It is also important that they realize what effect an economic or other change has on these priorities.

What Do Workers Want?—Other Findings

Studies are continuing on the important question of worker values. Table 2-3, which summarizes a variety of studies, reinforces the need for managers to assess the needs of their employees and to be sensitive to those needs.

Table 2-3   What Do Workers Want from Their Jobs?—Recent Findings

Job Reward	Supervisors[a]	Truckers[b]	Social Workers[c]	Doctors[d]	Nurses[e]
Advancement	3	5			
Autonomy			1	1	
Caring boss					3
Company philosophy	1			5	
Fringe benefits	5				6
Improved communication with boss					2
Job status				2	
Monetary compensation	2	1	3	3	1
More responsibility	4				
Nonisolation		2			
Teamwork with coworkers	6				
Work recognition					4
Work schedule		3	2		
Working conditions		4		4	5

[a]John S. McClenahen, "It's No Fun Working Here Anymore," *Industry Week,* 240 (1991), pp. 20–22.
[b]John D. Schultz, "Truckers Look to Returning Troops as Partial Solution to Driver Crises," *Traffic World,* 225 (1991), pp. 24–26.
[c]Beverly B. Butler, "Job Satisfaction: Management's Continuing Challenges," *Social Work,* 35 (1990), pp. 112–116.
[d]Suzanne B. Cashman, CindyLou Parks, Arlene Ash, David Hemingway, and William J. Bicknell, "Physician Satisfaction in a Major Chain of Investor Owned Walk-in Centers," *Health Care Management Review,* 15 (1990), pp. 47–57.
[e]Barbara B. Gray, "Are California Nurses Happy?" *California Nursing,* 13 (1991), pp. 12–17.
Note: 1 = most important; 6 = least important.

SUMMARY

People have many needs, all of which are continually competing. No one person has exactly the same mixture or strength of these needs as another. Some people are driven mainly by achievement, others are concerned primarily with security, and so on. Although we must recognize individual differences, we, as managers, cannot presume to decide which motives are most important to our employees. If we are to understand, predict, and control behavior, we must know what our employees really want from their jobs. It may be interesting to learn what employees in other organizations want from their jobs, but our primary concern should be to learn what our own workers want.

Managers have to know their people to understand what motivates them; they cannot just make assumptions. Even asking employees how they feel about something does not necessarily result in accurate needs assessment because individuals (both managers and employees) will act on the basis of their perceptions or interpretation of reality and not on the basis of reality itself. In fact, one of the reasons that we study the behavioral sciences is that they give us ways to get our perceptions closer and closer to reality. The closer we get our perceptions to a given reality, the higher the probability that we can have some impact on that particular piece of reality. Therefore, by bringing their perceptions closer and closer to reality—what their people really want—managers often can increase their effectiveness. As we continue our study and practice of the behavioral sciences in the following chapters, our ability to understand, predict, and control people, individually and in groups, will develop.

ENDNOTES

1. Kurt Lewin, "Behavior and Development as a Function of the Total Situation (1946)," pp. 239–240 in *Field Theory in Social Science,* Dorwin Cartwright (New York: Harper & Brothers, 1951). See also Gregory B. Northcraft and Margaret A. Neale, *Organizational Behavior: A Management Challenge,* 2nd ed. (Fort Worth: Dryden Press, 1994), p. 66.

2. Lewin used the expression E = Environment, whereas we have used S = Situation in keeping with the context of this book.

3. Lewin, "Behavior and Development as a Function of the Total Situation, (1946)," p. 239.

4. Sigmund Freud, *The Ego and the Id* (London: Hogarth Press, 1927). See also *New Introductory Lectures on Psychoanalysis* (New York: Norton, 1933).

5. Norman R. F. Maier, *Psychology in Industry,* 2nd ed. (Boston: Houghton Mifflin, 1955), p. 21.

6. Viktor E. Frankl, *Man's Search for Meaning* (New York: Washington Square Press, 1963), p. 154. See also Jerry L. Fletcher, *Patterns of High Performance: Discovering the Way People Work Best* (San Francisco: Berret-Koehler, 1993).

7. Tom Peters and Robert H. Watermann Jr., *In Search of Excellence: Lessons from America's Best Run Companies* (New York: Harper & Row, 1982), pp. 76, 80, 86.

8. Abraham H. Maslow, *Motivation and Personality* (New York: Harper & Row, 1954). See also Maslow, *Motivation and Personality,* 2nd ed. (New York: Harper & Row, 1970).

9. Leon Festinger, *A Theory of Cognitive Dissonance* (Stanford, CA: Stanford University Press, 1957); Stephen Kaplan, *Cognition and Environment: Functioning in an Uncertain World* (New York: Praeger, 1982).

10. Festinger, *A Theory of Cognitive Dissonance,* p. 155.

11. Freud, *The Ego and the Id.*

12. Maier, *Psychology in Industry,* pp. 83–91.

13. John A. C. Brown, *The Social Psychology of Industry* (Baltimore: Penguin Books, 1954), p. 252.

14. Roger Barker, Tamara Dembo, and Kurt Lewin, *Frustration and Aggression* (Iowa City: University of Iowa Press, 1942).

15. Brown, *The Social Psychology of Industry,* p. 253.

16. Maier, *Psychology in Industry,* pp. 88–90.

17. Brown, *The Social Psychology of Industry,* p. 254.

18. Dewey E. Johnson, *Concepts of Air Force Leadership* (Washington, D.C.: Air Force ROTC, 1970), p. 209.

19. J. Sterling-Livingston, "Pygmalion in Management," *Harvard Business Review,* September/October, 1988, pp. 81–89.

20. See John W. Atkinson, "Motivational Determinants of Risk-Taking Behavior," *Psychological Review,* 64, no. 6 (1957), p. 365.

21. Victor H. Vroom, "Leader." Pages 1527–1551 in *Handbook of Industrial and Organizational Psychology,* ed. Marvin D. Dunnette (Chicago: Rand McNally, 1976).

22. Martin L. Maehr and Larry A. Braskampt, *The Motivation Factor: A Theory of Personal Investment* (Lexington, MA: D. C. Heath, 1986).

23. Maslow, *Motivation and Personality.*

24. Clare W. Graves, "Human Nature Prepares for a Momentous Leap," *The Futurist,* April 1974, pp. 72–87.

25. Clayton Alderfer, "An Empirical Test of a New Theory of Human Needs," *Organizational Behavior and Human Performance*, May 1969, pp. 142–175.

26. Stephen P. Robbins, *Organizational Behavior*, 6th ed. (Englewood Cliffs, NJ, 1993), pp. 211–222.

27. Saul W. Gellerman, *Motivation and Productivity* (New York: American Management Association, 1963).

28. Peter F. Drucker, "How to Be an Employee," *Psychology Today*, March 1968, a reprint from *Fortune* magazine.

29. Gellerman, *Motivation and Productivity*, pp. 154–55.

30. Stanley Schachter, *The Psychology of Affiliation* (Stanford, CA: Stanford University Press, 1959).

31. Elton Mayo, *The Social Problems of an Industrial Civilization* (Boston: Harvard Business School, 1945); see also Mayo, *The Human Problems of an Industrial Civilization* (New York: Macmillan, 1933).

32. Vance Packard, *The Status Seekers* (New York: David McKay, 1959).

33. Gellerman, *Motivation and Productivity*, p. 151.

34. Alfred Adler, *Social Interest* (London: Faber & Faber, 1938).

35. Robert W. White, "Motivation Reconsidered: The Concept of Competence," *Psychological Review*, no. 5 (1959).

36. David C. McClelland, John W. Atkinson, R. A. Clark, and E. L. Lowell, *The Achievement Motive* (New York: Appleton-Century-Crofts, 1953); and McClelland, *The Achieving Society* (Princeton, NJ: D. Van Nostrand, 1961); John William Atkinson, *Motivation and Achievement* (New York: Halsted Press, 1974). See also Craig Pinder, "Concerning the Application of Human Motivation Theories in Organizational Settings," *Academy of Management Review*, 21 (1977), pp. 384–397.

37. Charles E. Whiting and E. Neal Gilbert, "Empowering Professionals," *Management Review*, June, 1993. See also David McClelland and David H. Burnham, "Power Is the Great Motivator," *Harvard Business Review*, 73, January/February 1995, pp. 126–130.

38. William F. Whyte, ed., *Money and Motivation* (New York: Harper & Row, 1955).

39. Gellerman, *Motivation and Productivity*, pp. 160–169.

40. Stephen C. Bushardt, Roberto Toso, and M. E. Schnake, "Can Money Motivate?" Pages 50–53 in *Motivation of Personnel*, ed. Timpe A. Dale (New York: KEND Publishing, 1986). See also Oren Harari, "The Missing Link in Performance," *Management Review*, 84 (March 1995), pp. 21–24.

41. "Why I Do This Job," *Business Week*, September 11, 1995, p. 8. See also Charles A. O'Reilly III and Jennifer A. Chatman, "Working Smarter and Harder: A Longitudinal Study of Managerial Success," *Administrative Science Quarterly*, 39 (December 1994), pp. 603–627.

42. M. Michael Markowich, "Does Money Motivate?" *Compensation and Benefits Review*, January–February, 1994.

43. *Ibid.* See also Connie Wallace, "The Fine Art of Using Money as a Motivator," *Working Woman*, January, 1990, pp. 126–128 and James E. Long, "The Effects of Tastes and Motivation on Individual Income," *Industrial and Labor Relations Review*, 48 (January 1995), pp. 338–351.

44. Lawrence Lindahl, "What Makes a Good Job?" *Personnel*, 25 (January 1949).

Chapter 3

Motivating

Behavioral science pioneers such as Elton Mayo (of the Harvard Graduate School of Business Administration), Douglas McGregor, Chris Argyris, George Homans, Frederick Herzberg, and Abraham Maslow have made such important contributions that their work continues to shape our understanding of human behavior. It is for this reason that we have included these important researchers in our discussion of what motivates people. ✧

THE HAWTHORNE STUDIES

Elton Mayo

In 1924, efficiency experts at the Hawthorne, Illinois, plant of the Western Electric Company designed a research program to study the effects of illumination on productivity. In the initial phases of the study, efficiency experts assumed that more light would result in higher output. Two groups of employees were selected: an experimental, or test, group that worked under varying degrees of light and a control group that worked under normal illumination conditions in the plant. As lighting power was increased, the output of the test group went up as anticipated. Unexpectedly, however, the output of the control group went up also—without any increase in light. When illumination was decreased to the level of moonlight with one test group, output increased even further. The illumination test ended in April 1927, when the researchers concluded that something other than illumination was affecting productivity.[1]

Determined to explain these and other surprising test results, the efficiency experts decided to expand their research at

Hawthorne. They felt that, in addition to technical and physical changes, some of the behavioral considerations should be explored.

The next phase of experiments started later in 1927 with a group of women who assembled telephone relays. For more than 1½ years during this experiment, the researchers improved the working conditions of the women by implementing such innovations as scheduled rest periods, company lunches, and shorter workweeks. Work output increased. Baffled by the result, the researchers then decided to take everything away from the women, returning the working conditions to the exact way they had been at the beginning of the experiment. This radical change was expected to have a negative psychological impact on the women and to reduce their output. Instead, their output increased to a new all-time high. Why?

The answers were found not in the production aspects of the experiment (changes in plant and physical working conditions) but in the human aspects. Because of the attention given them by experimenters, the women felt that they were an important part of the company. They no longer viewed themselves as isolated individuals, working together only in the sense that they were physically close to each other. Instead, they had become participating members of a congenial, cohesive work group. The relationships that developed elicited feelings of affiliation, competence, and achievement. These needs, which had long gone unsatisfied at the workplace, were now being fulfilled. The women worked harder and more effectively than previously. Pay was also an important factor. The women, paid on a piecework basis, were able to keep the pay benefits of increased productivity.

Elton Mayo, first for 2 days in 1928, then for 4 days in 1929, identified an interesting phenomenon. With guidance from Mayo, the researchers extended their research by interviewing more than 20,000 employees from every department in the company. Interviews were designed to help researchers find out what the workers thought about their jobs, their working conditions, their supervisors, their company, and anything that bothered them, and how those feelings might be related to their productivity. After several interview sessions, the researchers found that a structured question-and-answer-type interview was useless for eliciting the information they wanted. Instead, the workers wanted to talk freely about what they thought was important. So the predetermined questions were discarded, and the interviewer allowed the workers to say what they wanted to say.

The interviews proved valuable in a number of ways. First, they were therapeutic; the workers got an opportunity to express themselves. Many felt this was the best thing the company had ever done. The result was a wholesale change in attitude. Because many of their suggestions were being implemented, the workers began to feel that management viewed them as important, both as individuals and as a group; they were now participating in the operation and future of the company and not just performing unchallenging, unappreciated tasks.

Second, the implications of the Hawthorne studies signaled the need for management to study and understand relationships among people. In these studies, as well as in the many that followed, the most significant factor affecting organizational productivity was found to be the interpersonal relationships that are developed on the job, not just pay and working conditions. The researchers found that when informal groups identified with management, as they did at Hawthorne through the interview program, productivity rose. The increased productivity seemed to reflect the workers' feelings of competence—a sense of mastery over the job and work environment. The researchers also discovered that when the group felt that their own goals were in opposition to those of management, as often happened in situations where workers were closely supervised and had no significant control over the job or environment, productivity remained at low levels or was even lowered.

These findings were important because they helped answer many of the questions that had puzzled management about why some groups seemed to be high producers while others hovered at a minimal level of output. The findings also encouraged management to involve workers in planning, organizing, and controlling their own work in an effort to secure their positive cooperation.

Mayo saw the development of informal groups as an indictment of a society that treated human beings as insensitive machines who were concerned only with economic self-interest. As a result, workers had been expected to look at work merely as an impersonal exchange of money for labor. Work in American industry, according to Mayo, meant humiliation—the performance of routine, tedious, and oversimplified tasks in an environment over which one had no control. This environment denied satisfaction of esteem and self-actualization needs on the job. Instead, only physiological and safety needs were satisfied. The lack of avenues for satisfying other needs led to tension, anxiety, and frustration. Mayo called such feelings of helplessness *anomie*. This condition was characterized by workers' feeling unimportant, confused, and unattached—victims of their own environment.

Although anomie was a creation of the total society, Mayo felt its application was found in industrial settings where management held certain negative assumptions about the nature of people. According to Mayo, too many managers assumed that society consisted of a horde of unorganized individuals whose only concern was self-preservation or self-interest. It was assumed that people were primarily dominated by physiological and safety needs, wanting to make as much money as they could for as little work as possible. Thus, management organized work on the basic assumption that workers, on the whole, were a contemptible lot. Mayo called this assumption the *Rabble Hypothesis*. He deplored the authoritarian, task-oriented management practices that it created.

THEORY X AND THEORY Y

Douglas McGregor

The work of Mayo and particularly his idea of the Rabble Hypothesis may have paved the way for the development of the now classic Theory X–Theory Y by Douglas McGregor.[2] According to McGregor, the traditional organization—with its centralized decision making, hierarchical pyramid, and external control of work—is based on certain assumptions about human nature and human motivation (see Theory X, Table 3-1). These assumptions, which McGregor called *Theory X*, are very similar to the view of people defined by Mayo in the Rabble Hypothesis. Theory X assumes that most people prefer to be directed, are not interested in assuming responsibility, and want safety above all. Accompanying this philosophy is the belief that money, fringe benefits, and the threat of punishment motivate people.

Managers who accept Theory X assumptions attempt to structure, control, and closely supervise their employees. These managers feel that external control is clearly appropriate for dealing with unreliable and irresponsible people.

After describing Theory X, McGregor questioned whether this view of human nature is correct and if management practices based on it are appropriate in many situations today: Are not people in a democratic society, with its increasing level of education and standard of living, capable of more responsible behavior? Drawing heavily on Maslow's hierarchy of needs, McGregor concluded that Theory X assumptions about human nature, when universally applied, are often inaccurate and that management approaches that develop from these assumptions may fail to motivate many individuals to work toward organizational goals. Management by direction and control may not succeed, according to McGregor, because it is a questionable method for motivating people whose physiological and safety needs are reasonably satisfied and whose social, esteem, and self-actualization needs are becoming predominant. Management is interested in work, and work, according to McGregor, is as natural and can be as satisfying for people as play. After all, both work and play are physical and mental activities; consequently, there is no inherent difference between work and play. In reality, however, particularly under Theory X management, a distinct difference in need satisfaction is discernible. Whereas play is internally controlled by the individuals (they

Table 3-1 Assumptions About Human Nature That Underlie McGregor's Theory X and Theory Y

THEORY X	THEORY Y
1. Work is inherently distasteful to most people.	1. Work is as natural as play, if the conditions are favorable.
2. Most people are not ambitious, have little desire for responsibility, and prefer to be directed.	2. Self-control is often indispensable in achieving organizational goals.
3. Most people have little capacity for creativity in solving organizational problems.	3. The capacity for creativity in solving organizational problems is widely distributed in the population.
4. Motivation occurs only at the physiological and security levels.	4. Motivation occurs at the social, esteem, and self-actualization levels, as well as at the physiological and security levels.
5. Most people must be closely controlled and often coerced to achieve organizational objectives.	5. People can be self-directed and creative at work if properly motivated.

decide what they want to do), work is externally controlled by others (people have no control over their jobs). Thus, management and its assumptions about the nature of people have built in a difference between work and play that seems unnatural. As a result, people are stifled at work and look for excuses to spend more and more time away from the job in order to satisfy their esteem and self-actualization needs (provided they have enough money to satisfy their physiological and safety needs). Because of their conditioning to Theory X management, most employees consider work a necessary evil rather than a source of personal challenge and satisfaction.

In contrast, Theory Y organizations have cohesive work teams whose goals parallel organizational goals. In such organizations, there is high productivity, and people come to work gladly because work is inherently satisfying.

McGregor felt that management needed practices based on a more accurate understanding of human nature and motivation. Because of his feeling, McGregor developed an alternative theory of human behavior called *Theory Y*. This theory assumes that people are not, by nature, lazy and unreliable. It suggests that people can be basically self-directed and creative at work, if properly motivated. Therefore, it should be an essential task of management to unleash this potential in individuals. Properly motivated people can achieve their own goals best by directing their own efforts toward accomplishing organizational goals.

The impression that one might get from this discussion of Theory X and Theory Y is that managers who accept Theory X assumptions about human nature usually direct, control, and closely supervise people, whereas Theory Y managers are supportive and facilitating. We want to warn against drawing this conclusion, because it could lead to the trap of thinking that Theory X is "bad" and Theory Y is "good" and that everyone is independent and self-motivated rather than, as McGregor implies, that most people have the potential to be independent and self-motivated. This assumption of the potential self-motivation of people necessitates recognition of the difference between attitude and behavior.

Theory X and Theory Y are attitudes, or predispositions, toward people. Thus, although the "best" assumptions for a manager to have may be Theory Y, it may not be appropriate to behave consistently with those assumptions all the time. Managers may have Theory Y assumptions about human nature, but they may find it necessary to behave in a very directive, controlling manner (as if they had Theory X assumptions) with some people in the short run to help them "grow up" in a developmental sense, until they are truly Theory Y–acting people.

PATTERN A AND PATTERN B

Chris Argyris

Chris Argyris recognized the difference between attitude and behavior when he identified and discussed behavior patterns A and B in addition to Theory X and Y.[3] Pattern A represents the interpersonal behavior, group dynamics, and organizational norms that Argyris found in his research to be associated with Theory X; pattern B represents the same phenomena found to be associated with Theory Y. Pattern A individuals do not own up to feelings, are not open, reject experimenting, and do not help others to engage in these behaviors. Their behavior tends to be characterized by close supervision and a high degree of structure. Pattern B individuals own up to feelings, are open, enjoy experimenting, and help others to engage in these behaviors. Their behavior tends to be supportive and facilitating. The result is norms of trust, concern, and individuality.

As Argyris emphasized, "Although XA and YB are usually associated with each other in everyday life, they do not have to be. Under certain conditions, pattern A could go with Theory Y or pattern B with Theory X."[4] Thus, XA and YB are the most frequent combinations, but some managers, at times, may be XB or YA. Although XB managers have negative assumptions about people, they seem to behave in supportive and facilitating ways. We have found that this XB combination tends to occur for two reasons. These managers (although they think most people are lazy and unreliable) engage in supportive and facilitating behaviors either because they have been told or have learned from experience that such behavior will increase productivity or because they work for people who have created a supportive environment, and if they want to maintain their jobs they are expected to behave accordingly. On the other hand, YA managers (although they think people are generally independent and self-motivated) control and closely supervise people either because they work for controlling people who demand similar behavior from them or because they find it necessary to behave in a directive, controlling manner for a period of time. When they use pattern A behavior, these managers usually are attempting to help people develop the skills and abilities necessary for self-direction and thus are creating an environment in which they can become YB managers.

INFORMAL WORK GROUPS

George C. Homans

Management is often suspicious of strong informal work groups because of their potential power to control the behavior of their members and, as a result, the level of productivity. Where do these groups get their power to control behavior? George C. Homans developed a model of social systems that may be useful in finding an answer.[5]

There are three elements in a social system. *Activities* are the tasks that people perform. *Interactions* are the behaviors that occur between people in performing those tasks. And *sentiments* are the attitudes that develop between individuals and within groups. Homans argued that although these concepts are separate, they are closely related. In fact, as Figure 3-1 illustrates, they are mutually dependent. A change in any one of these three elements will produce some change in the other two.

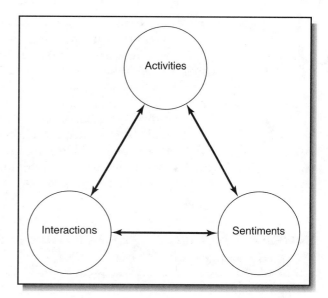

Figure 3-1
The Mutual
Dependency of
Activities,
Interactions, and
Sentiments

In an organization, certain activities, interactions, and sentiments are essential or required from its members if it is to survive. In other words, jobs (activities) have to be done that require people to work together (interactions). These jobs must be sufficiently satisfying (sentiments) for people to continue doing them. As people interact on their jobs, they develop sentiments toward each other. As people increase interaction with each other, it is important that positive sentiments be developed. The more positive the sentiment, the more people will tend to interact with each other. It can become an upward-spiraling process until some equilibrium is reached. As this upward-spiraling process continues, there is a tendency for the group members to become more alike in their activities and sentiments—in what they do and how they feel about things.

As they become more alike, the group tends to develop expectations or norms that specify how people in the group "might" tend to behave under specific circumstances. For example, a group of workers might have a norm that "you should not talk to Mary or help her any more than necessary." If the group is cohesive enough—that is, the group is attractive to its members and they are reluctant to leave it—then it will have little trouble in getting members to conform. People who deviate significantly from group norms usually incur sanctions from the group. "The group has at its disposal a variety of penalties, ranging from gentle kidding to harsh ostracism, for pressuring deviant members into line."[6] Group members may react in several ways. They may decide to continue to deviate from group norms. If the resulting pressure from their peers becomes too great, they may leave the group.

The influence that group pressures can have in achieving conformity in the perceptions and behavior of people is well documented. For example, Solomon E. Asch conducted a classic experiment in which groups of eight college men were each asked to match the length of a line with one of three unequal lines.[7] Seven members of each group were privately told to give the same incorrect answer. The uninstructed member was the last one asked to give his answer and was thus confronted with the dilemma of either reporting what he saw as being correct or reporting what all the others had said in order to be congruent with the group. Asch reported that "one-third of all the estimates were errors identical with or in the direction of the distorted estimates of the majority."[8] If pressure can cause distorted behavior in this kind of exercise, imagine what peer group pressure can induce with more subjective judgments.

It should be reiterated that strong informal work groups do not have to be a detriment to organizations. In fact, as Mayo identified at Hawthorne, these groups can become powerful driving forces in accomplishing organizational goals if they see their own goals as satisfied by working for organizational goals.

INCREASING INTERPERSONAL COMPETENCE

Chris Argyris

Although management based on the assumptions of Theory X is perhaps no longer widely appropriate, in the opinion of McGregor and others, it is still widely practiced. Consequently, large majorities of the people in the United States today are treated as immature human beings in their working environments. In attempting to analyze this situation, Chris Argyris compared bureaucratic-pyramidal values (the organizational counterpart to Theory X assumptions about people) that still dominate most organizations with a more humanistic-democratic value system (the organizational counterpart to Theory Y assumptions about people).

According to Argyris, bureaucratic or pyramidal values lead to poor, shallow, and mistrustful relationships.[9] Because these relationships do not permit the natural and free expression of feelings, they are phony or nonauthentic and result in decreased interpersonal competence. "Without interpersonal competence or a 'psychologically safe' environment, the organization is a breeding ground for mistrust, intergroup conflict, rigidity, and so on, which in turn lead to a decrease in organizational success in problem solving."[10]

If, on the other hand, humanistic or democratic values are adhered to in an organization, Argyris claimed that trusting, authentic relationships will develop among people and will result in increased interpersonal competence, intergroup cooperation, flexibility, and the like and should result in increases in organizational effectiveness. In this kind of environment, people are treated as human beings. Both organizational members and the organization itself are given an opportunity to develop to the fullest potential, and there is an attempt to make work exciting and challenging. Implicit in "living" these values is "treating each human being as a person with a complex set of needs, all of which are important in his work and in his life . . . and providing opportunities for people in organizations to influence the way in which they relate to work, the organization, and the environment."[11]

Argyris's Immaturity-Maturity Theory

The fact that bureaucratic-pyramidal values still dominate most organizations, according to Argyris, has produced many of our current organizational problems. While at Yale, he examined industrial organizations to determine what effect management practices have had on individual behavior and personal growth within the work environment.[12] According to Argyris, seven changes should take place in the personality of individuals if they are to develop into mature people.

First, individuals move from a passive state as infants to a state of increasing activity as adults. Second, individuals develop from a state of dependency upon others as infants to a state of relative independence as adults. Third, individuals behave in only a few ways as infants but as adults they are capable of behaving in many ways. Fourth, individuals have erratic, casual, and shallow interests as infants but develop deeper and stronger interests as adults. Fifth, the time perspective of children is very short, involving only the present, but as they mature, their time perspective increases to include the past and the future. Sixth, individuals as infants are subordinate to everyone, but they move to equal or superior positions with others as adults. Seventh, as children, individuals lack awareness of a "self," but as adults, they are not only aware of but they are able to control "self." Argyris suggests that these changes reside on a continuum and that the "healthy" personality develops along the continuum from "immaturity" to "maturity" (see Table 3-2).

These changes are only general tendencies, but they give some light on the matter of maturity. Norms of the individual's culture and personality inhibit and limit maximum expression and growth of the adult, yet the tendency is to move toward the "maturity" end of the continuum with age. Argyris would be the first to admit that few, if any, persons develop to full maturity.

In examining the widespread worker apathy and lack of effort in industry, Argyris questioned whether these problems were simply the result of individual laziness. He suggests that they are not. Argyris contends that, in many cases, when people join the workforce, they are kept from maturing by the management practices utilized in their organizations. They are given minimal control over their environment and are encouraged to be passive, dependent, and subordinate; therefore, they behave immaturely. The worker

Table 3-2 Argyris's Immaturity-Maturity Continuum

IMMATURITY ⟶ MATURITY	
Passive ——————————————————————— Active	
Dependent ————————————————————— Independent	
Behave in a few ways ——————— Capable of behaving in many ways	
Erratic shallow interests ——————— Deeper and stronger interests	
Short-time perspective ——————— Long-time perspective (past and future)	
Subordinate position ——————— Equal or superordinate position	
Lack of awareness of self ——————— Awareness and control over self	

in many organizations is expected to act in immature ways rather than as a mature adult. This does not occur only in industrial settings. In fact, one can even see it happening in many school systems, where most high school students are subject to more rules and restrictions and generally are treated less maturely than are students in elementary school.

According to Argyris, keeping people immature is built into the very nature of the formal organization. He argues that because organizations are usually created to achieve goals or objectives that can best be met collectively, the formal organization is often the architect's conception of how those objectives may be achieved. In this sense, the individual is fitted to the job. The design comes first. This design is based on four concepts of scientific management: task specialization, chain of command, unity of direction, and span of control. Management tries to increase and enhance organizational and administrative efficiency and productivity by making workers "interchangeable parts."

Basic to these concepts is the notion that power and authority should rest in the hands of a few at the top of the organization, and, thus, those at the lower end of the chain of command are strictly controlled by management or the system itself. Task specialization often results in oversimplification of the job so that it becomes repetitive, routine, and unchallenging. Leadership is directive and task-oriented. Decisions about the work are made by the manager, and the workers only carry out those decisions. This type of leadership evokes managerial controls such as budgets, some incentive systems, time-and-motion studies, and standard operating procedures, all of which can restrict the initiative and creativity of workers.

MOTIVATION-HYGIENE THEORY

Frederick Herzberg

We have noted that needs such as esteem and self-actualization seem to become more important as people develop. One of the most interesting series of studies that concentrates heavily on these areas was directed by Frederick Herzberg.[13] Out of these studies has developed a theory of work motivation that has broad implications for management and its efforts toward effective utilization of human resources.

Herzberg, in developing his motivation-hygiene theory, seemed to sense that scholars such as McGregor and Argyris were identifying important human behaviors. Knowledge about human nature, motives, and needs could be invaluable to organizations and individuals:

> To industry, the payoff for a study of job attitudes would be increased productivity, decreased absenteeism, and smoother working relations. To the individual, an understanding of the forces that lead to improved morale would bring greater happiness and greater self-realization.[14]

Herzberg set out to collect data on job attitudes from which assumptions about human behavior could be made. The motivation-hygiene theory resulted from the analysis of an initial study by Herzberg and his colleagues at the Psychological Service of Pittsburgh. This study involved extensive interviews with some 200 engineers and accountants from 11 industries in the Pittsburgh area. In the interviews, they were asked about what kinds of things on their job made them unhappy or dissatisfied and what things made them happy or satisfied.

In analyzing the data from these interviews, Herzberg concluded that people have two different categories of needs—which he called *hygiene factors* and *motivators*—that are essentially independent of each other and affect behavior in different ways. He found that when people felt dissatisfied with their jobs, they were concerned about the environment in which they were working. On the other hand, when people felt good about their jobs, this feeling had to do with the work itself. Herzberg called the first category of needs hygiene, or maintenance, factors: *hygiene* because they describe people's environment and serve the primary function of preventing job dissatisfaction; *maintenance* because they are never completely satisfied—they have to continue to be maintained. He called the second category of needs *motivators* because they seemed to be effective in motivating people to superior performance. Table 3-3 presents a summary of motivation and hygiene factors.

Hygiene Factors

Company policies and administration, supervision, working conditions, interpersonal relations, money, status, and security may be thought of as maintenance factors. These are not an intrinsic part of a job, but they are related to the conditions under which a job is performed. Herzberg related his original use of the word *hygiene* to its medical meaning (preventive and environmental). He found that hygiene factors produced no growth in worker output capacity; they only prevented losses in worker performance due to work restrictions. That is another reason why Herzberg called these maintenance factors.

Table 3-3 Motivation and Hygiene Factors

MOTIVATOR	HYGIENE FACTOR
THE JOB ITSELF	ENVIRONMENT
Achievement	Policies and administration
Recognition for accomplishment	Supervision
Challenging work	Working conditions
Increased responsibility	Interpersonal relations
Growth and development	Money, status, security

Motivators

Herzberg refers to factors that involve feelings of achievement, professional growth, and recognition that one can experience in a job that offers challenge and scope as motivators. Herzberg used this term because these factors seem capable of having a positive effect on job satisfaction, often resulting in an increase in one's total output capacity.

In recent years, motivation-hygiene research has been extended well beyond engineers and accountants to include every area of an organization, from top management to hourly employees. For example, in an extensive study at Texas Instruments, Scott Meyers concluded that Herzberg's motivation-hygiene theory "is easily translatable to supervisory action at all levels of responsibility. It is a framework on which supervisors can evaluate and put into perspective the constant barrage of 'helpful hints' to which they are subjected, and hence serves to increase their feelings of competence, self-confidence, and autonomy."[15]

Perhaps an example will further differentiate between hygiene factors and motivators and help explain the reason for classifying needs as Herzberg has done. Let us assume that an employee is highly motivated and is working at 90-percent capacity. The person has a good working relationship with the supervisor, is well satisfied with pay and working conditions, and is part of a congenial work group. Suppose the supervisor is suddenly transferred and replaced by a person who is difficult to work with, or suppose the employee finds out that someone whose work seems inferior is receiving more pay. How will these factors affect this individual's behavior? We know that performance or productivity depends on both ability and motivation. These unsatisfied hygiene needs (supervision and money) may lead to restriction of output. This decline in productivity may be intentional, or the employee may not be consciously aware of holding back. In either case, productivity will be lowered, as illustrated in Figure 3-2. In our illustration, even if the worker's

Figure 3-2
Effect of Dissatisfying Hygiene Factors

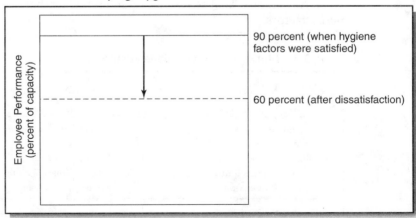

salary is adjusted well above expectations and the former supervisor returns, productivity will probably increase only to its original level.

Conversely, let us take the same employee and assume that dissatisfaction has not occurred; work is at 90-percent capacity. Suppose the person is given an opportunity to develop and satisfy motivational needs in an environment where there is freedom to exercise some initiative and creativity, to make decisions, to handle problems, and to take responsibility. What effect will this situation have on this individual? If the employee is able to fulfill the supervisor's expectations in performing these new responsibilities, that person may still work at 90-percent capacity but may have developed and grown in ability and may be capable now of more productivity, as illustrated in Figure 3-3. Capacity has increased.

Hygiene factors, when satisfied, tend to eliminate dissatisfaction and work restriction, but they do little to motivate an individual to superior performance or increased capacity. Enhancement of the motivators, however, will permit an individual to grow and develop, often increasing ability. Thus, hygiene factors affect an individual's willingness, and motivators affect an individual's ability.

The Relationship of Herzberg's Theory to Maslow's Theory

Maslow's theory is helpful in identifying needs or motives, and Herzberg's theory provides us with insights into the goals and incentives that tend to satisfy those needs, as illustrated in Figure 3-4. Thus, in a motivating situation, if you know the high-strength needs (Maslow) of the individuals you want to influence, then you should be able to determine what goals (Herzberg) you could provide in the environment to motivate those individuals. At the same

Figure 3-3
Effect of Satisfying Motivators

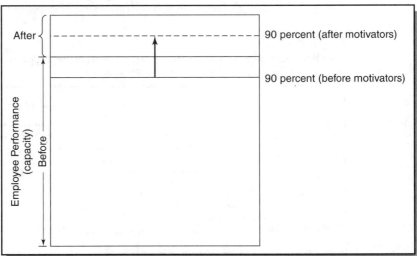

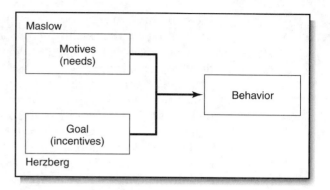

Figure 3-4
The Relationship of Maslow's and Herzberg's Theories to Motivation Situation

time, if you know what goals these people want to satisfy, you can predict what their high-strength needs are. That is possible because it has been found that money and benefits tend to satisfy needs at the physiological and security levels; interpersonal relations and supervision are examples of hygiene factors that tend to satisfy social needs; increased responsibility, challenging work, and growth and development are motivators that tend to satisfy needs at the esteem and self-actualization levels. Figure 3-5 shows the relationship we feel exists between the Maslow and Herzberg frameworks.

We believe that the physiological, safety, social, and part of the esteem needs are all hygiene factors. The esteem needs are divided because there are some distinct differences between status per se and recognition. Status tends to be a function of the position one occupies. One may have gained this position through family ties, and thus this position may not be a reflection of personal achievement or earned recognition. Recognition is gained through competence and achievement. It is earned and granted by others. Consequently, status is classified with physiological, safety, and social needs as a hygiene factor, whereas recognition is classified with esteem as a motivator.

It appears to us that McClelland's concept of achievement motivation is also related to Herzberg's motivation-hygiene theory.[16] People with high achievement

Figure 3-5
The Relationship Between Herzberg's Motivation-Hygiene Theory and Maslow's Hierarchy of Needs Theory

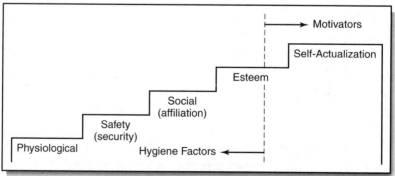

Chapter 3   Motivating

motivation tend to be interested in the motivators (the job itself). Achievement-motivated people want task-relevant feedback. They want to know how well they are doing on their job. On the other hand, people with low achievement motivation are more concerned about the environment. They want to know how people feel about them rather than how well they are doing.

Job Enrichment

Before Herzberg's work, many other behavioral scientists were concerned with worker motivation. For several years, there was an emphasis on what was termed "job enlargement" or "job rotation." This was believed to be an answer to the overspecialization that had characterized many industrial organizations. The assumption was that workers could gain more satisfaction at work if their jobs were enlarged, that is, if the number or variety of their tasks was increased.

Herzberg made some astute observations about this trend. He claimed that doing a snippet of this and a snippet of that does not necessarily result in motivation. Washing dishes, then silverware, and then pots and pans does no more to satisfy and provide an opportunity to grow than washing only dishes. What we really need to do with work, Herzberg suggested, is to enrich the job. Job enrichment means the deliberate upgrading of responsibility, scope, and challenge in work.

Example of Job Enrichment

Job enrichment may be illustrated by the experience an industrial relations superintendent had with a group of janitors. After a transfer to a new plant, the superintendent learned that the position responsibilities included supervising 15 janitors in a plant maintenance crew. There was no foreman over this crew. Reviewing the files one day, the superintendent noticed that there was a history of complaints about housekeeping around the plant. After talking to others and observing, it took the superintendent little time to confirm these reports. The janitors seemed to be lazy, unreliable, and generally unmotivated. They were walking examples of Theory X assumptions about human nature.

Determined to do something about the behavior of the janitors, the superintendent called a group meeting, discussed some of the problems, and asked the janitors, because they were the experts, for ideas. "Does anyone have a suggestion?" There was dead silence. The superintendent sat down and said nothing. The silence lasted for almost 20 minutes. Finally, one janitor spoke up, related a problem, and made a suggestion. Soon others joined in, and suddenly the janitors were involved in a lively discussion while the superintendent listened and jotted down their ideas. At the conclusion of the meeting, the suggestions were summarized with tacit acceptance by all, including the superintendent.

After the meeting, the superintendent referred any housekeeping problems to the janitors, individually or as a group. For example, when any cleaning equipment or material salespersons came to the plant, the superintendent did not talk to them—the janitors did. In fact, regular meetings continued to be held in which problems and ideas were discussed.

These changes had a tremendous influence on the behavior of the crew. They developed a cohesive productive team that took pride in its work. Even their appearance changed. Once a grubby lot, now they appeared at work in clean, pressed work clothes. All over the plant, people were amazed at how clean and well-kept everything had become. The superintendent was continually stopped by supervisors in the plant and asked, "What have you done to those lazy, good-for-nothing janitors, given them pep pills?" Even the superintendent could not believe what had happened. It was not uncommon to see one or two janitors running floor tests to see which wax or cleaner did the best job. Because they had to make all the decisions, including committing funds for their supplies, they wanted to know which were the best. Such activities, while taking time, did not detract from their work. In fact, the crew worked harder and more efficiently than ever before. This example illustrates several positive aspects of job enrichment. The tasks were redesigned so that the janitors would be responsible for the housekeeping of the plant—what is called *horizontal job expansion.* In addition, the janitors were given responsibility for making decisions regarding equipment, supplies, and methods—what is called *vertical job expansion*—previously reserved to higher management. Both horizontal and vertical job expansion are required to gain the greatest improvement in motivation and satisfaction.[17]

This example also illustrates that even at low levels in an organization, people can respond in responsible and productive ways to a work environment in which they are given an opportunity to grow and mature. People begin to satisfy their esteem and self-actualization needs by participating in the planning, organizing, motivating, and controlling of their own tasks.

MOTIVATION AND SATISFACTION

Edward E. Lawler III, a researcher, educator, and consultant, has examined the relationship between motivation and satisfaction because some managers may think these terms are similar if not synonymous. Lawler thinks they are not.

> They are, in fact, very different. Motivation is influenced by forward-looking perceptions concerning the relationship between performance and rewards, while satisfaction refers to people's feelings about the rewards they have received. Thus satisfaction is a consequence of past events while motivation is a consequence of their expectations about the future.[18]

Managers should be aware of this important difference. Attempts to improve future performance by focusing on past rewards and benefits demonstrates a lack of understanding of the character of satisfaction. Satisfaction is past-oriented; motivation is future-oriented. Managers wanting to improve future performance should use the concepts and techniques discussed in these pages to enhance motivation.

INTEGRATION OF FOUR MOTIVATION THEORIES

Figure 3-6 synthesizes four prominent theories of motivation and allows us to reach some general conclusions.

1. *People seek security.* There are certain "insecurity" needs fundamental to people's existence. If these needs are not addressed, people will put their main focus on job performance. We will come back to this point in chapter 8 when we discuss Situational Leadership's readiness dimension. We cannot neglect the security aspect of effective organizations.
2. *People seek social systems.* Whether we call this need relatedness, affiliation, interpersonal relations, or belongingness, we cannot neglect the sociability aspect of effective organizations.
3. *People seek personal growth.* Whether we call this self-actualization, advancement, growth, or need for achievement, "what is in it for *me*" is a powerful need. We cannot neglect the development aspect of effective organizations.

We believe that Figure 3-6 demonstrates that a leadership model must incorporate these three basic human need categories. The necessity of doing so was

Figure 3-6
Comparison of Four Theories of Motivation

Maslow	Alderfer	Herzberg	McClelland
Self-Actualization	Growth	Motivators	Need for Achievement
Esteem			
Social	Relatedness	Hygiene Factors	Need for Affiliation
Safety	Existence		
Physiological			

Source: Gregory B. Northcraft and Margaret A. Neal, *Organization Behavior: A Management Challenge,* 2nd ed., (Fort Worth: Dryden Press, 1994), p. 113.

affirmed by an interview presented in *Business Week:* "The job, certainly, is not dead. There's still a robust need for relationships between employer and employed that rely on stability, security, and shared economic interests. 'Man has always sought the company of people, and that will continue to be the driving force of organization,' says CEO Robert J. Saldich of Raychem Corp., one employer that is creatively confronting workplace changes."[19]

SELF-CONCEPT AND PERCEPTION

How do you see yourself when facing a leadership situation? Confident, self-assured, willing to accept the challenge? Or do you see yourself as hesitant, insecure, worried about what will happen? Your self-concept is a very important influence on your behavior. It colors the way you see the world, acting as your perceptual filter, and also shapes what you do to maintain your self-concept. Carl Rogers, an eminent psychologist, explained it this way. "People strive to maintain their concepts of themselves by engaging in behavior that is consistent with their goals, competencies, beliefs and values as they see them. . . . People also strive to enhance their self-concepts by learning and developing themselves toward some 'ideal-self.' . . . People generally make choices that are consistent with their self-concepts."[20]

Attribution Theory

We may assess another's behavior on the basis of whether we believe it was caused by an internal or an external influence. As Steve Robbins has suggested, "*internally* caused behaviors are those that are believed to be under the personal control of the individual. *Externally* caused behavior is seen as resulting from outside causes; that is, the person is forced into the behavior by the situation."[21]

Robbins suggests that there are three factors that help us determine behavior: distinctiveness, consensus, and consistency. Let's consider an example. One of your managers fails to get a very important contract. How do you judge the manager's performance? Table 3-4 provides some clues. Was this failure distinctive? Yes, very unusual. Would other experienced managers in a similar situation fail? Most likely. Was this failure consistent with previous

Table 3-4 Application of Attribution Theory

FACTOR	YES OR NO	INTERNAL	EXTERNAL
Unusual	Yes		X
Consensus	Yes		X
Consistent	No		X

performance? No. This was the first time. On the basis of this analysis, you attribute the failure to an external cause beyond the control of the manager. Subsequently, your investigation reveals that a competitor submitted an unusually low bid because it had excess capacity.

If, on the other hand, you had judged the manager's performance as not unusual for this person who consistently failed when others succeeded, you would have attributed the failure to an internal cause.

PUTTING IDEAS TOGETHER

Figure 3-7 puts together several of the ideas we have discussed, and it also serves as a preview for future chapters. The figure builds on both Lewin's and Maier's models as discussed in chapter 2; that is, behavior is caused by the interaction of personal and situational elements. As Rogers pointed out, our perceptions and expectancies are influenced by our self-concept within the context of the situation and lead to actions and outcomes. These outcomes influence the situation and ourselves.

Figure 3-7
How Behavior Results from Perceptions and Expectancies As Influenced by the Self-Concept

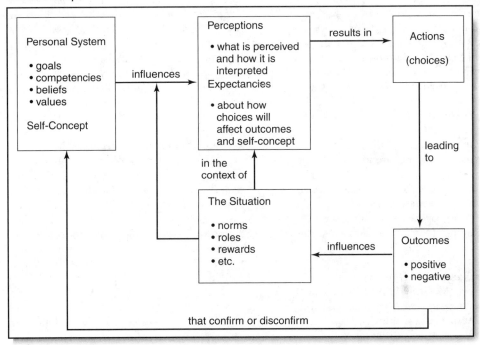

Source: Allan R. Cohen, Stephen L. Fink, Herman Gadon, and Robin D. Willits, *Effective Behavior in Organizations*, 6th ed., © 1995, Irwin. Reprinted by permission of the McGraw-Hill Companies.

SUMMARY

Two polar positions are evident in this chapter's discussion of motivating employees. At one extreme (and most people still think it is the most common extreme) are organizations that are dominated by Theory X assumptions about human nature, bureaucratic-pyramidal values, and pattern A behavior. Managers in these organizations think and act as if people are motivated only by physiological and safety needs and satisfying hygiene factors. Followers in these organizations tend to be passive, dependent, and childlike. At the other extreme are the "ideal" organizations with their Theory Y assumptions about human nature, humanistic-democratic values, and pattern B behavior. Managers in these organizations believe that people are motivated by affiliation, esteem, and self-actualization needs.

The differences between these two extremes are great, and, as Chris Argyris argues, the journey from XA to YB is not an easy one. Preparation for this journey requires analyzing and understanding, but real skills are also needed in directing, changing, and controlling behavior. Chapter 4 presents a framework for applying leader behavior that may help us "get on the road to start the journey."

ENDNOTES

1. For detailed descriptions of this research, see *Reflections on the Hawthorne Studies, 75 Years Later: Symposium Presented for the Management History Division*, 1999 Annual Academy of Management Meeting, Chicago, IL, August 9, 1999. Fritz J. Roethlisberger and William J. Dickson, *Management and the Worker* (Cambridge: Harvard University Press, 1939); T. N. Whitehead, *The Industrial Worker*, 2 vols. (Cambridge: Harvard University Press, 1938); Elton Mayo, *The Human Problems of an Industrial Civilization* (Salem, NH: Ayer Company, 1977). See also R. E. Dutton, "On Alix Carev's Radical Criticism of the Hawthorne Studies: Comment," *Academy of Management Journal*, 14 (September 1971), pp. 394–396; Randolph M. Hale, "Managing Human Resources: Challenge for the Future," *Enterprise*, June 1985, pp. 6–9.

2. Douglas McGregor, *The Human Side of Enterprise* (New York: McGraw-Hill, 1960). See also McGregor, *Leadership and Motivation* (Boston: MIT Press, 1966); Craig C. Pinder, *Work Motivation: Theory, Issues, and Applications* (Glenview, IL: Scott, Foresman, 1984).

3. Chris Argyris, *Management and Organizational Development: The Path from XA to YB* (New York: McGraw-Hill, 1971); Walter E. Natemeyer, ed., *Classics of Organizational Behavior* (Oak Park, IL: Moore Publishers, 1978); David R. Hampton, *Organizational Behavior and the Practice of Management* (Glenview, IL: Scott, Foresman, 1986).

4. Argyris, *Management and Organizational Development*, p. 12.

5. George C. Homans, *The Human Group* (New York: Harcourt, Brace & World, 1950).

6. Anthony G. Athos and Robert E. Coffey, *Behavior in Organization: A Multidimensional View* (Upper Saddle River, NJ: Prentice Hall, 1968), p. 101.

7. Solomon E. Asch, "Effects of Group Pressure upon the Modification and Distortion of Judgments," pp. 177–190 in *Groups, Leadership and Men*, ed. Harold Guetzkow (New York: Russell and Russell, 1963). Also in Dorwin Cartwright and Alvin Zander, *Group Dynamics*, 2nd ed. (Evanston, IL: Row, Peterson, 1960), pp. 189–200.

8. Asch, "Effects of Group Pressure," p. 181.

9. Chris Argyris, *Interpersonal Competence and Organizational Effectiveness* (Homewood, IL: Irwin, Dorsey Press, 1962), p. 43.

10. *Ibid.*, p. 43.

11. *Ibid.*

12. Chris Argyris, *Personality and Organization* (New York: Harper & Row, 1957); Argyris, *Interpersonal Competence and Organizational Effectiveness* (Homewood, IL: Irwin, Dorsey Press, 1962); and Argyris, *Integrating the Individual and the Organization* (New York: John Wiley & Sons, 1964).

13. Frederick Herzberg, Bernard Mausner, and Barbara Snyderman, *The Motivation to Work* (New York: John Wiley & Sons, 1959); and Herzberg, *Work and the Nature of Man* (New York: World Publishing, 1966). See also Richard M. Steers and Lyman W. Porter, *Motivation and Work Behavior*, 2nd ed. (New York: McGraw-Hill, 1979); Terence R. Mitchell, "Motivation: New Directions for Theory, Research and Practice," *Academy of Management Review*, January 1982, pp. 80–88. See also Renato Tagiuri, "Managing People: Ten Essential Behaviors," *Harvard Business Review*, 73 (January–February 1995), pp. 10–11.

14. Herzberg, Mausner, and Snyderman, *The Motivation to Work*, p. ix.

15. Scott M. Meyers, "Who Are Your Motivated Workers?" p. 64 in *Behavioral Concepts in Management*, David R. Hampton (Belmont, CA: Dickenson Publishing, 1968). Originally published in *Harvard Business Review*, January–February 1964, pp. 73–88. See also Charles M. Cumming, "Incentives That Really Do Motivate," *Compensation and Benefits Review*, 26 (May/June 1994), pp. 38–40; Michael M. Markovich, "Is Your Company's Revenue Greater Than Its Expenses? *HR Focus*, 71 (January 1994), pp. 4–6; and Donna Deeprose, "Operating with a Sense of Purpose," *Supervisory Management*, 40 (June 1995), p. 7.

16. David C. McClelland, John W. Atkinson, R. A. Clark, and E. L. Lowell, *The Achievement Motive* (New York: Appleton-Century-Crofts, 1953); and McClelland, *The Achieving Society* (Princeton, NJ: D. Van Nostrand, 1961). See also David McClelland and David H. Burnham, "Power Is the Great Motivator," *Harvard Business Review*, 73 (January/February 1995), pp. 126–130.

17. Edward E. Lawler III, *High Involvement Management* (San Francisco: Jossey-Bass, 1990), p. 32. See also Esther Bogin, "From Staff to Dream Team," *Financial Executive*, January/February 1995, pp. 54–56.

18. Lawler, *High Involvement Management*, p. 32. See also David Sharpley, "Exploring Work Behavior (PRISM: Profile Report on Individual Style and Motivation)," *Personnel Management*, 26 (August 1994), p. 53.

19. "The New World of Work," *Business Week*, October 17, 1994, p. 76. See also Don Merit, "What Really Motivates You?" *American Printer*, January 1995, p. 74; Orin Hari, "The Missing Link in Performance," *Management Review*, 84 (March 1995), p. 74.

20. Carl Rogers, quoted in Allan R. Cohen, Stephen L. Fink, Herman Gadon, and Robin D. Willits, *Effective Behavior in Organizations*, 6th ed. (Chicago: Irwin, 1995), pp. 201–203.

21. Stephen P. Robbins, *Organizational Behavior: Concepts, Controversies, and Applications*, 6th ed. (Upper Saddle River, NJ: Prentice Hall, 1993), p. 139.

Chapter 4

Leadership: An Initial Perspective

The successful organization has one major attribute that sets it apart from unsuccessful organizations: dynamic and effective leadership. Peter F. Drucker pointed out that managers (business leaders) are the basic and scarcest resource of any business enterprise.[1] ✧

Businesses are continually searching for effective leaders, and they are not easy to find. This shortage of effective leadership is not confined to business but is evident in the lack of able administrators in government, education, foundations, churches, and every other form of organization. Thus, when we decry the scarcity of leadership talent in our society, we are not talking about a lack of people to fill administrative positions. What we are agonizing over is a scarcity of people who are willing to assume significant leadership roles in our society and who can get the job done effectively.

LEADERSHIP DEFINED

According to George R. Terry, "Leadership is the activity of influencing people to strive willingly for group objectives."[2] Robert Tannenbaum, Irving R. Weschler, and Fred Massarik define leadership as "interpersonal influence exercised in a situation and directed, through the communication process, toward the attainment of a specialized goal or goals."[3] Harold Koontz and Cyril O'Donnell state that "leadership is influencing people to follow in the achievement of a common goal." [4]

A review of other writers reveals that most management writers agree with us in that leadership is the process of influencing the activities of an individual or a group in efforts toward goal achievement in a given situation. From this definition of leadership, it follows that the leadership process is a function of the leader, the follower, and other situational variables:

$$L = f(l,f,s)$$

It is important to note that this definition makes no mention of any particular type of organization. In any situation in which someone is trying to influence the behavior of another individual or group, leadership is occurring. Thus, everyone attempts leadership at one time or another, whether activities are centered on a business, educational institution, hospital, political organization, or family.

It should also be remembered that when this definition mentions leader and follower, one should not assume that we are talking only about a hierarchical relationship such as suggested by manager-coworker. Any time an individual is attempting to influence the behavior of someone else, that individual is the potential leader, and the person subject to the influence attempt is the potential follower, whether that person is the boss, a colleague (associate), a subordinate, a friend, a relative, or a group.

LEADERS AS VISION CREATORS

"Leadership is making what you believe in . . . happen."[5] We introduced the essence of leadership in chapter 1 as the efforts of courageous men and women making what they believed in happen under extremely challenging conditions. They had a vision and acted upon this vision to make their aspirations and the aspirations of others happen.

Leaders must know where they are going if they are to achieve their purposes. Today, just as thousands of years ago, without a vision, persons and organizations perish.[6] Therefore, leaders must be vision creators. This is an immensely powerful and far-reaching idea. Visioning defines leadership. It is fundamental to the process of leading organizations.

Warren Bennis observed that "the single defining quality of leaders is their ability to create and realize a vision."[7] Marshall Loeb said, "All the leaders I know have a strongly defined sense of purpose. And when you have an organization where the people are aligned behind a clearly defined vision or purpose, you get a powerful organization."[8] And Jack Welch, chief executive officer of General Electric, stated, "The effective leader leads through a vision, a shared set of values, a shared objective."[9] It is the responsibility,[10] one might even say the duty, of top management to create a vision for the organization and to articulate this vision so it turns into concrete strategies, solid management systems, and informed resource allocations that enable an organization to accomplish results.

Results are a key focus of this book. Initially, in chapters 4 through 14, the primary emphasis is on results from individual and group perspectives. In chapters 15 through 20, the emphasis shifts to more of a focus on organizations. For example, the discussion of organizational performance and the ACHIEVE model in chapter 15; the Building Commitments model in chapter 16; and approaches to planning and implementing change in chapter 17 are directly concerned with achieving results. Chapter 18, Leadership to Achieve Quality; chapter 19, The Organizational Cone; and chapter 21, Leadership Strategies for Organizational Transformation, bring all of the key elements of individuals, groups, and organizations together to suggest important ways of achieving peak performance.

Before we look at trait, attitudinal, and situational approaches to leadership, we must place organizational leadership into a broad context. We will do this by introducing two powerful models: the SOAR Peak Performance model and the Vision to Results (VTR) model. Each model, we believe, offers an important perspective that will highlight and interrelate many of the key variables affecting performance.

The SOAR Peak Performance Model

What determines the road to results—to successful performance—is a combination of interacting factors that can be represented by the SOAR Peak Performance model depicted in Figure 4-1. This model is an adaption of Norman R. F. Maier's classic Causal Sequence model that we first discussed in chapter 2. The SOAR Peak Performance model suggests that an interaction between the *Situation* and the *Organization* leads to *Activities* that ultimately lead to *Results*.

If an organization is going to SOAR to peak performance, the leader, as an integral part of the situation, must influence the organization's activities to achieve results. Let's now look at Figure 4-2, which adds *L* to the model to represent the *Leader*. The leader's influence potential is represented in this model by an equal sign to illustrate the increasingly indirect power of leaders. One might think of indirect power as similar to the force that the north poles of two magnets have on each other. The closer they come together, the more resistance there is between them, much like an organization's resistance to a leader's attempt to change it.

Leaders are currently facing a decrease in power. Laws, regulations, and changes in social norms, among many other factors, have restricted leaders' ability to influence. This conclusion is not made in a normative sense of good

Figure 4-1
The SOAR Peak Performance Model

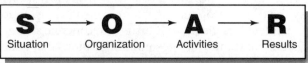

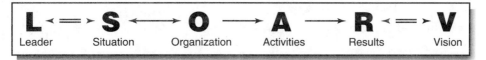

Figure 4-2
The SOAR Peak Performance Model (revised)

or bad, but as a fact of modern organizational life. At the same time, the situation has become increasingly complex and difficult to manage.

The leader, however, is but one of a myriad forces influencing the organization. From an external perspective, the organization is also affected by political, economic, social, technological, and environmental forces in the remote environment. Additional forces such as competitors and suppliers influence the operational environment. Further, within the business, contending forces such as culture help or hinder change. We will be discussing those matters in greater detail later. Given the effect of these many countervailing forces, the leader alone has insufficient power to influence an organization toward results. A leader's "magnetic" personality isn't enough; something more is needed to *pull* the organization toward results, and this is the role of *Vision* as depicted by the letter *V* in Figure 4-2. A leader's influencing push is not enough to achieve results; the pull of a powerful, impelling vision is required.

We have seen a similar idea in marketing where products and services are pushed through distribution channels, and advertising is used to stimulate customer demand to pull the products and services through the distribution channels toward them.

The SOAR Peak Performance model can be expanded into the Vision to Results model.

Vision to Results Model

The central framework discussed in this book is the Situational Leadership model, but we think it is important to look at achieving results from a strategic perspective. Just as a tapestry has a pattern that defines it, so does success. The key "pattern" words for tomorrow's success are:

- Vision
- Change
- Implementation
- Results

These four words are integral to the Vision to Results model developed in the following pages. It combines each of these characteristics in a process-oriented model composed of these key components.

- Vision
- Business idea—Organizational environment
- Strategy—Culture

- Goal—Teams
- Task—People
- Results

Many variables affect organizational performance, so the VTR model focuses on those variables that empirical research and managerial practice have identified as the most critical. At the top right of the model (see Figure 4-3), we identify a strategic vision; every organization has a driving vision, whether articulated or not, that determines its direction. Vision is a core part of a person (or organization), the inner being that reveals itself in thoughts, concepts, and dreams. Vision is conceiving of impossible things. Vision creates the potential for success and turns potential into profits . . . into results. Some may call this vision by different names such as will, purpose, charter, or goal. Whatever the name, there remains a picture of the future painted by the organization's core values and desires.

Figure 4-3
Vision to Results Through Leadership Actions

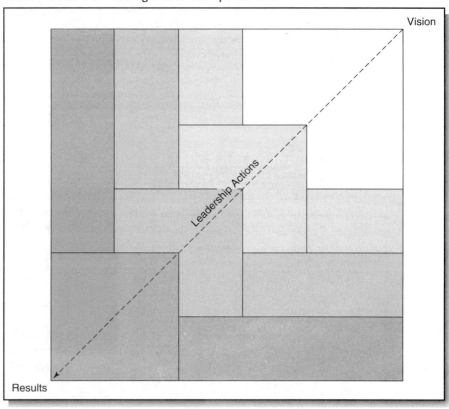

Johnson & Johnson, the health-care products company, is an example of an organization living the core values reflected in its credo:

We believe our first responsibility is to the doctors, nurses and patients, to mothers and fathers and all others who use our products and services. In meeting these needs, everything we do must be of high quality.[11]

This emphasis on core values led Johnson & Johnson to be named the top company in a nationwide reputation survey conducted by Harris Interactive Inc. and the Reputation Institute of New York.[12] Johnson & Johnson's chairman and chief executive officer explains how its reputation is guarded:

A lot of our companies want to be identified with J&J because the logo is so powerful, and on occasion we let them make it a tagline. But we use it very sparingly, because it belongs on products that evoke caring and gentleness. The last thing we want to do is confuse the customer about our image. . . . Johnson & Johnson is a trustmark, not a trademark. . . . Your reputation can be destroyed in an instant; if employees do anything to violate the consumer trust, they probably would not survive here.[13]

Returning to the model, we see in the lower-left corner the desired outcome of the vision—the results. This component tells us day-by-day how we are doing, in a tactical sense, to achieve the vision. Leadership turns visions into results!

The right side of the model (see Figure 4-4) is the planning (decision) side. Managers make decisions that spell out the mission (business ideas), strategies, goals, and tasks required to move the organization in the desired direction.

No matter how eloquent the plans, they must be implemented. Leadership is more than creating plans; it is achieving those plans. Most organizations focus on "what to do" and forget about "doing it." When you look at their plans, they are mostly structure. The main reason they do not work is that these plans neglect the influence of an organization's environment, culture, teams, and people (see Figure 4-5).

As we move diagonally from upper right to lower left (see Figure 4-6), we see that from Vision to Results moves through four levels. In level one, implementing business ideas in the internal and external environment is affected by the stakeholders, those persons, key players, or factors whose helping or hindering roles determine success or failure. Level two finds strategic initiatives carried out within the corporate culture, the way we do things around here. Level three suggests that goals are achieved by teams, and in level four, tasks are performed by people.

The business issues along the right side represent a decision process spelling out the "what" and "how" looking down and defining the "why" and "what" looking up.

The human issues along the top of the figure represent the influence process of leading the organization, regardless of level, toward the accomplishment of the right side.

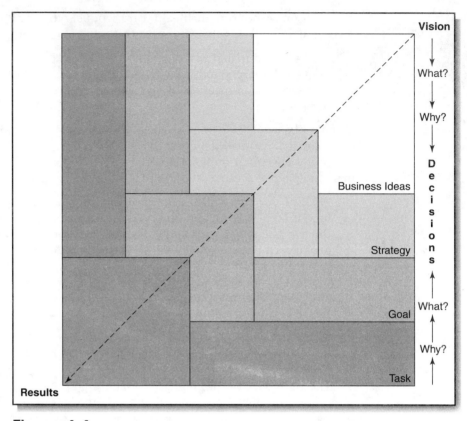

Figure 4-4
The Right-Hand Side—Decision Processes

The leadership challenges at each level as we move diagonally from right to left, top to bottom, in Figure 4-6 are:

1. Monitoring, refining, and establishing the vision, mission, and business ideas in light of the organization's environment
2. Energizing, attuning, and aligning the strategic initiatives and the culture
3. Connecting, unifying, and focusing teams toward their goals
4. Empowering, engaging, and enabling people for their tasks

This is illustrated by the "linking pin" boxes.

The leader's role today is that of a facilitating "linking pin" between the vision and results, between strategic issues and tactical issues, between the transformational and the transactional. It is not enough to simply watch over the decision-influence interface, no matter how well you do it. Leaders today must connect vision and results.

Oren Harari, professor at the University of San Francisco, management consultant, and frequent contributor to *Management Review,* published by the

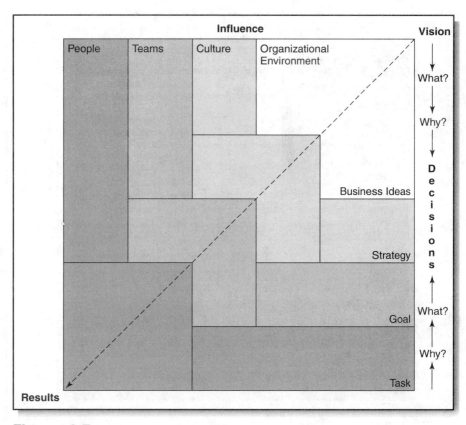

Figure 4-5
The Top Side—The Human Influence

American Management Association, sums up this connection in what he calls "three little words": inspire, shared, vision. He urges that the twenty-first century organization, to be effective, must have a "... coherent, comprehensive vision, a shared understanding and ownership of that vision, and an energy of inspiration that permeates and drives the vision."[14] How do effective leaders make this connection? It is through leadership.

LEGACIES OF THE PAST

Many distinguished authors and researchers have contributed to the rich legacy of modern leadership. Without the forward-looking visionaries of past generations (some of whom are listed in Table 4-1), we would not have the insights that we have today. And, as we review the contributions of these

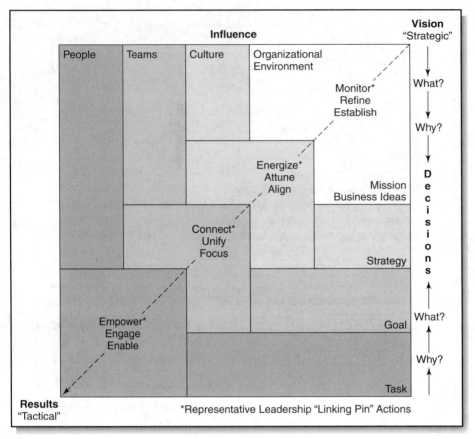

Figure 4-6
The Vision to Results (VTR) Model

Source: Adapted with permission of the Center for Leadership Studies, Inc. Copyright © 1996. All rights reserved.

visionaries from the perspective of the present, we should not be too hasty to criticize their efforts and their different approaches. They probably were applicable in their time.

In this book, we will take these insights, these visions from the past, and move with them to greater understanding that will help you create and accomplish a productive future. We want to help you "lead your best" in the twenty-first century.

SCHOOLS OF ORGANIZATIONAL THEORY

We have defined leadership as the process of influencing the activities of an individual or a group in efforts toward goal achievement in a given situation. In essence, leadership involves accomplishing goals with and through

Table 4-1   Significant Motivation and Leadership Theories and Models

Contributor	Theory or Model	Year of Publication of Significant Research
Taylor	Scientific Management	1911
Mayo	Hawthorne Studies	1933
Barnard	Executive Function	1938
Coch-French	Michigan Studies	1948
Stogdill	Ohio State Studies	1948
Homans	Human Group	1950
Maslow	Hierarchy of Needs	1954
McGregor	Theory X-Theory Y	1957
Tannenbaum-Schmidt	Continuum of Leader Behavior	1957
Blake-Mouton	Managerial Grid	1964
Argyris	Maturity-Immaturity	1964
McClelland	Achievement Theory	1965
Odiorne	Management By Objectives	1965
Herzberg	Motivation-Hygiene	1966
Likert	Systems 1–4	1967
Fiedler	Contingency Model	1967
Reddin	3-D Management Style	1967
Olsson	Management By Objectives	1968
Hersey-Blanchard	Situational Leadership	1969
Vroom-Yetten	Contingency Model	1973
House-Mitchell	Path-Goal	1974
Vroom	Expectancy Theory	1976
House	Charismatic Leadership	1977
Burns	Transformational Leadership	1978
Kerr-Jermier	Substitutes for Leadership	1978
McCall-Lombardo	Fatal Leadership Flaws	1983
Greenleaf	Servant Leadership	1983
Bennis-Nanus	Leadership Competencies	1985
Tichy-Devanna	Transformational Leadership	1986
Manz	Super Leadership	1989
Yukl	Integrating Leadership Model	1989
Covey	Principle-Centered Leadership	1991
Fisher	Leading Self-Directed Work Teams	1993
Johnson	SOAR Model	1994
Pansegrouw	Transformational Model	1995
Gyllenpalm	Organizational Cone	1995
Whetter-Cameron	Empowerment	1995
Tichy	Leadership Engine	1997
Ball	DNA Leadership	1997
Byham-Cox	Empowerment	1998
Fairholm	Values-Based Leadership	1998
Cohen	8 Universal Laws of Leadership	1998
Ulrich, Zenger, Smallwood	Results-Based Leadership	1999
Wheatley	Leadership and the New Science	1999

people. Therefore, a leader must be concerned about tasks and human relationships. Although using different terminology, Chester I. Barnard identified these same leadership concerns in his classic work *The Functions of the Executive* in the late 1930s.[15] These leadership concerns seem to be a reflection of two of the earliest schools of thought in organizational theory—scientific management and human relations.

Scientific Management Movement
Frederick Winslow Taylor

In the early 1900s, one of the most widely read theorists on administration was Frederick Winslow Taylor. The basis for his scientific management was technological in nature. It was felt that the best way to increase output was to improve the techniques, or methods, used by workers. Consequently, he has been interpreted as considering people as instruments or machines to be manipulated by their leaders. Accepting this assumption, other theorists of the scientific management movement proposed that an organization as rationally planned and executed as possible be developed to create more efficiency in administration and consequently increase production. Management was to be divorced from human affairs and emotions. The result was that the workers had to adjust to the management and not the management to the workers.

To accomplish this plan, Taylor initiated time-and-motion studies to analyze work tasks to improve performance in every aspect of the organization. Once jobs had been reorganized with efficiency in mind, the economic self-interest of the workers could be satisfied through various incentive work plans (piece rates and such).

The function of the leader under scientific management or classical theory was to set up and enforce performance criteria to meet organizational goals. The main focus of a leader was on the needs of the organization and not on the needs of the individual.[16]

Human Relations Movement
Elton Mayo

In the 1920s and early 1930s, the trend started by Taylor was to be replaced by the human relations movement, initiated by Elton Mayo and his associates. These theorists argued that in addition to finding the best technological methods to improve output, it was beneficial to management to look into human affairs. It was claimed that the real power centers within an organization were the interpersonal relations that developed within the working unit. The study of these human relations was the most important consideration for management and the analysis of organization. The organization was to be developed around the workers and had to take into consideration human feelings and attitudes.[17]

The function of the leader under human relations theory was to facilitate cooperative goal attainment among followers while providing opportunities for their personal growth and development. The main focus, contrary to scientific management theory, was on individual needs and not on the needs of the organization.

In essence, then, the scientific management movement emphasized a concern for task (output); the human relations movement stressed a concern for relationships (people). The recognition of these two concerns has characterized the writings on leadership ever since the conflict between the scientific management and the human relations schools of thought became apparent.

Looking specifically at leadership, we find that basic approaches to leadership have moved through three rather dominant phases: trait, attitudinal, and situational.

TRAIT APPROACHES TO LEADERSHIP

Before 1945, the most common approach to the study of leadership concentrated on leadership traits per se, suggesting that certain characteristics, such as physical energy or friendliness, were essential for effective leadership. These inherent personal qualities, like intelligence, were felt to be transferable from one situation to another. Because all individuals did not have these qualities, only those who had them would be considered potential leaders. Consequently, this approach seemed to question the value of training individuals to assume leadership positions. It implied that if we could discover how to identify and measure these leadership qualities (which are inborn in the individual), we should be able to screen leaders from nonleaders. Leadership training would then be helpful only to those with inherent leadership traits.

Reviews of research using this trait approach to leadership revealed few significant or consistent findings.[18] Eugene E. Jennings concluded that "fifty years of study have failed to produce one personality trait or set of qualities that can be used to discriminate leaders and nonleaders."[19]

This is not to say that certain traits won't hinder or facilitate leadership; the key is that no set of traits has been identified that clearly predicts success or failure. As Gary Yukl has observed,

In retrospect, it is apparent that many leadership researchers overreacted to the earlier pessimistic literature reviews by rejecting the relevance of traits entirely. However, Stogdill (1984) makes it clear that recognition of the relevance of leader traits is not a return to the original trait approach. The premise that some leader traits are absolutely necessary for effective leadership has not been substantiated in several decades of trait research. Possession of particular traits increases the likelihood that a leader will be effective, but [it does] not guarantee effectiveness, and the relative importance of different traits is dependent upon the nature of the leadership situation.[20]

What are some traits and skills found to be most characteristic of successful leaders? Yukl offered some suggestions, shown in Table 4-2.

Trait research is still continuing. Warren Bennis completed a 5-year study of 90 outstanding leaders and their followers. On the basis of this research, he identified four common traits, or areas of competence, shared by all 90 leaders.[21]

1. *Management of attention.* The ability to communicate a sense of outcome, goal, or direction that attracts followers
2. *Management of meaning.* The ability to create and communicate meaning with clarity and understanding
3. *Management of trust.* The ability to be reliable and consistent
4. *Management of self.* The ability to know one's self and to use one's skills within the limits of one's strengths and weaknesses

Bennis suggested that leaders empower their organizations to create an environment where people feel significant and are part of the community or team, where learning and competence matter, and where work is exciting. Leaders should also create an environment where quality matters and dedication to work energizes effort.[22]

Bennis updated these traits with seven characteristics of effective performance:

1. *Business literacy.* Does the manager know the business—the real feel of it?
2. *People skills.* Does the manager have the capacity to motivate, to bring out the best in people?
3. *Conceptual skills.* Does the manager have the capacity to think systematically, creatively, and inventively?
4. *Track record.* Has the manager done it before and done it well?

Table 4-2 Traits and Skills Found Most Frequently to Be Characteristic of Successful Leaders

TRAIT	SKILL
Adaptable to situations	Clever (intelligent)
Alert to social environment	Conceptually skilled
Ambitious and achievement-oriented	Creative
Assertive	Diplomatic and tactful
Cooperative	Fluent in speaking
Decisive	Knowledgeable about group tasks
Dependable	Organized (administrative ability)
Dominant (desire to influence others)	Persuasive
Energetic (high activity level)	Socially skilled
Persistent	
Self-confident	
Tolerant of stress	
Willing to assume responsibility	

Source: Leadership in Organizations, 3/E by Yukl, Gary, © 1998. Reprinted by permission of Prentice-Hall, Inc., Upper Saddle River, NJ.

5. *Taste.* Does the manager have the ability to pick the right people—not clones, but people who can make up deficiencies?

6. *Judgment.* Does the manager have the ability to make quick decisions with imperfect data?

7. *Character.* The core competency of leadership is character, but character and judgment are the qualities we know least about when trying to teach them to others.[23]

Negative Leadership Traits

As Yukl indicated, there may be negative traits that hinder a person from reaching leadership potential. In one study, John Geier found three traits that kept group members from competing for a leadership role.[24] Those three traits were, in order of importance, the perception of being uninformed, of being nonparticipants, or of being extremely rigid. Why were these traits so critical? Because the other group members believed that members who were uninformed, uninterested, or overly rigid would hinder the group's accomplishment of its goals. As an aside, isn't our educational system designed to make students more informed, more motivated, and less rigid? We think so.

Morgan McCall and Michael Lombardo examined differences between executives who went all the way to the top and those who were expected to go to the top but were "derailed" just before reaching their goal. Both winners and losers had strengths and weaknesses, but those who fell short seemed to have one or more of what McCall and Lombardo called "fatal flaws."

1. Insensitive to others: abrasive, intimidating, bullying style
2. Cold, aloof, arrogant
3. Untrustworthy
4. Overly ambitious: always thinking of next job, playing politics
5. Having specific performance problems with the business
6. Unable to delegate or build a team—overmanaging
7. Unable to staff effectively
8. Unable to think strategically
9. Unable to adapt to boss with different style
10. Overdependent on advocate or mentor[25]

The most frequent cause for derailment was insensitivity to others, but the most serious was untrustworthiness. Betrayal of trust—not following through on promises or double-dealing—was the one "unforgivable sin."[26]

Shelley Kirkpatrick and Edwin Locke in the *Academy of Management Executive* reinforced the views of Bennis, Yukl, and others:

> Recent research, using a variety of methods, has made it clear that successful leaders are not like other people. The evidence indicates that there are certain core traits which contribute to business leaders' success. . . . Leaders do not have to be great men or women by being intellectual geniuses or omniscient prophets to succeed, but they do need to have the "right stuff" and this stuff is not equally present in all people.[27]

Table 4-3 lists the traits Kirkpatrick and Locke say do matter.

Table 4-3 Leadership Traits That Do Matter

Drive: achievement, ambition, energy, tenacity, initiative
Leadership motivation (personalized versus socialized)
Honesty and integrity
Self-confidence (including emotional stability)
Cognitive ability
Knowledge of the business
Other traits: charisma, creativity, originality, flexibility

Source: Shelley A. Kirkpatrick and Edwin A. Locke, "Leadership: Do Traits Matter?" *Academy of Management Executive,* 5, no. 2 © 1991, p. 49. Reprinted by permission of Oxford University Press.

In summary, empirical research suggests that leadership is a dynamic process, varying from situation to situation with changes in the leader, the followers, and the situation. Therefore, although certain traits may help or hinder in a given situation, there is no universal set of traits that will ensure leadership success. The lack of validation of trait approaches led to other investigations of leadership. Among the most prominent areas were the attitudinal approaches.

ATTITUDINAL APPROACHES

The main period of the attitudinal approaches to leadership occurred between 1945, with the Ohio State and Michigan studies, and the mid-1960s, with the development of the Managerial Grid®.[28]

By attitudinal approaches, we mean approaches that use paper-and-pencil instruments such as questionnaires to measure attitudes or predispositions toward leader behavior. For example, the dimensions of the Managerial Grid—concern for production and concern for people—are attitudinal. *Concern* may be defined as a predisposition or feeling toward or against production and people. In this section, we will look specifically at three attitudinal approaches to leadership: the Ohio State studies; the Michigan studies, including Rensis Likert's work; and the Managerial Grid.

Ohio State Leadership Studies

The leadership studies initiated in 1945 by the Bureau of Business Research at The Ohio State University attempted to identify various dimensions of leader behavior.[29] The researchers, directed by Ralph Stogdill, defining leadership as the behavior of an individual when directing the activities of a group toward goal attainment, eventually narrowed the description of leader behavior to two dimensions: initiating structure and consideration. *Initiating structure* refers to "a type of leader behavior that describes the extent to which a leader is task oriented and directs subordinates' work activities toward goal achievement."[30] On the other hand, *consideration* refers to "a type of leader behavior that describes the extent to which a leader is sensitive to subordinates, respects their ideas and feelings, and establishes mutual trust."[31]

To gather data about the behavior of leaders, the Ohio State staff developed the leader behavior description questionnaire (LBDQ), an instrument designed to describe how leaders carry out their activities. The LBDQ contains 15 items pertaining to consideration and 15 to initiating structure. Respondents judge the frequency with which their leader engages in each form of behavior by checking one of five descriptions—always, often, occasionally, seldom, or never. Thus, consideration and initiating structure are dimensions of observed behavior as perceived by others. Examples of items used in the LBDQ for both of these dimensions are shown in Table 4-4.

Although the major emphasis in the Ohio State Leadership studies was on observed behavior, the staff did develop the leader opinion questionnaire (LOQ) to gather data about leaders' self-perceptions of their leadership style. The LBDQ was completed by leaders' followers, supervisors, or associates (peers), but the LOQ was scored by the leaders themselves.

In studying leader behavior, the Ohio State staff found that initiating structure and consideration were separate and distinct dimensions. A high score on one dimension does not necessitate a low score on the other. The behavior of a leader could be described as any mix of both dimensions. Thus, it was during these studies that leader behavior was first plotted on two separate axes rather than on a single continuum. Quadrants were developed to show various combinations of initiating structure and consideration, as illustrated in Figure 4-7.

Michigan Leadership Studies

Researchers at the University of Michigan conducted leadership studies, starting in 1945. In the early studies, there was an attempt to approach the study of leadership by locating clusters of characteristics that seemed to be related and by determining various indicators of effectiveness. The studies identified two concepts, which the researchers called *employee orientation* and *production orientation*.[32]

Leaders who were described as employee-oriented emphasized the relationships aspect of their job. They felt that every employee is important and

Table 4-4 Examples of LBDQ Items

CONSIDERATION	INITIATING STRUCTURE
The leader finds time to listen to group members.	The leader assigns group members to particular tasks.
The leader is willing to make changes.	The leader asks the group members to follow standard rules and regulations.
The leader is friendly and approachable.	The leader lets group members know what is expected of them.

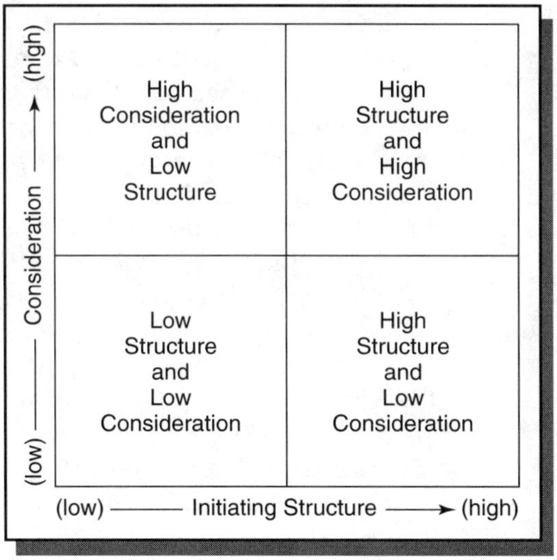
High Consideration and Low Structure
High Structure and High Consideration
Low Structure and Low Consideration
High Structure and Low Consideration
(low) —— Consideration ——→ (high)
(low) —— Initiating Structure ——→ (high)

Figure 4-7
The Ohio State Leadership Quadrants

took interest in everyone, accepting their individuality and personal needs. Production-oriented leaders emphasized production and the technical aspects of the job; employees are seen as tools to accomplish the goals of the organization. These two orientations parallel the democratic (relationship) and authoritarian (task) concepts of the leader behavior continuum of the Tannenbaum-Schmidt model to be presented in chapter 5.

Group Dynamics Studies

Dorwin Cartwright and Alvin Zander, summarizing the findings of numerous studies at the Research Center for Group Dynamics at the University of Michigan, claimed that group objectives fall into one of two categories: (1) the achievement of some specific group goal or (2) the maintenance or strengthening of the group itself.[33]

According to Cartwright and Zander, the type of behavior involved in goal achievement is illustrated by these examples: The manager "initiates action . . . keeps members' attention on the goal . . . clarifies the issue and develops a procedural plan."[34] On the other hand, typical behaviors for group maintenance are characterized by a manager who "keeps interpersonal relations pleasant . . . arbitrates disputes . . . provides encouragement . . . gives the minority a chance to be heard . . . stimulates self-direction . . . and increases the interdependence among members."[35] Goal achievement seems to coincide with the task concepts discussed earlier (production orientation), and group maintenance parallels the relationship concepts (employee orientation).

Research findings in recent years indicate that leadership styles vary considerably from leader to leader. Some leaders emphasize the task and can be described as authoritarian leaders; others stress interpersonal relationships and may be viewed as democratic leaders. Still others seem to be both task-oriented and relationship-oriented. There are even some individuals in leadership positions who are not concerned about either. No dominant style appears. Instead, various combinations are evident. Thus, task and relationship are not either-or leadership styles. They are separate and distinct dimensions that can be plotted on two separate axes.

Rensis Likert's Management Systems

Using the earlier Michigan studies as a starting place, Rensis Likert did some extensive research to discover the general pattern of management used by high-producing managers in contrast to the pattern used by the other managers. He found that "supervisors with the best records of performance focus their primary attention on the human aspects of their employees' problems and on endeavoring to build effective work groups with high performance goals."[36] These supervisors were called *employee-centered*. Other supervisors who kept constant pressure on production were called *job-centered* and were found more often to have low-producing sections. Figure 4-8 presents the findings from one study.

Likert also discovered that high-producing supervisors "make clear to their employees what the objectives are and what needs to be accomplished and then give them freedom to do the job."[37] Thus, he found that general rather than close supervision tended to be associated with high productivity. This relationship, found in a study of clerical workers, is illustrated in Figure 4-9. The figure shows that nine out of ten high-producing sections were led by first-line supervisors who used general supervision, whereas eight out of twelve low-producing sections were led by supervisors who used close supervision. Note that general supervision did not always result in high production or close supervision in low production. But, general supervision under the conditions described in this study had a higher probability of resulting in high production than did close supervision.

Likert and his colleagues' continuing research at the Institute for Social Research at the University of Michigan emphasized the need to consider both human resources and capital resources as assets requiring proper management attention. He found that most managers, when asked what they would

Figure 4-8
Employee-Centered Supervisors Are Higher Producers Than Are Job-Centered Supervisors

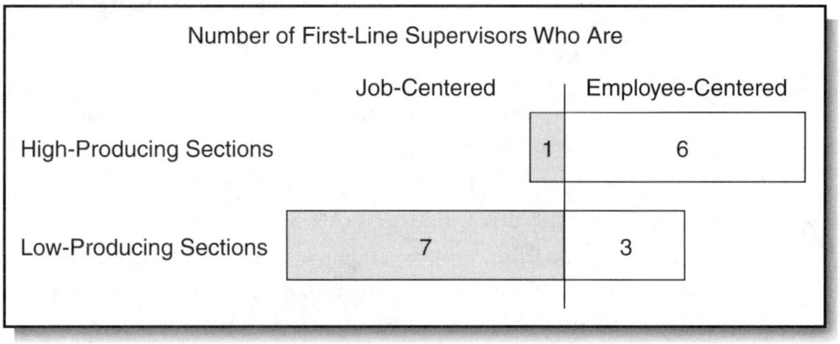

Number of First-Line Supervisors Who Are		
	Job-Centered	Employee-Centered
High-Producing Sections	1	6
Low-Producing Sections	7	3

Source: Rensis Likert, *New Patterns of Management,* © 1961, McGraw-Hill. Reprinted by permission of the The McGraw-Hill Companies.

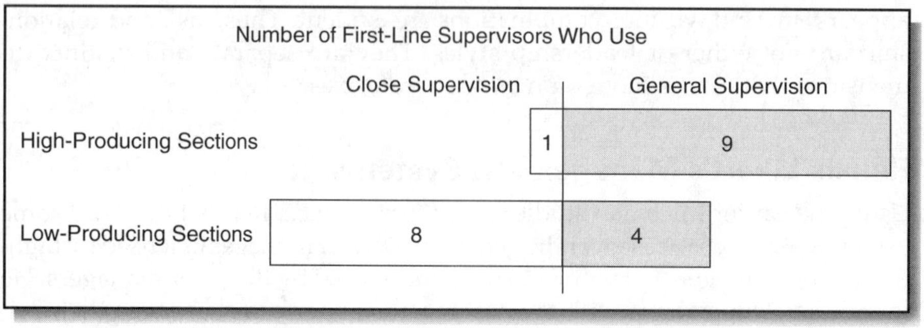

Number of First-Line Supervisors Who Use		
	Close Supervision	General Supervision
High-Producing Sections	1	9
Low-Producing Sections	8	4

Figure 4-9
Low-Producing Sections Are More Closely Supervised Than Are
High-Producing Sections

Source: Rensis Likert, *New Patterns of Management,* © 1961, McGraw-Hill. Reprinted by permission of The McGraw-Hill Companies.

do if they suddenly lost half of their plant, equipment, or capital resources, were quick to answer that they would depend on insurance or borrowed money to keep them in business. Yet, when these same managers were asked what they would do if they suddenly lost half of their human resources—managers, supervisors, and hourly employees—they were at a loss for words. There is no insurance against outflows of human resources. Recruiting, training, and developing large numbers of new personnel into a working team takes years. In a competitive environment, this task is almost impossible. Organizations are now realizing that their most important assets are human resources and that managing them is one of their most crucial tasks.

As a result of behavioral research studies of numerous organizations, Likert implemented organizational change programs in various industrial settings. These programs were intended to help organizations move from Theory X to Theory Y assumptions, from fostering immature behavior to encouraging and developing mature behavior, from emphasizing only hygiene factors to recognizing and implementing motivators.

Likert in his studies found that the prevailing management styles of organizations can be depicted on a continuum from system 1 through system 4. These systems might be described as follows:[38]

System 1
Management has no confidence or trust in employees and seldom involves them in any aspect of the decision-making process. The bulk of the decisions and the goal setting of the organization are made at the top and issued down the chain of command. Employees are forced to work with fear, threats, punishment, and occasional rewards. Need satisfaction is at the physiological and safety levels. The limited management-employee interaction that does take place is usually with fear and mistrust. Although the control process is highly concentrated in top management, an informal organization generally develops in opposition to the goals of the formal organization.

Chapter 4   Leadership: An Initial Perspective

System 2

Management has only condescending confidence and trust in employees, such as a master has toward the servants. The bulk of the decisions and goal setting of the organization are made at the top, but many decisions are made within a prescribed framework at lower levels. Rewards and some actual or potential punishment are used to motivate workers. Any interaction takes place with some condescension by management and fear and caution by employees. Although the control process is still concentrated in top management, some control is delegated to middle and lower levels. An informal organization usually develops, but it does not always resist formal organizational goals.

System 3

Management has substantial, but not complete, confidence and trust in employees. Broad policy and general decisions are kept at the top, but employees are permitted to make more specific decisions at lower levels. Communication flows both up and down the hierarchy. Rewards, occasional punishment, and some involvement are used to motivate workers. There is a moderate amount of interaction, often with a fair amount of confidence and trust. Significant aspects of the control process are delegated downward, with a feeling of responsibility at both higher and lower levels. An informal organization may develop, but it may either support or partially resist goals of the organization.

System 4

Management has complete confidence and trust in employees. Decision making is widely dispersed throughout the organization, although well integrated. Communication flows not only up and down the hierarchy, but among peers. Workers are motivated by participation and involvement in developing economic rewards, setting goals, improving methods, and appraising progress toward goals. There is extensive friendly management-employee interaction, with a high degree of confidence and trust. There is widespread responsibility for the control process, with the lower units fully involved. The informal and formal organizations are often one and the same. Thus, all social forces support efforts to achieve stated organizational goals.

In summary, system 1 is a task-oriented, highly structured authoritarian management style; system 4 is a relationship-oriented management style based on teamwork, mutual trust, and confidence. Systems 2 and 3 are intermediate stages between two extremes, which approximate closely Theory X and Theory Y assumptions.

To expedite the analysis of a company's current behavior, Likert's group developed an instrument that enables members to evaluate their organization in terms of its management system. This instrument is designed to gather data about a number of operating characteristics of an organization. These characteristics include leadership, motivation, communication, decision making, interaction and influence, goal setting, and the control process used by the organization. Sample items from this instrument are presented in Table 4-5.

Table 4-5 Examples of Items from Likert's Table of Organizational and Performance Characteristics of Different Management Systems

Organizational Variable	System 1	System 2	System 3	System 4
Leadership processes used Extent to which superiors have confidence and trust in subordinates	Have no confidence and trust in subordinates	Have condescending confidence and trust, such as master has to servant	Substantial but not complete confidence and trust; still wishes to keep control of decisions	Complete confidence and trust in all matters
Character of motivational forces Manner in which motives are used	Fear, threats, punishment, and occasional rewards	Rewards and some actual or potential punishment	Rewards, occasional punishment, and some involvement	Economic rewards based on compensation system developed through participation; group participation and involvement in setting goals, improving methods, and appraising progress toward goals
Character of interaction-influence process Amount and character of interaction	Little interaction and always with fear and distrust	Little interaction and usually with some condescension by superiors; fear and caution by subordinates	Moderate interaction, often with fair amount of confidence and trust	Extensive, friendly interaction with high degree of confidence and trust

Source: Rensis Likert, *The Human Organization* © 1967 McGraw-Hill. Reproduced with permission of McGraw-Hill Companies.

The complete instrument includes more than 20 such items. Various forms of this instrument have been adapted for specific situations. For example, a version for school systems is now available with forms for the school board, superintendent, central staff, principals, teachers, parents, and students.

In testing this instrument, Likert asked hundreds of managers from many different organizations to indicate where the most productive department, division, or organization they have known would fall between system 1 and system 4. Then, these same managers were asked to repeat this process and indicate the position of the least productive department, division, or organization they have known. Although the ratings of the most and the least productive departments varied among managers, almost without exception each manager rated the high-producing unit closer to system 4 than the low-producing unit. In summary, Likert found that the closer the management style of an organization comes to system 4, the more likely it will be to have a continuous record of high productivity. Similarly, the closer a management style comes to system 1, the more likely it is to have a sustained record of low productivity.

Likert used this instrument not only to measure what individuals believe are the current characteristics of their organization but also to find out what they would like management characteristics to be. Data generated from this use of the instrument with managers of well-known companies indicated a large discrepancy between the management system their company was currently using and the management system they felt would be most appropriate. System 4 was seen as being most appropriate, but few saw their companies as utilizing this approach. These implications have led to attempts by some organizations to adapt their management system to approximate more closely system 4. Changes of this kind are not easy. They involve a massive reeducation of all concerned, from the top management to the hourly workers.

Theory into Practice

One instance of a successful change in the management style of an organization occurred with a leading firm in the pajama industry.[39] After being unprofitable for several years, this company was purchased by another corporation. At the time of the transaction, the purchased company was using a management style falling between system 1 and system 2. Some major changes were soon implemented by the new owners. The changes that were put into effect included extensive modifications in how the work was organized, improved maintenance of machinery, and a training program involving managers and workers at every level. Managers and supervisors were exposed in depth to the philosophy and understanding of management approaching system 4. All of these changes were supported by the top management of the purchasing company.

Although productivity dropped in the first several months after the initiation of the change program, productivity increased by almost 30 percent within 2 years. It is not possible to calculate exactly how much of the increased productivity resulted from the change in management system, but it was apparent to the researchers that the impact was considerable. In addition to increases in productivity, manufacturing costs decreased 20 percent, turnover was cut almost in half, and morale rose considerably (reflecting a friendlier attitude of workers toward the organization). The company's image in the community was enhanced, and for the first time in years the company began to show a profit.

The implication throughout Likert's writings is that the ideal and most productive leader behavior for industry is employee-centered or democratic. Yet, his own findings raise questions as to whether there can be an ideal or single normatively good style of leader behavior that applies in all leadership situations. Notice that in Figures 4-8 and 4-9, one of the eight job-centered supervisors and one of the nine supervisors using close supervision had high-producing sections; also, three of the nine employee-centered supervisors and four of the thirteen supervisors who used general supervision had low-producing sections. In other words, in almost 35 percent of the low-producing sections, the suggested ideal type of leader behavior produced undesirable results, and almost 15 percent of the high-producing sections were supervised by the suggested "undesirable" style.

Similar findings and interpretations were made by Andrew Halpin and Ben Winer in a study of the relationship between aircraft commanders' leadership patterns and the proficiency rating of their crews.[40] Using the LBDQ, they found that eight of ten commanders with high proficiency ratings were described as using above average consideration and initiating structure and that six of seven commanders with low ratings were seen as below average in consideration and initiating structure. As Likert did, Halpin and Winer reported only that the leaders above average in both consideration and initiating structure are likely to be effective and did not discuss the two high-proficiency, low-consideration, low-initiating structure commanders and the one low-producing, high-initiating structure, high-consideration commander.

Evidence suggesting that a single ideal or normative style of leader behavior is unrealistic was provided by a study done in an industrial setting in Nigeria.[41] The results were almost the exact opposite of Likert's findings. In that country, the tendency was for job-centered supervisors who provide close supervision to have high-producing sections and for employee-centered supervisors who provide general supervision to have low-producing sections. Thus, a single normative leadership style does not take into consideration cultural differences, particularly customs and traditions as well as the level of education, the standard of living, or industrial experience. These are examples of cultural differences in the followers and the situations that are important in determining the appropriate leadership style to be used. Therefore, on the basis of the definition of the leadership process as a function of the leader, the followers, and other situational variables, a single ideal type of leader behavior seems unrealistic.

The Leadership Grid®
Robert R. Blake and Anne Adams McCanse

In discussing the Ohio State, Michigan, and Likert leadership studies, we concentrated on two theoretical concepts—one emphasizing task accomplishment and the other stressing the development of personal relationships. Robert R. Blake and Anne Adams McCanse modified these concepts in their Leadership Grid (formerly the Managerial Grid by Robert R. Blake and Jane S. Mouton) and have used them extensively in organization and management development programs.[42]

In the Leadership Grid, five different types of leadership based on concern for production (task) and concern for people (relationship) are located in four quadrants (see Figure 4-10) similar to those identified by the Ohio State

Figure 4-10
The Leadership Grid®

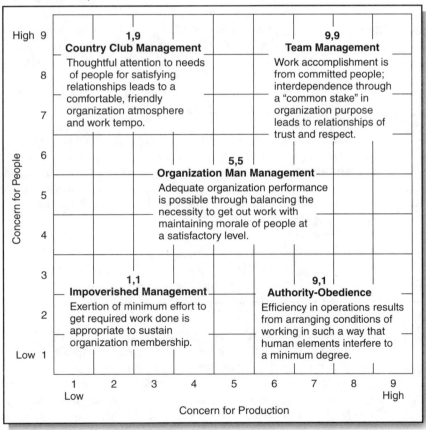

Source: The Leadership Grid figure for *Leadership Dilemmas—Grid Solutions* by Robert R. Blake and Anne Adams McCanse. (Formerly the Managerial Grid figure by Robert R. Blake and Jane S. Mouton) Houston: Gulf Publishing Company, p. 29. Copyright 1991 by R. R. Blake, J. C. Mouton, and A. Jane. Reproduced by permission of the owners.

studies (see Figure 4-7). Concern for production is illustrated on the horizontal axis. Production becomes more important to the leader as the rating advances on the horizontal scale. A leader with a rating of nine on the horizontal axis has a maximum concern for production. Concern for people is illustrated on the vertical axis. People become more important to leaders as their ratings progress up the vertical axis. A leader with a rating of nine on the vertical axis has maximum concern for people.

The five leadership styles are described as follows:

1, 1 Impoverished Management. Exertion of minimum effort to get required work done is appropriate to sustain organization membership.

1, 9 Country Club Management. Thoughtful attention to the needs of people for satisfying relationships leads to a comfortable, friendly organization atmosphere and work tempo.

9, 1 Authority-Obedience Management. Efficiency in operations results from arranging conditions of work in such a way that human elements interfere to a minimum degree.

5, 5 Organizational Man Management. Adequate organization performance is possible through balancing the necessity to get work out while maintaining morale of people at a satisfactory level.

9, 9 Team Management. Work accomplishment is from committed people; interdependence through a "common stake" in organization purpose leads to relationships of trust and respect.[43]

We want to point out one significant difference between the Leadership Grid and the Ohio State frameworks. "Concern for" is a predisposition about something, or an attitudinal dimension. Therefore, the Leadership Grid tends to be an attitudinal model that measures the values and feelings of a manager, whereas the Ohio State framework attempts to include behavioral concepts (items) as well as attitudinal items.

IS THERE A BEST STYLE OF LEADERSHIP?

Researchers such as Blake, Mouton, and McCanse and McGregor have argued that there is "one best" style of leadership—a style that maximizes productivity and satisfaction, growth and development in all situations—but further research in the last several decades has clearly supported the contention that there is no one best leadership style. Successful and effective leaders are able to adapt their style to fit the requirements of the situation. To amplify this idea, we must place the current state of leadership theory into perspective.

First, leadership theories, like the vast majority of behavioral science theories, have not been conclusively validated by scientific research. As Stephen

Robbins observed, "Simple and universal principles [of organizational be-havior] are avoided because there exist no simple and universal truths or principles that consistently explain organizational behavior."[44] But just be-cause research does not conclusively validate a behavioral science theory does not necessarily make it invalid. If it did, there probably wouldn't be any organizational behavior theories (or books such as this one, based on the be-havioral sciences). For example, as Robbins suggested in his appraisal of Maslow's hierarchy of needs, "Remember that there is a difference between finding 'insufficient evidence' for a theory and labeling it 'invalid.' It is clear that the available research does not support the Maslow theory to any signifi-cant degree. This does not imply that the theory is wrong, merely that it has not been supported."[45]

Solid "scientific" evidence supporting leadership theories may be lack-ing simply because leadership theories are, at this point, sets of empirical gen-eralizations that by their very nature cannot be "scientifically" tested. In its strictest sense, scientific testing requires controlling variables, and few vari-ables in an organization over time can be controlled. Likewise, anthropology and archaeology cannot be tested, but theories in those fields are nonetheless considered to be valid.

Perhaps the problem is that we have been expecting too much from so-called leadership theories. They really are not theories at all but, as we have suggested, descriptions of concepts, procedures, actions, and outcomes that exist. (This is why we refer to Situational Leadership as a model.)

The primary reason why there is no one best way of leadership is that leadership is basically situational, or contingent. All of the leadership theo-ries mentioned so far, and others, as well, that represent the mainstream of leadership thought are situational. As Robbins stated, "OB [organizational behavior] concepts are founded on situational conditions; that is, if X, then Y, but only under conditions specified in Z (the contingency variables)."[46] In other words, the effectiveness of a particular leadership style is contingent upon the situation in which it is used.

Effective managers must be able not only to determine the most appro-priate leadership style but also to correctly apply that style. As James Owens observed:

> managers expressed a virtual consensus that, based on their actual experience, each situation they handled demanded a different lead-ership style. No single style could suffice under the day-to-day, even minute-by-minute, varying conditions of different personali-ties and moods among their employees, routine process vs. chang-ing or sudden deadlines, new and ever-changing government regulations and paperwork, ambiguous roles of workers, wide ranges in job complexity from simple to innovation-demanding, changes in organizational structure and markets and task technolo-gies and so on. Contingency theory has come to mean, therefore, that the effective manager has, and knows how to use, many lead-ership styles as each is appropriate to a particular situation.[47]

Frances Hesselbein, past CEO of the Girl Scouts of America, put it quite eloquently also. "Leadership is a matter of how to be, not how to do it. And the one indispensible quality of leadership is personal integrity with a sense of ethics that works full-time."[48] But perhaps Ralph Stogdill said it best: "The most effective leaders . . . exhibit a degree of versatility and flexibility that enables them to adapt their behavior to the changing and contradictory demands made on them."[49]

PREVIEW

What are some of these "changing and contradictory demands"? How do they influence leadership? How does a potential leader diagnose the situation to determine the high-probability leadership style to use? These and many other important issues will be the subjects for chapter 5 and the following chapters.

ENDNOTES

1. Peter F. Drucker, *The Practice of Management* (New York: Harper & Row, 1954). See also Allen L. Appell, *A Practical Approach to Human Behavior in Business* (Columbus, OH: Merrill, 1984).

2. George R. Terry, *Principles of Management*, 3rd ed. (Homewood, IL, 1960), p. 493.

3. Robert Tannenbaum, Irwin R. Weschler, and Fred Massarik, *Leadership and Organization: A Behavioral Science Approach* (New York: McGraw-Hill, 1959).

4. Harold Koontz and Cyril O'Donnell, *Principles of Management*, 2nd ed. (New York: McGraw-Hill, 1959), p. 435.

5. Roland S. Barth, Senior Lecturer, Harvard University, quoted in Harold J. Burbach, "New Ways of Thinking for Educators," *The Education Digest*, March 1988, p. 3.

6. Proverbs 29:18. See also Neil H. Snyder, "Leadership and Vision," *Business Week*, 37 (January/February 1994), pp. 1–7.

7. Warren Bennis, *On Becoming a Leader* (Reading, MA: Addison-Wesley, 1989), p. 194. See also Marshall Loeb, "Where Leaders Come From," *Fortune*, September 19, 1994, p. 242; Gerald Egan, "A Clear Path to Peak Performance,"

People Management, v (May 18, 1995), pp. 34–35; and Gerald Kushel, *Reaching the Peak Performance Zone: How To Motivate Yourself and Others To Excel* (New York: AMACOM, 1994).

8. Marshall Loeb, "Where Leaders Come From," *Fortune*, September 19, 1994, p. 242.

9. Quoted in Bennis, *On Becoming a Leader*, p. 194.

10. Bennis, *On Becoming a Leader*, p. 194.

11. Ronald Alsop, "Johnson & Johnson (Think Babies!) Turns Up Tops," *The Wall Street Journal*, September 23, 1999, p. B1.

12. Ronald Alsop, "The Best Corporate Reputations in America. Just As in Politics, Trust, Reliability Pay Off over Time," *The Wall Street Journal*, September 23, 1999, p. B1.

13. Ronald Alsop, "Johnson & Johnson (Think Babies!) Turns Up Tops," *The Wall Street Journal*, September 23, 1999, p. B1.

14. Oren Harari, "Three Vital Little Words," *Management Review*, November 1995, p. 27.

15. Chester I. Barnard, *The Functions of the Executive* (Cambridge, MA: Harvard University Press, 1938).

16. Frederick W. Taylor, *The Principles of Scientific Management* (New York: Harper & Brothers, 1911).

17. Elton Mayo, *The Social Problems of an Industrial Civilization* (Boston: Harvard Business School, 1945), p. 23.
18. Cecil A. Gibb, "Leadership." In *Handbook of Social Psychology,* ed. Gardner Lindzey (Cambridge, MA: Addison-Wesley, 1954). See also Ralph M. Stogdill, "Personal Factors Associated with Leadership: A Survey of Literature," *Journal of Psychology,* 25 (1948), pp. 35–71.
19. Eugene E. Jennings, "The Anatomy of Leadership," *Management of Personnel Quarterly,* 1, no. 1 (Autumn 1961). See also Arthur G. Jago, "Leadership: Perspectives in Theory and Research," *Management Science,* March 1982, pp. 315–336.
20. Gary A. Yukl, *Leadership in Organizations,* 3rd ed. (Upper Saddle River, NJ: Prentice Hall, 1994), pp. 255–256.
21. Warren Bennis, "The Four Competencies of Leadership," *Training and Development Journal,* August 1984, pp. 15–19. See also Warren Bennis and Bert Nanus, Leaders, *The Strategies for Taking Charge* (New York: Harper & Row, 1986).
22. Bennis, "The Four Competencies of Leadership."
23. Adapted from Loeb, "Where Leaders Come From." pp. 241–242.
24. John G. Geier, "A Trait Approach to the Study of Leadership in Small Groups," *Journal of Communications,* December 1967.
25. Morgan W. McCall Jr. and Michael M. Lombardo, "What Makes a Top Executive?" *Psychology Today,* February 1983, pp. 26–31. See also Morgan M. McCall Jr. and Robert E. Kaplan, *Whatever It Takes: The Realities of Managerial Decision Making* (Upper Saddle River, NJ: Prentice Hall, 1990).
26. *Ibid.*
27. Shelley A. Kirkpatrick and Edwin A. Locke, "Leadership: Do Traits Matter?" *Academy of Management Executive,* 5, no. 2 (1991), pp. 49, 59.
28. Robert R. Blake and Jane S. Mouton, *The Managerial Grid III,* 3rd ed. (Houston, TX: Gulf Publishing, 1984). See also Robert R. Blake and Jane S. Mouton, "The Managerial Grid III," *Personnel Psychology,* 39 (Spring 1986), pp. 238–240.
29. Ralph M. Stogdill and Alvin Coons, eds., *Leader Behavior: Its Description and Measurement, Research Monograph No. 88* (Columbus: Bureau of Business Research, The Ohio State University, 1957). See also Fred E. Fiedler and Martin M. Chemers, "Improving Leadership Effectiveness," *Personnel Psychology,* 38 (Spring 1985), pp. 220–222.
30. Richard L. Daft, *Management,* 3rd ed. (Fort Worth: The Dryden Press, 1994), p. 484.
31. *Ibid.* See also Andrew W. Halpin, *The Leadership Behavior of School Superintendents* (Chicago: Midwest Administration Center, University of Chicago, 1959), p. 4.
32. Robert Kahn and Daniel Katz, "Leadership Practices in Relation to Productivity and Morale," Dorwin Cartwright and Alvin Zander, eds., *Group Dynamics: Research and Theory,* 2nd ed. (Evanston, IL: Row, Peterson, 1960). Many other studies are available from University of Michigan, Ann Arbor, MI, Institute for Social Research.
33. Dorwin Cartwright and Alvin Zander, eds., *Group Dynamics: Research and Theory,* 2nd ed. (Evanston, IL: Row, Peterson, 1960). See also Patrick R. Penland, *Group Dynamics and Individual Development* (New York: Dekker, 1974); Robert H. Guest, *Work Teams and Team Building* (New York: Pergamon, 1986).
34. Cartwright and Zander, *Group Dynamics,* p. 496. See also *Group Plannings and Problems—Solving Methods in Engineering Management,* ed. Shirley A. Olsen (New York: Wiley, 1982).
35. Cartwright and Zander, *Group Dynamics,* p. 497.
36. Rensis Likert, *New Patterns of Management* (New York: McGraw-Hill, 1961), p. 7.
37. *Ibid.,* p. 9.
38. Adapted from Rensis Likert, *The Human Organization* (New York: McGraw-Hill, 1967), pp. 197–211.
39. Lester Coch and John R. P. French Jr., "Overcoming Resistance to Change," *Human Relations,* 1, no. 4 (1948), pp. 512–532.
40. Andrew W. Halpin and Ben J. Winer, *The Leadership Behavior of Airplane Commanders* (Columbus: Ohio State Research Foundation, 1952).
41. Paul Hersey, unpublished research project, 1965.
42. Robert R. Blake and Anne Adams McCanse, *Leadership Dilemmas—Grid Solutions* (Houston: Gulf Publishing Company, 1991). See also Robert R. Blake and Jane S. Mouton, *The Managerial Grid* (Houston: Gulf Publishing, 1964); Blake and Mouton, "The Managerial Grid III,"

Personnel Psychology; Blake and Mouton, *The Versatile Manager: A Grid Profile* (Homewood, IL: Irwin, 1982); and Blake and Mouton, *The Secretary Grid: A Program for Increasing Office Synergy* (New York: AMACOM, 1983).

43. Blake and McCanse, *Leadership Dilemmas—Grid Solutions,* p. 29.

44. Stephen P. Robbins, *Organizational Behavior: Concepts, Controversies, and Applications,* 4th ed. (Upper Saddle River, NJ: Prentice Hall, 1989), pp. 11–12.

45. *Ibid,* p. 136.

46. Robbins, *Organizational Behavior,* 4th ed., p. 12.

47. James Owens, "A Reappraisal of Leadership Theory and Training," *Personnel Administrator,* 26 (November 1981), p. 81.

48. Frances Hesselbein, "Driving Strategic Leadership through Mission, Vision, and Goals," *The Planning Forum Network,* 7, no. 6 (Summer, 1994), pp. 4–5.

49. Ralph M. Stogdill, "Historical Trends in Leadership Theory and Research," *Journal of Contemporary Business,* Autumn 1974, p. 7.

Chapter 5

Leadership: Situational Approaches

The focus in situational approaches to leadership is on the observed behavior of leaders and their group members (followers) in various situations, not on any hypothetical inborn or acquired ability or potential for leadership. This emphasis on behavior and environment allows for the possibility that individuals can be trained to adapt their style of leader behavior to varying situations. Therefore, it is believed that most people can increase their effectiveness in leadership roles through education, training, and development. From observations of the frequency (or infrequency) of certain leader behavior in numerous types of situations, models can be developed to help leaders make some predictions about the most appropriate leader behavior for their current situation. For these reasons, in this chapter we will talk in terms of leader behavior rather than leadership traits, thus emphasizing the situational approach to leadership. ✧

SITUATIONAL APPROACHES TO LEADERSHIP

As we noted in the last chapter, current organizational behavior theory views leadership as well as other organizational behavior concepts and theories as situational, or contingent in nature. The views of Stephen Robbins and others cited in chapter 4 are not unique. Chester Schriesheim, James Tolliver, and Orlando Behling noted that "the literature supports the basic notion that a situational view is necessary to portray accurately the complexities of the leadership process."[1] Victor Vroom concurred, "I do not see any form of leadership as optimal for all situations. The contribution of a leader's

107

actions to the effectiveness of his organization cannot be determined without considering the nature of the situation in which that behavior is displayed."[2]

Peter Drucker, one of the fathers of modern management, has concluded that different people need to be led differently. There is no one right way to lead people, individually or in teams, organizations, or institutions. Drucker was influenced in this view by Abraham Maslow's work that we considered in chapter 2.[3]

Earlier we identified the three main components of the leadership process as the leader, the follower, and the situation. Situational approaches to leadership examine the interplay among these variables in order to find causal relationships that will lead to predictability of behavior. You will find a common thread among the situational approaches that we will elaborate upon in this and subsequent chapters: All situational approaches require the leader to behave in a flexible manner, to be able to diagnose the leadership style appropriate to the situation, and to be able to apply the appropriate style.

Although there are many situational models and theories, we will focus on five that have received wide attention in leadership research: the Tannenbaum-Schmidt Continuum of Leader Behavior, Fiedler's Contingency model, the House-Mitchell Path-Goal theory, Vroom-Yetten Contingency model, and the Hersey-Blanchard Tridimensional Leader Effectiveness model.

Tannenbaum-Schmidt Continuum of Leader Behavior

Robert Tannenbaum and Warren H. Schmidt's 1957 *Harvard Business Review* article "How to Choose a Leadership Pattern" was one of the initial and certainly one of the most significant situational approaches to leadership.[4] In this model, the leader selects one of seven possible leader behaviors depending upon the forces among the leader, follower, and situation. As Figure 5-1 indicates, the range of choices is between democratic, or relationship-oriented, behaviors and authoritarian, or task-oriented, behaviors. You will remember that these are dimensions from the Michigan and Ohio State studies, respectively.

Previous writers felt that concern for task tends to be represented by authoritarian leader behavior, and a concern for relationships is represented by democratic leader behavior. This feeling was popular because it was generally agreed that leaders influence their followers in either of two ways: (1) They can tell their followers what to do and how to do it or (2) they can share their leadership responsibilities with their followers by involving them in the planning and execution of the task. The former is the traditional authoritarian style, which emphasizes task concerns. The latter is the more nondirective democratic style, which stresses the concern for human relationships.

The differences in the two styles of leader behavior are based on the assumptions leaders make about the source of their power or authority and human nature. The authoritarian style of leader behavior is often based on the assumption that the power of leaders is derived from the position they occupy and that people are innately lazy and unreliable (Theory X). The democratic style assumes that the power of leaders is granted by the group they are to lead and that people can be basically self-directed and creative at work if

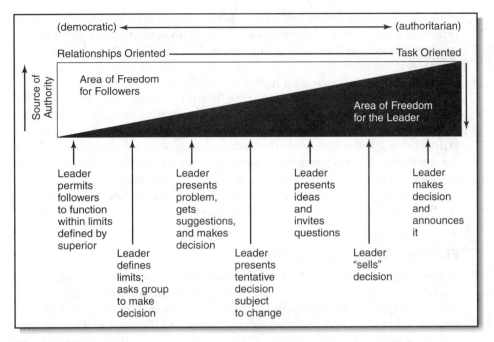

Figure 5-1
The Tannenbaum-Schmidt Continuum of Leader Behavior

Source: Reprinted by permission of *Harvard Business Review.* From How to Choose a Leadership Pattern, by Robert Tannenbaum and Warren H. Schmidt, May–June 1973. Copyright © 1973 by the President and Fellows of Harvard College. All rights reserved.

properly motivated (Theory Y). As a result, in the authoritarian style, all policies are determined by the leader; in the democratic style, policies are open for group discussion and decision.

There are a wide variety of styles of leader behavior between these two extremes. Tannenbaum and Schmidt depicted a broad range of styles as a continuum moving from authoritarian, or manager-centered, leader behavior at one end to democratic, or follower-centered, leader behavior at the other end, as illustrated in Figure 5-1. Tannenbaum and Schmidt now refer to these two extremes as manager power and influence and nonmanager power and influence.

Leaders whose behavior is observed to be at the authoritarian end of the continuum tend to be task-oriented and use their power to influence their followers; leaders whose behavior appears to be at the democratic end tend to be group-oriented and thus give their followers considerable freedom in their work. Often this continuum is extended beyond democratic leader behavior to include a laissez-faire style.[5] This style of behavior permits the members of the group to do whatever they want to do. No policies or procedures are established. Everyone is left alone. No one attempts to influence anyone else. Because there is no leader behavior, the laissez-faire style is not included in the continuum illustrated in Figure 5-1. In reality, a laissez-faire atmosphere represents an absence of formal leadership. The formal leadership role has been abdicated, and, therefore, any leadership that is being exhibited is informal and emergent.

In the 1973 reprint of their article in the *Harvard Business Review,* Tannenbaum and Schmidt commented that the interrelationships among leader, follower, and situation were becoming increasingly complex.[6] With this complexity, it becomes more difficult to identify causes and effects, particularly when more forces outside the traditional situation are exerting influence. As the world becomes more international, as more stakeholders come into play, and as more traditional customs, practices, and authorities are eroded, the leadership process becomes more difficult. Warren Bennis's "Where Have All the Leaders Gone?" is one astute commentary on this phenomenon.[7]

Fiedler's Contingency Model

Widely respected as the father of the contingency theory of leadership, Fred Fiedler developed the Leadership Contingency model. He suggested that three major situational variables determine whether a given situation is favorable to leaders: (1) their personal relations with the members of their group (leader-member relations), (2) the degree of structure in the task that their group has been assigned to perform (task structure), and (3) the power and authority that their position provides (position power).[8] Leader-member relations seem to parallel the relationship concepts discussed earlier; task structure and position power, which measure very closely related aspects of a situation, seem to be associated with task concepts. Fiedler defined the favorableness of a situation as "the degree to which the situation enables the leader to exert influence over the group."[9]

The most favorable situation for leaders to influence their groups is one in which they are well liked by the members (good leader-member relations), have a powerful position (strong position power), and are directing a well-defined job (high task structure); for example, a well-liked general making an inspection in an army camp. On the other hand, the most unfavorable situation for leaders is one in which they are disliked, have little position power, and face an unstructured task—such as an unpopular head of a voluntary hospital fund-raising committee.

In a reexamination of old leadership studies and an analysis of new studies, Fiedler concluded that:

1. Task-oriented leaders tend to perform best in group situations that are either very favorable or very unfavorable to the leader.
2. Relationship-oriented leaders tend to perform best in situations that are intermediate in favorableness.[10]

These conclusions are summarized in Figure 5-2. Fiedler has made an important contribution to leadership theory, particularly in his focus on situational variables as moderating influences. Fiedler's model has research support, particularly in its general conclusions represented in Figure 5-2. He may, in his single continuum of leader behavior, be suggesting that there are only two basic leader behavior styles, task-oriented and relationship-oriented. Most evidence indicates that leader behavior must be plotted on two separate axes rather than on a single continuum. Thus, a leader who is high on task behavior is not necessarily high or low on relationship behavior. Any combination of the two dimensions may occur.

House-Mitchell Path-Goal Theory

The Path-Goal theory builds upon two concepts that we looked at earlier—the Ohio State Leadership studies and the Expectancy Model of Motivation. You will recall that the Expectancy model focused on the effort-performance and the performance-goal satisfaction (reward) linkages. You will also remember that the key dimensions of the Ohio State model are initiating structure and consideration, and that the model suggested that the most effective leaders would be high on both the initiating structure and the consideration dimensions.

Robert House, who did much of his early leadership research at The Ohio State University, was interested in explaining the contradictions in the Ohio State model: for example, the situations in which initiating structure, consideration, or certain combinations of the two variables were not as effective as predicted. In other words, he was interested in explaining not only which style of leadership was effective, but also why. He was interested in those situations in which initiating structure was most appropriate and those situations where consideration was most appropriate.

Before we go further, it is important to state why this theory is called the path-goal theory. House and Mitchell explained it in this manner:

> According to this theory, leaders are effective because of their impact on [followers'] motivation, ability to perform effectively and satisfactions. The theory is called Path-Goal because its major concern is how the leader influences the [followers'] perceptions of their work goals, personal goals and paths to goal attainment. The theory suggests that a leader's behavior is motivating or satisfying

Figure 5-2
Leadership Styles Fiedler Concluded Are Appropriate for Various Group Situations

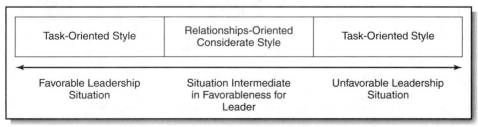

Task-Oriented Style	Relationships-Oriented Considerate Style	Task-Oriented Style
Favorable Leadership Situation	Situation Intermediate in Favorableness for Leader	Unfavorable Leadership Situation

Source: Adapted from Fred E. Fiedler, *A Theory of Leadership Effectiveness* (New York: McGraw-Hill, 1967), p. 14.

to the degree that the behavior increases [followers'] goal attainment and clarifies the paths to these goals.[11]

The Path-Goal theory relates very well to the Expectancy model and the Ohio State Leadership model. The Expectancy model tells us that "people are satisfied with their job if they think it leads to things that are highly valued [goal], and they work hard if they believe that effort [path] leads to things that are highly valued."[12] The leadership model is related because "subordinates are motivated [path] by leader behavior to the extent that this behavior influences expectancies [goal]."[13] Leaders do this best according to Path-Goal theory when they supply what is missing from the situation. If clarification is missing, then the leader should provide structure. If intrinsic and or extrinsic rewards are missing, then the leader should provide rewards. Richard Daft summarized this idea, "The leader's job is to increase personal payoffs to followers for goal attainment and to make the paths to these payoffs clear and easy to travel."[14]

These relationships are shown in Figure 5-3. The leader can be seen as clarifying the path on the left side of this figure while increasing rewards on

Figure 5-3
Leader Roles in the Path-Goal Model

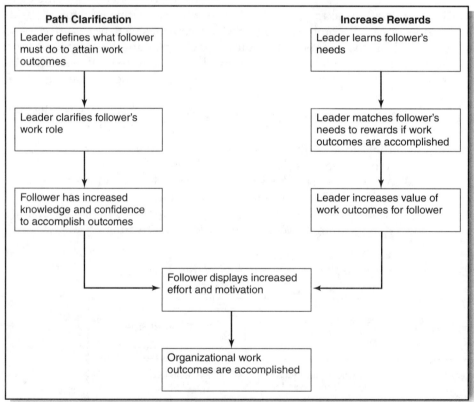

Source: Exhibit from MANAGEMENT by Richard Daft, copyright © 1994 by The Dryden Press, reprinted by permission of the publisher. Based on Bernard M. Bass, "Leadership: Good, Better, Best," *Organizational Dynamics*, 13 (Winter 1985), pp. 26–40.

the right side. The end result of these leader actions is follower increased effort and motivation leading to greater accomplishment of organizational work outcomes.

We have identified Path-Goal as a situational approach because different situations call for different leader behavior as shown in Figure 5-4. Let's start on the left side of this figure. Four situations are described calling for different leader behaviors. These behaviors, in turn, have a different impact on the follower and result in different outcomes. For example, in situation 2, if the follower is not meeting performance expectations in an ambiguous job, directive leadership spelling out more who, what, when, and how may serve to clarify work methods, procedures, and objectives. This clarification may lead to more effort, increased satisfaction and improved job performance. Path-Goal theory is an excellent example of the need to diagnose a situation before attempting a leadership intervention.

Vroom-Yetten Contingency Model

The Contingency model developed by Victor Vroom and Phillip Yetten is based on a model commonly used by researchers who take a contingency approach to leadership.[15] This model, shown in Figure 5-5, is based on the assumption that situational variables interacting with personal attributes or characteristics of the leader result in leader behavior that can affect organizational

Figure 5-4
Path-Goal Situations and Preferred Leader Behaviors

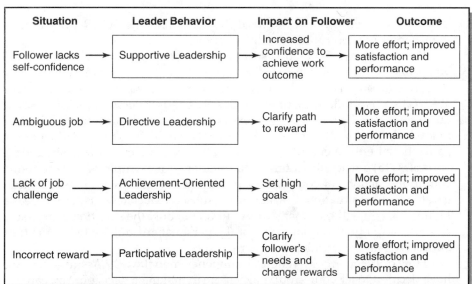

Source: Reprinted with permission from Richard L. Daft, *Management,* 3rd ed. (Fort Worth, TX: Dryden Press, 1993), p. 395. Adapted from Gary A. Yukl, *Leadership in Organizations* (Upper Saddle River, NJ: Prentice Hall, 1981), pp. 146–152.

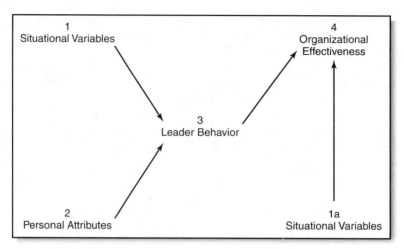

Figure 5-5
Schematic Representation of Important Variables Used in
Leadership Research

effectiveness. This change in the organization—because the organization is
part of the situation—can, in turn, affect the next leadership intervention.

This is a very familiar theme that we have visited before. You will recall
Lewin's model discussed in chapter 2:

$$B = f(P \Leftrightarrow S)$$

You will also recall Maier's Causal Sequence and the SOAR Peak Performance models introduced in earlier chapters.

Because Figure 5-5 blends several of the ideas we have already visited
and will be considering in our discussion of leadership, it is important that
we pause to look at it in some detail. Figure 5-5 assumes that situational variables (1) such as followers, time, and job demands, interacting with personal
attributes (2) of the leader, such as experience or communication skills, result
in leader behavior (3), such as a directive style of leadership, to influence organizational effectiveness (4) which is also influenced by other situational
variables (1a) outside the control of the leader—for example, world economic
conditions, actions of competitors, government legislation. We will look in
greater detail at situational variables in a subsequent chapter. Before we leave
Figure 5-5, you will note that it draws upon not only the situational approach
to leadership but also upon some of the personal attributes cited in the trait
approach that we considered earlier.

How does the Vroom-Yetten Contingency model work? Assume that you
have decided to let your group participate in making a decision. You can use
Figure 5-6 as a guide, by asking questions A through G in sequence. Table 5-1
describes the five different types of decision styles possible in this model.
Table 5-2 lists seven problem attributes (A through G) together with their

Figure 5-6
Vroom-Yetten Decision Model

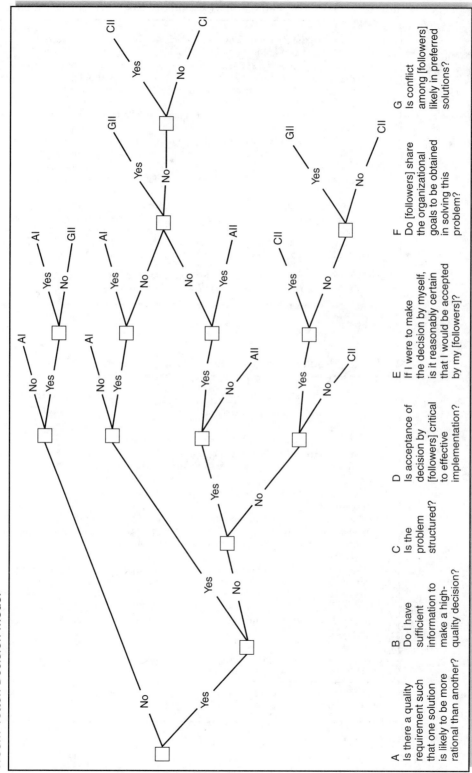

A
Is there a quality requirement such that one solution is likely to be more rational than another?

B
Do I have sufficient information to make a high-quality decision?

C
Is the problem structured?

D
Is acceptance of decision by [followers] critical to effective implementation?

E
If I were to make the decision by myself, is it reasonably certain that I would be accepted by my [followers]?

F
Do [followers] share the organizational goals to be obtained in solving this problem?

G
Is conflict among [followers] likely in preferred solutions?

Source: Reprinted from Leadership and Decision-Making, by Victor H. Vroom and Philip W. Yetton, © 1973, by permission of the University of Pittsburgh Press.

Table 5-1 Types of Managerial Decision Styles in the Vroom-Yetten Model

AI   You solve the problem or make the decision yourself, using information available to you at the time.

AII   You obtain the necessary information from your [follower(s)], then decide on the solution to the problem yourself. You may or may not tell your [followers] what the problem is in getting information from them. The role played by your [followers] in making the decision is clearly one of providing the necessary information to you, rather than generating or evaluating alternative solutions.

CI   You share the problem with relevant [followers] individually, getting their ideas and suggestions without bringing them together as a group. Then, you make the decision that may or may not reflect your [followers'] influence.

CII   You share the problem with your [followers] as a group, collectively obtaining their ideas and suggestions. Then, you make the decision that may or may not reflect your [followers'] influence.

GII   You share a problem with your [followers] as a group. Together you generate and evaluate alternatives and attempt to reach agreement (consensus) on a solution. Your role is much like that of chairperson. You do not try to influence the group to adopt "your" solution, and you are willing to accept and implement any solution that has the support of the entire group.

Source: Reprinted from Leadership and Decision-Making, by Victor H. Vroom and Philip W. Yetton, © 1973, by permission of the University of Pittsburgh Press.

Table 5-2 Problem Attributes Used in the Vroom-Yetten Model

PROBLEM ATTRIBUTES	DIAGNOSTIC QUESTIONS
A. The importance of the quality of the decision	Is there a quality requirement such that one solution is likely to be more rational than another?
B. The extent to which the leader possesses sufficient information/expertise to make a high-quality decision	Do I have sufficient information to make a high-quality decision?
C. The extent to which the problem is structured	Is the problem structured?
D. The extent to which acceptance or commitment on the part of [followers] is critical to the effective implementation of the decision	Is acceptance of the decision by [followers] critical to effective implementation?
E. The prior probability that the leader's autocratic decision will receive acceptance by subordinates	If I were to make the decision by myself, is it reasonably certain that it would be accepted by my [followers]?
F. The extent to which [followers] are motivated to attain the organizational goals as represented in the objectives explicit in the statement of the problem	Do [followers] share the organizational goals to be obtained in solving this problem?
G. The extent to which [followers] are likely to be in conflict over preferred solutions	Is conflict among [followers] likely in preferred solutions?

Source: Reprinted from Leadership and Decision-Making, by Victor H. Vroom and Philip W. Yetton, © 1973, by permission of the University of Pittsburgh Press.

Chapter 5 Leadership: Situational Approaches

corresponding diagnostic questions. You will note that these diagnostic questions are the same as those in Figure 5-6. Let's try an example.

Following the same process as in Figure 5-5, the manager should first diagnose the situational variables. Table 5-2 is very useful for this purpose and has been found to have a high success rate in improving decision quality. After asking these seven questions, the manager should refer to Figure 5-6 and work through this decision tree from left to right asking questions A through G. When the response indicates a type of decision, for example AI, then the manager should turn to Table 5-1 for a description of the appropriate decision style.

This model is a contingency model because the leader's possible behaviors are contingent upon the interaction between the questions and the leader's assessment of the situation in developing a response to the questions. Perhaps you recognized that the questions used the quality and acceptance aspects of decision making popularized by Norman R. F. Maier. The first three questions concern the quality or technical accuracy of the decision, and the last four concern the acceptance of the decision by the group members. The questions are designed to eliminate alternatives that would jeopardize the quality or the acceptance of the decision, as appropriate.

The Vroom-Yetten approach is important for several reasons. One is that it is widely respected among researchers in leadership behavior. Another reason is that the authors believe that leaders have the ability to vary their styles to fit the situation. This point is critical to acceptance of situational approaches to leadership. A third reason is that the authors believe that people can work to be developed into more effective leaders. Vroom has continued this productive research direction, most recently with Arthur Jago.[16]

Hersey-Blanchard Tridimensional Leader Effectiveness Model

In this leadership model, the terms *task behavior* and *relationship behavior* are used to describe concepts similar to *initiating structure* and *consideration* of the Ohio State studies. The four basic leader behavior quadrants are labeled high task and low relationship; high task and high relationship; high relationship and low task; and low relationship and low task (see Figure 5-7).

These four basic styles depict essentially different leadership styles. The leadership style of an individual is the behavior pattern, as perceived by others, that a person exhibits when attempting to influence the activities of those others. This may be very different from a person's own perception, which we shall define as *self-perception* rather than style. A person's leadership style involves some combination of task behavior and relationship behavior. The two types of behavior, which are central to the concept of leadership style, are defined as follows:

- *Task behavior.* The extent to which leaders are likely to organize and define the roles of the members of their group (followers) and to explain what activities each is to do and when, where, and how tasks are to be accomplished; characterized by endeavoring to establish well-defined

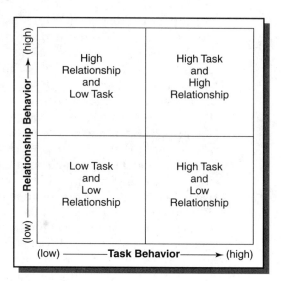

Figure 5-7
A Two-Dimensional Model: Basic Leader Behavior Styles Suggested by Hersey and Blanchard

patterns of organization, channels of communication, and ways of getting jobs accomplished.

- *Relationship behavior.* The extent to which leaders are likely to maintain personal relationships between themselves and members of their group (followers) by opening up channels of communication, providing socioemotional support, active listening, "psychological strokes," and facilitating behaviors.[17]

Effectiveness Dimension

The effectiveness of leaders depends on how appropriate their leadership style is to the situation in which they operate. Therefore, an effectiveness dimension should be added to the two-dimensional model. This three-dimensional model is illustrated in Figure 5-8.

In his "3-D Management Style Theory," William J. Reddin was the first to add an effectiveness dimension to the task concern and relationship concern dimensions of earlier attitudinal models such as the Leadership Grid.[18] Reddin, whose pioneering work influenced us greatly in the development of the Tridimensional Leader Effectiveness model presented here, felt that a useful theoretical model "must allow that a variety of styles may be effective or ineffective depending on the situation."[19]

By adding an effectiveness dimension to the task behavior and relationship behavior dimensions of the earlier Ohio State Leadership model, we are attempting in the Tridimensional Leader Effectiveness model to integrate the concepts of leader style with situational demands of a specific environment. When the style of a leader is appropriate to a given situation, it is termed effective; when the style is inappropriate to a given situation, it is termed ineffective.

If the effectiveness of a leader behavior style depends on the situation in which it is used, it follows that any of the basic styles may be effective or in-

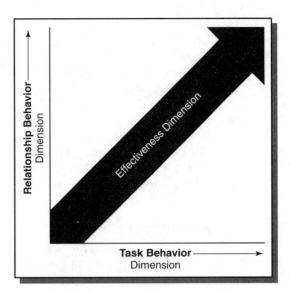

Figure 5-8
Adding an
Effectiveness
Dimension to the
Hersey-Blanchard
Dimensions of Task
and Relationship

Relationship Behavior
Dimension

Effectiveness Dimension

Task Behavior
Dimension

effective, depending on the situation. The difference between the effective and ineffective styles is often not the actual behavior of the leader, but the appropriateness of that behavior to the environment in which it is used. In reality, the third dimension is the environment. It is the interaction of the basic style with the environment that results in a degree of effectiveness or ineffectiveness. We call the third dimension *effectiveness* because in most organizational settings various performance criteria are used to measure the degree of effectiveness or ineffectiveness of a manager or leader. But we feel it is important to keep in mind that the third dimension is the environment in which the leader is operating. One might think of the leader's basic style as a particular stimulus, and it is the response to this stimulus that can be considered effective or ineffective. This point is important because theorists and practitioners who argue that there is one best style of leadership are making value judgments about the stimulus, whereas those taking a situational approach to leadership are evaluating the response or the results rather than the stimulus.

Let's use an example. A department head has been given an important promotion from one department to another, much larger department. What would be her most effective leadership style? Most likely, it would be the one that earned her the valued promotion—in this case, a high relationship-low task style. Will this style be effective in the new situation? It could be extremely effective or extremely ineffective or somewhere in between. The effectiveness of a given leadership style will depend on its relevance to the situation as seen by the leader's followers, superiors, or associates. Table 5-3 describes briefly one of the many different ways each style might be perceived as effective or ineffective by others.

A model such as the Tridimensional Leader Effectiveness model is distinctive because it does not depict a single ideal leader behavior style that is suggested as being appropriate in all situations. For example, the high task and high relationship style is appropriate only in certain situations. In basically crisis-oriented organizations, such as the military or the fire department, there is considerable evidence that the most appropriate style would be high task and low relationship, because under combat, fire, or emergency conditions success often depends on immediate response to orders. Time demands do not permit talking things over or explaining decisions. But once the crisis is over, other styles might become appropriate. For example, although the fire chief may have to initiate a high level of structure at the scene of a fire, upon returning to the firehouse it may be appropriate for the chief to engage in other styles while the staff is participating in ancillary functions such as maintaining the equipment or studying new fire fighting techniques.

Instrumentation

To gather data about the behavior of leaders, we developed two leader effectiveness and adaptability description (LEAD)[20] instruments for use in training settings: the LEAD Self and the LEAD Other. The LEAD Self contains 12 leadership situations in which respondents are asked to select from four alternative actions—a high task–low relationship behavior, a high task–high relationship behavior, a high relationship–low task behavior, and a low relationship–low task behavior—the one they feel most closely describes

Table 5-3 How the Basic Leader Behavior Styles May Be Seen by Others

BASIC STYLE	EFFECTIVE	INEFFECTIVE
High task and low relationship behavior	Seen as having well-defined methods for accomplishing goals that are helpful to the followers	Seen as imposing methods on others; sometimes seen as unpleasant and interested only in short-run output
High task and high relationship behavior	Seen as satisfying the needs of the group for setting goals and organizing work, but also providing high levels of socioemotional support	Seen as initiating more structure than is needed by the group and often appears not to be genuine in interpersonal relationships
High relationship and low task behavior	Seen as having implicit trust in people and as being primarily concerned with facilitating their goal accomplishment	Seen as primarily interested in harmony; sometimes seen as unwilling to accomplish a task if it risks disrupting a relationship or losing a "good person" image
Low relationship and low task behavior	Seen as appropriately delegating to followers decisions about how the work should be done and providing little socioemotional support where little is needed by the group	Seen as providing little structure or socioemotional support when needed by members of the group

Table 5-4   Sample Item from LEAD Self Instrument

SITUATION	ALTERNATIVE ACTIONS
Your followers, usually able to take responsibility, are not responding to your recent redefinition of standards.	A. Allow group involvement in redefining standards, but don't push. B. Redefine standards and supervise carefully. C. Avoid confrontation by not applying pressure. D. Incorporate group recommendations, but see that new standards are met.

their own behavior in that type of situation. An example of a situation-action combination used in the LEAD Self is shown in Table 5-4.

The LEAD Self was designed to measure self-perception of three aspects of leader behavior: (1) style, (2) style range, and (3) style adaptability. Style and style range are determined by four style scores, and the style adaptability (effectiveness score) is determined by one normative score. The LEAD Self was originally designed as a training instrument and should properly be used only in training situations and not, as some researchers have done, as a research instrument. The length of the scale (12 items) and time required (10 minutes) clearly reflect the intended function.

The LEAD Self provides data basically in terms of the leader's self-perception. This information is helpful, but to really know your leadership style—how you influence others—you must collect data from those you attempt to lead. We developed the LEAD Other to gather this important leadership style information in training situations. The LEAD Self is scored by leaders themselves, but the LEAD Other is completed by leaders' followers, superiors, or associates (peers). We will discuss both these instruments in more detail in chapter 12.

WHAT ABOUT CONSISTENCY?

Consistent leadership is not using the same leadership style all the time, but using the style appropriate for the followers' level of readiness in such a way that followers understand why they are getting a certain behavior, a certain style from the leader. Inconsistent leadership is using the same style in every situation. Therefore, if a manager uses a supportive high relationship–low task style with a staff member when that person is performing well and also when that staff member is performing poorly, that manager would be inconsistent, not consistent. Managers are consistent if they direct their followers, and even sometimes discipline them when they are performing poorly, but support and reward them when they are performing well. Managers are inconsistent if they smile and respond supportively all the time—whether their followers are doing their job well or not.

To be really consistent (in our terms), managers must behave the same way in similar situations for all parties concerned. Thus, a consistent manager would not discipline one follower when that person makes a costly mistake, but not another staff member, and vice versa. It is also important for managers to lead their followers the same way in similar circumstances even when it is inconvenient—when they don't have time or when they don't feel like it.

Some managers are consistent only when it is convenient. They may praise and support their people when they feel like it and redirect and supervise their activities when they have time. This attitude leads to problems. Parents are probably the worst in this regard. For example, suppose Wendy and Walt get upset when their children argue with each other and are willing to clamp down on them when it happens. However, there are exceptions to their consistency in this area. If they are rushing off to a dinner party, they will generally not deal with the children's fighting. Or, if they are in the supermarket with the kids, they will frequently permit behavior they would normally not allow because they are uncomfortable disciplining the children in public. Because children are continually testing the boundaries or limits of their behavior (they want to know what they can do and cannot do), Walt and Wendy's kids soon learn that they should not fight with each other except when Mom and Dad are in a hurry to go out or when they're in a store. Thus, unless parents and managers are willing to be consistent even when it is inconvenient, they may actually be encouraging misbehavior.

Another thing that frequently happens is that, instead of using appropriate leader behavior matched with follower readiness, performance, and demonstrated ability, leaders assign privileges on the basis of chronological age or gender. For example, a parent may permit an irresponsible 17-year-old son to stay out until 2:00 A.M. but make a very responsible 15-year-old daughter come home by midnight.

ATTITUDE VERSUS BEHAVIOR

One of the ideas behind the old definition of consistency was the belief that your behavior as a manager *must* be consistent with your attitudes. This idea bothered some people who were heavily involved with the human relations or sensitivity-training movement. They believed that if you care about people and have positive assumptions about them, you should also treat them in high relationship ways and seldom in directive or controlling ways.

We feel that much of this problem stemmed from the failure of some theorists and practitioners to distinguish between an attitudinal model and a behavioral model. For example, in examining the dimensions of the Managerial Grid (concern for production and concern for people) and Reddin's 3-D Management Style theory (task orientation and relationship orientation), one can see that all these dimensions appear to be attitudinal. Concern or orientation is a feeling or an emotion toward something. The same can be said about McGregor's Theory X and

Theory Y assumptions about human nature. Theory X describes negative feelings about the nature of people, and Theory Y describes positive feelings. These are all models that describe attitudes and feelings.

On the other hand, the dimensions of the Hersey-Blanchard Tridimensional Leader Effectiveness model (task behavior and relationship behavior) are dimensions of observed behavior. Thus, the Tridimensional Leader Effectiveness model describes how people behave, whereas the Managerial Grid, the 3-D Management Style theory, and Theory X–Theory Y describe attitudes or predispositions toward production and people.[21]

Although attitudinal models and the Tridimensional Leader Effectiveness model examine different aspects of leadership, they are not incompatible. A conflict develops only when behavioral assumptions are drawn from analysis of the attitudinal dimension of models such as the Managerial Grid and theories such as Theory X–Theory Y. First, it is very difficult to predict behavior from attitudes and values. In fact, it has been found that you can actually do a much better job of predicting values or attitudes from behavior. If you want to know what's in a person's heart, look at what that person does. Look at the person's behavior.

For example, assume that a manager has a very high concern for product quality. Does that tell you what that manager is going to do about it? No. One manager who has a high concern for product quality may say the following: "Don't even talk to me about quality. I don't want to make any changes right now." In other words, the person engages in avoidance or withdrawal behavior (low relationship behavior and low task behavior). Another manager who has a very high concern for product quality may meet with employees and tell them what to do, how to do it, when to do it, and where to do it (high task behavior and low relationship behavior). A third manager who has high concern for product quality might visit a department saying, "Gee, I'm sorry you have problems. Do you want to talk to me about it? Let's discuss it. Gosh, I'm sympathetic" (high relationship behavior and low task behavior). Finally, another manager who has a high concern for product quality might try to provide high amounts of both task behavior and relationship behavior in helping the department form self-managed teams.

What we're suggesting is that the same value set can evoke a variety of behaviors. You cannot easily predict behaviors from values. A look at one of the simplest models in the behavioral sciences may help to emphasize our point of view. The model is the S-O-R (a stimulus directed toward an organism produces some response). The trap that many humanistic trainers fall into is to suggest that we assess the effectiveness of management by looking at the stimulus, or the leadership style. In other words, they say there are good styles and bad styles. What we are saying is that if you are going to assess performance, you don't evaluate the stimulus, you assess the results—the response. It's here that we need to make assessments in terms of performance. This is exactly what we suggest. There is no best leadership style, or stimulus. Any leadership style can be effective or ineffective depending on the response that style gets in a particular situation. We also have to look at the impact the leaders have on the human resources. It's not enough to have a tremendous amount of productivity for the next 6 months. Your methods may upset your people, causing them to leave and join your competitors. You also have to be concerned about what impact you are having on your followers, on developing their competency and their commitment. So when we talk about response, or results, we're talking about output and impact on the human resources.

There is another reason to be careful about making behavioral assumptions from attitudinal measures. Although high concern for both production and people (9-9 attitude; see Figure 4-10) and positive Theory Y assumptions about human nature are basic ingredients for effective managers, it may be appropriate for managers to engage in a variety of behaviors as they face different problems in their environment. Therefore, the high task–high relationship style often associated with the Managerial Grid 9-9 team management style or the participative high relationship–low task behavior that is often argued as consistent with Theory Y may not always be appropriate.

For example, if a manager's employees can take responsibility for themselves, the appropriate style of leadership for working with them may be low task and low relationship. In this case, the manager delegates to those employees the responsibility of planning, organizing, and controlling their own operation. The manager plays a background role, providing socioemotional support only when necessary. In using this style appropriately, the manager would not be "impoverished" (low concern for both people and production). In fact, delegating to competent and confident people is the best way a manager can demonstrate a 9-9 attitude and Theory Y assumptions about human nature. The same is true for using a directive high task–low relationship style. Sometimes the best way you can show your concern for people and production (9-9) is to direct, control, and closely supervise their behavior when they are insecure and don't have the skills yet to perform their job.

SUMMARY

Empirical studies tend to show that there is no normative (best) style of leadership. Effective leaders adapt their leader behavior to meet the needs of their followers and the particular environment. If their followers are different, they must be treated differently. Therefore, effectiveness depends on the leader, the followers, and other situational variables. Anyone who is interested in effectiveness as a leader must give serious thought to both behavioral and environmental considerations.

ENDNOTES

1. Chester A. Schriesheim, James M. Tolliver, and Orlando C. Behling, "Leadership Theory: Some Implications for Managers," *MSU Business Topics*, 22, no. 2 (Summer 1978), pp. 34–40, in William E. Rosenbach and Robert L. Taylor, eds., *Contemporary Issues in Leadership* (Boulder, CO: Westview Press, 1984), p. 128.

2. Victor Vroom, "Can Leaders Learn to Lead?" *Organizational Dynamics*, 4 (Winter 1976).

3. Peter F. Drucker, "Management's New Paradigms," *Forbes*, October 5, 1998, pp. 152–530.

4. Robert Tannenbaum and Warren H. Schmidt, "How to Choose a Leadership Pattern," *Harvard Business Review*, May–June 1973. This is an

update of their original 1957 article, one of the landmarks in leadership research.

5. Kurt Lewin, R. Lippitt, and R. White identified laissez-faire as a third form of leadership style. See Lewin, Lippitt, and White, "Leader Behavior and Member Reaction in Three 'Social Climates,'" in *Group Dynamics: Research and Theory*, 2nd ed., Dorwin Cartwright and Alvin Zander, eds. (Evanston, IL: Row, Peterson, 1960).

6. Tannenbaum and Schmidt, "How to Choose a Leadership Pattern," (1973).

7. Warren G. Bennis, "Where Have All the Leaders Gone?" *Technology Review*, 758, no. 9 (March–April 1977), pp. 3–12.

8. Fred E. Fiedler, *A Theory of Leadership Effectiveness* (New York: McGraw-Hill, 1967). See also Fred E. Fiedler and Martin M. Chemers, "Improving Leadership Effectiveness," *Personnel Psychology*, 38 (Spring 1985), pp. 220–222; Fred E. Fiedler and Martin M. Chemers, *Improving Leadership Effectiveness: The Leader Match Concept* (New York: Wiley, 1984).

9. Fiedler, *A Theory of Leadership Effectiveness*, p. 13.

10. *Ibid.*, p. 14.

11. Robert J. House and Terence R. Mitchell, "Path-Goal Theory of Leadership," *Journal of Contemporary Business*, Autumn 1974, p. 81. See also Mark J. Knoll and Charles D. Pringle, "Path-Goal Theory and the Task Design Literature: A Tenuous Linkage," *Akron Business and Economic Review*, 17, no. 4 (Winter 1986), pp. 75–83.

12. House and Mitchell, "Path-Goal Theory of Leadership," p. 81.

13. *Ibid.*

14. Richard L. Daft, *Management*, 3rd ed. (Fort Worth, TX: Dryden Press, 1993), p. 493.

15. Victor H. Vroom and Philip W. Yetten, *Leadership and Decision Making* (Pittsburgh: University of Pittsburgh Press, 1973), p. 198.

16. Victor H. Vroom and Arthur Jago, *The New Leadership: Managing Participation in Organizations* (Upper Saddle River, NJ: Prentice Hall, 1988).

17. Because the model is an outgrowth of the Ohio State leadership studies, these definitions have been adapted from their definitions of initiating structure (task) and consideration (relationship): Ralph M. Stogdill and Alvin E. Coons, eds., *Leader Behavior: Its Description and Measurement*, *Research Monograph No. 88* (Columbus: Bureau of Business Research, Ohio State University, 1957), pp. 42–43.

18. William J. Reddin, "The 3-D Management Style Theory," *Training and Development Journal*, April 1967, pp. 8–17. See also Reddin, *Managerial Effectiveness* (New York: McGraw-Hill, 1970).

19. Reddin, "The 3-D Management Style Theory," p. 13.

20. The LEAD (formerly known as the leader adaptability and style inventory, LASI), first appeared in Paul Hersey and Kenneth H. Blanchard, "So You Want to Know Your Leadership Style?" *Training and Development Journal*, February 1974. LEAD instruments are distributed through Center for Leadership Studies, 230 W. 3rd Ave., Escondido, CA, 92025.

21. Fiedler, in his contingency model of leadership effectiveness (Fiedler, *A Theory of Leadership Effectiveness*), also tends to make behavioral assumptions from data gathered from an attitudinal measure of leadership style. A leader is asked to evaluate his least preferred coworker (LPC) on a series of semantic differential type scales. Leaders are classified as high or low LPC depending on the favorableness with which they rate their LPC.

Chapter 6

Determining Effectiveness

One of the most important issues facing the applied behavioral sciences is that of human productivity—the quality and quantity of work. Productivity concerns both effectiveness (the attainment of goals) and efficiency (resource costs, including those human resource costs affecting the quality of life). Our focus in this chapter will be primarily on effectiveness because, as Peter Drucker, a founding father of management theory, wrote, "Effectiveness is the foundation of success—efficiency is a minimum condition for survival after success has been achieved. Efficiency is concerned with doing things right. Effectiveness is doing the right things."[1] ✧

MANAGEMENT EFFECTIVENESS VERSUS LEADERSHIP EFFECTIVENESS

In discussing effectiveness, we must once again distinguish between management and leadership. As we discussed earlier, leadership is a broader concept than management. Management is thought of as a special kind of leadership in which the accomplishment of organizational goals is paramount. Leadership is an attempt to influence people, individually and in groups, for whatever reason. Influence and leadership may be used interchangeably. Not all leadership behavior is directed toward accomplishing organizational goals. In fact, many times when you are trying to influence someone else you are not even part of an organization. For example, when you are trying to get some friends to go someplace with you,

you are not engaging in management, but you certainly are attempting leadership. If they agree to go, you are an effective leader but not an effective manager. Even within an organizational setting, managers may attempt to engage in leadership rather than management because they are trying to accomplish personal goals, not organizational ones.

For example, a vice president may have a strong personal goal to become the company president. In attempting to achieve this goal, this executive may not be concerned with organizational goals at all, but only with undermining the plans of the president and other executives who may be contenders for the job. The vice president may accomplish this personal goal and, in that sense, be a successful leader. However, this individual cannot be considered an effective manager because these actions were probably disruptive to the effective operation of the firm.

Parkinson's "law" suggests a clear example of a person's placing personal goals before organizational goals. His law states that in bureaucracies, managers often try to build up their own departments by adding unnecessary personnel, more equipment, or expanded facilities.[2] Although this tendency may increase the prestige and importance of the managers, it often leads to "an organizational environment that is not only inefficient but also stifling and frustrating to the individuals who must cope with [it]."[3] Thus, in discussing effectiveness, we must recognize the differences between individual goals, organizational goals, leadership, and management.

SUCCESSFUL LEADERSHIP VERSUS EFFECTIVE LEADERSHIP

An attempt by an individual to have some effect on the behavior of another is called *attempted* leadership. This attempted leadership can be successful or unsuccessful in producing the desired response. A basic responsibility of managers in any type of organization is to get work done, with and through people, so their success is measured by the output or productivity of the group they lead. With that thought in mind, Bernard M. Bass suggested a clear distinction between successful and effective leadership or management.[4]

Suppose manager A attempts to influence individual B to do a certain job. A's attempt will be considered successful or unsuccessful depending on the extent to which B accomplishes the job. It is not really an either/or situation. A's success could be depicted on a continuum (see Figure 6-1) ranging from very successful to very unsuccessful, with gray areas in between that would be difficult to ascertain as either.

Let us assume that A's leadership is successful. In other words, B's response to A's leadership stimulus falls at the successful end of the continuum. We still do not know the whole story of effectiveness.

If A's leadership style is not compatible with the expectations of B, and if B is antagonized and does the job only because of A's position power, then we

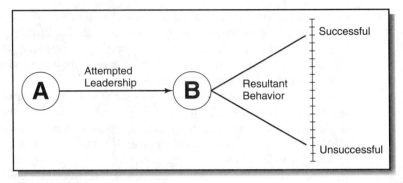

Figure 6-1
Bass's Successful Leadership Continuum

Source: Based on Bernard M. Bass, *Leadership, Psychology, and Organizational Behavior* (New York: Harper & Brothers, 1960), pp. 90, 448.

can say that A has been successful but not effective. B has responded as A intended because A has control of rewards and punishment—not because satisfying the goals of the manager or the organization also satisfies B's needs.

On the other hand, if A's attempted leadership leads to a successful response, and B does the job because it's personally rewarding, then we consider A as having not only position power, but also personal power. B respects A and is willing to cooperate, realizing that A's request is consistent with some personal goals. In fact, B sees these personal goals as being accomplished by this activity. This is what is meant by effective leadership, keeping in mind that effectiveness also appears as a continuum that can range from very effective to very ineffective, as illustrated in Figure 6-2.

Success has to do with how the individual or the group behaves. On the other hand, effectiveness describes the internal state, or predisposition, of an individual or a group, and thus it is attitudinal in nature. Individuals who are

Figure 6-2
Bass's Successful and Effective Leadership Continuum

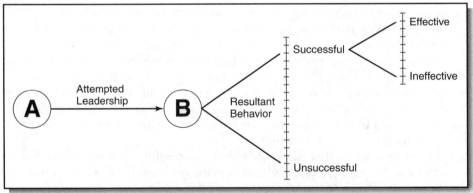

Source: Based on Bernard M. Bass, *Leadership, Psychology, and Organizational Behavior* (New York: Harper & Brothers, 1960), pp. 90, 448.

interested only in success tend to emphasize their position power and use close supervision. Effective individuals, however, will also depend on personal power and use more general supervision. Position power tends to be delegated down through the organization; personal power is generated upward from below through follower acceptance.

Fred Luthans, a professor of management at the University of Nebraska, conducted a 4-year observational study to determine the similarities and differences between successful managers (those who were rapidly promoted) and effective managers (those who had satisfied, committed employees and high-performing departments).[5] The study reported that successful managers spent more of their time and effort networking with others inside and outside the organization than did effective managers. Politicking and socializing occupied most of their time, with less time spent on the traditional activities of managing—planning, decision making, and controlling. In contrast, the effective managers spent most of their time in communications, that is, exchanging information and paperwork, and in human resource management (see Figure 6-3). These activities contributed most to the quality and quantity of their high-performing departments.

Less than 10 percent of the managers in the study sample were in both the top third of successful managers and the top third of effective managers. These managers were able to achieve a balanced approach in their activities; they networked and got the right job done. The study concluded that more attention needs to be paid to designing systems to reward and support effective managers, not those with the most successful political and social skills. By rewarding effectiveness, organizations will increase their abilities to compete and excel in rapidly changing market and environmental conditions.

In the management of organizations, the difference between successful and effective often explains why many supervisors can get a satisfactory level of output only when they are right there looking over a worker's shoulder. But as soon as they leave, output declines and often such things as horseplay and scrap loss increase.

This same phenomenon occurs in organizations that rely on phone conversations with service representatives for order placement. By monitoring incoming calls, the supervisor can rapidly determine if service representatives are answering calls quickly, correctly, and in a friendly fashion. If the representatives perceive the monitoring in a negative fashion and view the supervisor as ineffective, their performance can deteriorate when the monitoring is stopped. A supervisor who uses the monitoring as a tool to assist the representatives in achieving departmental goals and who rewards positive improvements in call answering and order placement will find that performance stabilizes or improves even when the monitoring is discontinued. The supervisor has used effective leadership to help the representatives meet department and corporate goals.

The phenomenon described applies not only to educational and business organizations but also to less formal organizations such as the family. If parents are successful and effective, have both position and personal power, their children accept family goals as their own. Consequently, if the husband and

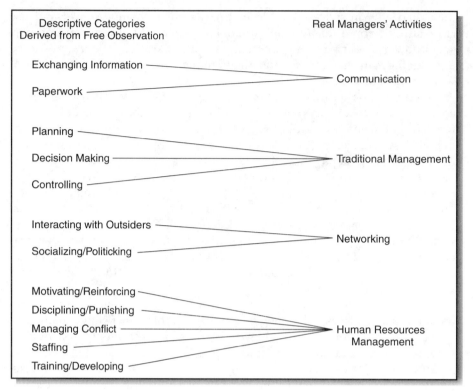

Figure 6-3
The Activities of Real Managers

Source: Reprinted, by permission of the publisher, from *Academy of Management Executive,* 1988, © Academy of Management. All rights reserved.

wife leave for the weekend, the children behave no differently than if their parents were there. If, however, the parents continually use close supervision and the children view their own goals as being stifled by their parents' goals, the parents have only position power. They maintain order because of the rewards and the punishments they control. If these parents went away on a trip, leaving the children behind, upon returning they might be greeted by chaos.

In summary, managers could be successful, but ineffective, having only a short-lived influence over the behavior of others. On the other hand, if managers are both successful and effective, their influence tends to lead to long-run productivity and organizational development. This really is what leadership and management are all about. In the words of *The Wall Street Journal,* "The first job of the manager is to make the organization perform."[6]

It should be pointed out that this successful versus effective framework is a way of evaluating the response to a specific behavioral event and not of evaluating performance over time. Long-term evaluation is not a result of a single leadership event but a summation of many different leadership events. The evaluation of a leader or an organization over time will be discussed in the following section.

WHAT DETERMINES ORGANIZATIONAL EFFECTIVENESS?

In discussing effectiveness, we have concentrated on evaluating the results of individual leaders or managers. These results are significant, but perhaps the most important aspect of effectiveness is its relationship to an entire organization. Here, we are concerned not only with the outcome of a given leadership attempt but also with the effectiveness of the organizational unit over a period of time. Rensis Likert identified three variables—causal, intervening, and end result—that are useful in discussing effectiveness over time.[7]

Causal Variables

Causal variables are those factors that influence the course of developments within an organization and its results or accomplishments. These independent variables can be altered by the organization and its management; they are not beyond the control of the organization, as are general business conditions. Leadership strategies, skills, and behavior; management's decisions; and the policies and structure of the organization are examples of causal variables.

Intervening Variables

Leadership strategies, skills, behaviors, and other causal variables affect the human resources or intervening variables in an organization. According to Likert, intervening variables represent the current condition of the internal state of the organization.[8] They are reflected in the commitment to objectives, motivation, and morale of members and their skills in leadership, communications, conflict resolution, decision making, and problem solving.

Output, or End Result, Variables

Output, or end result, variables are the dependent variables that reflect the achievements of the organization. In evaluating effectiveness, perhaps more than 90 percent of managers in organizations look at measures of output alone. Thus, the effectiveness of managers is often determined by net profits; the effectiveness of college professors may be determined by the number of articles and books they have published; and the effectiveness of basketball coaches may be determined by their win-loss records.

Many researchers talk about effectiveness by emphasizing similar output variables. Fred E. Fiedler, for example, in his studies evaluated "leader effectiveness in terms of group performance on the group's primary assigned task."[9] William J. Reddin, in discussing management styles, wrote in similar terms about effectiveness. He argued that the effectiveness of a manager should be measured "objectively by his profit center performance—maximum output, market share, or other similar criteria."[10]

There has been a move away from single-measure assessments of effectiveness. For example, Peter B. Vaill noted that organizational stakeholders are increasingly looking for "winning" in five categories of values.

- *Economic values.* Reflect what the firm's bottom line should be.
- *Technological values.* Reflect how the firm will do what it chooses to do.
- *Communal values.* Reflect the kind of "home" the firm will be for its employees.
- *Sociopolitical values.* Reflect the kind of neighbor the firm will be to its external constituencies.
- *Transcendental values.* Reflect what the firm means at a deeper level to its external constituencies.[11]

These five categories reflect a growing emphasis on organizational values.

A similar set was developed by professor Robert S. Kaplan and business consultant David P. Norton writing in the *Harvard Business Review*.[12] They suggested that businesses should concentrate on four perspectives in setting performance measures.

- *The customers' perspective.* How your customers see you.
- *The internal operations perspective.* What you must excel at.
- *The change perspective.* How you continue to improve and create value.
- *The financial perspective.* How you look to shareholders.

A third example is *Fortune* magazine's annual Corporate Reputations survey. The criteria *Fortune* uses are quality of management; quality of product or services; financial soundness; value as a long-term investment; use of corporate assets; innovativeness; community or environmental responsibility; and ability to attract, develop, and keep talented people.[13]

Returning to the Likert model, we might visualize the relationship between the three classes of variables as stimuli (causal variables) acting upon the organism (intervening variables) and creating certain responses (output variables), as illustrated in Figure 6-4.[14]

The causal variables largely produce the level or condition of the intervening variables, which in turn influence the end result variables. Attempts to improve the intervening variables directly will usually be much less effective than will attempts to improve them by changing the causal variables. The end result variables, also, can be improved most effectively by modifying the causal variables rather than the intervening variables.

Long-Term Goals versus Short-Term Goals

Intervening variables are concerned with building and developing the organization, and they tend to be long-term goals. This is the part of effectiveness that many managers overlook because it emphasizes long-term potential as well as short-term performance. This oversight is understandable because most managers tend to be promoted on the basis of short-term output variables, such as increased production and earnings, without concern for long-run potential and organizational development. This oversight creates an organizational dilemma.

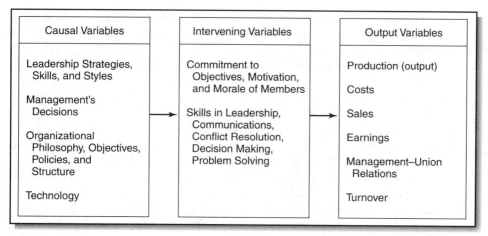

Figure 6-4
Relationship among Likert's Causal, Intervening, and Output Variables

Organizational Dilemma

One of the major problems in industry today is that there is a shortage of effective managers. Therefore, it is not uncommon for managers to be promoted in 6 months or a year if they are "producers." The basis on which top management promotes is often short-run output, so managers attempt to achieve high levels of productivity and often overemphasize tasks, placing extreme pressure on everyone, even when it is inappropriate.

We probably all have had some experience with coming into an office or a home and raising the roof with people. The immediate or short-run effect is probably increased activity. We also know that if this style is inappropriate for those concerned and if it continues over a long period of time, the morale of the organization will deteriorate. Some indications of deterioration of these intervening variables at work may be turnover, absenteeism, increased accidents, scrap loss, and numerous grievances. Not only the number of grievances but also the nature of grievances is important. Are grievances really significant problems, or do they reflect pent-up emotions due to anxieties and frustration? Are they settled at the complaint stage between the employee and the manager, or are they pushed up the hierarchy to be settled at higher levels or by arbitration? The organizational dilemma is that, in many instances, a manager who places pressure on everyone and produces in the short run is promoted out of this situation before the disruptive aspects of the intervening variables catch up.

There tends to be a time lag between declining intervening variables and significant restriction of output by employees under such a management climate. Employees tend to feel things will get better. Thus, when high-pressure managers are promoted rapidly, they often stay "one step ahead of the wolf."

The real problem is faced by the next manager. Although productivity records are high, this manager has inherited many problems. Merely the introduction of a new manager may be enough to collapse the slowly deteriorating intervening variables. A tremendous drop in morale and motivation leading almost immediately to a significant decrease in output can occur. Change by its very nature is frightening; to a group whose intervening variables are declining, it can be devastating. Regardless of this new manager's style, the current expectations of the followers may be so distorted that much time and patience will be needed to close the now apparent "credibility gap" between the goals of the organization and the personal goals of the group. No matter how effective this manager may be in the long run, senior management in reviewing a productivity drop may give the manager only a few months to improve performance. But as Likert's studies indicate, rebuilding a group's intervening variables in a small organization may take 1 to 3 years, and in a large organization it may take up to 7 years.

This dilemma is not restricted to business organizations. It is very common in school systems where superintendents and other top administrators can get promoted to better, higher paying jobs in other systems if they are innovative and implement new programs in their systems. One such superintendent brought a small town national prominence by putting every new and innovative idea being discussed in education into a school. In this process, there was almost no involvement or participation by the teachers, or by community administrators, in the decision making that went into these programs. After 2 years, the superintendent, because of these innovations, was promoted to a larger system with a $50,000-a-year raise. A new superintendent was appointed in the "old" system, but, almost before the new superintendent unpacked, turmoil hit the system with tremendous teacher turnover, a faculty union, and a defeated bond issue. As things became unglued, people were heard saying that they wished the old superintendent were back. And yet, in reality, it was the old superintendent's style that had eroded the intervening variables and caused the current problems.

Most people tend to evaluate coaches on win-and-loss records. Let's look at an example. Charlie, a high school coach, has had several good seasons. He knows if he has one more good season he will have a job offer with a better salary at a more prestigious school. Under these conditions, he may decide to concentrate on the short-run potential of the team. He may play only his seniors and have an impressive record at the end of the season. He will have maximized his short-run output goals, but the intervening variables of the team will have been neglected. If Charlie leaves this school and accepts another job, a new coach will find himself with a tremendous rebuilding job. Because developing the freshmen and sophomores and rebuilding a good team take time and much work, the team could have a few poor seasons in the interim. When the alumni and fans see the team losing, they might soon forget that old adage "It's not whether you win or lose, it's how you play the game" and consider the new coach a loser. "After all," they might say, "we had some great seasons with good old Charlie." They might not realize that good old Charlie concentrated only on short-run winning at the expense of building for the future. The problem is that the effectiveness of the new coach is being judged on the same games-won basis as his predecessor's. The new coach may be doing an excellent job of rebuilding and may have a winning season in 2 or 3 years, but the probability that the coach will be given the opportunity to build a future winner is low.

Problems don't occur just when leaders concentrate on output. For example, in *Twelve O'Clock High*, a classic World War II movie about the Air

Force, Frank Savage (played by Gregory Peck) is asked suddenly to take over a bomber group from a commanding officer whom everyone loved and respected. But his overidentification with and concern for his men result in an outfit that is not producing and is hurting the war effort.[15]

It should be clear that we do not think this is an either/or process. It is often a matter of determining how much to concentrate on each—output and intervening variables. Let's look at a basketball example. Suppose a women's team has good potential, with a large number of experienced senior players, but as the season progresses it does not look as if it is going to be an extremely good year. There comes a point in this season when the coach must make a basic decision. Will she continue to play her experienced seniors and hope to win a majority of her final games, or should she forget about concentrating on winning the last games and play her sophomores and juniors to give them experience, in hopes of developing and building a winning team for future years? The choice is between short-term and long-term goals. If the accepted goal is building the team for the future, then the coach should be evaluated on those terms and not entirely on the season's win-loss record. The art of achieving a balance is essential to effective leadership.

Although intervening variables do not appear on win-loss records, balance sheets, sales reports, or accounting ledgers, we feel that these long-term considerations are just as important to an organization as short-term output variables. Therefore, although difficult to measure, intervening variables should not be overlooked in determining organizational effectiveness. One of the instruments used by Likert to measure these variables was discussed in chapter 4 (see Table 4-5).

In summary, we feel that effectiveness is actually determined by whatever the manager and the organization decide are their goals and objectives, but they should remember that effectiveness is a function of:

1. Output variables (productivity/performance)
2. Intervening variables (the condition of the human resources)
3. Short-range goals
4. Long-range goals

INTEGRATION OF GOALS AND EFFECTIVENESS

The extent to which individuals and groups perceive their own goals as being satisfied by the accomplishment of organizational goals is the degree of *integration of goals.* When organizational goals are shared by all, this is what Douglas McGregor calls a *true* integration of goals.[16]

To illustrate this concept, we can divide an organization into two groups, management and employees. The respective goals of these two groups and the resultant attainment of the goals of the organization to which they belong are illustrated in Figure 6-5.[17] In this instance, the goals of management are

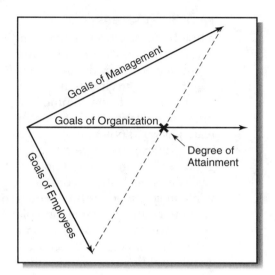

Figure 6-5
Directions of Goals
of Management,
Employees, and the
Organization—
Moderate
Organizational
Accomplishment

somewhat compatible with the goals of the organization, but they are not exactly the same. On the other hand, the goals of the employees are almost totally at odds with those of the organization. The result of the interaction between the goals of management and the goals of employees is a compromise, and actual performance is a combination of the two. It is at this approximate point that the degree of attainment of the goals of the organization can be pictured.

This situation can be much worse when there is little accomplishment of organizational goals, as illustrated in Figure 6-6. In this situation, there seems

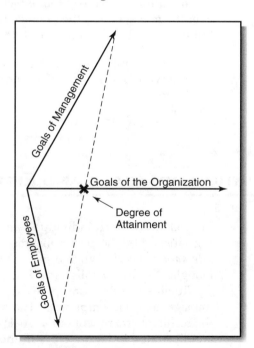

Figure 6-6
Little Organizational
Accomplishment

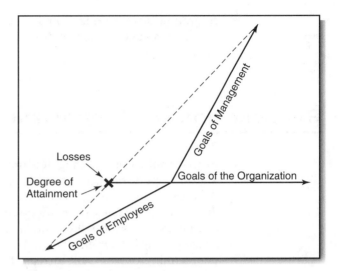

Figure 6-7
No Positive
Organizational
Accomplishment

to be a general disregard for the welfare of the organization. Both managers and workers see their own goals as conflicting with those of the organization. Consequently, both morale and performance will tend to be low, and organizational accomplishment will be negligible.

In some cases, the organizational goals can be so opposed that no positive progress is obtained. The result often is substantial losses, or draining off of assets (see Figure 6-7). In fact, organizations are going out of business every day for these very reasons.

The hope in an organization is to create a climate in which one of two things occurs. The individuals in the organization (both managers and employees) either see their goals as being the same as the goals of the organization or, although different, see their own goals as being satisfied as a direct result of working for the goals of the organization. Consequently, the closer we can get the individual's goals and objectives to the organization's goals and objectives, the greater will be the organizational performance, as illustrated in Figure 6-8.

One of the ways in which effective leaders bridge the gap between the individual's and the organization's goals is by creating a loyalty to themselves among their followers. They do this by being an influential spokesperson for their followers with higher management.[18] These leaders have little difficulty

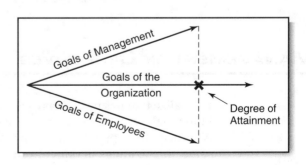

Figure 6-8
An Integration of the
Goals of
Management,
Employees, and the
Organization—*High*
Organizational
Accomplishment

communicating organizational goals to followers, and these followers find it easy to associate the acceptance of these goals with accomplishment of their own need satisfaction.

PARTICIPATION AND EFFECTIVENESS

In an organizational setting, it is urged that the criteria for an individual's or a group's performance should be mutually decided in advance. In making these decisions, managers and their employees should consider output and intervening variables, short-range and long-range goals. This process has two advantages. First, it will permit employees to participate in determining the basis on which their efforts will be judged. Second, involving employees in the planning process will increase their commitment to the goals and objectives established. Research evidence seems to support this contention.

One of the classic studies in this area was done by Lester Coch and John French in an American factory.[19] They found that when managers and employees discussed proposed technological changes, productivity increased and resistance to change decreased when these procedures were initiated. Other studies have shown similar results.[20] These studies suggest that involving employees in decision making tends to be effective in our society. Once again, we must remember that the success of using participative management depends on the situation. Although this approach tends to be effective in some industrial settings in the United States, it may not be appropriate in other cultures.

This argument was illustrated clearly when French, Joachim Israel, and Dagfinn Ås attempted to replicate the original Coch and French experiment in a Norwegian factory.[21] In this setting, they found no significant difference in productivity between work groups in which participative management was used and those in which it was not used. In other words, increased participation in decision making did not have the same positive influence on factory workers in Norway as it did in the United States. As did Hersey's replication of one of Likert's studies in Nigeria, this Norwegian study suggests that cultural differences in the followers and the situation may be important in determining the appropriate leadership style.

MANAGEMENT BY OBJECTIVES

We realize that it is not an easy task to integrate the goals and objectives of all individuals with the goals of the organization. Yet, it is not an impossible task. A participative approach to this problem, which has been used successfully in some organizations in our culture, is a process called management by objectives (MBO). The concepts behind MBO were introduced by Peter Drucker[22] in the early 1950s and have become popularized throughout the world, particularly through the efforts of George Odiorne[23] and John Humble.[24] Through their work and the efforts of others, managers in all kinds of organizational settings, whether they be industrial, educational, governmental, or military, are attempting to run their organizations with the MBO process as a basic underlying management concept.[25]

Management by objectives is basically

> a process whereby the senior and the junior managers of an enterprise jointly identify its common goals, define each individual's major areas of responsibility in terms of the results expected . . . and use these measures as guides for operating the unit and assessing the contribution of each of its members.[26]

This process in some cases has been successfully carried beyond the managerial level to include hourly employees. The concept rests on a philosophy of management that emphasizes an integration between external control (by managers) and self-control (by employees). It can apply to any manager or individual no matter what level or function, and to any organization, regardless of size.

The smooth functioning of this system is an agreement between a manager and an employee about that employee's own or group performance goals during a stated time period. These goals can emphasize either output variables or intervening variables or some combination of the two. The important thing is that goals are jointly established and agreed upon in advance. At the end of the time period, performance is reviewed in relation to accepted goals. Both the employee and the manager participate in this review and in any other evaluation that takes place. It has been found that objectives that are formulated with each person participating seem to gain more acceptance than those imposed by an authority figure in the organization. Consultation and participation in this area tend to establish personal risk for the attainment of the formulated objective by those who actually perform the task.

Before individual objectives are set, the common goals of the entire organization should be clarified, and, at this time, any appropriate changes in the organizational structure should be made: changes in titles, duties, relationships, authority, responsibility, span of control, and so forth.

Throughout the time period, what is to be accomplished by the entire organization should be compared with what is actually being accomplished; necessary adjustments should be made and inappropriate goals discarded. At the end of the time period, when the final mutual review of objectives and performance takes place, if there is a discrepancy between the two, efforts are initiated to determine what steps can be taken to overcome these problems. This step sets the stage for the determination of objectives for the next time period. The entire cycle of management by objectives is represented graphically in Figure 6-9.[27]

Many companies have found MBO to be a useful adjunct to achieving corporate effectiveness, but years of use have highlighted some of its

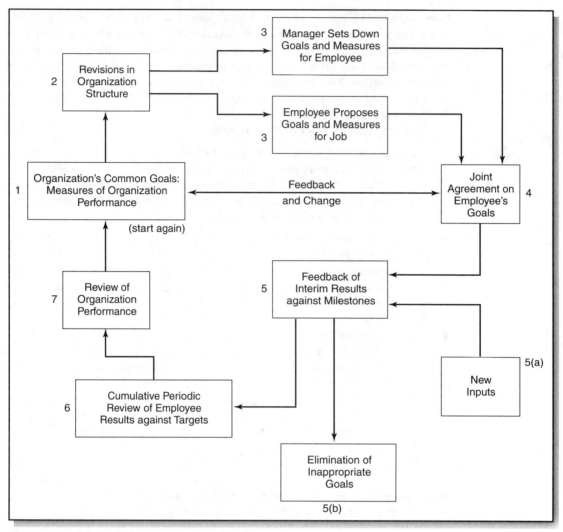

Figure 6-9
The Cycle of Management by Objectives

shortcomings. Employees may react to the implementation of an MBO program with distrust and skepticism; they may question why managers are interested in their input after years of giving orders.

After it is implemented, the MBO system can generate excessive documentation and paperwork. Goals of improved communication and planning can be lost in the shuffle of papers. Related to this is the problem of overemphasizing the grading and evaluating of employee performance in achieving MBO goals. MBO needs to focus on helping employees assist each other in improved performance.

Another problem of the MBO system can develop when managers set meaningless or easily achieved goals. Goals must be carefully monitored with an eye on overall corporate goals and objectives. Problems can also develop when the feedback process is slow and managers are unable to change or adapt their goals to meet rapidly changing conditions.

Management by objectives can be a powerful tool in gaining mutual commitment and high productivity for an organization in which this type of employee involvement is appropriate. However, the system must be developed, implemented, and managed with an understanding of the problems it can generate.

STYLE AND EFFECTIVENESS

Abundant research supports the argument that all the basic leader behavior styles can be effective or ineffective depending on the situation. Abraham K. Korman gathered some of the most convincing evidence that dispels the idea of a single best style of leader behavior.[28] Korman attempted to review all studies that examined the relationships between the Ohio State behavior dimensions of initiating structure (task) and consideration (relationship) and various measures of effectiveness, including group productivity, salary, performance under stress, administrative reputation, work group grievances, absenteeism, and turnover. In all, Korman reviewed more than 25 studies. In every case, the two dimensions were measured by either the leader opinion questionnaire (LOQ) or the leader behavior description questionnaire (LBDQ). The former is used to assess how leaders think they should behave in a given situation; the latter measures follower perceptions of leader behavior. Korman concluded that

> despite the fact that "Consideration" and "Initiating Structure" have become almost bywords in American industrial psychology, it seems apparent that very little is now known as to how these variables may predict work group performance and the conditions which affect such predictions. At the current time, we cannot even say whether they have any predictive significance at all.[29]

Thus, Korman found that consideration and initiating structure had no significant predictive value in terms of effectiveness. This finding suggests that because situations differ, so must leader style.

Fred Fiedler, in testing his contingency model of leadership in more than 50 studies covering a span of 16 years (1951–1967), concluded that both directive, task-oriented leaders and nondirective, human relations-oriented leaders are effective under some conditions. As Fiedler argued:

> While one can never say that something is impossible, and while someone may well discover the all-purpose leadership style or behavior at some future time, our own data and those which have come out of sound research by other investigators do not promise such miraculous cures.[30]

SUMMARY

The evidence is clear that there is no single all-purpose leader behavior style that is effective in all situations. Although our basic conclusion in this chapter is that the type of leader behavior needed depends on the situation, this conclusion leaves many questions unanswered for a specific individual in a leadership role. Such individuals may be personally interested in how leadership depends on the situation and how they can find some practical value in theory. To accommodate this type of concern, in chapter 7 we will discuss the environmental variables that may help a leader or a manager to make effective decisions in problematic leadership situations.

ENDNOTES

1. Peter F. Drucker, *Management: Tasks, Responsibilities, Practices* (New York: Harper & Row, 1973), p. 45.
2. C. Northcote Parkinson, *Parkinson's Law* (Boston: Houghton Mifflin, 1957).
3. Fred J. Carvell, *Human Relations in Business* (Toronto: Macmillan, 1970), p. 182.
4. Bernard M. Bass in *Leadership, Psychology, and Organizational Behavior* (New York: Harper & Brothers, 1960), pp. 88–89.
5. Fred Luthans, "Successful versus Effective Real Managers," *The Academy of Management Executive,* 11, no. 2 (May 1988), pp. 127–132.
6. *Wall Street Journal,* January 9, 1978, p. 12.
7. Rensis Likert, *The Human Organization* (New York: McGraw-Hill, 1967), pp. 26–29.
8. Rensis Likert, *New Patterns of Management* (New York: McGraw-Hill, 1961), p. 2.
9. Fred E. Fiedler, *A Theory of Leadership Effectiveness* (New York: McGraw-Hill, 1967), p. 9.
10. William J. Reddin, "The 3-D Management Style Theory," *Training and Development Journal,* April 1967. This is one of the critical differences between Reddin's 3-D management style theory and the Tridimensional Leader Effectiveness model. Reddin in his model seems to consider only output variables in determining effectiveness, whereas in the Tridimensional Leader Effectiveness model both intervening variables and output variables are considered.
11. Peter B. Vaill, "Managing As a Performing Art," page 221 in *The Manager's Bookshelf,* 3rd ed., Jon Pierce and John Newstrom (New York: Harper Collins Publishers, 1993).
12. Robert S. Kaplan and David P. Norton, "Putting the Balanced Scorecard to Work," *Harvard Business Review,* September–October 1993, p. 134.
13. Rahul Jacob, "Corporate Reputations," *Fortune,* March 6, 1995, pp. 54–64.
14. Adapted from Likert, *The Human Organization,* pp. 47–77.
15. This classic film is an excellent illustration of the concepts of motivation, Situational Leadership, and improving organizational performance.
16. Douglas McGregor, *The Human Side of Enterprise* (New York: McGraw-Hill, 1960). See also McGregor, *Leadership and Motivation* (Boston: MIT Press, 1966).
17. In reality, the schematics presented in the following pages are simplifications of vector analyses and therefore would be more accurately portrayed as parallelograms.
18. Saul W. Gellerman, *Motivation and Productivity* (New York: American Management Association, 1963), p. 265. See also Gellerman, *Management by Motivation* (New York: American Management Association, 1968).
19. Lester Coch and John R. P. French Jr., "Overcoming Resistance to Change," in *Group Dynamics: Research and Theory,* 2nd ed., Dorwin Cartwright and Alvin Zander, eds. (Evanston, IL: Row, Peterson, 1960).
20. See Kurt Lewin, "Group Decision and Social Change," pages 459–473 in *Readings in Social Psychology,* ed. G. Swanson, T. Newcomb, and E. Hartley (New York: Henry Holt, 1952).

21. John R. P. French Jr., Joachim Israel, and Dagfinn Ås, "An Experiment on Participation in a Norwegian Factory," *Human Relations,* 13 (1960), pp. 3–19.

22. Peter F. Drucker, *The Practice of Management* (New York: Harper & Row, 1964).

23. George S. Odiorne, *Management by Objectives: A System of Managerial Leadership* (New York: Pitman Publishing, 1965); Odiorne, *The Human Side of Management* (San Diego, CA: University Associates, 1987); Odiorne, *MBO II: A System of Managerial Leadership for the 80s* (Belmont, CA: Pitman, Learning, 1979); Odiorne, "The Managerial Bait-and-Switch Game," *Personnel,* 63, no. 3 (March 1986), pp. 32–37.

24. John W. Humble, *Management by Objectives* (London: Industrial Education and Research Foundation, 1967).

25. See also J. D. Batten, *Beyond Management by Objectives* (New York: American Management Association, 1966); Ernest C. Miller, *Objectives and Standards Approach to Planning and Control, AMA Research Study 74* (New York: American Management Association, 1966); and William J. Reddin, *Effective Management by Objectives: The 3-D Method of MBO* (New York: McGraw-Hill, 1971).

26. Odiorne, *Management by Objectives,* pp. 55–56.

27. *Ibid.,* p. 78.

28. Abraham K. Korman, "'Consideration,' 'Initiating Structure,' and Organizational Criteria— A Review," *Personnel Psychology: A Journal of Applied Research,* 19, no. 4 (Winter 1966), pp. 349–361.

29. *Ibid.,* p. 360.

30. Fiedler, *A Theory of Leadership Effectiveness,* p. 247.

Chapter 7

Diagnosing the Environment

The situational approach to leadership is built on the concept that effectiveness results from a leader's using a behavioral style that is appropriate to the demands of the environment. The key for managers or leaders is learning to *diagnose* their environment, the first of the three important leadership competencies. You will recall from chapter 1 that the remaining two are adapting and communicating.

This chapter will also discuss the special requirements of leading many different groups such as "the generations" and multicultural groups. ✧

ENVIRONMENTAL VARIABLES

The environment in an organization consists of the leader, that leader's follower(s), supervisor(s), associates, organization, job demands, and other variables such as time.[1] This list is not all-inclusive, but it contains some of the interacting components that tend to be important to a leader.[2] As illustrated in Figure 7-1, the environment a leader faces may have some other situational variables that are unique to it, as well as an external environment that has an impact on it.

Except for job demands, each of these environmental variables can be viewed as having two major components—style and expectations. Thus, our list of variables is expanded to include the following:

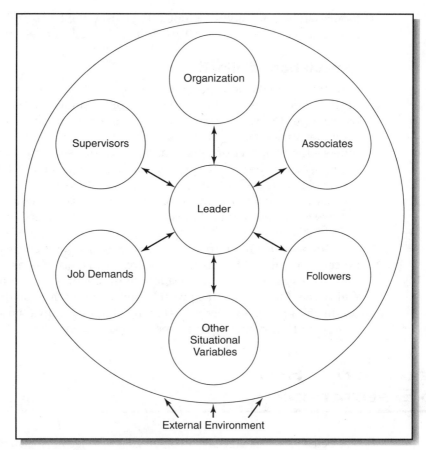

Figure 7-1
Interacting Components of an Organizational Setting

Leader's style   Leader's expectations
Followers' styles   Followers' expectations
Supervisors' styles   Supervisors' expectations
Associates' styles   Associates' expectations
Organization's style   Organization's expectations
Job demands
Other situational variables
External environment

Style Defined

As discussed in chapter 5, the *style* of leaders is the consistent behavior patterns that they use when they are working with and through other people, as perceived by those people. These patterns emerge as leaders are seen to respond in the same fashion under similar conditions; they develop habits of action that become somewhat predictable to those who work with them.

(Some writers, ourselves included, have used the terms *style* and *personality* interchangeably. In chapter 10, we will distinguish between those two terms.)

Expectations Defined

Expectations are the perceptions of appropriate behavior for one's own role or position or one's perception of the roles of others within the organization. In other words, the expectations of individuals define for them what they should do under various circumstances in their particular job and how they think others—their supervisors, peers, and followers—should behave in relation to their positions. To say that a person has shared expectations with another person means that each of the individuals involved perceives accurately and accepts a personal role and the role of the other. If expectations are to be compatible, it is important to share common goals and objectives. Although two individuals may have differing styles because their roles require different styles of behavior, it is imperative for an organization's effectiveness that they perceive and accept the institution's goals and objectives as their own.

The task of diagnosing a leader environment is very complex when we realize that the leader is the pivotal point around which all of the other environmental variables interact, as shown in Figure 7-1. In a sense, all these variables are communicating role expectations to the leader.

INTERACTION OF STYLE AND EXPECTATIONS

The behavior of managers in an organization, as Jacob W. Getzels suggested, results from the interaction of style and expectations.[3] Some managerial positions or roles are structured greatly by expectations; that is, they allow people occupying that position very little room to express their individual style. The behavior of an army sergeant, for example, may be said to conform almost completely to role expectations. Little innovative behavior is tolerated. Supervision of highly structured, routine jobs based on Theory X assumptions about human nature requires almost predetermined behavior by a manager (that is, close supervision).

The difference between structured and unstructured roles in terms of style and expectations is illustrated in Figure 7-2, where style is a larger component of the advertising agency manager's job than of the army sergeant's. Although the mix varies from job to job, behavior in an organization remains a function of both style and expectations and involves some combination of task and relationship behaviors.

Leader's Style and Expectations

One of the most important elements of a leadership situation is the style of the leader. Leaders develop their style over a period of time from experience, education, and training. Robert Tannenbaum and Warren Schmidt suggested that there are at least four internal forces that influence a manager's leader-

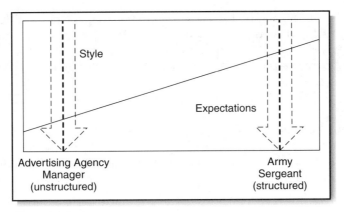

Figure 7-2
Style and Expectations as Related to Two Different
Positions or Roles

Source: Adapted from Jacob W. Getzels, "Administration As a Social
Process," p. 158 in *Administrative Theory in Education,* ed. Andrew W.
Halpin (Chicago: Midwest Administration Center, University of
Chicago, 1958).

ship style: value system, confidence in employees, personal inclinations, and
feelings of security in an uncertain situation.[4]

A manager's *value system* consists of the answers to such questions as:
How strongly does a manager feel that individuals should have a share in
making the decisions that affect them? How convinced is the manager that
the person who is paid to assume responsibility should personally carry the
burden of decision making? The strength of a manager's convictions on questions such as these will tend to affect that manager's leadership style, particularly in terms of the amount of direction or support that manager is willing
to provide for staff members.

Confidence in employees is often influenced by the manager's Theory X or
Theory Y assumptions about human nature. In other words, the amount of
control or freedom a manager gives to staff members depends on whether
that manager believes that people are basically lazy, unreliable, or irresponsible or that people can be creative and self-motivated in an environment, if
properly motivated. In addition, a manager's confidence in employees also
depends on feelings about the knowledge and competence of staff members
in a particular area of responsibility.

A manager's *personal inclinations* have an impact on leadership style. Some
managers are comfortable being directive (controlling and supervising). Others operate more comfortably in a team situation in which they provide some
direction or facilitate the interactions of team members. Still other managers
prefer to delegate and let staff members handle specific problems and issues.

Feelings of security in an uncertain situation have a definite impact on
the manager's willingness to release control over decision making to other
people in an uncertain environment. What might be involved here is the
manager's tolerance for ambiguity.

It is important to recognize that managers have different leadership styles, but it is also important to remember that style is not how leaders think they behave in a situation, but how others (most importantly, their followers) perceive their behavior. The importance of this concept is often difficult for leaders to understand. For example, if Jane's followers think that she is a firm, task-oriented leader, it will not matter that she thinks she is a democratic, relationship-oriented leader; her followers will behave according to how they perceive her. In this case, the followers will treat Jane as if she were a firm, task-oriented leader. Thus, leaders have to learn how they are coming across to others. Yet, this kind of information is difficult to obtain. People are often reluctant to be honest on this subject, especially in a supervisor-employee relationship.

Followers' Styles and Expectations

The styles of followers are an important consideration for leaders in appraising their situation. In fact, as Fillmore Sanford indicated, there is some justification for regarding the followers "as the most crucial factor in any leadership event."[5] Followers in any situation are vital, not only because individually they accept or reject the leader, but because as a group they actually determine whatever personal power that leader will have. If the follower decides not to follow, it really doesn't matter what the other elements in the situation are.

This is an important aspect of all levels of management. Victor H. Vroom uncovered evidence that the effectiveness of a leader is dependent to a great extent on the style of the individual workers.[6] Saul Gellerman also stressed the importance of the workers:

> Place a group with strong independence drives under supervisors who need to keep the group under their thumb, and the result is very likely to be trouble. Similarly, if you take a docile team who is accustomed to obedience and respect for their supervisors and place them under supervisors who try to make them manage their own work, they are likely to wonder uneasily whether the supervisors really know what they are doing.[7]

Tannenbaum and Schmidt argued that a leader can permit followers greater freedom if the following essential conditions exist:

- If the [followers] have relatively high needs for independence
- If the [followers] have a readiness to assume responsibility for decision making
- If they have a relatively high tolerance for ambiguity
- If they are interested in the problem and feel it is important
- If they understand and identify with the goals of the organization
- If they have the necessary knowledge and experience to deal with the problem
- If they have learned to expect to share in decision making.[8]

Even though managers would prefer to change their followers' styles, they may find that they must adapt, at least temporarily, to the followers' current behavior. For example, a supervisor who wants followers to take more responsibility and to operate under general rather than close supervision cannot expect this kind of change to take place overnight. The supervisor's current behavior, at least to some extent, must be compatible with the current expectations of the group, with planned change taking place over a long-term period. We have seen numerous examples of the need for this kind of diagnosis in schools where humanistic teachers have tried to turn over significant responsibility to students without recognizing that many of these students expect teachers to tell them what to do. This rapid change in style often produces irresponsibility rather than more student initiative.

Hyler Bracey has suggested that leaders need to "manage from the HEART":

- *Hear* and understand me.
- *Even* if you disagree with me, please do not make me wrong.
- *Acknowledge* the greatness within me.
- *Remember* to look for my good intentions.
- *Tell* me the truth with understanding.[9]

Managing from the HEART can promote increased honesty in supervisor-employee relationships, increase job satisfaction through personal empowerment, and give your organization a tangible competitive edge.

Leaders, especially leaders who are new in their position, should know the expectations that followers have about the way they should behave in certain situations. A predecessor's leader behavior style is still a powerful influence. If this style is different from the new leader's style, this difference may create an immediate problem.[10] Leaders must either change their style to coincide with followers' expectations or change follower expectations. Because the style of leaders often has been developed over a long period of time, it can be difficult for them to make any drastic changes in the short run. It may, therefore, be more effective if leaders concentrate on changing the expectations of their followers.

Supervisor's Style and Expectations

Another element of the environment is the leadership style of one's supervisor. By *supervisor*, we mean the leader's leader. Just about everyone has a supervisor of one kind or another. Most managers give considerable attention to supervising followers, but some do not pay enough attention to being a follower themselves. Yet, meeting the supervisor's expectations is often an important factor affecting one's style, particularly if one's supervisor is located close by. If a supervisor is very task-oriented, for example, the supervisor might expect follower(s) to operate in the same manner. Relationship-oriented behavior might be evaluated as inappropriate, without even considering results. This rigid thinking has become evident when first-line supervisors are sent to training programs to improve their human relations skills. Upon returning to the company, they try to implement some of these new ideas. But their own supervisors, who have not accepted these concepts, become impatient with the first-line supervisor's newfound concern for people: "Joe, cut out all that talking with the workers and get the work done." With such reactions, it would not take this first-line supervisor long to revert to the previous style, and in the future, it will be much more difficult to implement any behavioral change.

It is important for managers to know their supervisor's expectations, particularly if these managers want to advance in the organization. If they are seeking a promotion, they may tend to adhere to the customs and mores (styles and expectations) of the group to which they aspire rather than those of their peer group.[11] Consequently, their supervisors' expectations may become more important to them than those of the other groups with which they interact—their followers or associates.

The importance of the expectations of one's supervisor and the effect they can have on leadership style was vividly illustrated by Robert H. Guest in a case analysis of organizational change.[12] He examined a large assembly plant of an automobile company, Plant Y, and contrasted the situation under two different leaders. Under Stewart, the plant manager, working relationships at Plant Y were dominated by hostility and mistrust. His high task style was characterized by continual attempts to increase the push for productivity. As a result, the prevailing atmosphere was that of one emergency following on the heels of another, and the governing motivation for employee activity was fear—fear of being chewed out right on the assembly line, fear of being held responsible for events in which one had no clear authority, fear of losing one's job. Of the six plants in this division of the corporation, Plant Y had the poorest performance record, and it was getting worse.

Stewart was replaced by Cooley, who seemed like an extremely effective leader. Over the next 3 years, dramatic changes took place. In various cost and performance measures used to rate the six plants, Plant Y was now truly the leader; and the atmosphere of interpersonal cooperation and personal satisfaction had improved impressively over the situation under Stewart. These changes, moreover, were effected through an insignificant number of dismissals and reassignments. Using a much higher relationship style, Cooley succeeded in turning Plant Y around.

On the surface, the big difference was style of leadership. Cooley was a good leader. Stewart was not. But Guest pointed out clearly in his analysis that leadership style was only one of two important factors. The other was that, whereas Stewart received daily orders from division headquarters to correct specific situations, Cooley was left alone. Cooley was allowed to lead; Stewart was told how to lead.[13] In other words, when productivity in Plant Y began to decline during changeover from wartime to peacetime operations, Stewart's supervisors expected him to get productivity back on the upswing by taking control of the reins, and they put tremendous pressure on him to do just that. Guest suggested that these expectations forced Stewart to operate in a very crisis-oriented, autocratic way. When Cooley was given charge as plant manager, however, a hands-off policy was initiated by his supervisors. The fact that the expectations of top management had changed gave Cooley an opportunity to operate in a completely different style.

Associates' Styles and Expectations

A leader's associates, or peers, are those individuals who have similar positions within the organization. For example, the associates of a vice president for production are the other vice presidents in the company; the associates of a teacher would be other teachers. Yet, not all associates are significant for leaders; only those they interact with regularly have an impact on their style and effectiveness. The styles and expectations of one's associates are important when a leader has frequent interactions with them, such as a situation that involves trading and bargaining for resources.[14]

We mentioned managers who have a strong drive to advance in an organization. Some people, however, are satisfied with their current positions. For these people, the expectations of their associates may be more important in influencing their behavior than are those of their supervisors. College professors tend to be good examples. Often they are more concerned about the opinions of other professors or colleagues in their area of expertise than they are in the opinions of administrators.

Organization's Style and Expectations

The style and expectations of an organization are determined by the history and tradition of the organization, as well as by the organizational goals and objectives that reflect the style and expectations of current top management.

Over a period of time, an organization, much like an individual, becomes characterized by certain modes of behavior that are perceived as its style. The development of an organizational style, or corporate image, has been referred to as the process of *institutionalization*.[15] In this process, the organization is infused with a system of values that reflects its history and the people who have played vital roles in its formation and growth. Thus, it is difficult to understand Ford Motor Company without knowing the impact that Henry Ford had on its formation. Some organizations, for example, hold to the notion that the desirable executive is one who is dynamic, imaginative, decisive, and persuasive. Other organizations put more emphasis on the importance of the executive's ability to work effectively with people—human relations skills.[16]

Members of the organization soon become conscious of the value system operating within the institution and guide their actions from many expectations derived from those values. The organization's expectations are most often expressed in forms of policies, operating procedures, and controls, as well as in informal customs and mores developed over time.

Organizational Goals

The goals of an organization usually consist of some combination of output and intervening variables. As we discussed earlier, output variables are those short-run goals that can easily be measured, such as net profits, annual earnings, and win-loss records. On the other hand, intervening variables consist of those long-run goals reflecting the internal condition of the organization that cannot easily be measured, such as its capacity for effective interaction, communication, and decision making.

Joseph Batten, an author of fourteen books on leadership and quality management, summarized the relationship of an organization's values and expectations.

> Organizational policies, procedures, processes, and programs must be indivisibly rooted in the organization's philosophy, which is the basic repository of corporate vision and values, and which, in turn, pervades every part and person in the organization. It is important to note that in the absence of a coherent and cogent philosophy, mediocrity and a sense of drift abound.[17]

OTHER SITUATIONAL VARIABLES

Job Demands

Another important element of a leadership situation is the demands of the job that the leader's group has been assigned to perform. Fiedler called this situation *variable task structure*—the degree of structure in the task that the group has been asked to do.[18] He found that a task that has specific instructions on what leaders and their followers should do requires a different leadership style than an unstructured task with no prescribed operating procedure.[19] Highly structured jobs that need directions seem to require high task behavior, whereas unstructured jobs that do not need directions seem to favor relationship-oriented behavior.[20]

Time

Another important element in the environment of a leader is the time available for decision making. If a manager's office bursts into flames, he cannot seek opinions and suggestions from his followers or use other methods of involvement to determine the best way to leave the building. The leader must make an immediate decision and point the way. Therefore, short-time demands, such as in an emergency, tend to require task-oriented behavior. On the other hand, if time is not a major factor in the situation, there is more opportunity for the leader to select from a broader range of leadership styles, depending on the other situational variables.

The Generations

Managers will face the daunting challenge of leading employees who will be the essential resources of twenty-first century organizations. These employees can be categorized into several generations, each with special motivation needs. Rogene Baxter, Bridgewater Group, a Moraga, California management development firm, argues that managing employees is not a management issue, but a leadership issue.[21]

Generation G: Ages 54 and Older

Also known as the "Gray Generation," Rebecca Kuzins reported that these are the people near or beyond retirement age.[22] They love to work and feel they have very significant contributions to make. Many need to work to supplement a modest income. They are concerned, however, about being led by younger leaders. After being in authority positions most of their lives, it is difficult for them to be in a follower role. Those individuals, born between 1922 and 1943, continue to demonstrate such core values as "dedication, sacrifice, hard work, conformity, law and order, respect for authority, patience, delayed reward, duty before pleasure, adherence to rules, and honor."[23] They account for nearly 25 percent of the work population. This cohort demonstrates specific personality traits. They like consistency, uniformity, and things on a grand scale; they are disciplined conformers, past oriented, and history absorbed; they believe in hierarchy, logic, rules, law, and order; and spend conservatively. Having been heavily influenced by the manufacturing economy, their work ethic includes loyalty, dependability, and hard work to get things accomplished. They value obedience over individualism, respect of leaders and institutions, and tend to live in rural areas, suburbs, and small towns. Their workplace had traditionally been one with a hierarchical division of labor (i.e., executives at the top and workers at the bottom) which correlated with age and experience.[24]

Generation B: Ages 35 to 53

The "Baby Boomer" generation, having ridden the crest of several decades of prosperity, is now facing retirement. Some have retired early. Others find themselves with less retirement income than they had expected. Security is a critical issue with mergers, downsizing, pension plan changes, care of elderly parents, and many other challenging issues. "Where do I stand?" is a recurring question. They are perceived to be a generation of commitment. There are currently 81 million Baby Boomers in the United States.[25] In an article, Kim Clark referred to the "New Midlife" in which the biggest class of Boomers (42.5 million) hits 40, redefines middle age, and reshapes the nation.[26]

Ron Zemke, Claire Raines, and Bob Filipczak described this cohort as having been born between 1943 and 1960 at the end of the United States' rural, agrarian lifestyle. They believe in growth, expansion, and being stars of the show; are collaborative and cooperative; pursue personal gratification; and strive for health, optimism, wellness, involvement, and personal growth.[27]

There appears to be somewhat distinct differences between those born during the first half of the Boomer generation and those born during the second half. According to these authors, those born during the first half (i.e., "Yuppies") tend to be more idealistic, ambitious, and are economic achievers, with a "workaholic" nature driving them to succeed in ways that increase their status, prestige, and opportunities for control and power. However, the late Boomers born during the second decade tend to be less materialistic, spend more time with their families, and are more cynical about the belief that good work habits and a positive mental attitude will yield rewards in the workplace.[28]

Overall, Boomers represent about 50 to 55 percent of all workers.[29] They work in all types of industries and organizations with half in technical and production positions and about one-fourth in management. Boomers consider their "*work* ethic" as synonymous with their "*worth* ethic" and are the majority in the highest-paying jobs such as doctors, lawyers, and accountants. The remaining one-fourth work in sales and clerical positions. Work environment preferences are based on affiliation, consensus, team building, relationship building, and participative management. According to Kim Clark, the bodies of individuals in their 30s and 40s decline as their ability to use oxygen to power physical activities decreases, eyesight diminishes, muscles lose mass, hormones deplete, processing speed decreases, and the ability to cope with novel information deteriorates. Boomers worry that management might be thinking about replacing them with younger employees. "The spread of technology and the American culture's infatuation with youth are said to be creating a job market that increasingly rewards flexibility and speed over age and experience."[30]

Generation X: Ages 23 to 34

Dorina Lazo reported that there are 47 million "Xers" who are now the "hackers, business people, volunteers, and politicians who run the country."[31] Job satisfaction is a very important factor for this group. This cohort wants their work to matter and their work relationships to be positive experiences in their lives. These beneficiaries of technology want to be self-led. They want to know where the organization is going, vision is particularly important, and they want to contribute.

Zemke, Raines, and Filipczak described this cohort birth period from 1960 to 1980 as the "Xers" or Generation "I for invisible" or "L for lost" due to the fact that they have grown up in the shadow of the Boomers. This group has a demonstrated concern for survival, both economic and psychological. Their personalities are further described as self-reliant; seeking a sense of family; wanting balance; are informal, skeptical, and attracted to the "edge"; are technologically savvy and have a casual approach to authority.[32] Likewise, Claire Raines describes Xers as "good at change, comfortable with technology, independent, financially savvy, not intimidated by authority, and creative."[33]

Zemke, Raines, and Filipczak compared the first-half Generation X to the second half of the generation. They suggested that those born during the first half of the period were workers "no one wanted" who entered the workforce just as the traditional "understood" job contract was torn up and redrafted as a result of corporate downsizing efforts.[34] The second-half Xers were referred to as the "Gold Collar" workers who took advantage of the information technology function demands of companies needing qualified computer technicians and programmers. Members of this cohort were labeled "slackers" due to their different orientation to work which resulted from learning that work is no guarantee of survival when companies can release them from their positions without warning, logic, or an apology (i.e., downsizing, corporate takeovers, or buyouts). They also realized they were often put in entry-level positions that tended to be mindless, dull, and exhausting.[35]

It is interesting to note that according to these three authors, researchers have claimed that media exposure (i.e., photography, television, video, computers, and movies) has increased the average intelligence quotient (IQ) such that an individual taking an IQ test 30 years ago would have scored 20 points lower as compared to IQ tests designed for today's examinees.[36] Higher scores in visual acuity have been evidenced among children who have grown up with intense visual imagery. Additionally, technology has influenced cognitive changes in the ways individuals perceive and process information (i.e., parallel processing, which means doing many different things or handling multiple and diverse information at the same time).

Generation Xers demonstrate a nontraditional orientation about time and space and have often gone into technology-rich employment. They "work to live" and will not try to juggle the roles of parent, employee, or spouse at the price they perceive their parents paid for success.[37] They want positions with flexible work hours, where independence is encouraged, fun and humor are integrated into the work environment, and casual dress is the standard. Current trends for some employees to retire later means those younger employees will be managing older employees.

A few essential employees can determine the success or failure of the company in "information or knowledge" industries such as computer and software companies. For a firm to remain competitive, it must have committed employees. Therefore, a firm's ability to motivate its employees is critical to its success. Generation Xers will walk. There are just too many opportunities available.

Heather Neely, a Palo Alto, California, management consultant has identified a potential problem regarding the technologic age. Friction in the workplace has developed because technology has enabled Generation Xers to be technologically perceptive. This throws off the traditional dynamic in the workplace about respecting your elders. It is not a generation gap; it is a generation lap. Generation Xers are lapping their superiors in terms of their superior technological knowledge.[38]

There are also subsets of these generations; for example, "Generation N," the Hispanic population of Generation X. According to Lazo, these Xers struggle with language and cultural barriers that white Generation Xers never face. He refers to this cohort as the "movers and shakers" who have progressed from "realistic and pessimistic to realistic and guardedly optimistic" and are not afraid of risks.[39]

Generation Y: Ages 12 to 22

Also called the "Yes Generation," they might be referred to as the "S Generation" because they comprise so many of the service providers. Teens and those in their early 20s want to work to pay for cars, music, clothing, and other perceived necessities of life. They feel they are competent and they are. They want to feel responsible and most are very responsible. Dorina Lazo referred to this group as "Generation Why?" and reported that there are 38 million members in this group.[40]

Zemke, Raines, and Filipczak defined this cohort, born between 1980 and 2000, with alternative names such as "Nexters," "Y as in follows X," "N-Gen," for the Internet Generation or Nintendo Generation," "Millennials," "Echo Boomers," or "Generation 2001" for the first graduating class of the new millennium.[41] These young people are in their teens and many know more about digital technology than most of their parents. In the United States, this cohort is the first generation to grow up without expecting a strong nuclear family, as evidenced by the fact that more than 50 percent live in homes that do not include two parents. Girls are more involved in educational, sports, and career endeavors than in the previous generations. They acknowledge and talk openly about adult issues. They have learned to be advocates for their environment (i.e., recycling, global warming, endangered species, destruction of rain forests, racism, resistance of peer pressure, and acid rain). Many of these young people have turned to the Internet for support via Web sites and online chat rooms to give them a voice.[42]

Because 60 percent of households with children age 7 and under have personal computers, exposure to the Internet has influenced the learning of advanced motor, spatial, and strategy skills via game technology.[43] Diversity of races, religions, and backgrounds has provided the Nexters with greater exposure to, and acceptance of, multiculturalism. Although approximately one-third of all teens work 20 hours a week—usually in food service and light retail positions—as a group, they tend to be optimistic, civic minded, confident, sociable, diverse, value conscious, and achievement oriented. Over half plan to enter the workforce right after college in careers such as education and teaching, medicine, business, computer-related fields, law, and psychology.[44]

INFLUENCE OF THE GENERATIONS ON LEADERSHIP

Rogene Baxter suggests, "Managers and leaders need to understand people, whatever their age. They need to find out their skills, strengths, and whatever motivates them. They have to recognize that everyone is different and deal with each employee as an individual."[45]

What all of this means is that there is no one best approach to leadership. Each generation, for example, has special needs and wants. A "one-size-fits-all" approach just does not work. Leaders must tailor their leadership to the followers. A size 48-long suit will fit some, but not very many. Hence, a directive approach will fit some, but not many.

Generation G

This generation tends to demonstrate a command-and-control leadership style for decision making through clear and simple directives. Zemke, Raines, and Filipczak described this cohort as those who take charge, delegate, and make the most of their decisions based on specialized rules and roles. Their attributes include interpersonal pleasantry and dependability, although they may tend to be overbearing when directing others. They have well-developed skills, talents, experience, and wisdom. Younger leaders need to understand these concerns and lead with compassion and awareness. Leaders need to take time to discuss the issues, because frequently they are the same issues that the leaders themselves are facing. They need to collaborate with older employees to learn things they do not know and strive to keep employees motivated, productive, and employed.[46]

Elaine Fortier and Denise Brouillette, management consultants who specialize in intergenerational issues, have these suggestions for older employees reporting to younger managers:

- Sit down and discuss expectations right away.
- Age is not the issue; it is the attitude. The new generation does not want to hear you say, "I'll try." They want to hear, "I'll take care of it."
- Look for ways to cut through bureaucracy and red tape.
- Do not be put off by overambition.
- No matter what, keep up with the technology.[47]

Zemke, Raines, and Filipczak outlined several key principles a younger manager of a Generation G employee would benefit from considering. These considerations include not limiting older employees to full-time; taking time to properly orient employees regarding what to expect, what the policies are, and who's who; providing them with the "big picture" and history of the department; emphasizing long-term goals; training them in technology and not stereotyping them as "technophobes"; using the personal touch with handwritten notes; and providing some perks that symbolize status and rewards for their contributions.[48] Mentoring this group involves understanding that they will learn new skills once they recognize the necessity for change in terms of organizational goals through a tactful and respectful process of coaching, establishing rapport, discussion, problem agreement, and action.

Generation B

The book, *Generations at Work: Managing the Clash of Veterans, Boomers, Xers, and Nexters in Your Workplace,* described the leadership style of Baby Boomers as one in which their tendency is to be consensual, not hierarchical, and they participate in terms of understanding, listening, communicating, motivating, and delegating. Additionally, they often use rapport skills for protection, improvement, or betterment of themselves or overburdened others. Key principles for managing involve letting Boomers know their experience is valued, respected, and credit will be given for their accomplishments.[49] It is important to challenge them to excel and promote future growth and development of the organization. Assurance is required that the work environment is warm, supportive, and individuals are recognized as unique contributors to make a difference. Boomers need training in strategic planning, budgeting, and coaching skills and opportunities for developmental experiences and personal growth.

Generation X

Generation Xers have to be able to say, "This is where I am strong and this is where I am weak." Employers are learning that to create bottom-line results, they must create this type of environment to keep their best employees. This is particularly important for leading Generation Xers. The old chain-of-command system takes too long to get through the hierarchy and bureaucracy and micromanaging will not work. This generation of leaders must be skilled at supporting and developing a responsive team who can change direction, or projects, at a moment's notice.[50] They tend to challenge others' thinking, fairly and competently, and value information as a means of power. Additionally, they enjoy independent activities and "virtual teamwork" in the form of electronic communication.

Key principles for managing Generation Xers include acknowledging the fact that Xers want to have a life (i.e., maintain a healthy balance between work, family, and fun); reassurance that the quality of their work is more critical than the number of years of experience; incorporation of technology and innovation with a "hands-off" management approach; and the establishment of service departments for employees (i.e., transportation, child care, language skills). Generation Xers benefit from being provided information on a variety of corporate subjects, freedom to get their jobs done, knowledge of the organizational changes, availability of training through multiple resources and media, and responsibility for simultaneous tasks and projects.[51]

Claire Raines outlined the 10 things that managers of Xers do that annoy them: providing insignificant raises; giving insincere thank you's; assigning jobs they're not qualified or trained to do; allowing the workplace to be disorganized; creating a stressful environment with corporate visitations; saying, "Because I said so"; allowing unacceptable behavior from staff; ignoring Xers' opinions and ideas; failing to provide feedback; and micromanaging.[52] Generations Xers thrive on job sharing, cross training, internal promotion, flexible scheduling, relaxed dress code, regular staff meetings, involvement, and feeling like they can make a difference in a productive work atmosphere.

She further stated that the Xers' work ethic is different than most of their generation's G and B managers. In their work ethic, they are self-reliant and skeptical, seek balance between work and life, and are reluctant to commit personally and professionally. They demonstrate blurred life-stage boundaries (i.e., adolescence to independent adulthood), technical literacy, and one in three belongs to an ethnic minority as compared to one in four throughout the general population.[53]

Generation Y

Generation Y, or Nexters, should be evaluated on their demonstrated performance and moved along quickly being self led. This cohort brings the "can-do attitude of Generation G, the teamwork ethic of Generation B, and the technological practical understanding of Generation X" into the workforce.[54] Their resilience is one of their best assets and they are willing to work hard and set goals to achieve their dreams both professionally and politically. The basic principles for managing Nexters involves spending more time orienting and supervising them in the work environment, expanding team size, being sensitive to generation differences in workers, continuing their education and work skills development, and establishing mentor programs that include electronic mail connections. Leaders have to be flexible to adapt their style or approach, as the situation requires.

Leading Teams

It is important to point out that it is not always necessary for supervisors and employees within an organization to have similar styles. People do not have to have the same personalities to be compatible. What is necessary is that they share perceptions of each other's roles and have common goals and objectives. It is often more appropriate for chief executive officers to recruit key executives who can compensate for areas in which they have shortcomings than to surround themselves with aides who are all alike. And yet, there are large companies today that have created problems for themselves by using a testing and selection process that eliminates personalities not congruent with the norm. The usual process is to measure the values and styles of the top management and then select new people who are compatible with those patterns. The assumption is that if those people got to the top, their values and styles must be what are needed to be successful in the organization. When these norms become part of the screening process, what the organization is saying is that there is a best style, at least for this organization.

One of the reasons that hiring "likes" became popular is that it led to a more harmonious organization. For example, if we have the same set of values and behave in similar ways, will we tend to get along? Yes, because we will tend to be compatible. There will probably not be much conflict or confrontation. On the surface, this kind of screening appears to be very positive. Yet, we have found that this approach can lead to organizational or management "inbreeding," which tends to stifle creativity and innovation. To be effective in the long run, organizations need an open dialogue in which there is a certain amount of conflict, confrontation, and differing points of view to encourage new ideas and patterns of behavior. Without them, the organization will lose its ability to adjust to external competition. Organizations that have lost their competitive edge because of their prior policy of promoting only from within have almost been forced to hire some key people from the outside to encourage open dialogue.

What is often needed in organizations is more emphasis on team building in which people are hired who complement rather than replicate a manager's style. For example, Henry Ford, who was considered a paternalistic (authoritarian) leader, placed in key positions in the organization men who supplemented rather than duplicated his style. Henry Bennett, for one, acted as a hatchet man, clearing deadwood from the organization (high task). Another executive acted as a confidant to Henry (high relationship). While these styles differed considerably, Ford's success during that time was based on compatibility of expectations; each understood the other's role and was committed to common goals and objectives. John Byrne, writing on current management trends, reinforced teamwork as being the one important development in organizations that "many believe . . . will help restore a sense of community with the organization, the feeling of belonging shattered by waves of restructuring and downsizing."[55] Diversity is an important ingredient in creating the modern team. But, as Debra D. Richards, a communications manager observed, "There is still a network in place that feels more comfortable in promoting white men. That barrier is hard to break."[56] The barrier is being broken, however slowly. Organizations are coming to the realization that diversity will help them win in the global marketplace.

Other examples could be cited. This kind of team building is common in sports such as football. Assistant coaches not only may have different task roles—that is, line coach, backfield coach, and so forth—but they also may have different behavioral roles with the players. The same is true with principals and vice principals, and so on.

Other Environmental Variables

One could probably enumerate many more variables. For example, even the physical stature of a leader can affect the kind of style that leader can use. Take the example of the foreman in the steel mill who is 6 feet 6 inches tall and weighs over 250 pounds. He may be able to use a different style than a foreman 5 feet 4 inches tall weighing 98 pounds, because their followers' expectations about their behavior will probably be influenced by their leader's physical appearance. Gender may have a similar effect. Some men may respond to and interact with a female supervisor, associate, or follower very differently than with a male, and vice versa. The effect of gender undoubtedly is influenced by the amount of experience one has had in working with members of the opposite sex. But it certainly may be a situational variable worth examining in a leadership environment.

The kinds of environmental variables we have been discussing tend to be important whether one is concerned about an educational, an informal, or a business organization. But specific organizations may have additional variables unique to themselves that must be evaluated before determining effectiveness.

External Environment

Years ago, managers didn't worry much about the external environment because it didn't seem to affect them or their decisions. Today, it does. Organizations do not exist in a vacuum but are continually affected in numerous ways by changes in the external environment. (See chapter 4, the SOAR Peak Performance model.)

Most writers categorize the external environment, both domestic and global, into three subcategories: *remote* environment, *industry* environment, and *operating* environment.[57] Most organizations have little or no influence on or control over the economic, social, political, technological, and ecological factors in the remote environment. For example, organizations have little or no influence on currency exchange rates. They are takers of whatever the rates may be.

Organizations, depending on their size, may have more influence on industry factors such as barriers to entry into the industry, power of suppliers, power of buyers, availability of substitutes or complements, and the intensity of competitive rivalry.[58]

The operating environment, also known as the *task*, or *competitive*, environment, comprises such factors as competitors, creditors, customers, labor force, and suppliers.[59] Let's look at two trends in the operating environment. One trend is increasing family responsibilities. Nearly half of the workforce must care for a dependent, and well over two-thirds have daily domestic responsibilities. This is a very important trend for management. These responsibilities create significant work stress and, therefore, a greater need for family policies such as flexible work scheduling and dependent-care help.[60]

Another trend, downsizing, has affected many organizations. One of the negative aspects of this trend has been the loss of talent and valuable skills and knowledge caused by voluntary retirement programs. Employees have accepted this option enthusiastically, including those that the organization would like to retain. In some universities, for example, key departments have been reduced. Retiring employees see the process as a way to gain more freedom and still receive benefits from their former employer.[61]

We want to reinforce the point that we made in chapter 1 that in the last several decades organizations have been increasingly challenged by forces and events beyond their direct control. Consider the implications for today's leadership of such trends as increased globalization, concern for the environment, changing demographics and social mores, and the increasing widespread concern for the quality of working life and its relationship to worker productivity, participation, and satisfaction.

These and other societal changes make effective leadership in the future a more challenging task, requiring even greater sensitivity and flexibility than was ever needed before. Today's manager is more likely to deal with employees who resent being treated as subordinates, who may be highly critical of any organizational system, who expect to be consulted and to exert influence, and who often stand on the edge of alienation from the institution that needs their loyalty and commitment. In addition, [today's manager] is frequently confronted by a highly turbulent, unpredictable environment.[62]

Therefore, as Edith Weiner predicts, "Organizations that hope to survive in the next decade and beyond must seek out new perspectives. Too many are currently based on outdated interpretations of the world, its inhabitants, its social structures, and the ways that markets behave."[63]

DEVELOPING STRATEGIES

Changing Style

One of the most difficult changes to make is a complete change in the style of a person, yet industry invests many millions of dollars annually for training and development programs that concentrate on changing the style of its leaders. As Fiedler suggested:

> A person's leadership style reflects the individual's basic motivational and need structure. At best it takes one, two, or three years of intensive psychotherapy to effect lasting changes in personality structure. It is difficult to see how we can change in more than a few cases an equally important set of core values in a few hours of lectures and role playing or even in the course of a more intensive training program of one or two weeks.[64]

Fiedler's point is well taken. It is indeed difficult to effect changes in the styles of managers overnight. Although not completely hopeless, it is a slow and expensive process that requires creative planning and patience. In fact, Rensis Likert found that it takes from 3 to 7 years, depending on the size and complexity of the organization, to implement a new management theory effectively. Haste is self-defeating because of the anxieties and stresses it creates. There is no substitute for ample time to enable the members of an organization to reach a level of skillful and easy, habitual use of the new leadership style.[65]

What generally happens in current training and development programs is that managers are encouraged to adopt certain normative behavior styles. In our culture, these styles are usually high relationship–low task or high task–high relationship styles. Although we agree that there is a growing tendency for these two styles to be more effective than the high task–low relationship or low relationship–low task styles, we recognize that this is not universally the case even in our own culture. In fact, it is often not the case even within a single work group. Most people might respond favorably to the high relationship styles, but a few might react in a negative manner, taking advantage of what they consider a soft touch. As a result, certain individuals will have to be handled in a different way. Perhaps they will respond only to close supervision (a high task–low relationship style). Thus, it is unrealistic to think that any of these styles can be successfully applied everywhere. In addition to considering application, it is questionable whether every leader can adapt to one normative style.

Most training and development programs do not recognize these two considerations. Consequently, a foreman who has been operating as a task-oriented, authoritarian leader for many years is encouraged to change style—get in step with the times. Upon returning from the training program, the foreman will probably try to utilize some of the new relationship-oriented techniques. As long as things are running smoothly, there is no difficulty in using them. The minute an important issue or a crisis develops, however, the foreman tends to revert to the old basic style and vacillates between the new relationship-oriented style and the old task-oriented style, which has the force of habit behind it. The problem is that the style the foreman has used for a long time is not compatible with the new concepts.

This idea was supported in a study that General Electric conducted at one of its turbine and generator plants.[66] In this study the leadership styles of about 90 foremen were analyzed and rated as "democratic," "authoritarian," or "mixed." In discussing the findings, Saul W. Gellerman reported that

> the lowest morale in the plant was found among those men whose foremen were rated between the democratic and authoritarian extremes. The GE research team felt that these foremen may have varied inconsistently in their tactics, permissive at one moment and hard-fisted the next, in a way that left their men frustrated and unable to anticipate how they could be treated. The naturally autocratic supervisor who is exposed to human relations training may behave in exactly such a manner . . . a pattern which will probably make him even harder to work for than he was before being "enlightened."[67]

In summary, changing the style of managers is a difficult process and one that takes considerable time. Expecting miracles overnight will only lead to frustration and uneasiness for both managers and their employees. Consequently, we recommend that change in overall management style in an organization be planned and implemented on a long-term basis so that expectations can be realistic for all involved.

Changes in Expectations versus Changes in Style

Using the feedback model discussed in chapter 2 (see Figure 7-3), we can begin to explain why it is so difficult to make changes in leader style in a short period of time. As discussed earlier, when a person behaves in a motivating

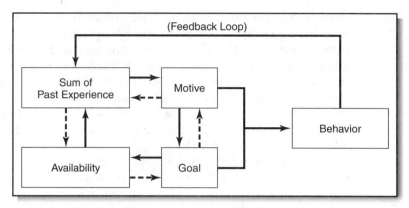

Figure 7-3
Feedback Model

situation, that behavior becomes a new input to the individual's inventory of past experience. The earlier in life that this input occurs, the greater its potential effect on future behavior. At that time, this behavior represents a larger portion of the individual's total past experience than the same behavior input will later in life. In addition, the longer a behavior is reinforced, the more patterned it becomes and the more difficult it is to change. That is why it is easier to make personality changes early in life. As a person gets older, more time and new experiences are necessary to effect a change in behavior.

As discussed in chapter 1, changes in behavior are much more difficult and time-consuming than are changes in knowledge and attitudes if force is not a factor. Because changes in expectations, in reality, are changes in knowledge and attitudes, these can be implemented more rapidly than can changes in style. In fact, changes in expectations may be accomplished merely by having leaders sit down and clarify what their behavior will be with the individuals involved. Once they understand their leader's style, followers can more easily adjust their expectations to it.

Changing Situational Variables

Recognizing some of the limitations of training and development programs that concentrate only on changing leadership styles, Fiedler suggested that "it would seem more promising at this time to teach the individual to recognize the conditions under which he can perform best and to modify the situation to suit his leadership style."[68] This philosophy, which he calls *organizational engineering*, is based on the following assumption: "It is almost always easier to change a man's work environment than it is to change his personality or his style of relating to others."[69] Although we basically agree with Fiedler's assumption, we feel that changes in both are needed, and both are difficult but possible. Fiedler is helpful, however, in suggesting ways in which a leadership situation can be modified to fit the leader's style. These suggestions are based on his leadership contingency model, which we discussed in chapter 5. As you will recall, that model lists three major situational variables that seem to determine whether a given situation is favorable or unfavorable to leaders: (1) *leader-member relations*—leader's personal relations with the members of their group; (2) *position power*—the power and authority that their position provides; and (3) *task structure*—the degree of structure (routine versus challenging) in the task that the group has been assigned to perform. The changes in each of these variables that Fiedler recommended can be expressed in task or relationship terms; each change tends to favor either a task-oriented or a relationship-oriented leader, as illustrated in Table 7-1.

With changes such as these, Fiedler suggested that the situational variables confronting leaders can be modified to fit their style. He recognized, however, as we have been arguing, that the success of organizational engineering depends on training individuals to be able to diagnose their own leadership style and the other situational variables. Only when they have accurately interpreted these variables can they determine whether any changes are necessary. If changes are needed, leaders do not necessarily have

Table 7-1 Changes in the Leadership Situation to Fit Leader's Task or Relationship Style

VARIABLE BEING CHANGED	CHANGE MADE	
	TASK LEADERS COULD BE GIVEN:	RELATIONSHIP LEADERS COULD BE GIVEN:
Leader-member relations	1. Followers who are quite different from them in a number of ways. 2. Followers who are notorious for their conflict.	1. Followers who are very similar to them in attitude, opinion, technical background, race, etc. 2. Followers who generally get along well with their superiors.
Position power of the leader	1. High rank and corresponding recognition, i.e., a vice presidency. 2. Followers who are two or three ranks below them. 3. Followers who depend on their leader for guidance and instruction. 4. Final authority in making all decisions for the group. 5. All information about organizational plans, thus making them expert in their group.	1. Little rank (office) or official recognition. 2. Followers who are equal in rank. 3. Followers who are experts in their field and are independent of their leader. 4. No authority in making decisions for the group. 5. No more information about organizational plans than their followers get, placing the followers on an equal footing with the leaders.
Task structure	1. A structured production task that has specific instructions on what they and their followers should do.	1. An unstructured policy-making task that has no prescribed operating procedures.

Source: Adapted from discussion in Fred E. Fiedler, *A Theory of Leadership Effectiveness* (New York: McGraw-Hill, 1967), pp. 255–256.

to initiate any in their own particular situation. They might prefer to transfer to a situation that better fits their style. In this new environment, no immediate changes may be necessary.

DIAGNOSING THE ENVIRONMENT— A CASE

Any of the situational elements we have discussed can be analyzed in terms of task and relationship. Let us take the case of Steve, a general foreman who has been offered a promotion to superintendent in another plant. In his current position, which he has held for 15 years, Steve has been extremely effective as a task-oriented manager responsible for the operation of several assembly-line processes.

Steve's first impulse is to accept this promotion in status and salary and move his family to the new location. But he feels it is important first to visit the plant and to talk with some of the people with whom he will be working. In talking with these people, Steve may gain insight into some of the important dimensions of this new position. An analysis of all these variables in terms of task and relationship could be summarized together, as illustrated in Figure 7-4. If Steve makes this type of analysis, he will have a well-informed basis for making his decision.

Figure 7-4
An Example of All the Environmental Variables Being Analyzed Together in Terms of Task and Relationship

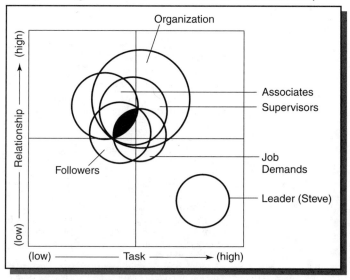

Source: Adapted from William J. Reddin, *The 3-D Management Style Theory, Theory Paper #6—Style Flex* (Fredericton, N.B., Canada: Social Science Systems, 1967), p. 6.

The circle designated for the leader represents Steve's primary leadership style (high task–low relationship), which has been reinforced over the past 15 years. The other circles represent the expectations of all the other environmental variables in terms of what is considered appropriate behavior for a superintendent. In this plant, most of the situational variables seem to demand a high task–high relationship or high relationship–low task superintendent. Unfortunately, Steve's style does not seem appropriate for any of the situational variables. Thus, if he accepts the job and makes no changes, there is a high probability that Steve will be ineffective. At this point, he has to make a decision. Several alternatives are available to him.

1. He can try to change his style of behavior, so that he can work effectively with the various situational variables in the new environment.
2. He can try to change some or all of the situational elements. For example, he can try to change the behavior and the expectations of his followers through training and development programs or coaching and counseling.
3. He can try to make some changes in both his own range of behavior and some or all of the situational elements, thus attempting in the long run to have the two move toward each other rather than concentrating only on changing one or the other.
4. He can reject the job and seek another superintendent's position in an environment in which his range of behavior is more compatible with the demands of the other situational elements.
5. He can remain in his current position, where he knows he has been effective and will probably continue to be.

William Reddin, in doing a similar analysis, would attempt to find an area in which the expectations of the organization, supervisors, associates, followers, and job demands intersected (the shaded area of Figure 7-4).[70] He would suggest that a leader might be able to be effective within that area. That averaging process, perhaps, could be used for a case such as Steve's in which the expectations of all the other situational variables are grouped closely together, but it would not be useful in other situations. And Steve still would not fit in.

Figure 7-4 is a powerful diagnostic tool because it can be used to analyze the "fit" of all of the environmental variables. For example, when the expectations of various key variables do not intersect, it is not possible for leaders to use a generalized style; leaders will have to use different styles with each of the important situational variables in their environment. Thus, Dorothy, a sales manager, may have to treat her supervisor differently from the way she treats any of her followers or associates. Even among the salespeople who report to her, she will probably have to treat some differently from others.

Although these examples have been written from the point of view of an individual, this type of analysis is just as important from an organization's point of view. It is vital that the people placed in key positions throughout the organization have the prerequisites for carrying out the organizational goals effectively. Management must realize that it does not follow that a person will be effective in one position merely because the person has been effective in another. Lawrence J. Peter writes about such assumptions. The Peter Principle is stated as follows: "In a hierarchy, every employee tends to rise to his level of incompetence."[71]

Peter Principle Vaccine

The "principle" expressed by Peter is not necessarily true. There are several ways an organization can develop an immunity to the problem. One method is to train and develop employees before promoting them. Training may often include, before promotion, delegating some responsibility, so that the person has an opportunity for some real experience that approximates the new position. High-performing companies see training as essential to competitiveness. For example, Motorola, convinced of training's importance, established its own university.[72] Another part of the solution is careful selection of those whose personality and expectations are appropriate for the new job, instead of having upward mobility depend only on good performance at the preceding level.

Training should be constant throughout employees' careers. Many managers mistakenly believe that qualifications alone will prepare new employees for their initial positions and might eventually allow them to advance in the organization. Patricia M. Buhler stressed that new employees, no matter how qualified, must be trained in the ways in which the organization operates. Employees from the time of their initial employment must see training and retraining as the only sure way they will advance and remain productive within the organization. Managers should never allow employees to fall behind their required skill levels. Training and retraining "keeps people the most valuable resource in the organization. . . . It is the responsibility of managers to share where the organization is going. Everyone tends to work a little harder when they know just what it is that they are working toward."[73] Training clearly immunizes an organization against the Peter Principle.

HOW CAN MANAGERS LEARN TO DEAL WITH ALL THESE ENVIRONMENTAL VARIABLES?

It would be impossible for managers to look at all the interacting variables discussed in this chapter every time they had to make a leadership decision. We think, however, there is one key variable—the relationship between the leader and the follower. We have found that if the follower decides not to follow, it really doesn't matter what the boss thinks, what the nature of the work is, how much time is involved, or what the other situational variables are.

ENDNOTES

1. These environmental variables were adapted from a list of situational elements discussed by William J. Reddin, *The 3-D Management Style Theory, Theory Paper #5—Diagnostic Skill* (Fredericton, N.B., Canada: Social Science Systems, 1967), p. 2.

2. Robert Tannenbaum and Warren H. Schmidt indicated that the appropriate leadership style to use in a given situation is a function of factors in the leader, the follower, and the situation. What constitutes the situation can vary in different environmental settings. See Tannenbaum and Schmidt, "How to Choose a Leadership Pattern," *Harvard Business Review,* March–April, 1957.

3. The introductory section here was adapted from a model that discusses the interaction of personality and expectations. See Jacob W. Getzels and Egon G. Guba, "Social Behavior and the Administrative Process," *The School Review,* 65, no. 4 (Winter 1957), pp. 423–441. See also Getzels, "Administration as a Social Process," in *Administrative Theory in Education,* ed. Andrew W. Halpin (Chicago: Midwest Administration Center, University of Chicago, 1958).

4. Tannenbaum and Schmidt, "How to Choose a Leadership Pattern."

5. Fillmore H. Sanford, *Authoritarianism and Leadership* (Philadelphia: Institute for Research in Human Relations, 1950).

6. Victor H. Vroom, *Some Personality Determinants of the Effects of Participation* (Upper Saddle River, NJ: Prentice Hall, 1960).

7. Saul W. Gellerman, *Motivation and Productivity* (New York: American Management Association, 1963).

8. Tannenbaum and Schmidt, "How to Choose a Leadership Pattern."

9. Adapted from Hyler Bracey, "Managing 'From the HEART' Produces Bottom-Line Results," *Journal of Career Planning and Employment,* Spring 1993.

10. Reddin, *The 3-D Management Style Theory, Theory Paper #5—Diagnostic Skill,* p. 4.

11. William E. Henry, "The Business Executive: The Psychodynamics of a Social Role," *The American Journal of Sociology,* 54, no. 4 (January 1949), pp. 286–291.

12. Robert H. Guest, *Organizational Change: The Effect of Successful Leadership* (Homewood, IL: Irwin, Dorsey Press, 1964). See also Robert Guest, Paul Hersey, and Kenneth Blanchard, *Organizational Change through Effective Leadership,* 2nd ed. (Upper Saddle River, NJ: Prentice Hall, 1986).

13. Guest, *Organizational Change.*

14. Reddin, *The 3-D Management Style Theory, Theory Paper #5—Diagnostic Skill,* p. 4.

15. Waino W. Suojanen, *The Dynamics of Management* (New York: Holt, Rinehart & Winston, 1966).

16. Tannenbaum and Schmidt, "How to Choose a Leadership Pattern."

17. Joseph Batten, "A Total Quality Culture," *Management Review,* May 1994, p. 61.

18. Fred E. Fiedler, *A Theory of Leadership Effectiveness* (New York: McGraw-Hill, 1967).

19. *Ibid.*

20. Edwin P. Hollander, *Leadership Dynamics: A Practical Guide to Effective Relationships* (New York: Free Press, 1978).

21. Rebecca Kuzins, "Young Boss, Older Worker, New Problem," *San Francisco Examiner,* March 7, 1999, p. W-16

22. *Ibid.*

23. Ron Zemke, Claire Raines, and Bob Filipczak, *Generations at Work: Managing the Clash of Veterans, Boomers, Xers, and Nexters in Your Workplace* (New York: American Management Association Publications Association, 2000), pp. 30–31.

24. *Ibid.,* pp. 49–50.

25. Dorina Kim Lazo, "Talking 'Bout My Generation," *The Fresno Bee,* February 6, 2000, Life, pp. E5–E6.

26. K. Clark, "The New Midlife," *U.S. News and World Report,* March 30, 2000, pp. 70–83.

27. Zemke, Raines, and Filipczak, *Generations at Work: Managing the Clash of Veterans, Boomers, Xers, and Nexters in Your Workplace,* p. 63.

28. *Ibid.,* pp. 71–74.

29. *Ibid.,* pp. 76–78.

30. Clark, "The New Midlife," *U.S. News and World Report,* p. 82.

31. Lazo, "Talking 'Bout My Generation," *The Fresno Bee.*

32. Zemke, Raines, and Filipczak, *Generations at Work: Managing the Clash of Veterans, Boomers, Xers, and Nexters in Your Workplace,* p. 93.

33. Claire Raines, *Beyond Generation X: A Practical Guide for Managers, 188 Tips, Tools, and Techniques that Narrow the Gap at Work* (Menlo Park, CA: Crisp Publications, 1997), p. 8.

34. Zemke, Raines, and Filipczak, *Generations at Work: Managing the Clash of Veterans, Boomers, Xers, and Nexters in Your Workplace,* pp. 103–105.

35. *Ibid.,* p. 111.

36. *Ibid.,* p. 112.

37. *Ibid.,* pp. 98–102.

38. Kuzin, "Young Boss, Older Worker, New Problem."

39. Lazo, "Talking 'Bout My Generation," *The Fresno Bee.*

40. *Ibid.*

41. Zemke, Raines, and Filipczak, *Generations at Work: Managing the Clash of Veterans, Boomers, Xers, and Nexters in Your Workplace,* p. 127.

42. Lazo, "Talking 'Bout My Generation," *The Fresno Bee.*

43. Zemke, Raines, and Filipczak, *Generations at Work: Managing the Clash of Veterans, Boomers, Xers, and Nexters in Your Workplace,* p. 136.

44. Louis Harris and Northwestern Mutual. "Generation 2001." Study conducted by Milwaukee-based Northwestern Mutual and New York City-based Louis Harris, 1998.

45. Kuzins, "Young Boss, Older Worker, New Problem." *San Francisco Examiner.*

46. Zemke, Raines, and Filipczak, *Generations at Work: Managing the Clash of Veterans, Boomers, Xers, and Nexters in Your Workplace,* p. 52.

47. Don Asher, "Younger Bosses Can Pose Problems for Older Workers," *San Francisco Examiner,* March 21, 1999, pp. W-5, 13.

48. Zemke, Raines, and Filipczak, *Generations at Work: Managing the Clash of Veterans, Boomers, Xers, and Nexters in Your Workplace,* pp. 55–58.

49. *Ibid.,* pp. 81–83.

50. *Ibid.,* p. 115.

51. *Ibid.,* pp. 118–123.

52. Raines, *Beyond Generation X: A Practical Guide for Managers, 188 Tips, Tools, and Techniques that Narrow the Gap at Work,* p. 2.

53. *Ibid.,* pp. 38–42.

54. Zemke, Raines, and Filipczak, *Generations at Work: Managing the Clash of Veterans, Boomers, Xers, and Nexters in Your Workplace,* p. 143.

55. John A. Byrne, "Paradigms for Post-Modern Managers," *Business Week,* November 5, 1992, pp. 62–63.

56. Quoted in Wendy Zeller, "Pioneer: The Race Battle Never Ends," *Business Week,* October 17, 1994, pp. 98, 100.

57. John A. Pearce II and Richard B. Robinson Jr., *Formulation, Implementation, and Control of Competitive Strategy,* 5th ed. (Burr Ridge, IL: Irwin, 1994), p. 62.

58. *Ibid.,* pp. 75–85. These factors were first identified by Michael E. Porter, "How Competitive Forces Shape Strategy," *Harvard Business Review,* March–April 1979, pp. 137–145.

59. Pearce and Robinson, *Formulation, Implementation, and Control of Competitive Strategy,* p. 62.

60. Susan Shellenbarger, "Work-Force Study Finds Loyalty Is Weak, Divisions of Race and Gender Are Deep," *Wall Street Journal,* September 3, 1993, pp. B1, 9.

61. Gene Carats, "Downsized Companies Feel the Downside of Early Retirement," *Business Week,* February 1, 1993.

62. Robert Tannenbaum and Warren H. Schmidt, "How to Choose a Leadership Pattern," *Harvard Business Review,* May–June 1973.

63. Edith Weiner, "Business in the 21st Century," *The Futurist,* March–April 1992.

64. Fiedler, *A Theory of Leadership Effectiveness,* p. 248.

65. Rensis Likert, *New Patterns of Management* (New York: McGraw-Hill, 1961), p. 248.

66. *Leadership Style and Employee Morale* (New York: General Electric Company, Public and Employee Relations Services, 1959).

67. Gellerman, *Motivation and Productivity,* p. 43.

68. Fiedler, *A Theory of Leadership Effectiveness,* p. 255.

69. *Ibid.*

70. William J. Reddin, *The 3-D Management Style Theory, Theory Paper #6—Style Flex* (Fredericton, N.B., Canada: Social Science Systems, 1967).

71. Lawrence J. Peter and Raymond Hull, *The Peter Principle: Why Things Always Go Wrong* (New York: Morrow, 1969).

72. John Rau, "Nothing Succeeds like Training for Success," *Wall Street Journal,* September 12, 1994, p. A14.

73. Patricia M. Buhler, "Are You Getting the Most Out of Your Employees?" *Supervision,* October 1990, pp. 14–16.

Chapter 8

Situational Leadership

The importance of a leader's *diagnostic ability* cannot be over-emphasized. Edgar H. Schein expressed it well: "The successful manager must be a good diagnostician and must value a spirit of inquiry. The abilities and motives of the people under the manager vary; therefore, managers must have the sensitivity and diagnostic ability to be able to sense and appreciate the differences."[1] In other words, managers must be able to identify clues in an environment. Yet even with good diagnostic skills, leaders may still not be effective unless they can adapt their leadership style to meet the demands of their environment. This is the second of the three important leadership competencies discussed in chapter 1. "[Leaders] must have the personal flexibility and range of skills necessary to vary [their] own behavior. If the needs and motives of [their followers] are different, they must be treated differently."[2] ✧

It is easy to tell managers that they *should* use behavioral science theory and research to develop the necessary diagnostic skills to maximize effectiveness. It is not easy to tell them *how* to use it. First, much of the research currently published in the field of applied behavioral sciences is not even understandable to many practicing managers; it often appears to be more an attempt to impress other researchers than to help managers to be more effective. Second, even if practitioners could understand the research, many would argue that it is impractical to consider every situational variable in every decision.

As a result, one of the major focuses of our work has been the development of a practical model that can be used by managers, salespeople, teachers, or parents to make the moment-by-moment decisions necessary to effectively influence other people. The result is Situational Leadership®. This approach uses as its basic data the perceptions and observations made by managers—parents in the home or supervisors on the job—on a day-to-day basis in their own environments.

Situational Leadership was developed by Paul Hersey and Kenneth H. Blanchard at the Center for Leadership Studies in the late 1960s.[3] Until 1982, Hersey and Blanchard worked together to continually refine Situational Leadership. After that time, Blanchard and his colleagues at Blanchard Training and Development (BTD) began to modify the original Situational Leadership model and developed diagnostic instruments and training materials to support their approach (called SLII®) in training seminars and presentations. The best description of this approach to Situational Leadership can be found in *Leadership and the One Minute Manager*.[4] The Situational Leadership model used in this book reflects the current thinking of Paul Hersey and the Center for Leadership Studies and does not include the changes to the model that Blanchard and his colleagues made in SLII.

SITUATIONAL LEADERSHIP

The Center for Leadership Studies

Situational Leadership is based on an interplay among (1) the amount of guidance and direction (task behavior) a leader gives; (2) the amount of socioemotional support (relationship behavior) a leader provides; and (3) the readiness level that followers exhibit in performing a specific task, function, or objective. This concept was developed to help people attempting leadership, regardless of their role, to be more effective in their daily interactions with others. It provides leaders with some understanding of the relationship between an effective style of leadership and the level of readiness of their followers.

Thus, although all the situational variables (leader, followers, senior management, associates, organization, job demands, and time) are important, the emphasis in Situational Leadership is on the behavior of a leader in relation to followers. As Fillmore H. Sanford indicated, there is some justification for regarding the followers "as the most crucial factor in any leadership event."[5] Followers in any situation are vital, not only because individually they accept or reject the leader, but because as a group they actually determine whatever personal power the leader may have.

It may be appropriate at this point to note the difference between a model and a theory. A theory attempts to explain why things happen as they do. As such, it is not designed to recreate events. A model, on the other hand, is a pattern of already existing events that can be learned and therefore repeated. For example, in trying to imagine why Henry Ford was motivated to mass produce automobiles, you would be dealing with a theory. However, if you recorded the procedures and sequences necessary for mass production, you would have a model of the process. Situational Leadership is a model, *not a* theory. Its concepts, procedures, actions, and outcomes are based on tested methodologies that are practical and easy to apply.

Chapter 4 emphasized that when discussing leader-follower relationships, we are not necessarily talking about a hierarchical relationship; that is, manager-employee. The same caution will hold during our discussion of Situational Leadership. *Thus, any reference to leader(s) or follower(s) in this model should imply potential leader and potential follower.* Although our examples may suggest a hierarchical relationship, the concepts presented in Situational Leadership should be applicable whether you are attempting to influence the behavior of an employee, your supervisor, an associate, a friend, a relative, or a group.

Basic Concept of Situational Leadership

According to Situational Leadership, there is no one best way to influence people. Which leadership style a person should use with individuals or groups depends on the readiness level of the people the leader is attempting to influence. Before we look at the application of the Situational Leadership model, it is important that we understand leadership styles as they are used in the model and the idea of follower readiness.

Our earlier discussion of different leadership theories in chapters 4 and 5 introduced us to our definition of *leadership style*—behavior by the leader as perceived by the followers. We also saw the ways that classifying leader behaviors developed, including the identification of task and relationship behavior.[6]

> *Task behavior* is defined as the extent to which the leader engages in spelling out the duties and responsibilities of an individual or group. These behaviors include telling people what to do, how to do it, when to do it, where to do it, and who is to do it.

High amounts of task behavior might be required, for instance, when you ask someone for directions. The person probably very precisely and clearly tells you what streets to take and what turns to make. You are told where to start and where to finish. It is important to notice that being directive does not mean being nasty or short-tempered. The person helping you might be very pleasant toward you, but the actions and statements are aimed at completing the task—that of helping you find your way. Task behavior is characterized by one-way communication from the leader to the follower. The person is not so much concerned with your feelings, but with how to help you achieve your goal.

> *Relationship behavior* is defined as the extent to which the leader engages in two-way or multiway communication. The behaviors include listening, facilitating, and supportive behaviors.[7]

High amounts of relationship behavior might be required when you reach an impasse with an assignment. You basically know how to do the assignment but need some encouragement to get you over the hump. The listening, encouraging, and facilitating a leader does in this example is an illustration of relationship behavior.

Task behavior and relationship behavior are separate and distinct dimensions. They can be placed on separate axes of a two-dimensional graph, and the four quadrants can be used to identify four basic leadership styles.[8] Figure 8-1 illustrates these styles. Plotting task behavior from low to high on the horizontal axis and relationship behavior from low to high on the vertical axis makes it possible to describe leader behavior in four ways, or styles.

As we discussed in chapter 5, the four quadrants shown in Figure 8-1 can be used as the basis for assessing effective leader behavior. No one style is effective in all situations. Each style is appropriate and effective depending on the situation.

The following descriptions apply to the four styles:

- *Style 1 (S1).* This leadership style is characterized by above-average amounts of task behavior and below-average amounts of relationship behavior.
- *Style 2 (S2).* This leadership style is characterized by above-average amounts of both task and relationship behavior.
- *Style 3 (S3).* This style is characterized by above-average amounts of relationship behavior and below-average amounts of task behavior.
- *Style 4 (S4).* This style is characterized by below-average amounts of both relationship behavior and task behavior.

The important information presented by this model is in the operational definitions of task behavior and relationship behavior presented earlier. In leadership situations involving the family, schools, or other settings, different words may be more appropriate than *task* and *relationship*—for example, *guidance* and *supportive* behavior or *directive* behavior and *facilitating* behavior—but the underlying definitions remain the same.

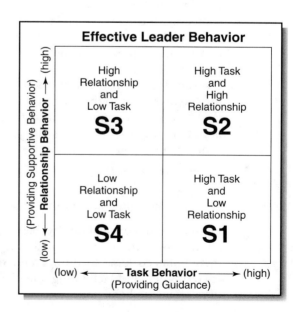

Figure 8-1
Leadership Styles

Source: Adapted from Paul Hersey, *Situational Selling* (Escondido, CA: Center for Leadership Studies, 1985), p. 20. Reprinted with permission.

Readiness of the Followers or Group

In chapter 7 we looked at the situation—the complex pattern of conditions that exist within a given environment. We also noted that there is no one best style of leadership; it depends upon the situation within which the attempt to influence takes place. The more leaders can adapt their behaviors to the situation, the more effective their attempts to influence will be. The situation, in turn, is influenced by the various conditions present.

Some of the primary factors in the situation that influence leader effectiveness include the following:

- Leader
- Followers
- Supervisor
- Key associates
- Organization
- Job demands
- Decision time

These variables do not operate in isolation. They are interactive. For example, style 1 is often referred to as "crisis leadership" because it is appropriate in times of crisis. The important thing to remember is that we should use it to *respond* to crises, not to create them. If we treat an organization as if it is in crisis, that's what we get—crisis. If we treat people like children, they will often begin to behave like children. This is one of the most important concepts in the field of applied behavioral sciences—the concept of the *self-fulfilling prophecy*. In working with others and helping them develop, leaders should have positive assumptions about followers' potential. Effective leaders believe that people have the potential to grow and that, given an opportunity, they can and will respond.[9]

We need to remind ourselves that the relationship between leaders and followers is the crucial variable in the leadership situation. If the followers decide not to follow, it doesn't matter what the supervisor or key associates think or what the job demands may be. *There is no leadership without someone following.*

In order to maximize the leader-follower relationship, the leader must first determine the task-specific outcomes the followers are to accomplish—on an individual and group basis. Without creating clarity on outcomes, objectives, subtasks, milestones, and so on, the leader has no basis for determining follower readiness or the specific behavioral style to use for that level of readiness.

Readiness Defined

Readiness in Situational Leadership is defined as the extent to which a follower demonstrates the ability and willingness to accomplish a specific task.

People tend to be at different levels of readiness depending on the task they are being asked to do. Readiness is not a personal characteristic; it is not an evaluation of a person's traits, values, age, and so on. Readiness is how ready a person is to perform a particular task. This concept of readiness has to do with specific situations—not with any total sense of readiness. All persons tend to be more or less ready in relation to a specific task, function, or objective that a leader is attempting to accomplish. Thus, a salesperson may be very responsible in securing new sales, but very casual about completing the paperwork necessary to close on a sale. As a result, it is appropriate for the manager to leave the salesperson alone in terms of closing on sales, but to supervise closely in terms of paperwork until the salesperson can start to do well in that area, too.

In addition to assessing the level of readiness of individuals within a group, a leader may have to assess the readiness level of the group as a group, particularly if the group interacts frequently in the same work area, as happens with students in the classroom. Thus, a teacher may find that a class as a group may be at one level of readiness in a particular area, but a student within that group may be at a different level. When the teacher is one-to-one with that student, the teacher may have to behave very differently than when working with the class as a group. In reality, the teacher may find a number of students at various readiness levels. For example, the teacher may have one student who is not doing the assigned work regularly, and when the work is turned in, it is poorly organized and not very well done. The teacher may have to initiate some structure and supervise that student closely. Another student, however, may be doing good work but may be insecure and shy. With that student, the teacher may not have to engage in much task behavior in terms of schoolwork, but may need to be supportive, to engage in two-way communication, and to help facilitate the student's interaction with others in the class. Still another student may be competent and confident in the schoolwork and thus can be given minimum assistance. So leaders have to understand that they may have to behave differently one on one with members of their group from the way they do with the group as a whole.

The two major components of readiness are *ability* and *willingness*.[10]

> *Ability* is the knowledge, experience, and skill that an individual or group brings to a particular task or activity.

The components of ability are demonstrated knowledge, skill, and experience. They are defined as follows:

- *Knowledge* is demonstrated understanding of a task.
- *Skill* is demonstrated proficiency in a task.
- *Experience* is demonstrated ability gained from performing a task.

When considering the ability level of others, one must be *task-specific*. A person who has a Ph.D. in music and 20 years of professional experience playing the piano may be of little help in the design of a new jet engine. It is essential to focus on the specific outcome desired and to consider the ability of the followers in light of that outcome.

> *Willingness* is the extent to which an individual or group has the confidence, commitment, and motivation to accomplish a specific task.

The components of willingness are demonstrated confidence, commitment, and motivation. They are defined as follows:

- *Confidence* is demonstrated assurance in the ability to perform a task.
- *Commitment* is demonstrated duty to perform a task.
- *Motivation* is demonstrated desire to perform a task.

Willingness is only one word that describes the issue. Sometimes, it isn't so much that people are really unwilling, it's just that they've never done a specific task before. Perhaps they don't have any experience with it, so they're insecure or afraid. In general, if it is an issue of never having done something, the problem is insecurity. The term *unwilling* might be most appropriate when, for some reason, the individuals have slipped, or lost some of their commitment and motivation. It might imply that they are regressing.

Even though the concepts of ability and willingness are different, it is important to remember that they are an *interacting influence system*. This means that a significant change in one will affect the whole. The extent to which followers bring willingness into a specific situation affects the use of their current ability. And it affects the extent to which they will grow and develop competence and ability. Similarly, the amount of knowledge, experience, and skill brought to a specific task will often affect confidence, commitment, and motivation. Readiness levels are the different combinations of ability and willingness that people bring to each task (see Figure 8-2).

The continuum of follower readiness can be divided into four levels.[11] Each represents a different combination of follower ability and willingness or confidence:

- *Readiness level 1 (R1)*. Unable and unwilling. The follower is unable and lacks commitment and motivation.

  or

  Unable and insecure. The follower is unable and lacks confidence.

- *Readiness level 2 (R2)*. Unable but willing. The follower lacks ability but is motivated and making an effort.

  or

  Unable but confident. The follower lacks ability but is confident as long as the leader is there to provide guidance.

Figure 8-2
Continuum of Follower Readiness

High	Moderate		Low
R4	R3	R2	R1
Able and Willing or Confident	Able but Unwilling or Insecure	Unable but Willing or Confident	Unable and Unwilling or Insecure

Source: Adapted from Paul Hersey, *Situational Selling* (Escondido, CA: Center for Leadership Studies, 1985), p. 27. Reprinted with permission.

- *Readiness level 3 (R3).* Able but unwilling. The follower has the ability to perform the task but is not willing to use that ability.

or

Able but insecure. The follower has the ability to perform the task but is insecure or apprehensive about doing it alone.

- *Readiness level 4 (R4).* Able and willing. The follower has the ability to perform and is committed.

or

Able and confident. The follower has the ability to perform and is confident about doing it.

Ron Campbell of the Center for Leadership Studies has expanded the continuum of follower readiness (see Figure 8-2) to include behavioral indicators of the four readiness levels. Each level represents a different combination of follower ability and willingness or confidence. As shown in Figure 8-3, indicators of a person at R1 *for that specific task* would be such behaviors as not performing the task to an acceptable level or being intimidated by the task.

Because it is important to assess whether a person is unable and unwilling or unable and insecure, Campbell further refined these readiness indicators to help differentiate between the two R1 readiness states. Specifically, an *unable and unwilling R1* would exhibit:

- Defensive, argumentative, complaining behaviors
- Late completion of tasks
- Performance only to exact request
- Intense frustration

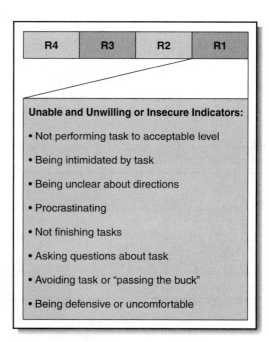

Figure 8-3
Readiness Level 1 (R1)

An *unable and insecure R1* would exhibit:

- Body language expressing discomfort: furrowed brow, shoulders lowered, leaning back
- Confused, unclear behavior
- Concern over possible outcomes
- Fear of failure

The following paragraphs will present indicators for the three remaining readiness levels. R2's indicators are illustrated in Figure 8-4. Specifically, an *unable but willing or confident R2* would:

- Speak quickly and intensely
- Seek clarity
- Nod head; make "yes, I know" type comments, seem eager
- Listen carefully
- Answer questions superficially
- Accept tasks
- Act quickly
- Be preoccupied with end results rather than incremental steps

R3's indicators are illustrated in Figure 8-5. Specifically, an *able but unwilling R3* would:

- Be hesitant or resistant
- Feel overobligated and overworked
- Seek reinforcement
- Be concerned performance is somehow punishing

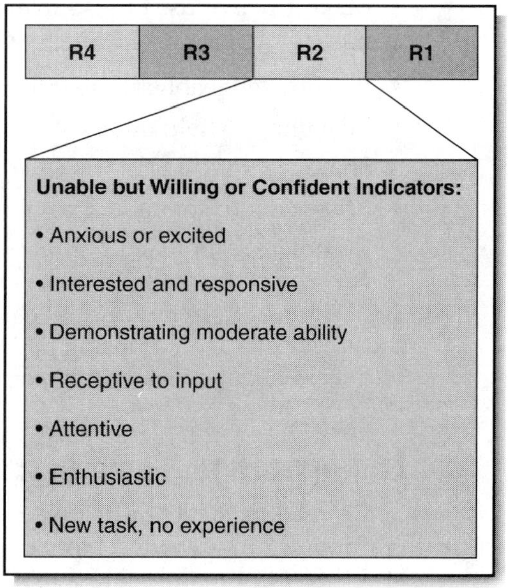

Figure 8-4
Readiness Level 2 (R2)

Source: Copyright © 1995, Center for Leadership Studies. All rights reserved.

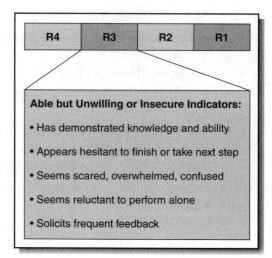

Figure 8-5
Readiness Level 3 (R3)

Source: Copyright © 1995, Center for Leadership Studies. All rights reserved.

An *able but insecure R3* would:

- Question own ability
- Focus on potential problems
- Lack self-esteem
- Encourage leader to stay involved

R4's indicators are illustrated in Figure 8-6. Specifically, an *able and willing or confident R4* would:

- Keep boss informed of task progress
- Make efficient use of resources
- Be responsible and results-oriented
- Be knowledgeable; share information to streamline operational tasks
- Be willing to help others
- Share creative ideas
- "Take charge" of tasks
- Complete responsibilities on time and perhaps early

These indicators are important clues to follower readiness. Just as a physician must use clues in diagnosing patient illness, leaders must be alert for clues in follower behavior as a critical step to correctly diagnosing readiness.

Going from R1 to R2 to R3

Some readers have difficulty understanding the development of followers from R1 to R2 to R3. How can one go from being insecure to confident and then become insecure again? The important thing to remember is that

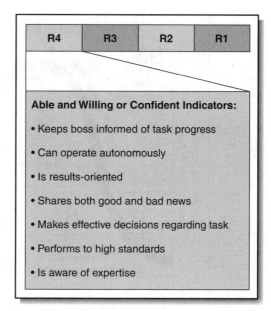

R4	R3	R2	R1

Able and Willing or Confident Indicators:

• Keeps boss informed of task progress

• Can operate autonomously

• Is results-oriented

• Shares both good and bad news

• Makes effective decisions regarding task

• Performs to high standards

• Is aware of expertise

Figure 8-6
Readiness Level 4 (R4)

Source: Copyright © 1995, Center for Leadership Studies. All rights reserved.

at the lower levels of readiness, the leader is providing the direction—the what, where, when, and how. Therefore, the decisions are *leader-directed.* At the higher levels of readiness, followers become responsible for task direction, and the decisions are *follower-directed* (self-directed). This transition from leader-directed to self-directed may result in apprehension or insecurity.

As followers move from low levels of readiness to higher levels, the combinations of task and relationship behavior appropriate to the situation begin to change. The curved line through the four leadership styles shown in Figure 8-7 represents the high probability combinations of task behavior and relationship behavior that correspond to the readiness levels directly below. To use the model, identify a point on the readiness continuum that represents follower readiness to perform a specific task. Then construct a perpendicular line from that point to a point where it intersects with the curved line representing leader behavior. This point indicates the most appropriate amount of task behavior and relationship behavior for that specific situation.

Note that the curved line never goes to either the lower-left or the lower-right corner. In both quadrants 1 and 4, there are combinations of both task and relationship behavior. Style 1 always has some relationship behavior, and style 4 always has some task behavior.

In selecting the combination of task behavior and relationship behavior with a high probability of success, you don't have to be exact. As you move away from the optimal combination, the probability of success gradually falls off, slowly at first and then more rapidly the farther away you move. Because of this, you don't need a direct hit—a close approximation keeps the probability of success high.

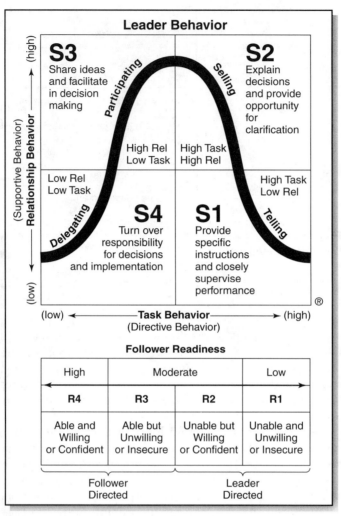

Figure 8-7
Situational Leadership Model

Source: Adapted from Paul Hersey, *Situational Selling* (Escondido, CA: Center for Leadership Studies, 1985), p. 19. Reprinted with permission.

Selecting Appropriate Styles
Matching Readiness Level 1 with Leadership Style 1—Telling

For a follower or group that is at readiness level 1 for a specific task, it is appropriate to provide high amounts of guidance but little supportive behavior. A word that describes this specific leadership style is *telling*—telling the followers what to do, where to do it, and how to do it. This style is appropriate when an individual or group is low in ability and willingness and needs direction. Other one-word descriptors for this leadership style include *guiding*, *directing*, or *struc-*

turing. Figure 8-8 summarizes the telling style and presents one-word descriptors of effective and ineffective approaches at readiness level 1.[12]

The appropriate leader behaviors for an *unable and unwilling R1* would be to:

- Directly state specific facts
- Positively reinforce small improvements
- Consider consequences for nonperformance
- Keep emotional level in check

For an *unable and insecure R1:*

- Provide task information in digestible amounts
- Be sure not to overwhelm follower
- Reduce fear of mistakes
- Help step by step
- Focus on instruction

Matching Readiness Level 2 with Leadership Style 2—Selling

The next range of readiness is readiness level 2. This is an individual or group that is still unable, but they're trying. They're willing or confident. The high probability styles are combinations of high amounts of both task and relationship

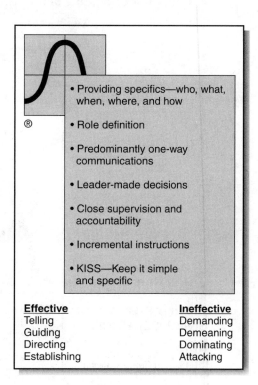

Figure 8-8
Style 1 (S1): HT/LR

- Providing specifics—who, what, when, where, and how
- Role definition
- Predominantly one-way communications
- Leader-made decisions
- Close supervision and accountability
- Incremental instructions
- KISS—Keep it simple and specific

Effective	Ineffective
Telling	Demanding
Guiding	Demeaning
Directing	Dominating
Establishing	Attacking

behavior. The task behavior is appropriate because people are still unable. But because they're trying, it is important to be supportive of their motivation and commitment.

This style is *selling*. It is different from telling in that the leader is not only providing the guidance but is also providing the opportunity for dialogue and for clarification in order to help the person "buy in" psychologically to what the leader wants. If a leader simply says, "Go stand by the door and keep people from coming through," that is *telling*. On the other hand, if the leader suggests, "I'd sure appreciate it if you would be willing to stand by the door to guide people around the classroom because people coming through here have been disruptive," this would be an example of *selling*. The follower can ask questions and get clarification, even though the leader has provided the guidance.

The definition of task behavior includes providing the "what, how, when, where, and who." The reason that "why" isn't included is that efforts to explain why bridge both task and relationship behaviors. One of the differences between telling and selling is that selling answers "why" questions. Other words for style 2 include *explaining, persuading,* and *clarifying.* Figure 8-9 summarizes the selling style and presents one-word descriptors of effective and ineffective approaches at readiness level 2.

The appropriate leader behaviors for an *unable but willing* or *unable but confident R2* would be to:

- Seek "buy-in" through persuading
- Check understanding of the task

Figure 8-9
Style 2 (S2): HT/HR

Source: Copyright © 1995, Center for Leadership Studies. All rights reserved.

- Providing who, what, when, where, how, and why
- Explain decisions and allow opportunity for clarification
- Two-way dialogue
- Leader-made decisions
- Explain follower's role
- Ask questions to clarify ability level
- Reinforce small improvements

Effective	**Ineffective**
Selling	Manipulating
Explaining	Preaching
Clarifying	Defending
Persuading	Rationalizing

- Encourage questions
- Discuss details
- Explore related skills
- Explain "why"
- Give follower incremental steps (not "run with it")
- Emphasize "how to"

Matching Readiness Level 3 with Leadership Style 3—Participating

Readiness level 3 would include a person or group that's able but has just developed ability and hasn't had an opportunity to gain confidence in doing it on their own. An example is the fledgling salesperson who goes out on a sales call for the first time without the sales manager.

Readiness level 3 could also be a person or group that was able and willing but for one reason or another is slipping in terms of motivation. Perhaps they're upset, mad at the supervisor, or just tired of performing this behavior and, therefore, are becoming unwilling.

In either case, the appropriate behavior would be high amounts of two-way communication and supportive behavior but low amounts of guidance. Because the group has already shown that they are able to perform the task, it isn't necessary to provide high amounts of what to do, where to do it, or how to do it. Discussion, supportive, and facilitating behaviors would tend to be more appropriate for solving the problem or soothing the apprehension.

In *participating*, the leader's major role becomes encouraging and communicating. Other descriptors for this style of leadership include *collaborating, facilitating*, and *committing*. Each of these terms implies high relationship, low task behaviors. Figure 8-10 summarizes the participating style and presents one-word descriptors of effective and ineffective approaches at readiness level 3.

The appropriate leader behaviors for an *able but unwilling R3* would be to:

- Share responsibility for decision-making with follower
- Feed follower's "need to know"
- Focus on results
- Involve follower in consequences of task to increase commitment and motivation

For an *able but insecure R3:*

- Combine leader-follower decision-making
- Determine next step
- Encourage and support
- Discuss apprehension

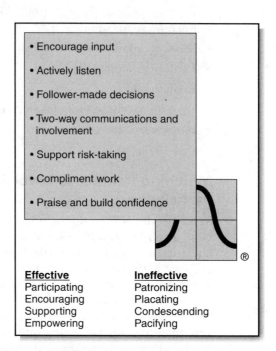

- Encourage input

- Actively listen

- Follower-made decisions

- Two-way communications and involvement

- Support risk-taking

- Compliment work

- Praise and build confidence

Figure 8-10
Style 3 (S3): HR/LT

Source: Copyright © 1995, Center for Leadership Studies. All rights reserved.

Effective	**Ineffective**
Participating	Patronizing
Encouraging	Placating
Supporting	Condescending
Empowering	Pacifying

Matching Readiness Level 4 with Leadership Style 4—Delegating

Readiness level 4 is where the individual or group is both able and willing or able and confident. They've had enough opportunity to practice, and they feel comfortable without the leader providing direction.

It is unnecessary to provide direction about where, what, when, or how because the followers already have the ability. Similarly, above-average amounts of encouraging and supportive behaviors aren't necessary because the group is confident, committed, and motivated. The appropriate style involves giving them the ball and letting them run with it.

This style is called *delegating.* Other words for this leadership style include *observing* and *monitoring.* Remember—some relationship behavior is still needed, but it tends to be less than average. It is still appropriate to monitor what's going on, but it is important to give these followers an opportunity to take responsibility and implement on their own.

One point to remember is that when an individual or group is *developing,* the issue is usually one of insecurity; when they are *regressing,* the issue is usually one of unwillingness. We will go into these ideas in greater detail in subsequent chapters. Figure 8-11 summarizes the delegating style and presents one-word descriptors of effective and ineffective approaches at readiness level 4.

The appropriate leader behaviors for an *able and willing or confident R4* would be to:

- Listen to updates
- Resist overloading

- Encourage autonomy
- Practice overall hands-off management; observe
- Reinforce follower-led communications
- Provide support and resources
- Delegate activities
- Encourage freedom for risk taking

Appropriate Leadership Styles

The appropriate leadership style for the four readiness designations—low (R1), low to moderate (R2), moderate to high (R3), and high (R4)—are telling (S1), selling (S2), participating (S3), and delegating (S4), respectively. That is, low readiness needs a telling style, low to moderate readiness needs a selling style, and so on. These combinations are shown in Table 8-1.

Situational Leadership not only suggests the high probability leadership style for various readiness levels, but it also indicates the probability of success of the other style configurations if a leader is unable to use the desired style. The probability of success of each style for the four readiness levels, depending on how far the style is from the high probability style along the prescriptive curve in the style of leader portion of the model, tends to be as follows:

- *R1.* S1 high, S2 2nd, S3 3rd, S4 low probability
- *R2.* S2 high, S1 2nd, S3 3rd, S4 low probability
- *R3.* S3 high, S2 2nd, S4 3rd, S1 low probability
- *R4.* S4 high, S3 2nd, S2 3rd, S1 low probability

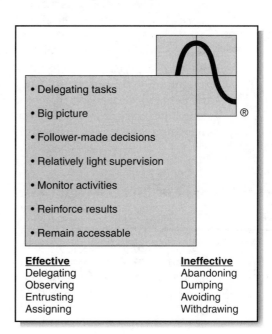

Figure 8-11
Style 4 (S4): LR/LT

Source: Copyright © 1995, Center for Leadership Studies. All rights reserved.

Table 8-1 Leadership Styles Appropriate for Various Readiness Levels

READINESS LEVEL	APPROPRIATE STYLE
R1, *Low Readiness* Unable and unwilling or insecure	S1, *Telling* High task-low relationship
R2, *Low to Moderate Readiness* Unable but willing or confident	S2, *Selling* High task-high relationship
R3, *Moderate to High Readiness* Able but unwilling or insecure	S3, *Participating* High relationship-low task
R4, *High Readiness* Able and willing or confident	S4, *Delegating* Low relationship-low task

In Situational Leadership, it is the *follower* who determines the appropriate leader behavior. The follower can get any behavior desired depending upon the follower's behavior. The follower's behavior determines the leader's behavior. What a marvelous thing we now have available to use at home, at the office, in any kind of interpersonal situation. For example, how much easier parenting would be if children were to realize that Mom and Dad do not determine and control their behavior; *they* control their own behavior and determine the behavior of Mom and Dad.

Why is it that a leadership style that may not be our "natural" style is frequently our most *effective* style? The reason is that we have worked at these learned styles, we have practiced and practiced those behaviors, and we have worked at them with some expert help. We have also paid attention to the details of applying these learned styles. We do not put the same amount of skill practice into our natural style as we do our learned styles. As a consequence, our natural styles are not as effective.

Situational Leadership is not a prescription with hard-and-fast rules. In the behavioral sciences, there are no rules. Situational Leadership as a major contribution to the behavioral sciences is attempting to improve the odds that managers will be able to become effective leaders.

APPLICATION OF SITUATIONAL LEADERSHIP

In using Situational Leadership, one should always keep in mind that there is no one best way to influence others. Rather, any leader behavior may be more or less effective depending on the readiness level of the person you are attempting to influence. Shown in Figure 8-12 is a comprehensive version of the Situational Leadership model that brings together our discussion of

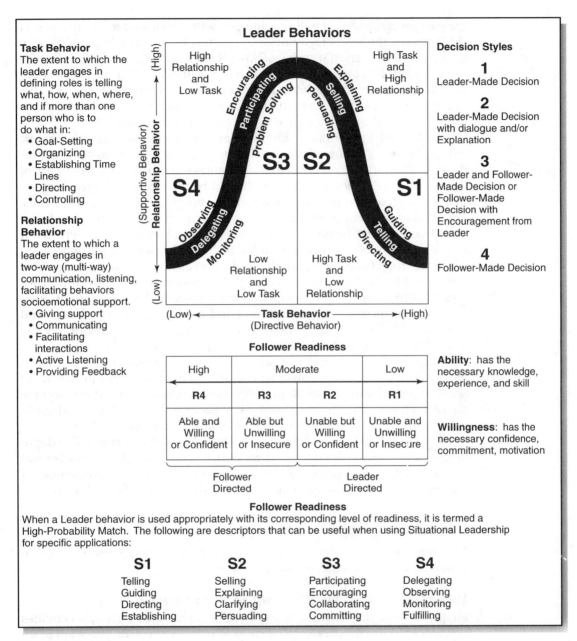

Task Behavior
The extent to which the leader engages in defining roles is telling what, how, when, where, and if more than one person who is to do what in:
- Goal-Setting
- Organizing
- Establishing Time Lines
- Directing
- Controlling

Relationship Behavior
The extent to which a leader engages in two-way (multi-way) communication, listening, facilitating behaviors socioemotional support.
- Giving support
- Communicating
- Facilitating interactions
- Active Listening
- Providing Feedback

Leader Behaviors

(High)

(Supportive Behavior)
Relationship Behavior

(Low)

High Relationship and Low Task

Encouraging
Participating
Problem Solving

Explaining
Selling
Persuading

High Task and High Relationship

S3 **S2**

S4 **S1**

Observing
Delegating
Monitoring

Guiding
Telling
Directing

Low Relationship and Low Task

High Task and Low Relationship

(Low) ◄——— **Task Behavior** ———► (High)
(Directive Behavior)

Decision Styles

1
Leader-Made Decision

2
Leader-Made Decision with dialogue and/or Explanation

3
Leader and Follower-Made Decision or Follower-Made Decision with Encouragement from Leader

4
Follower-Made Decision

Follower Readiness

	High	Moderate		Low
	R4	**R3**	**R2**	**R1**
	Able and Willing or Confident	Able but Unwilling or Insecure	Unable but Willing or Confident	Unable and Unwilling or Insecure

Follower Directed ⎵ Leader Directed

Ability: has the necessary knowledge, experience, and skill

Willingness: has the necessary confidence, commitment, motivation

Follower Readiness

When a Leader behavior is used appropriately with its corresponding level of readiness, it is termed a High-Probability Match. The following are descriptors that can be useful when using Situational Leadership for specific applications:

S1	**S2**	**S3**	**S4**
Telling	Selling	Participating	Delegating
Guiding	Explaining	Encouraging	Observing
Directing	Clarifying	Collaborating	Monitoring
Establishing	Persuading	Committing	Fulfilling

Figure 8-12
Expanded Situational Leadership Model

Source: Adapted from Paul Hersey, *Situational Selling* (Escondido, CA: Center for Leadership Studies, 1985), p. 35.
Copyright 1998 by Center for Leadership Studies. All rights reserved.

the past several pages. It will provide you with a quick reference to assist in (1) *diagnosing* the level of readiness; (2) *adapting* by selecting high probability leadership styles; and (3) *communicating* these styles effectively to influence behavior. Implicit in Situational Leadership is the idea that a leader should help followers grow in readiness as far as they are able and willing to go. This development of followers should be done by adjusting leadership behavior through the four styles along the leadership curve in Figure 8-12.

Situational Leadership contends that strong direction (task behavior) with followers with low readiness is appropriate if they are to become productive. Similarly, it suggests that an increase in readiness on the part of people who are somewhat unready should be rewarded by increased positive reinforcement and socioemotional support (relationship behavior). Finally, as followers reach high levels of readiness, the leader should respond not only by continuing to decrease control over their activities but also by continuing to decrease relationship behavior. People with high readiness do not need socioemotional support as much as they need greater freedom. At this stage, one of the ways leaders can prove their confidence and trust in these people is to leave them more and more on their own. It is not that there is less mutual trust and friendship between leader and follower—in fact, there is more—but less supportive behavior on the leader's part is needed.

Regardless of the level of readiness of an individual or group, change may occur. Whenever a follower's performance begins to slip—for whatever reason—and ability or motivation decreases, the leader should reassess the readiness level of this follower and move backward through the leadership curve, providing appropriate socioemotional support and direction.

These developmental and regressive processes will be discussed in depth in chapters 10 and 11. At this point, though, it is important to emphasize that Situational Leadership focuses on the appropriateness or effectiveness of leadership styles according to the *task-relevant readiness* of the followers.

Determining Appropriate Style

To determine what leadership style you should use with a person in a given situation, you must make several decisions.

What Objective(s) Do We Want to Accomplish?

First, you must decide what areas of an individual's or a group's activities you would like to influence. Specifically, what objective(s) do you want to accomplish? In the world of work, those areas would vary according to a group's responsibilities. For example, sales managers may have responsibilities in sales, administration (paperwork), service, and group development. Therefore, before managers can begin to determine the appropriate leadership style to use with a group, they must decide what aspect of that group's job they want to influence.

For example, the goal "to ship 100-percent of customer orders within 24 hours of order receipt" is too general and needs to be broken up into specific tasks that can be assigned to a group to accomplish the goal. Developed in association with a customer service unit, it would work like this:

1. The goal is summarized using trigger words, e.g., *prompt service.*
2. Tasks to accomplish the goal are identified by the people involved.
   a. Answering the phone
   b. Completing the order form
   c. Completing the packing order
   d. Shipping the order
   e. Adjusting service problems

What Is the Group's Readiness?

The sales manager must then diagnose the readiness of the group to accomplish these tasks. The key issue is, How ready or receptive is the group to accomplish these tasks? If the group is at a high level of readiness, only a low amount of leadership intervention will be required. If, on the other hand, the group is at a low level of readiness, considerable leadership intervention may be required.

What Leadership Action Should Be Taken?

The next step is deciding which of the four leadership styles (see Table 8-1) would be appropriate for the group. Suppose the manager has determined that the group's readiness level, in terms of accomplishing all of these tasks, is high—that is, the group is able and willing (R4). Using Table 8-1, the manager would know that when working with this group, a delegating (S4) style (low task–low relationship behavior) should be used. Some members of the group may be lower in readiness than the group as a whole with respect to specific tasks. For example, a team member may be R3 (able but insecure) with regard to responding to service problems on a new line of equipment. The manager would use an S3 (high relationship–low task) leadership style to build that member's confidence and self-esteem.

What Was the Result of the Leadership Intervention?

This step requires assessment to determine if results match expectations. As will be discussed in chapter 10, individuals and groups learn a little bit at a time. Development involves positively reinforcing successive approximations as the individual or group approaches the desired level of performance. Therefore, after a leadership intervention, the manager must assess the result through rechecking the objectives, rediagnosing readiness, and ascertaining if further leadership is indicated.

What Follow-up, If Any, Is Required?

If there is a gap between current performance and desired performance of the individual or group, then follow-up is required in the form of additional leadership interventions, and the cycle starts again. In a dynamic environment such as the leadership environment, follow-up is almost a certainty. Leadership under modern competitive conditions means hitting moving targets.

Tasks, readiness, and results are all continually changing; follow-up is a must. Leading is a full-time job that must be practiced every hour of every day.

Effective Task Statements

A well-formulated task statement contributes greatly toward the assessment of individual readiness. In contrast, vague and weakly formulated task statements make it difficult to accurately assess task readiness and can lead to unnecessary friction and conflict. Gustav Pansegrouw, president of P-E Corporate Services, a management consulting firm, found the following technique for writing task statements very useful, particularly from the follower's perspective. A key task for a customer order clerk may be stated as follows:

To answer the phone promptly.

Using this task statement as a guide, the manager may assess the clerk's task readiness level as R2, willing but unable. Using the same task statement as a guide, the clerk may assess the task readiness level as R4, willing and able.

This difference in task readiness assessment between manager and clerk is usually the result of different meanings attached to the word *promptly*. If the task was formulated in the following way, the two persons would have a much clearer understanding of the task.

To answer the phone on the first ring.

With such a specific statement of the task as a guide, it becomes much easier to assess task-relevant readiness. The probability of agreement between the two parties' assessments also increases.

The major difference between the two task statements just presented is that the second one contains a *clearly defined and measurable performance standard* for the task. The *expected performance* is thus an *integral part* of the task.

Of all the aspects of accomplishing tasks, individual readiness is the most critical. At any given time, each person is at a variety of task-specific readiness levels, depending on the tasks that must be performed. It is not that an individual is high or low in readiness, but that each person tends to be approximately ready according to a specific task.

It should be remembered that, although readiness is a useful concept for making diagnostic judgments, other situational variables—the supervisor's style (if close by), a crisis or time bind, the nature of the work—can be of equal or greater importance. Yet, the readiness concept is a solid benchmark for choosing the appropriate style with an individual or group at a particular time.

Direction of Readiness Change

Recent research at the Center for Leadership Studies has indicated that it is useful to measure not only a follower's general level of readiness, such as R1 or R2, but also the *direction* of this readiness. The primary reason is that there are important differences in leader behavior if the follower's readiness is increasing, decreasing, or static.

For example, place yourself in the role of leader in each of three situations. Recall that one aspect of your role as leader is to diagnose the follower's ability and willingness to respond to your efforts to implement a specific goal. In other words, how receptive is the follower in each of these situations to your leadership efforts?

- *Situation 1.* The follower's confidence, commitment, and motivation are low and are continuing to decline. Knowledge, experience, and skill remain marginal.

- *Situation 2.* The follower's knowledge, skill, and experience are increasing from an entry level, but confidence, commitment, and motivation remain low.

- *Situation 3.* Ability and willingness remain low; the follower is unable and insecure.

After reading the three situations, you can diagnose the appropriate readiness level by looking for the key elements of ability and willingness. Remember that ability has the three components of knowledge, experience, and skill; willingness has the three components of confidence, commitment, and motivation. One convenient way of assessing these components is to use a scale from + + + for a high level of readiness to − − − for a low level of readiness.

Suppose you have made the correct diagnosis that the follower is R1—unable and unwilling or insecure regarding the goal. You now want to diagnose the direction of the follower's readiness. Does the information in each situation show any elements that seem to be increasing, decreasing, or remaining static?

In situation 1, the follower is declining in readiness; in situation 2 the follower is increasing in readiness; in situation 3 the follower remains static or unchanged in readiness.

What is the implication of this analysis to your leadership efforts? In each situation, the follower's general level of readiness is R1. But does that mean that your leadership interventions should be the same? Probably not. Situation 1 suggests action to correct regressive behavior; situation 2 suggests continuing developmental behavior; and situation 3 suggests initiating developmental behavior. Each of these potential leadership interventions will be discussed further in chapters 10 and 11.

Instruments to Measure Readiness

To help managers and their followers make valid judgments about follower readiness, the Center for Leadership Studies has developed two readiness scale instruments: the *manager rating scale* and the *staff rating scale.*[13] Both leadership instruments measure job readiness (ability) and psychological readiness (willingness) on five behavioral dimensions.

In the manager rating scale, for example, the manager selects one to five of the staff member's major objectives or responsibilities and writes them on the form. Then, with respect to each major objective or responsibility, the manager rates the staff member on five job readiness dimensions and five psychological readiness dimensions, basing the rating on observations of the staff member's behavior. Two of the five items from the job readiness dimension and two of the five items from the psychological readiness dimension are illustrated in Figure 8-13. The ten items used on the complete form were selected after a pilot study from a pool of more than 30 indicators of each of the two dimensions. Note that behavioral indicators—e.g., "Has experience relevant to the job" and "Does not have experience relevant to the job"—are included.

In more recent work, the Center for Leadership Studies developed a Readiness Style Match rating form that permits managers and their staff members to rate leadership style and readiness on the same instrument. Figure 8-14 shows that integration. This instrument measures readiness using only one scale for each dimension—one measuring *ability* and the other measuring *willingness*.[14] In this instrument, a person's ability (knowledge, skill, and experience) is thought of as a matter of degree. That is, an individual's ability does not change drastically from one moment to the next. At any given moment, an individual has a little, some, quite a bit, or a great deal of ability.

Willingness (confidence, commitment, and motivation), however, is different. A person's motivation can, and often does, fluctuate from one moment to another. Therefore, a person is seldom, on occasion, often, or usually willing to take responsibility in a particular area.

The use of both a *manager's rating scale* and a *staff member scale* of the readiness style match is necessary to initiate a program combining Situational Leadership with *Contracting for Leadership Style*.[15] We will discuss that process in some detail in chapter 12.

Components of Leadership Style

Once managers have identified the readiness level of the individual or group they are attempting to influence, the key to effective leadership then is to bring to bear the appropriate leadership style. How can managers get a better handle on the behaviors of each of the four leadership styles?

Instruments to Measure Leader Behavior

To help managers and their staff members make better judgments about leadership style, the Center for Leadership Studies has developed two leadership scale instruments: *Leadership Scale: Perception by Manager* and *Leadership Scale: Perception by Staff Member*.[16] Both leadership instruments measure task and relationship behavior on five behavioral dimensions. The five task behavior dimensions and five relationship behavior dimensions are listed in Table 8-2.

After the five dimensions were established for both leader behaviors, behavioral indicators of the extremes of each of these dimensions were identified to help managers and their staff members differentiate between high and low amounts of each leader behavior. For example, with the task behavior dimension "organizing" on the staff member form, the end points of a rating scale were chosen to be "organizes the work situation for me" and "lets me organize the work situation." For the relationship behavior dimension "providing feedback," the end points of the rating scale were chosen to be

Figure 8-13 Representative Sections from Readiness Scale: Manager Rating Scale

Your name _____ Today's date _____

Your staff member's name _____ this person

		In performing the objective								
Job Readiness Dimensions	1. Past job experience	Has experience relevant to the job					Does not have experience relevant to the job			
		8	7	6	5	4	3	2	1	
	2. Job knowledge	Possesses necessary job knowledge					Does not have necessary job knowledge			
		8	7	6	5	4	3	2	1	
Psychological Readiness Dimensions	1. Willingness to take responsibility	Is very eager					Is very reluctant			
		8	7	6	5	4	3	2	1	
	2. Achievement motivation	Has a high desire to achieve					Has little desire to achieve			
		8	7	6	5	4	3	2	1	

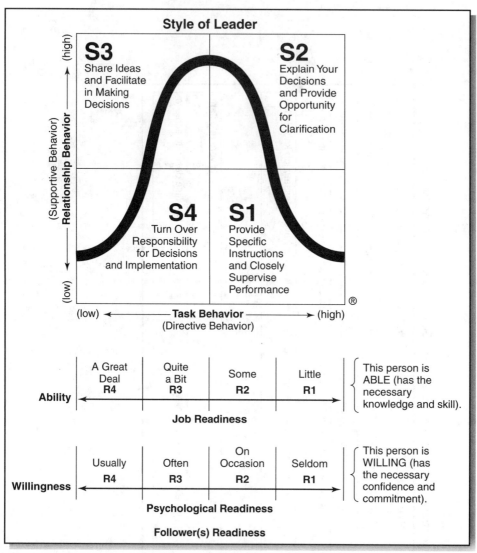

Figure 8-14
Defining Readiness and the Four Basic Leadership Styles

"frequently provides feedback on my accomplishments" and "leaves it up to me to evaluate accomplishments."

In the readiness style match instrument, each of the four basic leadership styles are described as shown in Figure 8-14:

- *Telling (S1).* Provide specific instructions and closely supervise performance.
- *Selling (S2).* Explain your decisions and provide opportunity for clarification.
- *Participating (S3).* Share ideas and facilitate in making decisions.
- *Delegating (S4).* Turn over responsibility for decisions and implementation.

Table 8-2 Task Behavior and Relationship Behavior Dimensions and Their Behavioral Indicators

TASK BEHAVIOR DIMENSION	BEHAVIORAL INDICATOR
	THE EXTENT TO WHICH A LEADER:
Goal setting	Specifies the goals people are to accomplish
Organizing	Organizes the work situation for people
Setting timelines	Sets timelines for people
Directing	Provides specific directions
Controlling	Specifies and requires regular reporting on progress

RELATIONSHIP BEHAVIOR DIMENSION	BEHAVIORAL INDICATOR
	THE EXTENT TO WHICH A LEADER:
Giving support	Provides support and encouragement
Communicating	Involves people in "give-and-take" discussions about work activities
Facilitating interactions	Facilitates people's interactions with others
Active listening	Seeks out and listens to people's opinions and concerns
Providing feedback	Provides feedback on people's accomplishments

SITUATIONAL LEADERSHIP IN VARIOUS ORGANIZATIONAL SETTINGS

We have found that Situational Leadership has application in every kind of organizational setting, whether it be business and industry, education, government, military, or even the family. The concepts apply in any situation in which people are trying to influence the behavior of other people.

The only problem we have found in working in various organizational settings is that some of the language has to be adapted to fit specific vocabularies. For example, we found that terms such as *task* and *relationship behavior* were meaningless to spouses who were not in a business environment. We soon realized that, in such family settings, it was much easier for parents and children to identify with "directive" behavior than with "task" behavior and with "supportive" behavior than with "relationship" behavior.

On the other hand, when working with trainers and facilitators who have had considerable personal growth experience, we found that *directive behavior* will often be considered a negative term. With these professionals, the word *guidance* is a good substitute for *directive behavior*. In using various labels for the two basic leader behaviors—task behavior and relationship behavior—we are not changing the definitions at all. Task behavior is essentially the extent to which a leader engages in one-way communication by explaining what each staff member is to do as well as when, where, and how tasks are to be accomplished. Relationship behavior, even when we call it supportive behavior, is still the extent to which a leader engages in two-way communication by providing socioemotional support and facilitating behaviors.

The reason it is important to modify the use of various words is that a key concept in all behavioral sciences is communication. If you're going to help people grow and develop, you have to learn to put frameworks, concepts, and research results into terminology that is acceptable to the groups you are attempting to influence. This has to be done if you want to have the highest probability of gaining acceptance and, therefore, affecting their growth.

Parent-Child Relationships

We have found an important application of Situational Leadership to the family and the parent-child relationship. The book *Situational Parenting*[17] is devoted completely to applying Situational Leadership to the family setting.

We suggest that when working with children (although they will need "different strokes even for the same folks"), in general, there is a pattern and movement in leadership style that works best over children's developmental years. Thus, when working with children who are low in readiness on a particular task, a directive parent style has the highest probability of success. This is especially true during the first few years of children's lives, when they are unable to control much of their own environment. This whole developmental process will be discussed in more depth in chapter 10.

Ineffective Parent Styles

One of the useful aspects of Situational Leadership is that one can begin to predict not only the leadership styles with the highest probability of effectiveness but also which styles tend to be ineffective in what circumstances. For instance, we can take three examples of parents who tend to use a single leadership style during the child's entire developmental period.

First, let us look at the parents who use a high directive–low supportive style (S1) throughout their children's developmental years: that is, "As long as you're living in this house, you'll be home at 10 P.M. and abide by the rules we've set." Two predictions might be made. The first one is that the children might pack their bags and leave home at the earliest opportunity. If they do not leave, they may succumb to their parents' authority and become very passive, dependent individuals throughout their lives, always needing someone to tell them what to do and when to do it.

A high probability result of a parent's using exclusively a style of high directive–high supportive behavior (S2) might be called the "mama's boy" or "daddy's little girl" syndrome. Even when the children get older, they may chronologically be adults, but they are still psychologically dependent on their parents to make decisions for them. Because most of the direction for their behavior and socioemotional support has been provided by their parents, these young people are unable to provide it for themselves.

What happens when parents are unfailingly supportive and never structure or direct any of their children's activities? The response to this high supportive–low directive style (S3) may be called a "spoiled brat" syndrome, for the children develop into individuals who have little regard for rules and little consideration for the rights of others.

As we mentioned in chapter 5, some people might question why it is inappropriate to use the same leadership style all the time—"After all, we've been told that consistency is good." This advice might have been given in the past, but, as we argue, according to Situational Leadership, consistency is not using the same style *all the time*. Instead, *consistency is using the same style for all similar situations*, but varying the style appropriately as the situation changes. Parents are consistent if they tend to discipline their children when they are behaving inappropriately and reward them when they are behaving appropriately. Parents are inconsistent if they smile and engage in other supportive behavior when their children are bad as well as when they are good. This discussion of consistency urges parents to remember that children are often at different levels of readiness in various aspects of their lives. Thus, parental style must vary as children's activities change.

Educational Setting

Educational settings provide us with numerous examples of Situational Leadership in operation.[18]

Teacher-Student Relationship

In an educational setting, Situational Leadership is being used in studying the teacher-student relationship. For example, Paul Hersey and two colleagues in Brazil, Arrigo L. Angelini and Sofia Caracushansky, conducted a study applying Situational Leadership to teaching.[19] In the study, an attempt was made to compare the learning effectiveness scores of students who attended a course in which a conventional teacher-student relationship prevailed (control subgroups) with the scores of students who attended a course in which Situational Leadership was applied by the same teacher (experimental subgroups). In the control group classes, lectures prevailed, but group discussions, audiovisual aids, and other participative resources were also used. In the experimental classes, the readiness level of students (willingness and ability to direct their own learning and provide their own reinforcement) was developed over time by a systematic shift in teaching style.

The teacher's style started at S1 (high task–low relationship), with the teacher in front of the class lecturing; then moved to S2 (high task–high relationship behavior), with the teacher directing the conversation of a group sitting in a circle; then to S3 (high relationship–low task), with the teacher participating in group discussions as a supportive, but nondirective, group member; and finally to S4 (low relationship–low task), with the teacher involved only when asked by the class. (The configuration of the class is depicted in Figure 14-2.) Student readiness developed slowly at first, with gradual decreases in teacher direction and increases in teacher encouragement. As the students demonstrated their ability not only to assume more and more responsibility for directing their own learning but also to provide their own reinforcement (self-gratification), decreases in teacher socioemotional support accompanied continual decreases in teacher direction.

In two experiments with this design, the experimental classes not only showed higher performance on content exams, but they were also observed to have a higher level of enthusiasm, morale, and motivation, as well as less tardiness and absenteeism.

Administrator-Governing Board Relationship

An important area for the top administrator (college president or school superintendent) in an educational institution is the relationship this person maintains with the governing board. Because these boards have the ultimate power to remove college presidents or superintendents when they lose confidence in their leadership, these administrators often tend to use a high relationship style (S3), providing only a limited amount of structure for these decision-making groups.[20] In fact, they sometimes seem to shy away from directing the activities of their board for fear of arousing their criticism. Situational Leadership questions this behavior.

Although the members of the governing board are often responsible, well-educated individuals, they tend to have little work experience in an educational setting. For example, in a survey of college trustees in New York State, it was found that less than 10 percent of the trustees serving on these boards had any teaching or administrative experience in an educational institution.[21] In fact, the large majority of the 1,269 trustees sampled were employed primarily in industry, insurance and banking, merchandising and transportation, medicine, and law. Virtually half acted as corporation officials with the rank of treasurer, director, or above. In addition to their involvement in other than educational institutions, these trustees tended to be overcommitted and were probably unable to give the time to university problems they would have liked to give. In fact, the most frequent dissatisfaction expressed by trustees was the lack of time to devote to the board.

The relative inexperience of the trustees and the heavy commitment elsewhere suggest that it may be appropriate for college presidents to combine with their high relationship behavior an increase of task behavior in working with their trustees. In fact, the responsibility for defining the role of trustees and organizing their work should fall on the college president. Henry Wriston, former president of Brown University, said it well:

> It may seem strange, at first thought, that this should be a president's duty. A moment's reflection makes it clear that it can [devolve to] no other person. Trustees are unpaid; they have no method of analyzing talents and making assignments. The president is in a position to do so.[22]

Administrator-Faculty Relationship

For an administrator working with experienced faculty, the low relationship–low task style (S4) characterized by a decentralized organizational structure and delegation of responsibility to individuals may be appropriate. The level of education and experience of these people is often such that they do not need their department chairperson to initiate much structure. Sometimes they tend to resent it. In addition, some faculty desire or need only a limited amount of socioemotional support (relationship behavior).

Often an effective leader style in working with faculty tends to be low relationship–low task, but certain deviations may be necessary. For example, during the early stages of a school year or a curriculum change, a certain amount of structure as to the specific areas to be taught, by whom, when, and where must be established. Once these requirements and limitations are understood by the faculty, the administrator may move rapidly back to the low relationship–low task style appropriate for working with experienced, responsible, self-motivated faculty.

Other deviations may be necessary. For example, a new, inexperienced teacher might need more direction and socioemotional support than more seasoned teachers until gaining experience in the classroom.

UNDERSTANDING EARLIER RESEARCH

Determining the Effectiveness of Participation

An analysis of studies in participation in terms of Situational Leadership suggests some interesting things about the appropriate use of participation.[23] Situational Leadership suggests that the higher the level of task-relevant readiness of an individual or group, the higher the probability that participation will be an effective management technique. The less task-relevant readiness, the lower the probability that participation will be a useful management practice.

Involvement and participation in decision making with people at extremely low levels of readiness might be characterized by a pooling of ignorance, or the blind leading the blind; therefore, directive leadership might have a higher probability of success. At the other end of the readiness continuum (extremely high levels of task-relevant readiness), some of these people tend to resist engaging in "group-think." They would prefer having the individual with the highest level of expertise in an area make the decisions. "Bill, how do you think we should go on this? It's your area." Thus, according to Situational Leadership, the probability that participation will be a successful management technique increases as one moves from low to moderate levels of readiness (from right to left on Figure 8-15). The probability of success then begins to plateau in potential effectiveness as one's followers become high in task-relevant readiness (at the left in Figure 8-15).

One further point about participation should be mentioned. Although participation tends to satisfy affiliation and esteem needs by giving people a chance to feel in on things and be recognized as important in the decision-making process, it does not necessarily satisfy the self-actualization need. The high-level need satisfaction most often occurs in a work environment where people are given a job that allows them an opportunity for achievement, growth and development, and challenge.

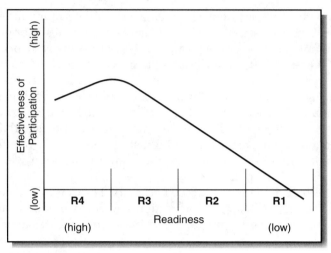

Figure 8-15
Participation As an Effective Management Technique

SUMMARY

Situational Leadership is based on an interplay among (1) the amount of guidance and direction (task behavior) a leader gives; (2) the amount of socioemotional support (relationship behavior) a leader provides; and (3) the readiness level that followers exhibit in performing a specific task, function, or objective.

Readiness has two main components: ability and willingness.

Ability is the knowledge, experience, and skill that an individual or group brings to a particular task or activity.

Willingness is the extent to which an individual or group has the confidence, commitment, and motivation to accomplish a specific task.

According to Situational Leadership, there is no one best way to influence people. The leadership style depends on the readiness level of the followers the leader is attempting to influence. The following chapters will help leaders select the high probability style to use in different situations.

ENDNOTES

1. Edgar H. Schein, *Organizational Psychology* (Upper Saddle River, NJ: Prentice Hall, 1965), p. 61.
2. *Ibid.*
3. Situational Leadership was first published by Paul Hersey and Kenneth H. Blanchard as "Life Cycle Theory of Leadership," in *Training and Development Journal*, May 1969.
4. Kenneth Blanchard, Patricia Zigarmi, and Drea Zigarmi, *Leadership and the One Minute Manager* (New York: William Morrow, 1985). For further information on SLII, contact Blanchard Training and Development, Inc., 125 State Place, Escondido, CA, 92029. See also appendix A, an adaptation of an article by Paul Hersey and Ken Blanchard, "Life Cycle

Theory of Leadership," published in the special 50th Anniversary Edition of *Training and Development*, January 1996.

5. Fillmore H. Sanford, *Authoritarianism and Leadership* (Philadelphia: Institute for Research in Human Relations, 1950).

6. The following section has been adopted from Paul Hersey, *Situational Selling* (Escondido, CA: Center for Leadership Studies, 1985), pp. 19ff.

7. *Ibid.*

8. *Ibid.*

9. *Ibid.*, p. 22.

10. *Ibid.*, pp. 25–26.

11. A pocket guide to Situational Leadership is available from the Center for Leadership Studies, Escondido, CA, 92025.

12. These ideas were developed by Ron Campbell, Center for Leadership Studies, Esondido, CA.

13. These two instruments, originally using the term *maturity*, were developed by Ronald K. Hambleton, Kenneth H. Blanchard, and Paul Hersey through a grant from Xerox Corporation. We are grateful to Xerox Corporation not only for providing financial support for the instrument development project but also for allowing us to involve many of their managers and employees in our development and validation work. In particular, we thank Audian Dunham, Warren Rothman, and Ray Gumpert for their assistance, encouragement, and constructive criticism of our work. The instruments are available through the Center for Leadership Studies, Escondido, CA.

14. These instruments, originally using the term *maturity*, were developed by Paul Hersey, Kenneth H. Blanchard, and Joseph Keilty. Information on these instruments is available through Center for Leadership Studies, Escondido, CA.

15. The integration of Situational Leadership with Contracting for Leadership Styles was first published as Paul Hersey, Kenneth H. Blanchard, and Ronald K. Hambleton, "Contracting for Leadership Style: A Process and Instrumentation for Building Effective Work Relationships," in *The Proceedings of OD '78*, San Francisco, CA, sponsored by University Associates/LRC. This presentation is available through the Center for Leadership Studies, Escondido, CA.

16. The initial versions of these leadership scales were developed by Paul Hersey, Kenneth H. Blanchard, and Ronald K. Hambleton. Information on these instruments is available through the Center for Leadership Studies, Escondido, CA.

17. Paul Hersey and Ronald Campbell, *Situational Parenting* (Escondido, CA: Center for Leadership Studies, 1999).

18. See Kenneth H. Blanchard and Paul Hersey, "A Leadership Theory for Educational Administrators," *Education*, Spring 1970.

19. Arrigo L. Angelini, Paul Hersey, and Sofia Caracushansky, "The Situational Leadership Theory Applied to Teaching: A Research on Learning Effectiveness," *Proceedings*, 9th World Training and Development Conference, Rio de Janeiro, Brazil, August 31–September 5, 1980.

20. Kenneth H. Blanchard, "College Boards of Trustees: A Need for Directive Leadership," *Academy of Management Journal*, December 1967.

21. F. H. Stutz, R. G. Morrow, and Kenneth H. Blanchard, "Report of a Survey," in *College and University Trustees and Trusteeship: Recommendations and Report of a Survey* (Ithaca, NY: New York State Regents Advisory Committee on Educational Leadership, 1966).

22. Henry M. Wriston, *Academic Procession* (New York: Columbia University Press, 1959), p. 78.

23. A classic study in the area of participation is Victor H. Vroom, *Some Personality Determinants of the Effects of Participation* (Upper Saddle River, NJ: Prentice Hall, 1960).

Chapter 9

Situational Leadership, Perception, and the Impact of Power

The concepts of leadership and power have generated lively interest, debate, and occasionally confusion throughout the evolution of management thought. The concept of power is closely related to the concept of leadership, for power is one of the means by which a leader influences the behavior of followers.[1] Given this integral relationship between leadership and power, leaders must not only assess their leader behavior in order to understand how they actually influence other people, but they must also examine their possession and use of power.[2] ✦

POWER DEFINED

We earlier defined leadership as an attempt to influence another individual or group and concluded that leadership is an influence process. *Power is influence potential*—the resource that enables a leader to gain compliance or commitment from others. Despite its critical importance, power is a subject that is often avoided, because power can have its seamy side, and many people want to wish it away and pretend it is not there. But power is a real-world issue. Leaders who understand and know how to use power are more effective than those who do not or will not use power. To successfully influence the behavior of others, the leader should understand the impact of power on the various leadership styles. In today's world, many sources of power within organizations have been legislated, negotiated, or administered away. Leaders now have less of some types of power to draw from, so it is important to use effectively what is available. Because power bases drive leadership styles, using them appropriately can enhance your effectiveness as a leader.[3]

In spite of the widespread usage of the term *power* in the management literature, there are many definitions.[4] James Hillman reports that power's "... rather innocent definition is simply the agency to act, to do, to be, coming from the Latin *potere*, to be able ... power can be defined as sheer potency or potentiality, not the doing, but the capacity to do."[5] David C. McClelland and David H. Burnham have defined power as "influencing others."[6] John B. Miner defined power as "... the ability to induce a person to do something he or she would not otherwise have done."[7] Miner goes on to write, "Influence is a broader concept, referring to anything a person does to alter the behavior, attitudes, values, feelings, and such of another person. ... Power is thus one form of influence."[8] Stephen P. Robbins suggests, "Power refers to a capacity that A has to influence the behavior of B, so that B does something that he or she would not otherwise do. This definition implies (1) a *potential* that need not be actualized to be effective, (2) a *dependence relationship*, and (3) that B has some *discretion* over his or her own behavior."[9]

We will use M. F. Rogers' simple definition of power as "the potential for influence."[10] Thus, power is a resource that may or may not be used. The use of power resulting in a change in the probability that a person or group will adopt the desired behavioral change is defined as "influence." Accepting Rogers' definition, we make the following distinction between leadership and power. As was suggested in chapter 4, leadership is defined as the process of influencing the activities of an individual or a group in efforts toward accomplishing a goal in a given situation. Therefore, leadership is simply any attempt to influence; power is a leader's influence potential. It is the resource that enables a leader to influence.

POWER: AN ERODING CONCEPT

If power is defined as influence potential, how does one describe authority? *Authority* is a particular type of power that has its origin in the position that a leader occupies. Thus, authority is the power that is legitimatized by virtue of an individual's formal role in a social organization.

Hundreds of years ago, serfs had no power; kings and queens had all the power. Their positions gave them ultimate authority. For years, managers were almost like kings and queens. They could make all the decisions. If they didn't like the way you looked or the way you combed your hair, they could fire you, and workers could do very little to stop such arbitrary action. Today, that is no longer the case. The balance of this chapter discusses modern concepts of power.

POSITION POWER AND PERSONAL POWER

One of the characteristics of leadership is that leaders exercise power. Amitai Etzioni discussed the difference between position power and personal power. His distinction resulted from his concept of power as the ability to induce or influence behavior. He claimed that power is derived from an organizational office, personal influence, or both. Individuals who are able to induce other individuals to do a certain job because of their position in the organization are considered to have position power; individuals who derive their power from their followers are considered to have personal power. Some individuals can have both position power and personal power.[11]

Where do managers get the position power that is available to them? Although Etzioni would argue that it comes from the organizational office of a manager, we feel it comes from above and, therefore, is not inherent in the office. Managers occupying positions in an organization may have more or less position power than their predecessor or someone else in a similar position in the same organization. *Position power* is the extent to which those people to whom managers report are willing to delegate authority and responsibility down to them. So position power tends to flow down in an organization; it is not a matter of the office's having power. This is not to say that leaders do not have any impact on how much position power they accrue. They certainly do. The confidence and trust they develop with the people above them will often determine the willingness of upper management to delegate down to them. And remember, whatever power is delegated downward can be taken back. We have all seen this occur on occasions when managers still have the same responsibilities, but all of a sudden their authority (to distribute rewards and sanctions) to get the job done in the way they once did is taken away.

Personal power is the extent to which followers respect, feel good about, and are committed to their leader and to which they see their own goals as being satisfied by the goals of their leader. In other words, personal power is the extent to which people are willing to follow a leader. As a result, personal power in an organizational setting comes from below—from the followers—and so flows up in an organization. Thus, we must be careful when we say that some leaders are charismatic or have personal power that flows from them. Personal power is not inherent in the leader. If it were, managers with personal power could take over any department and have the same commitment and rapport they had in their last department. We know that they can't. Although managers certainly can influence the amount of personal power they have by the way they treat their people, it is a volatile kind of power. It can be taken away rapidly by followers. Make a few dramatic mistakes and see how many people are willing to follow. Personal power is a day-to-day phenomenon—it can be earned and it can be taken away.

Etzioni suggested that the best situation for leaders is when they have both personal power and position power. But, in some cases, it is not possible to build a relationship on both. Then, the question becomes whether it is more important to have personal power or position power. Happiness and human relations have been culturally reinforced over the past several decades. With this emphasis, most people would pick personal power as being the most important. But there may be another side of the coin.

In his sixteenth-century treatise *The Prince,* Machiavelli presented an interesting viewpoint when he raised the question of whether it is better to have a relationship based on love (personal power) or fear (position power).[12] Machiavelli, as did Etzioni, contended that it is best to be both loved and feared. If, however, one cannot have both, he suggested that a relationship based on love alone tends to be volatile, short-lived, and easily terminated when there is no fear of retaliation. On the other hand, a relationship based on fear tends to be longer-lasting, because the individual must be ready to incur the sanction (pay the price) before terminating the relationship. This is a difficult concept for many people to accept. One of the most difficult roles for leaders—whether they be a supervisor, teacher, or parent—is disciplining someone about whom they care. Yet, to be effective, leaders sometimes have to sacrifice short-term friendship for long-term respect if they are interested in the growth and development of the people with whom they are working. Machiavelli warned, however, that one should be careful that fear does not lead to hatred. For hatred often evokes overt behavior in terms of retaliation, undermining, and attempts to overthrow.

In summary, position power can be thought of as the authority, which is delegated down, to use rewards and sanctions. Personal power is the cohesiveness, commitment, and rapport between leaders and followers. It is also affected by the extent to which followers see their own goals as being the same, similar to, or at least dependent upon the accomplishment of the leader's goals.

Although personal and position power are distinct, they are an interacting influence system. Often, followers are affected by their perception of the leader's ability to provide rewards, punishments, and sanctions and of the leader's influence up the organization. Also, the extent to which people above you in the organization are willing to delegate position power is often dependent on their perception of the followers' commitment to you. So it is not sufficient just to have either position or personal power alone—you need to work at gaining both.

Selling Within Your Own Organization

It is important to keep in mind that no matter where you are within your organization, you are trying to influence people.[13] If you are managing, you can use both position power and personal power to influence the people who report directly to you. When attempting to influence your supervisor, senior executives, and associates, however, you must depend almost exclusively on personal power. Therefore, you are selling. When you have little or no position power, you must learn to develop rapport through personal power,

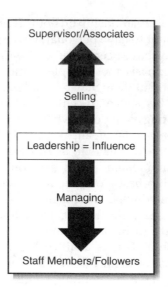

Figure 9-1
Selling Up/Managing
Down

Source: Adapted from Paul
Hersey, *Situational Selling*
(Escondido, CA: Center
for Leadership Studies,
1985), p. 15. Reprinted
with permission.

because it is through this trust and confidence that an effective relationship
can be built. Figure 9-1 illustrates this important idea. Keep in mind that
power is a real-world issue. People who understand and know how to use
power are more effective than those who do not or will not. Recognition of
the fact that all managers are in the business of selling is an important aspect
of this understanding.

ADDITIONAL BASES OF POWER

Although position power and personal power are important and useful concepts in examining power, they are limited because they force you to divide
"the pie" into just two pieces. R. L. Peabody named four categories of power
on the basis of statements of questionnaire respondents in a police department, a welfare office, and an elementary school: power of legitimacy (laws,
rules, policies); of position; of competence (professional and technical expertise); and of person.[14]

A study by A. C. Filley and A. J. Grimes identified 11 reasons why an individual would seek a decision from another on various work-related matters in a professional organization.[15] These reasons, from most frequently to
least frequently mentioned, were responsibility and function (the person is
responsible for the particular matter); formal authority (the person is in a position to make decisions generally); control of resources (the person controls
money, information, and so on); collegial (a group of peers has the right to be
consulted); manipulation (the person can get the decision made in the manner desired); default or avoidance (the person is available and will deal with
the problem); bureaucratic rules (the rules specify the person to consult); traditional rules (custom, tradition, or seniority specify the person to consult);

equity (the person is a fair decision maker); friendship (the person is personally liked); and expertise (the person has superior knowledge of the subject).

Many other power base classification systems have been developed,[16] but the framework devised by J. R. P. French and B. Raven[17] appears to be the most widely accepted. They proposed that there are five bases of power: coercive power, expert power, legitimate power, referent power, and reward power.

Later, Raven, collaborating with W. Kruglanski,[18] identified a sixth power base—information power. Hersey and Marshall Goldsmith modified some of the definitions of French, Raven, and Kruglanski and proposed a seventh base of power—connection power.[19]

The Perception of Power

In the following discussion of power bases, we use the word *perceived* in such instances as "coercive power—the perceived ability to provide sanctions." We do this because the key issue in the concept of power is that it is not based on the reality of how much power the manager has but rather on the followers' perception of that power. Truth and reality evoke no behavior. All behavior is based on people's perception and interpretation of truth and reality. For example, when a couple has a fight, it does not matter whether the cause was real or imagined—it was just as much of a fight. It is the perception others hold about power that gives people the ability to influence.

We operate using psychological maps. The caution that one must make is that no matter how hard we work or how detailed our psychological map, no matter how much information and specificity we have in our psychological map, the map is not the territory. The closer and closer we match our psychological map to the territory, however, the higher the probability that we will be able to operate effectively within that territory.

Get the Information Out

People must not only perceive you as having power, they must also see you as able and willing to use it. It's not enough to have access to power; you have to let people know you're willing to use it. Information has value only when you get it out to the end user in a fashion that can be understood and accepted. If you don't blow your own horn, somebody else will use it as a spittoon.

Consider a father examining his son's report card and suffering mild cardiac tremors as he sees a solid column of Ds. Outraged that a product of his genes could so disgrace the family, he confronts his son: "Dave, this just won't do. I can't tolerate these grades, and if you don't show me an immediate turnaround, you're going to be grounded!" Six weeks later, Dave brings home another report card. This time the Ds are written in red ink with exclamation points. The father says, "David, get in here! I'm really upset, and now you have no choice at all. Hit those books hard or you're definitely going to be grounded!"

Next time, it's the same, except that the teacher has added some pointed remarks about Dave's inattentive behavior in class. Dave's father turns crimson, crumples his beer can, and shouts, "David Ralph, this is it . . . last chance city . . . you're in real trouble with the old man now!" What has Dave learned? That his father, who has the ability to ground him, won't use the power! Because of his father's reluctance to follow through with his threatened punishments, Dave knows that all he has to do is take the heat for 6 minutes and he's off the hook for 6 weeks!

Power is a matter of perception—use it or lose it!

Readiness, Styles, and Power Bases

The relationship between readiness, leadership style, and the power base that drives that style will be explained from the aspects of managing and leading.

Coercive Power—The Perceived Ability to Provide Sanctions, Punishment, or Consequences for Not Performing

Followers at readiness level R1 need guidance. Too much supportive behavior with people who are not performing may be perceived as permissive or as rewarding the lack of performance. Without some coercive power to drive the telling style, attempts to influence will be ineffective. Followers need to know that if they do not respond, there may be some costs, sanctions, or other consequences. These may take the form of a reprimand, cut in pay, transfer, demotion, or even dismissal.

Managers often erode their coercive power by not following through. They may have the ability to impose sanctions but for one reason or another be unwilling to do so. This reluctance to use sanctions can result in a loss of power. Another way to erode coercive power is by not differentiating in the use of sanctions on the basis of performance. If people feel they will be punished regardless of performance, coercive power has little impact.

It is even possible to "talk" coercive power away. A manager begins a performance appraisal interview with a low performer by saying, "Now, look, both of us know that you've been here over 20 years and I can't fire you." In just a few words, the manager has stripped away any coercive power the follower might have perceived.

Connection Power—The Perceived Association of the Leader with Influential Persons or Organizations

Connection power is an important driver for telling and selling leadership styles. Usually, followers at R1 and R2 want to avoid the sanction or gain the favor they associate with powerful connections. The important issue is not whether there is a real connection, but whether there is a perception of a real connection.

For example, a first-level supervisor may be regarded as having limited power. But, if that supervisor is married to a relative of the company president, the perceived connection may provide added influence with others in the organization.

Reward Power—The Perceived Ability to Provide Things That People Would like to Have

Reward power is enhanced if managers are seen as having the ability to give appropriate rewards. Followers who are unable but willing (R2) are most likely to try on new behaviors if they feel increases in performance will be rewarded. Rewards may include raises, bonuses, promotions, or transfers to more desirable positions. They may also include intangibles such as a pat on the back or feedback on accomplishment. In the final analysis, managers get what they reward.

A significant amount of reward power has been legislated, negotiated, and administered away. We find that this is true in the classroom as well as in almost every organization. Yet, managers themselves often erode the power that remains by making promises they don't keep. For example:

> *Salesperson:* I did it! I made the 15 percent over quota with room to spare. When am I going to get that 10-percent bonus?
> *Sales Manager:* I'm sorry, but economic conditions are such that we'll have to postpone it for awhile. But don't worry, if you keep up the good work, I promise I'll make it up to you.

Other managers erode their reward power by "hoping for A but rewarding B."[20] An example might be an organization that gives all salespeople a 10-percent cost-of-living adjustment and yet the difference between reward for average sales and outstanding sales is only 1 or 2 percent. In this case, "hanging around" for another year is significantly rewarded. This practice often results in high performers losing their motivation and commitment or looking outside the company for opportunities. The problem with power derived from rewards is that rewards will often run their course. The manager will be left with an employee who is no longer motivated through the use of rewards and an organization that can no longer provide rewards.

Legitimate Power—The Perception That It Is Appropriate for the Leader to Make Decisions Because of Title, Role, or Position in the Organization

Legitimate power can be a useful driver for the selling and participating styles. Followers who are both unable and unwilling (low readiness) couldn't care less about whether someone's title is manager, regional manager, or vice president. And followers high in readiness are far less impressed with title or position than they are with expertise or information. But followers in the moderate ranges of readiness can often be influenced if they feel it is appropriate for a person in that position or with that title to make that decision. For example, a salesperson might comment to a peer about the department's recent reorganization: "Pat should be making those kinds of decisions . . . that's what the sales manager gets paid to do."

Referent Power—The Perceived Attractiveness of Interacting with the Leader

In attempting to influence people who are able but insecure or unwilling (R3), high relationship behavior is necessary. If people have a confidence problem, the manager needs to encourage. If they have a motivation problem, the manager needs to discuss and problem solve. In either case, if the manager has not taken time to build rapport, attempts to participate may be perceived as adversarial rather than helpful. Confidence, trust, and rapport are important in influencing people. If a follower feels that the manager will provide encouragement and help when it is needed, it can make an important difference in the success of the influence attempt. Referent power is based on the manager's personal traits. A manager high in referent power is generally liked and admired by others because of personality. It is this liking for, admiration for, and identification with the manager that influences others.

Information Power—The Perceived Access to, or Possession of, Useful Information

The styles that tend to effectively influence followers at above-average readiness levels, R3 and R4, are participating and delegating. Information power is helpful in driving these styles. This power source has grown in importance during the high-tech explosion, with the emphasis on data storage and data retrieval.

Information power is based on perceived access to data. This is different from expert power, which is the understanding of or ability to use data. For example, one study found that secretaries in a major corporate office had a significant amount of information power but little expert power in some technical areas. They were able to help gain or prevent access to information but in a few technical areas had little expertise themselves.

Expert Power—The Perception That the Leader Has Relevant Education, Experience, and Expertise

Followers who are competent and confident require little direction or supportive behavior. They are able and willing to perform on their own. The driver for influencing these followers is expert power. With followers who are able and willing, leaders are more effective if they possess the expertise, skill, and knowledge that followers respect and regard as important. An apt example is Al Smith, former governor of New York State. When he was a freshman legislator, he spent his late nights studying the New York State budget instead of attending the many social events. As Tom Peters, well-known author and commentator on the management scene, described it, "His matchless command of the fine print [of the budget] launched an extraordinary career."[21]

IS THERE A BEST TYPE OF POWER?

The French and Raven initial classification system motivated a number of scholars to try to answer the following question: Given the wide variety of power bases available to the leader, which type of power should be emphasized in order to maximize effectiveness? In any attempt to answer this question, it is important to remember the definition of effectiveness. As stated in chapter 6, organizational effectiveness, as well as leader effectiveness, is a function of both output variables and intervening variables.

K. R. Student studied 40 production groups in two plants of a company that manufactured home appliances.[22] Employees rated the extent to which they complied with their foremen because of each of the five French and Raven power bases. Legitimate power was found to be the strongest reason for compliance, followed by expert power, reward power, referent power, and last, coercive power.

Student also related the foremen's power base utilization (as perceived by the workers) to a number of measures of performance. He found that legitimate power, although most important among the reasons for compliance, was not related to the performance of the work groups. Reward and coercive power were positively related to some performance measures (suggestions submitted, supply cost performance) but negatively related to others (average earnings, maintenance cost performance). Expert and referent power were significantly and positively related to four and five measures of performance, respectively, and thus emerged as the two most effective bases of supervisory power. Student explained these results by suggesting that expert and referent power are qualitatively different from legitimate, reward, and coercive power. Expert and referent power are considered idiosyncratic in character and dependent on an individual's unique role behavior; legitimate, reward, and coercive power are organizationally determined and designed to be equal for supervisors at the same hierarchical level. Implicit in Student's conclusions is the contention that followers are more responsive to and satisfied with a leader whose influence attempts are not based entirely on position-based power (that is, legitimate, reward, and coercive).

Similar results were obtained in a study by J. G. Bachman, C. G. Smith, and J. A. Slesinger.[23] Data were obtained from 36 branch offices of a national sales organization. Each office was managed by a single office supervisor. Employees were asked to rank each of the five power bases according to the extent to which it was a reason for compliance. These results were then correlated with satisfaction and performance measures. Legitimate and expert power again emerged as first and second in importance, followed by referent, reward, and coercive power, in that order.

In those offices in which referent and expert power predominated, performance and satisfaction were high. In those offices in which reward power was high, performance tended to be poor, and there was marked dissatisfaction. Coercive and legitimate bases of power were associated with dissatisfaction, but they were unrelated to performance.

The findings of Student and Bachman and others were included in a comparative study of five organizations by Bachman, D. G. Bowers, and P. M. Marcus.[24] In addition to the appliance firm and the sales organization, other organizations examined were 12 liberal arts colleges, 40 agencies of a life insurance company, and 21 work groups of a large midwestern utility company. A ranking procedure was used to ascertain the strength of the supervisors' power bases in the colleges and the utility company; an independent rating procedure for each power base was used with the life insurance agencies.

Expert and legitimate power were again the most important reasons for complying with supervisors in all three organizations. Expert power was most important, and legitimate power, second, in the colleges and insurance agencies. The order was reversed in the utility company. Referent power was third in importance in the colleges, fourth in the insurance agencies, and fifth in the utility companies. Reward power was third in importance in the utility company and the agencies and fourth in the colleges. Finally, coercive power was least important in the colleges and the insurance agencies and fourth in the utility company.

Expert and referent power were again strongly and positively related to satisfaction in these three additional organizations, whereas reward and legitimate power were not strongly related to the satisfaction measures. Coercive power was consistently related to dissatisfaction. Performance data were obtained from the insurance agencies but not from the colleges or utility company. Expert and reward power were positively related to insurance agency performance measures, and coercive, legitimate, and referent power yielded nonsignificant correlations.

J. M. Ivancevich and J. H. Donnelly studied salespersons' perceptions of their managers' power bases in 31 branches of a large firm that produces food products.[25] The employees were asked to rank the power bases in order of importance for compliance. Expert power was most important, followed by legitimate, reward, referent, and coercive power. Referent and expert power were positively related to performance; reward, legitimate, and coercive power showed no relationship.

R. J. Burke and D. S. Wilcox conducted a study of leader power bases and follower satisfaction in six offices of a large public utility company.[26] A 1-to-5 ranking method was used. Expert power emerged as most important, followed by legitimate, coercive, referent, and reward power. Referent and expert power were associated with greatest satisfaction; legitimate and reward power were intermediate; and coercive power was associated with least satisfaction.

D. W. Jamieson and K. W. Thomas conducted a study of power in the classroom. Data were collected from high school, undergraduate, and graduate students on their teachers' bases of power, and results were correlated with several measures of student satisfaction.[27] For the high school students, legitimate power was most important, followed by coercive, expert, referent, and reward power. The undergraduate students viewed coercive power as most important, followed by legitimate, expert, reward, and referent power. The graduate students perceived expert power as the strongest, followed by legitimate, reward, coercive, and referent power. Coercive power was

Chapter 9   Situational Leadership, Perception, and the Impact of Power

Figure 9-2
The Impact of Power
Bases at Various
Levels of Readiness

strongly and negatively associated with satisfaction among all three groups; the other four power bases yielded nonsignificant results.

In summarizing a review of the most important research relating supervisory power bases to follower satisfaction and performance, Walter Natemeyer made the following general conclusion: Although expert and legitimate power bases appear to be the most important reason for compliance, and expert and referent power bases tend to be often strongly and consistently related to follower performance and satisfaction measures, the results are not clear enough to generalize about a best power base.[28] In fact, the results suggest that the appropriate power base is largely affected by situational variables. In other words, leaders may need various power bases, depending on the situation.

Power Bases and Readiness Level

Hersey, Blanchard, and Natemeyer suggest that there is a direct relationship between the level of readiness of individuals and groups and the kind of power bases that have a high probability of gaining compliance from those people.[29] Situational Leadership views readiness as the ability and willingness of individuals or groups to take responsibility for directing their own behavior in a particular situation. Thus, it must be reemphasized that readiness is a task-specific concept and depends on what the leader is attempting to accomplish.

As people move from lower to higher levels of readiness, their competence and confidence to do things increase. The seven power bases appear to have significant impact on the behavior of people at various levels of readiness, as seen in Figure 9-2.

INTEGRATING POWER BASES, READINESS LEVEL, AND LEADERSHIP STYLE THROUGH SITUATIONAL LEADERSHIP

Situational Leadership can provide the basis for understanding the potential impact of each power base. It is our contention that the readiness of the follower not only dictates which style of leadership will have the highest probability of success, but that the readiness of the follower also determines the power base that the leader should use in order to induce compliance or influence behavior.

The Situational Use of Power

Even if the leader is using the appropriate leadership style for a given readiness level, that style may not be maximizing the leader's probability of success if it does not reflect the appropriate power base. Therefore, just as an effective leader should vary leadership style according to the readiness level of the follower, it may be appropriate to vary the use of power in a similar manner. The power bases that may influence people's behavior at various levels of readiness are pictured in Figure 9-3.

Figure 9-3 shows a relationship only between power bases and readiness level. There also appears to be a direct relationship between the kind of power bases a person has and the corresponding leadership style that will be effective for that person in influencing the behavior of others at various readiness levels.

Coercive Power

A follower low in readiness generally needs strong directive behavior in order to become productive. To engage effectively in this telling style, the leader may have to use coercive power. The behavior of people at low levels of readiness seems to be influenced by the awareness that costs will be incurred if they do not learn and follow the rules of the game. Thus, sanctions—the perceived power to fire, transfer, demote, and so on—may be an important way that a leader can induce compliance from people who are unable and unwilling. The leader's coercive power may motivate the followers to avoid the punishment or "cost" by doing what the leader tells them to do.

Connection Power

As a follower begins to move from readiness level R1 to R2, directive behavior is still needed, but increases in supportive behavior are also important. The telling and selling leadership styles appropriate for these levels of readiness may become more effective if the leader has connection power. The

Figure 9-3
Power Bases Necessary to Influence People's Behavior at Various Levels of Readiness

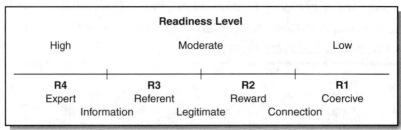

Chapter 9   Situational Leadership, Perception, and the Impact of Power

possession of this power base may induce compliance because a follower at these readiness levels tends to aim at avoiding punishments or gaining rewards available through the powerful connection.

Reward Power

A follower at a low to moderate level of readiness often needs high amounts of supportive behavior and directive behavior. This selling style is often enhanced by reward power. Because individuals at this readiness level are willing to try on new behavior, the leader needs to be perceived as having access to rewards in order to gain compliance and reinforce growth in the desired direction.

Legitimate Power

The leadership styles that tend to influence effectively those at both moderate levels of readiness (R2 and R3) are selling and participating. Legitimate power seems to be helpful in effective use of these styles. By the time a follower reaches these moderate levels of readiness, the power of the leader has become legitimized. That is, the leader is able to induce compliance or influence behavior by virtue of the leader's position in the organizational hierarchy.

Referent Power

A follower at a moderate to high level of readiness tends to need little direction but still requires a high level of communication and support from the leader. This participating style may be effectively utilized if the leader has referent power. This source of power is based on good personal relations with the follower. With people who are able but unwilling or insecure, this power base tends to be an important means of instilling confidence and providing encouragement, recognition, and other supportive behavior. When that occurs, followers will generally respond in a positive way, permitting the leader to influence them because they like, admire, or identify with the leader.

Information Power

The leadership styles that tend to motivate followers effectively at above-average readiness levels (R3 and R4) are participating and delegating. Information power seems to be helpful in using these two styles. People at these levels of readiness look to the leader for information to maintain or improve performance. The transition from moderate to high readiness may be facilitated if the follower knows that the leader is available to clarify or explain issues and provide access to pertinent data, reports, and correspondence when needed. Through this information power, the leader is able to influence people who are both willing and able.

Expert Power

A follower who develops to a high level of readiness often requires little direction or support. This follower is able and willing to perform the tasks required and tends to respond most readily to a delegating leadership style and expert power. Thus, a leader may gain respect from and influence most readily a person who has both competence and confidence by possessing expertise, skill, and knowledge that this follower recognizes as important.

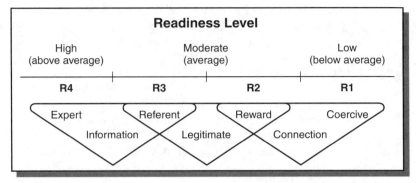

Figure 9-4
Power Bases Necessary to Influence People at Various Readiness Levels

An easy way to think about sources of power in terms of making diagnostic judgments is to draw a triangle, as shown in Figure 9-4, around the three power bases necessary to influence below-average, average, and above-average levels of readiness.

A way to examine the high probability power base for a specific readiness level is to draw inverted triangles, as shown in Figure 9-5. Note that R1 and R4, the extreme readiness levels, include only two power bases instead of three.

Developing Sources of Power

Although these seven power bases are potentially available to any leader as a means of influencing the behavior of others, it is important to note that there is significant variance in the powers that leaders may actually possess. Some leaders have a great deal of power; others have very little. Part of the variance in actual power is due to the organization and the leader's position in the organization (position power), and part is due to individual differences among the leaders themselves (personal power), as shown in Figure 9-6.

The power bases that are most relevant at the below-average levels of readiness tend to be those that the organization or others can bestow upon the leader. The power bases that influence people who are above average in readiness must, to a large degree, be earned from the people the leader is at-

Figure 9-5
Power Bases Necessary to Influence People's Behavior at Specific Levels of Readiness

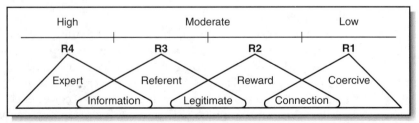

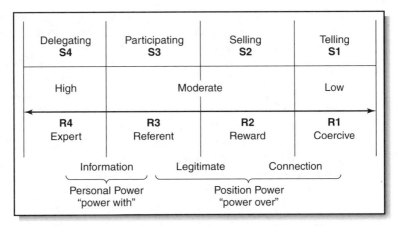

Figure 9-6
Summary of Relationships among Power Bases, Readiness
Level, and Leadership Style

tempting to influence. Therefore, we suggest that position power and the phrase "power over" are most descriptive with coercive, connection, reward, and legitimate power bases; and we suggest that personal power and the phrase "power with" more accurately describe the effect on behavior from referent, information, and expert power.

Sources of Power

Just as some leaders start off with little power and gradually build and develop various power sources, other leaders gradually let their power bases erode and lose them. Why? Before we answer that question, managers need to understand what the sources of position and personal power are.

As we discussed earlier, position power can be thought of simply as the authority that is delegated down in an organization. Managers do, however, have some impact on how much position (coercive, connection, reward, and legitimate) power they get. The extent to which they develop rapport, confidence, and trust between themselves and senior management will determine how willing those above will be to delegate power. In that sense, position power is something that a manager has to earn on a day-to-day basis.

The same can be said about personal power, except that the personal (reward, information, and expert) power that managers possess depends on the confidence and trust those managers generate from the people they are attempting to influence. For example, people might think that some leaders have charisma and other leaders don't. Leaders don't have charisma; followers give leaders charisma. We have all seen that phenomenon with elected officials. They are often carried into office because of their charisma, but when their actions do not gain general approval, they may lose their charisma overnight. Again, this is not to say that managers do not have some impact on how much personal power they get, but it's something that they have to earn on a day-to-day basis.

Position power and personal power bases together constitute an interaction-influence system. That is, power does not develop in a vacuum. Each power base tends to affect each of the other power bases. Thus, the extent to which people are willing to grant personal power to a manager depends a great deal on their perception of a leader's ability to provide rewards, punishment, or sanctions (position power). At the same time, the willingness of managers above a leader to delegate position power is often determined by the extent to which they perceive that leader as being liked and respected and having information and expertise (personal power) with their people. Keep in mind that we did not say how much personal power or position power affects whether leaders will be delegated authority or treated with respect. As we have noted before, it is the perception that others have of those power bases that is crucial. So, the key word, perhaps, in the whole area of the behavioral sciences is *perception.*

Eroding Sources of Power

Because leaders have only a limited amount of power available to them, one would hope for their sake that they would hold on to whatever power bases they have. Yet, some leaders who start off with significant power gradually lose their power bases and let them erode. The key to avoiding such erosion is using your power bases. For example, a leader could have a significant amount of coercive power but gradually lose it by threatening. If a leader continually threatens followers with some kind of punishment, but never delivers the punishment, the people will start to think that the leader really does not have any coercive power. Similarly, leaders can lose their reward power if everyone gets the same reward whether they perform or not, or just because they have seniority in the industry, or are older in the family. Some parents establish age requirements when kids can get to do things. "When you're 13, you'll be able to stay out past 10 P.M. When you're 16, you'll be able to stay home alone." The problem with using age as a factor in determining when people can do things is that all they have to do is get older. When age is used as the determining factor, reward power as a parent or a leader is lost. What is happening is that people are getting rewards for being older, not for being more ready to take responsibility.

Connection power can be eroded when people begin to see that the sponsor or connection does not make any disciplinary interventions or provide any favors or sanctions. In other words, to be maintained, connection power needs occasional interventions from the sponsor. Managers can lose their legitimate power by not making decisions that people think they ought to make, given their position. Erosion of this power base can also occur if a manager continually makes decisions that are not fruitful. After a while, their staff members will no longer look to them to make decisions even if they have the title of senior research scientist or department chairman.

This process also works with referent power. When you give "strokes" to those who are performing and the same strokes to those who are not performing, you begin to erode your referent power. If people do not have to earn strokes, then you no longer have referent power.

Leaders also have to be careful about eroding their information and expert power, particularly if they give away expertise and information to people whose goals are not organizational goals. If you give away too much information and knowledge, eventually those people will not need you. The only way you can get around this problem is to continually develop new information and new expertise so that they have to come back to the source.

If leaders let their power bases erode, they will also reduce the effectiveness of their leadership attempts. For example, an effective telling (S1) leadership style depends on having some coercive power. If leaders are not seen as being able to deliver punishments and sanctions, their use of that style is limited.

The same can be said about a selling (S2) style. Without some control over rewards, leaders are seen as not able to reinforce or reward increased performance as people grow and develop their skills.

A participating (S3) style won't work if people don't like and respect a manager. If a manager has let reward power erode because the manager hasn't been responsive to people, then a participative, high relationship style is going to be seen not as a reward, but as a punishment. Suppose a manager has ignored and left a staff member alone for a long time, then suddenly, when that person's family life begins to deteriorate, the manager tries to comfort and console the staffer. Because the manager has eroded available referent power, these supportive leadership attempts are not seen as rewards, but as sanctions and punishments. Time with the boss is not seen as a positive situation.

A manager who is supervising highly competent and motivated people needs to have some expert power to make any kind of significant intervention. If the manager has eroded information and expert power, the possibility of influencing these people in any significant way will be very limited.

Willingness to Take a Power Role

As we just noted, a person desiring a leadership role must also be willing to assume the responsibilities of that role. This means gaining and exercising power. Managing, supervising, and leading are all influencing behaviors. If a person is unwilling or unable to exercise power, any attempt to manage, supervise, or lead is doomed to failure.

Katherine Benzinger provided some special insights into the process of gaining and using power.[30] We will spend the next few paragraphs summarizing her important contributions.

Benzinger defined power as "the ability to get your way."[31] She noted that there are important differences between personal and organizational power. In the former, a person has freedom of choice as far as who to influence, and the size of the group is much smaller. In the latter, a person is not free to choose coworkers and supervisors, and there are many more people in the group. These differences are very significant, particularly in the way men and women approach these differences. Men, Benzinger observed, have been trained since childhood—particularly in athletic groups—to develop trust and respect among fellow group members, even those they may personally dislike. Women, on the other hand, when confronted with an unpleasant situation, may choose to either avoid the threatening person or to accommodate that person. We have equated leadership with influence but, as Benzinger correctly concluded, accommodation does not influence. Therefore, "The first difference between personal and organizational power is: 'In seeking organizational power, you must consciously try to build the trust and respect of your coworkers.'"[32]

Benzinger suggested that women have a tendency to rely on experience: that is, to seek a family-sized group such as their own staff or peer group as a power base. If they had control of their own staff, women believe, they would be perceived as competent and doing an effective job. But this scenario neglects contextual power—power external to one's immediate staff. Men, in Benzinger's view, assume that they have control of their immediate staff and place their primary focus of power on persons external to their unit or department. This brings up the second difference between personal and organizational power. "The second difference is the need to develop influence with a large number of people."[33]

Do You Want Power?

Benzinger suggested that "If . . . you want to climb a career ladder or influence your organization significantly, you must not only understand power, you must seek it actively and skillfully. . . . To protect yourself from frustration and burnout, you must therefore decide consciously whether you want power and are willing to do what it takes to acquire it."[34] She suggests two guidelines that are related to our previous discussion.

1. *Earning power requires a very substantial time commitment.* If you are not willing to invest the time, perhaps gaining power is not right for you.
2. *Gaining power in organizations requires confrontation.* If you are not willing to play "King of the Mountain" to get on top and stay on top, then you may not wish to seek power.[35]

Once you have decided to acquire power, you may wish to consider Benzinger's 12-step strategy:

1. Learn and use your organization's language and symbols.
2. Learn and use your organization's priorities.
3. Learn the power lines.
4. Determine who has power and get to know those people.
5. Develop your professional knowledge.
6. Develop your power skills.
7. Be proactive.
8. Assume authority.
9. Take risks.
10. Beat your own drum.
11. Meet [your supervisor's] needs.
12. Take care of yourself.[36]

Benzinger concluded this list with a worthwhile personal note: "You may discover that being powerful is not as exhausting as some people might have you believe. What's more, you might discover having power is fun—it gets things you want done."[37]

OTHER VIEWS ON DIFFERENCES BETWEEN MEN AND WOMEN MANAGERS

Other authors have commented on differences between men and women managers. Judy Rosener, in a *Harvard Business Review* article, noted that "men are more likely to use power that comes from their organizational position and formal authority, [whereas women] ascribed their power to personal characteristics like charisma, interpersonal skills, hard work, or personal contacts rather than to organizational stature."[38]

Sue Shellenbarger, however, suggests that care must be taken not to stereotype men or women too rigidly in these roles. She notes that a workforce study financed by 15 companies and foundations found that no differences existed in the way men and women managed, as viewed by those they managed. Women were sometimes seen as more sympathetic, which view, in and of itself, might be an inherent stereotype. With the workforce moving toward having more women managers, organizations should take note of this and other studies that identify few if any differences between men and women managers.[39]

WHAT ABOUT EMPOWERMENT?

One of the most written-about management themes in recent years is employee empowerment. The theme is an extension of delegation and suggests that managers can carve off slices from their lump of authority and distribute them to employees. The results, in William J. Ransom's view, are "more rewarding than you can imagine when accomplished. You will gain more time to do the projects that only you can do. Your associates will become better at their tasks and operations will function more smoothly . . . workers will become happier and more capable."[40]

Joy Day, managing principal in the consulting firm of Colby Day & Day, relates empowerment to developing an ownership attitude among a work group. She suggests that such an attitude can generate a productivity increase of 30 percent or more that is sustainable year after year. Her steps for creating such an attitude are:

- *Identify your starting point.* Who are true contributors and who are the slackers? It is important to get the right players on your team.

- *Educate.* Employees must have comprehensive knowledge of the organization including finances, sales, and operations if they are to contribute.

- *Share the secrets.* Share what is really happening.

- *Create a daily score.* If employees know the score, they can make adjustments required to improve performance.
- *Ensure operational consistency.* Enforce operational standards to assure quality. Employees must meet customers' expectations.
- *Experiment with every element of the process/product over time in a methodical, documented way.* This is a proven approach to process improvement.
- *Tell stories about what your department and organization are doing and what they are about.* Stories give zest to the numbers.
- *Give more loyalty to your employees: After all, they are your partners now.* If you expect loyalty, you must give loyalty—*first.*
- *Expand the decision-making responsibility of your staff.* You have established guidelines through the preceding steps; now is the time to trust your partners.
- *Party hearty.* Celebrate the successes, and taste the vinegar of failure.
- *Volunteer as a group.* Charity commitments add meaning to your mutual efforts.[41]

Oren Harari, a frequent contributor to the American Management Association's *Management Review,* has a somewhat different view of empowerment.

> Your goal is not to empower, but to liberate. . . . Liberation involves freeing people from organizational constraints (including you) that inhibit their willingness to take proactive action and accountability. Power is a feeling, an experience. It is the consequence of liberation. To put it crudely, one successful manager was quoted as follows: "You know what good leadership is? Tell 'em the rules of the game, train the dickens out of them, and then get out of the way." That's liberation. Feelings of power will follow.
>
> All this empowerment stuff is a con because you cannot confer power on human beings. You cannot make anyone powerful. What you can do is create a condition where people will feel powerful, a condition where people choose to create power for themselves.[42]

We believe that these seemingly contradictory views of empowerment are correct in their context. If you consider delegating authority as setting freedom-of-action boundaries, then Harari's idea of liberation has value. Employees should be given freedom of decision-making action within prescribed, delegated boundaries. Delegation has always had limits; that is what differentiates it from abdication. If, on the other hand, you see authority as setting forth specific policies and guidelines, then the empowerment approach is more meaningful. You delegate authority to take specific actions.

We would be more inclined to support Harari's liberation view if the follower's readiness level suggests a delegating leadership style. The follower, as we will see in our discussion of contracting for leadership style in chapter 12, determines what the area of freedom will be. For a follower at readiness level R1, the area would be very small; for a follower at readiness level R4, it would be rather large, but not infinite. This is what we mean when we say, "Let the individual or group run with the ball—*but within the playing field."*

THE POWER PERCEPTION PROFILE

To provide leaders with feedback on their power bases so that they can determine which power bases they already have and which they need to develop, Hersey and Natemeyer developed the power perception profile.[43] There are two versions of this instrument: one measures self-perception of power and the other determines an individual's perception of another's power.

Development of the Power Perception Profile

The power perception profile contains 21 forced-choice pairs of reasons often given by people when asked why they do things that a leader suggests or wants them to do.

After completing the power perception profile, respondents are able to obtain a score of the relative strength of each of the seven bases of power. This score represents the perception of influence for themselves or some other leader.

One of the shortcomings of most forced-choice instruments is that they provide comparisons only between items or categories, but they do not offer any perspective on the overall scope of the concepts. In other words, a leader might score high or low on a certain power base when compared with each of the other power bases, but no indication is given of how that power base score compares with the score another leader might receive. For example, even if a leader's score on coercive power is low in relation to the other six power bases, the leader may be relatively high in coercive power when compared with other leaders the respondent has known. To correct this deficiency, the power perception profile goes one step further than most forced-choice questionnaires and asks respondents to compare the leader with other leaders they have known, in reference to each of the seven power bases.

Uses of the Power Perception Profile

The power perception profile can be used to gather data in actual organizational settings or any learning environment—for example, student or training groups. In learning groups, the instrument is particularly helpful in groups that have developed some history—that is, they have spent a considerable amount of time interacting with each other analyzing or solving cases, participating in simulations or other training exercises, and so on. In this kind of situation, it is recommended that the group fill out one instrument together, using a particular member as the subject and arriving at a consensus on each of the items on the instrument. During each discussion, the person whose power bases are being examined should play a nonparticipant role. That person should not ask any questions or attempt to clarify, justify, or explain actions. An appropriate response might be, "Could you tell me more about that?" or "I'd like to hear more on that point." Then, at the end of the group's assessment, the person whose power bases were being examined is given an opportunity to respond to the group's discussion. This process is repeated until every participant has had a turn to get feedback from the group.

If the power perception profile is being used to gather data in an organization, each organizational member from whom perceptions are desired should fill out a separate instrument. In this case, it is strongly suggested that the leaders not collect the data themselves. Instead, a third party who has the trust and confidence of all involved—such as a representative from personnel or human resources—should administer the questionnaire. It is also important to assure respondents that only generalized data will be shared with the leader, not the scores from any particular instrument. These suggestions are important because if leaders collect their own data, even if the instruments are anonymous, there is a tendency for some respondents to answer according to what they feel the leaders do or do not want to hear. Thus, to help establish a valid database, leaders may want to have their data gathered by a third party.

Another value of understanding power bases is important to mention. If you understand which power bases tend to influence a group of people, you have some insight into who should be given a particular project assignment or responsibility. The person you assign to a particular task should have the power bases and be comfortable in using the appropriate leadership styles that are required in a particular setting. If someone really wants an assignment and doesn't have the appropriate power bases, it's a problem of self-development. You can work out a program to build that power base or appropriate style. What all this means is that we can increase the probability of success of a particular manager if we understand the territory—if we know what power bases and corresponding leadership styles are needed to influence the people involved in the situation effectively. That's the whole concept of team building. We will be talking about that subject in much greater depth in later chapters.

SUMMARY

Whether a leader is maximizing effectiveness is not a question of style alone; it is also a question of what power bases are available to that leader and whether those power bases are consistent with the readiness levels of the individual or group that the leader is trying to influence. Dynamic and growing organizations are gradually moving away from reliance on power bases that emphasize "power over" and are moving toward the use of power bases that aim at gaining "power with." It is important to keep in mind that many times this change, by necessity, will be evolutionary rather than revolutionary.

ENDNOTES

1. R. M. Stogdill, *Handbook of Leadership* (New York: Free Press, 1974).
2. Many of the concepts in this chapter were first published in Paul Hersey, Kenneth H. Blanchard, and Walter E. Natemeyer, "Situational Leadership, Perception, and the Impact of Power," *Group and Organizational Studies*, 4, no. 4 (December 1979), pp. 418–428.
3. Adapted from Paul Hersey, *The Situational Leader* (Escondido, CA: Center for Leadership Studies, 1985), p. 27.
4. This section on defining power and other concepts originated with Walter E. Natemeyer, *An Empirical Investigation of the Relationships between Leader Behavior, Leader Power Bases, and Subordinate Performance and Satisfaction*, an unpublished dissertation, University of Houston, August 1975.
5. James Hillman, *Kinds of Power* (New York: Currency-Doubleday, 1995), p, 97.
6. David C. McClelland and David H. Burnham, "Power is the Great Motivator," *Harvard Business Review*, January-February 1995, p. 134.
7. John B. Miner, *Organizational Behavior* (New York: Random House, 1988), p. 481.
8. *Ibid.*
9. Stephen P. Robbins, *Essentials of Organizational Behavior*, 4th ed. (Upper Saddle River, NJ: Prentice Hall, 1994), p. 152.
10. M. F. Rogers, "Instrumental and Infra-Resources: The Bases of Power," *American Journal of Sociology*, 79, 6 (1973), pp. 1418–1433.
11. Amitai Etzioni, *A Comparative Analysis of Complex Organizations* (New York: Free Press, 1961).
12. Niccolo Machiavelli, "Of Cruelty and Clemency, Whether It Is Better to Be Loved or Feared," *The Prince and the Discourses* (New York: Random House, 1950), chapter 17.
13. This section is adapted from Paul Hersey, *Situational Selling* (Escondido, CA: Center for Leadership Studies, 1985), pp. 14–15.
14. R. L. Peabody, "Perceptions of Organizational Authority: A Comparative Analysis," *Administrative Quarterly*, 6 (1962), pp. 463–482.
15. A. C. Filley and A. J. Grimes, "The Bases of Power in Decision Processes," *Reprint Series 104* (Industrial Relations Research Institute, University of Wisconsin, 1967).
16. K. D. Beene, *A Conception of Authority* (New York: Teachers College, Columbia University, 1943).
17. John R. P. French and B. Raven, "The Bases of Social Power," in *Studies in Social Power*, D. Cartright (Ann Arbor: University of Michigan, Institute for Social Research, 1959).
18. B. H. Raven and W. Kruglanski, "Conflict and Power," pages 177–219 in *The Structure of Conflict*, ed. P. G. Swingle (New York: Academic Press, 1975).
19. Paul Hersey and Marshall Goldsmith, "The Changing Role of Performance Management," *Training and Development Journal* (April 1980).
20. Steven Kerr, "On the Folly of Rewarding A, While Hoping for B," *Academy of Management Journal*, 18 (1975), pp. 769–783. Reprinted with commentary in *The Academy of Management Executive*, 9, no. 1, (February 1995), pp. 7–14 and an informal survey, "More on the Folly," pp. 15–16.
21. Tom Peters, "Power: Get It and Use It with These 13 Secrets," *Star Tribune*, August 2, 1994, p. 2D.
22. K. R. Student, "Supervisory Influence and Work-Group Performance," *Journal of Applied Psychology*, 52, no. 3 (1968), pp. 188–194.
23. J. G. Bachman, C. G. Smith, and J. A. Slesinger, "Control, Performance, and Satisfaction: An Analysis of Structural and Individual Effects," *Journal of Personality and Social Psychology*, 4, no. 2 (1966), pp. 127–136.
24. J. G. Bachman, D. G. Bowers, and P. M. Marcus, "Bases of Supervisory Power: A Comparative Study in Five Organizational Settings," in *Control in Organizations*, Arnold S. Tannenbaum (New York: McGraw-Hill, 1968).
25. J. M. Ivancevich and J. H. Donnelly, "Leader Influence and Performance," *Personnel Psychology*, 23, no. 4 (1970), 539–549.
26. R. J. Burke and D. S. Wilcox, "Bases of Supervisory Power and Subordinate Job Satisfactions," *Canadian Journal of Behavioral Science* (1971).
27. D. W. Jamieson and K. W. Thomas, "Power and Conflict in the Student-Teacher Relationship," *Journal of Applied Behavioral Science*, 10, no. 3 (1974).

28. Natemeyer, *An Empirical Investigation of the Relationships between Leader Behavior, Leader Power Bases, and Subordinate Performance and Satisfaction.*
29. Hersey, Blanchard, and Natemeyer, "Situational Leadership, Perception, and the Impact of Power."
30. Katherine Benzinger, "The Powerful Woman," *Hospital Forum* (May–June 1982), pp. 15–20.
31. *Ibid.*, p. 15.
32. *Ibid.*, pp. 15–16.
33. *Ibid.*, p. 16.
34. *Ibid.*, pp. 16–17.
35. *Ibid.*
36. *Ibid.*, pp. 18–20.
37. *Ibid.*, p. 20. For a related discussion, see Jane Covey Brown and Rosabeth Moss Kanter, "Empowerment: Key to Effectiveness," *Hospital Forum*, May–June 1982, pp. 6–12.
38. Judy B. Rosener, "Ways Women Lead," *Harvard Business Review,* November–December 1990, pp. 119–125.
39. Sue Shellenbarger, "Work-Force Study Finds Loyalty Is Weak, Divisions of Race and Gender Are Deep," *Wall Street Journal,* September 3, 1993, pp. B1, 9.
40. William J. Ransom, "There Is Profit in Empowerment," *Industrial Engineering,* February 1992.
41. Joy Day, "Getting the Edge: The Attitude of Ownership," *Supervision,* June 1999, pp. 3–5, 8.
42. Oren Harari, "Stop Empowering Your People," *Management Review,* November 1993, pp. 26–29.
43. This instrument was developed by Paul Hersey and Walter E. Natemeyer. Published by the Center for Leadership Studies, Escondido, CA, 92025.

Chapter 10

Situational Leadership: Training and Development

In chapter 4, we stated that in evaluating performance, a manager ought to consider both output (productivity) and intervening variables (the condition of the human resources). We urged that both these factors should be examined in light of both short- and long-term organizational goals. If the importance of intervening variables is accepted, then one must assume that one of the responsibilities of managers, regardless of whether they are parents in the home or managers in a business setting, is developing the human resources for which they are responsible. Managers need to devote time to nurture the leadership potential, motivation, morale, climate, commitment to objectives, and the decision-making, communication, and problem-solving skills of their people. Thus, an important role for managers is the development of the task-relevant readiness of their followers. ✧

We think it is vital to emphasize this developmental aspect of Situational Leadership. Without emphasizing this aspect, there is a danger that managers could use Situational Leadership to justify the use of any behavior they wanted. Because the concept contends that there is no "best" leadership style, the use of any style could be supported merely by saying "the individual or group was at such-and-such readiness level." Thus, although close supervision and direction might be necessary initially when working with individuals who have had little experience in directing their own behavior, it should be recognized that this style is only a first step. In fact, managers should be rewarded for helping their people develop and be able to assume more and more responsibility on their own. For example, in some progressive companies in which we have worked, we have been able to introduce a new policy, which essentially states: No managers will be promoted in this organization unless they do at least two things. First, they have to do a good job in what they are being asked to do—that is, good "bottom-line" results (output variables). Second, they have to have a ready replacement who can take over their job tomorrow (intervening variables).

This means that using a leadership style with a high probability of success for working with a given level of readiness is not really enough. These managers may be accomplishing their goals, but their responsibilities should not stop there. Besides achieving goals, managers must develop their human resources (their followers).

INCREASING EFFECTIVENESS

Rensis Likert found that employee-centered supervisors who use general supervision tend to have higher-producing sections than job-centered supervisors who use close supervision.[1] We emphasize the word *tend* because there are exceptions, which are evident even in Likert's data. What Likert found was that employees generally respond well to their supervisor's high expectations and genuine confidence in them and try to justify the supervisor's expectations of them. Employees with high performance will reinforce their supervisor's high trust for them; it is easy to trust and respect people who meet or exceed your expectations.

Cases and other evidence available from scientific research reveal:

- What managers expect of their followers and the way they treat their followers largely determine the followers' performance and career progress.
- A unique characteristic of superior managers is their ability to create high performance expectations that followers fulfill.
- Less effective managers fail to develop similar expectations, and, as a consequence, the productivity of their followers suffers.
- Followers, more often than not, appear to do what they believe they are expected to do.

When people respond to the high expectations of their managers with high performance, we call that the *effective cycle,* as illustrated in Figure 10-1.

Yet, as we pointed out earlier, the concentration on output variables as a means of evaluating effectiveness tends to lead to short-run, task-oriented leader behavior. This style, in some cases, does not allow much room for a trusting relationship with employees. Instead, employees are told what to do and how to do it, with little consideration expressed for their ideas or feelings. After a while, the employees respond with minimal effort and resent-

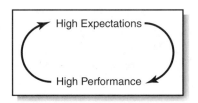

Figure 10-1
Effective Cycle

High Expectations

High Performance

ment; these behaviors lead to low performance. Reinforced by low expectations, it becomes a vicious cycle, which we call the *ineffective cycle.* Many other examples could be given that result in this all-too-common problem in organizations, as shown in Figure 10-2.

These cycles are depicted as static, but in reality they are dynamic. The situation tends to get better or worse. For example, high expectations result in high performance, which reinforces the high expectations and produces even higher productivity. It almost becomes an upward-spiraling effect, as illustrated in Figure 10-3. In many cases, this spiraling effect is caused by an increase in leverage created through the use of the motivators. As people perform, they are given more responsibility and opportunities for achievement, growth, and development.

This spiraling effect can also occur in a downward direction. Low expectations result in low performance, which reinforces the low expectations and produces even lower productivity. It becomes a downward-spiraling effect, as shown in Figure 10-4. If this downward spiraling continues long enough, the cycle may reach a point where it cannot be turned around in a short period of time because of the large reservoir of negative experience that has built up in the organization. Much of the focus and energy are directed toward perceived problems in the environment, such as interpersonal relations and respect for supervision rather than toward the work itself. Reaction to deteriorating hygiene factors takes such forms as hostility, undermining, and slowdown in work performance. When this happens, even if a manager actually changes behavior, the credibility gap based on long-term experience is such that the response is still distrust and skepticism rather than change.

One alternative that is sometimes necessary at this juncture is to bring in a new manager from the outside. The reason this has a high probability of success is that the sum of the past experience of the people involved with the new manager is likened to a "clean slate," and thus new manager behaviors are seen as more believable: Change in employee behavior is more likely to occur. This was evident in the case of Plant Y described by Robert Guest, which was discussed in chapter 7. The ineffective cycle had been in a

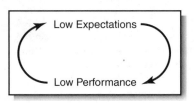

Low Expectations

Low Performance

Figure 10-2
Ineffective Cycle

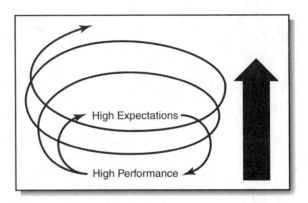

Figure 10-3
Upward-Spiraling
Effect of the Effective
Cycle

downward spiral far past the point where Stewart would have had an opportunity to make significant changes. But, with the introduction of a new manager, Cooley, significant changes were possible.

Breaking the Ineffective Cycle

Although new managers may be in a good position to initiate change in a situation that has been spiraling downward, they still do not have an easy task. Essentially, they have to break the ineffective cycle. There are at least two alternatives available to managers in this situation. Either they can fire the low-performing personnel and hire people whom they expect to perform well, or they can respond to low performance with high expectations and trust.

The first choice is not always possible because competent replacements are not readily available or the people involved have some form of job security (civil service or union tenure), which means they cannot be fired without considerable cost in time, energy, and trouble.

The latter choice for managers is also difficult. In effect, the attempt is to change the expectations or behavior of their people. It is especially difficult for managers to have high expectations and trust for people who have shown no indication that they deserve either. The key, then, is to change appropriately.

From our work with Situational Leadership, we have identified two cycles that managers can use for changing or maximizing the task-relevant readiness of their followers—the developmental cycle and the regressive

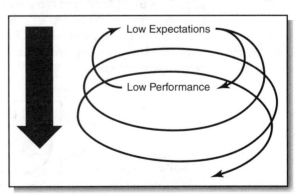

Figure 10-4
Downward-Spiraling
Effect of the
Ineffective Cycle

cycle. In this chapter we will discuss the developmental cycle. In chapter 11, we will present the regressive cycle.

DEVELOPMENTAL CYCLE

The role managers play in developing the readiness level of their people is extremely important. Too often, managers do not take responsibility for the performance of their people, especially if they are not doing well. If they're having problems, often managers will say, "I have an example of a Peter Principle," and not take responsibility for the poor performance. It has been our experience that managers who have to fire someone or find a place to hide them (this is what Peter called a "lateral arabesque"), or who are downright worried about someone's performance, should look in the mirror. In most cases, the biggest cause of the performance problem is looking back at them. Managers are responsible for making their people "winners," and this is what the developmental cycle is all about. Managers are involved in the developmental cycle any time they attempt to increase the current readiness level of an individual or group in some aspect of their work. In other words, the developmental cycle is a growth cycle.

WHAT'S IN IT FOR THE MANAGER?

When followers are at low levels of readiness, the manager must take the responsibility for the "traditional" management functions such as planning, organizing, motivating, and controlling.[2] The manager's role is that of supervisor of the group. However, when managers develop their people and have followers at high levels of readiness, the followers can take over much of the responsibility for these day-to-day traditional management functions. The manager's role can then change from supervisor to the group's representative in the next level of the organization.

If they develop followers who can take responsibility for their own tasks on a day-to-day basis, managers can invest their time in the "high-payoff" management functions, the "linking-pin" activities that enhance the group's performance. These functions include acquiring resources necessary for maximizing the group's productivity, communicating both horizontally and vertically, and coordinating the group's efforts with those of other departments to improve overall productivity. The manager, instead of getting trapped in minutiae, has time for long-range strategic planning and creativity.

Initially, close supervision and direction are helpful when working with individuals who have little experience in directing their own behavior. The manager recognizes that this style is only a first step. In order to maximize their potential in the high-payoff functions, managers must change their style and take an active role in helping others grow. The development of followers depends not only on the manager's behavior, but also on values and expectations.

What Do We Want to Influence?

The first question managers have to ask when they are thinking about developing their people is: What area of my employees' work do I want to influence? In other words, what are their responsibilities or goals and objectives? A foreman, for example, might want to influence productivity, quality, waste, absenteeism, accident rate, and so on. A university department chair might want to affect the faculty's writing and research, teaching, and community service.

Once the objectives or responsibilities are identified and understood, managers must clearly specify what constitutes good performance in each area, so that both managers and employees know when performance is approaching the desired level. What does a good sales record mean? Does it mean a certain number of sales made or dollar volume of sales? What is meant by "developing your people" or "being a good administrator"? Managers have to specify what good performance looks like. Just telling a person "I want you to review credit histories" is not as helpful as saying, "I want you to review the credit histories of our ten largest customers this week and give me a one-page report on each by Friday afternoon." For managers and staff members to know how well someone is doing, good performance has to be clearly specified. Managers cannot change and develop their followers' behavior in areas that are unclear.

How Is the Person Doing Now?

Before beginning the developmental cycle with an individual in a work situation, the manager must decide how well that person is doing right now. In other words, what is the person's readiness level right now in a specific aspect of the job? How able is the person to take responsibility for specific behavior? How willing or motivated is the person? As was discussed earlier, people do not have a degree of readiness in any total sense. How can we know what a person's readiness level is in a given situation?

Determining Readiness

In assessing the readiness level of an individual, we will have to make judgments about that person's ability and willingness. Where do we get the information to make these judgments? We can either ask the person or observe the person's behavior. We could ask a person such questions as, "How well do you think you are doing at such and such?" or "How do you feel about doing that?" or "Are you or are you not enthusiastic and excited about it?" Obviously, with some people, asking for their own assessment of their readiness won't be productive. However, it has been surprising how even young children are able to share that kind of information. Phil and Jane learned that when they used to ask their 2-year-old daughter, Lee, to do something. Often Lee would reply, "I can't want to!" When translated, what Lee was really saying is, "I'm both unable and unwilling to do what you want me to do." If Lee's parents still wanted her to do it, they soon learned that they had to direct and closely supervise her behavior in this area (S1—"telling"). As children get older, they can play an even more significant role in determining their own readiness level. That process will be discussed in much more detail in chapter 12.

You might be wondering whether people will always tell their managers the truth or just tell what is necessary to keep the manager off their backs. Managers who doubt what their people tell them about their ability or willingness to do something can simply observe the staff members' behavior. Ability can be determined by examining past performance. Has the person done well in this area before or has performance been poor? Does the staff member have the necessary knowledge to perform well in the area or does that person not know how to do what needs to be done?

Willingness can be determined by watching a person's behavior in a particular case. What is the person's interest level? Does the person seem enthusiastic or interested? What is the person's commitment to this area? Does the person appear to enjoy doing things in this area or merely anxious to get them over with? Is the person self-confident and secure in this area, or does the person lack confidence and feel insecure? Remember that people can be at any of four levels of readiness in each of their various areas of responsibility. A person's readiness level gives us a good clue as to how to begin any further development of that individual. If a manager wants to influence a staff member in an area in which the person is both unable and unwilling (low readiness level), the manager must begin the developmental cycle by directing, controlling, and closely supervising (telling) the staff member's behavior. If, however, the person is willing (motivated) to do something, but not able to do it (low to moderate readiness), the manager must begin the cycle by both directing and supporting (selling) the desired behavior. If the person is able to do something without direction, but is unwilling to do it or is insecure (moderate to high readiness), the manager is faced with a motivational problem. Individuals reluctant to do what they are able to do are often insecure or lacking confidence. In this case, the manager should begin the developmental cycle by using a supportive style (participating) to help the individual become secure enough to do what the individual already knows how to do. Finally, if staff members are both able and willing to direct their own behavior (high readiness), we can merely delegate responsibility to them and know that they will perform well. When that occurs, there is no need for beginning the developmental cycle. The person already has a high degree of readiness in that area.

Increasing Readiness

Managers are engaged in the developmental cycle any time they attempt to increase the task-relevant readiness of an individual or group beyond the level that individual or group has previously reached. In other words, the developmental cycle is a growth cycle.

To explain fully how the developmental cycle works, let us look at an example. Suppose a manager has been able to diagnose the environment and finds that the task-relevant readiness of a staff member is low (R1) in the area of developing a departmental budget. If the manager wants the staff member to perform well in this area without supervision, the manager must determine the appropriate leadership style for starting the developmental cycle. As can be seen in Figure 10-5, once this manager has diagnosed the readiness level of the follower as low, the appropriate style can be determined by drawing a straight line from a point on the readiness continuum to where it meets the curved line in the style-of-leader portion of the model. In this case, it would be appropriate to start the developmental cycle by using a directive, telling style (S1). What would a telling style look like in this situation?

It would involve several things for the manager. First, the manager would have to tell the staff member exactly what was involved in developing a departmental budget—taking inventory, processing personnel and materials requests, comparing current costs with last year's budget, and so on. Second, the manager would begin to show the staff member how to do each of the tasks involved. Thus, telling in a teaching situation involves "show and tell"; the staff member must be told what to do and then shown how to do it. Although this telling style is high on direction and low on support, the manager is not necessarily being unfriendly to the staff member. Low supportive

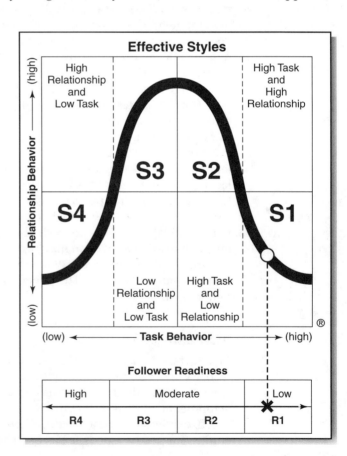

Figure 10-5
Determining an Appropriate Leadership Style

behavior in this situation merely means that the manager is not patting the staff member on the back before the member has earned it. Till then, the manager emphasizes explaining the what, when, where, and how of the job.

If the manager uses an S1 telling style in this situation, the departmental budget will probably be done fairly well, because the manager is working closely with the staff member. But if this same manager or leader assumes a responsibility to increase the task-relevant readiness of the follower, then the manager has to be willing to take a risk and begin to delegate some responsibility to the followers. This is particularly true when supervising an individual or group that has not assumed much responsibility in the past. Yet, if one is going to develop people—children in the home, employees on the job—one has to take that risk. Although taking a risk is an inherent part of the developmental cycle, managers have to keep the degree of risk reasonable; it should not be too high. For example, suppose a mother wants to teach her 8-year-old daughter how to wash the dishes. The risk is a few broken dishes. It would be wise, then, to start the daughter off on old dishes, or even plastic dishes, rather than Grandma's priceless bone china. It's not a question of whether to take a risk or not; it's a matter of taking a calculated risk.

Successive Approximations

If a manager asks a staff member to do something the member has never been taught to do and expects good performance the first time, and doesn't offer any help to the staff member, the manager has set the person up for failure and punishment. Thus begins the widely used "tell, leave alone, and then 'zap'" approach to managing people. The manager tells the staff member what to do (without bothering to find out if the person knows how to do it), leaves the staff member alone (expecting immediate results), and then yells at and "zaps" the staff member when the desired behavior does not follow.

If the manager in our budget example used that approach, the events might look something like this. The manager might assume that anyone could prepare the departmental budget. So the manager tells the staff member to prepare the budget and have it within 10 days. Not bothering to analyze whether the staff member is able or willing to prepare the budget alone, the manager gives the order and then goes about his own responsibilities. When the staff member produces the budget 10 days later, the manager finds all kinds of mistakes and problems with it and screams and yells at the staff member about the poor quality of the work.

Managers should remember that no one (including themselves!) learns how to do anything all at once. We learn a little bit at a time. As a result, if a manager wants someone to do something completely new, the manager should reward the slightest progress the person makes in the desired direction.

Many parents use this process without really being aware of it. For example, how do you think we teach a child to walk? Imagine if we stood Eric up and said, "Walk," and then, when he fell down, we spanked him for not walking. Sound ridiculous? Of course. But it's not really any different from the manager's anger with the staff member about the poorly prepared budget. A child spanked for falling down will not try to walk because the child knows falling down leads to punishment. At this point, Eric is not even sure what his legs are for. Therefore, parents usually first teach children how to stand up. If the child stays up even for a second or two, his parents get excited and hug and kiss him, call his grandmother, and the like. Next, when the child can stand and hold onto a table, his parents again hug and kiss him. The same happens when he takes his first step, even if he falls down. Whether or not his parents know it, they are positively rewarding the child for small accomplishments as he moves closer and closer to the desired behavior—walking.

Thus, in attempting to help an individual or group develop—to get them to take more and more responsibility for performing a specific task—a leader must first delegate some responsibility (not too much or failure might result); and second, reward as soon as possible any behavior in the desired direction. This process should continue as the individual's behavior comes closer and closer to the leader's expectations of good performance. What would relationship behavior look like in this situation?

Relationship behavior would involve providing encouragement (positive strokes) and reinforcement. Positive reinforcement is anything that is desired or needed by an individual whose behavior is being reinforced. Whereas reducing task behavior precedes the desired behavior, relationship behavior, or positive reinforcement, follows the desired behavior and increases the likelihood of its recurring. It is important to remember that reinforcement must immediately follow any behavior in the desired direction. Reinforcement at a later time will be of less help in getting the individual or group to do something they've never done before on their own.

This two-step process of (1) reducing the amount of direction and supervision and (2) after adequate performance follows, increasing socioemotional support (relationship behavior) is known as *positively reinforcing successive approximations.*

Suppose a manager wanted to change leadership style with an individual from point A to point C along the curved line or curvilinear function of Situational Leadership, as illustrated in Figure 10-6. Step 1 would be to delegate some responsibility by decreasing task behavior to point B. This is a risky step, because the manager is turning over the direction and the supervision of some of the tasks to the follower. If the follower responds well to the increased responsibility, then it is appropriate to engage in step 2—positively reinforcing this behavior by increasing socioemotional support (relationship behavior) to the higher level point C, as shown in Figure 10-6.

A leader must be careful not to delegate too much responsibility too rapidly. Doing so is a common error. Delegating responsibility before the follower can handle it may be setting the follower up for failure and frustration that could prevent that person from wanting to take additional responsibility in the future. The process is often started off by good intentions. The manager provides direction and structure but then moves too quickly to a "leave-alone" leadership style. This abrupt movement from telling to delegating assumes that telling is learning. The manager is likely to return to style 1 rapidly in a punitive way if the job is not getting done.

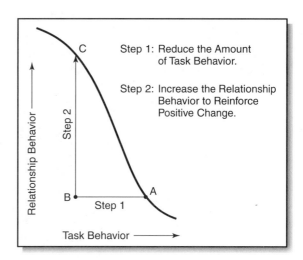

Figure 10-6
Two-Step Process of the Developmental Cycle

In addition, a manager should not increase socioemotional support (relationship behavior) without first getting the desired performance; in other words, a manager should not positively reinforce nonperformance. A manager who does may be viewed as a soft touch. That is why the manager in our example does not immediately move from point A to point C along the curved line in Figure 10-6. If the manager moved from point A to point C without some evidence that the individual could assume responsibility at Point B, it would be like giving the reward before the person had earned it. It would be like paying a person $20 an hour right now who at present is worth only $5 an hour. For many people, if you gave them $20 an hour up front, there would be very little incentive to improve their performance. Thus, the leader should develop the readiness of followers slowly on each task that they must perform, using less task behavior and more relationship behavior as they become more willing and able to take responsibility. When an individual's performance is low on a specific task, one must not expect drastic changes overnight.

If the manager (in our example) finds that the follower is unable to handle that much added responsibility when task behavior is decreased to point B, the manager might have to return to a moderate level of direction (where the follower is able to take responsibility) somewhere between point A and point B. This new level of task behavior is indicated by point B′ in Figure 10-7. If the follower is now able to be effective at that level, then the manager can appropriately increase socioemotional support (relationship behavior) to point C′. Although this level of socioemotional support is less than depicted at point C, it is appropriate to the amount of task behavior that the follower, at that time, is able to assume.

As shown in Figure 10-8, this two-step process—cutting back structure and then increasing socioemotional support if the follower can respond to the additional responsibility—tends to continue in small increments until the individual is assuming moderate levels of readiness. This continual decreasing

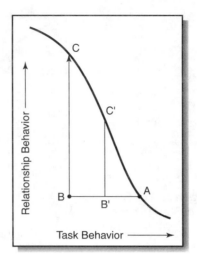

Figure 10-7
Adjustment When
Growth Expectation
is Too High

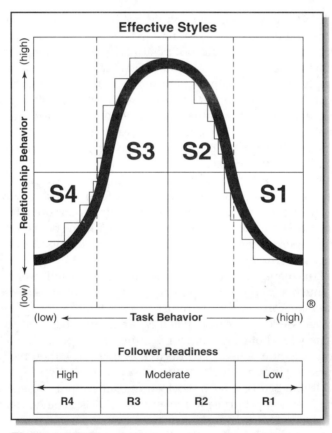

Figure 10-8
Developmental Cycle As People Develop over Time.
"Steps" along the Curve Represent Successive
Approximations.

of task behavior does not mean that the individual will have less structure, but that the structure can now be internally provided by the follower, rather than being externally imposed by the leader.

An interesting phenomenon occurs in the developmental cycle when the high point of the curvilinear function in the leadership style portion of the model is reached. This is where the function crosses the mean, or average, of task behavior. Past this point, a leader who is appropriately using leadership style 3 or style 4 is supervising people at moderate to high levels of readiness (R3 and R4). At that time, the process changes and becomes one whereby the leader not only reduces structure (task behavior), but, when the followers can handle their responsibility, reduces socioemotional support as well. This continuation of the successive approximation process is illustrated by the downward steps in Figure 10-8.

Sometimes the following question is raised: Doesn't the reduction of socioemotional support mean that there is a lack of confidence and trust between manager and follower? In reality, when a manager reduces the amount of socioemotional support and structure appropriately, it indicates that there is more mutual trust and confidence between the leader and the followers.

This relationship suggests that as people change, their motives and needs hierarchy often change, too. For example, people who have low levels of readiness tend to view increased socioemotional support and facilitating behavior as positive reinforcement. In fact, leaving them too much on their own would create insecurities and help reinforce fear and anxiety. As a result, this low relationship behavior could be perceived as punishment rather than reward.

On the other hand, as people move to high levels of readiness, they do not require as much encouragement. As people become high on task-relevant readiness, one way the leader can demonstrate confidence and trust in the follower(s) is to leave them more and more on their own. Just as socioemotional support from the leader tends to be positive reinforcement for persons with low levels of readiness, too much socioemotional support or relationship behavior for people at high levels of readiness is not seen as a reward. In fact, this supportive behavior is often seen as dysfunctional and can be interpreted by these high-readiness people as a lack of confidence and trust on the part of the leader.

Time and the Developmental Cycle

There is no set blueprint in terms of the amount of time necessary to develop an individual or group. A manager may be doing very well to move a group from readiness level 1 to level 2 over a period of 18 months to 2 years. On the other hand, within that group there may be an individual or several individuals who will develop much more rapidly than the group as a whole. Thus, time is a function of the complexity of the job being performed and the performance potential of the individual or group. For example, one might take someone on a specific task through the total cycle—from low to high levels of readiness—in a matter of minutes. And yet, in other tasks with that same individual, the readiness development process may take a much greater amount of time. In fact, it could take weeks, months, or even years to move through the complete cycle in terms of appropriate leadership style from telling (S1) to delegating (S4). A short developmental process might be, for example, teaching a child to tie her shoes.

If the child has not made any attempt to learn to tie her shoes, the parent needs to provide some high task behavior for the child. The child has low readiness on this task, so the parent should explain what to do, how to do it, and where to do it. In essence, the parent must move into the early stages of coaching and counseling by holding the child's hands while guiding her through the motions of tying a shoelace. As the child begins to show the ability to do some shoe-tying functions, the parent reduces the amount of telling behavior and increases, to some extent, supportive behavior. "That's fine! Good! You're getting it!" And perhaps, in a matter of minutes, the behavior of the parent may change from a highly structured style to just being nearby, providing a moderate amount of structure but also high levels of verbal and nonverbal supportive and facilitative behavior. In another few minutes, the parent may leave the child to practice alone while staying close enough to make an intervention if there should be some regression. Thus, in a matter of 10 to 15 minutes, the parent has taken the child in that specific task of shoe tying from style 1 through styles 2 and 3 to almost a complete delegation of that function to the child in a manner characteristic of style 4. This does not mean that the parent's style with that child should now always be style 4. It just means that in that specific task (shoe tying), the most appropriate style to use with that child is style 4.

CHANGING READINESS THROUGH BEHAVIOR MODIFICATION

In our discussion of the developmental cycle, we made reference to behavior modification and, in particular, the concept of positively reinforcing successive approximations. This section will elaborate on some other concepts from this behavioral science field and attempt to show how these concepts provide guidelines for changing one's leadership style with shifts in readiness.

Behavior modification is a useful tool for managers and leaders because it can be applied in almost all environments. Although it may involve a reassessment of customary methods for obtaining compliance and cooperation, it has relevance for persons interested in accomplishing objectives through other people. This may not be the case with some methods of psychotherapy.

For example, one form of psychotherapy is based on the assumption that to change behavior one must start with the feelings and attitudes within an individual. The problem with psychotherapy from a practitioner's viewpoint is that it tends to be too expensive and is appropriate for use only by professionals. One way of illustrating the main difference between these two approaches is to go back to a portion of the basic motivating situation model as illustrated in Figure 10-9. The figure shows that both psychotherapy and behavior modification are interested in affecting behavior. The emphasis in psychotherapy is on analyzing the reasons underlying behaviors that are often the result of early experiences in life. Behavior modification concentrates on observed behavior and uses goals or rewards outside the individual to modify and shape behavior toward the desired performance.

Behavior modification theory is based on observed behavior and not on internal unobserved emotions, attitudes, or feelings. Its basic premise is that behavior is controlled by its immediate consequences. Behavior can be increased, suppressed, or decreased by what happens immediately after it occurs. Because probabilities are difficult to work with, we use observations of the subsequent frequency of the behavior as a measure of the effectiveness of a consequence. Five of the major concepts of reinforcement that help one to make behavioral changes are positive reinforcement, punishment, negative reinforcement, extinction, and schedule of reinforcement. In our discussions in this chapter, we have and will continue to emphasize positive reinforcement and schedule of reinforcement. In the next chapter, we will examine punishment, negative reinforcement, and extinction.

Positive Reinforcement

Positive reinforcement, as mentioned earlier, can be anything that is desired or needed by the individual whose behavior is being reinforced. A positive reinforcer tends to strengthen the response it follows and make that response more likely to recur.

Figure 10-9
Comparison of Psychotherapy and Behavior Modification

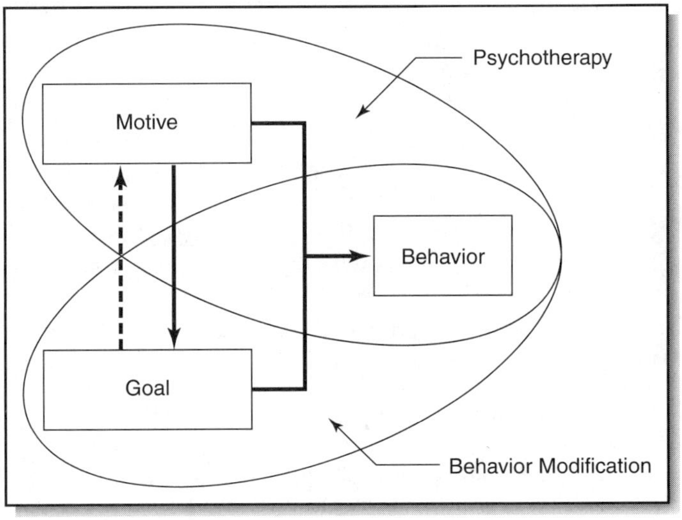

To increase the probability that desirable behavior will occur, reinforcement should immediately follow the response. Reinforcement at a later time may be of less help in making the desired behavioral change.

Individualizing Reinforcement

Reinforcement depends on the individual. What is reinforcing to one person may not be reinforcing to another. Money may motivate some people to work harder. But others may find the challenge of the job to be the most rewarding aspect of the situation. In addition, the same individual at different times will be motivated by different things, depending on current need satisfaction. Thus, at one time an individual might respond to praise as a reinforcer, but at another time that same individual might not respond to praise but be eager for more responsibility. Managers must recognize the dangers of over-generalizing and not only look for differences in their people but also be aware of the various fluctuations in need satisfaction within a person.

For a desirable behavior to be obtained, the slightest appropriate behavior exhibited by the individual in that direction must be rewarded as soon as possible. This is the basic premise for the concept of positively reinforcing successive approximations of a certain response. For example, when an individual's performance is low, one cannot expect drastic changes overnight, regardless of changes in expectations for the individual or the type of reinforcers (rewards) used.

A child learning some new behavior is not expected to give a polished performance at the outset. So, as parent, teacher, or supervisor, we use positive reinforcement as the behavior approaches the desired level of performance. Managers must be aware of any progress of their employees so as to be in a position to reinforce this change appropriately.

This approach is compatible with the concept of setting short-term goals rather than final performance criteria and then reinforcing appropriate progress toward the final goals as they are met. In setting goals, it is important that they be difficult but obtainable so that the individual proceeds along a path of gradual and systematic development. Eventually, this individual will reach the point of a polished performance.

The type of consequence individuals experience as a result of their behavior will determine the speed with which they approach the final performance. Behavior consequences can be either positive (money, praise, award, promotion); negative (scolding, fines, layoffs, embarrassment); or neutral. The difference between positive and negative consequences is important to reiterate. Positive consequences tend to result in an increase in the rewarded behavior in the future. Negative consequences merely disrupt and suppress ongoing behavior. Negative consequences tend to have neither a lasting nor a sure effect on future behavior.

Schedule of Reinforcement

Once a manager has someone engaging in a new behavior, it is important that the new behavior not be extinguished over time. To ensure that the behavior continues, managers must schedule reinforcement in an effective way.

Most experts agree that there are two main reinforcement schedules: continuous and intermittent.[3] *Continuous reinforcement* means that the individuals being changed are reinforced each time they engage in the desired new pattern. With *intermittent reinforcement*, on the other hand, not every desired response is reinforced. Reinforcement either can be completely random or it can be scheduled.

How is the concept of reinforcement related to Situational Leadership? In the early stages of a developmental cycle, whenever a manager delegates some responsibility to a person at a low level of readiness and that person responds well, the manager should provide reinforcement. That is, every time the manager cuts back on task behavior and the staff member responds well, the manager should immediately increase relationship behavior appropriately. This kind of reinforcement should continue until the manager's style is between selling and participating and the readiness of the person shifts toward readiness level 3. At that time, the manager should begin periodically to reinforce, so that the manager's decreased support and direction will not be seen by the staff member as punishment. When the style of a manager moves toward the delegating style, the person's behavior is self-reinforcing, and external strokes from the manager are significantly reduced. In sum, the developmental cycle moves from continual reinforcement to periodic reinforcement to self-reinforcement.

Consistency in Reinforcement

In chapter 5, consistency was defined as behaving the same way in similar circumstances. This practice is very important when it comes to reinforcement. Many managers are reinforcing or supportive of their people only when they feel like it. Although that's probably more convenient for managers, it is not helpful if they want to have an impact on other people's behavior. Managers should know when they are being supportive and should be careful not to be supportive when their people are performing poorly. Be consistent! Only good behavior or improvement—not just any behavior—should be rewarded.

SUMMARY

The ultimate goal of the developmental process discussed in this chapter is to shift people toward self-management so that they can eventually assume responsibility for motivating their own behavior. This ultimate goal is mentioned to reassure people who have some real doubts about the use of reinforcement. Some readers may say, "People should be motivated by a desire to succeed or the desire to please people around them, not by a hoped-for reward," or "This sounds like bribery to me," or "If I use positive reinforcement with people, won't they always expect rewards for every little thing they do?"

Although we have shared similar concerns in the past, our experience in observing people in organizations has been reassuring. We have found that people who are reinforced when they are first learning new behaviors and performance areas and then are gradually allowed to be more and more on their own turn out to be self-motivated people who have high productivity.

ENDNOTES

1. Rensis Likert, *New Patterns of Management* (New York: McGraw-Hill, 1961), p. 7.
2. This section is adapted from Paul Hersey, *The Situational Leader* (Escondido, CA: Center for Leadership Studies, 1985), pp. 92–94.
3. *Skinner for the Classroom: Selected Papers* (Champaign, IL: Research Press, 1982).

Chapter 11

The Situational Leader and Constructive Discipline

In the last chapter, we discussed how to develop readiness and independence in people through the use of positive reinforcement and changing leadership styles. You should be aware, however, that for one reason or another, people's performance may begin to slip. And one of the most difficult challenges managers face is working with performance problems. That's because discipline is often viewed as a negative intervention. But the origin of the word *discipline* is a "disciple"; *disciple* is a learner. ✧

Unfortunately, in our culture many people interpret discipline as punishment. But it doesn't always have to be punishment. The problem-solving nature of *constructive discipline* differentiates it from punitive discipline. As such, constructive discipline is designed to be a learning process that provides an opportunity for positive growth. Effective managers use constructive discipline when people slip in readiness.[1] In this chapter, we will attempt to help managers determine what needs to be done when this happens.

THE REGRESSIVE CYCLE

Managers may need to make a regressive intervention when their followers begin to behave less willingly than they have in the past. Thus, in a developmental cycle, managers are attempting to increase the task-relevant readiness of an individual or group beyond where it has been in the past. The regressive cycle involves an intervention that leaders need to make when an individual or a group is becoming less effective. Thus, in a regressive cycle, managers must use a leadership style appropriate to the current level of readiness rather than the style that might have been effective when the individual or group was at a higher level of readiness.

Decreases in readiness are often the result of what might be called "high-strength competing responses" in the environment. These responses are competing with the goals of the leader or the organization and, therefore, have become higher-strength needs to the followers in terms of their behavior.

Decreases in readiness occur for a variety of reasons. Followers can have problems with the supervisor, problems with coworkers, suffer burnout, boredom, and have other problems on or off the job. These are just a few of the things that can have a negative impact on people's performance. Let's take an example of a performance problem.

While consulting with a large research and development laboratory, one of us (Hersey) worked with a manager who was responsible for supervising John, one of the most motivated scientists on the staff. John was so committed to his job that it was not unusual to see a light under his laboratory door at eight o'clock in the evening. John often worked on weekends. He probably had more patents and made more contributions to the overall program than any other person in the laboratory.

Observations indicated that John's manager was behaving appropriately in using a low relationship–low task style (S4) for John's high readiness level (R4). Thus, rather than operating as John's supervisor, the manager was behaving more as John's representative to higher levels in the organization. John's manager was attempting to maximize John's potential by engaging in such "linking-pin" activities as acquiring necessary resources and coordinating his activities with the activities of other staff members. Although John was at a high level of readiness in this organizational setting, we learned that John's behavior was seen in a different light in his interactions in another organization—his family. In that organizational setting, his wife saw his behavior of long hours and weekends at work as an indication that he no longer cared about her and their young daughter. So, in his wife's eyes, John was behaving at a low readiness level. As a result, John went home one evening and found a note from his wife in which she told him that she had packed her bags and taken their daughter away to start a new life. John was shocked by his wife's action; he had perceived his own behavior quite differently from the way she did. He felt that he was attempting to provide for his wife and child.

On the job, with these family problems now on his mind, John's effectiveness began to decrease. It has been said many times that you should leave your family problems at home and your job problems at work, but in reality we tend to carry problems both ways. Problems at home affect our behavior in the work environment, and problems at work affect our home environment. This was certainly true in John's case. As his concerns for his family began to take effect, his performance as a scientist began to shift from readiness

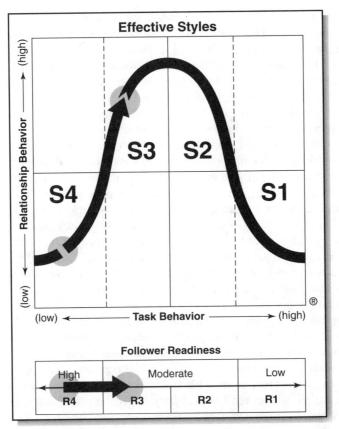

Figure 11-1
An Example of a Regressive Cycle Intervention

level 4 into level 3, as shown in Figure 11-1. Although his work emphasized technical competency, his declining psychological readiness was now affecting his performance. John did not seem to be able to cope with his problems at home. This meant that to maximize performance, John's manager had to shift behavior from style 4 to style 3 to deal with this lowering readiness level (Figure 11-1). As a result, a moderate increase in direction and structure as well as significant increases in socioemotional support, two-way communication, and the willingness to listen actively and be supportive (relationship behavior) were necessary. At this point, the situation was still more of a problem to the follower than to the leader. But the high-relationship intervention by the manager seemed to help the situation.

Once John was able to cope with his problem and put it into perspective, it was possible for his manager to move directly back to style 4. This story illustrates one of the basic differences between a developmental cycle and a regressive cycle. In a regressive cycle, once an appropriate intervention has been made, the leader may often move back to the former leadership style without going through the process of positively reinforcing successive approximations. This is because the follower has previously demonstrated an ability to function at this level. If John's performance had continued to decline, however, the situation clearly would have become a problem to both leader and follower and would have demanded an eventual shift by the manager to a high task–high relationship style (S2).

In another example, Henry, a construction engineer, was operating as a project consultant; that is, he had a special expertise that was useful for a variety of projects. As a result, rather than being assigned to a specific project, he worked with a half-dozen projects at different construction sites. Because his readiness level was extremely high, his boss was also treating him appropriately in a style 4 manner. His supervisor was acting more as a linking pin with the rest of the organization than as his supervisor.

This style was effective until Henry began to take an active interest in golf. As a result of this new high-strength competing response, Henry could no longer be reached after two o'clock in the afternoon. It took several months for his supervisor to discover Henry's unavailability, because his coworkers just assumed that he was at one of the other construction sites. The supervisor finally became aware of Henry's behavior and discovered that his golfing was impeding progress at some of the construction sites. As a result, Henry's readiness level as a project consultant in terms of the accomplishment of organizational goals had moved from readiness level 4 to readiness level 1, particularly between two and five in the afternoon. Thus, it became appropriate for the supervisor to shift his leadership style from S4 to S1 to deal with this drastic change in readiness. What might be called a *disciplinary intervention* was necessary to redefine roles and expectations for Henry. Once the manager "unfroze" Henry's new pattern, he shifted his style back to S4. This was possible, once again, because Henry had been at a high readiness level earlier. Thus, it may not be necessary for a manager to positively reinforce successive approximations before moving back to a previously appropriate style. Often in a disciplinary intervention, all managers have to do is get the attention of their followers to get them moving back in the right direction.

The regressive cycle should be taken one step at a time. If we are letting individuals operate on their own (delegating) and performance declines, we should move to participating and support their problem solving. If we are being supportive, but not directive (S3), and performance declines, we should move to selling, continuing to engage in two-way communication but also being more directive (S2). If we are providing both task and relationship behavior (S2) and performance declines, we should move to telling (S1) and reduce some of our supportive behavior and increase direction and supervision. In both the regressive and developmental cycles, we should be careful not to jump from delegating (S4) to selling (S2) or telling (S1), or from telling to participating (S3) or delegating. Making a drastic shift backward in leadership styles is one of the common mistakes managers make. It sets up the leave-alone-and-zap style of management—an approach that is not only disruptive to the relationship a manager has with a staff member, but is also disruptive to that person's growth and development.

Relationship Between Ability and Willingness in the Developmental and Regressive Cycles

Sometimes we are asked, "How can a person go from 'unable but willing or confident' (R2) to 'able but unwilling or insecure' (R3)?" Figure 11-2 answers that question. As people grow in their task-specific readiness, the behaviors they need from the leader also change. Followers who are performing at readiness levels 1 and 2 need structure and guidance in order to perform well and grow. They also need increased supportive behavior as they move from R1 to R2 as reward and reinforcement for their efforts.

Often, managers will observe followers moving from being unable and insecure, R1, to unable but confident, R2. They perform well as long as the leader is there providing direction. But as people grow and are given responsibility to accomplish tasks on their own, there is usually some apprehension with taking charge the first few times. Insecurity increases as the follower moves from R2 to R3. This is the realm of *follower-directed behavior* versus *leader-directed behavior.*

Think about the first time you had to make a presentation in front of a group. Even though you practiced in front of a mirror and on videotape, you probably had some "butterflies" and insecurity just before the moment of truth. But after you had made a few successful presentations, you became both able and confident about performing on your own. Your insecurity came about, in part, because the leader was not right there to bail you out when you got in trouble.

Figure 11-2 further clarifies the ability and willingness issues. Performance slippage in the short run is usually a willingness problem. It is not that an individual's or a group's ability has deteriorated significantly, but it is the use of ability that is causing the performance slippage. It is a motivation problem, not an ability problem. So if performance starts to slip, the person may be giving verbal and nonverbal cues about being upset with the boss, with a peer, with the organization about not getting an expected raise or promotion, or whatever it happens to be. The person's mental attitude is now focused on personal troubles rather than work requirements. If there are problems at home, the same things may occur.

As illustrated in Figure 11-2, first comes the decline in willingness, as shown by the top gray line, followed by a decline in performance, shown by the bottom darker line. There is a lead-lag relationship. There is another related point. During the developmental cycle, issues of confidence or insecurity predominate psychological readiness; during the regressive cycle, issues of willingness and commitment predominate.

SOME THINGS TO REMEMBER WHEN DISCIPLINING AN INDIVIDUAL

If a disciplinary intervention is called for, how can it be carried out effectively? As just discussed, it is important to use a leadership style appropriate

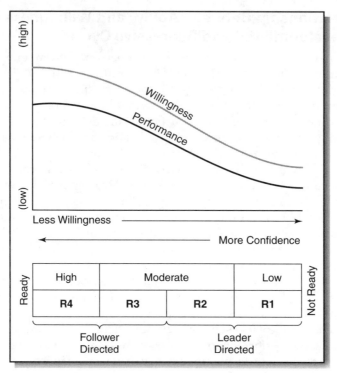

Figure 11-2
Relationship Between Willingness and Performance
in the Regressive Cycle; Confidence and Performance
in the Development Cycle

for the follower's *current* level of readiness; doing so may involve using different styles for the same person at different times. Here are a few other helpful guidelines.[2]

Making the Intervention Timely

Problem solving needs to be done in a timely manner. The sooner the intervention, the better the chance of stopping the performance slippage. The longer a manager waits, the more directive the intervention will have to be. Therefore, a manager may risk a follower's becoming anxious, frustrated, or resentful. Even an appropriate directive intervention may lead to attempts to get out from under the manager or to get the manager out.

For example, Mary, the office manager, expects all employees to maintain good attendance records. For the last 3 months, however, Susan, a data-entry clerk, has repeatedly arrived for work late and has failed to come to work twice. The other office staff have been complaining among themselves about Susan's behavior and have mentioned their complaints to Mary. Mary knows that Susan has had problems with child care and has decided to wait and see if Susan's behavior will improve. The weeks pass, and Susan continues to arrive late for work. Mary has finally had enough and decides to let Susan really have it when Susan finally gets to the office today. Susan may then feel "zapped," feel bitter toward Mary, and not focus on her real problem of poor attendance.

If Mary had intervened earlier, a participative style would probably have been enough to turn the problem around. But now, the highly structured style is necessary and creates resentment in Susan. This is a trap that managers fall into when making disciplinary interventions. First, they engage in "ostrich" leadership by sticking their heads in the sand and hoping the problem will go away. And then, when it doesn't, they get angry and zap the follower.

By timing interventions appropriately and treating people appropriately for the level at which they are *currently* performing, managers can begin to take a proactive approach to problem solving, as opposed to just reacting to each new crisis.

Unless discipline occurs close to the misbehavior or the poor performance, it won't be helpful in influencing future behavior. Some managers are "gunnysack" discipliners. That is, they store up observations of poor behavior, and then one day when the bag is full, they charge in and "dump everything on the table." Often, managers wait until the yearly performance review. That is why some people call an annual performance review program NIHYYSOB—"Now I have you, you S.O.B." Managers using the NIHYYSOB performance review tell their people all the bad things they have done over the last months or year. Manager and employee usually end up arguing about the "facts," and the employee doesn't really hear what is wrong. This is a version of the leave-alone-and-zap form of discipline. If managers would only intervene early, they could calmly deal with one behavior at a time, and the person could "hear" the feedback.

Varying the Emotional Level

The emotional level of the intervention is different for constructive discipline than it is for developing people. When developing people, you are attempting to expand the current ability of the follower. Therefore, it helps to keep the emotional content of a development intervention at a low level. People often misinterpret Situational Leadership because they think a telling style involves raising your voice or losing your temper. Actually, style 1 can be a very soft and caring approach by providing the needed demonstration of how to do things. It would be inappropriate to shout or get angry at people who are developing. That approach would only make them feel insecure and would discourage them from learning.

But when followers choose not to use their current ability, and constructive discipline is appropriate, you can raise the emotional content to a moderate level. This helps to get people's attention, lets them know that you are aware of the performance problem, and tells them that you care. It also helps to "unfreeze" the inappropriate behavior so that change can take place.

Focusing on Performance

The next thing to consider in working with constructive discipline is *don't attack personality—focus on performance*. If you attack personality and the person becomes angry, the probability of your successfully working with the person will be much lower. Imagine a manager's starting off a disciplinary intervention with, "I just told you that a week ago. Can't you remember to do anything, you dumb so and so?" Such an approach will only raise the emotional level of other people; it won't get them to focus on the problem. If the focus is on performance, not on personality, both leader and follower can talk about the problem and solve it.

Be Specific, Do Your Homework

Being specific about performance problems is important. When using constructive discipline, be careful of *glittering generalities*. Often managers perform all the other aspects of constructive discipline well. They use an appropriate leadership style for their people's readiness levels; they have good timing, keep a moderate emotional profile, and focus on performance. But their intervention sounds like this: "Look, you're just not doing the kind of job we both know you're capable of; now let's get back on track." Then the manager is bewildered or gets angry when the follower doesn't understand.

These kinds of glittering generalities don't get the job done. You have to do your homework before the intervention and gather specific details that may be useful in problem solving. With specific information, the interventions might sound like, "Productivity is down 14 ½ percent"; "Scrap loss is up 6 ½ percent"; or "Project Z is 5 days late and we've got three other departments depending on us for that component." Specificity allows the manager and followers, together, to work on developing a solution.

Harry Levinson, a well-known management consultant, agrees with this approach. He offers three general principles to follow when delivering bad news.

1. Don't be apologetic—expressing sorrow or sympathy is one thing, but you should never apologize for facing facts, calling the shots, and making tough decisions (not every decision you make is going to make people happy).
2. Be honest. . . . sound the alarm early and lead people to redirect themselves voluntarily.
3. Be constructive and, when possible, get and follow suggestions from your employees to make them feel more a part of the process.[3]

Keep It Private

The last thing to remember is to keep disciplinary interventions private. As a guideline, it's a good idea to praise people in public and problem solve in private. If you address followers about problems when others are around, you run the risk of having them more concerned about being seen "catching hell" than with solving the problem. Discussing problems in private tends to make it easier to get your points across and to keep the other person focused on the problem-solving process.

Leaders should also refrain from discussing the problems that they may be having with an employee with other employees. Discussing such problems may lead an employee to think, "What is the leader saying about me to other employees behind my back."

Punishment and Negative Reinforcement

Punishment, as we discussed earlier, is a negative consequence. A negative consequence tends to weaken the action it immediately follows; that is, it prevents the recurrence of that behavior. It is a stimulus that an individual "will reject, if given a choice between the punishment and no stimulus at all."[4] As punishment suppresses the behavior that brought it (the punishment) on, *negative reinforcement* strengthens the response that eliminates the punishment.

An example of both punishment and negative reinforcement may be helpful. Suppose that, whenever a manager brings the work group together to share some new information with them, Bill, one of the employees, usually pays little attention and often talks to people around him. As a result, he is uninformed and his manager is irritated. The manager decides to punish Bill's whispering behavior by stopping in the middle of a sentence and looking at Bill whenever she sees him talk. The unexpected silence (a negative consequence, or punishment) causes the whole work group to focus on what stopped the manager's sharing of information (Bill's talking). The silence from the manager and having all eyes on him are uncomfortable to Bill (punishment). He stops talking and starts listening to his manager, who resumes her discussion. His manager's use of a negative consequence, or punishment (silence and look), weakened and suppressed Bill's whispering behavior. At the same time, it operated as negative reinforcement in strengthening his listening, the behavior that took the punishment away (his manager stops looking at him and starts talking).

A manager must be careful in using punishment because one does not always know what a person will do when punished. For example, suppose a manager reprimands (punishes) Al, an employee, for sloppy work. If Al settles down, figures out what he has done wrong, and begins working carefully (negative reinforcement), the punishment has been helpful. After having this good experience, the manager might try the same technique with Mary, another employee who is doing sloppy work. But rather than making Mary behave more carefully, the punishment (reprimand) causes her to work even more sloppily, and she begins to become disruptive in other areas. Thus, whereas Al shaped up with a reprimand, Mary became more troublesome after the same intervention.

Another important point to keep in mind when using punishment is that punishment shows one what *not* to do, but it does not show one what *to* do. This distinction was vividly pointed out by John Huberman in a case study about a Douglas-fir plywood mill in which the management had continually used punitive measures to deal with sloppy workmanship and disciplinary problems.[5] Although punishment seemed to stop the inappropriate behavior for the moment, it had little long-term effect. Top management finally analyzed the system while preparing to double its capacity. They were amazed that

> *Not a single desirable result could be detected.* The people who had been disciplined were generally still among the poorest workers; their attitude was sulky, if not openly hostile. And they seemed to be spreading this feeling among the rest of the crew.[6]

This reality and the findings that "85 percent of all those who entered the local prison returned there within 3 years of their release"[7] made management seriously question their use of punishment. Eventually, they worked out a new and highly effective system, which Huberman called "discipline without punishment." One of the main ingredients of the new method was that rather than a punitive approach to unsatisfactory work or a discipline problem, a six-step process was initiated that clearly spelled out appropriate behavior, told employees what to do, and placed "on the employee the onus" of deciding whether the employee wished (or was able) "to conform to the requirements of a particular work situation."[8]

It is essential in a disciplinary intervention for task behavior to follow immediately. That is, once an intervention has been made, the manager must identify the new behavior that is to replace the undesired behavior. Only when that occurs can positive reinforcement be used to increase the likelihood that the new behavior will continue.

Extinction

When reinforcement is withheld after a behavior occurs, the behavior is said to be *on extinction.* Punishment tends only to suppress behavior; extinction tends to make it disappear. Extinguishing a response requires that there be *no* consequence of behavior. For example, suppose a child learns that he can get his parents' attention, and usually whatever else he wants, by stomping up and down and crying. If the parents don't want that kind of behavior, they can extinguish it by not responding to the child (in either a positive or a negative way). After a while, as the child sees that stomping and crying get him nothing, he will stop behaving that way to get what he wants. People seldom continue to do things that provide no positive reinforcement.

Although extinction can help eliminate undesirable behavior, one should be careful not to use it unintentionally. Let's look at an example. Imagine that Ernest, who had been doing sloppy work, is now working carefully and neatly because his manager has been praising (rewarding) him for everything he does right. But, suddenly, the manager stops rewarding Ernest for neat work. Ernest goes for perhaps a week or two working neatly with no reward. He may not be able to tell us what is different, but gradually his behavior gives us a clue. He soon begins to try other behaviors. He becomes less careful and neat. If there are no negative consequences (punishment), within days he will have reverted to his earlier behavior of doing sloppy work. In essence, neatness and carefulness will have been extinguished.

People seldom continue to do things that do not provide positive reinforcement, either through external reward or internal satisfaction. Ernest did not find working carefully or neatly as rewarding in itself. The intervention by his manager helped his task readiness, but Ernest was not psychologically ready enough in this job (and he may never become so if it is a boring and unsatisfying job) to be left alone and not periodically reinforced for his neatness and carefulness.

In addition to its effect on the continuation of a particular behavior, extinction also can sometimes have an emotional impact. We could predict, for example, with an excellent chance of being correct, that Ernest will become surly, will complain more than before, or will have problems getting along with his coworkers. Emotional behavior usually accompanies extinction when reinforcement or punishment is withheld.

Parents often extinguish behaviors unintentionally when they pay attention only when their children are behaving poorly. If parents pay little or no attention when the children are behaving appropriately, they, in a sense, put that behavior on extinction. A child who wants attention (a reward) from the parents may be willing to endure what the parents think is punishment to get it. So, in the long run, the parents might be reinforcing the very behavior they do not want and extinguishing more appropriate behavior.

Leaders in all kinds of settings must beware of positively reinforcing inappropriate behavior; yet it happens all the time. Have you ever given a crying child a piece of candy? The child may eat the candy and stop crying. But the next time the child wants a piece of candy (or your attention), he will know exactly how to get it—by crying. You made the mistake of positively reinforcing inappropriate behavior.[9]

This phenomenon does not happen just at home; it is very common in the world of work. For example, a manager's work group had responded well to a high task–low relationship style of always spelling out tasks specifically and dealing firmly with anyone who did not demonstrate appropriate behavior. Now suddenly this style is not achieving results, and followers are being disruptive and making unreasonable demands. What should the manager do? The first impulse of most managers is to think "Maybe I've been too hard on them" and begin to give in to their demands. Perhaps the manager should have increased relationship behavior earlier and moved to a high task–high relationship leadership style, but doing so now may be perceived as positively reinforcing inappropriate behavior—every time the work group wants something, they will become disruptive. Positively reinforcing inappropriate behavior generally results in more unwanted behavior.

When to Use Punishment or Extinction

In essence, what we are saying is that leaders must think before they behave because they never know what they may or may not be reinforcing. This is particularly true when it comes to using punishment and extinction. Yet, these concepts can be useful in helping managers to effectively "unfreeze" inappropriate behavior so that they can begin to reinforce positively more desirable behavior. In using punishment or extinction, however, it is important to know what behavior you want to change and to communicate that in some way to the person(s) with whom you are working. To determine when to use punishment and when to ignore (extinguish by withholding reinforcement), managers need to estimate how long the undesirable behavior has been occurring. If the behavior is new, ignoring it (extinction) may get results and cause a person to abandon an inappropriate behavior. But if the behavior has been occurring for some time, it may be necessary to suppress this behavior through some form of punishment until some desirable behavior has a chance to become strong enough as a result of positive reinforcement to replace the undesirable behavior. As we discussed in chapter 2, the larger the reservoir of experience a person has in a particular behavior, the more difficult the behavior will be to change and, thus, the harder the initial intervention may have to be before positive reinforcement can be used effectively to strengthen a new behavior.

An Example of Using Behavior Modification

Consider the behavior of Tony, a new employee right out of high school. Tony can be described as a very aggressive and competitive individual. During his first day on the job, he argues over tools with another young employee. To make certain that a manager would be sure of what to do about Tony's behavior and to summarize our discussion of behavior modification, we present here some steps that managers can use in attempting to change employee behavior.[10]

- *Step 1.* Identify (for yourself and then with Tony) the behavior to be changed and the new behavior that is to replace the old. Discover what Tony would consider to be positive reinforcement and punishment. Devise a strategy to get the new behavior, and determine the way you will positively reinforce it.

- *Step 2.* Attempt to find out whether the old behavior (arguing over tools) is such a strong behavior that you need to suppress it through punishment or whether it is a new enough behavior that a lack of any kind of reinforcement will extinguish it. If you decide to use punishment, determine what it will be. Remember, this punishment could operate as negative reinforcement and thus strengthen the behavior that removes the punishment. So be careful!

- *Step 3.* Develop a strategy to get Tony to practice the new behavior and positively reinforce it on a regular schedule. As soon as Tony has practiced the new behavior so that it is more likely to occur than the old behavior, change to an intermittent schedule of reinforcing the new behavior (make the intervals between reinforcement increasingly longer) so that new behavior will resist extinction.

In examining these steps, one could get the impression that the manager is dominating the process with little if any involvement from Tony. According to Situational Leadership, this approach may be appropriate in working with people at low levels of readiness, such as a new and inexperienced employee like Tony. But, as the readiness level of the people that a manager supervises begins to increase, this process of change becomes much more of a collaborative process. As we will discuss in chapter 12, the extent of involvement of people in the change process will vary from situation to situation.

PROBLEMS AND THEIR OWNERSHIP— WHO'S GOT THE PROBLEM?

As we have been suggesting in this chapter, effective managers are not only able to develop the readiness of their people, but they also are able to spot "slippage" in readiness and intervene early enough to turn the situation around. How can managers know when to intervene? What should they look for?

As a simple guideline, whenever managers receive feedback—either verbal (one of their people tells them) or nonverbal (they observe the performance of one of their people)—indicating that a person is having a problem in some area, it's time to think about stepping in. A *problem* exists when there is a difference between what someone is doing and what that person's manager and that individual believe is really happening. Thus, detecting problems is all-important in determining what areas of a person's job require attention.

Thomas Gordon, in his book *P.E.T., Parent Effectiveness Training*, contends that one of the most important steps in becoming effective in rearing responsible self-motivated children is determining whether their behavior is acceptable or unacceptable to their parents as well as to themselves.[11] Once the acceptance question has been answered, then "who owns the problem" in terms of a child's behavior can be identified. Although the work of Gordon originated from observations of parents and teachers, the concepts behind the ownership of problems apply to any organizational setting in which a leader is trying to influence the behavior of others.

Problem Ownership and Situational Leadership

Let us look at problem ownership in the context of Situational Leadership. If managers can identify who has the problem, then they are in a position to assess readiness level, determine the leadership style that has the best chance of success, and decide how to intervene with followers (see Figure 11-3). The four problem situations described next combine these elements.

1. *The manager has the problem.* In this situation, the follower's behavior is a problem to the manager but not to the follower. The follower's readiness level is R1 because the follower sees no problem. The appropriate leadership style for the manager is telling (S1). For managers to rid themselves of these problems, they must provide followers with structure in the form of direction regarding the task.

2. *The manager and the follower have the problem.* This situation involves the follower's behavior when it is a problem for both the manager and the follower. The follower's readiness level is R2 because the follower

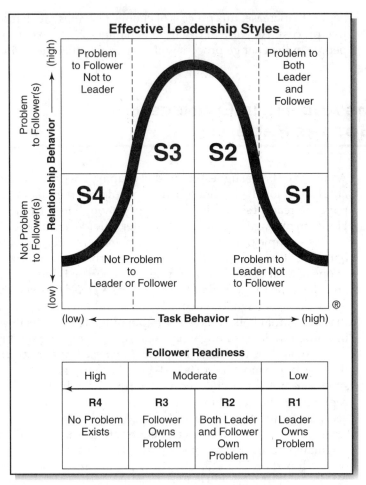

Figure 11-3
Four Problem Situations

needs some direction. Further, because the follower owns part of the problem, some relationship behavior in terms of two-way communication and facilitating behavior is also necessary. The appropriate leadership style is selling (S2) because the follower needs both direction and support to carry out the task.

3. *The follower has the problem.* Here, the follower's behavior is a problem for the follower but not for the manager. The follower's readiness level is R3 because the follower needs support and encouragement from the manager. The appropriate leadership style is S3, a participating style to facilitate two-way communication. The tragedy is that managers often treat this problem situation as if it were a problem to neither. If management intervention is not made somewhat soon, the problem could become a serious problem for the follower, the manager, and the organization.

4. *Neither the manager nor the follower has the problem.* In this situation, there are no problems requiring attention. Followers involved in this situation are R4, a high level of readiness. The most appropriate leadership style is delegating (S4), because the manager's job is to monitor the situation so that no problems will form.

Let's look at some examples of how this concept might be used as a diagnostic tool. William, a commodities trader in a large exchange, has always executed trades and recorded exchanges according to the high standards developed by his company. Because he is operating within guidelines, his behavior is not a problem to his manager or his company. But William's behavior may be a problem to himself; his best friends on the exchange floor have been involved in some questionable practices and are pressuring him to take part. If William's manager treats this situation as if it were a problem to neither and leaves William alone, the situation could quickly become a problem for both. Because of the pressures from his peers on the exchange floor, a lack of active listening and support by William's manager could move William toward the same behavior his peers are practicing. Thus, by not making a high-relationship intervention at the appropriate time, William's manager could create a problem for his company that did not exist earlier.

If the situation is one in which the behavior of the employee is a problem to the manager but not to the employee, the manager does not have to provide facilitating behaviors. For example, if the problem involves personal friends visiting the employee during working hours, the manager merely needs to provide the employee with an understanding of what the rules are (an S1 intervention). The employee, who doesn't see the situation as a problem, does not want to spend 15 or 20 minutes discussing it.

Another situation might be one in which no one has a problem. For example, a teacher assigns 15, 20, or 25 pages of reading for the next day. The students say nothing; the assignment doesn't strike them as a problem. All they want to know is what the teacher expects; they don't want to sit around and talk about it. But if the teacher says the assignment is 100 pages, the situation might quickly become a problem to both the students and the teacher. Now the teacher has to engage in selling behavior rather than telling. The teacher has to open up channels of communication and discussion and engage in facilitating behaviors. The teacher has to get the students to understand the "why" of the large assignment and have them "buy in" psychologically to the decision. The teacher might say, "A top lecturer is coming this week. That's why I'm making a heavy assignment for tomorrow. I want you to be prepared. Later in the week we'll have no reading assignment." In other words, the teacher attempts to make some trades to facilitate interaction but is still trying to get the students to buy into the decision.

As the discussion and examples suggest, the integration of Situational Leadership with Thomas Gordon's problem ownership approach can be very helpful in determining the appropriate leadership style in various situations. Remember, even if the follower's behavior is acceptable to the leader, the leader may still have to take action if the follower needs support and encouragement to keep up the good work. If the follower's behavior is unacceptable to the leader, a more directive intervention is needed to turn the situation around. How direct the intervention must be (just telling or selling) depends on whether the follower also sees this behavior as a problem and "owns the problem," too. If leaders are going to help their people grow and develop into self-motivated individuals, they must gradually let them think for themselves and solve their own problems.

POSITIVE DISCIPLINE

Another model of dealing with employees who fail to meet performance goals or who violate organizational rules is called *positive discipline*.[12] Developed by Eric L. Harvey, this approach to employee discipline follows three simple and direct steps:

1. Warn the employee orally.
2. Warn the employee in writing.
3. If steps 1 and 2 fail to resolve the problem, give the employee a day off, *with pay.*

The model removes punishment from the disciplinary process and places responsibility for appropriate performance on the employee. In the first two steps, the manager focuses on the specific discrepancy between the employee's actual and expected performance and the business reasons why the performance expectation must be met. The manager describes why meeting the performance standard is important and works to gain the employee's agreement to change behavior and meet the standard. The employee is reminded that proper performance and behavior are the individual's responsibility, not the manager's. Hostile or defensive employee reactions are met with mature and adult explanations of the specific discrepancy and the standard that needs to be met.

If the employee fails to change after the first two steps are taken, the manager moves to step 3. During the day off with pay, which is referred to as a "decision-making leave," the employee is expected to be thinking about remaining in the organization. The leave communicates to the employee that, "Your job is on the line. What are you going to do about it?" The suspension from work highlights the seriousness of the situation; being paid for the day removes employee hostility and reinforces the organization's honest desire to help the individual take responsibility for meeting organizational expectations. Upon returning to work, the employee tells the manager of the decision—to make the required changes and continue employment, or to quit. If the problems continue upon the employee's return, the employee is then terminated.

The model is based on the belief that an organization and its managers have the right to establish reasonable and appropriate standards; to point out discrepancies when they occur; and to let the individual decide whether or not to perform and meet those standards. Responsibility for performance is placed on the employee, not on the manager or the organization.

SUMMARY

This chapter offered suggestions for developing strategies for disciplining followers constructively. Leaders must remove themselves from the traditional job of directing, controlling, and supervising their followers and assist them in learning to stand on their own and achieve individual effectiveness in the demanding work environment.

The goal of constructive discipline is to make problem solving a positive, growth-oriented opportunity instead of a punitive experience. It is important to:

- Use a leadership style appropriate for your follower's *current* level of readiness.
- Make the intervention timely.
- Use an appropriate emotional level.
- Focus on performance, not personality.
- Be specific, do your homework.
- Keep the intervention private.

Managers who keep these factors in mind when making disciplinary interventions find that discipline need not be destructive, but can be a part of a helping relationship.

ENDNOTES

1. Adapted from Paul Hersey, *The Situational Leader* (Escondido, CA: Center for Leadership Studies, 1985), p. 114.
2. Adapted from Paul Hersey, *Situational Selling* (Escondido, CA: Center for Leadership Studies, 1985), pp. 115–120.
3. Harry Levinson, "Getting Past the Bad News," *Management Review,* September 1993, p. 4.
4. R. L. Solomon, "Punishment," *American Psychologist,* 19 (1964), p. 239.
5. John Huberman, "Discipline without Punishment," *Harvard Business Review,* May 1967, pp. 62–68.
6. *Ibid.,* pp. 64–65.
7. *Ibid.,* p. 65.
8. *Ibid.*
9. Taken from an enjoyable popular article on this subject by Alice Lake, "How to Teach Your Child Good Habits," *Redbook Magazine,* June 1971, pp. 74, 186, 188, 190.
10. These steps were adapted from seven steps identified by Madeline Hunter, *Reinforcement Theory for Teachers* (El Segundo, CA: TIP Publications, 1967), pp. 47–48.
11. Thomas Gordon, *P.E.T., Parent Effectiveness Training* (New York: Peter H. Wyden, 1970).
12. Eric L. Harvey, "Discipline versus Punishment," *Management Review,* March 1987, pp. 25–29.

12

Building Effective Relationships

In the last two chapters, our emphasis was on helping leaders develop people to their fullest potential. This development process involves shifting one's leadership style forward and backward (according to Situational Leadership) and utilizing various degrees of direction and support as followers increase or decrease in readiness or developmental level. Shifting of leadership style requires leaders to be flexible, to be able to adapt to various situations. Are most leaders able to be that flexible, or do they tend to be limited to only one or two leadership styles? How will changes in a leader's style affect followers' perceptions of the leader's intentions? ✧

The first question is something that has been examined at the Center for Leadership Studies for almost 3 decades through the use of Leader Effectiveness and Adaptability Description (LEAD) instruments.[1] Answering the second question was an important impetus in the creation of the Contracting for Leadership Style[2] process developed to increase the effectiveness of management by objectives (MBO), a formal leader-follower negotiation system.[3]

LEAD INSTRUMENTATION

The LEAD instrument developed at the Center for Leadership Studies was designed to measure three aspects of leader behavior:

264

1. Style
2. Style range, or flexibility
3. Style adaptability

The *leadership style* of an individual is the behavior pattern that a person exhibits when attempting to influence the activities of others—as perceived by those others. This may be very different from the leader's perception, which we will define as *self-perception* rather than style. Comparing one's self-perception of leadership style with the perceptions of others can be very useful, particularly because one's self-perception may or may not reflect one's actual leadership style, depending on how close a person's perceptions are to the perceptions of others. For this reason, two LEAD instruments were developed: LEAD Self and LEAD Other. The LEAD Self measures self-perception of how an individual behaves as a leader; the LEAD Other reflects the perceptions of a leader's followers, supervisors, and peers or associates.[4]

Leadership Style

Our extensive research over many years has revealed that all leaders have a *primary* leadership style, and most have a *secondary* leadership style. A leader's primary style is defined as the behavior pattern used most often when attempting to influence the activities of others, in other words, a favorite. A leader's secondary style is the leadership style that a person tends to use on occasion. All leaders have one primary leadership style; that is, they tend to use one of the four basic leadership styles described in Situational Leadership more often than not in leadership situations. However, they may have no secondary leadership style, or up to three secondary styles.

Style Range, or Flexibility

Style range is the extent to which leaders are able to vary their leadership styles. Leaders differ in their ability to vary their style in different situations. Some leaders seem to be limited to one basic style and tend to be effective only in situations in which their styles are compatible with the environment. Other leaders are able to modify their behavior to fit any of the four basic styles; still others can utilize two or three styles. Flexible leaders have the potential to be effective in a number of situations.

The style range of a leader can be illustrated in terms of task and relationship behavior, as shown in Figure 12-1. The area of the circle indicates the range of style. If the area is small, as in A, then the range of behavior of the leader is limited; if the area is large, as in B, the leader has a wide range of behavior.

Leadership situations vary in the extent to which they make demands on flexibility. William Reddin cited some of the conditions that demand, in his terms, low and high flexibility. For example, conditions that demand low flexibility include low-level managerial jobs, established tasks, and little environmental change. Conditions that demand high flexibility are the opposite: high-level managerial jobs, innovative tasks, and rapid environmental change, the types of trends discussed in chapter 1.[5]

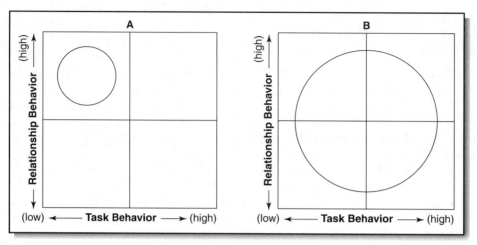

Figure 12-1
Style Range in Terms of Task Behavior and Relationship Behavior

Style Adaptability

Style range indicates the extent to which leaders are able to vary their style; *style adaptability* is the degree to which they are able to vary their style *appropriately* to the demands of a given situation, according to Situational Leadership. Let's contrast style adaptability with style range. Leaders with style adaptability can make whatever style (or styles) they use fit a given situation. People who have a narrow style range can be effective over a long period of time if they remain in situations in which their style has a high probability of success; however, they cannot be said to have style adaptability. Conversely, people who have a wide range of styles may be ineffective if they use a style that is not appropriate for the demands of the situation. These people, too, cannot be said to have style adaptability. Thus, *a wide style range will not guarantee effectiveness; style range is not as relevant to effectiveness as style adaptability.*

For example, in A in Figure 12-1, the leader has a dominant relationship style with no flexibility (a narrow range); in B, the leader has a wide range of leadership styles because the leader is able to use all four leadership styles on various occasions. In this example, A may be effective in situations that demand a high relationship–low task style, such as in coaching or counseling situations. In B, the potential exists to be effective in a wide variety of instances, but the B style range will not guarantee effectiveness. B's style will be effective only if the leader uses the style appropriate to the situation, that is, has style adaptability.

Flexibility: A Question of Willingness

The importance of a leader's *diagnostic ability* cannot be overemphasized. It is the key to adaptability. One of the questions raised at the beginning of the chapter comes up again: Are most leaders able to be that flexible, or do they tend to be limited to only one or two leadership styles?

It has been our experience that there are few, if any, leaders who cannot learn to use all four basic leadership styles. In fact, people use those behaviors almost every day. At least once a day, you probably tell somebody what to do and watch the person closely (style S1), explain what you want somebody to do and permit the person to ask clarifying questions (style S2), share ideas with people and support their efforts (style S3), and turn over responsibility to someone to "run with the ball" (style S4).

Learning to use the four basic styles is not the issue; the question is one of willingness. Anyone has the ability, but if the person does not want to learn, then there is not much that you can do. "You can lead a horse to water, but you can't make it drink."

When people are willing to learn to use all the leadership styles, we have found an interesting phenomenon. When people learn to use a leadership style that previously was not even considered a secondary style, the compensating style often becomes their most effective style. Although this style may never become comfortable, it can become the most effective, in many cases, because it has been learned. Leaders know a lot more about their learned styles than about their natural style because they have practiced them consciously. People often use their comfortable or primary leadership styles by the "seat of their pants." This is true not only in terms of leadership styles, but also in many other areas of their lives.

For example, suppose you are a golfer who enjoys and excels at hitting a drive; however, you realize that the "drive is for show, but the putt is for the dough," so you decide to take lessons in putting. If you consciously make an effort and take lessons and practice to become a good putter, very often it is this part of the game that becomes your most effective weapon. You would still be more comfortable hitting the ball off the tee, but because you have practiced putting, it is now the strongest part of your game.

The same goes for leaders. Your primary style is often one that you do not have to think about using. But once you learn other styles through conscientious study and practice, these compensating styles can be your most effective. Thus, we find that willingness—not ability—is the main issue in terms of style flexibility.

Is There Only One Appropriate Style?

The concept of adaptability implies that the effective leader is able to use the right style at the right time. What if a leader makes a good diagnosis and then is unwilling or is unable to use the "best" style? Is that leader doomed to failure? Situational Leadership not only suggests the high probability leadership styles for various readiness levels, but also indicates the probability of success of the other styles if the leader is unwilling or unable to use the "desired" style. The probability of success of each style for the four readiness levels is shown in Table 12-1.

As Table 12-1 indicates, the "desired" style always has a "second-best" style choice; that is, a style that would probably be effective if the highest

Table 12-1 Matching Readiness Level with the Leadership Style Most Likely to Work Well

READINESS	"BEST" STYLE	"SECOND-BEST" STYLE	"THIRD-BEST" STYLE	LEAST EFFECTIVE STYLE
R1 Low	S1 Telling	S2 Selling	S3 Participating	S4 Delegating
R2 Low to moderate	S2 Selling	S1 Telling or S3 Participating		S4 Delegating
R3 Moderate to high	S3 Participating	S2 Selling or S4 Delegating		S1 Telling
R4 High	S4 Delegating	S3 Participating	S2 Selling	S1 Telling

probability style could not be used. You will notice that at the low to moderate (R2) and moderate to high (R3) readiness levels there are two "second-best" style choices: Which one should be used depends on whether the readiness of the individual is getting better, indicating that the leader should be involved in a developmental cycle (chapter 10), or getting worse, revealing that a regressive cycle is occurring (chapter 11). If the situation is improving, participating (at R2) and delegating (at R3) would be the best second choices, but if things are deteriorating, telling (at R2) and selling (at R3) would be the most appropriate backup choices.

Table 12-1 also suggests that telling and delegating are the risky styles because one of the two is always the lowest probability style. Even so, later in this chapter we will discuss why it is important for leaders to learn to use these styles effectively.

Use of LEAD Instrumentation

When staff members at the Center for Leadership Studies diagnose an organization, part of that diagnosis often involves use of the LEAD instruments. The process consists of having managers throughout the organization complete the LEAD Self instrument (how they perceive their own leadership style). At the same time, each of these managers' employees, supervisor, and several associates or peers fill out the LEAD Other instrument. Once the data have been analyzed, a LEAD Profile is prepared for each individual manager. The profile gives managers an opportunity to see if there is any significant difference between how they perceive their own leadership style and how others in the environment perceive their style.

The purpose of distributing and analyzing the LEAD Self and LEAD Other data is to determine if there is any discrepancy between self-perception and the perception of others. A useful framework, the *Johari Window* (taken from the first names of its authors), developed by Joseph Luft and Harry Ingham, is used to analyze that data and feed it back to participating managers.[6]

The Johari Window is used in our consulting to depict leadership personality, not overall personality, as it is sometimes used. The difference between leadership personality and leadership style in this context is that leadership personality includes self-perception and the perception of others. However, leadership style consists only of an individual's leader behavior as perceived by others, that is, supervisors, employees, associates, and so on. Thus, leadership personality equals self-perception plus perception of others (style).

According to this framework, leaders engage in some attitudes or behaviors that they themselves know about. This *known to self* area includes their knowledge of the way they are coming across—the impact they are having on the people they are trying to influence. At the same time, part of the leader's personality is *unknown to self;* that is, in some areas leaders are unaware of how they are coming across to others. It may be that their followers have not given them feedback, or it may be that a leader has not been alert enough to pick up on some verbal or nonverbal feedback.

We can also look at leadership personality that includes behaviors and attitudes *known to others* in a leader's organizational setting, as well as areas *unknown to others.* In terms of what is known and unknown to self and known and unknown to others, we can create four areas that constitute the total window, as depicted in Figure 12-2.

The arena that is known to self and also known to others in any specific organizational setting is called the *public arena*—it is known to all (the leader and others) within that organizational setting.

	Known to Self	Unknown to Self
Known to Others	Public	Blind
Unknown to Others	Private	Unknown

Figure 12-2
The Johari Window

The arena that is unknown to self (the leader), but is known to others, is referred to as the *blind arena*. It might be unknown to the leader because followers have been unwilling to share feedback with or communicate ("level") with that leader. Or perhaps the leader is not able or does not care to see verbal and nonverbal cues.

The arena that is known to self but unknown to others is referred to as the *private arena*. It may be private because the leader has been unwilling to share or disclose it to others in the organizational setting. Or it may be private because the others are not picking up on the nonverbal and verbal cues provided by the leader.

The last arena, unknown to self and unknown to others, is called the *unknown*. In Freudian psychology this would be referred to as the subconscious or unconscious.[7] As you will recall from chapter 2, Freud likened personality to an iceberg. A certain portion of a leader's personality is above the surface—that is, it is noticeable. Anyone who looks in that direction can hardly help but see the basic size, consistency, makeup, and configuration. But much of this iceberg exists beneath the surface, and unless we make conscious efforts to probe and understand, we will really never have any insight into it. Yet, much of that part of a leader's personality referred to as unknown may be having an impact on the kinds of behaviors in which a leader engages when trying to influence the behavior of others.

Feedback

Two processes affect the configuration of the four arenas of the Johari Window. The first, which operates in the direction illustrated in Figure 12-3, is called *feedback*. This is the extent to which others in the organizational setting are willing to share with the leader, to be open, and to level with the leader. It is also the extent to which the leader attempts to perceive the verbal and nonverbal information provided by others. As can be seen in Figure 12-3, the

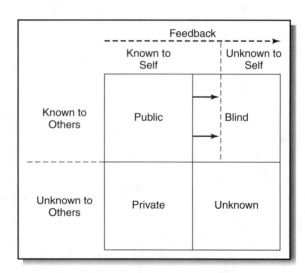

Figure 12-3
Effect of Feedback on the Johari Window

more relative feedback that takes place within an organization, the more the public arena of a leader begins to extend into and displace the blind arena, and, thus, the smaller that leader's blind area becomes.

Disclosure

The other process that affects the shape of the Johari Window is *disclosure*. This is the extent to which leaders are willing to share with others information about themselves.

The way we use the term *disclosure* is different from the way others in the field often use it. First, the most relevant disclosure is not what people say about themselves but rather how they behave. It is not words that mean, it is people that mean. And if you want to understand people better, you really have to look at their behavior to gain relevant insights into their values and what their behavior represents.

Second, we think disclosure is appropriate in organizations only when it is organizationally relevant. This is a different way of viewing disclosure than is urged by some people in the sensitivity training and personal growth field, who feel all disclosure is appropriate. In fact, some contend that it is appropriate for a leader or manager in an organizational setting to be open and disclose as much as possible and that the organization should process that data. Our experience from numerous organizational development interventions suggests that two of the scarcest resources in any organizational setting are time and energy. Therefore, if people disclosed almost everything about themselves within the organizational setting and others took time to process these various agendas, there would not be much time left to accomplish other organizational goals and objectives. We feel disclosure is important and helpful in organizations as long as it contributes to the operation of the organization.

In the process of disclosure, the more organizationally relevant the information that leaders disclose about the way they think or behave, the more the public arena opens into the private arena and the smaller that arena becomes, as shown in Figure 12-4.

Self-Perception versus Style

When we do an organizational diagnosis, the data from the LEAD Self, as we explained, denote self-perception. In terms of the Johari Window, the self-perception of leaders would represent what is known to them about their leadership style and would include both their public and private arenas. This self-perception of leadership style can be measured using the LEAD Self. On the other hand, an individual's leadership style would represent what is known to others and would include on the Johari Window both that person's public and blind arenas. Leadership style can be measured using the LEAD Other. The relationship between self-perception, leadership style, and the Johari Window is presented in Figure 12-5.

One of the interesting phenomena that we have discovered at the Center for Leadership Studies is that we can predict the shape of the public arena

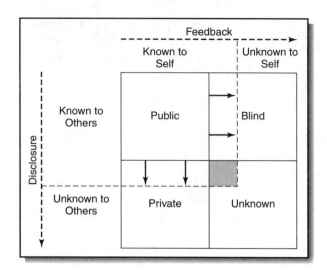

Figure 12-4
Effect of Feedback
and Disclosure on
the Johari Window

within the Johari framework. For instance, if there is a great discrepancy between self-perception and the way others perceive a manager (style), the public arena in that manager's Johari Window will tend to be very small, as illustrated in Figure 12-6.

But if there is no significant difference between self-perception and the perception of others within a leader's organizational setting, the public arena in that person's leadership Johari Window would be large, as illustrated in Figure 12-7. LEAD data can actually measure the shape of the arenas in a per-

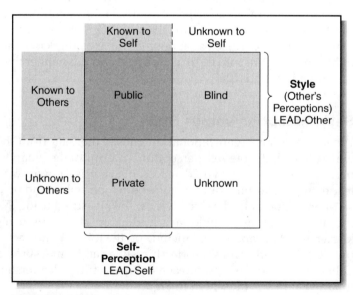

Figure 12-5
Self-Perception and Other Perception (Style)

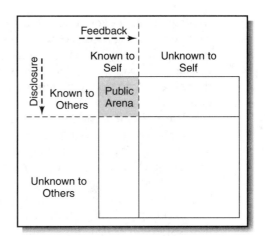

Figure 12-6
Public Arena When
There Is a Large
Discrepancy in
Perceptions

son's leadership Johari Window in each of the organizational settings in which that person operates.

For example, a manager responsible for three departments may find that in department A, where there is good feedback and disclosure, the public arena is very large. In department B, where there is very little contact, and thus infrequent feedback and disclosure, the public arena might be small. Finally, in department C, where there is average interaction, the public arena might be moderate in size.

Is It Too Late?

In reading about communication problems, managers might be feeling discouraged or even guilty. Maybe they have a problem employee or a child or two and are thinking they really have done a poor job as a manager or parent. Yet, as Wayne Dyer so aptly argued in his book *Your Erroneous Zones*, guilt is a useless feeling.[8]

> It is by far the greatest waste of emotional energy. Why? Because, by definition, you are feeling immobilized in the current over something that has already taken place, and no amount of guilt can ever change history.[9]

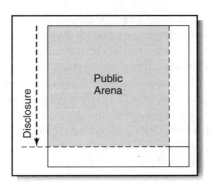

Figure 12-7
Public Arena When
There Is a Small
Discrepancy in
Perception

Managers can never redo what they should have done at an earlier time. Maybe you have made some mistakes. But that was yesterday; what are you going to do today? Today is the beginning of the rest of your life as a leader, manager, or parent. It is never too late to turn a situation around, as long as there is enough time. We mention time because it is a key factor. Let us try to explain from a child-rearing point of view.

The earlier in a child's life a parent attempts to have an impact, the greater will be that parent's potential influence on the child's future behavior. During the early years, an intervention by a parent represents a substantial portion of the child's sum of experience in that area of the child's life; the same intervention later can never carry the same weight. In addition, the longer the behavior is reinforced, the more patterned it becomes, and the more difficult it is to change. That's why as a child gets older, it takes more time and more new experiences to bring about a change in behavior. Think of it this way: One drop of red food coloring in a half-pint bottle of clear liquid may be enough to change drastically the appearance of the total contents. But the same drop in a gallon jug may make little, if any, noticeable difference.

If our children are now teenagers—young adults—it is still possible, though difficult, to bring about some change in their behavior. Now it becomes a matter of economics: How much time are we willing to invest in implementing such a change?

Let's take an extreme case. Suppose a teenage son is discovered by his parents to be taking drugs and in trouble with the law. What can his parents do now? One choice is to feel guilty and try to make up for past mistakes by putting all kinds of time in with the son now. But the son might resent all this attention from his parents after having been left on his own for so long. If the son doesn't resent the sudden attention from his parents, then it becomes an economic question: Our children have unlimited needs, but we have limited time. Where can we put in the most effective time with the biggest payoff?

If the parents have plenty of time and decide to attempt to change their son's behavior (even though it's an old pattern), the concepts presented in this book should provide some helpful hints as to where and how to begin. Probably they will have to do some telling (S1) and selling (S2), both of which are time-consuming. But with some concentrated effort, the parents can probably have an impact on this boy's behavior.

Before parents throw themselves into a change effort with one of their children, it's a wise idea to consider what impact this attention will have on the other children in the family. By devoting all their time and energy to one problem, the parents may unwittingly create other problems. If all the parents' time is spent on this teenage son, the other children may get the impression that the only way to get time with mom and dad is by getting into trouble (in effect, the parents have put all the other children's good behavior on extinction). Soon one problem child will have mushroomed into other problem children. Therefore, it's important always to look at the big picture and allot time accordingly.

The lesson to be learned in this example as a manager is to "get your shots in early" with your people. Rescue and salvage work are tough and time-consuming and often come too late to do much good.

Another point of importance concerns the types of stress placed on a manager. Elaina Zucker identified severe managerial stress as "that headache behind your left eye, the stiff neck, the quivering hands—these are the signs that stress is setting in."[10] Like guilt, stress does nothing to help a manager with the work and may, in fact, be detrimental. Zucker suggests making a list of things that cause stress—e.g., bad lighting, a certain employee, the trip to work—and reviewing the list periodically to ascertain if these stressors can be either eliminated or somewhat alleviated. Just being aware that you are becoming stressed is helpful. Learning to cope with stress by altering your perspective and dealing with it in a positive manner are important weapons a stressed manager can use to reduce tension.

Barbara Mackoff offered other strategies for reducing stress. Most involve friends and family outside of work. Mackoff suggests conscientiously not bringing work home, avoiding "talking shop" at the dinner table and other social times, and seeking friends who won't be impressed with your business savvy. Rather, you should make your life outside of work just as important, if not more important, than work itself, and you should treat it as such.[11]

LEAD PROFILES

As was indicated earlier, LEAD data are gathered in organizations to give managers feedback on how they perceive their own leadership style as compared with how others see their style. Once a manager has learned that employees perceive that one style or another is used most of the time with them, what does it all mean?

Sample

In this section, we will examine and interpret some of the common profiles that we have found from analysis of LEAD Self and LEAD Other data accumulated at the Center for Leadership Studies.[12] The information was generated from a LEAD sample of over 20,000 leadership events from 14 cultures. A "leadership event" occurs when we have data not only in terms of self-perception (LEAD Self), but also the perception of others (LEAD Other) in that leadership environment. Of these respondents, we interviewed some 2,000 middle managers from industry and education; of that number, we conducted more than 500 in-depth interviews. The interviews included not only the leaders in terms of self-perception, but also a sample of the leaders' followers and their perceptions of the leaders' styles.

Two-Style Profile

In our in-depth interviews, the emphasis was on what we call "two-style pro-files." A two-style profile includes either (1) a basic style that encompasses two of the four possible configuration styles or (2) a basic style and a sup-porting style.

It is suggested that as feedback is given on the specific two-style profiles, you keep in mind what you know about your own leadership style. If you think you have a one-style profile (you tend to use only one primary leader-ship style with little flexibility), then you need to remember that your profile represents only a portion of the two-style profile. If you think you have a three- or four-style profile (you have more than one supporting style in ad-dition to your primary style), you may have to integrate the feedback that will be given to you into several of the two-style profiles. It must be pointed out that unless you have gathered specific data on how your leadership style is perceived by others, your perception of your own leadership style is only that—your perception.

Wide Flexibility

We have found in working with people who have a wide range of styles that even though their effectiveness score may be low, a shorter period of time is needed to increase their effectiveness than is needed with people who have a smaller range of behavior. If people are engaging in a wide range of behav-ior, all you have to do to make a significant change in their effectiveness is to change their knowledge and attitude structure—in other words, teach them diagnostic skills. On the other hand, much more time is necessary for people who have had no experience in using a variety of styles to become comfort-able in using different styles.

Reference to Situational Leadership

We will be referring to Situational Leadership throughout the discussion of the two-style profiles. The basic framework is reproduced for your use in Figure 12-8.

Style Profile 1-3

People who are perceived as using predominately styles 1 and 3 (see Fig-ure 12-9) fall into what is called the Theory X–Theory Y profile. What we have found is that people who have a style profile 1-3, with little flexibility to styles 2 and 4, generally view their followers with either Theory X or Theory Y as-sumptions about human nature. They see some people as lazy, unreliable, and irresponsible. The only way to get anything out of these people is to co-erce, reward and punish, and closely supervise them. Other people they see very positively as creative and self-motivated; the only thing they have to do with these people is to provide socioemotional support. In fact, in interview-ing managers with this profile, we have found that they talk about individu-

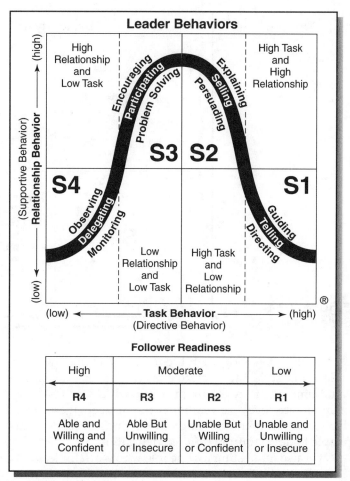

Figure 12-8
Situational Leadership Model

als they supervise as "good people" or "bad people," "with me" or "against me." Their followers, when interviewed, tend to agree. They see their managers as labeling people, and thus being very supportive (S3) with people they see in their "camp," but closely supervising, controlling (S1), and even punishing people whom they perceive as against them.

One of the interesting things that occurs with this style profile is that it often becomes a self-fulfilling prophecy. A manager with this style takes people who are at moderate readiness levels (R2) and either moves them up to moderate to high (R3) or moves them down to low levels of readiness (R1). Thus, this manager tends to be effective working with low levels of readiness or moderate to high levels of readiness.

A problem with this style is that the leaders who adopt it often are doing little to develop the potential of the people they don't like; they keep them locked into low levels of readiness by always relying on S1 (high task–low

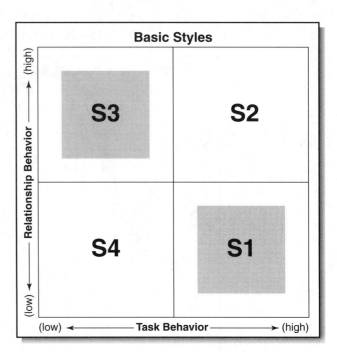

Figure 12-9
Style Profile 1-3

relationship behavior) with them. They lack the interim behaviors between style 1 and style 3 to operate effectively in the developmental cycle. At the same time, their style 3 (high relationship–low task behavior) with people of moderate levels of readiness might keep these people psychologically dependent on them too long. These kinds of leaders do not seem to allow people to develop fully through delegation.

It is also interesting that people who work for leaders with this style profile claim that if there is any change in their leader's style with them, it usually occurs in a movement from style 3 to style 1. In other words, it is very difficult if you are being treated in a style 1 fashion by these leaders ever to receive style 3 types of behavior from them. But it is not too difficult to move from receiving style 3 behaviors to receiving style 1 behaviors. All you have to do is make some mistakes and these leaders tend to respond with highly structured behavior.

Style Profile 1-4

People who are perceived as using mainly styles S1 and S4 (see Figure 12-10) have some similarity to the Theory X–Theory Y profile of style 1-3 leaders. But rather than assessing people on whether they are good or bad in terms of personal attachment to them, the sorting mechanism for this kind of leader often becomes competency. When interviewed, these managers suggest that if you are competent you will be left alone; but if you are incompetent, they will "ride you" and closely supervise your activities.

Their style is either telling or delegating. A leader with this style is effective at crisis interventions. This is the kind of style we might look for to make an in-

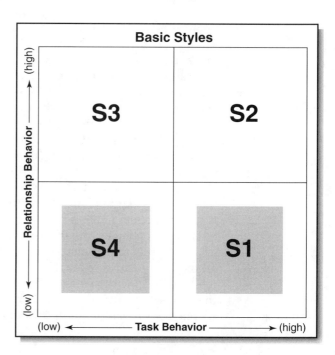

Figure 12-10
Style Profile 1-4

tervention into an organization with severe problems and little time to solve them. This kind of leader is quite capable of making disciplinary interventions, going in and turning around a situation, and, it is hoped, moving people back to a higher level of readiness. But again, much like the style 1-3 profile, this type of leader lacks the developmental skills to take people from low levels of readiness and develop them into higher levels of readiness.

An interesting thing occurs when leaders with this type of profile are introduced into a group with a normal distribution of readiness. What tends to happen is that the leader treats people in such a way that they either progress in their readiness or they regress, so that now, rather than a normal distribution of readiness levels, followers are clustered at the high end (R4) and low end (R1) of the readiness continuum. Once again, this style becomes a self-fulfilling prophecy.

Styles S1 and S4 are considered the "risky styles." We say "risky" because if they are used inappropriately, they can result in a great deal of crisis. For instance, if someone is supervising a group at a very low level of readiness and uses style S4, leaving people on their own, there is a high probability that the environment is going to deteriorate and serious problems will result. On the other hand, if you have an extremely high level of readiness among your followers and you are attempting to use style S1 interventions, you are likely to generate much resentment, anxiety, and resistance, which may lead to what Machiavelli referred to as attempts to undermine, overthrow, or get out from under the leader; that is, hatred rather than fear. Although styles S1 and S4 are risky styles, if you are going to maximize your role as leader, you have to be willing to take the risk and use these styles when the situation is appropriate. One warning is that if you feel style 1 or style 4 is needed in a situation, you should be careful in your diagnostic judgments before you make these kinds of interventions.

You need to learn to make style S1 interventions for the following reasons. First, they are effective interventions when beginning the process of developing the task-relevant readiness of people with low readiness levels. Second, this style is often necessary in making disciplinary interventions. On the other hand, S4 is often necessary if you are going to allow people to reach self-actualization by satisfying their need for achievement and desire to maximize their potential.

Learning to use style S4 is important. In any of the organizations for which we work, there are at least two prerequisites for promotion. The first is that managers have to do an outstanding job in their current position. In other words, their output in terms of that organization has to be high. The second prerequisite is that they have to have a ready replacement—someone who is ready and able to take over their responsibilities. To have this kind of ready replacement, managers must have at least one key follower with whom they are able to use style S4 and delegate significant responsibilities. If they do not, the probability of their having a ready replacement is very low.

Style Profile 2-3

People who are perceived as using predominantly styles S2 and S3 (see Figure 12-11) tend to do well working with people of average levels of readiness. However, they find it difficult to handle discipline problems and work

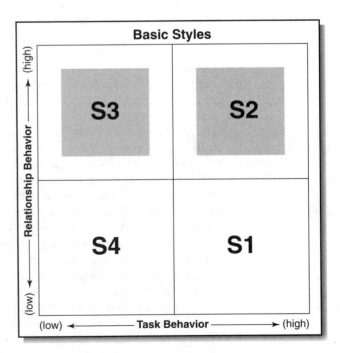

Figure 12-11
Style Profile 2-3

Chapter 12 Building Effective Relationships

groups at low levels of readiness (R1), and they also find it difficult to delegate with competent people to maximize their development. This style tends to be the most frequently identified style in the United States and other countries that have a high level of education and extensive industrial experience. Managers in some of the emerging cultures tend to have a more structured style profile (S1 and S2).

This style leader (S2-S3) tends to be effective more often than not, because most people in work settings usually fall into readiness levels R2 and R3. We find far fewer people, on the whole, at readiness levels R1 and R4.

If styles S1 and S4 are considered the "risky styles," then S2 and S3 are considered the "safe styles." Neither S2 nor S3 is ever likely to result in a crisis. The style profile S2-S3 is excellent for working with individuals at moderate levels of readiness, but if leaders with this profile are going to maximize their potential as leaders, they need to learn to use styles S1 and S4 when necessary.

Style Profile 1-2

People who are perceived as using predominantly styles S1 and S2 (see Figure 12-12) tend to be able to raise and lower their socioemotional support or relationship behavior, but they often feel uncomfortable unless they are "calling the shots"; that is, when they are providing the structure and direction. We found that this style profile tends to be characteristic of engineers who have become supervisors of other engineers, but who tend to be reluctant to give up their engineering; salespersons who have become sales managers yet still love to sell; and teachers who have become administrators, but still want

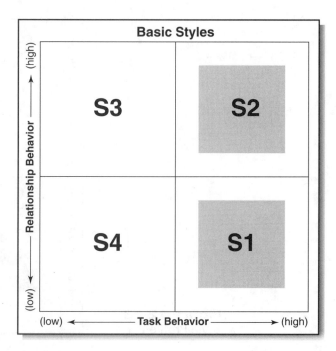

Figure 12-12
Style Profile 1-2

to be directing the activities of students. These leaders often project in interviews that "no one can do things as well as I can," and this often becomes a self-fulfilling prophecy.

The style profile S1-S2 tends to be effective with low to moderate levels of readiness. It is often an extremely effective style for people engaged in manufacturing and production, where managers have real pressures to produce, as well as with leaders in crisis situations, where time is an extremely scarce resource. But when the crisis or time pressure is over, leaders with this style often are not able to develop people to their fullest potential. And this remains true until they learn to use styles S3 and S4 appropriately.

Style Profile 2-4

People who are perceived as using mainly styles S2 and S4 (see Figure 12-13) usually have a primary style of S2 and a secondary style of S4. This style seems to be characteristic of managers who do not feel secure unless they are providing much of the direction, as well as developing a personal relationship with people in an environment characterized by two-way communication and socioemotional support (high relationship behavior). Only occasionally do these people find a person to whom they feel comfortable delegating. And when they do delegate, their choice may not be able to handle the project. Thus, such a person may not be able to complete the task or may come to the manager for help because the person is used to the leader's providing direction and socioemotional support. The reason that style profile S2-S4 leaders tend not to be successful in delegating is that they generally move from style S2 to style S4 without moving through style S3. Let's look at an example.

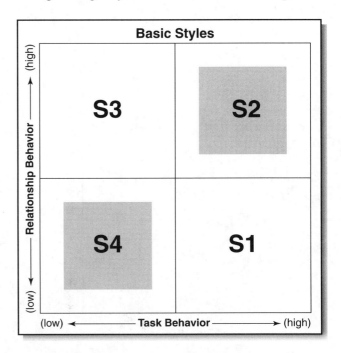

Figure 12-13
Style Profile 2-4

Chapter 12   Building Effective Relationships

Suppose Mac, a supervisor, usually directs and closely supervises (high task behavior) your activities, but you also have a good rapport with this supervisor and open communication, and you receive socioemotional support from these interactions (high relationship behavior). One day Mac puts a couple of projects on your desk and tells you that they must be completed in a couple of weeks. Then you don't see Mac for the next 2 weeks. You would probably respond to that behavior from Mac as if it were a punishment rather than a reward. You might respond by saying, "What's Mac giving me all this work for?" and "Mac must not care about me much anymore because I never see him now!" So rather than suddenly shifting from style S2 to S4, managers with this style—if they are going to be effective in delegating—have to learn to move from selling (S2) through participating (S3) and then to delegating (S4).

Style Profile 3-4

People who are perceived as using predominantly styles 3 and 4 (see Figure 12-14) tend to be able to raise and lower their socioemotional support or relationship behavior, but they often feel uncomfortable if they have to initiate structure or provide direction for people. Thus, although this style profile is appropriate for working with moderate to high levels of readiness, it tends to create problems with people who are decreasing in readiness and need a regressive intervention or with inexperienced people who require more direction during the early phases of the developmental cycle.

We have found style profile S3-S4 to be characteristic of certain types of individuals or groups. For example, one group is women who have recently

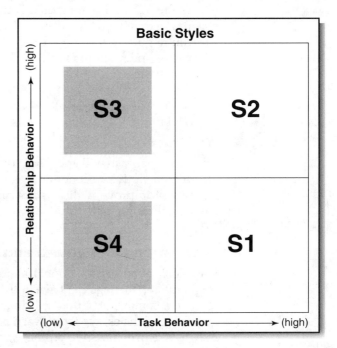

Figure 12-14
Style Profile 3-4

been promoted into significant middle-management positions. In interviewing these women, we have noted that before they were promoted, top management had not given them opportunities to engage in much telling (S1) or selling (S2) leader behavior; that is, they had little practice in initiating structure within the organizational setting. As a result, the only way they had an impact in the past was by raising or lowering socioemotional support. We found that with very little training these women responded quickly to trying on some of the other styles. It was just a matter of exposing them to concepts such as Situational Leadership to get them to feel comfortable trying these new behaviors. The tragedy is that women and other minorities restricted from management positions often have not received this training prior to promotion. Yet they may find that they are dealing with people who need direction and supervision. When they initially use a high relationship (S3) style, it is much more difficult to use other styles later, even though they now understand that they are appropriate.

Maximizing Your Management Staff

Felice Schwartz reinforced the need to give women more opportunities in her *Harvard Business Review* article. "If women are as smart, capable, and eager to exercise their skills as men are, all of which you say you believe, then why are the highest two levels in your company almost exclusively male domains? Ignore the matter of what is right or wrong. What does that segregation, intended or not, cost you? How are you hurt?"[13]

1. You're not mobilizing your best people at the top.
2. You're not maintaining quality at every level.
3. You're treating a big portion of your employees as deadweight.
4. You're putting a lid on the contributions individual women can make.
5. You're undervaluing promising people who wish to take a role in family caregiving.
6. You're wasting recruiting and training money.
7. You're failing to create beacons for the best women entering the workplace.
8. You are failing to capitalize on a tremendous opportunity.

This new approach will appeal to your stockholders, more than half of whom are women, both for economic reasons and reasons of principle. Your public image will improve, which is not an insignificant issue. Today, companies compete through their values as well as their products.[14]

Implications for Growth and Development

If we look at an organizational hierarchy from very low levels to what we might call top management, we find that effective managers at each level tend to have a somewhat different primary style profile. Before looking at these general tendencies, we must warn that although managers at a given level may have a primary style profile, *effective* managers at all levels use all of the styles, as appropriate. We have discussed this point repeatedly, but it deserves special emphasis.

We have found that effective managers at the lower levels (see Figure 12-15) tend to have style profile S1-S2. The reason is that at these lower levels of management (in industry, the general foremen and first- and second-line supervisors), there is an emphasis on productivity—getting the work out. At the other end of the management hierarchy, however, effective top managers tend to engage in more participating and delegating. The reason seems to be that as you move up in an organizational hierarchy, the greater is the probability that the subordinates who report directly to you will have a high level of task-relevant readiness. So you can see that as you progress through an organization, you learn to engage in styles S3 and S4, as well as those styles that might be effective at lower ends of the hierarchy (styles S1 and S2). Thus, we have found in working with manufacturing organizations that, although it may be appropriate for first-line supervisors to have a basic style of S1 and a supporting style of S2, when those people get promoted, it would be more appropriate if they had a basic style of S2 with supporting styles in S1 and S3. At this new supervisory level, they are no longer managers of hourly employees, but they have now become managers of managers.

Another interesting observation in terms of the management hierarchy is that it is the middle managers who really have to wear "both hats"—they need the most flexibility. They have to be able to provide the structured style S1 and style S2 interventions when appropriate, but they also must be able to use participating (S3) and delegating (S4) styles when necessary. It is interesting to think of this phenomenon in terms of the Peter Principle.

Figure 12-15
Style Profiles for Different Levels of Management

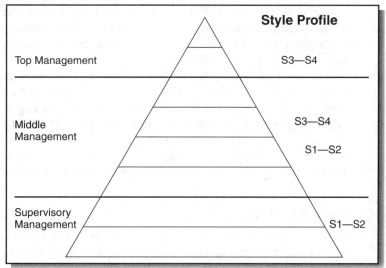

As you will recall, the Peter Principle states: "In a hierarchy, every employee tends to rise to his level of incompetence."[15] What we find in our work at the Center for Leadership Studies is that this is *not* a principle; it does not hold as a universal truth. In fact, as we suggested in chapter 7, one might think of the Peter Principle vaccine as being the appropriate training and development or experience before moving up to the next level of the hierarchy. Better than training and development *after* being appointed to the new position is having worked for a supervisor who is willing to delegate responsibilities and provide on-the-job experience for future higher-level positions. Another interesting observation is that, although the Peter Principle is not really a principle, it occurs often enough to merit some attention. There certainly is a tendency for people to reach their level of incompetency. Often, when we interview people who are in a position they are having trouble handling, it turns out that they have the technical skills and conceptual skills required. In most cases, their incompetence is a result of not having the human skills. Many times they are not able to adapt their leadership style to the new environment.

Although this lack of flexibility does occur, we have found in working with managers in a variety of settings and cultures that given some training in Situational Leadership, they seem willing and able, almost without exception, to expand their style range. They are able to take on new leadership styles effectively. The most important criterion here is motivation—people have to want to learn. If they want to, most people have the capacity to increase their style range and adaptability. This assumption is an important difference between our approach and the thinking of some other people in the field, such as Fred Fiedler.[16] Fiedler contends that if a leader's style is not appropriate to a given situation, what really needs to be done is either change the leader or change the job demands to fit the style of the leader. We feel that that approach implies Theory X assumptions about human nature; yet our work suggests strongly that the potential of people to operate under Theory Y assumptions is there to be tapped. Although lack of flexibility does occur, we have found that managers in a variety of settings and cultures, once exposed to training in Situational Leadership, are willing and able, almost without exception, to expand their range and adaptability.

One concluding thought before leaving this section: One of the major results of the current organizational resizing is compression of middle management. The result of this compression or reduction is expanding roles of both top management and supervisory management. We find that the primary roles of both top management and supervisory management are expanding toward styles S2 and S3. Once again, however, we must remind ourselves that effective managers at all levels use all of the styles, as appropriate.

Team Building

If managers have a narrow range of behavior, one way that they can expand their flexibility (without changing their own behavior) is by carefully choosing the people they gather around them. If leaders are careful to bring into the organization key followers who complement their leadership style rather than replicate it, the organization may develop a wider range of potential styles that can be brought to bear on the contingencies they face. As we warned in chapter 7, to avoid personality conflict and to increase the likelihood of building on the strength of others, leaders select subordinates who understand each others' roles and have the same goals and objectives, even though their styles might be somewhat different.

Determining the Leadership Style of a Manager

At the beginning of the chapter, we raised the following question: How will changes in a leader's style affect followers' perceptions of the leader's intentions? From our experience, once managers begin to share Situational Leadership with their key followers and clarify what is expected of them, this question no longer becomes an issue. Managers no longer are the sole determiners of the style they use with their people. Their key staff now play a vital role. If the managers are not practicing situational leaders, the key staff start to realize that it is *their* behavior (not the manager's) that determines the leadership style to be used with them. Thus, if everyone in a management team knows Situational Leadership, the key staff realize how they can keep their manager off their backs. All they have to do is perform in responsible ways—ways that everyone has agreed are appropriate—and their manager will be supportive (S3) or leave them alone (S4). But, if they do not produce and perform in responsible ways, they know their manager will watch them more closely. They will know why they are getting that kind of treatment from their manager, and they will know how they can get their manager to treat them in a more supportive way again—by getting back on track. It must be remembered though that this approach is effective only if managers are consistent (that is, they treat their people the same way in similar circumstances) even when it is inconvenient or unpopular with their people.

Thus, Situational Leadership is a vehicle to help managers and their staff understand and share expectations in their organizational setting. If people know what is expected of them, they can gradually learn to supervise their own behavior and become responsible, self-motivated individuals.

CONTRACTING FOR LEADERSHIP STYLE

The process that was developed at the Center for Leadership Studies for sharing Situational Leadership with key staff and helping to enlarge everyone's public arena (in Johari Window terms) is called "Contracting for Leadership Style." This process is a helpful addition to a management by objectives (MBO) program.

Of all the management concepts and techniques developed over the past several decades, few have received such widespread attention as management by objectives. Theoretically, MBO, discussed in chapter 6, offers tremendous potential as a participatory management approach, but problems have developed in implementation. Consequently, although many attempts have been made to utilize MBO, ineffective implementations have occurred. As a result, success stories do not occur as often as anticipated by theorists who have written about MBO or practitioners who have applied it. One reason is that often the role of the leader in helping followers accomplish objectives is not clearly defined in MBO.

What often happens in the MBO process is that once a leader and follower have negotiated and agreed upon goals and objectives for the follower, the leader may or may not engage in the appropriate leader behavior that will facilitate goal accomplishment for the follower. For example, if the leader leaves the follower completely alone, the leader will be unaware until the next interim performance evaluation period that this low relationship–low task leadership style is appropriate for accomplishing objectives in areas where the follower has had significant experience, but inappropriate when the follower lacks sufficient technical skill and know-how in a particular area. Conversely, if, after negotiating goals and objectives, a leader continually hovers over and directs the activities of the followers, this high task–low relationship style might alienate followers working in areas where they are competent and capable of working alone. Problems may occur when a leader uses too much of any one style.

Adding the Contracting Process

In terms of Situational Leadership, once a leader and follower have agreed upon and contracted certain goals and objectives for the follower, the next logical step would be negotiation and agreement about the appropriate leadership style that the leader should use in helping the follower accomplish each of the objectives. For example, an individual and the leader may agree on five objectives for the year. After this agreement, the next step would be the negotiation of leadership style. In areas where the person is experienced and has been successful in accomplishing similar objectives over a period of time, the negotiated leadership contract might be for the leader to give the follower considerable freedom. In this case, rather than directing and closely supervising behavior, the role of the leader would be to make sure that the resources necessary for goal accomplishment are available and to coordinate the results of this project with other projects being supervised. With another goal, the follower might be working on a new project with little prior experience, while the leader does have some expertise in this area. In this case, the follower and leader might negotiate significant structure, direction, and supervision from the leader until the follower is familiar with the task. Different leadership styles may be appropriate at different times, depending on the follower's readiness in relation to the specific task involved.

Two things should be emphasized in discussing the negotiation of leadership style. First, it should be an open contract. Once style has been negotiated for accomplishing a particular goal, it can be opened for renegotiation by either party. For example, an individual may find on a particular task that working without supervision is not realistic. At this point, the follower may contact the leader and set up a meeting to negotiate for more direction. The leader, at the time, may gather some data that suggest that the style being used with an individual on a particular task is not producing results. The leader in this case can ask for a renegotiation of style.

Second, when a negotiation over leadership style occurs, it implies a shared responsibility if goals are not met. For example, if a follower has not accomplished the agreed-upon goals and the leader has not provided the contracted leadership style or support, the data then become part of the evaluation of both people. This means that if a leader has contracted for close supervision, help cannot be withheld from a follower (even though the leader may be busy on another project) without the leader's sharing some of the responsibility for lack of accomplishment of that goal.

Making the Process Work

Initially, as people were exposed to Situational Leadership concepts and began to apply them in daily leader and follower interactions, they sought some general ways to judge similarities and differences between leadership styles and follower expectations.

An Example—Contracting for Leadership Styles in a School

Some interesting results of the Contracting for Leadership Style process occurred in an elementary school in eastern Massachusetts. In many school systems, the principal of a school is required by school policy to visit each classroom a certain number of times each year. This visitation policy is dysfunctional for principals who recognize that their teachers vary in their experience and competence and, therefore, have varying needs for supervision from the principal. If a principal decides to schedule visitations according to a perception of the competence of the teachers, problems often occur with teachers at either end of the extreme. Left alone, a highly experienced teacher may be confused by the lack of contact with the principal and may even interpret it as a lack of interest. At the same time, an inexperienced teacher may interpret the frequent visits of the principal as a sign of lack of trust and confidence. In both cases, what the principal does may be interpreted as negative by the teachers.

These problems were eliminated in this elementary school when the principal shared Situational Leadership with the staff and then attempted to negotiate what the principal's leadership style should be with each of the teachers. It was found that when low relationship–low task leadership style was negotiated between the principal and teachers because both agreed that these teachers were capable of working on their own, infrequent visits from the principal were perceived by the teachers as a reward rather than a punishment.

The same thing held true at the other end of the continuum. When negotiation for leadership style took place with inexperienced teachers (who realized that the system was designed to help teachers learn to work on their own), these teachers were less reluctant to share anxieties about certain aspects of their teaching. If the negotiation led to initial close supervision and direction, the teachers were able to view this interaction as positive, not punitive, because it was a temporary style and demonstrated the principal's interest in helping them operate on their own.

Using the Readiness Style Match

A useful instrument has been developed at the Center for Leadership Studies. The instrument formalizes the process of implementing Contracting for Leadership Style. It's called the Readiness Style Match. As discussed in chapter 8, the Readiness Style Match measures readiness using two dimensions: (1) *ability*, or job readiness and (2) *willingness*, or psychological readiness. The rating form also describes precisely the four basic leadership styles. The description of those styles and the two readiness scales are depicted in Figure 12-16.

As indicated in Figure 12-16, a person's ability (knowledge and skill) is thought of as a matter of degree. That is, an individual's ability does not change drastically from one moment to the next. At any given moment, an individual has a little, some, quite a bit, or a great deal of ability. Willingness (confidence and commitment), however, is different. A person's psychological readiness can, and often does, fluctuate from one moment to another. Therefore, a person is seldom, on occasion, often, or usually willing to take responsibility in a particular area.

Combining establishing objectives and reaching consensus on performance criteria in a traditional MBO program with a similar process for negotiating the appropriate leadership style that a manager should use to facilitate goal accomplishment in a specific task area can be accomplished through the following steps.

1. *Establish objectives and performance criteria.* Manager and staff member independently establish objectives and performance criteria for the staff member.
2. *Reach agreement on objectives and performance criteria.* Manager and staff member come together to reach agreement on objectives and performance criteria.
3. *Introduce Situational Leadership.* Both manager and staff member are introduced to Situational Leadership, if they have not already been exposed to the concept (which can be accomplished by reading chapter 8 of this book).
4. *Complete Readiness Style Match.* Manager and staff member independently complete a Readiness Style Match rating form. The staff member records the primary and secondary leadership styles that the manager has been using on each of the agreed-upon goals and objectives. The manager does the same, indicating what leadership style has been used with the staff member on each of the agreed-upon goals and objectives. If the staff member has never had a particular objective area before, no past leader-

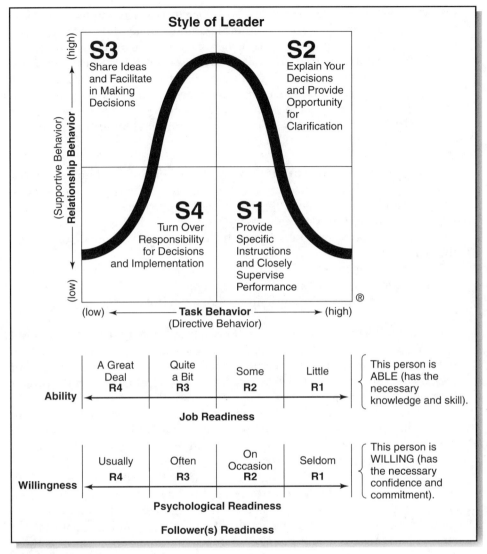

Figure 12-16
Defining Readiness and the Four Basic Leadership Styles

ship style can be diagnosed. After analyzing leadership style, both the staff member and manager make judgments on the ability and the willingness of the staff member to accomplish each of the goals and objectives established at the desired performance level without any supervision. In other words, the staff member participating in this process would analyze the leadership style that the manager has been using, as well as self-assessment judgments of the readiness level. At the same time, the manager would be analyzing the readiness level of the staff member as well as making leadership style self-assessment judgments.

5. *Meet to share data from Readiness Style Match.* Manager and staff member meet and share the data from their Readiness Style Match rating forms. It is recommended that they consider one objective or responsibility at a time. The purpose of sharing data is to agree upon the readiness level and appropriate leadership style that can be utilized with the staff member to maximize performance. During this process, both manager and staff member should bring their calendars. Once they have determined the appropriate leadership style to make this commitment and turn it into behavior, they will require scheduled meetings.

For example, in a particular objective area, any one of the four leadership styles may have been agreed upon as appropriate. If the staff member is inexperienced and insecure about performing in a particular area, a telling (S1) style would be appropriate for the manager to use. If this is the case, they should schedule frequent meetings so that the manager can work closely with the staff member.

If the staff member is willing but inexperienced in a particular area, the manager should utilize a selling (S2) style. This would involve scheduling meetings to work with the staff member, but not as frequently as under S1 supervision.

If the staff member is able in a particular area but is a little insecure about working completely alone, a participating (S3) leadership style would be appropriate. That may involve meeting periodically over lunch so that the staff member can show the manager what has been accomplished and the proper support and encouragement can be given.

If the staff member is able and willing to perform at the desired level in a particular objective area, no meetings are necessary unless called by the staff member. In this case, performance review can occur on an infrequent basis.

If the Contracting for Leadership Style process is utilized, the frequency of performance review will change depending on the ability and the willingness of the staff member to perform at the desired level without supervision. As stated earlier, if this process is used, the negotiation of leadership style should be an open contract and imply shared responsibility if goals are not met. In particular, if a staff member is improving in a particular area, there should be a renegotiation of leadership style to a less directive leadership style. At the same time, if a staff member's performance is not being maximized utilizing a particular leadership style, that will signal the need to move back to a more directive style. A give-and-take process should occur between leader and follower.

The readiness style match matrix, part of the Readiness Style Match, is useful in providing insight into whether your manager is using "overleadership"—you have high levels of readiness, but your manager is using telling and selling styles to a greater degree than necessary. "Underleadership" is where you have low levels of readiness, but your manager is using participating and delegating styles more than is appropriate. A high probability style match would be when the style(s) of your manager tends to correspond with the readiness level(s) you exhibit.

One warning should be given in using the Contracting for Leadership Style process and the Readiness Style Match rating forms. When managers go through that process, their public arena in the Johari Window becomes very large. Very little about what these managers think and feel about the staff member is unknown to that staff member, and vice versa. Feedback and disclosure become an ongoing process. If managers do not want their people to know what they think and feel about them, then they should be careful about using the described process. With some people, they might want to remain much less open. When managers make that choice, they must remember that with those people, the blind and private arenas in their Johari Window will be large. In some cases, that may very well be appropriate.

SUMMARY

This chapter has discussed three aspects of leader behavior: (1) style, (2) style range, or flexibility, and (3) style adaptability. We also looked at the use of LEAD instruments to diagnose these three aspects. The Johari Window was introduced as an approach to self-perception and the perception of others. The chapter concluded with discussion of a number of two-style profiles and the Contracting for Leadership Style process.

ENDNOTES

1. LEAD (formerly known as the Leader Adaptability and Style Inventory, LASI) is based on the Situational Leadership model. The first publication of this LEAD instrument appeared in Paul Hersey and Kenneth H. Blanchard, "So You Want to Know Your Leadership Style?" *Training and Development Journal*, February 1974. Copies of the LEAD Self and LEAD Other instruments can be ordered from the Center for Leadership Studies, Escondido, CA 92025.

2. This contracting process first appeared in Paul Hersey and Kenneth H. Blanchard, "What's Missing in MBO?" *Management Review*, October 1974. Much of the discussion that follows was taken from that article.

3. George S. Odiorne, *The Human Side of Management* (San Diego, CA: University Associates, 1987).

4. The LEAD Other is the same instrument as the LEAD Self but written so that a subordinate, superior, or peer could fill it out on a leader. Instruments are available from the Center for Leadership Studies, Escondido, CA, 92025.

5. William J. Reddin, *The 3-D Management Style Theory, Theory Paper #6—Style Flex* (Fredericton, N.B., Canada: Social Science Systems, 1967), p. 6.

6. Joseph Luft and Harry Ingham, "The Johari Window, A Graphic Model of Interpersonal Awareness," *Proceedings of the Western Training Laboratory in Group Development* (Los Angeles: UCLA, Extension Office, 1955). A more up-to-date version of the framework is presented in Joseph Luft, *Group Process: An Introduction to Group Dynamics*, 2nd ed. (Palo Alto, CA: National Press Book, 1970).

7. Sigmund Freud, *The Ego and the Id* (London: Hogarth Press, 1927).

8. Wayne W. Dyer, *Your Erroneous Zones* (New York: Funk & Wagnalls, 1976).

9. This statement is adapted from a quotation by Dorothy Canfield Fisher that Dyer referred to in *Your Erroneous Zones*, p. 195.

10. Elaina Zucker, "5 Tips for Managing a Stressful Job," *Nursing*, May 1993.

11. Barbara L. Mackoff, "Leave the Office Behind," *Public Management*, June 1992.

12. The analysis of LEAD data was first presented in Paul Hersey, *Situational Leadership: Some Aspects of Its Influence on Organizational Development*, Ph.D. dissertation, University of Massachusetts, 1975.

13. Felice N. Schwartz, "Women As a Business Imperative," *Harvard Business Review*, March–April 1992, p. 108.

14. *Ibid.*, p. 111.

15. Lawrence J. Peter and Raymond Hull, *The Peter Principle: Why Things Always Go Wrong* (New York: Morrow, 1969). See also Peter, *The Peter Plan: A Proposal for Survival* (New York: Morrow, 1976); Peter, *Peter's Quotations: Ideas for Our Time* (New York: Morrow, 1977).

16. Fred E. Fiedler, "Engineer the Job to Fit the Manager," *Harvard Business Review*, 51 (1965), pp. 115–122. See also Fiedler, *Leader Attitudes and Group Effectiveness* (Westport, CN: Greenwood, 1981); Fiedler and Martin M. Chemers, *Improving Leadership Effectiveness: The Leader Match Concept* (New York: Wiley, 1984).

Chapter 13

Effective Communication

Very early in this book, we defined leadership as an attempt to influence, for whatever reason. We also noted that leadership and influence might be used interchangeably. You will also recall that we discussed the three basic competencies in influencing as (1) *diagnosing*—being able to understand the situation you are attempting to influence; (2) *adapting*—being able to adapt your behavior, and the other things that you have control over, to the contingencies of the situation; and (3) *communicating*—being able to put the message in a way that people can easily understand and accept. In this chapter, we will explore different areas of effective communication by showing the importance of effective communication, explaining the three basic communication models, defining and describing the functions and types of nonverbal communication, and then briefly introducing the aspects of organizational and intercultural communication. ✧

HOW IMPORTANT IS EFFECTIVE COMMUNICATION?

All the evidence clearly shows that written and oral communication skills are critical not only in obtaining a job, but also in performing effectively on the job. For example, in a study reported in *Personnel*, a survey questionnaire was sent to the personnel managers of 175 of the largest companies in a western state.[1] One of the key questions in the study concerned the factors and skills most important in helping graduating business students obtain employment. Written and oral communication skills were the two most important factors or skills in obtaining employment.

This trend has continued. In a more recent study of MBAs, Kimberly F. Kane writes that strong interpersonal and communication skills appear to be of primary importance in the hiring decision.

> Nearly two-thirds (of recruiters surveyed) thought MBAs have fully satisfactory skills and knowledge in their specialty areas. However, fully half thought MBAs were lacking to some degree in both interpersonal and written communications skills—the very skills reported to be the most important hiring criteria. One-third reported that MBAs were lacking in some degree in oral communication skills.[2]

But what is the relationship between oral and written communication skills and performance on the job?

Most chief operating officers (COOs) rate employee communication skills as vital, using such phrases as "extremely important," "very important," or "tops."[3] Other COOs state "There is a direct correlation between employee communication and profitability" and "I find that making good profits really goes hand in hand with having good communication." Perhaps the importance of good communication is best summarized by a senior executive who noted:

> The best business plan is meaningless unless everyone is aware of it and pulling together to achieve its objectives. Good communications are the lifeblood of any enterprise, large or small. Communications are essential to keep our entire organization functioning at maximum levels and to make the most of our greatest management resource—our people.[4]

> Other surveys have confirmed that communication is a skill desired by the business world (Curtis, Winsor, and Stephens, 1989; DiSalvo, 1980; DiSalvo, Larsen, and Seller, 1978; Hanna, 1978). The study by Curtis, Winsor, and Stephens included (among other questions) asking the American Society of Personnel Administrators to assess the skills necessary for successful job performance and the skills necessary for managerial success. The responses showed that the top two skills for successful job performance were interpersonal/human relations skills and the top two skills for managerial success were the abilities to work one-on-one and to gather accurate information. These skills are dynamic skills requiring the ability to analyze the entire situation in context.[5]

How can we, as leaders and potential leaders, improve our communication competency? We will begin by looking at the basics of communication, starting with the three basic communication models. The first two are static models. The third is a dynamic, interactive model that represents communication in leadership situations.

COMMUNICATION MODELS

The Linear Model

There are three basic ways, as suggested by Barnlund (1970), to show how human beings communicate. The first is the *linear model*, shown in Figure 13-1, which shows commmunicative events as one-sided activities from the leader, on the left, to the follower, on the right. People begin this process by *encoding* their thoughts into *symbols*. Symbols are things that represent something else. For example, corporate logos and computer icons *in and of themselves* do not mean anything, yet they represent the corporation or a computer program or file. A person seeing an older gentleman with a goatee and a shock of white hair in an oval on the top of a red-and-white-striped container realizes that this person is not alive on the cardboard, but represents Kentucky Fried Chicken. The words on this page, for example, are symbolic of thoughts and ideas.

Once the symbols are created, they are then formed into a *message* that can be one symbol or a set of symbols. The message is then placed into a *channel* for distribution. The message can consist of either verbal or nonverbal communication, or it can be a combination of both. *Verbal* communication refers only to words. Leaders should be aware that words can be perceived as powerful or powerless. Powerless language choices include hedges ("I *think* it will work"), gap-filling sounds (the use of "ums" and "ers"), tag questions ("We need your help, *don't you think so?*"), and disclaimers (I would do that, *but I am not the boss."*) Bradac, Wiemann, and Schafer (1994) point out that numerous studies have shown that a person who uses power*ful* language is perceived as

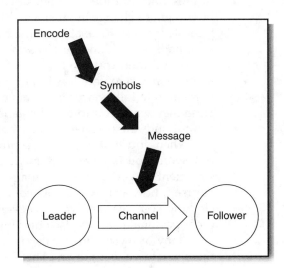

Figure 13-1
Linear
Communication
Model

competent, dynamic, and attractive versus a person who uses hedges and other power*less* language choices.

Nonverbal Cues

All other aspects of communication are *nonverbal* cues. Nonverbal cues have four basic functions: They supplement the verbal by accenting or adding emphasis to certain words (making a powerful gesture); they can substitute for verbal cues (smile or frown); they can contradict the verbal cues (saying, "This will work" while sweating, twisting a foot back and forth, and looking for an emergency exit); and they regulate the verbal cues. Regulation occurs by increasing the pitch at the end of a sentence that forms a question, pausing and looking at someone to await a response, holding up a hand to stop verbal interaction, and leaving a room to end a verbal interaction.

There are also many types of nonverbal cues. Appearance and body orientation, face and eye behavior, gestures, the use of touch and distance behavior, posture, and movement can all be perceived as showing an interest or a lack of interest in a communicative act. Let's look at some examples of how nonverbals help or hinder your leader effectiveness.

The physical environment and the use of time are key powerful nonverbal cues. Who has not sat outside of an office waiting for an interview that invariably is later than arranged? This is a message about power and control. And then, when presented to the interviewer, you were placed in a chair slightly lower than the interviewer, with a table or a large desk positioned between you. Regardless of what was said in the interview, these different types of nonverbal cues may have lead to nervousness or elation based on your perception of the events.

How you enter an office, how you support your message through gestures and facial expressions, how you imply interest and vitality through eye contact, and other nonverbal behaviors affect other people's reactions to you. In turn, the nonverbal cues of followers serve as windows to their emotions, desires, and attitudes. Changes in a follower's body postures and gestures often signal a change in readiness. Movement toward the front of a chair may indicate interest. Relaxation of the body may reflect acceptance. Mirroring of your nods, smiles, and gestures could also indicate acceptance.

As a leader, you should also understand how followers view space and its relationship to you. It is important to monitor how you position yourself in relation to followers. People have levels of comfort when it comes to how close they want you to be. The general rule is, if you are making them uncomfortable, then change, either by moving closer or by moving farther away.

When you first encounter a prospective follower, before you say your first word you have already made a statement about yourself. Part of this statement involves body language in terms of how confidently you carry yourself, how you walk, and your general manner. Part of it involves the clothing you wear and your accessories. Grooming, neatness, hairstyle, and other personal features also enter into the equation.

Many of these nonverbals are under your direct control. You can make them what you want them to be. To the extent possible, your attire and general appearance should reflect a sense of personal dignity and self-worth. They should be appropriate to your followers' environment and should reflect your personal and your organization's values.[6]

Paralanguage

Paralanguage is another type of nonverbal cue that includes the pitch, rate, volume, and the use of pauses. Your voice is a highly versatile instrument. Through it, you can convey enthusiasm, confidence, anxiety, urgency, serenity, and other states of mind and intent. The ability of the voice to affect how something is said is known as *paralanguage*. Timing when you speak, increasing or decreasing voice intensity, pausing, and varying pitch and other aspects of speech patterns can increase your ability to influence. By closely attending to the followers' paralanguage, you can pick up clues about your progress in influencing your followers.

The Interactional Model of Communication

We have introduced the linear model of human communication and have defined and explained such important terms as encoding, symbols, message, channels, verbal, and nonverbal communication. The main problem with the linear model is that the follower is not involved. This model does not explain face-to-face communication, but it does represent other one-way communicative acts such as billboards, television, flyers, and signs. Does an employee actually read the organization's newsletter? Do the organization's employees accept its vision? The linear model is based on hope—hope that the follower understands the communication. How can we illustrate face-to-face communication in the everyday workplace to show some response from the follower?

The follower must be involved in some response to the message. The interactional model does just this (see Figure 13-2). After receiving the message, the follower then *decodes* the message to ascertain some form of meaning for the message. By translating the symbols (Quality Is Job One; Be All That You Can Be), the follower then has an opportunity to create a message to return to the leader. After decoding, the follower can encode symbols that can be placed in the form of a message and give *feedback* to the leader. Feedback may involve verbal or nonverbal cues and, with the examples given previously, the responses could include: "I believe in quality—I'll buy a Ford"; "I'll be at the recruiting station in the morning." The leader can then reshape or change a return message and send another to the follower.

This turn-taking is akin to what Galanes, Adams, and Brilhart call ". . . a tennis game. The server sends the message, the receiver lobs a response back. This is misleading because communication is a multidirectional transactional process."[7]

What does this model represent with respect to communication in the workplace? E-mail? Telephone calls? Paging someone? Even if there is no response from the follower, the lack of a response is feedback to the leader. The key to creating a model that best explains face-to-face human communication

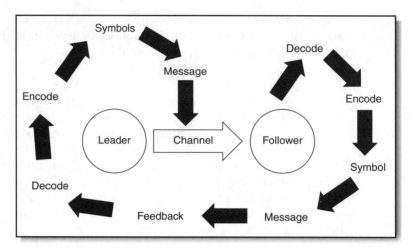

Figure 13-2
Interactional Communication Model

is to show that the responses of the other person involved are continual. This process is known as the *transactional communication model*.

The Transactional Communication Model

This model (see Figure 13-3) gives us our best understanding of face-to-face human communication. Because we are constantly encoding and decoding messages when talking face-to-face with another person, this model best explains the communication process. As shown in Figure 13-3, the channel is now a two-headed arrow representing an ongoing process between the leader and follower and contains three new elements not seen in the previous two models. The first of these is *noise*.

External and Internal Noise

External noise is noise that occurs outside the brain of the decoder. Examples include your stomach growling during a meeting, a tree growing and blocking your company's sign, watching a newsbreak on television, or being interrupted by a phone call and not paying attention to the caller. All of these things are external noise because they can distract from the communication. An effective leader must be aware of possible external factors that could interfere with the communication and act accordingly to minimize those factors. For example, instead of talking next to a punch press, an effective leader would find a quieter place to communicate with the followers.

Internal noise can be created in at least four different ways. First, internal noise occurs because we each have a brain. If a person is talking at 125 words per minute and you have the ability to listen effectively at 200 words per minute and the ability to think at a much higher word per minute rate, your brain decides to use the "free" word per minute spaces to do other things.

Paul Cameron, a professor at Wayne State University in Detroit, conducted a study with 85 college sophomores. An associate made a loud noise

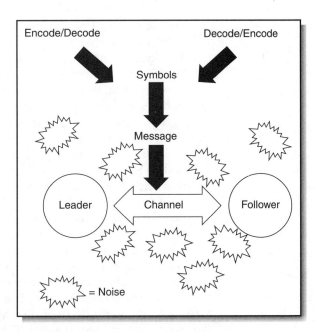

Figure 13-3
Transactional
Communication
Model

21 times during professor Cameron's lectures over the length of the course. The students had been told that they needed to encode their thoughts at that time. The results reported to the American Psychological Association showed that 20 percent of the students were reminiscing about something, 20 percent were pursing romantic thoughts, 20 percent were actually paying attention, 12 percent were actively listening, and the rest were worrying, daydreaming, thinking about lunch, or thinking about religion. In other words, 88 percent of this population were not actively involved in the lecture due to internal noise. Imagine what occurs during a committee meeting.

Second, external noises can also cause internal noise. Your stomach or another person's stomach growling may produce thoughts in the brain that cry out for lunch instead of paying attention to the discussion. The overwhelming smell of perfume or cologne may cause multiple reactions in your brain, from romance to revulsion. If you are focused on a breaking news story, you may not remember a phone conversation. And, there may be so much noise on, for example, the factory floor that the follower would not even bother to listen.

The third way internal noise can be created is through the perception process of individuals involved in the communication. Every person has a distinct method for selecting, organizing, and interpreting verbal or nonverbal cues (Coon, 1992). For example, a person hears the term "leader" during a presentation. This term may evoke different thoughts in different people. A person who disliked a previous leader would interpret the term in a negative way; a person who admired a previous leader would think of the term positively. Internal noise can then be created as the former person would begin to think of the disliked leader; the other person would begin to think of the admired leader with *neither* paying any attention to the communicative acts occurring around them.

The fourth way internal noise can be created is through the perceptual process. People do not behave on the basis of truth and reality. Their behavior is evoked from their *perception* and *interpretation* of truth and reality. These perceptions and interpretations are the product of information taken in through the senses: sight, hearing, smell, taste, and touch. So much information comes in that people cannot attend to it all. Through selective awareness, psychological maps are formed from only part of the information. Behavior is based on these maps. And the maps affect what people perceive. Communication effectiveness is enhanced if you understand the way people map their psychological worlds.

People use their psychological maps to make decisions, to get around in life. However, the map is not the territory. It is based upon perceptions of that territory. And these perceptions differ from person to person.[8]

Here is an example of how perception affects behavior. Some friends made a reservation at a seaside restaurant that has a world famous view of the ocean and the crashing surf. Their reservations were for 7:00 P.M., but they arrived a little early. To their dismay, they watched as other groups entered the restaurant and were seated. Time passed, and it was now 7:10 P.M. Convinced that they had been snubbed or ignored by the management of the restaurant, they were about to make an angry complaint to the maitre d' when he approached. "May I seat you now?" he said, as he led them to one of the best tables, where they had a spectacular view. "I am sorry for the delay, but the previous party just wouldn't leave!" The friends' perception was opposite of what was really happening. Instead of snubbing them, the restaurant management was doing its best to seat them at a table with an excellent view. Had the situation been explained earlier, they would not have been so impatient, and they would have perceived the situation entirely differently.

Semantic Noise

In the context of communication, the perceptual process creates *semantic* noise, also known as *word noise*. Ogden and Richards (1949), in their classic text *The Meaning of Meaning*, created a triangle (see Figure 13-4) that shows:

> When we speak, the symbolism we employ is caused partly by the reference we are making and partly by social and psychological factors—the purpose for which we are making the reference, the proposed effect of our symbols on other persons, and our own attitude.
>
> When we hear what is said, the symbols both cause us to perform an act of reference and to assume an attitude which will, according to the circumstances, be more or less similar to the act and the attitude of the speaker.[9]

We see or hear an object and then think about how to categorize or define the symbol or object, and we name that symbol or object. All of this occurs while we study the context of the situation, including who or what transmitted the symbol or object, deciding our relationship with the person or thing involved,

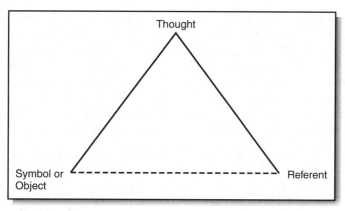

Figure 13-4
Triangle of Meaning

Source: C. K. Ogden and I. A. Richards, *The Meaning of Meaning* (1949), p. 10.

checking our past experiences with the symbol or object, and many other things that go into the brain in a split second.

The bottom of the triangle has a dotted line showing that for most symbols or objects, there is no direct referent. Corporations would like to think that this is not true as evidenced by the amount of money spent to create logos or ideas so that customers would immediately identify the name for a symbol or object. However, a yellow shaped "M" can still represent something other than McDonalds, a peace sign is not a rabbit head, and a ram's head can be a referent for the Rocky Mountains instead of Dodge. Very effective symbols, frequently repeated, can be quickly identified. An octagonal red sign with a white stripe around the border with large white letters that spell S-T-O-P does the job most of the time.

Problems occur when one of two conditions is present. If there are multiple referents for a symbol or object, a follower may use one that the speaker did not intend to be used. An executive may urge the organization to become more efficient. What does efficient mean? Faster? Better output? Less time off? More cost-effective? Followers may interpret the executive's remarks as a signal for future layoffs, although the executive was urging watching the expenses to avoid future layoffs—one simple word, two opposite interpretations.

A classic example of too many referents was experienced by Chevrolet when it marketed the Nova in Spanish-speaking countries. Nova in Spanish means, "No go," which not only shows semantic noise, but also shows a direct relationship to sales.

The second way that semantic noise may occur is when there is no referent for a symbol or object. The music associated with "Intel Inside" is widely known. However, if a person is not computer literate, the music has no referent. A person joins a new company. The slang, terms, and abbreviations used in the company must be taught to the new employee or semantic noise will occur.

Jay A. Conger, of McGill University, reinforces the need for careful word selection, use of paralanguage, and nonverbal behavior to inspire others.

Leadership, as we noted in chapter 1, is more than having technical and conceptual skills; leadership involves capturing the hearts and minds of followers.

Conger cites the well-known story of two stonemasons to support his view of the motivational aspect of leadership. When one of the stonemasons was asked what he was doing, the reply was: "I am cutting stone." When the other mason was asked, his reply was: "I am building a great cathedral." Leaders must build "great cathedrals" with their communications. Conger's guidelines for more expressive, inspirational leadership include:

1. Craft your organization's mission statement around the basic deeply held values, beliefs, and societal purposes of the organization.
2. Use key elements of the organization's culture, e.g., stories, analogies, metaphors, when you are communicating the mission into action.
3. Use rhetorical techniques such as paralanguage and nonverbal behavior.
4. Show your emotions to reflect your personal feelings and concern.[10]

Conger summarizes his views of the leader as a communicator: "It is important that . . . leaders see their role as 'meaning makers.' They must pick from the rough materials of reality to construct pictures of great possibilities. . . . If you, as a leader, can make an appealing dream seem like tomorrow's reality, your [employees] will freely choose to follow you."[11]

This section of the chapter has looked at external and internal noise. Effective leaders need to understand that they cannot influence others if the message they are sending is interrupted or disregarded due to these common factors. Leaders must create the appropriate environment to diminish external noise and clarify terminology to decrease internal noise. Once this is accomplished, leaders will be able to meet two key goals in the communication process: influence and effectiveness. The leader can measure the influence of the communication through the amount of action or change in the receiver caused by the message. The fit between the message received and the readiness of the receiver to accept it will determine whether the leader exerts positive or negative influence. Effectiveness can be evaluated by how closely the influence of the message reflects the intentions of the sender: In other words, is the receiver influenced in the manner intended by the leader? Effectiveness, therefore, is a measure of reception coupled with understanding.

Communication is much more difficult when there is a difference of opinion between employee and supervisor than there is when they agree. Laura Carrol has developed a program for employees to use when they wish to communicate a problem to an employer or coworker or to get a negative situation resolved. The series of steps she has outlined concern effective communication. Foremost is the idea of creating a thought process that fosters an understanding of what the problem is and how best it can be resolved. She suggests that the employee see the problem from the other person's point of view and make certain that the "facts" of the situation are true from both viewpoints. If this can be done, then there exists a level, nonjudgmental, playing field from which solutions can arise without hurt feelings and misgivings. This is what the communication process is all about: respect for yourself, your ideas, and those of the other person.[12] The key for an effective leader to accomplish these goals is to be aware of their own internal noise and the role it can play with their own listening abilities.

Leaders spend more time communicating than doing any other single activity; yet, studies summarized in Table 13-1 show that many have not had a great deal of training in developing their ability to communicate effectively. Research also shows that people spend about 45 percent of their communication time listening. Even so, the average listener understands and retains only about half of what is said immediately after a presentation. And within 48 hours, this level drops off to 22 percent.

Active Listening

Active listening can allow a leader to become a more effective communicator. Communication is not only a process of sending messages. A leader must also be skilled in receiving, or listening to, messages. A manager may spend as much as 75 percent of work time in face-to-face communication.[13] As much as half of that time may be spent listening.[14] Human physiology influences our ability to listen accurately and actively. We speak at an average pace of 125 words per minute, but our brain is able to listen at a speed of 400 to 600 words per minute. Because the brain can listen faster than we can speak, a "listening gap" occurs for the average person. The gap allows the mind to wander to thoughts unrelated to those being expressed by the speaker and influences the ability of the receiver to accurately hear the message being sent.

Anthony Alessandra identified four types of listeners[15]: the nonlistener, the marginal listener, the evaluative listener, and the active listener. The nonlistener and the marginal listener hear the words being spoken but are preoccupied, uninterested, or busy preparing their next statement. These listeners are concerned with neither the message nor the context in which it is being presented. The evaluative listener makes a sincere attempt to listen by paying attention to the speaker but makes no effort to understand the intent of the speaker's message. This listener hears the words but not the feelings and meaning of what is being said.

The active listener hears and understands the message. The active listener's full attention is on the content of the message and the intention of the speaker.

Table 13-1 Communication Skills Training (Average Person)

SKILL	YEARS OF TRAINING	EXTENT USED IN ADULT LIFE
Writing	14	Little
Reading	8	Some
Speaking	1	Quite a bit
Listening	0	A great deal

Active listening is a skill that can be learned through daily practice and use. Carl Rogers, who popularized the term *active listening,* proposed five guidelines you can use to perfect your technique.

1. *Listen for the content of the message.* Make an effort to hear precisely what is being said.
2. *Listen for the feelings of the speaker.* Try to perceive the speaker's feelings about what is being said through the way that the message is delivered.
3. *Respond to the feelings of the speaker.* Demonstrate to the speaker that you recognize and understand the feelings being expressed.
4. *Note the speaker's cues, both verbal and nonverbal.* Attempt to identify mixed messages and contradicting messages the speaker may be expressing.
5. *Reflect back to the speaker what you think you are hearing.* Restate to the speaker in your own words what you think the speaker said. Allow the speaker to respond to further clarify the message being sent.[16]

C. Glenn Pearce reinforces the importance of effective listening. "The ability to listen effectively is a predictor of managerial success."[17] This was the conclusion of researchers at Cornell University, who also found a correlation between effective listening and position within an organization, especially that of "top-level" management.[18] Through effective, active listening, the leader can develop better relationships between management and staff, can increase the establishment of clear and concise goals that are understood by all, and can decrease the chance of communication misunderstandings progressing to complex and costly problems.

Developing these skills is not easy. Becoming an effective, active listener takes much skill and practice. It cannot be acquired; it must be achieved. Most participants in listening skills seminars do not improve in these skills until after the second or third course, indicating that effective listening, as is true of almost any skill, comes only with practice and a determination to learn.

Pacing, Then Leading

Leaders, as we have seen, influence from both personal power and position power. You can begin building personal power by establishing rapport. Part of establishing rapport is being able to communicate effectively in a way that is comfortable for people you are attempting to influence. To make people feel comfortable, you have to get in step with them—pace with them.

In order to understand how to establish rapport, you should keep some key concepts in mind:

- *Rapport.* Being attuned to other people verbally or nonverbally so that they are comfortable and have trust and confidence in you.
- *Pacing.* Establishing rapport by reflecting what others do, know, or assume to be true (doing something similar, matching some part of their ongoing experience).
- *Leading.* Getting other people to pace with you (attempting to influence them to consider other possibilities).
- *Having behavioral adaptability.* Having enough range in your own behavior to pace with the person or persons with whom you are interacting.

Chapter 13   Effective Communication

The secret of establishing rapport with people is pacing. To pace with other people, you need to adapt to match their behavior—to get "in sync" with them so that they feel comfortable with you. This means getting in alignment with their words, their voice characteristics, and their nonverbals.[19]

When you have established rapport with people, they are more apt to follow your lead. The general pattern can be thought of in this way:

> When you're interacting with other people, you're either pacing—doing something similar—or leading—having them pace with you. If your primary objective is to gain acceptance, then pacing may be enough. But if your objective is to influence them to consider other alternatives, then you must also lead. Managers can sometimes lead first and then pace to get results, since they often have position power.[20]

How to Test for Rapport

Sometimes, it is useful to test the level of rapport you have established. In the following example, the salesperson attempts to lead the customer to a buying decision after pacing with the customer through the early part of the sales process.

Salesperson: [attempting to lead customer: leaning forward and showing interest] Tom, we've agreed that increasing sales is important. Our program has demonstrated a significant impact on that objective. You viewed turnover as the major problem your marketing group is currently facing. Our training program, through its emphasis on professionalism, can impact that directly.

Customer: [accepting lead: leaning forward, partially mirroring the salesperson's posture] Yes, cutting down on our turnover would be a positive step in cost containment.

Salesperson: [continuing to lead: sensing that they now have rapport and are in agreement and alignment at both the verbal and nonverbal levels] You might consider conducting some pilot programs. Although our minimum order is 200 units, training 100 new hires with the 5-day design and 100 experienced representatives with a combination of the other designs would give you a chance to evaluate actual results.

If the customer continues to pace, then the salesperson can keep leading.

In the following example, the customer does not respond on a verbal or nonverbal basis. The key here is to return to pacing to reestablish comfort and rapport.

Salesperson: [attempting to lead: leaning forward and showing interest] Are we in agreement that turnover is the major problem your marketing group is currently facing?

Figure 13-5
Influencing from Personal Power: The Pace-Lead Process

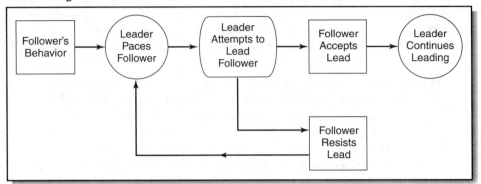

Customer: [resisting lead: remaining in the same posture] I'm not so sure. The real issue might be our advertising program.

Salesperson: [returning to pacing: mirroring customer's posture] I can understand how advertising can impact your sales.

In summary, the general rules of pacing, as shown in Figure 13-5, are (1) if your boss, associates, or followers go with your lead, continue to lead; (2) if your boss, associates, or followers resist your lead, go back to pacing—and look for new opportunities to lead.

ORGANIZATIONAL COMMUNICATION

Organizations have unique communication systems the leader can use to communicate effectively and efficiently. All members of an organization have an inherent desire to know what is occurring in their workplace; information is gained through communication with others.

Organizations communicate externally with their environment and internally through specific systems. Researchers have identified five basic internal organizational communication systems: downward communication, upward communication, horizontal communication, the grapevine, and networks.[21] These five systems can be grouped into informal and formal channels of communication. Informal channels allow information to be carried outside of the formal communication channels. The grapevine and networks are informal communication channels. The other three systems are formal communication channels. They are planned and established by the organization.

Downward communication is the most common communication system used in an organization. Communication flows from a manager to a follower.

The means of communication most frequently used is writing; the following types of information are conveyed through this system.

1. *Specific task directives.* Describes the best way to complete a task.
2. *Job rationale.* Defines a job and relates it to organizational goals and objectives.
3. *Organizational policies and objectives.* Changes in policies and objectives need to be communicated to employees.
4. *Performance feedback.* Rates an employee's performance and ways to improve.
5. *Information of an ideological nature.* Explains organizational goals.

Distortion of communication in this system can occur if a manager attempts to restrict or monitor the amount and type of information passed to employees. Monitoring is part of a manager's role and is not necessarily detrimental to the organization.

Upward communication is characterized by communication from the subordinate to the manager and can be verbal, nonverbal, or written. Upward communication provides management with feedback about current issues and problems, with day-to-day information about progress toward meeting organizational goals, and with information about the effectiveness of downward communication. A sincere and trusting relationship between a manager and employees increases the accuracy of information passed in this system. Active listening can be used by the effective leader in this system to ensure honest and clear communication. Encouraging followers to discuss bad as well as good news will help build trust and confidence in the manager's ability.

Communication between a manager and peers or between coworkers is called *horizontal communication.* This system is less formal than the two vertical types of systems and usually involves problem solving and the coordination of workflow between peers or groups. Because horizontal communication is under limited control by managers, information can be widely spread and exchanged rapidly in times of crisis. Horizontal communication also forms a useful link in decision-making for task coordination and provides emotional and social support to individual organizational members.

The *grapevine* communication system is often neglected by managers but can be found in any organization. Grapevines grow primarily to meet organizational members' innate need for information. Although information is often incomplete, it is 70 percent to 90 percent accurate in content and travels at an extremely rapid pace. The grapevine acts without conscious direction or thought; it will carry any information at any time, anywhere in the organization. Both managers and followers have links into the grapevine system.

The effective leader sees the positive and negative value of the grapevine system. It can let a manager gain insights into employee attitudes, provide a release valve for employee emotions, and help spread useful information. Negative aspects of the grapevine system include rumor carrying, untruths, and irresponsible communication. The grapevine grows most vigorously in organizations where secrecy, poor communication by management, and autocratic leadership behaviors are found. Adopting a proactive communication policy and integrating the grapevine into more formal communication systems can help decrease negative aspects of the grapevine system.[22]

Networks are the second informal communication system in an organization. Networks are patterned after regular interactions of organizational members and are composed of various groups of people. Networks link the other organizational communication systems. Members who take work breaks together and socialize outside of work form strong networks. Network characteristics and actions are reflective of small groups, with members serving as opinion leaders, gatekeepers, and bridges to other networks. Networks can encourage strong identification with work and serve as essential socializing units.

The influential leader understands the communication systems inherent in an organization. Through the use of effective communication, including active listening, the leader can work with the systems to achieve organizational goals.

PATTERNS OF COMMUNICATION

One of the most important considerations in determining whether to use a participative or directive change strategy or some combination of the two is how communication patterns are structured within a group or organization prior to implementing a change.[23] Two of the most widely used ways of structuring communications, illustrated in Figure 13-6, are the star and the circle.

The arrowhead lines represent two-way communication channels. In the circle, each person can send messages to a colleague on either side, and, thus, the group is free to communicate all around the circle. In other words, nothing in the structure of the communication pattern favors one group member

Figure 13-6
Two Ways of Structuring Communications

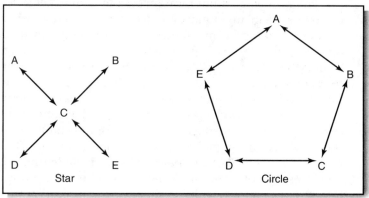

Star

Circle

over another as leader. In essence, this depicts an open, democratic organization in which there is participation in decision making by all members. In the star communication pattern, however, one individual (C) is definitely in a leadership position; C can communicate with the other four members of the group, and they can communicate with C but not with each other. This group represents an autocratic structure, with C acting as the manager. Either of these groups might be analogous to groups of department heads, each having a department, but all reporting eventually to the same manager. In both patterns, A, B, D, and E are department heads and C is the manager.

Is There a "Best" Pattern of Communication?

Once these two patterns of communication have been identified, the usual question arises about which is the best pattern. Some classic experiments conducted by Alex Bavelas attempted to answer that question.[24] In particular, Bavelas was interested in determining how each of these communication patterns affected the efficiency of a group's performance as well as the group's morale.

In one experiment, two groups were put to work in the star and circle patterns. Sets of five marbles were given to each of the five group members. The marbles of each set had different colors, but one color was common to all sets. The two groups were to discover the common color. When that had been accomplished, the task was completed. In essence, it was the star, or autocratic, pattern against the circle, or democratic, pattern.

The autocratic star pattern was much faster. Its four followers simply had to describe their marbles to the leader. After noting the common color, the designated leader sent correct information back. In trial after trial, the star group arrived at correct answers in an average of about 30 to 40 seconds. The circle group took 60 to 90 seconds. The star group was not only faster but also used fewer messages and developed more efficient ways of solving problems. In addition, group members respected their communication pattern.

The star pattern, although fast, tended to have a negative effect on morale. Although group members had a high opinion of their communication pattern or organization, they had a low opinion of themselves except for the leader (C). With each ensuing trial, they felt less important and more dissatisfied. In fact, on one occasion the leader received a message, "Enough of this game; let's play tic-tac-toe." On other occasions, messages were torn up or written in French or Spanish; yet, on the whole, the group still was faster and more productive than the circle group.

The circle could be described as slow, inaccurate, but happy. It developed no system for working on problems, and no one leader seemed to emerge. Although members were openly critical of the organization's productivity, they seemed to enjoy the tasks. No one attempted sabotage by, for example, sending messages in a foreign language.

In terms of performance, everything seemed to be in favor of the autocratic groups, until Bavelas created a so-called emergency. He changed the marbles. Instead of simple solid colors, each group was given odd-colored marbles that were difficult to describe. The task, as before, was to find out which marble all members of the group had in common. The new marbles required close observation to tell one from another. In fact, two group members could be looking at identical marbles and describe them quite differently.

Because morale was good in the circle group, members pulled together in the "emergency" and were able to solve the problem. On the other hand, the star pattern group members looked to the leader to solve the problem with little commitment from them.

The new task confused both groups. Errors mounted, and it took 10 minutes or more to solve the problem. Yet, eventually, the circle seemed to adapt to the crisis and after a number of trials had restored its efficiency completely. On the other hand, the star could not seem to cope with it, taking twice as much time and committing three to four times as many errors as the circle.

Why was the star communication pattern normally faster? Essentially, because it was a one-way communication system dominated by a single leader. With this communication pattern, an orderliness was imposed on the group that eliminated extra messages. In the circle, no such clear organization existed. Each group member could communicate with two people. Because they had this kind of mobility, they seemed to get around more and thus spend more time. Because the members of a circle group sent more messages, however, they could take advantage of more checkpoints and, thus, could locate and correct more of their errors.

Members of the circle group had more chance to participate and take responsibility. They were less dependent on one person because they could check with another member. Thus, they were more satisfied and happy. The leader (C) in the star also felt quite happy and satisfied, probably for the same reasons as the members of the circle pattern—C was given responsibility and had several sources of information and checkpoints. In essence, C was independent and powerful.

In summary, these experiments suggest that the mere structure of communication patterns can influence how people feel and act in terms of independence, security, and responsibility. This same structure also can influence the total operational efficiency of a group in terms of speed, accuracy, and adaptability. In essence, the structure seems to influence the way people feel in one direction and their speed and accuracy in another. Although the two communication patterns discussed have been described as if they were either/or structures, in reality, the design for an effective organization may need to incorporate both. For example, with an experienced staff, a manager might find it most appropriate to structure the communication pattern in a democratic, freewheeling manner, as in the circle. However, with inexperienced personnel, the manager might find it appropriate to operate in a more autocratic manner, as in the star pattern. These groups may be at different levels of commitment, motivation, and ability to take responsibility, and, therefore, different kinds of communication patterns are needed.

INTERNATIONAL BUSINESS COMMUNICATION

Computers, telephones, modems, satellites, fax machines, and airplanes have eliminated the time and distance barriers once faced by business leaders. Successful companies see the world, not their local area or nation, as the competitive arena. Exchanging ideas and information, leading, motivating, negotiating, and decision making are based on the ability of a manager from one culture to communicate effectively with managers and employees in other cultures.

Communication difficulties can occur when differences in culture and background lead to a misunderstanding. These difficulties will not disappear. "By 2010, managers will have to handle greater cultural diversity with subtle human relations skills."[25] With the very good possibility that employees will come from several different cultures with varied and often differing management styles, a manager in 2010 will not only have to make difficult decisions but also use various communication techniques and media.

Attribution, the judgments we make about the characteristics and behavior of others, plays an important role in cross-cultural communication. Three factors affect the attributions or judgments we make: perception, stereotyping, and ethnocentrism. *Perception* is the mental process we use to select, organize, and evaluate stimuli from the external environment to mold them into a meaningful experience. We have more difficulty perceiving a person's behavior when we are unfamiliar with their language or their culture. *Stereotyping* is a mental form of organizing information about behavioral norms for members of a particular group. Effective stereotyping can assist you in understanding, communicating, and acting appropriately in new situations, but stereotyping can lead to poor communication if the stereotypes we have are inaccurate. *Ethnocentrism* occurs when members of a particular group believe that their cultural values, habits, and beliefs are superior to those of all other groups. Ethnocentrism can lead to complete communication breakdowns. Awareness of these three factors and active work to eliminate cultural biases facilitate effective international communication.

Nonverbal communication—gestures, the meaning of time and space, and facial expressions—also varies among cultures. For example, the American "OK" gesture with thumb and forefinger touching in a circle means money to the Japanese, zero to the French, and an obscenity to Brazilians.[26] Cultures have unwritten rules regarding, for example, the distance one stands or sits from another in a face-to-face interaction and how waiting lines are formed and maintained.[27] The use of time also varies among cultures. Americans are clock watchers and value punctuality. Indonesians do not place the same value on time; an Indonesian businessperson could arrive 30 minutes after an agreed-upon appointment time and still not be considered late.

Japanese and U.S. companies are becoming more frequent business partners and, as a result, executives from the two countries often must work together. The prudent organization must deal consciously with cultural differences before effective communication can take place.[28] The Japanese culture has many traditions and beliefs that a U.S. company should follow when working with the Japanese. For example, some unique aspects of conducting a meeting that should be recognized are:

- Forms of address
- Greetings
- Gestures
- Personal contact
- Negotiation protocol
- Gifts[29]

Differences in sentence structure, word meaning, and tense also create communication difficulties when translating messages from one language to another. Even within the same language, words can have different meanings; for example, what belongs on the head of an American (a bonnet), is part of a car in England.

Awareness of attributions we make about a person from another culture, understanding of cultural norms and behaviors, and the use of resources to bridge cultural and language gaps will aid the leader in achieving effective and influential international communication. But we need not look across oceans to realize that the differences in cultures among people must be acknowledged and addressed. The culturally diverse workforce in the United States makes the need apparent.

SUMMARY

Many studies have demonstrated that interpersonal skills and written and oral communication skills are requisites of effective leaders. These skills are vital in gaining meaningful jobs and performing well in these jobs. In the words of Irving S. Shapiro:

> One important day-to-day task for the CEO [chief executive officer] is communication—digesting information and shaping ideas, yes, but even more centrally, the business of listening and explaining. Decisions and policies have no effect nor any real existence unless they are recognized and understood by those who must put them into effect. . . . It sounds banal to say that a CEO is first and foremost in the human relations and communication business—what else could the job be?—but the point is too important to leave to in-

ference. No other item on the chief executive's duty list has more leverage on the organization's prospects.[30]

The transactional model of communication, with its emphasis on teams, best explains the type of communication needed in today's workplace.

ENDNOTES

1. Gary L. Benson, "On the Campus: How Well Do Business Schools Prepare Graduates for the Business World?" *Personnel,* July–August 1983, pp. 63–65. See also "Can We Talk? Can We Ever?" *Fortune,* July 11, 1994, p. 54.
2. Kimberly F. Kane, "MBAs: A Recruiter's-Eye View," *Business Horizons,* January/February, 1993, p. 69.
3. Louis C. Williams Jr., "What 50 Presidents and Chief Executive Officers Think about Employee Communication," *Public Relations Quarterly,* Winter 1978, p. 7. See also James Bredin, "Short and Simple: Eschew Jargon and Wordiness," *Industry Week,* September 19, 1994, p. 18; Federick Moss, "Perceptions of Communication in the Corporate Community," *Journal of Business and Technical Communication,* January 1, 1995, p. 63; and Deborah Britt Roebuck, Kevin W. Sightler, and Christina Christenson Brush, "Organizational Size, Company Type, and Position Effects on the Perceived Importance of Oral and Written Communication Skills," *Journal of Managerial Issues,* Spring 1995, pp. 97–116.
4. "Listening Your Way to the Top," *Graduating Engineer,* Winter 1980. See also Sandra A. Miller, "Controlling How Others See You Is Good Business," *The CPA Journal,* October 1994, pp. 75–76.
5. Robert Powell and Mary Jane Collier, "Public Speaking Instruction and Cultural Bias," *American Behavioral Scientist,* Vol. 34, No. 2, November/December 1990, pp. 245-46.
6. George Walter, "Communicating Clearly," *Profitable Telemarketing Audiocassette Program,* Tape No. 2 (Chicago: Nightengale-Conant Corporation, 1984). See also Bonnie J. Sparks, "Make the Right Moves with Body Language," *Real Estate Today,* June 1994, pp. 35–38.
7. G. J. Galanes, K. Adams, and J. K. Brilhart, *Communicating in Groups.* 4th ed. (Boston: McGraw Hill, 2000).
8. Byron A. Lewis and R. Frank Pucelik, *Magic De-Mystified* (Lake Oswego: Metamorphous Press, 1982), pp. 11–49.
9. C. K. Ogden and I. A. Richards, *The Meaning of Meaning: A Study of the Influence of Language upon Thought and of the Science of Symbolism* (London: Routledge and Kegan Paul, 1949), p. 10.
10. Jay A. Conger, "Inspiring Others: The Language of Leadership," *Academy of Management Executive,* 5, no. 1 (1991), pp. 31–45.
11. *Ibid.,* p. 44.
12. Laura Carrol, "A 10-Step Strategy for Issue Resolution," *HR Focus,* December 1993, p. 19.
13. Tom W. Harris, "Listen Carefully," *Nation's Business,* 77 (1989) p. 78. See also Jay T. Kippen and Thad B. Green, "How the Manager Can Use Active Listening," *Public Personnel Management,* Summer 1994, pp. 357–359; and Donald J. McNerney, "Improve Your Communication Skills," *Human Resource Focus,* October 1994, p. 22.
14. Donald W. Caudill and Regina Donaldson, "Effective Listening Tips for Managers," *Administration Management,* 47 (1986), pp. 22–24.
15. Anthony J. Alessandra, "How Do You Rate As a Listener?" *Data Management,* February 1986, pp. 20–21.
16. Carl Rogers, *Client-Centered Therapy: Its Current Practice, Implications, and Theory* (Boston: Houghton Mifflin, 1951).
17. C. Glenn Pearce, "How Effective Are We As Listeners?" *Training & Development,* April 1993, p. 15.
18. Study by Judi Brownell, "Research Capsules," *Training and Development,* April 1993, p. 79.
19. Jerry Richardson and Joel Margulis, *The Magic of Rapport* (San Francisco: Harbor Publishing, 1981), pp. 19–59.
20. John Grinder and Richard Bandler, *The Structure of Magic II* (Palto Alto: Science and Behavior Books, 1976), pp. 4–6.

21. J. L. DiGaetani, ed., *The Handbook of Executive Communication* (Homewood, IL: Dow-Jones Irwin, 1986). See also P. V. Lewis, *Organizational Communication: The Essence of Effective Management* (New York: John Wiley, 1987).

22. A. Zaremba, "Working with the Organizational Grapevine," *Personnel Journal,* July 1988, pp. 38–42.

23. Kenneth H. Blanchard and Paul Hersey, "The Importance of Communication Patterns in Implementing Change Strategies," *Journal of Research and Development in Education,* 6, no. 4 (Summer 1973), pp.66–75.

24. Alex Bavelas, "Communication Patterns in Task-Oriented Groups." In *Group Dynamics: Research and Theory,* ed. Dorwin Cartwright and Alvin Zander (Evanston, IL: Row, Peterson, 1953).

25. "A Day in the Life of Tomorrow's Manager: He or She Faces a More Diverse, Quicker Market" (The Second Century), *The Wall Street Journal,* March 20, 1989, pp. B1, 3.

26. Joseph H. Singer, "How to Work with Foreign Clients," *Public Relations Journal,* October 1987, pp. 35–37.

27. Rose Knotts, "Cross-Culture Management: Transformations and Adaptation," *Business Horizons,* January–February 1989, pp. 29–33.

28. Richard G. Linowes, "The Japanese Manager's Traumatic Entry into the United States: Understanding the American-Japanese Cultural Divide," *Academy of Management Executive,* 7, no. 4 (November 1993), pp. 21–37.

29. Anne Stewart, "Communication Protocols," *CIO,* July 1994, pp. 100–102.

30. Irving S. Shapiro, "Executive Forum: Managerial Communication: The View from Inside," *California Management Review,* Fall 1984, p. 157.

Chapter 1

Leading Effective Teams

One of the realities of organizational behavior is that we must work with others to accomplish our aspirations. No matter how much we value and protect our individuality, almost all of our goals can be achieved in this way. Although the following description was presented more than 3 decades ago, it is probably even more true today. ✧

> The paradox of modern man is that only as the individual joins with his fellows in groups and organizations can he hope to control the political, economic, and social forces which threaten his individual freedom. This is especially true now that massive social groupings—in nations and combinations of nations—are the order of the day. Only as the individual in society struggles to preserve his individuality in common cause with his fellows can he hope to remain an individual.[1]

It is, therefore, important to be able to apply behavioral science principles and concepts to make teams more effective. In this chapter, we will describe how Situational Leadership, through an understanding of helping and hindering roles, can accomplish this goal.

IMPORTANT DEFINITIONS

Before we continue, it is important that we define key terms. You will recall that we defined leadership in chapter 1 as a behavior that occurs whenever one person attempts to influence the behavior of an individual or group, regardless of the reason. This broad definition covers many different settings, from families to formal organizations. *Group* is also a very broad term. There are, perhaps, as many definitions of group as there are definitions of leadership. This lack of common definition creates problems in terms of communicating, diagnosing, and being able to think through strategies for change. To help reduce this confusion, we suggest this working definition. A *group* is two or more individuals interacting, in which the existence of all (the existence of the group as a group) is necessary for the needs of the individual group members to be satisfied.

An important point to keep in mind is that individual need satisfaction may be quite different for each member of the group. This is the ingredient that is missing from most definitions of groups. One of the principal problems with most definitions is the assumption that group members have common goals and purposes. There are many examples of groups devoid of common goals or purposes. For example, you may have three people in a group who have very different needs. One person may have joined the group because of a need for power; another because of the need for interaction with other people, a social need; a third may have joined because of a need for status, for esteem. The individual group members do not necessarily have to have common needs, goals, or purposes; the key is that the satisfaction, at least in part, of these individual needs is dependent upon the accomplishment of group goals. The degree to which individual need satisfaction is achieved differentiates effective from ineffective groups. When the needs are harmonious, the group is probably effective. When they are not, the group is probably ineffective. Common, or at least harmonious, goals or purposes are, therefore, not criteria of groups, but of *effective* groups.

A group without clear-cut objectives lacks guidelines for the behavior of its members. For the group to be productive, it must have goals that are understood by all participants. Progress toward these goals is the best way to measure effectiveness. Research has consistently shown that group productivity is highest in those groups in which techniques are used that simultaneously further the attainment of group goals and bring fulfillment of the needs of individual group members.

Figure 14-1 illustrates the goal alignment of group members at the four basic readiness levels of Situational Leadership. At readiness level 1, which we call "chaos," there is no alignment. Group members have widely differing and frequently opposing goals. Then, as the group develops through readiness levels 2 and 3, it becomes, in readiness level 4, a "self-managing group" that is both able and willing to work with little external supervision.

The group leader's role changes throughout this developmental process. Consider Figure 14-2, which uses the leadership style, or upper portion, of the Situational Leadership model. Group members are depicted by the letter *M*. At readiness level 1, the leader's role is one of defining and structuring. The leader is outside the group. When the group is at readiness level 2, the leader's role becomes one of clarifying, as illustrated by the leader's being in the center of the group. At readiness level 3, the leader's role is one of involving and providing support. In this role, the leader is part of the group

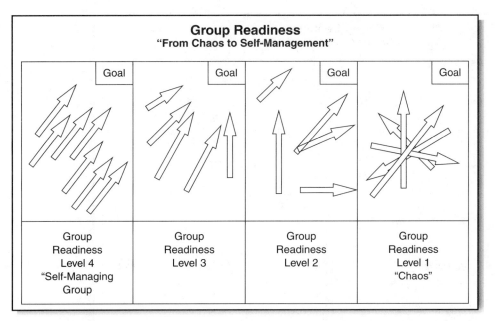

Figure 14-1

Goal Alignment at Different Group Readiness Levels

Source: Adapted from "Team Leadership," *Executive Summary* (Escondido, CA: Leadership Studies International, 1991).

circle. Last, at readiness level 4, the leader is once again outside the group, empowering it and providing needed resources, but the relationship of group members has changed.

What is the difference between groups and organizations? Again, it is not commonality of goals or purposes. Do owners, managers, first-line supervisors, and line workers have the same goals? Not in very many organizations.

Our definition of an *organization* is a group that has stated and formal goals. Organizations exist for various reasons and have different organizational goals. *Organizational goals* are targets toward which input, process, and output are directed; for example, make a 10-percent return on investment, help conquer hunger, or increase sales 20-percent during the current fiscal year.[2]

There is a third important type of association—a collection. Which of the three entities (group, organization, collection) has the best chance of having common goals? A collection. Twenty-seven people standing on a corner waiting for a bus have a common goal—everyone is waiting for the bus. Interdependence is not necessary. Suppose you are swimming across San Francisco Bay from Oakland to San Francisco. Another swimmer comes alongside. Are the two of you a group? No, you are a *collection* because you only have a common goal—to get to San Francisco. There is no interdependence. If, however, you start to interact, give encouragement, support each other so that the existence of both of you is necessary for the satisfaction of both of your individual needs, then you have a group. Now suppose that, having reached San Francisco, you decide to meet three times a week in Oakland to swim to San

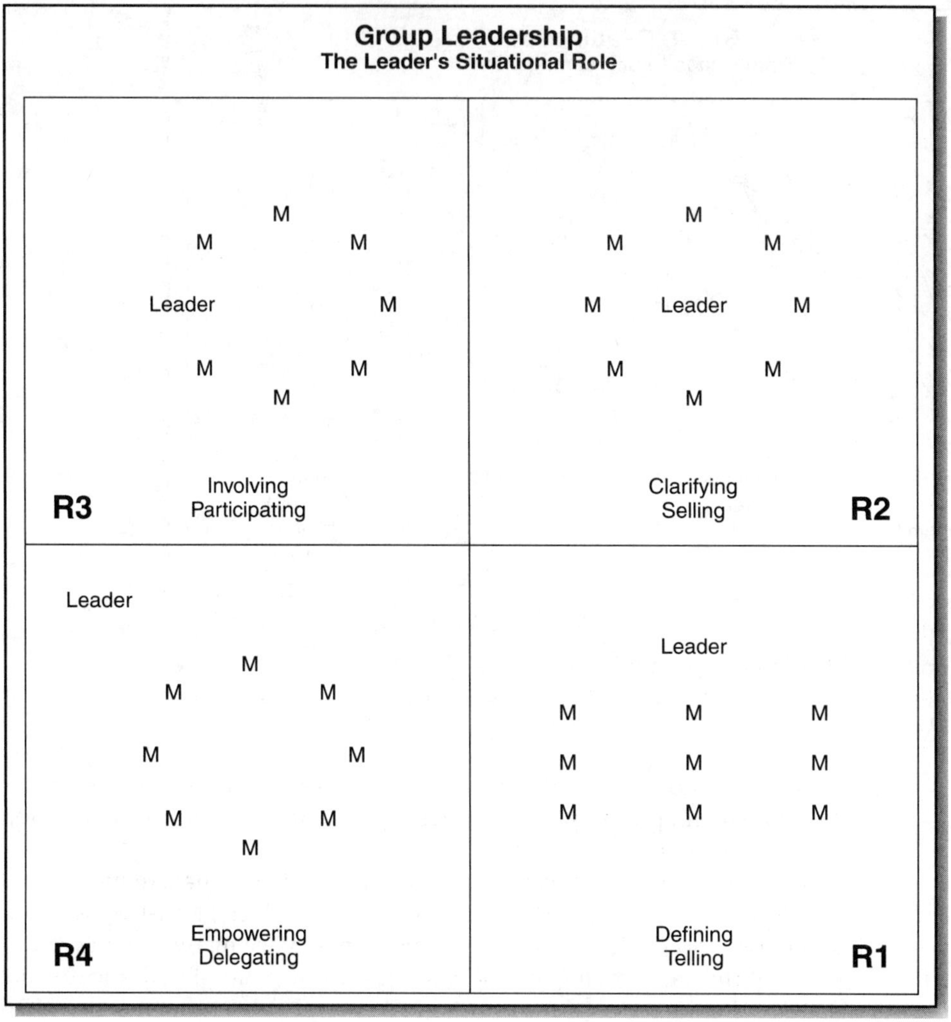

Group Leadership
The Leader's Situational Role

M M M Leader M M M M **R3** Involving Participating	M M M M Leader M M M M Clarifying Selling **R2**
Leader M M M M M M M M **R4** Empowering Delegating	Leader M M M M M M M M M Defining Telling **R1**

Figure 14-2
The Leader's Situational Role in Groups (M = member)

Francisco to get in shape. Now you are an organization because you have stated or formal goals. Do you necessarily share the same goal? No, but you both agree on the formal, stated goals.

A fourth term that we have been using in this chapter is *team*. A *team* is a formal work group.

Let us summarize these definitions:

- *Collection.* Two or more individuals with common goals.
- *Organization.* Two or more individuals who have stated and formal goals.
- *Group.* Organization in which the existence and interdependence of all is necessary for the satisfaction of individual needs.
- *Team.* A formal work group.

Team will be used for the balance of the chapter for three reasons: One, the major emphasis will be on formal work groups—teams. Two, the term is used frequently in settings other than work, e.g. athletic *teams*. Three, *team* is used for motivation, e.g. "Let's work as a *team*."

TEAMS AS A COMPETITIVE STRATEGY

Organizations today are under tremendous pressure to survive in a competitive environment. One of the most consistently successful strategies to improve performance has been the use of teams and teamwork. Many companies have found that teamwork has increased productivity, increased revenues, decreased absenteeism, and decreased turnover. Results achieved by companies through teamwork include the following:

- Monarch Marking Systems, a manufacturer of labeling, identification, and tracking equipment, reduced the size of the assembly area by 70 percent, reduced past-due shipments 90 percent, and doubled productivity.
- Texas Instruments increased revenues per employee by over 50 percent.
- Dallas/Fort Worth-based GTE Directories' publication teams increased production of telephone directories 158 percent from 1994 to 1998, while decreasing errors by 48 percent.
- An 11-member team at Xerox Manufacturing Operation in Webster, NY, discovered problems with a product and generated a first-year savings of $266,000.[3,4]

In addition to increasing corporate performance, membership in a team benefits the individual. Employees who work in teams report that they experience greater job satisfaction, collaborate better with others, have increased pride and ownership in their job, and experience higher self-esteem.[5] According to Jon Katzenback and Douglas Smith, consultants with McKinney & Company, the use of teams benefits the organization and team members because:

- Projects assigned to a team are more likely to be accomplished than those assigned to an individual.
- Teams can and do make practical and reasonable decisions provided there are concrete, measurable goals by which to judge their performance, and the teams are given timely, meaningful feedback.
- Rewards and punishment are more effective in swaying individual performance when given by a work group rather than a single superior.
- Working as a team member is preferred by many employees, particularly those who resent being bossed.

- Work teams can effectively handle inventory, scheduling, quality assurance, and other disciplines typically reserved for members of management.

- Management costs are often lower when teams are used in a business or industrial operation because employee-to-supervisor ratios can be reduced to as much as 50 to 1.[6]

Teams are used typically in manufacturing organizations, but their use has spread widely into service and other types of companies. The Association of Quality & Participation's National Team Excellence Award has noted in the last 4 years that 30 to 40 percent of teams applying for this award are in service organizations.

We will close this section with a quote from W. H. Weiss:

Teamwork is like a salad: Individually, each ingredient may be tasty and fresh, but they will certainly not add up to a gourmet experience. Put together in the right way, the ingredients enhance one another to produce startling results. Each ingredient retains its character and strengths, but contributes to a more exciting and effective overall result.[7]

Let's now examine some of the obstacles that may prevent "startling results."

OBSTACLES TO EFFECTIVE TEAM PERFORMANCE

Why are many organizations having difficulty forming effective work teams such as interdisciplinary teams?[8] One reason is that labor and management lack shared values.[9] Another is because the structure and function of problem-solving teams was not established according to behavioral science concepts and techniques.[10] Too often, problem-solving teams focus too much on participation as the only problem-solving mode and neglect other, potentially better possible modes. When problem-solving teams have been effective—much as in the teams cited in the Plant Y study by Guest, Hersey, and Blanchard (see chapter 7)—it is because values were shared, and the teams were structured to take advantage of all of the team problem-solving modes. Only then can teams reach their full potential payoff both in terms of goal achievement and quality of life—the true components of productivity.[11]

Another important impediment to achieving team effectiveness is a lack of leadership skill. By this, we mean skill in the leadership role—the role of providing proactive influence and receiving feedback from team members. Skill is needed because your role as a leader is paradoxically both simple and complex. Team leadership is simple, because effectively functioning teams tend to harness a natural synergy that gives them momentum, allowing you to step aside and let the team work on its own. Team leadership is complex, because your relationships with team members are dynamic and constantly changing, depending on the situation, goals, and the environment.

Some managers think that by simply extending leadership concepts that work so well with one-on-one situations they can effectively manage a team. There are many similarities between leading individuals and leading teams, but team leadership requires more leadership skill because of the simple-complex considerations discussed earlier. Peter Drucker summarized the essential difficulty of leading a team: "Management is about human beings. Its task is to make people capable of *joint performance,* to make their strengths effective and their weaknesses irrelevant."[12]

Teams (formal work groups) are increasingly becoming productivity engines, but, as Brian Dumaine suggests, like engines, they require care and maintenance.[13] Organizations that are willing to invest in matching the right type of team to the right situation are experiencing a very high return on their investment. Why? According to Philip Condit, president of Boeing, "Your competitiveness is your ability to use the skills and knowledge of people most effectively, and teams are the best way to do that."[14] Dumaine describes five species in the kingdom of teams:

- *Problem-solving teams.* Attack a problem and then disband.
- *Management teams.* Coordinate work from different functions.
- *Work teams,* including the most advanced species, *self-managed teams,* do the daily work.
- *Virtual teams.* Use advanced communications to exchange ideas and roles.
- *Quality circles.* Consist of workers and supervisors who meet periodically to address problems. This species may be becoming extinct.[15]

The word *team* is often used to describe all types of working arrangements. A true team is "a small number of people with complementary skills who are equally committed to a common purpose, goals, and working approach for which they hold themselves mutually accountable."[16] Teams are usually formed for one of the following purposes:

- To recommend an action; for example, to study a specific problem and come up with solution(s).
- To make or do something; for example, to refine operations in a specific department in manufacturing, service, or selling.
- To mange a specific function; for example, to administer and control an entire organization.[17]

Dumaine offers four guidelines for the most effective use of teams:

1. *Use the right team for the job.* For example, problem-solving teams should be disbanded once the job is done.
2. *Create a hierarchy of teams.* There must be an organizational structure of teams to facilitate coordination and communication.
3. *Build trust.* For example, you can't build team spirit if the team's task is to eliminate team member jobs.
4. *Address "people" issues.* A significant investment must be made in building and maintaining teams if they are going to work.[18]

A study of technology and the process of change (reengineering of an organization) pointed toward effective team leadership as being critical in effecting change. "Success [in achieving change], it turns out, is . . . dependent on clear senior management leadership and vision, and the training and involvement of a cross-functional group of employees."[19]

INDIVIDUALS AND TEAMS

Although much of the previous discussion has focused on one-on-one leadership, it is important to remember that the Situational Leadership model is equally applicable whether you are working with a team or with an individual. Certainly, there are some complicating factors when you are working with teams, but you still have to apply the three basic competencies in influencing—diagnosing, adapting, and communicating. It is also important to remember that you may have to deal with individual team members differently when you are in a one-on-one situation than when you are working with the entire team. Individual team members may be at different levels of readiness from the entire team. Team leaders need to be aware of intrateam dynamics and the need to diagnose not only the behavior of individuals but the behavior of the team as a team.

Just as individuals may be at different levels of readiness, so may teams. For example, most graduate classes are at a high level of readiness. Class members are there because they want to be, and they bring considerable academic and work experience to the class. There might be some insecurity because some of the material is new or especially difficult, but on balance, most graduate classes are at an R3 to R4 readiness level.

A team consisting of managers attending a training seminar might be at a lower readiness level. They have made a considerable investment in time, transportation costs, and fees to attend the seminar, and they are probably very willing. But, because they are attending the training seminar to learn new knowledge and skills, they are probably somewhat unable. It is also true that individuals in the team may be higher or lower than the team, as a whole, in readiness.

LEADERSHIP IN A TEAM ENVIRONMENT

Now that we have defined some important terms, we can extend the Situational Leadership model to the team environment. The use of the Situational Leadership model centers around five well-designed and interrelated questions:

1. What objective do we want to accomplish?
2. What is the team's readiness in the situation?
3. What intervention should the leader make?

4. What was the result of this leadership intervention?
5. What follow-up, if any, is required?

Let's apply each of these steps to team leadership.

What Objective Do We Want to Accomplish?

The manager must first determine the task-specific outcome the team is to accomplish. Without creating clarity on outcomes, objectives, subtasks, milestones, and so on, the manager has no basis for determining team readiness or the specific behavioral style to use for that level of readiness.

Objectives are just parts of the desired road to goal achievement. They must be integrated with the organization's vision, mission, and business objectives, as we discussed in chapter 4. One illustration of a task-specific objective for a team is: "To make specific recommendations on how to reduce web-press paper waste by 2 percent."

What Is the Team's Readiness in the Situation?

Once an objective has been stated, the manager must then diagnose the team's readiness to accomplish the objective. Some clues may be found using Figure 14-3.

Readiness level 1. This team resembles "Pick-Up Sticks" in terms of its orientation toward the specific objective. In this "forming" stage, uncertainty and lack of goal and role clarity are evidenced by a strong need for definition of the objective. The entire team is unable and unwilling or insecure in reference to the specific objective.

Readiness level 2. This team is "coming around," but teams at this "storming" stage are often divided with intrateam dissonance and competition for recognition and influence. The team as a whole is unable, but willing and confident, in reference to the specific objective.

Readiness level 3. This team is "coming together," with team cohesion very important at this "norming" stage. Adjustments are made between individuals and factions, and informal leaders and experts emerge. The team itself is now demonstrating ability with modest accomplishments, but it is still unwilling or insecure in its efforts toward accomplishing the objective.

Readiness level 4. This team acts "as one" and shows strong evidence of functional role-relatedness, esprit, synergy, and high levels of performance. The team is now a team: able, willing, and confident in relation to the objective.

We mentioned earlier that individual members of teams may be at different levels of readiness. It is almost certain that, even in teams at an R4 level, there will be some individual team members at a lower level. The team leader, as well as other members of the team, needs to increase these members' readiness.

How else can a manager measure readiness? A convenient way is to assess a team's ability and willingness. Ability includes knowledge, experience, and skill; willingness includes confidence, commitment, and motivation. The manager can use a Likert-type scale ranging from + +, representing a high

R4	R3	R2	R1
Able and Willing or Confident	Able and but Unwilling or Insecure	Unable But Willing or Confident	Unable and Unwilling or Insecure
Goal  "As One"	Goal 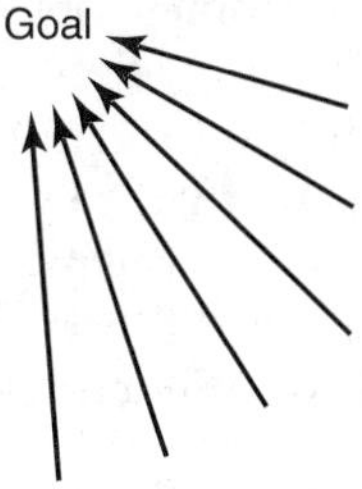 "Coming Together"	Goal 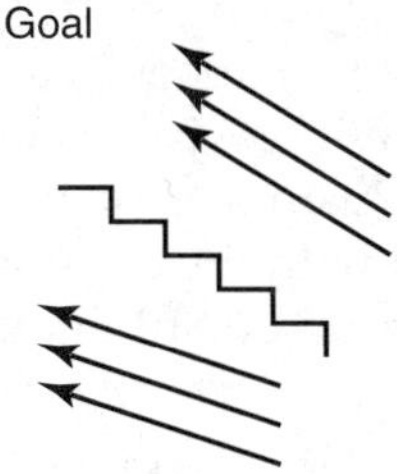 "Coming Around"	Goal  "Pick-Up Sticks"
Perform	**Norm**	**Storm**	**Form**
Functional Role-Relatedness "Self-Managing Team"	Team Cohesion	Intrateam Dissonance	Uncertain "Chaos"
Esprit Performance Synergy	Emergence Adjustment	Competence for Recognition and Influence	Need for Goal and Objective Definition

Figure 14-3
Indicators of Team Readiness

Source: Used by permission of the copyright holder, The Center for Leadership Studies, Escondido, CA, 92025. All rights reserved.

degree of readiness regarding the factor, to − −, representing a low degree of readiness. The range would be the following:

$$\text{Very High } (+\,+) \text{ to Very Low } (-\,-)$$

For example, the factor, knowledge, could range from very high to very low.

What Intervention Should the Leader Make?
After the team's readiness has been diagnosed, the leader is now prepared to use the appropriate style. But what style? Figure 14-4 provides guidance. In using Figure 14-4, take special note of the center 2×2 matrix showing the leader's position in relation to the team.

Chapter 14   Leading Effective Teams

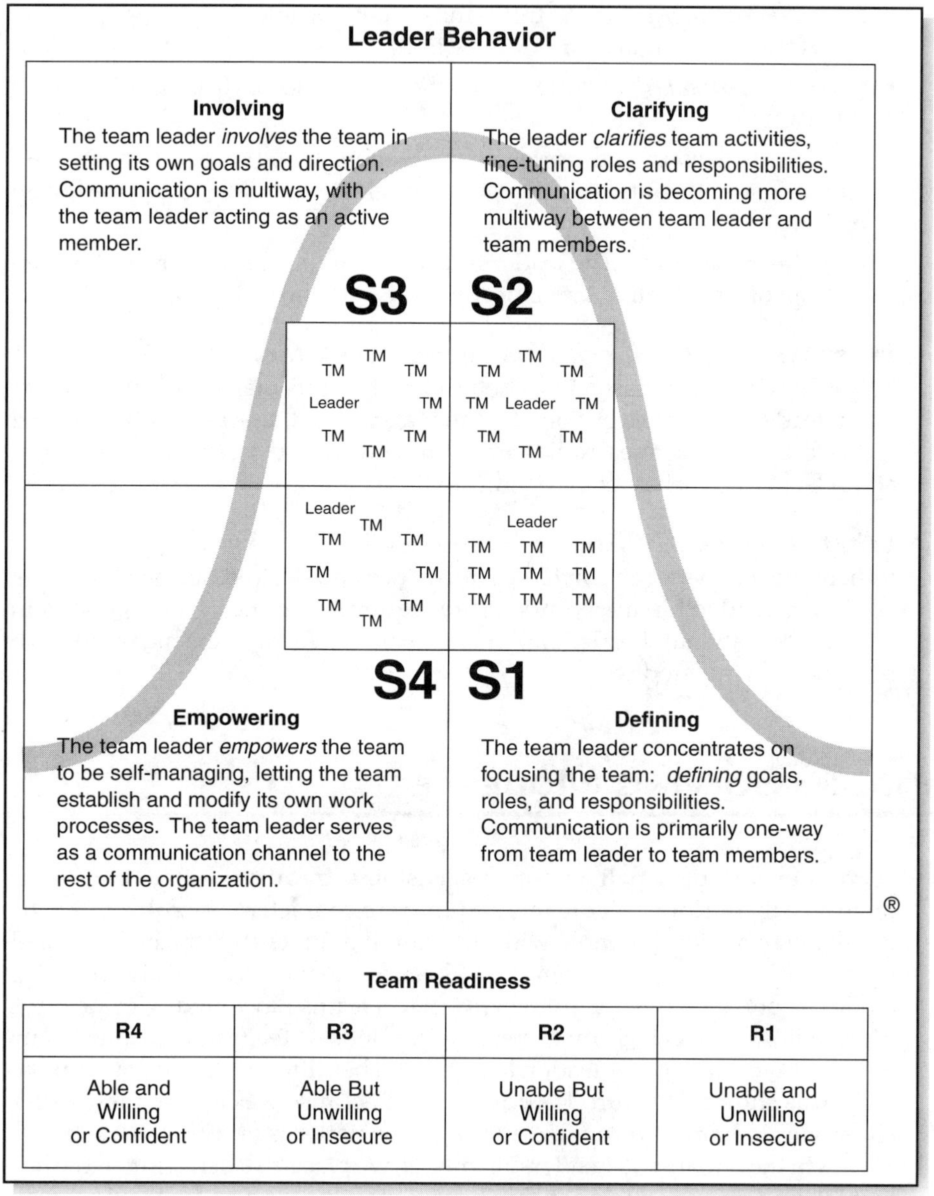

Leader Behavior

Involving
The team leader *involves* the team in setting its own goals and direction. Communication is multiway, with the team leader acting as an active member.

Clarifying
The leader *clarifies* team activities, fine-tuning roles and responsibilities. Communication is becoming more multiway between team leader and team members.

S3	S2

<table>
<tr><td>

	TM	
TM		TM
Leader		TM
TM		TM
	TM	

</td><td>

	TM	
TM		TM
TM	Leader	TM
TM		TM
	TM	

</td></tr>
<tr><td>

Leader		
	TM	TM
TM		TM
TM		TM
	TM	

</td><td>

	Leader	
TM	TM	TM
TM	TM	TM
TM	TM	TM

</td></tr>
</table>

S4	S1

Empowering
The team leader *empowers* the team to be self-managing, letting the team establish and modify its own work processes. The team leader serves as a communication channel to the rest of the organization.

Defining
The team leader concentrates on focusing the team: *defining* goals, roles, and responsibilities. Communication is primarily one-way from team leader to team members.

®

Team Readiness

R4	R3	R2	R1
Able and Willing or Confident	Able But Unwilling or Insecure	Unable But Willing or Confident	Unable and Unwilling or Insecure

Figure 14-4
Leadership in a Team Environment

- *Style 1—Defining.* This is a "front-and-center" position. Defining goals and objectives is of primary importance in this role.
- *Style 2—Clarifying.* This role makes the leader the "indispensable hub" of the team.
- *Style 3—Involving.* The leader is an unequal member of the team (contributing and the formal leader) but has a lessening role in day-to-day operations.
- *Style 4—Empowering.* The leader is away from the daily "spin" of the team in more of a facilitating or connecting role with the rest of the organization.

What Was the Result of This Leadership Intervention?

This step requires assessment to determine if results match expectations. After a leadership intervention, the manager must assess results through rechecking the objectives, rediagnosing readiness, and ascertaining what task and relationship behaviors are indicated.

What Follow-Up, If Any, Is Required?

If there is a gap between current performance and desired performance, then additional leadership interventions are required; and the cycle begins again.

The Situational Leadership model can be further extended to team problem-solving modes.

TEAM PROBLEM-SOLVING MODES

Teams develop personalities—mores, customs, traditions—that tend to differentiate them from other teams and that are characteristic of them. It is the collective behavior of people within a team that gives it its special personality, its individuality as a team. Just as leaders have styles—patterns of behavior as perceived by the followers—so do teams have modes, or patterns, of behavior as perceived by others. We can look at team modes in the same way that we can look at leadership styles. The different modes of team behavior, as shown in Figure 14-5, are helpful because we can use these different modes to help us recognize and organize patterns of team behavior.

As in the Situational Leadership model, we place task behavior on the horizontal, or X, axis, and relationship behavior on the vertical, or Y, axis. A team that is facing a situation that requires significant amounts of task behavior—lots of what, when, where, and how information—and that doesn't have a lot of time for relationship behavior—dialogue and discussion—is in the crises mode. This mode can be used appropriately for problem solving. In fact, the very nature of many crisis situations makes this the best approach for problem solving. The danger is that many organizations use this mode inappropriately and treat every situation as a crisis, just as some individuals treat every situation as a telling situation whether or not it is.

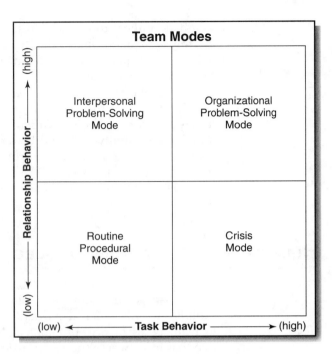

Figure 14-5
Team Problem-
Solving Modes

The organizational problem-solving mode, when used appropriately, requires high amounts of both task and relationship behavior. In this type of situation, considerable emphasis must be placed on structuring team activities, as well as motivating team members.

For example, eight teachers met with the principal and the superintendent of a school district. The job at hand was to revise the general curriculum. The curriculum had been neglected in the past because energies had been directed toward student disciplinary problems. At the meeting, the superintendent and principal both spelled out what needed to be done. The principal then elicited ideas from each team member and encouraged dialogue among the team members. By giving the team content, structure, and a motivating process, the principal assured a productive team meeting.

In the interpersonal problem-solving mode, a high relationship–low task approach is appropriate. For example, if, after a team is given a problem, cliques develop that serve to disrupt the team, relationship behaviors need to be used to increase interaction of all team members.

When appropriately used, the routine procedural mode requires low task and low relationship behaviors. For example, a team of managers finds that they need to reassemble an important report before an early meeting the next day. The clerical staff has gone home. They quickly decide who is going to do what task and play what role. The emphasis is on getting the job done through performing the assigned roles with a minimum of structuring activities and socioemotional support.

In all of these modes, the focus must be on producing quality decisions in a timely manner. Quality decisions have no value if they are not timely. You may be highly skilled at picking the winners of Saturday's football games on Monday morning, but by then it's too late to do you any good.

A characteristic of effective teams is that they can move rapidly and easily from one mode to another. We enrich the ability of the team to respond to different situations and face different problems and contingencies if we build into them the ability and fluidity to move from one mode to another. Adaptability is very important. It is a product of growth and development. Mental receptiveness to the concept of change is the essence of adaptability, a virtue needed by persons in any team.

HELPING AND HINDERING ROLES

Individuals within teams play roles—the individual behavior each member exhibits. It is not that a particular role by itself is helping or hindering to team performance, but that a high-performing team member plays a role that in a given situation contributes to maximizing the productivity of the team. This is the same principle that underlies leadership styles. A particular style is not intrinsically good or bad. The key is whether it is appropriate to the situation.

For some time, the literature has given us lists of helping roles and lists of hindering roles. When these roles are researched, however, we find that the same roles are helping in some situations and hindering in others. So it is not that any combination of behavior by itself is a helping or hindering role, but it is the particular role in a particular contingency that makes the determination.

If we are to be effective in teams, all of us need to be able to adapt our roles to the needs of the team. We need to get rid of the idea that certain behaviors are always good and certain behaviors are always bad. There are behaviors that tend to be functional in some situations and dysfunctional in others.

In our extensive work with organizations in helping them improve their quality circles and other productivity programs, the material in Figure 14-6 has been particularly useful in giving people insights into roles they are and should be exhibiting in team settings. You will note that it is organized in much the same way as the Situational Leadership model, with the dimensions of task behavior and relationship behavior. It is a *taxonomy of influence.* Each style, S1 to S4, represents a *behavioral competency.* Within each competency, there are two categories of behavior—one helping and one hindering. These categories are further divided into indicators of the types of behavior an individual could engage in under each category.

Some people seem to be fairly predictable in the hindering roles they play. They frequently enter into a series of "transactions" when interacting with the team. Because of their importance, we will include brief illustrations of some of the psychological games associated with hindering roles.

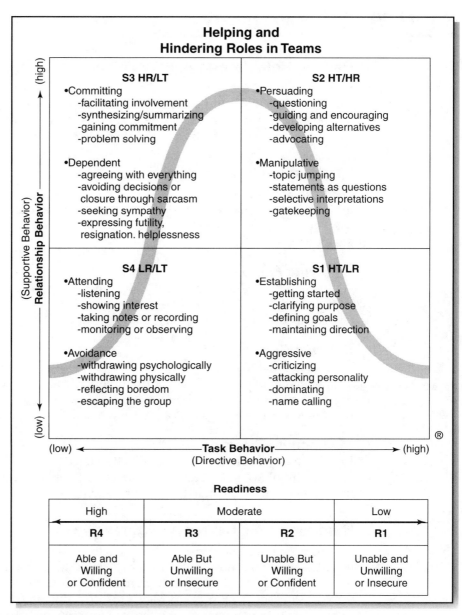

Figure 14-6
Helping and Hindering Roles in Teams

S1 (HT/LR) Competency

Helping Role Category: Establishing

Helps start the team along new paths. Proposes tasks and goals, defines problems, helps set rules, and contributes ideas. May suggest a plan of attack to handle a problem. Interprets issues and helps clear up ambiguous ideas or suggestions. Focuses attention on the alternatives and issues before the team.

Establishing Indicators

Getting Started

Initiating action. Suggesting roles, structure, or procedures for the team to use. For example, "I suggest we go once around the table. Each of us will have an opportunity to give input."

Clarifying Purpose

Stating why the team has been called together. Ensuring commonality of the intended result. "We are not here to play games. We have a responsibility to develop a workable strategic plan for our company."

Defining Goals

Specifying what is needed to fulfill the team's purpose; the steps necessary for attainment of the purpose. For example, "To meet budget guidelines, we must submit our plan by December first and within the target of two and a half million. The first step is to agree on the line items."

Maintaining Direction

Keeping the team on track; focusing on the stated goals and purpose. For example, "I think we're missing the point. We are not here to redefine the company's mission, we are here to agree on funding for each of the line items."

Hindering Role Category: Aggressive

Asserts personal dominance and attempts to get own way regardless of others. May react with hostility toward aspects of the problem or toward individuals who appear to be blocking progress. May criticize either directly or through sarcasm and innuendo. May refuse to cooperate by rejecting all ideas or by interrupting, monopolizing the conversation, or acting as an authority. May also engage in other aggressive behaviors such as bullying, ridiculing ideas, and boasting.

Aggressive Indicators

Criticizing

Downgrading, putting down, or otherwise finding fault with the suggestions or input of others. For example, "You keep coming up with these bright sayings. Why don't you try to sell them to *Readers' Digest?*"

Attacking Personality

Focusing on someone's personal attributes instead of the performance issue or problem the team is facing. For example, "That's one of the dumbest things I've heard. Why do you keep coming up with such stupid comments?"

Dominating

Taking "air time" and blocking other team members' opportunity to make suggestions. For example, "Just be quiet a minute. I've got something to say."

Name Calling

Stereotyping. Using labels that generalize about a person or team in a demeaning manner. For example, "You staff types really don't know what is going on in this company."

Games Played by Aggressive People

Uproar

Begins with some form of critical statement that triggers an attack-defense series of transactions. The game ends with team members arguing in loud voices.

"See What You Made Me Do" or "If It Weren't For You"

Using blaming games. The purpose is to transfer ownership or accountability for an error to another person, usually in a forceful, attacking manner. The message is: "My lack of influence [or the team's ineptness] is your fault."

S2 (HT/HR) COMPETENCY

Helping Role Category: Persuading

Requests the facts and relevant information on the problem. Seeks out expressions of feelings and values. Asks for suggestions, estimates, and ideas. Responds openly and freely to others. Encourages and accepts contributions of others, whether expressed verbally or nonverbally.

Persuading Indicators

Questioning

Asking questions for the sake of clarity and shared understanding of a point. Productive questioning enhances team process and quality of content. For example, "Of your training objectives, which one do you consider to be the most important?"

Guiding and Encouraging Responses

It isn't sufficient to ask good questions. It is also people's willingness to respond that helps bring out information and insights into their feelings and values. For example, "That is an excellent idea. Please tell us more about it."

Developing Alternatives

Creating options. Coming up with various interpretations or multiple conclusions or strategies for consideration. For example, "Perhaps we should look at the financial plan from a 'best case–worst case' set of scenarios."

Advocating

Suggesting that the team pursue one suggestion or alternative over another. For example, "Because we seem to be stuck for a next step, I'd like to suggest that we talk about the Johnson Tool acquisition next."

Hindering Role Category: Manipulative

Responds to a problem rigidly and persists in using stereotypical responses. Makes repeated attempts to use solutions that are ineffective in achieving team goals. Selectively interprets data so as to validate personal opinions and censure nonsupportive input. Responds to personal motives, desires, and aspirations to the exclusion of the public agenda. Attempts to lure others into joining position. Evaluates communication context. Judges remarks before they are understood and cross-examines others on their input.

Manipulative Indicators

Topic Jumping

Getting off course, such as in discussion about X, suddenly bringing up Y. Or, hairsplitting—focusing on and debating one detail so much that it is taken out of context and becomes a topic of its own. For example, "I agree that a business plan is important, but I think it is time that we rethink our company's mission statement."

Statements As Questions

Saying something in question form or a one-liner that is actually a statement of justification or criticism. For example, "Don't you think it's time you got this meeting going again? We're not getting anything accomplished here."

Selective Interpretations

Twisting what was said to discredit someone's point or taking a point out of context. For example, "That may be true, but we have never been successful in introducing a product without television advertising."

Gatekeeping

Hearing what one wants to hear. Attempting to control the input to match one's own assessment of significance and responding accordingly. For example, "Thank you for your suggestion." (writes it down) "That is interesting." (does not write it down) "Worthwhile idea." (writes it down)

Games Played by Manipulative People

Blemish

Becoming the team's nitpicker. Sifting through positive contributions looking for the chink in the armor and focusing on existing weak points.

Corner

Maneuvering other people through a series of seemingly plausible questions into a situation in that, no matter what they do, they never come out right.

Now I've Got You

Listening carefully to what is said, even questioning to get information, then pouncing on whoever makes a mistake or steps into a trap you've set.

S3 (HR/LT) COMPETENCY

Helping Role Category: Committing

Helps to ensure that all members are part of the decision-making process. Shows relationships between ideas. May restate suggestions to pull them together. Summarizes and offers potential decisions for the team to accept or reject. Asks to see if the team is nearing a decision. Attempts to reconcile disagreements and facilitate the participation of everyone in the decision. Helps keep communication channels open by reducing tension and getting people to explore differences.

Committing Indicators

Facilitating Involvement

Making sure that people are getting enough time to provide input. Making efforts to tap into the resources that are available in the team. For example, "Come on, fella, you're doing a fine job. Nobody wants to cut into what you have to say."

Synthesizing/Summarizing

Taking a variety of inputs and putting them into a new idea. Integrating what people say into a holistic framework. Summarizing existing ideas. For example, "If we take Joe's idea for a redesigned package and Mary's suggestion for in-store promotion, we may be able to launch the product introduction 2 months ahead of schedule."

Gaining Commitment

Tapping into the team to ensure members are on board and buying into the team's progress or results. Securing a shared sense of ownership. For example, "How many of you are willing to sign on to our commitment to ship 50,000 units by November first?"

Problem Solving

Dealing with problems affecting team commitment near the point of implementation. If there is skepticism, offer proof; if there is misunderstanding, clarify; if there is a drawback, be creative; procrastination, create a sense of urgency; if there is a solution not within the team's scope of authority, identify who is in authority, ask for support, and make suggestions. For example, "We have not been making very good progress. If we are going to wind this up today, we have to reach agreement before lunch on this personnel evaluation system."

Hindering Role Category: Dependent

Reacts to people as authority figures. May acquiesce to anyone who is seen as an overt leader. Abdicates problem solving to others and expects someone else to lead to the solution. Unwilling to use leadership resources available within self or others. Attempts to escape tension through diversions or the inappropriate use of humor. Easily embarrassed and vulnerable to criticism. Often apologizes for given input. Requires constant encouragement to participate. Seeks sympathy.

Dependent Indicators

Agreeing with Everything

Deferring to others. Suppressing one's feelings. Appears to agree with all members on all issues. For example, "No, I guess you're right. I'm out of ideas."

Avoiding Decisions or Closure Through Sarcasm

Making an inappropriate attempt at humor that keeps issues open when the team could be making a decision. For example, "Did you hear the story about the . . ."

Seeking Sympathy

Attempting to gain attention or concessions from other team members through sulking, looking dejected, or similar behaviors. Using such behaviors as manipulative ploys to gain influence. For example, "You always make my department take more than our share of the cuts. Why do we always have to give in? Why do we have to be punished?"

Expressing Futility, Resignation, or Helplessness

Snapping your gum, drawing, playing paper-and-pencil games, and doing things that distract team members and demonstrate noninvolvement. Announcing all the reasons why something is wrong or will not work. The aim is to convince others that the team is powerless and lacks control. For example, "Management is never going to listen to our ideas anyway. It is just another waste of time."

Games Played by Dependent People

Ain't It Awful

Presenting superficial concern for and commitment to the team's efforts when really attempting to thwart those efforts through statements such as: "It will take too much work" or "There'll be no support" or "No one ever listens to us."

Wooden Leg

Trying to avoid accomplishment, accountability, work, or to gain sympathy. Using some contrived or exaggerated handicap as an excuse for not being able to fulfill good intentions.

Poor Me

Behaving in a way that reinforces some form of self-pity and self-negation. The game is played to gain sympathy. Griping continues, but the person makes no real effort to change or improve the situation.

S4 (LR/LT) Competency

Helping Role Category: Attending

Listens as well as speaks. Easy to talk to. Encourages input from team members and tries to understand as well as be understood. Records input for use later. Demonstrates a willingness to become involved with other people. Takes time to listen and avoids interrupting.

Attending Indicators

Listening

Remaining silent, maintaining eye contact, and paying attention to what is being said with the purpose of understanding, not of agreeing. For example, "I've been listening very carefully, and it seems Tom has some very good points."

Showing Interest

Communicating in a way that shows one is involved in the team's process and concerned with its workings. The communication is usually nonverbal and is a type of emotionally neutral reinforcement. For example, leaning forward, visibly concentrating on discussions.

Taking Notes (For Oneself) or Recording (For the Team)

Keeping some form of registered evidence of the team's inputs, activities, and decisions that will make them accessible at a later point. For example, "I've made some notes and I'd like to say something."

Monitoring or Observing

Auditing or examining the team. Paying special attention to the impact things have on the team's progress or performance. For example, showing alertness during discussions.

Hindering Role Category: Avoidance

Retreats emotionally in thought or physically. Daydreams, avoids the topics, or remains indifferent. Engages in individualistic activity that has little or nothing to do with team activity. May withdraw from the team. Scoffs at team effort, rolls eyes in disgust, or demonstrates aloofness nonverbally. Will occasionally preplan a means to leave the team early.

Avoidance Indicators

Withdrawing Psychologically

Being unresponsive, withdrawn, seemingly checked out from the team's activities—preoccupied with thoughts other than the issues before the team. For example, trying not to be involved in the team's activities—looking intently at pictures, and so on.

Withdrawing Physically

Stationing oneself away from the team. Creating a physical distance between oneself and the team's activities. For example, getting up from the team discussion area and walking over to the windows, a few feet away.

Reflecting Boredom

Pouting, physically conveying the message "I'd rather not be here." Being an active competing response for the team. For example, slouching in the chair and appearing uninterested.

Escaping the Team

Physically leaving the environment, planning to be late, intentionally absenting oneself from the team. For example, phone rings as secretary makes prearranged call. "Sorry, folks, have to leave to take care of some important business."

Games Played by Avoidance People

Harried

Appearing too overworked or busy to meet deadlines and commitments. To sustain the game and maintain this image, the player will take on and even solicit added responsibilities. This overload provides the basis for permission to be late, to leave meetings before the team comes to closure, and to turn over unfinished work with incomplete instructions to other team members—guilt-free and with justification.

Kick me

Making a mistake, that is, coming to work late or unprepared and hoping that someone in the team will provide the desired kick—criticism, questions, and so on. This kick provides the payoff the player seeks. An eventual result is that the person will probably withhold contributions or withdraw psychologically or physically from the team.

Withdrawing psychologically or physically from the team can be an outcome of any of these games. Although this may give the hinderer some short-term satisfaction, it undermines the team process.

SUMMARY

These are some of the behavioral indicators reflecting helping and hindering roles in each of the four competencies. They are illustrations of the types of activities that contribute to or detract from functional and constructive team problem solving. We want to emphasize again that these roles are not by themselves helping or hindering—there are no generic helping or hindering roles. A role may be helping or hindering depending upon the situation. Your awareness of these roles will make a very real contribution toward increasing your effectiveness in teams.

One last thought. This chapter has shown that the management of teams requires the special challenge of leading individuals to become more than their individual selves. As Jon Katzenbach and Douglas K. Smith suggest, "In the end, the wisdom of teams is within the team itself. It is not in creating the high-performance organization, managing transformational change, enforcing corporate performance ethics, or inspiring new dimensions of leadership. It is in a small team of people so committed to something larger than themselves that they will not be denied."[20]

ENDNOTES

1. David Krech, Richard S. Crutchfield, and Egerton L. Ballachey, *Individual in Society* (New York: McGraw-Hill, 1962), p. 529.
2. Sam Certo, *Principles of Modern Management: Functions and Systems* (Dubuque, IA: Brown, 1983).
3. Elisa Mendzela, "Effective Teams," *The CPA Journal*, September 1997, p. 2.
4. Carla Joinson, "Teams at Work," *HR Magazine*, May 1999, p. 32.
5. Charles L. Parnell, "Teamwork," *Vital Speeches of the Day*, September 14, 1996, p.46–49.
6. Quoted in W. H. Weiss, "Teams and Teamwork," *Supervision*, July 1998, 59, no. 7, p. 9.
7. Mendzela, p. 62.
8. Joycee Ranney and Mark Deck, "Making Teams Work: Lessons from Leaders in New Product Development," *Planning Review,* July/August 1995, pp. 6–12.
9. John Cunniff, "Involving People in a New Work Contract," *The Fresno Bee*, November 12, 1995, p. C6.
10. Joycee Ranney and Mark Deck, "Making Teams Work: Lessons from Leaders in New Product Development." See also Shoichi Suzawa, "How the Japanese Achieve Excellence," *Training and Development Journal*, May 1985, pp. 110–117; Howard J. Klein and

Paul W. Mulvey, "Two Investigations of the Relationships among Group Goals, Goal Commitment, Cohension, and Performance," *Organizational Behavior and Human Decision Processes,* January 1995, pp. 44–53; and Anne M. O'Leary-Kelly, Joseph J. Martocchio, and Dwight D. Frink, "A Review of the Influence of Group Goals on Group Performance," *Academy of Management Journal,* October 1994, pp. 1285–1301.

11. Guest, Hersey, and Blanchard, *Organizational Change through Effective Leadership,* 2nd ed. (Upper Saddle River, NJ: Prentice Hall, 1986).

12. Peter F. Drucker, "The New Realities: In Government and Politics" In *Economics and Business-In Society and World View* (New York: Harper Collins, 1990).

13. Brian Dumaine, "The Trouble with Teams," *Fortune,* September 5, 1994, pp. 86–92.

14. *Ibid.*

15. *Ibid.*

16. *Ibid.*

17. W. H. Weiss, p. 9.

18. Katzenbach and Smith quoted in W. H. Weiss, p. 9.

19. Dummaine, pp. 86–92. Tim R. Furley, Jennifer L. Garlitz, and Michael L. Kelleher, "Applying Information Technology to Reengineering," *Planning Review,* November–December, 1993, pp. 22–25, 55. See also Steve H. Barr and Edward J. Conlon, "Effects of Distribution of Feedback in Work Teams," *Academy of Management Journal,* June 1994, pp. 641–655; W. Jack Duncan, "Why Some People Loaf in Teams While Others Loaf Alone," *Academy of Management Executive,* 8, pp. 641–655; and Glenn M. Parker, *Cross-Functional Teams: Working with Allies, Enemies, and Other Strangers* (San Francisco: Jossey–Bass, 1994).

20. Jon R. Katzenbach and Douglas K. Smith, *The Wisdom of Teams* (New York: Harper Collins, 1994), p. 259.

Chapter 15

Implementing Situational Leadership: Managing People to Perform

This and the next chapter will build upon significant aspects of Situational Leadership in bottom-line approaches to managing people to perform. As we discussed in the opening paragraphs of chapter 1, management must be results based. Regardless of how a leadership or management concept might appear to be initially, the most fundamental issue is, Does it contribute to organizational productivity? This is what we mean by effective management. We will return to this point very shortly. ✧

Our approach in these chapters is to draw upon some of the most significant contributions to effective management in recent years, using as a focus Situational Leadership. In this chapter, we begin with a satellite model of organizational performance (see Figure 15-1) and then follow up with several tactical or operational approaches to enhancing organizational performance, with a special emphasis on quality management. Although the approaches in these chapters may differ in terminology and in specific areas of emphasis, they all are related to Situational Leadership and the achievement of organizational productivity through effective leadership and management.

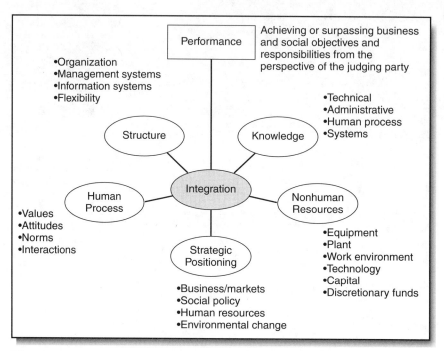

Figure 15-1
Satellite Model of Organizational Performance

Source: Reprinted by permission of the publisher, from Alan A. Yelsey, "Strategies and Actions for Improving Organizational Performance," *Academy of Management Review,* June 1984, pp. 45, 46. © 1984 Academy of Management, New York. All rights reserved.

ORGANIZATIONAL PERFORMANCE

We need to remind ourselves through a strategic model that organizational performance is the product of many factors, as shown in Figure 15-1.[1] This model identifies several of the most important factors, including organizational structure, knowledge, nonhuman resources, strategic positioning, and human process. A *strategy* is a broad, integrated plan of action to accomplish organizational goals; in our frame of reference, the goal is to improve human productivity. Because a strategy is an integrated plan, all of the factors or variables are interrelated. And they all contribute to *performance*, which is defined in the model as achieving or surpassing business and social objectives and responsibilities from the perspective of the judging party. *Integration* is not only essential to meeting current business and social needs but, as Figure 15-2 suggests, it is essential to the change process necessary to meet future business and social needs of the organization.[2]

Although all of these factors are important and are certainly worthy of study, our primary emphasis in this book is on human resources. This emphasis is justified because increasing attention is being directed toward hu-

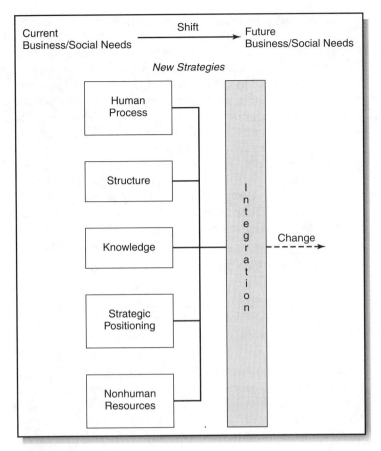

Figure 15-2
Positioning for Future Performance

Source: Reprinted by permission of the publisher, from Alan A. Yelsey, "Strategies and Actions for Improving Organizational Performance," June 1984, pp. 45, 46. © 1984 Academy of Management, New York. All rights reserved.

man resources, not only in their traditional roles, but also in their influence on the other key performance factors.[3] For example, Ian MacMillan and Randall Schuler suggested that "focusing on a firm's human resources could provide a significant opportunity to secure a sustained edge over competitors."[4] This is an interesting idea. Using superior human resources as a competitive weapon in improving organizational performance is certainly a new dimension in the management of organizational behavior. But how can organizations use human resources as strategic weapons?

MacMillan and Schuler found that companies have gained an edge by either capturing or developing greater shares of critically needed human resource skills or by making better use of existing human resources. Neither can be done in isolation. There must be very close coordination between human resources planning and the other performance factors.

Increasingly, human resources managers will come under pressure to anticipate the major gaps in key skills needed for the firm.... The role of human resources management (HRM) in developing strategy will become critical. Clearly these managers are best equipped to identify the key skills that can be applied to create the competitive edge, and clearly they can play a major role in managing any transfer of skills to the strategic target, as well as assure the quality and quantity and continuity of the existing in-house skills. So it becomes vital for the HRM staff to become involved in the strategic process—not only in the traditional sense as a support function that assures the availability of human resources to support the strategic effort, but also as an aggressive participant that helps identify significant strategic advantages based on the corporation's existing human resources or to identify areas in which emerging skill needs can be preempted ahead of competitors.[5]

Questions MacMillan and Schuler recommend be asked include:

1. Which human resources in the company are unequivocally excellent?
2. How must HRM practices be applied to motivate the employees who possess the key skills?
3. What strategic targets could be pursued?
4. What strategic thrusts will be critical in the industry chain in the future?[6]

Their main argument that "companies can gain a competitive advantage through their human resources by making sure that employees both have the appropriate skills and are suitably motivated"[7] is the same argument that we have been using for more than 30 years. Managing people to perform can make a significant difference. We hope that the approaches presented in this and subsequent chapters will give you useful ideas in your own human resources management.

Figure 15-3 shows another useful model, developed by Clay Carr, a Defense Logistics Agency senior manager. The two most critical elements are motive and goal. In Carr's terms, "This is based on a straightforward assumption about human action in general and organizational performance in particular; individuals who set goals and are motivated to achieve those goals will attempt to achieve them regardless of any other factors.... All performance factors are not created equal. An individual's goal and motives for accomplishing that goal dominate the other factors."[8] This approach is fully consistent with our conclusions in chapters 2 and 3.

Goals

Carr defines a goal as "a different state of affairs that the individual [or organization] actively seeks to achieve."[9] He notes that this definition implies three important distinctions:

1. A goal is not a requirement.
2. A goal is not a desire.
3. Formal goals and real goals are different entities.

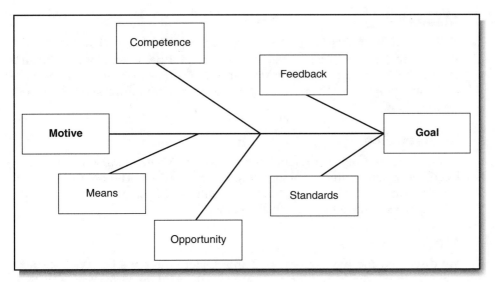

Figure 15-3
The Seven Factors of Performance

An example will clarify these distinctions. A manager tells the branch that sales will increase 10 percent during the next fiscal year. At this point, this statement is only the manager's requirement, desire, and formal goal. It is not a real goal because it has not been accepted by those who have to accomplish it. Furthermore, it has not been translated into the tasks that individuals must perform in combination with others so that the goal can be reached.

Standards

Standards are important because they tell when the goal was accomplished. Without standards, it is anyone's opinion whether the goal was reached. The standard answers the question, When do I know that I am successful?

Feedback

Goals, standards, and feedback are intertwined. Feedback reports both the quality and quantity of progress toward reaching a goal that is defined by standards. Feedback is particularly important when we consider "real" goals—goals that are accepted by employees as meaningful and worthwhile.

Katie, the district manager, observed Mac, a store manager, using a calculator. When she asked him what he was doing, Mac replied, "I am totaling every sale we make to see how close I am to reaching my daily sales goal." It wasn't Katie's goal or the owner's goal; it was Mac's goal. Mac had combined goal, standard, and feedback because it was a real goal.

Means

"What resources do I have to help me accomplish this goal successfully?" Without the means, the job-specific tasks cannot be done. If your machine can't be calibrated, if your computer program is flawed, if you can't hire the personnel you need, if you don't have access to vital information, you can't do the job.

Competence

Competence is a key ingredient in performance. A person must do more than learn about something; a person must be able to do it. The important question is, "Do I have the competence that will permit me to perform the job-related tasks required to achieve the goal?"

Motive

We discussed motive in chapters 2 and 3. Here the issue is, "Why would I want to do it; what's in it for me?" Managers facilitate performance motivation. How? Among the ideas that we have previously visited are money incentives, recognition, challenging goals, achievable standards, feedback, freedom to do the job including the time to do it, the necessary resources, and removal of disincentives.

Opportunity

Two factors contribute to the lack of opportunity to perform: time and eligibility. Higher priority tasks get more attention and consume available time. If employees are hindered from performing because supervisors don't believe in quality or customer satisfaction, they will be effectively blocked from *eligibility* to perform.

These seven factors are closely related. Like a three-legged stool, when one or more of the legs is missing, it is off balance. Organizational performance can easily be off balance, with the result that goals are not accomplished and standards are not met.

IMPROVING PRODUCTIVITY (AND QUALITY)

Productivity is the ratio of the output of goods and services divided by the input or resources used to produce those goods and services. Like all ratios, it can be improved by increasing the output, decreasing the input, or both. Joel Ross presents this idea in the productivity wheel illustrated in Figure 15-4. He makes the point that improvement has focused on technology and capital equipment to reduce the input of labor cost while using industrial engineering techniques to improve output. He goes on to make the important observation that "both of

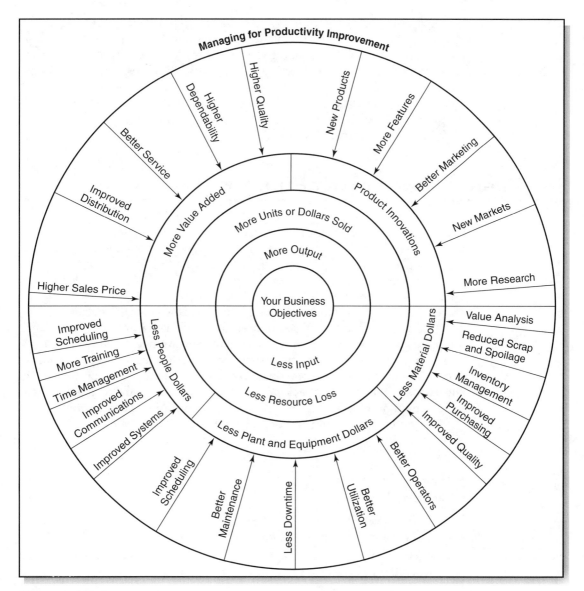

Figure 15-4
The Productivity Wheel

Source: Reprinted with permission from Joel E. Ross, *Total Quality Management*, 1999. Copyright CRC Press, Boca Raton, Florida.

these approaches are still appropriate, *but the current trend is toward better use of the potential available through human resources* [emphasis added]."[10]

Figure 15-4 illustrates this observation. On the output side, better service, higher quality, better marketing, improved distribution, and so on lead to more value added and product innovations, which lead to more units sold or dollars of revenue gained, to more output, to achieving business objectives.

On the input side, more training, better utilization, inventory management, and so on lead to less people dollars, less plant and equipment dollars, and less material dollars. These lead to less resource loss, less input, and greater achievement of business objectives. Figure 15-4 demonstrates that almost every action and technique for improving productivity depends on the management of organizational behavior. Essentially, it all comes down to this basic premise: Leader-follower interaction is the most important factor in organizational effectiveness.

360-DEGREE ASSESSMENT PROCESS

The 360-degree assessment process, sometimes called a *multisource* or *multirater tool*, is being used with increasing frequency for evaluating employee performance. "About 90 percent of Fortune 100 companies are estimated to use some form of multisource evaluation . . ."[11] The 360-degree feedback is a full-circle evaluation of an employee's performance by evaluating an ". . . employee's skills, abilities, styles, and job-related competencies."[12]

A common practice in 360-degree feedback is to have the employee complete a self-assessment, as well as having several peers, followers, supervisors, and customers complete instruments. Traditionally, a typical evaluation was completed by one person who assessed an employee's performance. The use of 360-degree feedback can help eliminate the halo effect of one great achievement or mistake that may occur during traditional evaluations.

Pros and cons to using 360-degree feedback are as follows:

Pros
- Lessens discrimination.
- Decreases bias in evaluations.
- Identifies areas that need improvement.
- Gathers information from different organizational levels.
- Offers an in-depth look at the raters' behavior patterns and the difference between their perceptions and the organization's view.
- Presents the employee's strengths and weaknesses.

Cons
- Feedback can hurt.
- People can be malicious with criticism.
- There may be conflicting opinions (Who's right and who's wrong?).
- The employee may choose friends to give feedback.
- Are people being truthful in their responses?
- Too many surveys in a short period of time can lead to burnout and inaccurate feedback.[13]

Consultants typically analyze the data and either present it to the employee in writing or face-to-face. The consultant can meet face-to-face to discuss and clarify information and help the employee develop strategies and goals to help change the undesirable behavior(s) that were found.

A follow-up assessment should be done after 6 months with another survey to determine whether the behavior-changing strategies worked and the goals were achieved.

Mary Vinson has made several recommendations to improve the feedback method's chances of producing change.

- Feedback must be anonymous and confidential.
- The employee must have been in that position for at least 6 months.
- A feedback expert should interpret the feedback.
- Feedback should not be used to determine salaries or promotion.
- Feedback providers should be given the chance to provide written descriptions as well as numerical data.
- The instrument should be reliable, valid, and based on statistical methods.
- Feedback should not be used with too many employees in one area at a time because it may cause "survey burnout."[14]

Stephen R. Covey, chairman of Covey Leadership Center and best-selling author of *Principle-Centered Leadership* and *7 Habits of Highly Effective People,* has related 360-degree feedback to empowerment.

> Within a culture of high trust, the entire organization can participate in a system of regular written and verbal 360-degree feedback. If the desired results have been clearly defined and other elements of a win-win agreement are in place, trustworthy people know better than anyone else how they are performing. People don't need their supervisors to judge their performance; they can judge themselves.
>
> When employees have no system of feedback except annual performance appraisals, the information comes too late, too general and from the wrong source to be truly empowering. "How am I doing in meeting your needs?" should be a question to all stakeholders that every employee and organization should be able to answer regularly.[15]

THE ACHIEVE MODEL

Background

A common problem that occurs in the management process is that many managers tend to be effective in letting followers know *what* performance problems exist, but they are not as effective in helping followers determine *why* those problems exist. In other words, many managers are strong in problem identification but are much weaker in problem analysis, or diagnosis.

In order to be most effective in evaluating and solving performance problems, managers need to determine why problems have occurred. The *ACHIEVE* model was designed by Paul Hersey and Marshall Goldsmith to help managers determine why performance problems may have occurred and then develop change strategies aimed at solving those problems.[16]

In developing a model for analyzing human performance problems, Hersey and Goldsmith had two primary goals in mind: to determine the key factors that can influence staff members' performance and to present these factors in a way that can be used and remembered by practicing managers.

The first step in the development of the ACHIEVE model was to isolate the key factors that influence performance management. Earlier work by John W. Atkinson indicated that performance is a function of motivation and ability.[17] Put in simple terms, the idea is that the follower has to have a certain degree of willingness to do the job and the skills necessary to complete the task. Lyman Porter and Edward Lawler expanded this idea by including role perception, or job understanding. They noted that followers can have all the willingness and skills needed to do the job but will not be effective unless there is a clear understanding of what to do and how to do it.[18]

Jay Lorsch and Paul Lawrence approached the topic from a different perspective and concluded that performance was not merely a function of attributes possessed by the individual, but also depended on the organization and the environment.[19] Individuals can be highly motivated and have all the skills to do the job, but they will be effective only if they get needed organizational support and direction and their work fits the needs of their organizational environment.

The ACHIEVE model uses two more factors in the performance management equation. The first factor is *feedback*, which means that the followers need to know not just what to do but also how well they are doing it on an ongoing basis. Feedback includes day-to-day coaching and formal performance evaluation. The other performance management factor is *validity*. In today's environment, managers need to be able to document and justify decisions that affect people's careers. Valid personnel practices have become a legal necessity in the United States. In analyzing performance, managers need to continually check for validity in all personnel practices, such as job analyses, recruitment, appraisal, training, promotion, and dismissal.

Hersey and Goldsmith isolated seven variables related to effective performance management: (1) ability; (2) understanding; (3) organizational support; (4) motivation; (5) performance feedback; (6) validity; and (7) environment. Next, they put these factors together in a manner that managers could easily remember and use. One technique for making items on a list easy to remember (such a technique is called a *mnemonic device*) is to make their first letters form a common word, an acronym. A seven-letter word that is synonymous with "to perform" is *achieve*. Substituting *incentive* for the motivation factor, *clarity* for understanding, *help* for organizational support, and *evaluation* for performance feedback gives the mnemonic ACHIEVE.

- Ability
- Clarity

- Help
- Incentive
- Evaluation
- Validity
- Environment

Using the ACHIEVE Model

In using the ACHIEVE model, the manager evaluates how each factor will affect the current or potential performance of followers for a given task. Then the manager should take the steps that "fit" the unique cause(s) of the performance problem. The seven factors in the ACHIEVE model, along with typical problem-solving alternatives, are listed next.

A—Ability (Knowledge and Skills)

In the ACHIEVE model, the term *ability* refers to the follower's knowledge, experience, and skill—the ability to complete the specific task successfully. It is important to remember that individuals are not universally competent. Key components of ability include task-relevant education (formal and informal training that facilitates the successful completion of the specific task); task-relevant experience (work experience that contributes to the successful completion of the task); and task-relevant skills (proficiencies that enhance the successful completion of the task). In analyzing follower performance, the manager should ask, Does this follower have the knowledge, skill, and experience to complete this task successfully?

If the person has an ability problem, solutions may include specific training, coaching, formal educational courses, or reassignment of specific duties or responsibilities. These alternatives should be considered from the viewpoint of cost effectiveness.

C—Clarity (Understanding or Role Perception)

Clarity refers to an understanding and acceptance of what to do, when to do it, and how to do it. To have a thorough understanding of the job, the follower needs to understand clearly what the major goals and objectives are, how they should be accomplished, and their priority (which objectives are most important at what times).

If the follower has a problem in clarity, or understanding, there may well be a problem in the performance-planning phase. In many cases, oral agreement on objectives is not enough. The manager should ensure that all objectives are formally recorded. The follower should be encouraged to ask questions for further clarification.

H—Help (Organizational Support)

The term *help* refers to the organizational help, or support, that the follower needs to effectively complete the task. Some organizational support factors include adequate budget and personnel, suitable equipment and facilities, and necessary support from other departments.

If there is a lack of help, or organizational support, managers should clearly identify where the problem exists. If the problem is lack of money, human resources, equipment, or facilities, the manager should see whether the necessary resources can be acquired in a cost-effective manner. If the resources cannot be acquired, the manager may have to revise objectives to avoid holding followers responsible for circumstances beyond their control.

I—Incentive (Motivation or Willingness)

The term *incentive* refers to the follower's task-relevant incentive—the motivation to complete the specific task under analysis in a successful manner. In evaluating incentive, one must remember that people are not equally motivated to complete all tasks. Followers tend to be more motivated to successfully complete tasks that bring them either intrinsic or extrinsic rewards than to complete tasks that do not reward them personally.

If the follower has an incentive problem, the first step is to check the use of rewards and punishments. The follower should clearly understand that performance on this task is related to pay, promotion, recognition, and job security. Research indicates that managers sometimes hope that followers will engage in certain behaviors even if those behaviors go unrewarded.[20] People have a natural tendency to pursue tasks that are rewarded and to avoid tasks that are not. Rewards can be tangible or intangible; feedback on performance, such as recognition or a pat on the back, can be an important part of the overall incentive system.

E—Evaluation (Coaching and Performance Feedback)

Evaluation refers to informal day-to-day performance feedback as well as formal periodic reviews. An effective feedback process lets followers know, on a regular basis, how well they are doing the job. It is unrealistic to expect followers to improve performance if they are unaware that performance problems exist. People should know how they are being evaluated on a regular basis before their formal periodic evaluation occurs. Many performance problems can be caused by a lack of necessary coaching and performance feedback.

If there is an evaluation problem, it may be caused by the lack of day-to-day feedback on both effective and ineffective performance. Many managers tend to focus on the bad news and forget to recognize when things are going well. Recognition for a job well done can be a vital part of the ongoing evaluation process. It can increase motivation, and it costs the organization very little.

One method that helps to highlight extremes in performance is the "significant incident" process, which includes formally documenting highly positive or negative performance. This practice ensures that the follower receives feedback that is part of the formal record.

V—Validity (Valid and Legal Personnel Practices)

The term *validity* refers to the appropriateness and legality of human resources decisions made by the manager. Managers need to make sure that decisions about people are appropriate in light of laws, court decisions, and company policies. Managers should make sure that personnel practices do not discriminate against any specific group or individual, and they should be aware that organizations need valid and legal performance evaluations, training and promotion criteria, and so on.

If there is a validity problem, managers should know that the trend of the law in management is clear: Personnel decisions need to be documented and justified on the basis of *performance-oriented* criteria. Managers uncertain about validity issues should discuss them with human resources or the organization's legal office. For example, shifting demographics of the modern workforce seem to indicate that current estimates of what constitutes "middle age" are much older than they were just a decade ago. Lydia Bronte cautions managers to avoid the "tremendous age bias and the discounting of experience" of this increasingly able and older workforce.[21] Laws are continually changing to address this situation, and managers must constantly check the validity of their decisions, particularly in this age of corporate downsizing and workforce reduction.

E—Environment (Environmental Fit)

The term *environment* refers to the external factors that can influence performance even if the individual has all the ability, clarity, help, and incentive needed to do the job. Key elements of the environmental factors include competition, changing market conditions, government regulations, suppliers, and so on.

If there is an environmental problem beyond their control, followers should not be rewarded or reprimanded for performance. In short, followers should be expected to perform at a level consistent with the limitations of their environment.

PERFORMANCE MANAGEMENT

Performance management integrates the Situational Leadership concept and the ACHIEVE model. The three major steps in implementing performance management are performance planning, coaching to reinforce performance plans and to develop followers, and conducting the formal performance review.

1. *Performance planning.* Setting objectives and directions for followers at the beginning of a planning period and developing plans for achieving those objectives.
2. *Coaching.* Day-to-day feedback and development activities aimed at enhancing performance plans.
3. *Performance review.* Overall evaluation of performance for the specific planning period.

The situational approach to performance management enables managers to individualize performance planning, coaching, and review by choosing managerial techniques that fit the unique situation faced by each of their followers.

Performance Planning

Many traditional management by objectives (MBO) approaches indicate that managers and followers should always develop objectives in a joint decision-making process. Situational Leadership suggests that degrees of joint decision making may be appropriate for followers at moderate readiness levels (R2 or R3) but not as appropriate with followers who have very high or very low readiness levels (R4 or R1).

In cases where followers have low readiness levels for setting certain goals, managers may be better off setting the goals and communicating them to the low-readiness level follower. In cases where follower readiness is extremely high regarding a particular task, followers may take the key role in the goal-setting process. If the follower is at a very high readiness level, it may be acceptable (and even desirable) for the follower to take the major leadership responsibility in setting more specific objectives. In summary, Situational Leadership suggests that managers should involve followers in the performance-planning process at a level consistent with the follower's readiness concerning the task under discussion.

Another use of Situational Leadership in the performance-planning process involves the idea of Contracting for Leadership Style (see chapter 12). In setting objectives, it is not enough for the manager and follower to determine what objectives should be achieved; it is also useful for them to agree upon their respective roles in the achievement of those objectives. Managers and followers should agree up front on the degree of managerial involvement expected for each specific task. Managers should let followers know where structure and direction can be expected and where delegation may be appropriate. By clarifying their roles in the performance-planning process, both managers and followers can help avoid unnecessary stress and surprises in the implementation phase.

One weakness of many MBO-type systems is that the manager and follower negotiate only for what the follower is going to contribute. The ACHIEVE system suggests that the manager and follower also need to get a clear idea of what needed support the organization is going to contribute. Using the ACHIEVE model in performance planning, the manager can deal with questions such as, Does the follower have the ability to do the job? Does the follower clearly understand what to do and how to do it? What degree of support is needed from the organization? Is there a process for ongoing coaching and feedback?

The ACHIEVE model gives the manager a clear analysis of performance potential. If any problems appear to exist, the manager should address those problems before the individual is assigned specific objectives. For example, if the manager feels that the follower lacks ability, necessary training should occur before the follower starts unsuccessfully trying to achieve the objective.

An analysis of each performance factor in the ACHIEVE model before the follower starts to work increases the probability of setting challenging, realistic objectives. Special attention should be paid to the validity factor. If performance objectives have been set in a way that may unfairly discriminate against any individual or group, the human resources staff may be contacted and the objectives changed.

Coaching

Managers can develop a situational approach to coaching by actually using the leadership styles contracted for during the performance-planning process. In coaching, Situational Leadership helps managers make clear connections between their leadership styles, the objectives set in the performance-planning process, and the follower's readiness level for achieving each specific objective.

One serious problem managers have in coaching is the lack of sufficient analysis before making a coaching intervention.[22] Managers can use the ACHIEVE model to analyze performance problems quickly before deciding what remedial actions to take.

Performance problems need to be faced as early as possible—before they turn into disasters. Managers observing a problem in its early stages often refrain from taking action because they hope the problems will go away. They very seldom do. With the ACHIEVE model, the manager has a quick mental checklist for day-to-day problem solving that can be used without formal meetings, documents, or office appointments. After using the ACHIEVE model to diagnose a unique problem, the manager can dramatically increase the probability of making a problem-solving intervention that fits the situation faced by the follower.

Performance Review

In the final performance appraisal meeting between manager and follower, there should be no surprises. If the manager has done a thorough job of performance planning and day-to-day coaching, both parties should see this meeting as a review of what happened during the planning and coaching periods. The manager can use Situational Leadership to determine the degree of follower involvement in the formal review process.

Managers may want followers at high readiness levels to complete self-evaluations, which can be discussed before final managerial ratings. Followers at moderate readiness levels may require a joint decision-making process, with the degree of follower direction depending on readiness level for each specific goal. Followers at low readiness levels may require a directive review, with most of the information going from the manager to the follower. Managers can use a situational approach to avoid the issue of determining what levels of follower participation in reviews are "good" or "bad." The Situational Leadership framework allows followers to engage in the degree of participation that works for their particular review.

In the final performance review, managers can use the ACHIEVE model to analyze why performance results did or did not meet the standards set in the performance-planning process. After the causes of performance problems have been determined by the manager and follower, developmental strategies can be designed to fit the specific performance problems that have occurred. The ACHIEVE model can help the manager attain specific performance-related data that can be used in future training, transfer, and personnel decisions. The ACHIEVE model also helps managers decide whether failure to meet performance standards was due to a lack of follower performance or to managerial, organizational, or environmental problems.

SUMMARY

Performance management builds upon the basic philosophy of Situational Leadership. There is no one best way to solve human resource problems. The manager should use the problem-solving strategy that best fits the needs of followers in their unique situations. Performance management provides managers with easy-to-use guidelines for analyzing work situations, determining why performance problems may exist, and choosing solution strategies to fit the problems faced by their followers. Another significant benefit of the situational approach to performance management is that it provides an effective framework that trainers can use for developing managers in performance planning, coaching, and performance review.

ENDNOTES

1. Alan A. Yelsey, "Strategies and Actions for Improving Organizational Performance," *Academy of Management Review,* June 1984, p. 25.
2. *Ibid.,* p. 26.
3. See, for example, the increasing importance of human resources in "Human Resources Managers Aren't Corporate Nobodies Anymore," *Business Week,* December 2, 1987, pp. 58–59. See also William A. Medlin, "Managing People to Perform," *The Bureaucrat,* Spring 1985, pp. 52–55; Jac Fritz Enz, "Human Resource: Formulas for Success," *Personnel Journal,* 64, no. 10 (October 1985), pp. 52–60; Philip H. Mirvis, "Formulating and Implementing Human Resource Strategy," *Human Resource Management,* 24, no. 4 (Winter 1985), pp. 385–412.
4. Ian C. MacMillan and Randall S. Schuler, "Gaining a Competitive Edge through Human Resources," *Personnel,* April 1985, p. 24. See also Dave Ulrich, "Human Resource Planning As a Competitive Edge," *Human Resource Planning,* 9, no. 2 (1986), pp. 41–49.
5. MacMillan and Schuler, "Gaining a Competitive Edge through Human Resources," p. 27.
6. *Ibid.,* p. 28.
7. *Ibid.,* pp. 28–29.
8. Clay Carr, "The Ingredients of Good Performance," *Training,* August 1993, p. 528.
9. *Ibid.*
10. Joel E. Ross, *Principles of Total Quality* (Delray Beach, FL: St. Lucie Press, 1999), p. 335.
11. Leanne Atwater and David Waldman. "Accountability in 360-Degree Feedback," *HRMagazine,* May 1998, p. 96.
12. Mary N. Vinson, "The Pros and Cons of 360-Degree Feedback: Making It Work," *Training & Development,* April 1996, p. 11.
13. *Ibid.*
14. *Ibid.*
15. Stephen R. Covey, "Principle-Centered Leadership," *QualityDigest,* February 1999.
16. This has been a primary research objective at the Center for Leadership Studies. This section on the ACHIEVE model is adapted from Paul Hersey and Marshall Goldsmith, "A Situational Approach to Performance Planning," *Training and Development,* 34 (November 1980), pp. 38–40.
17. John W. Atkinson, *An Introduction to Motivation* (New York: Van Nostrand, 1958).

18. Lyman Porter and Edward Lawler, *Managerial Attitudes and Performance* (Homewood, IL: Irwin, 1968). See also Charles R. Gowen, "Managing Work Group Performance by Individual Goals and Group Goals for an Interdependent Group Task," *Journal of Organizational Behavior*, 7, no. 3 (Winter 1986), pp. 5–27.

19. Jay Lorsch and Paul Lawrence, "The Diagnosis of Organizational Problems." In *Organizational Development: Values, Processes, and Technology*, Newton Margulies and Anthony P. Raia (New York: McGraw-Hill, 1972).

20. Steven Kerr, "On the Folly of Hoping for A While Rewarding B," *Academy of Management Journal*, 4 (1975), pp. 76–79. See also Thomas Kemper, "Motivation and Behavior, A Personal View," *Journal of General Management*, 9, no. 3 (Fall 1983), pp. 51–57; Martin Gevans, "Organizational Behavior: The Central Role of Motivation," *Journal of Management*, 12, no. 2 (Summer 1986), pp. 203–222.

21. Lydia Bronte, "Longevity and the Future of the Workplace," *Planning Forum Network*, 7, no. 6 (Summer 1994), p. 7.

22. Ferdinand Fournies, *Coaching for Improved Work Performance* (New York: Van Nostrand, 1978).

Chapter 16

Implementing Situational Leadership: Building Commitments

Making decisions that stick and building commitments are two of the most important activities a manager can perform. Both are essential to managerial success. In this chapter, we will first look at how Situational Leadership applies to making good decisions, an indispensable skill at every level of management. We will then examine a major contribution of the management consulting firm of Keilty, Goldsmith, and Boone—building commitments—which uses Situational Leadership as an important aspect of their approach.[1] ✧

MAKING EFFECTIVE DECISIONS

Managers spend much of their time reviewing and acting on the proposals of associates, upper management, and technical personnel. Therefore, it is common to hear some managers spoken of as "decisive" or as "having business sense." Unfortunately, it is also common to hear other managers spoken of as "wishy-washy" or as "lacking prudent judgment." That's why your chances for current success and future career advancement are helped if you can (1) make the right decisions in areas you control and (2) submit sound recommendations when requested by your supervisor.[2]

Viewed in a vacuum, decision making seems like a fairly straightforward process. There appear to be simple steps for collecting and analyzing data, weighing alternatives, testing possible solutions, and arriving at a course of action.

But the world rarely cooperates so conveniently. Real-life decisions are usually called for in a pressure-packed environment of inadequate input, conflicting information, budget restraints, time squeezes, scarce resources, and many other elements that cloud the issues and threaten the quality of decisions. Even so, poor decision making is not likely to be excused because of the complexities of the manager's workload. The manager needs a simple and logical framework for making decisions that stick.

Situational Leadership can serve as the framework. Just as your diagnosis of follower readiness can determine the high probability leadership style, it can also indicate which style of decision making is most apt to succeed in a given situation.

Figure 16-1 not only describes four problem-solving situations but also suggests four basic decision-making styles—authoritative, consultative, facilitative, and delegative. Each decision-making style has a high probability of getting results, depending on the readiness of the followers and the situation.

Decision Style

Authoritative decision making applies in situations where the manager has the necessary experience and information to reach a conclusion, and followers do not possess the ability, willingness, or confidence to help. In this case, the manager should make the decision without seeking assistance.[3]

The authoritative style requires directive leader behavior. Followers are usually not actively involved in determining the course of action. Therefore, they hear little about the decision until the manager announces it. Authoritative decisions are commonly communicated with phrases such as "I've decided that . . ." and "Here's what we're going to do."

What kinds of circumstances require leader-made authoritative decisions? Suppose that your background in product development is all that is needed to set the budget for next year's research program. You've managed your department for 4 years. You know the goals set for your work group. You are aware of all budgeting policies governing staff, supplies, travel, and so on. Further, your followers know little about budgeting and are new to your department (R1 for most tasks). They are still learning the basics and are not ready to assist you in making this decision. Therefore, you need to make this decision yourself. Your experience in this area assures you that (1) your conclusion has a high probability of being correct, and (2) your proposed budget has a high probability of being accepted by your supervisor.

Authoritative decisions are also required in cases where you are the only source of information or expertise. If a coworker suddenly begins choking—even though your knowledge of first aid is limited—you may be the *only*

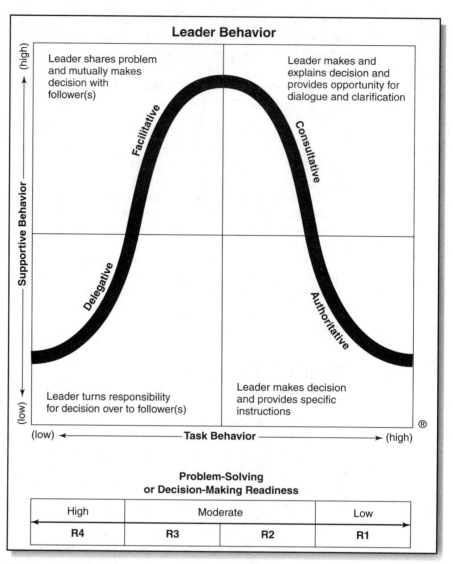

Leader Behavior

(high)

Supportive Behavior

(low)

Leader shares problem and mutually makes decision with follower(s)

Facilitative

Delegative

Leader makes and explains decision and provides opportunity for dialogue and clarification

Consultative

Authoritative

Leader turns responsibility for decision over to follower(s)

Leader makes decision and provides specific instructions

(low) ◄──────── **Task Behavior** ────────► (high)

®

**Problem-Solving
or Decision-Making Readiness**

High	Moderate		Low
R4	R3	R2	R1

Figure 16-1
Problem-Solving and Decision-Making Styles

available resource. Your experience may not provide all the answers you need, but there are no alternatives.

Consultative decision making is a valuable strategy when the manager recognizes that the followers also possess some experience or knowledge of the subject and are willing, but not yet able to help. In this case, the best strategy is to obtain their input before making the decision.

When using the consultative approach, the manager selects those followers who can help to reach a decision and asks their assistance with phrases such as "What do you know about . . ." and "I'd like some information on . . ." The manager may or may not share all aspects of the problem. After hearing from the followers, *the manager makes the final decision.*

Suppose you are a marketing manager and are considering a new ad campaign for one of your company's products. Two members of your staff have some experience in this area, so you ask their assistance in determining the product market strategy.

Your consultative strategy has two immediate benefits. First, by enlisting the cooperation of your somewhat knowledgeable resources, you increase the likelihood that your decision will be correct. Second, by giving your followers a chance to contribute, you reinforce their motivation and help them identify more closely with the goals of your department.

A word of caution: Whenever you bring others into the decision-making process, you must make the ground rules very clear. Followers low to moderate in readiness (R2) can be included in the process, but they are not ready to run with the ball. A consultative decision is still leader-made. To avoid misunderstandings, you should let your people know that you'll weigh their input carefully but may not follow their advice in reaching a decision.[4]

Facilitative decision making is a cooperative effort in which manager and followers work together to reach a shared decision. In situations where followers are moderate to high in readiness (R3), the manager can enlist their help with phrases such as: "Let's pool our thoughts and decide on . . ." or "We've got a problem and I'd like your opinion." The implication is that these followers are capable of sharing the authority to decide what should be done.

For example, let us assume that both you and your assistant have been through project management situations before. You know how the scheduling and work assignments should be handled. Your assistant can administer "process" items such as communications, record keeping, reporting procedures, and so forth. Your best approach is to work together in deciding how the new project should be set up. In this case, you are effectively committing yourself to a shared decision-making process—a perfectly good leadership style when dealing with an able, but not yet confident, follower.[5]

Finally, *delegative* decision making is used with followers high in readiness (R4) who have the experience and information needed to make the proper decision or recommendation. In situations where delegation is appropriate, the manager can look forward to a high level of performance simply by saying: "You know this subject. Work on it and let me know what you come up with."

For example, your plant supervisors are old pros who know how to schedule their swing shifts so that all your requirements are met. Although you could accomplish this task yourself, you recognize that your people are self-motivated and capable of self-direction in this specific situation. Therefore, your high probability strategy is to delegate this task to them and await their decision.[6]

As a general rule, you can select the appropriate decision-making style by using Situational Leadership to determine "who owns the decision."

- If none of your followers have experience or information in the specific area, they cannot own any part of the decision. You should make the *authoritative* decision by yourself and tell them what to do.

- If your followers have some knowledge of the subject, they may be capable of contributing to (but not making) the final decision. You should seek their help in a *consultative* manner and make your decision after considering their input.

- If your followers have quite a bit of experience, they can take some of the responsibility for making the decisions. You should use a *facilitative* strategy to share the decision-making process with them.

- If your followers have a thorough understanding of the subject and a willingness to deal with it, you should use a *delegative* style. Give them the ball and let them run with it.

It is important to remember that, although you may choose to give others a degree of authority in making decisions, the ultimate responsibility is yours alone. However, that's usually no problem for the manager who uses a logical approach to guide the decision maker's process. Followers are usually most likely to approve, follow, and support the decisions of someone who knows not only where to go but also the best way to get there!

DECISION MAKING AND LEADER LATITUDE

The LaJolla-based management consulting firm of Keilty, Goldsmith, and Boone has adapted the Situational Leadership model to an approach to decision making that combines the leader's decision-making latitude with follower readiness. As illustrated in Figure 16-2, the basic decision-making styles of *directing* (high task–low relationship), *guiding* (high task–high relationship), *supporting* (low task–high relationship), and *delegating* (low task–low relationship) are the results of the various combinations of leader latitude and follower readiness dimensions. The four degrees of leader decision-making latitude are L1 (little or no latitude), L2 (low to moderate latitude), L3 (moderate to high latitude), and L4 (high latitude). The four degrees of follower decision-making readiness are R1 (low), R2 and R3 (moderate), and R4 (high), as in Figure 16-1.

Keilty, Goldsmith, and Boone illustrate the relationships in Table 16-1. This table integrates decision-making style, characteristics of the decision, decision-making latitude, follower decision-making readiness, and the characteristics of effective design makers. Working through this table in much the same way you would work through a decision-logic table will help you improve your decision-making skills.

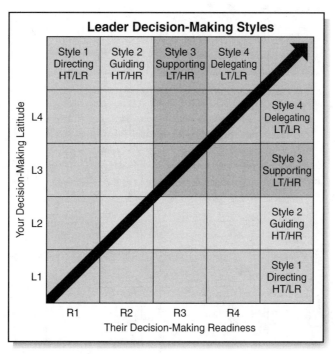

Figure 16-2
Selecting Your Decision-Making Style

BUILDING COMMITMENTS

Keilty, Goldsmith, and Boone have performed extensive research in identifying and defining the qualities that make managers successful, and helping their clients apply those qualities within their own corporation or organization. As frequently happens, some individuals are admired and respected for the way they manage others, but the reasons for their success are not always apparent. Building on the work of McKinsey and Company, the internationally respected management consulting firm, and through their experience with many excellent companies and managers, they have developed valuable insights and a very useful model concerning managerial excellence, the Five Key Commitments model, shown in Figure 16-3. The essential qualities and relationships necessary for successful management can be explained and understood in terms of commitment, a characteristic common to all individuals recognized for managerial excellence.

Managers carry out their tasks in an interpersonal world. Other people continually view the manager's manner, bearing, and conduct. From their observations, they form impressions of the manager's values, beliefs, and attitudes. Excellent managers make a powerful and positive impression on others because they blend a set of positive beliefs with an equally appropriate set of

Table 16-1 Decision-Making Characteristics

Your Decision-Making Style	Characteristics of the Decision	Your Decision-Making Latitude	Their Decision-Making Readiness	Characteristics of Effective Decision Makers
Style 1, Directing High task and low relationship (HT/LR)	The decision is made by you or from top down with little input from them	**L₁, Little or None** Decision is already made Decision is nonnegotiable Examples: rules, regulations, clearly defined procedures	**R₁, Low** They lack the motivation, ability, or understanding to make the decision	Makes the rules clearly understood Levels with people on what is not negotiable Gives specific direction when it is needed Maintains tight controls when necessary
Style 2, Guiding High task and high relationship (HT/HR)	The decision is primarily made by you or with with high input from them	**L₂, Low to Moderate** Decision can be changed but will be made from top down Examples: decisions on strategy implementation	**R₂, Moderate** They want to be involved, but lack the ability and understanding to make the decision	Gives orientation to people in new assignments Build's people's understanding and ability Takes time to answer questions and explain decisions Provides coaching and guidance when needed
Style 3, Supporting Low task and high relationship (LT/HR)	The decision is primarily their responsibility with high input from you	**L₃, Moderate to High** Decision must involve you but need not be controlled by you Examples: decisions requiring your feedback to higher management	**R₃, Moderate** They have the ability and understanding to make the decision with high input from you	Collaborates appropriately in setting objectives Encourages participation in decision making when appropriate Provides support when needed Builds and maintains people's confidence
Style 4, Delegating Low task and low relationship (LT/LR)	The decision is their responsibility with little input from you	**L₄, High** Decision can legitimately be made by them Examples: their defined job responsibilities	**R₄, High** They are willing and have the ability to make the decision with little input from you	Delegates when possible Lets others make decisions when appropriate Encourages others to take as much responsibility as they can handle Gives people the freedom to do their job well

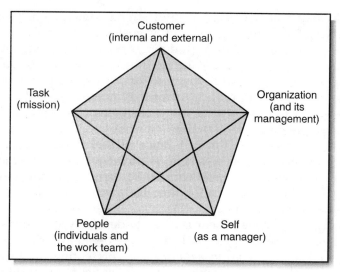

Figure 16-3
The Five Key Commitments Model

positive behaviors. These beliefs and actions form "commitments." The most effective managers share a fundamentally similar set of five commitments. These are:

- Commitment to the customer
- Commitment to the organization
- Commitment to self
- Commitment to people
- Commitment to task

Separately, each commitment is extremely important to effective management. Together, these commitments form the essential framework for long-term achievement of managerial excellence. True excellence seems to result from genuine dedication and positive service in all five areas of commitment.

Commitment to the Customer

The first and probably most important management commitment focuses on the customer. Excellent managers strive to provide useful service to customers. A customer is defined as anyone who rightly should benefit from the work of a manager's unit. For some managers, their work directly affects the external customer. For other managers, the essential customer is internal. For example, employees in one unit often serve members of another unit in the same organization. Whether the customer is primarily external or internal, the key to this commitment is service. The two primary ways in which an excellent manager demonstrates strong commitment to the customer are serving the customer and building customer importance.

Serving the customer boils down to consistent, conscientious dedication to customer needs. This requires responsiveness to customers through continually encouraging and listening to input from the people who use the manager's services or products. Clear, current identification of customer needs is necessary to genuinely serve the customer. In addition to knowing the customer and the needs of the customer, the excellent manager acts to solve customer problems in a timely manner. "Research has estimated that four out of five quality improvement efforts initiated by North American companies have either failed or experienced false starts," according to Tom Keiser, president of the Forum Corporation. He and many others point the finger of responsibility at upper management. "Why do so many companies stumble? . . . Top management is often underinvolved in the effort. When they delegate the effort to lower levels of the organization, it inevitably fails."[7]

Building customer importance means presenting the customer in a positive manner to those who actually provide service to the customer. The customer is not always appreciated by others within an organization. In fact, some employees view the customer as a necessary evil. To these employees, the customer is the source of most problems and often is viewed as someone to be tolerated. Excellent managers build customer importance by (1) clearly communicating the importance of the customer to employees, (2) treating the customer as a top priority, and (3) prohibiting destructive comments about the people who use their work group's products or services.

Robert Wayland and Paul Cole offer the following examples of principles an organization should adopt to acquire and retain loyal customers.

- Customers are assets. Understand, nurture, and protect their lifetime value.
- Products come and go; customers are forever (you hope!).
- Know what you are really selling. Focus on the total customer experience, not just the sale.
- Customers relate to people, not companies. Empowered employees excite customers.
- Expectations are more important than explanations. Point your customer information system forward, not backward.
- Customers are known by the company they keep. Build a strong brand.[8]

Ed Ojdana calls the commitment to customer

> the underlying prerequisite . . . Regardless of which strategic imperative your company pursues, success depends on satisfying the customer. Find a need and satisfy it. It sounds simple, yet the battlefield is strewn with failed products and companies that somehow did not meet customer expectations. The two most common shortcomings are not asking the customer what he or she wants

and forgetting that relative customer perceptions are what count. Studies of innovation over the last 20 to 30 years have clearly identified customers—as opposed to in-house new product development groups—as the major source for new product ideas.[9]

Gary Neilson suggests that the commitment to customer includes "Putting yourself in the customer's shoes and evaluate performance in customer terms. The best process profiles are prepared from the customer's perspective."[10]

Eisuke Toyama, president of Nissan Canada, also explains customer commitment:

> Customer Satisfaction is the new buzzword for business success. And with good reason . . . [The] ability to satisfy customers in a global marketplace will separate the winners from the losers.
>
> . . . Leadership in customer satisfaction became the guiding principle behind all of Nissan's business strategies. Nissan would never again distance itself from customers. Instead, our corporation would differentiate itself on customer satisfaction and establish itself as the leader in meeting customer needs and wants. Our research clearly shows that dealers with the highest customer satisfaction rating are also the most profitable. More than any other, this single point illustrates the importance of our global commitment to customer satisfaction. Long-term customer loyalty is the key to profitability.
>
> In its purest form, customer satisfaction is an unbroken chain of events that stretches from one end of the organization to the other. Your organization's definition of a customer should be expanded to include internal customers—such as staff, colleagues, dealers and suppliers . . . .
>
> To enhance customer satisfaction, you must serve both internal and external customers well. Successful organizations will focus on constantly improving the level of service they provide to both.[11]

Commitment to the Organization

The second management commitment focuses on the organization. Effective managers personally project pride in their organizations. They also instill the same pride in others. A manager positively demonstrates this commitment in three ways: building the organization, supporting higher management, and operating by the basic organizational values.

Building the organization is achieved by constantly presenting the organization in a positive way. Most people lose their motivation if they are ashamed of where they work or are embarrassed by what they do. They want to be part of something positive. The excellent manager builds support for what the organization does and effectively prevents destructive comments.

Supporting higher management is essential to the loyalty any organization needs in order to function. Excellent managers add value to the organization by showing and inspiring this necessary loyalty. These managers view their position in the organization as involving a dual responsibility (see Figure 16-4). The first responsibility is to actively challenge and lead "up" in the organization. The excellent manager takes decisions from above in the organization, makes them work, and expects others to do likewise. This manager does not blame higher management or pass the buck. The excellent manager's behavior strengthens the organization's ability to implement decisions and achieve objectives.

Operating by the basic organizational values clearly communicates the importance of what the organization stands for. A difficult aspect of managerial excellence is living the values of the organization, especially when those values are challenged during trying times. If an organization has a clearly defined and communicated set of basic beliefs, it is the manager's responsibility to function in a manner consistent with those fundamental beliefs. Managers are the clearest models of what the organization stands for. The excellent manager lives up to this challenge and this commitment.[12]

Commitment to Self

The third management commitment focuses on the manager personally.[13] Excellent managers present a strong, positive image of others. They act as a positive force in all situations. This attitude is not to be mistaken as self-serving or selfish. Excellent managers are seen as individuals who combine strength with a sense of humility. Commitment to self is evidenced in three specific activities: demonstrating autonomy, building self as a manager, and accepting constructive criticism.

Figure 16-4
The Roles of the Manager

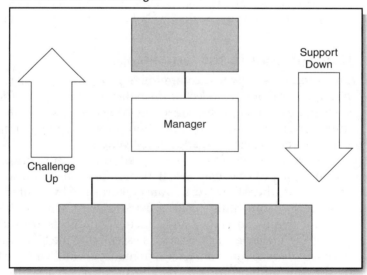

Demonstrating autonomy is an important dimension for an effective manager. Within their own organizational units, excellent managers act as though they are running their own business. They take responsibility and ownership for decisions. They stand up for personal beliefs. When taking risks, they are reasonable and more concerned with achieving excellence than with "playing it safe."

Building self as a manager deals with the self-image a manager projects to others. Excellent managers appear confident and self-assured. They act on the basis of total integrity. They do not belittle or overplay their own accomplishments. It becomes obvious to others that these managers belong in their jobs. Excellent managers live up to the faith others place in them. They act on the basis of honesty and expressly behave with exceptional integrity.

Accepting constructive criticism forms a balance with the first two aspects of a positive commitment to self. Many people act autonomously and worthy of their positions. It is the truly excellent manager who remains receptive to criticism or comment in order to become even better. Excellent managers demonstrate long-term ability to admit mistakes, encourage and accept constructive criticism, and avoid recrimination and adverse reaction. In other words, after receiving personal feedback, excellent managers do not "shoot the messenger" or discount the message. It is not easy to graciously accept criticism. However, the ability to listen and act positively to improve oneself is essential to sustain personal excellence over time.

Commitment to People

The fourth management commitment focuses on the work team and individual group members. Excellent managers display a dedication to the people who work for them. This commitment denotes the manager's use of the proper style of leadership to help individuals succeed in their tasks. Figure 16-5 reinforces the developmental process of matching leadership style to the ability and motivation of individuals. Positive commitment to people is demonstrated daily by a manager's willingness to spend the necessary time and energy working with people. Specifically, three vital activities constitute this commitment: showing positive concern and recognition, giving developmental feedback, and encouraging innovative ideas.

Showing positive concern and recognition focuses on the positive aspects of making people feel and act like winners by rewarding and reinforcing their performance. It also involves the creation of an environment in which people treat each other with courtesy and respect. For example, destructive comments concerning other people are not acceptable.

Giving developmental feedback is a realistic method of dealing with individual performance failure or setback. People sometimes fail to live up to positive expectations. The excellent manager is willing to intervene when performance does not meet established standards. Using honest feedback, the excellent manager works with the individual to reestablish realistic performance goals. Also, the manager is willing to take the time to guide and coach the individual to improve performance.

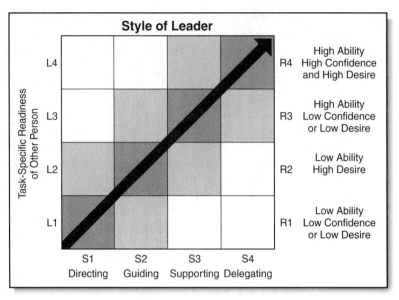

Figure 16-5
Using the Leadership Style That Fits

Encouraging innovative ideas demonstrates interest in others and stimulates individual and group progress. This positive action is often the difference between successful work teams and those that stagnate or disintegrate. The excellent manager taps into the full capacity of people through such common sense actions as listening to others' ideas, providing opportunities to test ideas, and directing the credit for a successful idea to its originator. These actions tend to create a desirable atmosphere of confidence, accomplishment, and trust.

Part of this commitment to people includes recognizing diversity within your workforce and addressing its issues openly and with compassion. James Houghton, chairman of Corning Inc., predicts:

> Unless [corporate America] wants to have a very limited pool of talent available we must learn to value and encourage a truly diverse workforce. Companies who do allow women, minorities, and foreign nationals to grow and contribute their potential (i.e., smashing the glass ceiling) will have a distinct competitive advantage. Our diversity as a nation can really work for us if we let it.[14]

Commitment to the Task

The fifth management commitment concentrates on the tasks that need to be done. Successful managers give meaning and relevance to the tasks people perform. They provide focus and direction, assuring successful completion of tasks. The durability of a manager's excellence is demonstrated through the sustained high performance of the organizational unit managed. This commitment is achieved by keeping the right focus, keeping it simple, being action-oriented, and building task importance.

Keeping the right focus refers to maintaining the proper perspective on tasks. The excellent manager concentrates everyone's attention on what is most important. This is determined through knowledge and support of the organization's overall mission. The manager consistently ties individual objectives into larger organizational goals.

Keeping it simple entails breaking work down into achievable components while avoiding unnecessary complications and procedures. The excellent manager fully considers objectives, tasks, and human capabilities, thus restraining the natural tendency to try to accomplish too much. Focus is clearly centered on major objectives within organizational priorities.

Being action-oriented is simply described as accomplishing. Excellent managers get things done. They execute. They maintain positive momentum. Realistic deadlines are set and met. People are encouraged to take action, and a sense of positive direction and accomplishment results.

Building task importance is the element that completes the fabric of managerial excellence. The excellent manager plays up the importance of the work. Excellence in task achievement is an expected result. Continuous excellence becomes the hallmark of the manager and the group.

Managerial Excellence

Consistently applied, the five commitments are the keys to effective management. The manager is the critical link among the commitments. The excellent manager takes a personal perspective with regard to the five commitments (see Figure 16-6).

The excellent manager is central to the process of developing and sustaining commitments. By taking personal responsibility and acting as a positive force, the manager can strongly influence the organization and its people, tasks, and customers. The active involvement and personal integrity of excellent managers flow to others. Excellent companies have long realized that "they are their people." What separates the excellent companies from the rest appears to be that they simply are made up of a greater number of individual managers acting as models of excellence.

These excellent managers recognize that their own task is to build specific commitments to the customer, organization, key tasks, people, and themselves. For each commitment, they build proper attitudes and demonstrate positive caring and concern. Building commitments becomes the responsibility of every employee, not just the manager. The excellent manager lives by the five commitments and works in concert with others to build commitments. Table 16-2 outlines specific behaviors characteristic of the excellent manager in each of the five commitments. Sustaining and replicating excellence is a reinforcing cyclical process based on the five key commitments (see Figure 16-7).

Fundamentally, these commitments are built through dedication and service. When the excellent manager demonstrates genuine dedication and

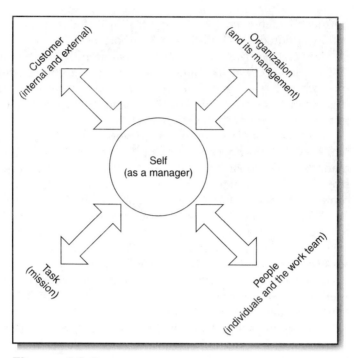

Figure 16-6
The Central Perspective of the Manager

Table 16-2   What Does the Excellent Manager Do?

COMMITMENT TO THE CUSTOMER
(internal and external)
THE EXCELLENT MANAGER:
Serves the Customer
Knows who the customers are.
Is dedicated to meeting the needs of people who use the organization's
  services or products.
Encourages and listens to input from the people who use the
  organization's services or products.
Acts to solve customers' problems in a timely manner.
Builds Customer Importance
Consistently treats the users of the organization's products or services as a
  top priority.
Clearly communicates the importance of the people who use the
  organization's products or services.
Does not allow destructive comments about the people who use the
  organization's products or services.
Is more committed to customers' long-term satisfaction than the
  organization's short-term gain.

COMMITMENT TO THE ORGANIZATION
(and its management)
THE EXCELLENT MANAGER:
Builds the Organization
Knows and supports the mission of the overall organization.
Discourages destructive comments about the organization.

Table 16-2 (continued)

Is honest and positive in describing organizational benefits.

Inspires pride in organization.

Supports Higher Management

Describes higher level managers in a positive way.

Avoids destructive comments about higher level managers.

Personally supports higher level management decisions.

Does not pass the buck or blame higher level management.

Operates by the Basic Values

Understands the basic values of the organization.

Manages using the basic values of the organization.

Encourages others to operate using the basic values of the organization.

Takes corrective action when basic organizational values are compromised.

COMMITMENT TO SELF

(as a manager)

THE EXCELLENT MANAGER:

Demonstrates Autonomy

Stands up for personal beliefs.

Takes responsibility and ownership for decisions.

Takes reasonable risks in trying out new ideas.

Is more concerned with achieving excellence than playing it safe.

Builds Self As a Manager

Shows a high degree of personal integrity in dealing with others.

Presents self in a positive manner.

Demonstrates confidence as a manager.

Avoids destructive self-criticism.

Accepts Constructive Criticism

Is willing to admit mistakes.

Encourages and accepts constructive criticism.

Acts on constructive advice in a timely manner.

Does not discourage people from giving constructive criticism.

COMMITMENT TO PEOPLE

(individuals and the work team)

THE EXCELLENT MANAGER:

Shows Positive Concern and Recognition

Consistently shows respect and concern for people as individuals.

Gives positive recognition for achievement without discomfort to either party.

Adequately rewards and reinforces top performance.

Makes people feel like winners.

Avoids destructive comments about people at work.

Gives Developmental Feedback

Effectively analyzes performance.

Develops specific plans when performance needs improving.

Strives to improve people's performance from acceptable to excellent.

Gives developmental performance feedback in a timely manner.

Encourages Innovative Ideas

Encourages suggestions for improving productivity.

Provides opportunities for others to try out new ideas.

Acts on ideas and suggestions from others in a timely manner.

Avoids taking credit for the ideas of others.

COMMITMENT TO THE TASK

(mission)

THE EXCELLENT MANAGER:

Keeps the Right Focus

Knows and supports the mission of the overall organization.

Ties individual objectives to larger organizational goals.

Concentrates on achieving what is most important.

Places greater emphasis on accomplishing the mission than following
   procedures.

Table 16-2 (continued)

Keeps It Simple
Keeps the work simple enough to be understood and implemented.
Breaks work into achievable components.
Encourages efforts to simplify procedures.
Avoids unnecessary complications.
Is Action-Oriented
Communicates a positive sense of urgency about getting the job done.
Emphasizes the importance of day-to-day progress.
Encourages taking action to get things done.
Concentrates on meeting deadlines.
Builds Task Importance
Is committed to excellence in task achievement.
Makes the task meaningful and relevant.
Encourages suggestions for improving productivity.
Does not downplay the importance of the work.

service to employees, they demonstrate a dedication and commitment to their tasks. This dedication to task excellence forms the basis for a strong dedication and service to the customer. The net result is that the customer benefits. As the customer profits, so does the organization. Customers maintain the organization's health and vitality through the same kind of dedication and loyalty to the organization. An organization experiencing continued customer loyalty is then in a position to build loyalty and dedication to its management by providing the tools for management's continued success. Long-term excellence is not a mystery. It is the result of building commitments.

Figure 16-7
The Commitments As a Reinforcing Cycle

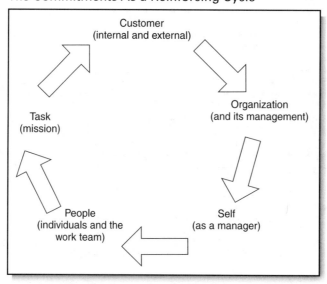

ENDNOTES

1. C. Patrick Fleenor, David L. Kurtz, and Louis E. Boone, "The Changing Profile of Business Leadership," *Business Horizons,* 26, no. 4 (July/August 1983), pp. 43–46.
2. Mohammad A. Yaghi, "The Behavioral Model: A New Approach to Decision Making," *Pakistan Management Review,* 23, no. 2 (Fall 1982), pp. 39–49.
3. Joseph Steger, George Manners, and Thomas Zimmerer, "Following the Leader: How to Link Management Styles to Subordinate Personality," *Management Review,* 71, no. 10 (October 1982), pp. 22–28.
4. Waldon Berry, "Group Problem Solving: How to Be Efficient Participants," *Supervisory Management,* 28, no. 6 (June 1983), pp. 13–19. See also Edwin A. Locke, David M. Schweiger, and Gary P. Latham, "Participation in Decision Making," *Organizational Dynamics,* 14, no. 3 (Winter 1986), pp. 65–79.
5. Colin Eden and John Harris, *Management Decision and Decision Analysis* (New York: Wiley, 1975). See also Robert Hollmann and Maureen F. Ulrich, "Participative and Flexible Decision Making," *Journal of Small Business Management,* 21, no. 1 (January 1983), pp. 1–7.
6. Patrick J. Montana and Deborah F. Nash, "Delegation: The Art of Managing," *Personnel Journal,* 60, no. 10 (October 1981), pp. 784–787. See also Charles D. Pringle, "Seven Reasons Why Managers Don't Delegate," *Management Solutions,* 31, no. 11 (November 1986), pp. 26–30.
7. Thomas C. Keiser and Douglas A. Smith, "Customer-Driven Strategies: Moving from Talk to Action," *Planning Review,* 21, no. 5 (1993), pp. 25–28, 32.
8. Robert E. Wayland and Paul M. Cole, "Turn Customer Service into Customer Profitability," *Management Review,* July 1994, pp. 22–24.
9. Ed Ojdana, "Service, Quality, Innovation: Strategic Imperatives for the 90s," *The Planning Forum Network,* 4, no. 9 (September 1991), p. 1.
10. Gary Neilson, "Delivering Quality through Business Processes," *The Planning Forum Network,* 5, no. 4 (April 1992), pp. 2, 9.
11. Eisuke Toyama, "Customer Service Turns Nissan Fortunes Around," *The Planning Forum Network,* 4, no. 12 (December 1991), pp. 2–3, 6.
12. Andrew M. McCosh, *Management Decision Support Systems* (New York: Wiley, 1978).
13. This section is based on J. Keith Murnighan, "Group Decision Making: What Strategies Should You Use?" *Management Review,* 70, no. 2 (February 1981), pp. 55–62.
14. James R. Houghton, "Leadership's Challenge: The New Agenda for the 90s," *The Planning Forum Network,* 6, no. 6 (Summer 1992), p. 1.

Chapter 17

Planning and Implementing Change

Mark Twain once said, "The only person who likes change is a baby with a wet diaper!" Like it or not, in the dynamic society surrounding today's organizations, the question of whether change will occur is no longer relevant. Change will occur. It is no longer a choice. Instead, the issue is, How do managers and leaders cope with the inevitable barrage of changes that confront them daily in attempting to keep their organizations viable and current? Although change is a fact of life, if managers are to be effective, they can no longer be content to let change occur as it will. They must be able to develop strategies to plan, direct, and control change. ✧

In a survey of 400 executives from Fortune 1000 companies, 79 percent of the executives interviewed reported "the pace of change at their companies as 'rapid' or 'extremely rapid' and 61 percent believed the pace will pick up in the future."[1] In contrast, most executives reported that they did not have formal plans for dealing with change. In addition, "62 percent believed they have a conservative or reluctant approach to change," and "more than 75 percent said that American managers resist change because they are 'too short-term oriented,' they 'don't like to lose control of people or events,' they have 'a vested interest in the status quo,' and they 'do not know what to do about change.' "[2]

This resistance to change is contradictory to the manager's primary role as a leader. You will recall that in chapter 1 we defined leadership as influencing the behavior of others, individually and in groups. Influencing means moving from one behavior to another; in other words, change. In chapter 4, we shared Warren Bennis' definition of leadership as the process of creating and implementing a vision. To be a leader, therefore, implies that you must learn to love change because it is intrinsic to the leadership process. Leaders must overcome their resistance to change and become *change managers.*

To be effective managers of change, leaders must have more than good diagnostic skills. Once they have analyzed the demands of their environment, they must be able to adapt their leadership style to fit these demands and develop the means to *change* some or all of the other situational variables

GENERAL FRAMEWORK FOR UNDERSTANDING CHANGE

Managers who are interested in implementing some change in their group or organization need a road map for change. The road map developed by Beckhard and Harris shown in Figure 17-1 is regarded as being among the best by prominent behavioral scientists such as Edgar Schein, professor emeritus at the Sloan School of Management, MIT.[3] Furthermore, it is supported strongly by research. Let us take a journey using this road map to understand the change process.

Diagnosis (Why Change?)

The first, and in some ways the most important, stage of any change effort is diagnosis. The central issue is identifying the *need* to change. Broadly defined, the skills of diagnosis involve techniques for asking the right questions, sensing the environment of the organization, establishing effective patterns of observation and data collection, and developing ways to process and interpret data. In diagnosing for change, managers should attempt to find out (a) what is *actually* happening now in a particular situation; (b) what is *likely* to be happening in the future if no change effort is made; (c) what would people *ideally* like to be happening in this situation; and (d) what are the *blocks,* or restraints, stopping movement from the actual to the ideal?

There are at least three steps in the diagnostic process: point of view, identification of problem(s), and analysis.

Point of View

Before beginning to diagnose in an organization, you should know through whose eyes you will be observing the situation—your own, those of your boss, your associates, your followers, an outside consultant, or others.

Ideally, to get the full picture you should look at the situation from the points of view of the people who will be affected by any changes. Reality, however, sometimes restricts such a broad perspective. At any rate, you should be clear about your frame of reference from the start.

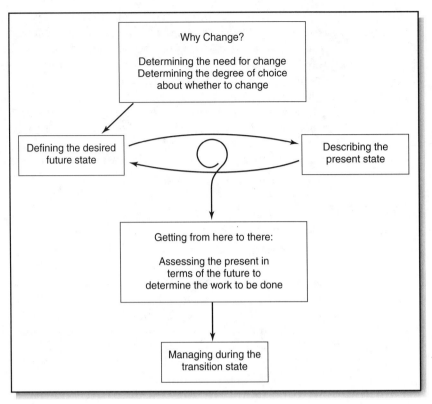

Figure 17-1
A Map of the Change Process

Source: R. Beckhard/R. Harris, ORGANIZATIONAL TRANSITIONS (Figure 4.1—page 31). © 1987, 1977, Addison Wesley Longman Inc. Reprinted by permission of Addison Wesley Longman.

Identification of Problem(s)

Any change effort begins with the identification of the problem(s). A problem in a situation exists when there is a discrepancy between what is actually happening (the *real*) and what you or someone who hired you (point of view) would like to be happening (the *ideal*). For example, in a given situation, there might be tremendous conflict among individuals in a work group. If this kind of conflict is not detrimental, there may be no problem. Until you can explain precisely what you would like to be occurring and unless that set of conditions is different from the current situation, no problem exists. On the other hand, if you would ideally like this work group to be harmonious and cooperative, then you have a problem—there is a discrepancy between the real and the ideal. *Change efforts involve attempting to reduce discrepancies between the real (actual) and the ideal.* It should be pointed out that change efforts may not always involve attempting to move the real closer to the ideal. Sometimes, after diagnosis you might realize that your ideal is unrealistic and should be brought more in line with what is actually happening.

It is in problem identification that the concepts and theoretical frameworks presented in this book begin to come into play. For example, two important potential areas for discrepancy are, in Rensis Likert's terms, end-result variables and intervening variables. These were discussed in chapter 6.

In an examination of *end-result variables,* the question becomes: Is the organization, work group, or individual doing an effective job in what it was asked to do; that is, production, sales, teaching the three Rs, and so on? Are short-term goals being accomplished? How does the long-term picture look? If performance is not what it should be, there is an obvious discrepancy.

If performance is a problem, you might want to look for discrepancies in the *intervening variables,* or condition of the human resources. For example, is there much turnover, absenteeism, or tardiness? How about grievances, accident rate, and such? The concepts that you have been studying in this book can generate diagnostic questions for the change situation you are examining, such as:

- What leadership, decision-making, and problem-solving skills are available? What is the motivation, communication, commitment to objectives, and climate (morale)? (Likert, chapter 4)

- What is the readiness level of the people involved? Are they willing and able to take significant responsibility for their own performance? (Hersey and Blanchard, chapter 8)

- What need level seems to be most important for people right now? (Maslow, chapter 2)

- What are the hygiene factors and motivators? Are people getting paid enough? What are the working conditions? Is job security an issue? How are interpersonal relations? Do people complain about the manager? Are people able to get recognition for their accomplishments? Is there much challenge in the work? Are there opportunities for growth and development? Are people given much responsibility? (Herzberg, chapter 3)

Good theory is just organized common sense. Therefore, use the theories and questions presented here to help you sort out what is happening in your situation, what might need to be changed, and the degree of choice about whether to change.

Analysis—An Outgrowth of Problem Identification

Problem identification flows almost immediately into analysis. Once a discrepancy (problem) has been identified, the goal of analysis is to determine why the problem exists. The separation between problem identification and analysis is not always that clear, however, because identifying areas of discrepancy is often a part of analysis.

Once a discrepancy has been identified in the end-result variables or intervening variables, the most natural strategy is to begin to examine what Likert calls causal variables—the independent variables that can be altered or changed by the organization and its management, such as leadership or management style, organizational structure, and organizational objectives. In other words, can you identify what in the environment might have caused the discrepancy? Again, different theorists come to mind and stimulate various questions.

- What is the dominant leadership style being used? How does it fit with the readiness level of the people involved? (Hersey and Blanchard, chapter 8)
- What are the prevailing assumptions about human nature adhered to by management? How well do those assumptions match the capabilities and potential of the people involved? (McGregor, chapter 3)
- Are people able to satisfy a variety of needs in this environment? How do the opportunities for need satisfaction compare with the high-strength needs of the people involved? (Maslow, chapter 2)
- How do the expectations of the various situational variables compare with the leadership style being used by management? (Hersey and Blanchard, chapter 7)

Implementation—Getting from Here to There

The implementation process involves the following: identifying alternative solutions and appropriate implementation strategies; anticipating the probable consequences of each of the alternative strategies; and choosing a specific strategy and implementing it.

This stage of the change process involves the translation of diagnostic data into change goals and plans, strategies, and procedures. Questions such as the following must be asked: How can change be effected in a work group or organization, and how will it be received? What is adaptive, and what is resistant to change within the environment?

Once your analysis is completed, the next step is to determine alternative solutions to the problem(s). Hand in hand with developing alternative solutions is determining appropriate implementation strategies. Three approaches are helpful in the implementation process: Lewin's change process and force field analysis and Schein's idea of psychological safety.

Lewin's Change Process

In examining change, Kurt Lewin identified three phases of the change process—unfreezing, changing, and refreezing.[4]

Unfreezing

The aim of *unfreezing* is to motivate and make the individual or the group ready to change. It is a thawing-out process in which the forces acting on individuals are rearranged so that now they see the need for change. According to Schein, when drastic unfreezing is necessary, the following common elements seem to be present: (1) The individuals being changed are physically removed from the accustomed routines, sources of information, and social relationships; (2) all social supports are undermined and destroyed; (3) the individuals being changed are demeaned and humiliated so that they will see their old attitudes or behavior as unworthy and thus be motivated to change; (4) reward is consistently linked with willingness to change and punishment with unwillingness to change.[5]

In brief, unfreezing is the breaking down of folkways, customs, and traditions—the old ways of doing things—so that individuals are ready to accept new alternatives. In terms of force field analysis, unfreezing may occur when either the driving forces are increased or the restraining forces are reduced.

Changing

Once individuals have become motivated to change, they are ready to be provided with new patterns of behavior. This process is most likely to occur by one of two mechanisms: identification or internalization.[6] *Identification* occurs when one or more models are provided in the environment—models from whom individuals can learn new behavior patterns by identifying with them and trying to become like them. *Internalization* occurs when individuals are placed in a situation in which new behaviors are demanded of them. They learn these new behavior patterns not only because they are necessary for survival, but also because new high-strength needs are induced by coping behavior.

> Internalization is a more common outcome in those influence settings where the direction of change is left more to the individual. The influence that occurs in programs such as Alcoholics Anonymous, in psychotherapy or counseling for hospitalized or incarcerated populations, in religious retreats, in [some kinds of] human relations training, . . . and in certain kinds of progressive education programs is more likely to occur through internalization or, at least, to lead ultimately to more internalization.[7]

Identification and internalization are not either/or courses of action. Rather, effective change is often the result of combining the two into a strategy for change.

Compliance is sometimes discussed as another mechanism for inducing change.[8] It occurs when an individual is forced to change by the direct manipulation of rewards and punishment by someone in a power position. In this case, behavior appears to have changed when the change agent is present, but it is often dropped when supervision is removed. Thus, rather than discussing force or compliance as a mechanism of changing, we should think of it as a tool for unfreezing.

Refreezing

The process by which the newly acquired behavior comes to be integrated as patterned behavior into the individual's personality or ongoing significant emotional relationships is referred to as *refreezing*. According to Schein, if the new behavior has been internalized while being learned, "this has automatically facilitated refreezing because it has been fitted naturally into the individual's personality. If it has been learned through identification, it will persist only so long as the target's relationship with the original influence model persists, unless new surrogate models are found or social support and reinforcement are obtained for expressions of the new attitudes."[9]

This statement highlights how important it is for an individual engaged in a change process to be in an environment that continually reinforces the desired change. The effect of many training programs has been short-lived when the person returns to an environment that does not reinforce the new patterns or, even worse, is hostile toward them.

Force Field Analysis

Force field analysis, a technique developed by Kurt Lewin, assumes that in any situation there are both driving and restraining forces that influence any change that may occur.[10] *Driving forces* are those forces affecting a situation that are pushing in a particular direction; they tend to initiate a change and keep it going. In terms of improving productivity in a work group, encouragement from a supervisor, incentive earnings, and competition may be examples of driving forces. *Restraining forces* are forces acting to restrain or decrease the driving forces. Apathy, hostility, and poor maintenance of equipment may be examples of restraining forces against increased production. *Equilibrium* is reached when the sum of the driving forces equals the sum of the restraining forces. In our example, equilibrium represents the current level of productivity, as shown in Figure 17-2.

This equilibrium, or current level of productivity, can be raised or lowered by changes in the relationship between the driving and the restraining forces. For illustration, let us look at the dilemma of the new manager who takes over a work group in which productivity is high, but whose predecessor drained the human resources (intervening variables). The former manager had upset the equilibrium by increasing the driving forces (that is, being

Figure 17-2
Driving and Restraining Forces in Equilibrium

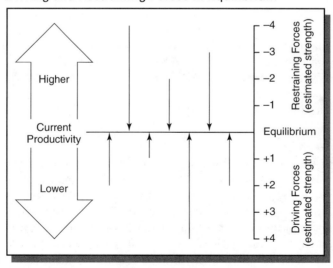

autocratic and keeping continual pressure on workers) and thus achieving increases in output in the short run. By doing this, however, the manager fostered new restraining forces, such as increased hostility and antagonism. At the time of the former manager's departure, the restraining forces were beginning to increase, and the results manifested themselves in turnover, absenteeism, and other restraining forces, which lowered productivity shortly after the new manager arrived. Now a new equilibrium at a significantly lower productivity is faced by the new manager.

Now just assume that our new manager decides not to increase the driving forces but to reduce the restraining forces. The manager may do this by taking time away from the usual production operation and engaging in problem solving and in training and development. In the short run, output will tend to be lowered still further. However, if commitment to objectives and technical know-how of the group are increased in the long run, they may become new driving forces, and, along with the elimination of the hostility and apathy that were restraining forces, will now tend to move the balance to a higher level of output.

Managers are often in a position in which they must consider not only output but also intervening variables, not only short-term but also long-term goals in diagnosing these interrelationships. Force field analysis is also useful in analyzing the various change strategies that can be used in a particular situation.[11]

Once you have determined that there is a discrepancy between what is actually happening and what you would like to be happening in a situation—and have done some analysis on why that discrepancy exists—then force field analysis becomes a helpful tool. Before embarking on any change strategy, it seems appropriate to determine what you have going for you in this change effort (driving forces) and what you have going against you (restraining forces). We have found that if managers start implementing a change strategy without doing that kind of analysis, they can get blown out of the water and not know why. An example might help.

In August, an enthusiastic superintendent of schools and his assistant took over a suburban school district outside a large urban area in the Midwest. Both were committed to changing the predominant teaching approach used in the system from a teacher-centered approach in which the teachers always tell the students what to do, how to do it, when to do it, and where to do it (high task–low relationship style) to a child-centered approach in which students play a significant role in determining what they are to do (low relationship–low task style).

To implement the changes they wanted, the two administrators hired a business manager to handle the office and the paperwork. They themselves essentially had no office. They put telephones in their cars and spent most of their time out in the schools with teachers and students. They spent 15 to 18 hours a day working with and supporting teachers and administrators who wanted to engage in new behavior. Then suddenly, in January, only 6 months after they had been hired, the school board called a special meeting and fired both administrators by a seven-to-two vote.

They could not believe what had happened. They immediately started a court suit against the school board for due process. They charged that the board had served as both judge and jury. In addition to the court actions, the administrators became educational martyrs and hit the lecture tour to talk about the evils of schools. During one of their trips, the assistant superintendent was asked to participate in a graduate seminar on the management of change. The class at that time was discussing the usefulness of force field analysis. The administrator, who did not know Lewin's theory, was asked to think about the driving and restraining forces that had been present in the change situation. In thinking about the driving forces that were pushing for the change they wanted, the administrator was quick to name the enthusiasm and commitment of the top administrators, some teachers, and some students, but really could not think of any other driving forces. When asked about the number of teachers and students involved, the administrator suggested that they were a small but growing group.

In thinking about restraining forces, the assistant superintendent began to mention one thing after another. The assistant said that they had never really had a good relationship with the mayor, chief of police, or editor of the town paper. These people felt that the two administrators were encouraging permissiveness in the schools. In fact, the town paper printed several editorials against their efforts. In addition, the teachers' association had expressed concern that the programs being pushed were asking the teachers to assume responsibilities outside their contract. Even the parent-teachers association (PTA) had held several meetings because of parent concerns about discipline in the schools. The administrator also reported the fact that the superintendent had been hired by a five-to-four vote of the board and that some supporters had been defeated in the November election. In general, the assistant superintendent implied that the town had been traditionally very conservative in educational matters, and on and on.

Figure 17-3 suggests the relationship between driving and restraining forces in this change situation. As can be seen, even with adding some board members as driving forces and not mentioning some teachers and students as restraining forces, the restraining forces for changing this school system from a teacher-centered approach to a child-centered approach not only outnumbered but easily outweighed the driving forces. As a result, the restraining forces eventually overpowered the driving forces and pushed the equilibrium even more in the direction of a teacher-centered approach.

Here are a few guidelines for using force field analysis to develop a change strategy.

1. If the driving forces far outweigh the restraining forces in power and frequency in a change situation, managers interested in driving for change can often push on and overpower the restraining forces.
2. If the restraining forces are much stronger than the driving forces, managers interested in driving for change have two choices. First, they can give up the change effort, realizing that it will be too difficult to implement. Second, they can pursue the change effort, but concentrate on maintaining the driving forces in the situation while attempting, one by one, to change each of the restraining forces into driving forces or

Figure 17-3
Driving and Restraining Forces in an Educational Change Example

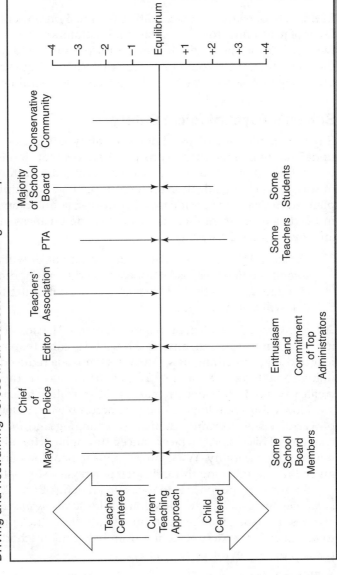

somehow to immobilize each of the restraining forces so that they are no longer factors in the situation. The second choice is possible, but very time-consuming.

3. If the driving forces and restraining forces are fairly equal in a change situation, managers probably will have to begin pushing the driving forces, while at the same time attempting to convert or immobilize some or all of the restraining forces.

In this school example, the situation obviously represented an imbalance in favor of restraining forces, yet the administrators acted as if the driving forces were clearly on their side. If they had used force field analysis to diagnose their situation, they would have seen that their change strategy was doomed until they took some time to try to work on the restraining forces.

Schein's Psychological Safety

Edgar Schein's idea of psychological safety is a major contribution to the understanding of the change process. We know that significant change means the casting off of old rules and procedures and the putting on of new ones. It means, for each organization undergoing change, a complete rethinking of its plans from vision to specific tasks. However, as an organization "unfreezes," in Lewin's term, from the old ways of doing business, it faces two types of anxiety, suggested by Schein:

> [**Anxiety 1**] . . . is associated with inability or unwillingness to learn something new because it appears too difficult or disruptive.
> [**Anxiety 2**] . . . is the induced anxiety of continuing to do something that will lead to failure.[12]

Anxiety 1 is caused by fear of changing; anxiety 2 is caused by fear of not changing. For change to occur, anxiety 2 must be greater than anxiety 1; that is, the fear of doing something new (anxiety 1) must be reduced, and the fear of *not* doing something new (anxiety 2) must be increased. Top management must create psychological safety in making the transition to a new course of action.

How can psychological safety be accomplished? One method is to use a powerful vision to *reduce* the fear of changing and *increase* the fear of not changing. This vision can be enhanced through portrayals of the change's potential and feasibility. What might appear nebulous and indistinct can be given life and meaning through such portrayals, simulations, or scenarios.

Because our purpose is to focus on anxieties 1 and 2, the approach must *build confidence* in the new direction while *increasing anxiety* about the *current*, business as usual, way of operating. In addition, the approach must be easy to use to avoid anxiety resulting from using the method itself. In summary, the two phases in the process are:

- **Phase 1.** Increase anxiety 2 (fear of *not changing*).

- **Phase 2.** Decrease anxiety 1 (fear of *changing*).

For example, a firm that has been using traditional technology for 2 decades has sales, market share, and a pretax cash flow near the industry average. In the past 3 years, sales growth has slowed as competitors have adopted new technology. This competitive pressure has resulted in drastically reduced pretax cash flow. When the bank notified it that its line of credit might not be renewed, the firm undertook a searching review of its business operations.

Complicating the decision process was the issue of environmental concerns. The new technology they needed would not only require the purchase of new manufacturing equipment, but also would require the purchase of air-purification equipment to reduce undesirable emissions. How could this firm address these issues using the anxiety 1–anxiety 2 approach?

Phase 1 was to take another look at their cash flow projections. These projections confirmed their bank's analysis. Business as usual would lead to bankruptcy. *This phase increased the fear of not changing (anxiety 2).*

The next phase included examining the impact of installing the new technology, again using cash flow projections. The projections showed that the new technology plus needed environmental equipment would pay for themselves, and *the fear of change (anxiety 1) was reduced.*

Options for change must be developed in such a way that, if found feasible, they can add confidence to the change decision. At the very least, a firm may be faced with the fact that given the analysis in phase 1, there is just no other alternative but to adopt new business strategies.

Force field analysis can also be employed to increase or decrease each of the anxieties. An analysis of factors that might help lead to increased sales—e.g., new markets, higher margins, developing an expanded sales force, creating new advertising approaches, and opening new distribution channels—might serve to reduce the fear of change, that is, reduce anxiety 1.

We can make the following conclusions about the change process:

1. In order for an organization to change, it must go through an "unfreezing" step.
2. This unfreezing involves two anxieties: Anxiety 1 is the fear of changing; anxiety 2 is the fear of not changing.
3. For an organization to unfreeze, anxiety 1 must be decreased and anxiety 2 must be increased.
4. Anxiety 2 issues should be addressed before anxiety 1 issues.
5. Anxieties can be further analyzed using established techniques such as force field analysis.

FIRST-ORDER AND SECOND-ORDER CHANGE

One way of approaching change for the purpose of diagnosis is to look at it from the perspective of two different frameworks. This approach is important because change does not always occur in a stable environment. Organizations have experienced revolutionary changes in technology, competition, and socioeconomic conditions; some changes have destroyed old industries and created new ones. Leaders need to recognize and understand the two frameworks in which change can occur.

The change process most managers are familiar with is continuous, or *first-order, change*—change that occurs in a stable system that itself remains unchanged. The change processes previously discussed in this chapter focus on managing first-order change. These changes are necessary for a business to grow and thrive in a competitive environment.

Discontinuous, or *second-order, change* occurs when fundamental properties or states of the system are changed.[13] The fall of communism and the introduction of democratic and free market principles in Eastern Europe and the former Soviet Union are examples of the cataclysmic upheaval of second-order change. Some industries currently experiencing the magnitude of second-order change include telecommunications, financial services, and health care, as discontinuous changes restructure the industry, relocate its boundaries, and change the bases of competition.

Figure 17-4 identifies current change theories and their relationship to first- and second-order change.[14] *Adaptation theories* maintain that individual firms monitor their environments continuously and make purposeful adjustments to them. *Incrementalism* refers to organizational changes in new products, structures, and processes; resource dependence mechanisms see organizational change as a response to external dependencies such as suppliers, markets, or governmental policies.

Figure 17-4
Models of Change within Organizations and Industries

	First-Order Change	Second-Order Change
Firm Level	Adaptation	Metamorphosis
	Focus: Incremental change within organizations	Focus: Frame-breaking change within organizations
	Mechanisms: • Incrementalism • Resource dependence	Mechanisms: • Life-cycle stages • Configuration transitions
Industry Level	Evolution	Revolution
	Focus: Incremental change within established industries	Focus: Emergence, transformation, and decline of industries
	Mechanisms: • Natural selection • Institutional isomorphism	Mechanisms: • Punctuated equilibrium • Quantum speciation

Source: Adapted from *Strategic Management Journal,* Meyer, Brooks, and Goes, 1990. © Wiley and Sons Limited. Reproduced with permission.

Evolution theories describe the first-order changes that industries experience. *Natural selection* mechanisms view the entry and exit of firms in an industry as the primary method of evolution. *Institutional isomorphism* occurs when organizations change to conform to the norms of the industry environment.

As firms experience various stages of the organizational life cycle, they experience *metamorphosis,* second-order change. Metamorphosis differs from adaptation in that the entire firm goes through a transformation and emerges with a different configuration and strategic intent. An example of this type of change can be seen when a visionary inventor with a small business brings in a professional management team, and the small business metamorphoses into a growing firm with a different organizational structure and competitive focus. The change is transforming for the members of the small business.

Revolutionary change occurs when an entire industry is restructured and reconstituted during a brief period of quantum change that is preceded and followed by a long period of stability. *Quantum speciation,* a term from biology, has been proposed as a mechanism through which new organizational forms emerge during a revolution. The breakup of AT&T into "baby bells" and the introduction of new competitors into long-distance telecommunications companies is an example of second-order revolutionary change in an industry.

Most organizational changes you initiate as a leader will occur on a level of first-order change. You should also understand the opportunities presented by second-order change and work to meet the challenges this type of change can create.

CHANGE CYCLES

Levels of Change

There are four levels of change: knowledge changes, attitudinal changes, individual behavior changes, and group or organizational performance changes.

Changes in *knowledge* tend to be the easiest to make; they can occur as a result of reading a book or an article or hearing something new from a respected person. *Attitudes* differ from knowledge in that they are emotionally charged in a positive or negative way. The addition of emotion often makes attitudes more difficult to change than knowledge.

Changes in *individual behavior* seem to be significantly more difficult and time-consuming than either of the two previous levels. For example, managers may have knowledge about the advantages of increased follower involvement and participation in decision making and may even feel that such participation would improve their performance; however, they may be unable to delegate or share decision-making responsibilities significantly with followers. This discrepancy between knowledge, attitude, and behavior may be a result of their own authoritarian leader-follower past. This experience has led to a habit pattern that feels comfortable.

Individual behavior is difficult enough to change, but implementing change within *groups* or *organizations* is even more complicated. The leadership styles of one or two managers might be effectively altered, but drastically changing the level of follower participation throughout an entire organization might be a very time-consuming process. At this level, you are trying to alter customs, mores, and traditions that have developed over many years.

Levels of change become very significant when you examine two different change cycles—the participative change cycle and the directive change cycle.[15]

Participative Change

A participative change cycle is implemented when new knowledge is made available to the individual or group. It is hoped that the group will accept the data and will develop a positive attitude and commitment in the direction of the desired change. At this level, an effective strategy may be to involve the individual or group directly in helping to select or formalize the new methods for obtaining the desired goals. This step is group participation in problem solving.

The next step will be to attempt to translate this commitment into actual behavior. This step is significantly more difficult to achieve. For example, it is one thing to be concerned about increased follower participation in decision making (attitude), but another thing to be willing actually to get involved in doing something (behavior) about the issue. An effective strategy may be to identify the informal and formal leaders among the work group(s) and concentrate on gaining their behavioral support for the desired change. Once the behavior of the group leaders has been changed, organizational change may be effected as other people begin to pattern their behavior after those persons whom they respect and perceive in leadership roles. This participative change cycle is illustrated in Figure 17-5.

Directive Change

We have all probably been faced with a situation similar to the one in which there is an announcement on Monday morning that "as of today all members of this organization will begin to operate in accordance with Form 10125." This is an example of a directive change cycle. It is through this change cycle that many managers in the past have attempted to implement such innovative ideas as management by objectives, job enrichment, and the like.

This change cycle begins when change is imposed on the total organization by some external force, such as higher management, the community, or new laws. In turn, the change will affect individual behavior. The new contacts and modes of behavior create new knowledge, which tends to develop predispositions toward or against the change. The directive change cycle is illustrated in Figure 17-6.

In cases in which change is forced, the new behavior sometimes creates the kind of knowledge that develops commitment to the change, and the change begins to resemble participative change as it reinforces individual

Chapter 17   Planning and Implementing Change

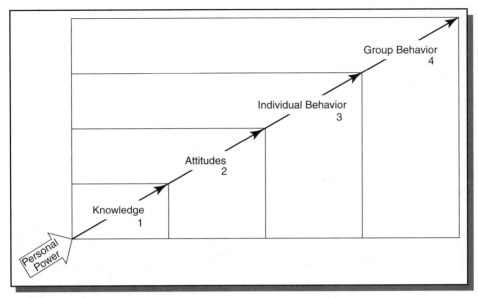

Figure 17-5
Participative Change Cycle

and group behavior. The hope is that "if people will only have a chance to see how the new system works, they will support it." This is illustrated in Figure 17-6 by the dashed line. The sequence goes from group behavior, individual behavior, to knowledge and then back to attitudes.

Figure 17-6
Directive Change Cycle

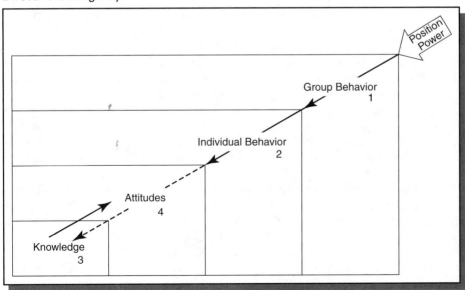

Is There a "Best" Strategy for Change?

Given a choice between the polarities of directive and participative change, most people would tend to prefer the participative change cycle. But, just as we have argued that there is no best leadership style, there also is no best strategy for implementing change. Effective change agents are identified as those who can adapt their strategies to the demands of their unique environment. Thus, the participative change cycle is not a better change strategy than the directive change cycle, and vice versa. The appropriate strategy depends on the situation, and there are advantages and disadvantages to each.

Advantages and Disadvantages of Change Cycles

The participative change cycle tends to be more appropriate for working with individuals and groups who are achievement-motivated, seek responsibility, and have a degree of knowledge and experience that may be useful in developing new ways of operating—in other words, people with moderate to high task-relevant readiness. Once the change starts, these people are highly capable of assuming responsibilities for implementation of the desired change. Although these people may welcome change and the need to improve, they may become very rigid and opposed to change if it is implemented in a directive (high task–low relationship) manner. A directive change style is inconsistent with their perceptions of themselves as responsible, self-motivated people who should be consulted throughout the change process. When they are not consulted and change is implemented in an authoritarian manner, conflict often results. Examples occur frequently in organizations in which a manager recruits or inherits a competent, creative staff that is willing to work hard to implement new programs and then proceeds to bypass the staff completely in the change process. This style results in resistance and is inappropriate to the situation.

A directive change style might be appropriate and productive with individuals and groups who are not ambitious, are dependent, and are unwilling to take on new responsibilities unless forced to do so. In fact, these people might prefer direction and structure from their leader to being faced with decisions they are not willing or experienced enough to make. Once again, diagnosis is all-important. It is just as inappropriate for a manager to attempt to implement change in a participative manner with a staff that has never been given the opportunity to take responsibility and has become dependent on its manager for direction as it is to implement change in a forceful manner with a staff that is ready to change and willing to take responsibility for implementing it.

There are other significant differences between these two change cycles. The participative change cycle tends to be effective when induced by leaders who have personal power; that is, they have referent, information, and expert power. On the other hand, the directive cycle necessitates that a leader have significant position power; that is, coercive, connection, reward, and legitimate power. Managers who decide to implement change in an authoritarian, coercive manner would be wise to have the support of their superiors and other sources of power or they may be effectively blocked by their staff.

A significant advantage of the participative change cycle is that once the change is accepted, it tends to be long-lasting. Since everyone has been involved in the development of the change, each person tends to be highly committed to its implementation. The disadvantage of participative change is that it tends to be slow and evolutionary—it may take years to implement a significant change. An advantage of directive change, on the other hand, is speed. Using position power, leaders can often impose change immediately. A disadvantage of this change strategy is that it tends to be volatile. It can be maintained only as long as the leader has position power to make it stick. It often results in animosity, hostility, and, in some cases, overt and covert behavior to undermine and overthrow.

In terms of force field analysis, the directive change cycle could be utilized if the power of the driving forces pushing for change far outweighed the restraining forces resisting change. On the other hand, a directive change cycle would be doomed to failure if the power of the restraining forces working against the change was greater than the power of the driving forces pushing for the change.

A participative change cycle that depends on personal power could be appropriate in either of the cases just described. With frequent and powerful driving forces pushing for change in a situation, a leader might not have to use a high task, directive change cycle because the driving forces are ready to effect the change and do not have to be forced to engage in the new desired behavior. At the same time, when the restraining forces could easily overpower the driving forces, managers would be advised to begin with participative change techniques designed gradually to turn some of the restraining forces into driving forces or at least immobilize their influence in the situation. In other words, when the odds are against you and you have little power, your best bet would be to try to moderate the forces against the change rather than to try to force change.

These two change cycles have been described as if they were either/or positions. The use of only one of these change cycles exclusively, however, could lead to problems. For example, if managers introduce change only in a directive, high task–low relationship manner without any movement toward participative change, members of their staff—if they decide to remain—may react in one of two ways. Some may fight the managers tooth and nail and organize efforts to undermine them. Others may buckle under to their authority and become very passive, dependent staff members, always needing the manager to tell them what to do and when to do it before doing anything. These kinds of people say yes to anything the manager wants and then moan and groan and drag their feet later. Neither of these responses makes for a very healthy organization. At the other extreme, managers who will not make a move without checking with their staff and getting full approval also can immobilize themselves. They may establish such a complicated network of "participative" committees that significant change becomes almost impossible. Thus, in reality, the question is, "What is the proper blend of the directive and participative change cycles in this situation?" Rather than, "Which one should I use?"

Change Process—Some Examples

To see the change process in operation, consider these examples:

A college basketball coach recruited Bob Anderson, a 6 foot 9 inch center, from a small town in a rural area where 6 feet 6 inches was a good height for a center. This fact, combined with his deadly turnaround jump shot, made Anderson the rage of his league and enabled him to average close to 30 points a game.

Recognizing that Anderson was a bit short for a college center, the coach hoped that he could make him a forward, moving him inside only when they were playing a double pivot. One of the things the coach was concerned about, however, was how Anderson, when used in the pivot, could get his jump shot off when he came up against other players ranging in height from 6 feet 11 inches to more than 7 feet. He felt that Anderson would have to learn to shoot a hook shot, which is much harder to block, if he were going to have scoring potential against this kind of competition. The approach that many coaches would use to solve this problem would probably be as follows: On the first day of practice, the coach would welcome Anderson and then explain the problem to him as he had analyzed it. As a solution, he would probably ask Anderson to start to work with the varsity center, Steve Cram, who was 6 feet 11 inches and had an excellent hook. "Steve can help you start working on that new shot, Bob," the coach would say. Anderson's reaction to this interchange might be one of resentment, and he would go over and work with Cram only because of the coach's position power. After all, he might think to himself, "Who does he think he is? I've been averaging close to 30 points a game for 3 years now, and the first day I show up here the coach wants me to learn a new shot."

So he may start to work with Cram reluctantly, concentrating on the hook shot only when the coach is looking but taking his favorite jump shot when not being observed. Anderson is by no means unfrozen, or ready to learn to shoot another way.

Let us look at another approach the coach might use to solve this problem. Suppose that on the first day of practice he sets up a scrimmage between the varsity and the freshmen. Before he starts the scrimmage, he takes big Steve Cram, the varsity center, aside and tells him, "Steve, we have this new freshman named Anderson who has real potential to be a fine ball player. What I'd like you to do today, though, is not to worry about scoring or rebounding—just make sure every time Anderson goes up for a shot, you make him eat it. I want him to see that he will have to learn to shoot some other shots if he is to survive against guys like you." So when the scrimmage starts, the first time Anderson gets the ball and turns around to shoot, Cram leaps up and stuffs the ball right down his throat. Time after time this occurs. Soon, Anderson starts to engage in some coping behavior, trying to fall away from the basket, shooting from the side of his head rather than from the front in an attempt to get his shot off. After the scrimmage, Anderson comes off the court dejected. The coach says, "What's wrong, Bob?" Bob replies, "I don't know, coach, I just can't seem to get my shot off against a man as big as Cram. What do you think I should do?" "Well, Bob," says the coach, "why don't you go over and start working with Steve on a hook shot. I think you'll find it much harder to block. And, with your shooting eye, I don't think it will take long for you to learn." How do you think Anderson would feel about working with Cram now? He'd probably be enthusiastic and ready to learn. Being placed in a situation in which he learns for himself that he has a problem will go a long way in unfreezing Anderson from his past patterns of behavior and preparing him for making the attempt at identification. Now he'll be ready for identification. He has had an opportunity to internalize his problem and is ready to work with Steve Cram.

Often the leader who has knowledge of an existing problem forgets that until the people involved recognize the problem as their own, it is going to be difficult to change their behavior. Internalization and identification are not either/or alternatives, but they can be parts of developing specific change strategies appropriate to the situation.

Another example of the change process in operation can be seen in the military, particularly in the induction phase. In a few short months, the military is able to mold inductees into an effective combat team. This feat is not an accident. Let us look at some of the processes that help accomplish this change.

The most dramatic and harsh aspect of the training is the unfreezing phase. All of Schein's four elements of drastic unfreezing are present. Let us look at some specific examples of these elements in operation.

1. The soldiers are *physically removed from their accustomed routines, sources of information, and social relationships.*
2. The DI (drill instructor) *undermines and destroys all social supports.* "Using their voices and the threat of extra PT [physical training], the DI . . . must shock the recruit out of the emotional stability of home, girlfriend, or school."[16]
3. *Demeaning and humiliating experiences* are commonplace during the first 2 weeks of the training as the DIs teach inductees to *see themselves as unworthy and thus be motivated to change* into what the DIs want a soldier to be.
4. Throughout the training, *reward* is consistently *linked with willingness to change and punishment with unwillingness to change.*

Though the soldiers go through a severe unfreezing process, they quickly move to the changing phase, first identifying with the DI and then emulating informal leaders as they develop. "Toward the end of the third week, a break occurs. What one DI calls 'that five percent—the slow, fat, dumb, or difficult' have been dropped. The remaining [soldiers] have emerged from their first week vacuum with one passionate desire—to stay with their platoon at all costs."[17]

Internalization takes place when the recruits, through their forced interactions, develop different high-strength needs. "Fear of the DI gives way to respect, and survival evolves into achievement toward the end of training. 'I learned I had more guts than I imagined' is a typical comment."[18]

Because the group tends to stay together throughout the entire program, it serves as a positive reinforcer, which can help to refreeze the new behavior.

BRINGING CHANGE THEORIES TOGETHER

The preceding theories should help a manager determine some alternative solutions to the identified problem(s) and suggest appropriate implementation strategies. For example, let us reexamine the case of our enthusiastic school administrators who wanted to humanize the schools in their system and change the predominant teaching approach from teacher-centered to child-centered. As we suggested, if they had done a force field analysis, they would have realized that the restraining forces working against this change far outweighed the driving forces in power and frequency. The analysis would have suggested that a directive, coercive change strategy would have been ineffective for implementing change, because significant unfreezing had to occur before the restraining forces against the change could have been immobilized or turned into driving forces. Thus, a participative change effort probably would have been appropriately aimed at reeducating the restraining forces by exposing them in a nonthreatening way (through two-way communication patterns) to new knowledge directed at changing their attitudes and eventually their behavior.

Although this approach might be appropriate, it also must be recognized that it will be time-consuming (4 to 7 years). The superintendent and his assistant just might not be willing to devote that kind of time and effort to this change project. If they are not, then they could decide not to enter that school system or to charge on in a coercive, directive manner and be ready for the consequences. Or, they could choose their action from a number of other alternatives that may have been generated.

CHANGE PROCESS— RECOMMENDED ACTION

After suggesting various alternative solutions and appropriate implementation strategies, a leader or manager interested in change should anticipate the probable consequences (both positive and negative) of taking each of the alternative actions. Remember:

1. Unless there is a high probability that a desired consequence will occur and that the consequence will be the same as the conditions that would

exist if the problem were not present, then you have not solved the problem or changed the situation.

2. The ultimate solution to a problem (the change effort) may not be possible overnight, and, therefore, interim goals must be set along the path to the final goal (the solving of the problem).

The end result of analysis (which includes determining alternative solutions) should be some recommended action that will decrease the discrepancy between the actual and the ideal. Although action is the end result, you must remember that action based on superficial analysis may be worse than no action at all. Too frequently, people want to hurry on to the action phase of a problem before they have adequately analyzed the situation. The importance of the analysis part cannot be given too much emphasis—a good analysis frequently makes the action obvious.

SUMMARY

The focus in this book has been on the management of human resources, and, as a result, we have spent little time on how technical change can have an impact on the total system. Our attempt in this example was to reiterate that an organization is an "open social system"; that is, all aspects of an organization are interrelated; a change in any part of an organization may have an impact on other parts or on the organization itself. Thus, a proposed change in any part of an organization must be carefully assessed in terms of its likely impact on the rest of the organization

ENDNOTES

1. The survey was conducted by the Gallup Organization and commissioned by Proudfoot Change Management, a division of an international consulting firm. It was reported in Barbara Ettorre, "Buddy, Can You Spare Some Change!" *Management Review,* January 1994, p. 5.
2. *Ibid.*
3. Edgar H. Schein, *The Corporate Culture Survival Guide* (San Francisco: Jossey-Bass Inc., 1999), p. 132.
4. Kurt Lewin, "Frontiers in Group Dynamics: Concept, Method, and Reality in Social Science; Social Equilibria and Social Change," *Human Relations,* 1, no. 1 (June 1974), pp. 5–41.
5. Edgar H. Schein, "Management Development As a Process of Influence." Page 110 in *Behavioral Concepts in Management*, David R. Hamp-

ton (Belmont, CA: Dickinson Publishing, 1968). Reprinted in *Industrial Management Review,* 2, no. 2 (May 1961), pp. 59–77.
6. The mechanisms are taken from Herbert C. Kelman, "Compliance, Identification and Internalization: Three Processes of Attitude Change," *Journal of Conflict Resolution,* (1958), II, no. 1, pp. 51–60.
7. Schein, "Management Development As a Process of Influence," p. 112.
8. See Kelman, "Compliance, Identification and Internalization."
9. Schein, "Management Development As a Process of Influence," p. 112.
10. Kurt Lewin, "Frontiers in Group Dynamics: Concept, Method, and Reality in Social Science; Social Equilibria and Social Change," *Human Relations,* 1, no. 1 (June 1947), pp. 5–41.

11. *Ibid.*
12. Edgar H. Schein, in an invited address to the World Economic Forum, February 6, 1992, Davos, Switzerland.
13. Paul Watzlawick, John Weakland, and Richard Fisch, *Change: Principles of Problem Formation and Problem Resolution* (New York: Norton, 1974).
14. Alan D. Meyer, Geoffrey R. Brooks, and James B. Goes, "Environmental Jolts and Industry Revolutions: Organizational Responses to Discontinuous Change," *Strategic Management Journal*, 11 (1990), pp. 93–110.
15. Paul Hersey and Kenneth H. Blanchard, "Change and the Use of Power," *Training and Development Journal,* January 1972. See also Chris Argyris, *Strategy, Change and Defensive Routines* (Cambridge, MA: Ballenger Publishing, 1985).
16. "Marine Machine," *Look Magazine,* August 12, 1969.
17. *Ibid.*
18. *Ibid.*

Chapter 18

Leadership to Achieve Quality

Many companies are currently experiencing very difficult market conditions because of the management revolution that we discussed in chapter 1. But the present, in retrospect, will be viewed as a time of favorable conditions because of the growth of smart, aggressive worldwide competitors. Today's managers are actively seeking ways of gaining an edge. Unfortunately, many are adopting quick fixes and relying on tools and techniques that have little long-term effect. Using such remedies is analogous to trying to eradicate dandelions by cutting off their heads. The technique has only temporary success because the roots of the problem remain. ✧

Improving product and service quality has been a standard strategy for gaining global market share. But time is of the essence. The competitive arenas of the twenty-first century will see contenders battling over issues that are above and beyond quality.[1]

We have included a chapter on quality for two primary reasons. First, quality is an essential contributor to organizational results. "There is no doubt that relative perceived quality and profitability are strongly related. Whether the profit measure is return on sales or return on investment, businesses with superior product/service offerings will clearly outperform those with inferior quality."[2]

This statement is supported by researchers Vinod Singthal and Kevin Hendricks, Georgia Institute of Technology and the College of William and Mary, respectively. Their conclusion was that, compared to a control group, TQM award winners averaged a 44 percent higher stock price return, a 48 percent higher growth in operating income, and a 37 percent higher growth in sales. Award winners also outperformed the control group with regard to operating margins, employee growth, and growth in assets."[3]

The second reason is that the role of leadership is particularly important in implementing quality. We can see its importance in the ISO (International Organization for Standardization) 9000-2000 and the Malcolm Baldrige National Quality Award that is given annually to U.S. business, education, health care, and not-for-profit organizations. The award's purpose is threefold:

- To help improve organizational performance practices and capabilities.
- To facilitate communication and sharing of best practices information among U.S. organizations of all types.
- To serve as a working tool for understanding and managing performance, and guiding planning and training.

The award's criteria are built upon a foundation of core values and concepts and include the critical role of leadership, as illustrated in Figure 18-1.

The criterion, Visionary Leadership, expresses many of the fundamental ideas that we have presented in this book, ideas that should apply to all leaders throughout an organization.

> An organization's senior leaders need to set directions and create a customer focus, clear and visible values, and high expectations. The directions, values, and expectations should balance the needs of all of your stakeholders. Your leaders need to ensure the creation of strategies, systems, and methods for achieving excellence, stimulating innovation, and building knowledge and capabilities. The values and strategies should help guide all activities and decisions of your organization. Senior leaders should ensure and motivate your entire workforce and should encourage involvement, development and learning, innovation, and creativity by all employees.
>
> Through their ethical behavior and personal roles in planning, communicating, coaching, developing future leaders, review of organizational performance, and employee recognition, your senior leaders should serve as role models, reinforcing values and expectations and building leadership, commitment, and initiative throughout your organization.[4]

In this chapter we avoid referring to specific quality efforts such as Total Quality Management, Total Quality Control, or Continuous Quality Improvement[5] because we believe that a quality mindset must be so pervasive throughout an organization that a single or even multiple programs will not suffice. The literature is clear that for quality to become an operationally effective part of an organization, it must permeate the entire organization. One way to make quality part of an organization's mindset is to employ the seven quality implementation phases that we discuss in this chapter: start-up; awareness and education; selecting performance targets; reinforcing implementation; liberating employees; measuring and monitoring ongoing perfor-

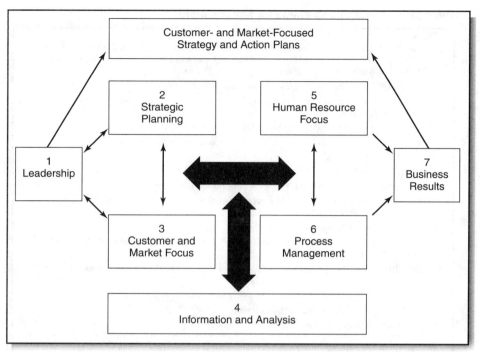

Figure 18-1
Baldrige Criteria for Performance Excellence Framework: A Systems Perspective

Source: Malcolm Baldrige National Quality Award Program 2000: Criteria for Performance Excellence (Gaithersburg, MD: U.S. Department of Commerce, 2000), p. 6.

mance, and adjusting performance targets for continuous improvement.[6] These seven steps complete the circle of Dr. W. Edwards Deming's continuous improvement cycle: PDCA (Plan, Do, Check, Act). Dr. Deming is widely regarded as one of the most important pioneers in the quality movement. His "14 Points for Management" shown in Table 18-1 have been adopted by many firms including the Ford Motor Company.[7]

PHASE 1—START-UP: CREATING THE VISION

You will recall that in chapter 4 we agreed with Warren Bennis that *creating a vision* is one of the two factors that define leadership. The other factor is achieving that vision. Therefore, it is vital that organizations achieve sustainable long-term profitability through customer satisfaction. High-performing businesses achieve their vision through the integration and continuous improvement of their functions and processes.

Table 18-1 Deming's 14 Points for Management

1. Create and publish to all employees a statement of the aims and purposes of the company or other organization. The management must demonstrate constantly their commitment to this statement.
2. Learn the new philosophy, top management and everybody.
3. Understand the purpose of inspection, for improvement of processes and reduction of cost.
4. End the practice of awarding business on the basis of price tag alone.
5. Improve constantly and forever the system of production and service.
6. Institute training.
7. Teach and institute leadership.
8. Drive out fear. Create trust. Create a climate for innovation.
9. Optimize toward the aims and purposes of the company the efforts of teams, groups, and staff areas.
10. Eliminate exhortations for the workforce.
11. (a) Eliminate numerical quotas for production. Instead, learn and institute methods for improvement.
    (b) Eliminate MBO (management by objectives). Instead, learn the capabilities of processes and how to improve them.
12. Remove barriers that rob people of pride of workmanship.
13. Encourage education and self-improvement for everyone.
14. Take action to accomplish the transformation.

Source: James R. Evans and James W. Dean, Jr., *Total Quality: Management, Organization and Strategy* (Cincinnati, OH: South-Western College Publishing, 2000), p. 51.

W. Edwards Deming, one of the founders of the quality movement, suggests that organizations must have an overriding *competitive vision,* a mindset that transcends programs, tools, and techniques and that addresses fundamental issues. Quality must become the passion of the entire organization. If quality does not become, as Tom Peters asserts, "the religion, organizing logic, and culture of the firm, but instead gets stalled as internal programs run by technocrats,"[8] it will fail. Quality will fail because the efforts are, in Harvard Business School Professor Rosabeth Moss Kanter's words, "mounted as programs, unconnected to business strategy, rigidly and narrowly applied, and expected to bring about miraculous transformations in the short term without management lifting as much as a finger."[9]

Quality must become a core value; you must believe in quality as you do other deep-seated values—from your soul. Just as values are persistent and long term, the implementation of quality is a multiyear process. We have observed repeatedly that it takes between 5 and 7 years before quality is solidly ingrained.[10]

Another way of describing this idea is to suggest that organizations need lifetime nourishment if they are to develop and prosper, not a quick bite of a fashionable tool or technique. They also must be willing to pay the price, to make the commitment. Unfortunately, management systems such as quality management and business process reengineering are increasingly being described as tools and techniques.[11] Characterizing quality management as a tool or technique is inappropriate. A tool is used to do work; a technique is a step-by-step way of performing work. A tool, no matter how expensive, can be added to or taken away from the work processes without fundamentally affecting the organization's culture.

Similarly, a technique can be modified without having a fundamental impact on the organization's basic ways of doing things. When management systems are characterized as tools and techniques, there is a tendency for opponents to call them fads or, as *The Wall Street Journal* called them, "trendy practices,"[12] thus decreasing their credibility. Calling quality management a tool or technique is inviting what one author described as "management's 'Program of the Month.' As one employee said, 'TQM is like kidney stone management. It may hurt for a while, but eventually it passes.'"[13]

What some have done by characterizing quality management as a tool or technique is to give the impression that it can be used and discarded with little or no impact on an organization. This characterization is unacceptable. Tools and techniques are of value only when used in support of a quality mindset. Regrettably, managers are now finding a dazzling array of so-called tools and techniques on the menu (the current management literature). Seemingly, all a manager has to do to receive nourishment for better performance is to place an order from menu selections such as benchmarking, integrated value chain analysis, scenario planning, and business process reengineering. Ordering is the easy part. Turning food into nourishment is the hard part. The tantalizing food might contain only empty calories, devoid of meaningful sustenance. The analogy of the human body is appropriate because organizations, like human bodies, are constantly being used up and need to be replenished. Every day, organizations are consumers of people, supplies, funds, and other resources. But quick fixes do not lead to meaningful changes for either organizations or people. Weight management, for example, requires a permanent change of lifestyle to be successful. Organizations need a permanent change also.

We believe that a quality organization's performance begins with creating and implementing a vision of quality. A quality mindset must be expressed in an organization's vision and mission statements. The importance of visioning was affirmed in a study that addressed the question, "What are the most important success factors for a reengineering effort?" The results, depicted in Table 18-2, are revealing. Senior management leadership and the closely associated factor, clear vision, were easily the most important key success factors. Looking specifically at implementation issues, "If there is one vital ingredient for a successful TQM effort . . . it is the CEO's visible and unreserved commitment to TQM. Without it, other managers will hang back."[14]

Let's focus on one aspect of quality, customer satisfaction, or in Deming's words, "customer delight." As he explained more than 3 decades ago:

> What you need are customers that are more than happy. You need customers that boast about your product. Just to have the customer satisfied is not enough. Just to meet specifications—what you think the customer requires—you'll have to do better than that. [It is]

Table 18-2 Key Success Factors for Reengineering, by Percentage of Respondents Mentioning

Factor	Percentage
Senior management leadership	82%
Clear vision	60%
Employee training	41%
Recipe for reengineering	36%
Cross-functional teams	31%
Financial resources	24%
Information technology	15%
Other	10%

Source: Oxford Associates' Survey of Fortune 500 Companies (Furney, Garlitz, Kelleher, 1993).

very important to have customers who brag about buying your product or service. Just to be satisfied—that will not keep you in business.[15]

When results are not achieved, it is easy to go back and blame the manager. A more productive approach is to examine the root causes of the poor results. For example, what were the activities leading to poor results, what caused these activities, and so forth? Focusing on behaviors and activities is a more productive way of identifying root causes.

Solectron Corporation of California provides custom manufacturing services to electronics original equipment manufacturers. It is a world-class example of taking care of customers. Walt Wilson, president of Solectron Americas, has observed, "Our stated corporate belief, 'customer first,' has always been our guiding principle, and every one of our associates understands that. Our teams follow the will of their customers. Whether it is a customer-focus team or a team of workers on the assembly line, the team knows its customer's needs and how to provide the best service. Our people believe in putting their heart and soul into building these products. That is why we are successful."[16] How successful?

- The company has received two Malcolm Baldrige National Quality Awards and an *Industry Week* Best-Managed Company Award.
- Net sales rose 29 percent and net income, before accounting changes, rose 59 percent in the last quarter of 1999.
- Twenty-three percent annual revenue growth.
- Less than 3 percent annual labor turnover.
- Less than 7 parts per million in-plant defect rate on manufactured components and finished products.[17]

The following sections deal with implementing the activities that promote increasing customer delight.

PHASE 2—AWARENESS: SHARING THE VISION AND SOLICITING FEEDBACK

In this phase, the quality vision is communicated to principal stakeholders: owners, managers, and employees. Then feedback from these stakeholders is solicited. Figure 18-2 illustrates the need to integrate all of the organization's activities around a "customer-driven" master plan. Figure 18-2 was developed by total quality researchers at GOAL/QPC, a leading research and publishing firm, with the assistance of General Motors, Ford, Hewlett-Packard, and other large organizations that have implemented quality programs. Communication with and feedback from the entire organization are absolutely critical.

Figure 18-2
Wheel Model: Customer-Driven Master Plan

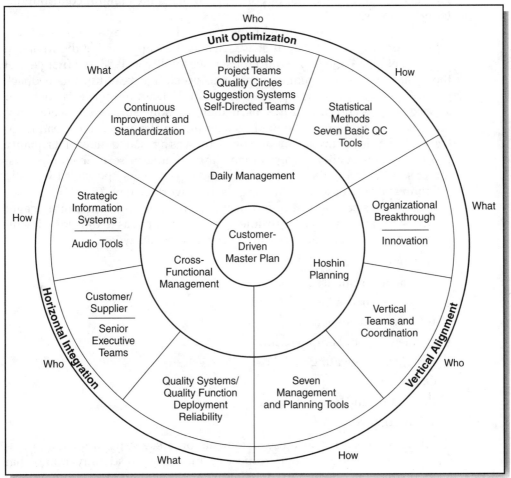

Source: "GOAL/QPC TQM." In *Health Care Research Report,* 1992.

Chapter 18   Leadership to Achieve Quality

Feedback from Employees

Feedback is necessary to see if employees understand the road the company wants to travel. One company encouraged employee feedback by using the following contest:

> We want to run our business not just to satisfy customers, but to do everything we can to make sure that our customers are DELIGHTED to do business with us. This means we want our customers to be captivated, ecstatic, elated, enraptured, enthralled, exhilarated with our service and quality! How can we do this? A contest will start today with prizes for suggestions for achieving TOTAL CUSTOMER DELIGHT! Write your suggestions, put them in a sealed envelope, and turn them in before the end of the month.

The employees in this company submitted many excellent suggestions that not only served as a check to see that everyone was sharing the same vision, but also gave employees an opportunity to make meaningful contributions to the business.

L. L. Bean, the well-known Maine mail-order company, used feedback in two important ways.[18] The first was when they applied for the Malcolm Baldrige National Quality Award for service quality in 1988, the first year of the award. No service quality award was given that year, but the feedback given from the application process caused L.L. Bean to revisit its customer service policies and procedures, particularly making sure orders were properly filled the first time. The Baldrige committee also urged L.L. Bean to increase its employee involvement. The result was a restated view of its quality process, "Total quality involves managing an enterprise to maximize customer satisfaction in the most efficient and effective way possible by totally involving your people in improving the way work is done."[19]

L.L. Bean's second use of feedback was the development of a manager feedback for improvement instrument. The first step was to develop nine dimensions of a total quality climate. These dimensions were:

- Aspiring and focused
- Ethical and compassionate
- Customer-focused and -aligned
- Effective and efficient
- Challenging and empowering
- Open and innovating
- Objective
- Rewarding and developing
- Team-oriented[20]

Employees responded to these statements on a seven-point scale and discussed the results with their respective managers to identify issues that needed attention. The important issues were refined into plans of action. The process was integrated into each manager's performance review.

Did employee feedback make a difference? Return on sales increased 80 percent, returns for quality went down by 25 percent, lost-time injuries decreased 40 percent, and work-in-progress cycle time improved 332 percent.[21]

Feedback from Internal Customers

In almost every organization, there are internal as well as external customers. As products and services flow through an organization, the output from one department becomes the input to another. The second department is an *internal customer* of the first. It is just as essential to obtain feedback from internal customers as it is from *external customers.* For example, a hospital's X-ray department serves not only external customers—e.g., patients and their health care providers—but also internal customers, those departments that need the X-rays for diagnoses and further patient treatment. The Sentara Norfolk (Virginia) General radiology department learned that it took 40 steps and 3 days for a written evaluation of an X-ray. Meanwhile, patients and the medical staff waited. After a simple review of the process, the X-ray team reduced the turnaround time to less than 12 hours, and it is still being reduced. This achievement won the team the *USA Today*/Rochester Institute of Technology Quality Cup.[22]

One of the most important aspects of implementing quality is the "customer for life" idea. This idea suggests that a customer is worth much more than a single transaction; a customer in terms of potential future business may represent hundreds of thousands of future sales dollars. Dealing with customers from this perspective makes customer delight even more critical.

PHASE 3—SELECTING PERFORMANCE TARGETS: BUSINESS OBJECTIVES AND CRITICAL SUCCESS FACTORS

This phase concerns focusing an organization's future direction by refining its vision and mission statements into business objectives. The relationship among vision, mission, and business objectives may be characterized as a road. A vision is the destination at the end of the road. The mission statement defines the composition, width, and other elements of the road. Business objectives are signposts along the way.

How do you know you are making progress without specific objectives, especially those objectives that are critical to the sustained profitability of the company? You don't. You must check your reference points. Each organization has critical operations. At Field Container Company, making a sheet-fed press ready for the next job is critical because each press costs at least $300 per hour to run.[23] Field Container was at the industry's average cycle time of 1½ hours per color. Therefore, a six-color job would take 9 hours to "make-ready." After being taught some cycle-time reduction skills and analyzing videotapes of the process, the press crew reduced make-ready time to 4 hours and has adopted a new target of 1 hour. In an adjacent facility, a team has reduced make-ready on a different press from 4 hours to 1 hour and is aiming for ½ hour.[24]

PHASE 4—REINFORCING IMPLEMENTATION: ACHIEVE IMMEDIATE SUCCESSES

This phase involves identifying areas where immediate successes can be achieved as a means of reinforcing implementation.

Indicators of Progress

There are several aspects to this phase. One is that management must be in the results business. There must be highly visible indicators of immediate progress. Chuck Holland, founder of QualPro, a management consulting firm, has suggested, "If quality improvement is to even take root, let alone flourish, it must achieve bottom-line results immediately. If you do not hit home runs upfront in the quality-improvement effort, it will fail. [Dramatic successes early on] are the most important factors for long-term improvement."[25]

How can you identify an area to implement quality? The social change model developed by Alan Rowe and colleagues can help a manager determine how change will be perceived by the stakeholders (persons who have an interest in, or "stake" in, the outcome) and how management can cope with possible resistance. "The purpose of the model is to identify the target area for introducing change and the best means of communicating the plan. Management must make clear to those involved why the proposed change is necessary and how it can be accomplished."[26]

Before implementing the change, the manager should perform force field analysis that will identify the key players, their resisting or supporting positions, and the magnitude of their influence. You may wish to review the discussion of force field analysis in the previous chapter. It is also important for the manager to assess sources of power, such as personal power, that can be brought to bear and to have a clear understanding of the social problem that needs to be changed.

Principles of Noneconomic Decision Making

We suggest that managers consider using the three principles of noneconomic decision making: changeability, separability, and growth. These principles are so important that we will outline them in some detail.

Changeability
Select the easiest possible relevant change within the organization.[27] The idea here is to find a change that is not only easy to implement in terms of necessary skills, but that also will only minimally disrupt the usual roles in the organi-

zation. For example, it is easier to change the pass routes of wide receivers in football than to covert wide receivers into new roles as tight ends.

A related idea is find a change that will have a high probability of acceptance. A consultant hired to evaluate the systems and procedures of a multiple chain company asked nine store managers individually what they would do if they had the authority and resources to make any change. They each suggested the same procedure. Therefore, it was easily implemented because it had such a high level of acceptance. The key questions that need to be asked are:

- What change is possible? Can it be introduced? Is it acceptable?
- What change is the easiest to make with the human resources available?[28]

Separability

Select a target area that is isolated from outside pressure. Make a modification in one store where implementation can be controlled rather than trying to modify all stores at the same time.[29]

Growth

Begin a change in such a way that it can be extended to other areas. If a seed is planted in one store, nurtured and cared for so it takes root and grows, it eventually will bear fruit in hard dollars. Management can then take the cuttings and plant them in other stores.[30]

PHASE 5—LIBERATING EMPLOYEES: GIVING EMPLOYEES THE ABILITY TO IMPLEMENT THE SYSTEM

This phase changes the management structure of a company by giving employees the authority necessary to delight customers. Some authors have suggested that the way to do this is to empower employees.[31] Oren Harari, however, has suggested an alternative view by urging managers to stop empowering their people. He suggests that a manager's "goal is not to empower, but to liberate. . . . All of this empowerment stuff is a con because you cannot confer power on human beings. You cannot make anyone powerful. What you can do is to create a condition where people will feel powerful, a condition where people choose to create power for themselves."[32] How can this work?

Settlement of Claims

In the dry-cleaning business, liberating employees to execute the customer delight strategy means freeing employees to make adjustments. One of the most demotivating factors for counter personnel is dealing with irate customers. Some customers who come in to pick up their dry-cleaned garments after they have had a difficult day use the dry-cleaning counter persons as convenient targets for their frustration. Quality cleaning is expensive and for businesspeople an unavoidable expense. These two factors seem to make some customers upset. They take it out on the counter persons who, although innocent, bear the criticism because they are the most available targets.

There are two types of adjustment problems. One is not making an adjustment when one is necessary, and the other is making an adjustment when one is not necessary. Many cleaning problems, such as color loss, are the result of manufacturers' errors; others are attempts by scam artists to rip off the cleaners. A few are genuine problems caused by the cleaners.

Counter persons in one company were free to adjust any claim up to 50 dollars. A claim form would be completed and a receipt obtained from the customer. Customers could have the option of cash or one and one-half times the value of the claim in free cleaning. The store would retain the garment for inspection by the manager.

Claims above 50 dollars would be referred to the store manager. Damaged garments would be sent to the International Fabricare Institute (IFI) technical lab. If the cause was determined to be a manufacturer's defect, the garment would be returned to the customer, together with a copy of the lab report. If the cause was store error, the customer would be paid the depreciated value of the garment according to standards established by the IFI or one and one-half times the full value in credit at the customer's option. These general guidelines were subject to modification by the plant supervisor—e.g., immediate settlement of the claim if the damage was caused by the store. This liberal credit policy was viewed as a form of advertising and was monitored to stay within 0.25 percent of gross sales.

Pledge Adjustments

As part of a company's pledge to their customers that all garments would be "ready to wear when promised," they also announced that "If we do not keep our pledge, you don't pay." This pledge was part of the company's desire to "Under Promise—Over Deliver." The company's quality systems were designed to clean and finish garments *before* they were promised and to deliver more quality and value than the customer expected.

This pledge, however, meant that counter persons were required to make adjustments when the pledge wasn't kept—e.g., a shirt with a button missing so it was not "ready to wear." Unless counter persons were liberated to fulfill the promise to provide free cleaning or additional services when the pledge wasn't kept, the pledge was meaningless. Counter persons were specifically authorized to make these adjustments and to keep a simple record for follow-up purposes. Employee freedom, in the areas of claims settlements and pledge adjustment, was critical to improving employee morale and to the effective implementation of customer delight.

Phase 6—Measuring and Monitoring Ongoing Performance: Tracking Implementation Progress

This phase carries out two of the basic tenets of management—*measure* and *monitor* your expectations as part of the journey. Briefly, inspect what you expect. In this regard, Tom Peters quoted Soshitsu Sen XV: "A monk once asked his master, 'no matter what lies ahead, what is the Way?' The master quickly replied, 'The Way is your daily life.'"[33] A company must make quality the Way. One company adopted two approaches in measuring and monitoring the Way: performance ratios and daily sales charts.

Performance Ratios

Several years ago, the company developed a series of performance ratios for laundry, dry cleaning, alterations, and other company functions. These were based on a work-in:labor ratio. Analysis of critical success factors in the industry and in the company revealed that this relationship was the most critical. Over the years, the company decided on targets of 4.0 for laundry and 3.2 for dry cleaning—e.g., work-in divided by the labor necessary to process the work-in. Adjustments were made for training new employees, equipment downtime, and other such factors.

The usefulness of these ratios is that the financial performance of an individual store is directly related to the target ratio. By feeding back the ratio to individual stores on a weekly basis and analyzing the factors affecting the ratio, company management increased profitability.

Daily Sales Charts

Store managers plot daily cash sales and work-in on a simple graph. This graph is a portrait of the store's performance. If the portrait looks good, customers are being delighted; if it doesn't, they aren't. Employee behavior must result in sales. As a means of reinforcement, the store is given a bonus of 5 percent of the year-to-year monthly sales increase payable every quarter. For example, if third quarter 2000 sales are $30,000 larger than third quarter 1999 sales, the store receives $1,500 to be divided among store employees as they decide.

Does this work? A store manager was observed on the last day of the month adding her sales as the day went on. When asked what she was doing, she replied, "Tracking my sales." When we can get to the point where *company* sales become "*my*" sales, then liberation is working.

Monitoring process improvement works. Sunny Fresh Foods, Monticello, Minnesota, is a manufacturer of further processed egg products such as refrigerated and frozen egg products. It was the 1999 Malcolm Baldrige National Quality Award recipient in the Small Business Category. Sunny Fresh uses a weekly Key Indicator Report to assess short-term performance. These reports, tied to core values, key strategies, and long-term goals, are examined for trends and are used as a basis for fact-based action plans. Has this made a difference?

- Market share has increased to over 20 percent. Market share rank has increased from 14th in 1988 to second in 1999.
- Return on gross investment has tripled in the past several years.
- All facilities score in the "excellent" range in American Sanitation Institute audits.
- Total waste was reduced 21 percent during a 2-year period where production increased 10 percent.[34]

PHASE 7—ADJUSTING PERFORMANCE TARGETS FOR CONTINUOUS IMPROVEMENT

We live in a very dynamic world of intrinsic change. Continuous improvement means new product and service standards. These standards then become the baseline for future continuous improvements.

The manager of one division of a national farm equipment manufacturer used "10% Better" as the continuous improvement target from the previous year's results. Productivity, safety, scrap, and other production-related targets were set "10% Better." Once achieved, these new targets became the standards for the next year.

A specialty printing company distanced itself from its competitors by increasing its financial targets 2 to 3 percent per year. Using data from the National Association of Printers and Lithographer's annual statistics for its market segment, the firm set its initial target as double the sales per employee of the average firm. Achieving this target, in turn, meant purchasing the highest quality, labor-saving equipment, training its employees, and implementing process efficiencies. The result of adjusting performance targets for continuous improvement was the highest profitability among competitive firms.

SUMMARY

Ron Heidke, Vice President and Director of Corporate Quality at Eastman Kodak, captured our thoughts:

> Successful processes require three components: skill, knowledge and will. . . . There is a definite need for strong leadership but not everybody can step into the leader's role and give a world-class

performance. Managers need to learn the kind of leadership that is required and they must perfect it over many long, hard years. . . . The future [of quality] is to become ingrained in the very fabric of the way we live and operate such that people won't talk about it anymore. They will just be doing it. It will no longer be perceived as the "program of the month" or a passing fancy; it will just be the way we do our work.[35]

To accomplish Heidke's and our goal, organizations need an approach to change that pervades every aspect, the very fabric of their existence. Quality must be an ongoing process to meet dynamic, ever-changing customer requirements. Transformational leadership, discussed in the next chapter, is such an approach.

ENDNOTES

1. Gary Hamel and C. K. Prahalad, *Competing for the Future* (Boston: Harvard Business School Press, 1994), p. 14.
2. Robert D. Buzzell and Bradley T. Gale, *The PIMS Principles: Linking Strategy to Performance* (New York: The Free Press, 1987), p. 107.
3. "TQM is Alive," *Quality*, Wheaton, 1999, pp. 1–2.
4. *Malcolm Baldrige National Quality Award Program 2000: Criteria for Performance Excellence* (Gaithersburg, MD: U.S. Department of Commerce, 2000), p. 2.
5. Harry Costin, "Exploring the Concepts Underlying TQM," *Readings in Total Quality Management* (Fort Worth: Dryden Press, 1994), p. 8; and William J. Kolarik, *Creating Quality: Concepts, Systems, Strategies, and Tools* (New York: McGraw-Hill, 1995), p. 5.
6. Adapted from Lawrence Holpp, "Making Choices: Self-Directed Teams or Total Quality Management?" *Training*, May 1992, p. 73. See also Judy D. Olian and Sara L. Rynes, "Making Total Quality Work: Aligning Organizational Processes, Performance Measures, and Stakeholders," *Human Resources Management*, 30, no. 3 (Fall 1991), pp. 303–333.
7. James R. Evans and James W. Dean, Jr. *Total Quality: Management, Organization and Strategy* (Cincinnati, OH: South-Western College Publishing, 2000), p. 51.
8. Tom Peters, quoted in "Strategic Planning," *Total Quality*, 5, no. 10 (October 1994), p. 1.
9. Rosabeth Moss Kanter, quoted in "Strategic Planning," *Total Quality*, 5, no. 10 (October 1994), p. 1.
10. Kolarik, *Creating Quality*, p. 827. See also Rhonda K. Reger, Loren T. Gustafson, Samuel M. Demarie, and John V. Mullane, "Reframing the Organization: Why Implementing TQM Is Easier Said Than Done," *Academy of Management Review*, 19, no. 3 (1994), pp. 565–584.
11. *Management Tools and Techniques: An Executive's Guide, 2000* (Boston: Bain & Company, 1999).
12. *The Wall Street Journal*, June 6, 1993, pp. A1, 6.
13. Thomas C. Keiser and Douglas A. Smith, "Customer-Driven Strategies: Moving from Talk to Action," *Planning Review*, 21, no. 5 (1993), pp. 25–32.
14. Michael Barrier, "Small Firms Put Quality First," *Nation's Business*, May 1992, pp. 22–32.
15. Mary Walton, *The Deming Management Method* (New York: Perigee Books, 1986), pp. 29–30.
16. John S. McClenahen, "Solecton Corporation," *Industry Week*, 1998, p. 69.
17. *Ibid.*, pp. 68–72. See also *Yahoo! Finance Market Guide, http://finanace.Yahoo.com,* February 14, 2000.
18. Dawn Anfuso, "L.L. Bean's TQM Efforts Put People before Success," *Personnel Journal*, July 1994, pp. 72–83.
19. *Ibid.,* p. 75.
20. *Ibid.,* p. 83.
21. *Ibid.*

22. Joseph Cosco, "Service with a Smile," *Journal of Business Strategy,* 1994, pp. 58–59.
23. Paul Froiland, "Quality in a Box," *Training,* February 1994, p. 63.
24. *Ibid.*
25. Quoted in Tracy Benson, "A Business Strategy Comes of Age," *Industry Week,* May 3, 1993, p. 42.
26. Alan J. Rowe, Richard O. Mason, Karl E. Dickel, Richard B. Mann, and Robert J. Mockler, *Strategic Management: A Methodological Approach,* 4th ed. (Reading, MA: Addison-Wesley, 1994), p. 513.
27. *Ibid.,* p. 514.
28. *Ibid.,* p. 516.
29. *Ibid.*
30. *Ibid.,* pp. 516–517.
31. Michael J. Showalter and Judith A. Mulholland, "Continuous Improvement Strategies for Service Organizations," *Business Horizons,* July–August 1992, p. 84.
32. Oren Harari, "Stop Empowering Your People," *Management Review,* November 1993, p. 26.
33. Tom Peters, "Paying Attention to the Journey Rather Than the Destination," *Business Journal,* May 31, 1993, p. 7.
34. News Release, Sunny Fresh Foods, 11/23/99.
35. Catherine Romano, "Report Card on TQM," *Management Review,* January 1994, p. 25.

Chapter 19

Leadership Strategies for Organizational Transformation

Why is organizational transformation important? You will recall that in chapter 1 we described a world in transformation. In all spheres of activity, we have entered a period of rapid, large-scale, and discontinuous change. Geopolitically, a new mosaic of nations, countries, and political systems is forming and reforming. Socially, the human race has been subjected to forces of cataclysmic proportions in areas such as health, welfare, and even physical safety. The technological explosion seems to be sweeping everybody along on a surprise-a-minute roller-coaster ride. The whole world has become one business arena, forcing all of us into new and qualitatively different ways of thinking and doing. ✧

In such a dynamic environment, it is inevitable that organizations of all shapes, sizes, and types will also undergo major change and upheaval. Organizational transformations have become the order of the day, and with them has come the potential for crises and chaos—or for new freedoms and better ways of living. The scope and the scale of change require leadership at a level and of a quality never experienced before. How are we as leaders to respond? One important response in the face of these great challenges

This chapter was contributed by Gustav Pansegrouw. Copyright© 2001 by Gustav Pansegrouw and the Center for Leadership Studies. All rights reserved.

415

and threatening periods of uncertainty is *transformational leadership*. This chapter was contributed by Gustav Pansegrouw.

CHARACTERISTICS OF ORGANIZATIONAL TRANSFORMATION

According to Richard Beckhard, one of the pioneering practitioners and researchers in the field of organizational development, a transformation represents a vital organizational change.[1] Transformation is characterized by certain features that clearly differentiate it from other types of change. First, according to Beckhard, it involves substantial and discontinuous change to the shape, structure, and nature of the organization, rather than incremental adjustments and fine-tuning of the current situation. One example of a discontinuous change would be when a firm changes from being production-driven to being customer-driven. Another would be a merger of two organizations. In both instances, the shape of the organization can be expected to change radically. An organization transforming from a production orientation to a customer orientation will need to drastically decentralize and delegate authority. In a merger, entirely new roles and working relationships will be created.

A second characteristic of transformation is that the need for change is caused by forces external to the organization rather than forces inside the organization. A typical example would be when an organization changes from a functional to a divisional structure in response to market forces or industry pressures in the form of competitor actions or regulatory changes. Currently, globalization is one of the most powerful external forces for organizational transformation.

A third distinguishing feature of transformation is that the change is deep and pervasive, rather than shallow and contained. The change affects all parts of the organization and involves many levels. Decentralization, downsizing, and the geographic relocation of functions and activities exemplify changes that transform structural relationships deeply and pervasively.

Finally, transformation requires significantly different, and even entirely new, sets of actions by the members of the organization, rather than more or less of existing behavior patterns. Examples are changes to the norms and core values of an organization that are brought about through acquisition, deregulation, and privatization or through a drastic strategic repositioning such as shifting from a production-efficiency focus to a customer-service strategy. An organizational transformation is thus characterized by the fact that the organization as a whole has to do substantially new and different things rather than only some people having to do more or less of the same thing.

A transformation starts beyond the current organization in that it deals with changes in the external environment; it includes realignment of the mission, strategy, structure, and systems; and it requires re-creation of the culture and behavioral processes of the organization as a whole.[2]

TRANSFORMATIONAL LEADERSHIP

Studies of successful and unsuccessful organizational transformations have emphasized the decisive role of leadership in these situations and have given rise to the concept of *transformational leadership,* which is also termed *visionary leadership, strategic leadership,* or *charismatic leadership.* This new leadership arena involves specific leadership behaviors, actions, and strategies that are required to bring about organizational transformation. Table 19-1 summarizes the characteristics of transformational leadership that have been proposed by various authors. These studies spanning more than a decade show that the concept of transformational leadership does not alter the basic definition of leadership presented in chapter 1—i.e., the process of influencing the activities of an individual or a group in efforts toward goal achievement in a given situation. It does, however, highlight the specific actions that the leader should perform in a transformation. On the basis of the strategies and characteristics presented in Table 19-1, let's summarize the key leadership actions for bringing about organizational transformation. It should be noted that these summary statements do not necessarily depict a sequential flow of events or a sequential process. Rather, we have attempted to emphasize *critical leadership incidents* for organizational transformation as reported by the cited authors in a brief, easy-to-use format. A sequential process model appears in a recent work of Nadler.[3]

Personal Commitment to the Transformation by the Leadership

The leadership of the organization must be fully committed to the transformation, and the commitment must be visible to other organizational members and external stakeholders (key players).

Firm, Relentless, and Indisputable Communication of the Impossibility of Maintaining the Status Quo

The leadership must forcefully communicate the *failure* of the status quo. This must be done in such a way that a critical mass of members will want to change. You will recall the Schein model in chapter 17 that emphasized the importance of increasing the anxiety of not changing and decreasing the anxiety of changing. This process requires:

- Firm statements backed by credible evidence that the status quo is untenable because of circumstances and trends external to the organization.
- Clear indications that the failure of the status quo is final and irreversible.

Table 19-1 Transformational Leadership Strategies and Characteristics

Bennis and Nanus (1985)	Tichy and Devanna (1986)	Kouzes and Posner (1987)	Nadler and Tushman (1989)	Conger (1989)	Nevis et al. (1996)
Attention through vision	Recognizing the need for revitalization	Challenging the process	Envisioning	Detecting unexploited opportunities and deficiencies in the current situation	Persuasive communication
Meaning through communication	Creating a new vision	Inspiring a shared vision	Energizing	Communicating the vision	Participation
Trust through positioning	Institutionalizing change	Enabling others to act	Enabling	Building trust	Expectancy
Deployment of self		Modeling the way	Structuring	Demonstrating the means to achieve the vision	Role modeling
		Encouraging the heart	Controlling		Structural rearrangement
			Rewarding		Extrinsic rewards
					Coercion

Sources: Edwin C. Nevis, Joan Lancourt, and Helen G. Vasallo, *International Revolutions* (San Francisco: Jossey Bass, 1996); Warren Bennis and Burt Nanus, *Leaders: The Strategies for Taking Charge* (New York: Harper & Row, 1985); Noel M. Tichy and Mary Anne Devanna, *The Transformational Leader* (New York: John Wiley and Sons, 1986); James M. Kouzes and Barry Z. Posner, *The Leadership Challenge* (San Francisco: Jossey Bass, 1987); Jay Conger, *The Charismatic Leader* (San Francisco: Jossey Bass, 1989); David A. Nadler and Michael Tushman, "Leadership for Organizational Change." In *Large Scale Organizational Change*, ed. Allen M. Mohrman, Jr., Susan Albers Mohrman, Gerald E. Ledford, Jr., Thomas G. Cummings, Edward E. Lawler III and Associates (San Francisco: Jossey Bass, 1989).

Clear and Enthusiastic Communication of an Inspiring Vision of What the Organization Could Become

The leadership must persistently communicate a clear picture of the future state of the organization in a way that this vision is shared and supported by the members of the organization, individually and collectively. This communication requires:

- A clear and vivid value-based vision created by an appropriate mix of rational analysis, intuition, and emotional involvement.
- Repeated communication of the vision, beliefs, and values to the members of the organization in a way that inspires and excites them and touches their hearts and minds with a sense of urgency.

Timely Establishment of a Critical Mass of Support for the Transformation

The leadership must identify the key players and power holders in the organization and in its operating environment and obtain their support for the change. Obtaining support requires:

- Acknowledging the power that key players in and outside the organization have.
- Discussing with them the failure of the status quo, presenting them with the vision of the future and the values accompanying it, and convincing them of the need to change.
- Showing personal and organizational benefits to be achieved and involving them in decisions and implementation.

Acknowledging, Honoring, and Dealing With Resistance to the Transformation

The leadership must acknowledge resistance to the change and deal with it as a necessary stage in the process of abandoning the status quo and embracing the new vision with its beliefs and values. Dealing with resistance requires:

- A willingness to listen.
- Some tolerance and patience.
- Clarification and repetition of the need to change and the benefits of the transformation.

Defining and Setting Up an Organization That Can Implement the Vision

The leadership must design and put into action an organization that will be congruent with the new beliefs and values. Leadership must be willing to risk the introduction of structural changes and the acquisition and allocation of resources that will secure the competence and commitment to make the transformation work and that will put into place appropriate systems of organization for the transformation including:

- Modeling and anchoring the required beliefs and values in appropriate new roles and actions.
- Implementing strategies, structures, and systems including a power network that is clearly aligned to, and supportive of, the actions that need to be accomplished in order to realize the vision and enact the new beliefs and values.
- Replacing key staff, or staff in key positions, who are not suited to the change.
- Introducing education, training, and retraining in the actions required by the transformation and specifically by the new beliefs and values.
- Implementing a reward system that will reinforce actions that are congruent with the new set of beliefs and values.

Regular Communication of Information about Progress and Giving Recognition and Reward for Achievements

The leadership must communicate to the organization how the transformation is progressing, announce and celebrate achievements, openly share setbacks, and encourage the risk-taking behavior required to implement the vision. This step requires:

- Regular publication of achievements and face-to-face feedback sessions.
- Emphasizing, recognizing, and consistently rewarding the gains made toward the implementation of the vision, the beliefs, and the values.

Transformational leadership thus includes both the dramatic, courageous, and emotionally stirring actions and the mundane, ongoing day-to-day transactions that are integral to life in organizations. Putting all of this together, we define transformational leadership as:

> A deliberate influence process on the part of an individual or group to bring about a discontinuous change in the current state and functioning of an organization as a whole. The change is driven by a vision based on a set of beliefs and values that require the members of the organization to urgently perceive and think differently and to perform new actions and organizational roles.

Let's examine this definition in some detail.

A Deliberate Influence Process
The leadership is very conscious of what they want to bring about, and they have a specific plan, at least initially, of how they want to bring about the transformation. Their actions are premeditated rather than spontaneous.

On the Part of An Individual or Group

This phrase specifies that the leadership may be an individual or a group within the organization.

To Bring About a Discontinuous Change

The term *discontinuous* is used in deliberate contrast to the term *incremental*. A transformation is a clear break from the past and the present. The acid test for a discontinuous change is analysis of future critical success factors. If these factors are not qualitatively different from the current critical success factors, the change is probably only incremental.

In the Current State and Functioning

State refers to the *performance* of the organization, such as the health of the organization. *Functioning* includes the internal and external *interactive patterns* as reflected in organizational structures and systems.

Of An Organization As a Whole

Transformational leadership is pervasive in terms of both the horizontal and vertical dimensions of the organization, and it is also systemic in that it sees the organization as a system to be changed.

The Change is Driven by a Vision Based on a Set of Beliefs and Values

The development and pursuit of a belief- and value-anchored vision is the distinguishing feature of transformational leadership. The vision, in terms of being a belief- and value-infused picture or representation of what the organization as an entity could become, is also the clearest signal that the change to come is discontinuous. The vision, and particularly the set of underlying beliefs and values, is, in effect, a control mechanism for ensuring the type of activities required to achieve the future state.

That Requires the Members of the Organization to Urgently Perceive and Think Differently and to Perform New Actions and Organizational Roles

Transformational leadership aims at instilling new behaviors in most members of the organization and without exception requires new role sets and role behaviors in the classic interpretation of the concept of role, as used in the behavioral sciences. Although we have put the emphasis on new actions as the observable result, we also include in the concept new ways of perceiving and thinking as the precursors toward observable behavior. Transformational leadership is also invariably characterized by an urgency; time is important, and because a transformation more often than not is a response to an organizational crisis, the new actions are urgently required.

No One "Ideal" Way for Organizational Transformation

The caution for leaders who wish to transform their organizations is not to idealize a given set of key actions as the one best way of bringing about transformations.[4] A cookbook approach tends to disregard the differences that exist from one situation to another. What may have worked well in one transformation situation may not work at all in another. There is always the danger that leadership recipes, collected from a variety of successful "meals," may be put together in a list that then becomes touted as the one best way, or best recipe, for attempting all organizational transformations irrespective of situational differences.

The Situational Leadership for Transformation model states that any combination of or all of the preceding leadership actions may be appropriate or inappropriate for bringing about a transformation, depending on the situation in which they are used. The most important situational factor is the "fit" between the leadership actions and the organization in terms of the organization's readiness for transformation. This view is consistent with our discussion in chapter 8. Of the many important situational factors the leader may consider, the relationship between the leader and the follower is the most critical. In this context, the relationship is between the leader and the organizational entity.

Organizational Readiness for Transformation

The inherent complexity of organizational behavior on the one hand and the scale of change involved in transformation on the other warn against an oversimplification of the concept of *readiness for transformation*—a concept that has not received sufficient attention in the field of organizational change and transformation.[5]

In our view, organizational readiness for transformation is a function of, or is determined by, the *culture* of the organization. Although organizational culture is itself a complex phenomenon with many interpretations, there is some agreement in the literature that the primary element of organizational culture is shared basic assumptions, or beliefs, about how to cope with the two fundamental problems that all groups and organizations face: survival and adaptation to the external environment, and the internal integration and coordination of organizational functioning.[6] A shared basic assumption, or belief, consists of cognitive, emotional, motivational, and behavioral components that are so taken for granted that as a rule they are seldom confronted or challenged by organizational members. When a shared assumption is held in an organization, it defines for the members what they should pay attention to, what meaning they should attach to environmental trends and organizational events, what action preferences and motivations they should have, and how they should react emotionally to issues inside and outside the organization.

In one sense, basic assumptions are the analytic, interpretive, decision-making, and coping frameworks, or models, that members of the organization share. They play a major role in providing meaning to events in and around the organization. Basic assumptions function as *coping mechanisms* in that they determine what information and events the organization will pay attention to, how they will be interpreted, and how they will be acted on. As such, basic assumptions are *ability factors* of organizational culture—they make the organization more or less able to cope with events. However, basic assumptions also reflect the preferences and motivational orientations, or models, that the members of the organization share. They play a major role in determining priorities and guidelines for selection and choice with regard to ends and means. Basic assumptions thus also function as *motivational mechanisms* in that they determine what the organization will strive for and how it will be achieved. As such, basic assumptions are also *willingness* factors of organizational culture—they make the organization more or less willing to pursue certain ends (and means to ends) rather than others.

Basic assumptions, or beliefs, often operate outside of awareness, and they may be viewed as a collective mindset that guides the organizational processes of interpretation, action preferences, and emotional reactions. The need for congruence created by shared assumptions is often so powerful that it may even bring about denial, projection, and other forms of distortion of events in and around the organization.[7]

We suggest that the more the basic assumptions, or belief systems, reflect a *learning culture,* the higher the organizational readiness for transformation will be. The past decade has witnessed an ever-increasing emphasis on the need for organizations to develop a learning culture as the only way to sustain a competitive advantage over the long term in an increasingly complex and turbulent environment. A learning culture is characterized by continuous learning from experiences and by learning how to learn.[8]

The basic assumptions, or beliefs, that characterize a learning culture can be described along two dimensions: flexibility with regard to the external environment ability and organizational commitment willingness.[9]

Flexibility with regard to the external environment includes the following organizational characteristics:

- Risk-seeking behavior
- Tolerance of ambiguity
- Ease in uncertain situations
- Inquisitiveness, scientific interest, experimentation
- High frequency of interaction with external environment
- Active customer information gathering
- Entrepreneurial orientation, innovation alertness
- Functional orientation

Organizational commitment consists of organizational characteristics such as:

- Sharing of goals, responsibilities, and information, supportive and "we" feelings, participative mindset
- Mission and goal orientation, results orientation
- Congruence and internal consistency, systemic integration
- Opportunities for creativity, freedom of ideas, individualism

The shared basic assumption that contrasts with, or is opposite to, flexibility with regard to the external environment is *rigidity with regard to the status quo.* The shared basic assumption that contrasts with organizational commitment is a *parochial orientation.* Integrating the concepts discussed so far allows us to develop the model of organizational readiness for transformation shown in Figure 19-1. This model presents four types of culture, each representing a different level of organizational readiness for transformation.

OR-4: The Learning Culture

Basic assumptions reflect flexibility with regard to the external environment and organizational commitment. This culture is able and willing to deal with organizational transformation. The ability is reflected in a versatility to effectively cope with any demands presented by the external environment. The

Figure 19-1
Organizational Readiness (OR) for Transformation Model

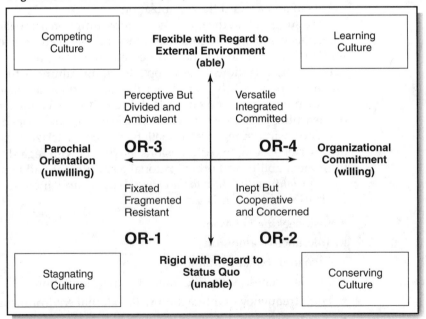

willingness is demonstrated by the integrated way in which the organization functions and by high levels of commitment to the organization as a whole and its continued well being.

OR-3: The Competing Culture

Basic assumptions reflect flexibility with regard to the external environment, but the organization has a parochial, or vested-interest, orientation. This culture is able, but unwilling to deal with organizational transformation. The ability is expressed as perceptiveness with regard to the demands of the external environment. The unwillingness is manifested as the divided way in which the organization functions and an ambivalence about the benefits that the transformation may bring about for the various vested-interest groups and role players in the organization.

OR-2: The Conserving Culture

Basic assumptions reflect a rigidity with regard to the status quo but also show an organizational commitment. This culture is unable, but willing to deal with organizational transformation. The inability is displayed by an ineptness in dealing with the demands of the external environment. The willingness is demonstrated by the cooperative way in which the organization functions and by a concern for the viability of the organization as a whole.

OR-1: The Stagnating Culture

Basic assumptions reflect a rigidity with regard to the status quo and parochialism. This culture is both unable and unwilling to deal with organizational transformation. The inability is expressed as a fixation on the status quo and apathy toward the demands of the external environment. The unwillingness is reflected in the fragmented functioning of the organization and in a resistance to any actions that may jeopardize vested interests and parochial preferences.

TRANSFORMATIONAL LEADERSHIP ACTIONS

Earlier in this chapter, we summarized the key leadership actions and models for bringing about organizational transformation, as reported by various authors. An analysis of these models and actions leads us to conclude that the leadership actions that leaders can use to bring about transformation can be divided into two types: structuring actions and inspiring actions.

Operationally, the leadership actions are defined as follows:

Structuring actions. The extent to which the leader engages in shaping new beliefs and value-based actions by providing information about the status quo, specifying the desired future state, defining and forming the required organization, and providing appropriate human and material resources. When using structuring actions, the leader is attempting to influence by creating a physical and psychological environment that reduces the choice of possible organizational behaviors to those required by the transformation.

It is important to remember that structuring actions may be viewed as a continuum, ranging from low amounts to high amounts of structuring behavior. A leader who presents only information on the inadequate functioning of the organization is providing a low amount of structuring behavior. Conversely, a leader who not only communicates the failure of the status quo but also restructures the organization, replaces key people, introduces new management systems, and develops different criteria for organizational effectiveness is engaging in high amounts of structuring behavior. Structuring actions, to be successful, require sufficient position power.

> *Inspiring actions.* The extent to which the leader engages in exciting organizational members by persuading and encouraging; discussing and clarifying; facilitating, processing, developing, and reinforcing the beliefs and new value-based actions that are required by the transformation. A leader uses inspiring actions to attempt to influence by persuasive and motivational communications that activate and induce the organizational actions required by the transformation.

Inspiring actions also fall on a continuum of low to high amounts. A leader who matter-of-factly tries to communicate a vision to the whole organization during an annual convention speech is demonstrating a low amount of inspiring behavior. On the other hand, a leader who passionately and frequently communicates the vision and values, discusses and clarifies the benefits of a new order, and also models, facilitates, encourages, and reinforces the new ways of doing things as required by the transformation is providing high amounts of inspiring actions. Inspiring actions, to be successful, require sufficient personal power.

In summary, structuring actions aim at limiting the range of new actions and constrain choice to those roles and actions required by the intended transformation. Inspiring actions aim at motivating organizational members, building their desire for the intended transformation, and inducing the behavior and roles it requires.

Transformational Leadership Strategies

The relative amounts of structuring and inspiring actions combine in an interactive influencing system to form four basic leadership strategies.

- *Enforcing strategies (S1).* Destroy the status quo and implement the new structure. Moderate to high amounts of structuring actions (HS) and moderate to low amounts of inspiring actions (LI).

- *Enabling strategies (S2).* Envision the future and develop the required actions and roles. Moderate to high amounts of structuring actions (HS) and moderate to high amounts of inspiring actions (HI).

- *Enlisting strategies (S3).* Facilitate commitment and participate in decisions and implementation. Moderate to low amounts of structuring actions (LS) and moderate to high amounts of inspiring actions (HI).

- *Endorsing strategies (S4).* Sponsor the transformation and monitor progress. Moderate to low amounts of structuring actions (LS) and moderate to low amounts of inspiring actions (LI).

THE SITUATIONAL LEADERSHIP FOR TRANSFORMATION MODEL

The Situational Leadership for Transformation model (SLT) is presented in Figure 19-2. In this model, the four quadrants, S1, S2, S3, and S4, represent the four basic transformational leadership strategies as derived from the relative amounts of structuring and inspiring actions. The structuring and inspiring actions are represented on two interacting dimensions. The four levels of readiness, OR-1, OR-2, OR-3, and OR-4, together with the descriptors for each level, are shown below the transformational leadership strategies. The curved line through the four transformational leadership strategies represents the high probability combination of structuring behavior and inspiring behavior. To use the model, identify a point on the organizational readiness continuum that represents organizational readiness to perform a specific transformation. Then draw a perpendicular line from that point to a point where it intersects with the curved line representing transformational leader behavior. This point indicates the most appropriate amount of structuring behavior and inspiring behavior for that specific level of organizational readiness.

We suggest that you use the same five-step implementation process described in chapter 8 when you implement the Situational Leadership for Transformation model. You should first determine whether the change being considered qualifies as a transformation. It must be a discontinuous change as defined earlier in this chapter. For instance, you may be considering changing from a production-efficiency to a customer-satisfaction paradigm. The next step is to determine the readiness level of your organization by assessing the organizational ability and organizational willingness for transformation. Third, the Situational Leadership for Transformation model should be used to select and implement the appropriate transformational leadership strategy in terms of the mix of structuring and inspiring actions for the diagnosed level of organizational readiness. Fourth, the result of the transformational leadership strategy should be assessed. And fifth, depending upon the assessment, the cycle should begin again, or no further action should be taken at this time.

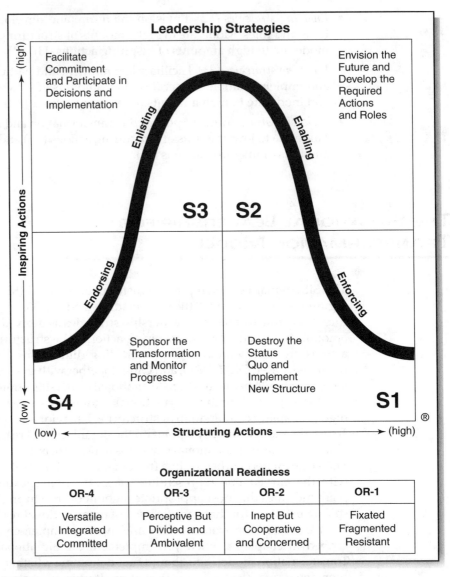

Figure 19-2
Situational Leadership for Transformation Model (SLT)

The appropriate transformational leadership strategies for each level of organizational readiness are as follows:

OR-1, Fixated, Fragmented, and Resistant/S1, Enforcing Strategy

"Destroy the status quo and implement new structure." The leader needs to engage in moderate to high amounts of structuring actions with below-average amounts of inspiring actions. Essential actions will include:

- Relentlessly, firmly, and repetitively presenting factual information that clearly and indisputably shows the impossibility of maintaining the status quo.
- Disconfirming all attempts to deny, rationalize, or refute the negative information about the status quo.
- Specifying and asserting the desired future state in terms of required performance criteria and critical success factors, modeling the belief systems, values, and actions required by the transformation.
- Replacing people who do not have the potential to develop the skills, insights, experience, and values required by the transformation with individuals from inside and outside the organization who are more suited to the change.
- Acquiring and reallocating the resources such as money, time, power, and rewards that will be required and shaping those roles and management systems that need to be aligned to, and that will support, the future state.

OR-2, Inept but Cooperative and Concerned/S2, Enabling Strategy

"Envision the future and develop the required actions and roles." The leader needs to engage in moderate to high amounts of both structuring and inspiring actions. Essential actions will include:

- Persuasive, enthusiastic, and inspiring communication of the vision including the new beliefs and values to all parts of the organization; advocating the vision, beliefs, and values in discussions with individuals and groups; explaining and reinforcing the benefits of the transformation and expressing confidence in accomplishing the vision.
- Modeling, clarifying, and reinforcing the beliefs, values, and actions that will fit the transformation.
- Interacting with, encouraging, and supporting those members and groups that show understanding and concern.
- Instituting performance enhancement systems built on the required beliefs and values (e.g., customer service, total quality).
- Educating and training the future key players specifically, and the organization in general, in the insights, understanding, and skills needed to implement and achieve the vision and enact the values.
- Replacing people who do not have the skills, beliefs, insights, experience, and values required by the change with individuals from inside and outside the organization who are more suited to the change.
- Acquiring the physical resources such as money and materials that will be required.
- Restructuring and reorganizing those parts and systems of the organization that need to be realigned to the future state.

OR-3, Perceptive but Divided and Ambivalent/S3, Enlisting Strategy

"Facilitate commitment and participate in decisions and implementation." The leadership needs to engage in moderate to high amounts of inspiring actions and below-average amounts of structuring actions. Essential actions will include:

- Expressing confidence and placing trust in the skills, insights, experience, and values of the organization and its overall capability to cope effectively with the change.
- Involving individuals and groups in the creation and communication of a clear vision and shared beliefs and values and the benefits they will offer the organization.
- Repeated and enthusiastic processing of the vision, the beliefs, and the value set with individuals and groups, clarifying and reinforcing the benefits of the transformation and dealing with uncertainties and doubt.
- Interacting with individuals and groups to facilitate self-management and joint restructuring of elements such as roles, objectives, structures, and systems that will effectively implement the transformation, accomplish the vision, and enact the values.
- Providing assistance in allocating and utilizing the resources needed by individuals and specific groups to implement the actions that are required.

OR-4, Versatile, Integrated, and Committed/S4, Endorsing Strategy

"Sponsor the transformation and monitor progress." The leadership needs to engage in below-average amounts of both structuring and inspiring actions. Essential actions will include:

- Trusting and inviting individuals and groups to contribute significantly to the creation of the vision, beliefs, and values for the future.
- Monitoring the decisions and plans for the design and implementation of the strategies, structures, and systems required.
- Being available for advice, opinion, support, and sanction.
- Linking with the external environment and stakeholders to facilitate the achievement of the transformation.

POWER BASES FOR TRANSFORMATIONAL LEADERSHIP

In chapter 9, we discussed the importance of power and the integral relationship between leadership and power. Where leadership is defined as an attempt to influence the activities of others, individually and in groups, power may be defined as the leader's influence potential. Leaders must thus not only assess their leader behavior, or style, to understand and improve their influence with or over the members of their organization, but they must also assess their possession and use of power, especially in transformational leadership. The task of bringing about discontinuous change and getting organizational members to enact a new set of values in their work actions and organizational roles demands, above all, the skillful use of leadership and power.

In recent years, many academics, writers, and practicing managers have emphasized both the reality of power in organizational life and the fundamental need for power in leadership and change management.[10] Nevertheless, the concept of power has a negative connotation for some leaders, probably because of an unwarranted narrow association of the term with images of coercion and suppression. Coercive power is only one of several kinds of power that may be used by a leader in bringing about organizational transformation (see chapter 9).

The appropriate power bases for specific organizational readiness levels and leadership strategies are shown in Table 19-2. Notice that in transformational leadership situations, all four of the transformational leadership strategies need a foundation of legitimate, expert, and connection power. These power bases may be seen as the general power bases that underpin the effectiveness of all leadership strategies throughout, and at any stage of, a transformation.

Legitimate power is probably the most critical. If the leaders who are initiating and attempting the transformation are not seen as legitimate, as not

Table 19-2 Power Bases for Organizational Readiness Levels and Transformational Leadership Strategies

OR-4	OR-3	OR-2	OR-1
Versatile Integrated Committed	Perceptive But Divided and Ambivalent	Inept But Cooperative and Concerned	Fixated Fragmented Resistant
S4	**S3**	**S2**	**S1**
Endorsing Strategy Information Power	Enlisting Strategy Reward and Referent Power	Enabling Strategy Referent and Reward Power	Enforcing Strategy Coercive Power

Legitimate
+
Expert
+
Connection
Power

having the right to lead the transformation, their efforts will come to nothing. The condition that most often precipitates the need for a transformation is a crisis of poor organizational performance, and the current leadership is inevitably associated with the development of the crisis. Their consequent loss of legitimate power is the main reason why, in most transformations, the leaders who are charged to bring it about are newly recruited from outside the organization or the existing power network of the institution.

Expert power provides the leadership with credibility in terms of being perceived as having relevant knowledge and experience and knowing what needs to be done and how to do it—throughout the entire process.

Connection power provides the leadership with a network of additional reserves, or sources, of power on which to draw if required. Connection power can augment and strengthen any or all of the other power bases and is often the reason why outside consultants are called in to assist with the transformational process.

With the general power bases in place, it is appropriate now to look at the specific power bases that individually, or in combinations, serve to facilitate the implementation of a specific leadership strategy for a given organizational readiness level.

OR-1, Fixated, Fragmented, and Resistant/S1, Enforcing Strategy: Coercive Power

Given the characteristic behavior patterns associated with OR-1, the leadership, through structuring actions, will need to institute high amounts of radical physical and perceptual change in a relatively short period of time to enforce the required new ways of perceiving, thinking, and acting. To achieve these changes in the face of apathy, fragmented organizational functioning, and resistance, the leader needs coercive power as the base from which to execute the enforcing strategies.

OR-2, Inept but Cooperative and Concerned/S2, Enabling Strategies: Referent and Reward Power

The unfreezing achieved through the proper use of the enforcing strategies sets the scene for the enabling strategies. The OR-2 characteristics of ineptness coupled with cooperative organizational functioning and a concern for the viability of the organization call for the strong emphasis on high amounts of both structuring and inspiring actions of the enabling strategy.

This strategy, especially the communication of the vision, beliefs, and values for the future, is greatly enhanced by a referent power base. Referent power, otherwise known as *charisma*, is the critical power base for high amounts of inspiring actions. The leadership will also need reward power with which to encourage and reinforce the demonstrated new ways of perceiving and thinking and the new behavior patterns that will develop as a result of the enabling programs. Because the willingness element at OR-2 is characterized by anxiousness and receptiveness, the high amounts of structuring actions can be enhanced by reward power rather than coercive power.

OR-3, Perceptive but Divided and Ambivalent/S3, Enlisting Strategy: Reward and Referent Power

At OR-3, the organization and key staff are characterized by perceptiveness, but they also exhibit divided organizational functioning and ambivalence toward the transformation. The need for the change is accepted, but there is doubt or skepticism about the viability and benefits of the transformation. The enlisting strategy utilizes the learning ability of the organization to facilitate commitment and to develop a participatory implementation of the vision for the future. These strategies create opportunities to overcome the ambivalence and skepticism through high amounts of inspiring actions. The inspiring actions now consist of clarifying, advocating, and involving, rather than the compelling leadership communication of vision, beliefs, and values. Reward power enables the leadership to show and clarify individual and organizational benefits stemming from the transformation and to commit to providing those benefits. Reward power is the critical power base of the enlisting strategy. Referent power, in the form of identification with the leadership, remains a very important additional power base.

OR-4, Versatile, Integrated, and Committed/S4, Endorsing Strategy: Information Power

At OR-4, the organization and key staff are versatile and function as an integrated and committed system. The role of the leadership is really that of letting the organization get on with the transformation through the use of an endorsing strategy with emphasis on low amounts of both structuring and inspiring actions. Because the organization at OR-4 will be taking charge of the structuring and inspiring actions in a self-leading fashion, the leadership's role will shift to one of being available for advice, acting as a sounding board from time to time, and fulfilling a linking-pin function with the stakeholders. Endorsing strategies are enhanced by information power; that is, the leadership either is a source of or is an access channel to information that may be required during the planning and execution of the transformation.

SUMMARY

The Transformational Leadership strategies presented in Figure 19-2 can be used to implement the seven specific phases described in chapter 18. It is probable that the earlier phases will require more structuring strategies and the later phases will require more inspiring strategies. The appropriate strategy, however, will be determined by the organization's readiness to implement that phase. Each phase is, likely, in reality, a "situation."

ENDNOTES

1. Richard Beckhard, "The Executive Management of Transformational Change." Pages 89–90 in *Corporate Transformation*, ed. Ralph H. Kilman, Teresa Joyce Couin and Associates. (San Francisco: Jossey Bass, 1989).

2. See also chapter 17: First-Order and Second-Order Change, pages 387–389.

3. David A. Nadler, *Champions of Change* (San Francisco: Jossey Bass, 1998), p. 74.

4. Edwin C. Nevis, Joan Lancourt, and Helen G. Vassallo, *International Revolutions* (San Francisco: Jossey Bass, 1996), pp. 42–43.

5. Beckhard and Harris use the concept of readiness to describe a system's or subsystem's attitudes toward the intended change. These authors identify capability as a second, apparently independent, factor to consider. See Richard Beckhard and Rueben T. Harris, *Organizational Transitions: Managing Complex Change* (Reading, MA: Addison-Wesley, 1977), pp. 24–25. See also Anton J. Cozijnsen and William J. Vrakking, *Organisatie—diagnose en Organizatie verandering* (Alphen aan den Rijn: Samson Bedrijfs Informatie, 1992), pp. 76–82. These authors use innovation capacity as their central concept. It is clear, however, that the term *innovation* is used in the context of a large-scale organizational change rather than in the sense of introducing a single innovation. See also Vrakking and Cozijnsen, *Management—Technieken bij Effectief Innovering* (Deventer Kleuver Bedrijfswetenskappen, 1992).

6. Edgar H. Schein, *Organizational Culture and Leadership* (San Francisco: Jossey Bass, 1992), pp. 17–26. See also Edward J. Dwyer, "More Lessons in Leadership for Organizational Managers: From Tempest to Transformation," *Training and Development*, 48, (March 1994), p. 41.

7. Schein, *Organizational Culture and Leadership*.

8. Dave Ulrich, Mary Ann Von Glinow, and Todd Jick, "High Impact Learning: Building and Diffusing Learning Capability," *Organizational Dynamics*, Autumn 1993, pp. 53–54. See also Chris Argyris and D. Schon, *Organizational Learning: A Theory of Action* (Reading, MA: Addison-Wesley, 1978); Peter Senge, *The Fifth Discipline: The Art and Practice of the Learning Organization* (New York: Doubleday, 1991); Anne Perkins, "The Learning Mind-Set," *Harvard Business Review*, March–April 1994, pp. 11–12.

9. These characteristics are adopted from a checklist for assessing organizational culture or innovativeness by Vrakking and Cozijnsen. See Vrakking and Cozijnsen, *Management*, p. 73. See also Robert Clement, "Culture, Leadership, and Power: The Keys to Organizational Change," *American Demographics*, January 1994, pp. 42–45. For a similar list of characteristics of a learning organization culture, see also Schein, *Organizational Culture and Leadership*, pp. 364–366.

10. Jeffrey Pfeffer, *Power in Organizations* (Marshfield, MA: Pitman, 1981). See also Henry Mintzberg, *Power in and around Organizations* (Upper Saddle River, NJ: Prentice Hall, 1983); John P. Kotter, *Power and Influence—Beyond Formal Authority* (New York: The Free Press, 1985); Ronald G. Harrison and Douglas C. Pitt, "Organizational Development: A Missing Political Dimension." Pages 65–85 in *Power, Politics, and Organizations*, ed. Andrew Kakabadse and Christopher Parker (London: John Wiley and Sons, 1984).

Chapter 20

The Organizational Cone

It is often difficult to see how all the terms, concepts, and steps used in the management literature are interconnected and influence one another. To help his consulting clients see and understand these relationships more clearly when working with them to reach peak performance, Swedish management consultant, Bo Gyllenpalm, has developed the Organizational Cone model, which will be described and discussed in this chapter. We believe that the Organizational Cone is a significant new contribution to understanding organizational relationships. ✧

VISION

All organizations, whether in sports, business, or other settings, are started by someone with an idea. Many people get ideas to start something, but few of these ideas are turned into successful events. The idea often begins with a vague desire to do something that challenges us and others. To become a success, this idea has to grow in intensity to the point where it is not just a passing fancy, but something that we really want to do. Such an idea creates energy, which, if strong enough, will compel us to act. Once we have a sense of what we want the organization to look like, feel like, and be like, we have actualized the idea. The idea then becomes a unique image of the future, usually referred to as a *vision*.

To turn this vision into results, the leader needs assistance from others. The vision has to be articulated so that others see in it the possibility of realizing their own hopes and dreams. Images or inner pictures must be created in the followers' minds that are similar to

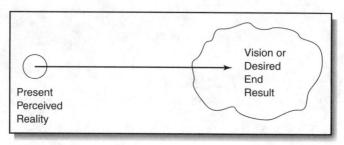

Figure 20-1
Creative Energy
Source: Copyright © 2000 by Bo Gyllenpalm. All rights reserved.

the images in the leader's, but at the same time a little different. The differences arise because of our perceptions. We all interpret what we hear and see in different ways. These interpretations are influenced by our experience, the situation we find ourselves in at the moment of communication, our dreams, our hopes, and our ambitions. Peter Senge wrote:

> A shared vision is not an idea. It may be inspired by an idea, but once it goes further—if it is compelling enough to acquire the support of more than one person—then it is no longer an abstraction. . . . It is, rather, a force in people's hearts, a force of impressive power.[1]

Creative energy, or as Senge calls it, *creative tension*[2], comes from seeing clearly where we want to be, our *vision*, and telling the truth about where we are, our *current reality*. Without vision, there is no creative tension. Creative tension cannot be generated from current reality alone. The natural energy for changing the reality comes from holding a picture of what might be that is more important to people than what is. This idea is shown in Figure 20-1.

These pictures in people's minds are not the same, but the more similarities there are, the more energy will be directed toward the organization's purpose and desired results.

Shared visions emerge from personal visions. If many people are having personal visions that partly overlap others' visions, a commonly shared vision will develop that attracts and excites them. They are then likely to put their energy to work to achieve their desired future results. Before most of us do anything, we ask ourselves, "What's in it for me?" If the answer convinces us that there is something in it for "me" that we really desire, we put our energy to work.

ENERGY

To move toward the desired future, we need energy. Without energy, there will be no movement. To create the energy needed, you can use two types of fuel: negative and positive. *Negative energy* is generated when someone feels threatened, afraid, or experiences some kind of pain, either physiological or psychological. The reaction generated is called *fight or flight*. This energy is generated as long as we feel the threat or pain. People will comply and do what is absolutely necessary, but the energy dissipates fast if the pain or threat is not kept at a high level. This type of "negative fuel" is often used in organizational change efforts. People are told that if they do not change or accept new ways of working, they will be punished or lose their jobs because the organization might lose its competitive advantage and go out of business.

Positive energy is generated when people can see something in their minds that really attracts and excites them. It may be the idea of saving for and buying a new car or the idea of attracting and building an interesting and rewarding relationship with a new partner or a team of people. This "positive fuel" is often longer lasting and will continue to be generated as long as the inner positive image is vividly experienced. This type of energy makes people commit to do whatever is necessary to make possible what they want.

Creation of a peak performing organization requires that each member see in the shared vision something that attracts their full interest and desire. The members' perceptions of the vision may not be exactly the same. If the visions are overlapping and interwoven, the "energy vectors" form a cone, as illustrated in Figure 20-2.

In most organizations, there are several cones guiding the energy. Each department or division should have its own clear purpose, vision, and direction. Even within a department or division, there might be teams with special purposes and visions. The more focused the energy for achieving the desired results, the more focused the cone will be. In Figure 20-3, the energy from the different departments on the left are not overlapping; thus, considerable energy is wasted. This situation is quite common in many large organizations where the energy vectors go in all different directions.

The best results are obtained when there is some overlap between the different departments/teams such as shown on the right in Figure 20-3.

To create energy, you should imagine yourself having reached the goal. The feelings of excitement and joy generate the energy necessary to go for the desired goals. The goals themselves are not the important thing. If the focus is clear and the vision is compelling, people in the organization will be committed, know what to do, and will make decisions on their own without interference from the managers. They can use their full creativity and energy to work toward the desired results. In today's swiftly changing world, it is

Figure 20-2
Shared Vision
Source: Copyright © 2000 by Bo Gyllenpalm. All rights reserved.

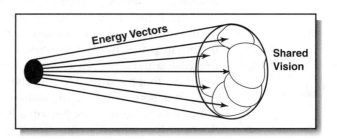

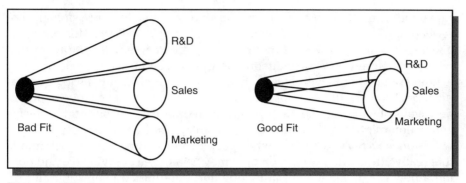

Figure 20-3
Examples of Good and Bad Fits

impossible to give instructions to control the behavior of all members in an organization. To be motivated, individuals need to use their talent and creativity and see the possibility of growing and developing. You cannot expect people to move toward the goal in a straight line. However, you should expect movement toward the shared goal or vision.

Vision Triggers

A vision trigger is a statement, a slogan, a picture, or something that creates strong feelings and a desire to do something or to be part of something. A good vision trigger creates the energy necessary for the process that will take us from where we are now to the more attractive future state we desire. Martin Luther King's "I have a dream" speech was a trigger that created significant action and reactions.

Another strong vision trigger was used by Jack Welch, CEO of GE, when he started the big change process at GE. "We should only be in businesses where GE can be number one or number two in the world market."

Focusing and Directing the Energy

Leaders must make sure the cone is focused and well defined. When necessary, the leader should change the direction of the energy and expand or contract the size of the cone, depending on the situation and the available resources. If someone starts acting outside the cone, the leader should find out why. It may be because the person has recognized that there is a change in the environment, such as new technology or new competition. In this case, the organization may have to redirect the energy to stay competitive. In Figure 20-4, a person, "X", is acting outside the cone and convinces the other members that a redirection is in the best interest of the organization.

When someone is acting outside the cone, it may also be because something has changed in the person's life. Something has happened that has influenced this person's value set, attitudes, or situation, and now the person

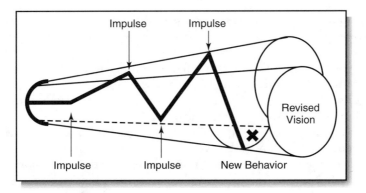

Figure 20-4
Revised Vision

Source: Copyright © 2000 by Bo Gyllenpalm. All rights reserved.

does not want to follow the established norms and does not have the same values, attitudes, or beliefs as the rest of the organization. This change usually is triggered by some personal change such as a divorce, a first child, or a new partner. Perhaps the person is asking, "What do I want out of life? What is important for me?" The person may find that the current situation—for example, working late hours and on weekends—is not satisfactory. The person's values or attitudes may have changed, or the person may no longer accept the current shared vision or ways to work. The person then has to decide whether it is worth continuing to be a member of this organization. If people cannot be persuaded to change their visions, the best thing for all parties concerned is that individuals find another group with whom they can share a vision.

If people start acting outside the cone, others who are loyal and share the vision will start asking themselves "Why is Tom breaking the rules?" They may say, "If Janet does it, I can do a few things outside the cone that interest me." Soon the cone opens up or disintegrates, the organization loses energy, and it will not be able to reach peak performance.

In many organizations where there is no clear vision to attract and guide people, the energy vectors are going in all directions. People may work very hard, but few of them will ever reach their desired results, peak perform, and make their personal or the organizational vision come true. Douglas McGregor wrote that the more aligned individual goals were with the organization, the better the results would be.[3]

Theoretically, the most efficient energy usage is not a cone, but a laser beam. However, a laser beam would mean that people are doing or envisioning exactly the same thing, and there would be no creativity and no development. The opening up of the cone represents a possible future situation, and there are many different possibilities and room for creative new ideas. Creation of a peak-performing organization requires that the energy be focused and directed toward the organization's primary goal or vision. This is especially important when there needs to be a change in the direction.

MISSION, PURPOSE, AND STAKEHOLDERS

When an organization is small or newly started, the focus is usually clear and commonly shared by the stakeholders—the key players needed to reach the organization's primary goal or persons who want to influence the organization. They are the owners, executives, employees, unions, customers, suppliers, community or environmental organizations, and so on. They are the people who want to be part of or influence the organizational vision, who clearly see that there is something in it for them if they join.

In order to help people see these benefits, someone or a group of people need to define the purpose or mission of the organization. A good mission statement explains the basic purpose of the operations. It illustrates how the organization differs from others in the same industry and identifies the scope of the operations in product, service, and market terms. The mission is the basis for setting the priorities, strategies, and plans. The mission is interpreted by the stakeholders and turned into personalized visions. The leaders should ask: What meaning does the organizational mission or purposes trigger in the stakeholders? What is in it for them? What is their interpretation of visions or images of the future? A very strong meaning for stakeholders must be created and communicated, a meaning that triggers energy and commitment to strive for peak performance. To get action and commitment, you need to create a strong emotional vision or desire to be part of the organization. Tom Peters, coauthor of one of the best-selling business books of all time, *In Search of Excellence*, describes this emotion as passion, one of the three essentials for organizational success: vision, passion, and action.[4]

STRATEGY, MINDSET, AND CULTURE

Visions and missions alone are not enough to create peak performance. Decisions need to be made about how to get there—in other words, strategic choices. Strategies, by themselves, do not create results either. Strategies are only decisions, and these decisions or choices have to be interpreted by the people who will implement them. The interpretation is influenced by our mindset or mental models, as Peter Senge calls them. Our mindset is the program in our mind that receives, interprets, and handles all the information we receive 24 hours a day. Our mindset determines our behavior, reactions, and emotions, everything we do both physically and emotionally. The mindset is not static but is evolving all the time.

The base of our mindset is our heredity combined with all our experiences in life, both real and imagined. A very important part is our self-esteem that influences our self-confidence, which, in turn, decides how we will act in different situations in life. Our environment or culture is the set of important understandings (often unstated) that members in a society or organization have in common. Culture guides individual and collective behavior. Culture consists of basic beliefs, values, and norms. Basic beliefs and values define what is right and what is wrong; what is important and what is unimportant; what is beautiful and what is not. Norms prescribe how to behave under different circumstances, how to treat different questions. Culture influences how decisions are made, the style of management, and relations and behavior patterns in the organization. Culture is created through different happenings, rituals and ceremonies, powerful persons, myths, and stories. It is also influenced by the use of material objects and the look and arrangement of physical settings.

The importance of basic values is to show what is rewarded and what is sanctioned in the organization. Values can arise from the organization or from individuals. Examples of business values are:

- Quality is important.
- Cost-effectiveness is important.
- Being the market leader is important.
- Customer service is important.

Examples of individuals' values are:

- The right to try and to fail is important.
- Safety is important.
- Teamwork is important.

A norm can be characterized as a "driving rule" for behavior. Norms are established by how the basic values are interpreted and followed. Relationships, the organizational structure, and the system can also establish norms. They can be negative or positive. Examples of negative norms are:

- Take no risks.
- Follow instructions without deviation to be safe.
- If you make a mistake, you will be punished.

Some examples of positive norms are:

- You should take risks.
- You are personally responsible.
- Change means personal development.

Negative norms can generate negative feelings and emotions that often block creativity and growth. Positive norms create positive feelings and emotions that make people dare to take on challenging tasks and stretch themselves. One of top management's most important strategic tasks, together with creating and communicating visions and the organization's purpose, is to establish and make sure the basic values of the organization are followed, and positive norms are created.

The existing organizational culture is the result of implemented decisions and events that have shaped the organization's way of thinking and operating.

Every new strategic decision is an attempt to influence the culture or the organization's way of performing to achieve the desired results. If the culture does not support the new strategies, most of the time the strategies will never be implemented. The organizational culture must be "in tune with" or attuned to the strategy.

Goals, Processes, and Team Spirit

Goals

Once the strategies have been developed, they need to be separated into operational goals. This is done on a team level. You will recall from chapter 14 our earlier definition of a team: two or more people interacting, in which the existence of all (the existence of the team as a team) is necessary for the needs of individual members to be satisfied. We frequently belong to more than one team. If a team does not have a clear, well-defined, measurable goal, it is difficult for team members to use their energy effectively. Imagine how long members of a soccer team would generate energy and direct it effectively if there were no clear rules and a clearly stated goal. To reach goals and peak perform, people also need a common understanding and acceptance of each other's strengths and weaknesses, shared values, and norms of behavior; this common understanding and acceptance is what we call *team spirit*.

Processes

To build a peak performing team, work rules and work processes have to be established, and the team must agree with them. How should decisions be made? Who should report to whom and how should information be communicated? How should disagreements or conflicts be handled? All sorts of routines and work processes must be discussed.

To reach goals and enable the team to peak perform, the team leader or leaders should help create what anthropologists call a "productive workscape." The culture and the set of interconnecting and mostly unwritten rules that organize behavior define a workscape.

> When you have the right people who share the same values, goal, and purpose and give them opportunities and incentives to excel in a supportive environment in which they feel free (empowered) to contribute as a team, then the workscape will be productive.[5]

Team Spirit

A productive workscape helps create a good team spirit and generates energy. Factors such as visionary thinking, collective self-confidence, high self-esteem, barrier-breaking goals, and a positive psyche affect a winning team spirit. Barrier-breaking goals are important for individuals as well as teams to reach peak performance.

As we discussed in chapters 2 and 3, goal setting is important for motivation. Willy Railo and his colleagues identified three types of goals: barrier-breaking goals, realistic goals, and safety goals.[6] Safety goals are what their name implies. You can feel safe if you reach these modest goals. You can put them out of your mind, because you do not have to think about what will happen if you do not achieve them. Realistic goals are based on an analysis of what is possible to achieve under normal circumstances. If you are satisfied with realistic goals, there is a chance that you are setting your goals too low. Goals can act as a brake. Thoughts and activities that can lead the team past the goal are blocked. We seem to have a built-in resistance (mental block) for going past a level that is not fully accepted by the mind. Barrier-breaking goals can act as icebreakers. Resistance is broken down, and the way to higher goals is opened.

Team spirit can be considered a subculture in an organization. There is not one organizational culture, just as there is not one team in an organization. There are as many cultures as there are teams. When aggregated, these subcultures constitute the organizational culture. This is why it is so difficult to change the organizational culture. To affect change, you have to influence each team, and you can do so only in day-to-day, multiway interactions among team members.

ROLES, TASKS, AND RELATIONS

The real action takes place when individuals perform different tasks, alone or as part of a team. A task may be the input for a new task to be performed by someone else on a team, on another team, or by someone or a team outside the organization. A task is never done for its own sake. All tasks should have some connection or relation to other tasks being performed in order to reach peak performance and be executed at the same high quality standard. An alternative for the term *tasks* would be to say the different *roles* people often take and the several jobs they perform in the organization. In most organizations, there are power and political plays occurring all the time, and, to be effective, you must be aware of and able to direct these processes.

THE ORGANIZATIONAL CONE MODEL

We have discussed in this chapter many terms and ideas found in the management literature. Most of these are not new; we have visited them previously in other chapters. The Organizational Cone model, Figure 20-5, was

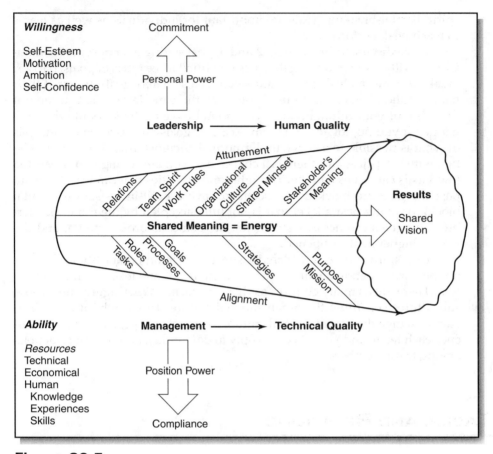

Willingness

Self-Esteem
Motivation
Ambition
Self-Confidence

Commitment

Personal Power

Leadership ⟶ Human Quality

Attunement

Relations Team Spirit Work Rules Organizational Culture Shared Mindset Stakeholder's Meaning

Shared Meaning = Energy

Tasks Roles Processes Goals Strategies Purpose Mission

Alignment

Results

Shared Vision

Ability

Resources
Technical
Economical
Human
  Knowledge
  Experiences
  Skills

Management ⟶ Technical Quality

Position Power

Compliance

Figure 20-5
The Organizational Cone Model

developed as a way of bringing these terms and ideas together to help organizations reach peak performance.

Management—Position Power—Compliance

The lower part of the cone deals with formulating the mission or defining the purpose of the organization or team, making strategic decisions, setting goals, and assigning tasks to be performed. These are usually called *management issues*. Management was defined in chapter 1 as the process of working with and through individuals and groups and other resources to accomplish organizational goals. Management has the responsibility to ensure that the organization has enough ability, technical facilities, and financial and human resources needed to produce peak performance. Management is a function built on access to position power, or the authority or right to make decisions about the use of resources, the right to use rewards, punishment, or different types of sanctions to get people to perform. Using position power can get people to comply but not always be committed, which is necessary for peak performance. Fostering commitment requires leadership.

Leadership—Personal Power—Commitment

The upper part of the cone deals with the willingness to achieve the common results; willingness includes the self-esteem, motivation, ambition, and self-confidence of the people to want to use their energy toward the shared goals. To influence these factors, we need leadership. As we also discussed in chapter 1, leadership can be defined as influencing the behavior of an individual or group. In chapter 8, we discussed readiness as the combination of willingness and ability to perform a specific task. To successfully influence people and to increase their readiness level, you need personal power, defined in chapter 9 as the extent to which people respect, feel good about, and are committed to their leader. We know that there are many persons inside and outside an organization who influence the behavior of others. Not all of them are managers. Leadership is necessary to get people committed to organizational goals.

To successfully create a peak performance, you need strong management, that is, knowledgeable, experienced, skillful managers who know the business inside and out and who are able and willing to make the right strategic decisions and make sure those decisions are implemented. You also need strong leadership: people who can influence the behaviors, norms, values, attitudes, and the willingness of the whole organization to peak perform. The best situation occurs when the same person fills the role of both these functions.

Alignment and Attunement in a Chaotic Environment

The bottom parts of the cone—the mission or purpose, strategies, goals, and tasks and roles—should be aligned and directed toward the vision or final performance. The more aligned they are with the vision and the organizational purpose, the higher the possibility of reaching peak performance. However, alignment is not enough to create peak performance. The relations, the team spirit, culture, shared mindset, and stakeholders have to be attuned to the tasks, goals, strategies, and mission or purpose. The more alignment and attunement there are, the more energy will be generated and focused toward achieving the desired shared results of creating a peak performance and peak experience for the stakeholders.

The organizational cone should not be regarded as a static, mechanistic "thing" but could better be thought of as a dynamic, living organism filled with different fields that influence its behavior. Quantum physics and Chaos Theory have given us new insights into organizational dynamics. For an organization to stay vital and competitive in the current chaotic world, it must be constantly willing to learn and develop new skills and behaviors. Field theory states that fields are unseen structures, occupying space and becoming known to us through their effects. However, as Margaret Wheatley said, space is never empty. If we do not fill the organizational space with coherent messages, people will bump up against contradicting fields that are created unintentionally. Only through open and honest conversations can these fields be aligned and attuned. She went on to say:

> This is no simple task. Anytime we see a system in apparent chaos, our training urges us to interfere, to stabilize and shore things up. However, if we trust the workings of chaos, we will see that the dominant shape of our organizations can be maintained if we retain clarity about the purpose and direction of the organization. If we succeed in maintaining focus, rather than hands-on control, we also create the flexibility and responsiveness that every organization craves. What leaders are called upon to do in a chaotic world is to shape their organizations through concepts, not through elaborate rules or structures . . . . Meaning or purpose serves as a point of reference. As long as we keep purpose in focus in both our organizational and private lives, we are able to wander through the realms of chaos, make decisions about what actions will be consistent with our purpose, and emerge with a discernible pattern or shape to our lives. [7]

Effective leaders create a compelling vision of what the final state can look like, feel like, and be like. A strong and compelling vision will create a shared meaning, generate energy, and guide the way—help the organization make the right choices toward the future desired state and help create peak performance. As Abraham Maslow suggested:

> Let us think of life as a process of choices, one after another. At each point are a progression choice and a regression choice. There may be movement toward defense, toward safety, toward being afraid; but over on the other side, there is the growth choice. To make the growth choice, instead of the fear choice, a dozen times a day is to move a dozen times a day toward self-actualization.[8]

If we can make the organization members overcome fear and pain by creating a shared meaning, they will make the growth choices more often. We make an enormous number of choices every day; most we are not aware of making. Many of these choices are preprogrammed and are made without reflection. These choices help or hinder the organization's actions to reach peak performance.

TIME FRAME AND ROOM FOR CREATIVITY

Let's start by looking at the narrow part of the cone, at the individual task level where the daily action take place. Here, the cone has to be rather narrow. The tasks, roles, and relations must be well defined, clear, understood, and supported by the individuals. If there is too much confusion here, the action will not produce good or desired results.

At the next level, the team level, the cone is a bit wider. Here we look at goals like annual budgets and results. To achieve these results, it is important that the processes are working, that we have enough resources, and that working rules are understood and clear to create a good team spirit. Here there is more freedom and the possibility to be creative.

At the next level, the cone is even wider. Here we are talking about implementing new strategies, a process involving changing the culture and forming a shared mindset, which usually takes several years. The possible strategies and actions are usually numerous and leave room for creativity. As you move along the timeline, the focus becomes more diffused, as you try to see further into the future.

QUALITY—CUSTOMER EXPECTATION AND PERCEPTION

To create a successful organization with the potential to peak perform, you need three fundamental components: an interesting product or service, an excellent delivery system, and customers. These concepts are illustrated in Figure 20-6.

The first thing to do is find customers. Customer focus is one of the areas necessary for today's fast-changing society. You have to know who your customers are and how to catch and focus their attention on what you are offering. You need an attractive product or service with the potential to evoke the customers' and stakeholders' interest. You also need an excellent delivery system that makes it easy and fun for the customers to buy. If the customers perceive it to be difficult or unpleasant to buy from an organization, chances to create peak performance are very small. The "moment of truth" is created when the three parts meet and start interacting. If a positive interaction is created, chances are high there will be peak performance.

Customers have some conscious or unconscious expectation of what they will experience when they deal with an organization. Their expectations are based on experience, what they have heard from others, and many other factors even as basic as how they feel that particular day. If their perception of the products and services they received is higher than their expectations, they will assess what they have received as high quality.

As shown in Figure 20-6, perception is influenced by two factors: the technical part, or *what* is delivered, and the human part, *how* it is delivered. The technical quality must fulfill basic customer-perceived needs. High quality is experienced when the human component is excellent, when customers feel well taken care of, and when they perceive it as easy to buy from an organization.

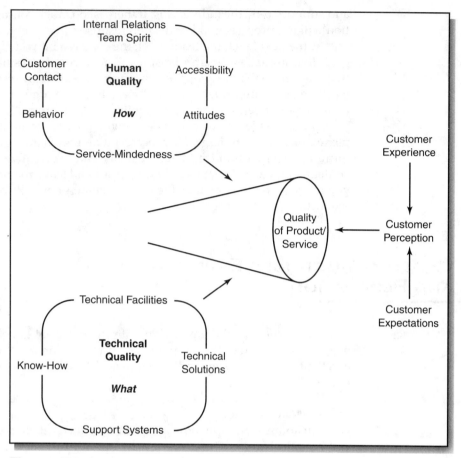

Figure 20-6
Delivering Quality Products and Services
Source: Copyright © 2000 by Bo Gyllenpalm. All rights reserved.

Customers are very sensitive to the atmosphere in an organization. If they feel tension among the staff, that the people serving them are not interested, or if it is difficult to get in contact with the organization, then the perceived quality is low, no matter how high the technical quality. There may be problems with the product or service. However, if the staff takes care of these problems without difficulty or irritation and rectifies problems, customers will probably perceive this as a high-quality organization. Technical aspects of a product or service can be replicated. The real competitive edge is created through the human delivery system and high team performance, which is much harder to replicate.

Let's return to the Organizational Cone model, Figure 20-5, to relate it to what we have been discussing. Technical quality is a management responsibility. Management has to make sure that there are enough technical facilities, technical solutions, support systems, and expertise to deliver technical quality. The human aspects—internal relations and team spirit, accessibility, attitudes, service-mindedness, behavior, and customer contact—require leadership and personal power. *Management* can generate some of these human qualities through position power, but they will get them without much commitment. If the people producing or delivering the products or services are not willing to use their knowledge, experience, and skills, there will be no peak performance. Human quality comes from leadership that is built on personal power. Leadership, the central focus of this book, is the key.

Thus, to create peak performance you need to have access to both position and personal power and be willing to use the power when needed to reach the goals. In many organizations, the power play is often misused and misunderstood. If you earn and have access to enough personal power, people around you will accept your use of position power even when they do not like it. It must not be used too much, as personal power erodes very quickly and has to be earned constantly.

SUMMARY

This chapter has presented several ideas of what can influence the creation of a peak performing organization. To create and direct its energy and make the organization perform at a peak, a manager/leader needs to do the following:

1. Define a purpose or mission, alone or with a team, and passionately communicate this purpose to create a shared vision that conveys meaning to the different stakeholders.
2. Make strategic choices or decisions to create the possibility of peak performance by making sure the required human, technical, and financial resources are available.
3. Set challenging and barrier-breaking performance goals, communicate clear expectations, and place rigid demands on oneself and on others.
4. Create and activate a productive, coherent, and shared mindset to stimulate, guide, and encourage organization members to stretch, expand, and go beyond their comfort zone.
5. Build strong performance ethics by creating disciplined work processes and rules and be willing to use both personal and position power when needed to make sure the work processes and rules are implemented and followed.
6. Define clear roles, delegate tasks, support, and care enough to help team members grow and develop through direct and honest feedback.

If all of the fields of energy in an organization can be brought to interact in a constructive way and are focused and directed toward a shared vision, fantastic results can be accomplished!

ENDNOTES

1. Peter M. Senge, *The Fifth Discipline* (New York: Bantam Doubleday Dell Publishing Group, 1990), p. 206.
2. Peter M. Senge, et al., *The Dance of Change* (New York: Doubleday Random House, Inc., 1999), p. 16.
3. Douglas McGregor, *The Human Side of Enterprise* (New York: McGraw-Hill, 1960).
4. Tom Peters and Nancy Austin, *A Passion for Excellence* (New York: Harper & Row, 1985).
5. Oscar G. Mink, Keith Q. Owen, and Barbara P. Mink, *Developing High-Performance People: The Art of Coaching* (Reading, MA: Addison-Wesley, 1993).
6. Willy Railo, Hakan Matson, and Jon-Ivar Johansen, *Forst till Framtiden,* 3rd printing (Oslo, Norway: Railo International A/S, 1992).
7. Margaret J. Wheatley, *Leadership and the New Science* (San Francisco: Berrett-Koehler Publishers, Inc., 1992), p. 56, 133, 136.
8. Abraham Maslow, *The Farther Reaches of Human Nature* (New York: Penguin Books, 1976), p. 44.

Chapter 21

Synthesizing Management Theory: Integrating Situational Leadership with the Classics

All the theories, concepts, and empirical research presented in earlier chapters have made a contribution to the field of management. They have relevance in diagnosing an environment, in making some predictions, and in planning for changes in behavior. These viewpoints have often appeared to be like threads, each thread unique unto itself. ✧

Our attempt in this book has been to weave these independent viewpoints into a holistic fabric to increase significantly the usefulness of each in diagnosis and prediction. In this last chapter, we will attempt to integrate these theories, using the Situational Leadership model together with other models, as synthesizing frameworks to portray their compatibility rather than their differences.

SITUATIONAL LEADERSHIP AND MASLOW'S AND HERZBERG'S THEORIES OF MOTIVATION

In developing the model of the motivating situation (chapter 2), we contended that motives directed toward goals result in behavior. One way of classifying high-strength motives is Maslow's Hierarchy of Needs (chapter 2).[1] Goals that tend to satisfy these needs can be described by Herzberg's hygiene factors and motivators (chapter 3).[2] Both of these frameworks can be integrated into Situational Leadership in terms of their relation to various readiness levels and the appropriate leadership styles that have a high probability of satisfying these needs or providing the corresponding goals, as illustrated in Figure 21-1.

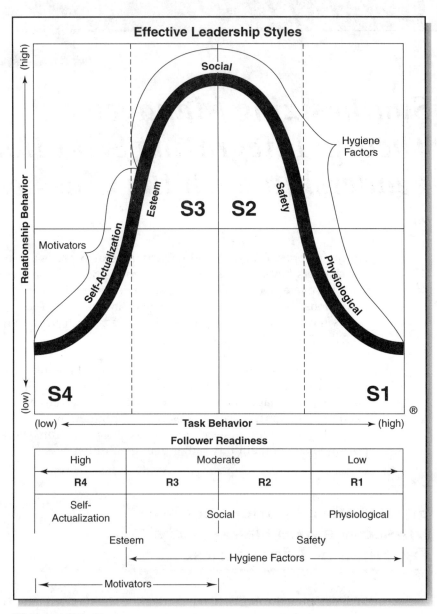

Figure 21-1
Relationship between Situational Leadership and Maslow's Hierarchy of Needs and Herzberg's Motivation-Hygiene Theory

It should be stressed that the relationship of Maslow's theory to the readiness levels in Situational Leadership is not necessarily a direct correlation; it is an integrative benchmark to use in attempting to make better decisions for managing human resources. As a result, styles suggested as appropriate for one need level might not be exclusively for that level; other styles may also satisfy those needs to some degree. This caution will hold true throughout our discussions in this chapter.

After examining Figure 21-1, one can begin to identify the styles that tend to be appropriate for working with people motivated by the various high-strength needs described by Maslow. At the same time, leadership styles S1, S2, and S3 tend to be consistent with satisfying hygiene factors, whereas styles S3 and S4 seem to facilitate the use of motivators.

SITUATIONAL LEADERSHIP AND McGREGOR'S, LIKERT'S, AND ARGYRIS'S THEORIES

McGregor's Theory X and Theory Y (chapter 3), Likert's Management Systems (chapter 4), and Argyris's Immaturity-Maturity Continuum[3] (chapter 3) blend easily into Situational Leadership, as illustrated in Figure 21-2.

In essence, Likert's System 1 describes behaviors that have often been associated with Theory X assumptions. According to these assumptions, most people prefer to be directed, are not interested in assuming responsibility, and want security above all. The assumptions and the corresponding System 1 behaviors seem to be consistent with the immature end of Argyris's continuum. System 4 illustrates behaviors that have often been associated with Theory Y assumptions. A Theory Y manager assumes that people are not lazy and unreliable by nature and thus can be self-directed and creative at work if properly motivated. These assumptions and the corresponding System 4 behaviors seem to correspond to the mature end of Argyris's continuum. System 1 is a task-oriented, highly structured authoritarian management style. System 4 is based on teamwork, mutual trust, and confidence. Systems 2 and 3 are intermediate stages between these two extremes.

In general, the tendency among people is to consider Theory X managers as engaging primarily with task behaviors in highly structured ways and Theory Y managers primarily as using relationship behaviors. This is not always accurate. Theory X and Theory Y are managers' *assumptions* about the nature of people and do not necessarily translate directly into leader *behaviors*. There are examples of both Theory X and Theory Y managers who use all four of the leadership styles.

In one example, Jim, a Theory X manager, calls a staff meeting and asks for participative (S3) solutions to a problem. In reality, Jim may keep everyone at the meeting until they agree with his own predetermined ideas for a

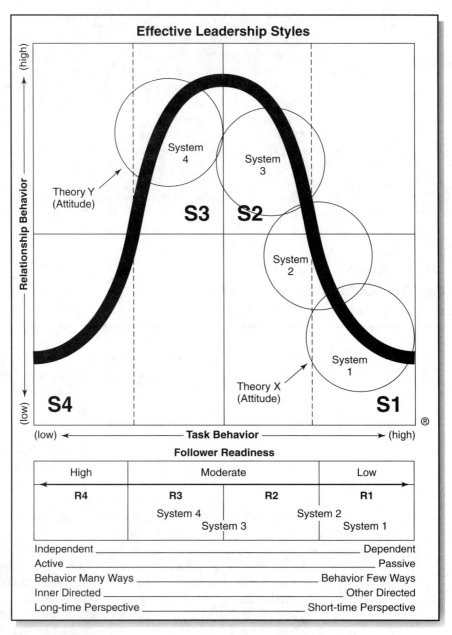

Figure 21-2
Relationship Between Situational Leadership and McGregor's Theory X
and Theory Y, Argyris's Maturity-Immaturity Continuum, and Likert's
Management Systems

solution. Jim's behavior may appear to be participative, but his assumptions are that only his own answer is acceptable.

In another instance, Sharon, a Theory X manager with a wide span of control, does not have sufficient time to closely supervise all of the people who report to her. Therefore, she uses close supervision (S1) with those people she perceives as major problems and, by necessity, leaves the others on their own (S4).

In a third example, Mike, a Theory Y manager, may demonstrate supportive (S2) behaviors in explaining his decisions to his employees. But his behavior may be manipulative rather than "selling" and may be more closely related to his personal objectives than to the goals of the organization or his people.

On the other hand, Mary, a Theory Y manager who has learned to diagnose employee levels of readiness, may be found to use all four leadership styles effectively. With people at below-average levels of readiness, she provides the necessary guidance and close supervision (S1). She gives direction to people whose abilities are improving (S2) and encouragement to those whose confidence is growing (S3). She delegates appropriately to motivated and competent employees who are capable of functioning on their own (S4).

SITUATIONAL LEADERSHIP AND ARGYRIS'S, SCHEIN'S, McCLELLAND'S, AND McGREGOR'S THEORIES

As illustrated in Figure 21-3, four theories can also be integrated into the Situational Leadership model: Argyris's concept of examining A behavior (structured) and B behavior (unstructured) patterns with McGregor's Theory X and Theory Y;[4] Schein's four assumptions about human nature and their implied managerial styles;[5] and McClelland's achievement motive.[6] Argyris contends that most often structured, controlling, A behavior patterns are associated with Theory X assumptions about human nature and that unstructured, nondirective, B behavior patterns are associated with Theory Y assumptions. But, as discussed in chapter 5, there is an important difference between attitude and behavior. The relationship between Theory X and Theory Y assumptions and A behavior and B behavior patterns is not necessarily a one-to-one relationship. Thus, as Argyris points out, you can find managers who have the predictable XA combination, but there are also some YA managers. Although both types of managers will tend to use styles S1 and S2, their assumptions or attitudes are not the same. The same holds true for YB and XB managers. Their behavior is similar (S3 and S4), but their assumptions are different.

In his book *Organizational Psychology,* Schein discussed four assumptions about people and their implied managerial styles: (1) rational-economic; (2) social; (3) self-actualizing; and (4) complex. These assumptions can help

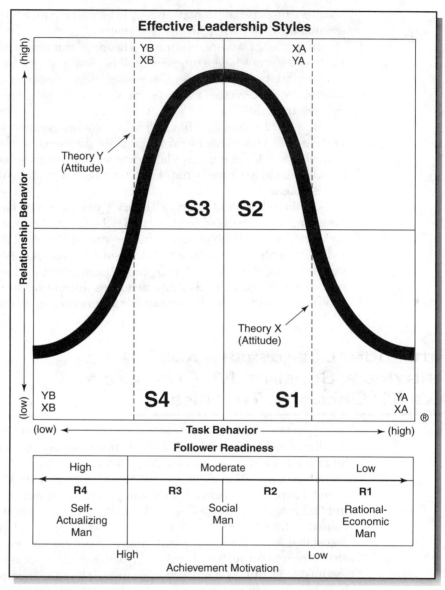

Figure 21-3
Relationship between Situational Leadership and Argyris's A and
B Behavior Patterns, McGregor's Theory X and Theory Y, Schein's
Four Assumptions About People and Their Implied Managerial
Strategies, and McClelland's Achievement Motive

us further integrate the work of Argyris, McClelland, and McGregor into Situational Leadership, as seen in Figure 21-3.

The assumptions underlying rational-economic people are very similar to those depicted by McGregor's Theory X. In essence, people are seen as primarily motivated by economic incentives: passive beings to be manipulated, motivated, and controlled by the organization, and irrational beings whose feelings must be neutralized and controlled. These assumptions imply a managerial strategy that places emphasis on efficient task performance and would be consistent with styles S1 and S2.

With social people come the assumptions that human beings are basically motivated by social needs; they seek meaning in the social relationships on the job and are more responsive to these than to the incentives and the controls of the organization. The managerial strategy implied for social people suggests that managers should not limit their attention to the task to be performed but should give more attention to the needs of the people. Managers should be concerned with the feelings of their people and, in doing so, must often act as the communication link between the employees and higher management. In this situation, the initiative for work begins to shift from leader to follower, with the leader tending to engage in behaviors related to styles S2 and S3.

Self-actualizing people are seen as seeking meaning and accomplishment in their work as their other needs become fairly well satisfied. As a result, these people tend to be primarily self-motivated, capable of being very self-directed, and willing to integrate their own goals with those of the organization. With self-actualizing people, managers need to worry less about being considerate to them and more about how to enrich their jobs and make them more challenging and meaningful. Managers attempt to determine what will challenge particular workers—managers become catalysts and facilitators rather than motivators and controllers. They delegate as much responsibility as they feel people can handle. Managers are now able to leave people alone to structure their own jobs and to provide their own socioemotional support through task accomplishment. This strategy is consistent with an S4 style appropriate for working with people of high levels of readiness (R4).

According to Schein, people are really more complex than rational-economic, social, or self-actualizing. In fact, people are highly viable, are capable of learning new motives, are motivated on the basis of many different kinds of needs, and can respond to numerous different leadership styles. Complex individuals tax the diagnostic skills of managers and, as Situational Leadership implies, effective managers must change their style appropriately to meet various contingencies.

According to McClelland, achievement-motivated people have certain characteristics in common. They like to set their own goals, especially moderately difficult, but potentially achievable ("stretching") goals. In addition, they seem to be more concerned with personal achievement than with the rewards of success. As a result, they like concrete task-relevant feedback. They want to know the score. As illustrated in Figure 21-3, low achievement motivation tends to be associated with readiness levels R1 and R2, and high achievement motivation tends to be associated with readiness levels R3 and R4.

Situational Leadership and the Leadership Grid

In chapter 5, we discussed Blake and McCanse's Leadership Grid and presented the differences between attitudinal and behavioral models. You may want to revisit those discussions where we pointed out that the Grid is an attitudinal model whereas Situational Leadership is a behavioral model.

We do not reject the Grid's 9-9 leadership style; but, we believe that all leaders should have a high concern for results and a high concern for people. Figure 21-4 shows how Situational Leadership carries out this concern through a variety of leadership styles. Because of a concern for people and results, a Situational Leader wants to use the most appropriate leader behavior for the level of follower readiness in any given situation. The two models are complementary.

Situational Leadership, the Leadership Grid, and Likert's Causal, Intervening, and Output Variables

If we add Likert's causal, intervening, and output variables to Figure 21-4, we get Figure 21-5. You may remember that Likert classified leadership strategies, skills, and styles as causal variables (see Figure 6-4). These are best associated with the Situational Leadership model. Intervening and output variables are best associated with the Grid. These relationships are not hard and fast, but they tend to illustrate similarities among Situational Leadership, the Grid, and Likert's variables.

Situational Leadership and Power Bases

In chapter 9, we discussed seven power bases: coercive, connection, reward, legitimate, referent, information, and expert. As is illustrated in Figure 21-6 and supported by the work of Hersey, Blanchard, and Natemeyer, Situational Leadership can provide the basis for understanding the potential impact of each power base.[7] In fact, in chapter 9 it was argued that the readiness of the follower not only dictates which style of leadership will have the highest

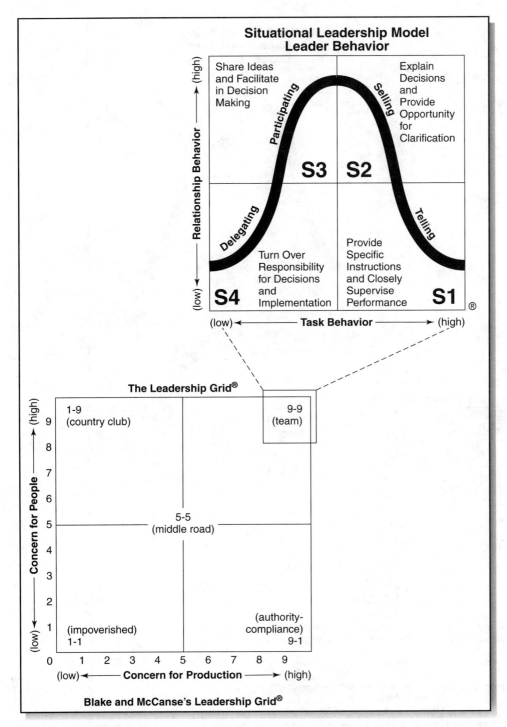

Figure 21-4
Relationship of Situational Leadership to the Leadership Grid

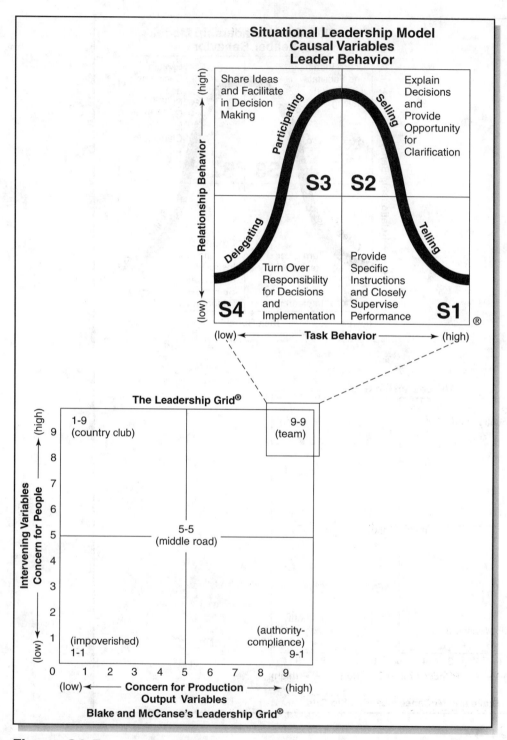

Figure 21-5
Relationship of Situational Leadership, the Managerial Grid, and Likert's Causal, Intervening, and Output Variables

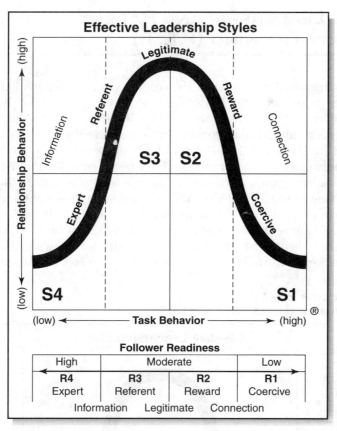

Figure 21-6
Relationship between Situational Leadership and
Power Bases

probability of success, but that the readiness of the follower also determines the power base that the leader should have in order to induce compliance or influence behavior.

As is suggested in Figure 21-6, a follower low in readiness (R1) generally needs strong directive behavior in order to become productive. Effective use of this S1 style often requires coercive power. As a follower begins to move from readiness level R1 to R2, directive behavior is still needed, and increases in supportive behavior are also important. The S1 and S2 leadership styles appropriate for these levels of readiness may become more effective if the leader has connection power and reward power. Legitimate power seems to be helpful to the S2 and S3 leadership styles that tend to influence moderate levels of readiness (R2 and R3). Referent power enhances the high supportive, but low directive, S3 style required to influence a moderate to high level of readiness. Information and expert power seem to be helpful in using the S3 and S4 styles that tend to motivate followers effectively at above-average readiness levels (R3 and R4).

Situational Leadership and Parent Effectiveness Training (P.E.T.)

As discussed in chapter 11, the work of Gordon on parent effectiveness training (translated into leader-follower terminology) and the related discussion of problems[8] integrate well into Situational Leadership (see Figure 21-7.) Gordon suggests that people's behavior can either be acceptable or unacceptable to leaders. If the behavior of the follower is acceptable to the leader, the leader can use an S3 or S4 style. If the behavior of the follower is unacceptable to the leader, an S1 or S2 leadership style is appropriate. To differentiate further among S1 and S2, and S3 and S4 styles, a leader must be able to determine "who owns the problem." As Figure 21-7 illustrates, if the behavior of the follower is acceptable and not a problem to either the leader or the follower (no problem exists), then an S4 style is appropriate. If that same acceptable behavior is a problem to the follower—that is, the follower lacks understanding or motiva-

Figure 21-7
Situational Leadership and P.E.T.

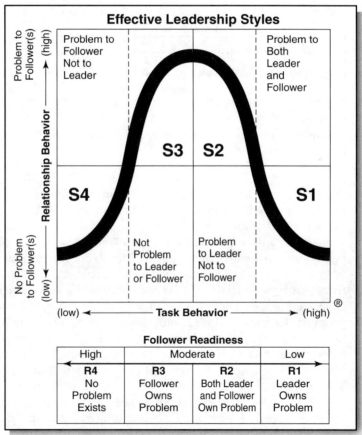

tion to continue the acceptable behavior for long periods of time—but not to the leader (the follower owns the problem), the appropriate leadership style to be used with that follower is S3. If a follower's behavior is unacceptable (and a problem) to both follower and leader, then an S2 style should be used. And, finally, when the follower's behavior is unacceptable and a problem to the leader, but not a problem to the follower (the leader owns the problem), an S1 leadership has the highest probability of changing that behavior.

SITUATIONAL LEADERSHIP AND CHANGE

Whenever you talk about initiating change (chapter 17), a first step is to determine the readiness level of the people with whom you are working. If they are low in readiness—dependent and unwilling to take responsibility for the change—they will tend to require more unfreezing (Lewin)[9] than if you are working with people who are moderate or high in their readiness levels. As illustrated in Figure 21-8, leadership styles S1 and S2 tend to play a major role

Figure 21-8
Relationship between Situational Leadership and the Process of Change

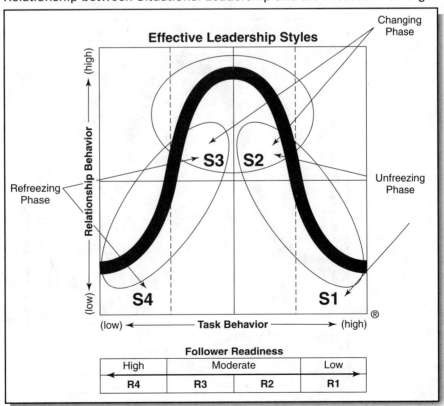

in terms of unfreezing; the emphasis in S2 and S3 styles is on the change process; and S3 and S4 stress the refreezing process.

One of the techniques used to increase readiness is behavior modification[10] (chapter 10), as illustrated in Figure 21-9. When working with people at low readiness levels, leaders at first tend to cut back on structure, giving individuals an opportunity to take some responsibility. When leaders get the smallest approximation of higher levels of readiness, they must immediately increase their socioemotional support as positive reinforcement. This stairlike process (cut back on structure and then increase socioemotional support) continues until the change or changes start to become a habit as the people develop. At that point, leaders tend also to cut back on reinforcement as they move toward S4 and a low relationship–low task style. If done earlier, this cutback on socioemotional support would appear as punishment to people at low or moderate levels of readiness. But to people of high readiness, the fact that their leader tends to leave them alone is positive reinforcement, not only in terms of the task, but also in terms of socioemotional support.

As illustrated in Figure 21-10, S1 and S2 styles seem to be consistent with the behaviors associated with a directive change cycle; S3 and S4 are more representative of a participative change cycle.[11] In a participative change cycle,

Figure 21-9
Situational Leadership and Behavior Modification

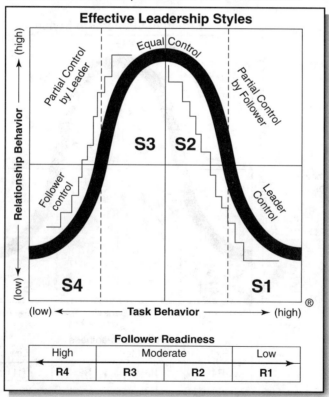

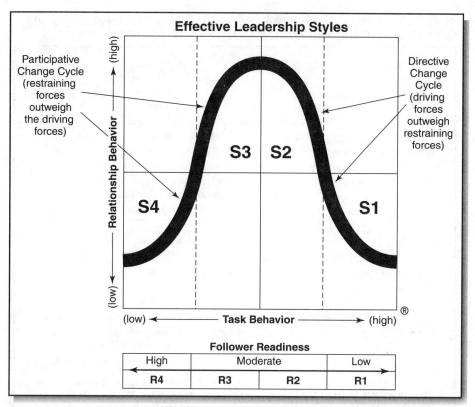

Effective Leadership Styles

Participative
Change Cycle
(restraining
forces
outweigh
the driving
forces)

Directive
Change
Cycle
(driving
forces
outweigh
restraining
forces)

Relationship Behavior (high) (low)

S3   S2

S4   S1

(low) ← Task Behavior → (high) ®

Follower Readiness

High	Moderate		Low
R4	R3	R2	R1

Figure 21-10
Relationship between Situational Leadership, Change Cycles, and Force
Field Analysis

the change begins at the knowledge level and eventually moves to the organizational level; the directive change cycle starts with changes in the organization and gradually moves toward changes in knowledge and attitudes.

As also shown in Figure 21-10, S1 and S2 styles tend to be appropriate for building on strong driving forces; S3 and S4 styles seem appropriate for attempting to overcome restraining forces (chapter 17).[12] In increasing the driving forces, the emphasis seems to be on short-term output; when attempting to eliminate restraining forces, the concern is more with building intervening variables and concentrating on long-term goals. It should be emphasized that these are only tendencies and benchmarks, and under certain conditions other styles might be appropriate.

SUMMARY

Table 21-1 integrates the summary material presented in this chapter. The table indicates how many of the theories discussed throughout this book are related to the various readiness levels and their corresponding appropriate leadership style.

Table 21-1 Relationship Between Leadership Styles, Readiness Levels, and Other Organizational Behavior Theories, Concepts, and Research

READINESS OF FOLLOWERS (THEREFORE HIGH PROBABILITY)	STYLE OF LEADER
(R1) LOW READINESS "UNABLE AND INSECURE OR UNWILLING . . . "	**(S1) HT/LR TELLING** "PROVIDE SPECIFIC INSTRUCTIONS AND CLOSELY SUPERVISE . . . "
Physiological-safety hygiene factors Rational-economic man Low achievement motivation Leader "owns the problem"	Theory X (attitude) XA/YA System 1/System 2 Coercive and connection power Unfreezing, changing (coercion) Directive change cycle
(R2) LOW TO MODERATE READINESS "UNABLE BUT CONFIDENT OR WILLING . . . "	**(S2) HT/HR SELLING** "EXPLAIN YOUR DECISION AND PROVIDE OPPORTUNITY FOR CLARIFICATION . . . "
Safety-social hygiene factor Rational-economic man/social man Low achievement motivation Both leader and follower "own the problem"	Theory X (attitude) XA/YA System 2/System 3 Connection, reward, and legitimate power Equal control contracting Unfreezing, changing (identification) Directive or participative change cycles
(R3) MODERATE TO HIGH READINESS "ABLE BUT INSECURE OR UNWILLING . . . "	**(S3) HR/LT PARTICIPATING** "SHARE IDEAS AND FACILITATE DECISION MAKING . . . "
Social-esteem hygiene factors and motivators Social or self-actualizing man High achievement motivation Follower "owns the problem"	Theory Y (attitude) YB/XB System 3/System 4 Legitimate, referent, information power Changing-refreezing (internalization) Participative or directive change cycles
(R4) HIGH READINESS "ABLE AND CONFIDENT OR WILLING . . ."	**(S4) LR/LT DELEGATING** "TURN OVER RESPONSIBILITY FOR DECISIONS AND IMPLEMENTATION . . . "
Esteem—self-actualization motivators Self-actualizing person High achievement motivation No problem exists	Theory Y (attitude) YB/XB System 4 Information, expert power Refreezing Participative change cycle

REFLECTIONS AND CONCLUSIONS

Much is still unknown about human behavior. Unanswered questions remain, and further research is necessary. Knowledge about motivation, leader behavior, and change will continue to be of great concern to practitioners of management for several reasons: It can help improve the effective leadership of human resources; it can help in preventing resistance to change, restriction to output, and personnel disputes; and often it can lead to a more productive organization.

Our intention has been to provide a conceptual framework that may be useful to you in applying the conclusions of the behavior sciences. The value that a framework of this kind has is not in changing one's knowledge, but in changing one's behavior in working with people.

We have discussed three basic competencies in influencing: *diagnosing*—being able to understand and interpret the situation you are attempting to influence; *adapting*—being able to adapt your behavior and the resources you control to the contingencies of the situation; and *communicating*—being able to put the message in such a way that people can easily understand and accept it. Each of these competencies is different and requires a different developmental approach. For example, diagnosing is cognitive or of the mind in nature and requires thinking skills; adapting is behavioral in nature and requires behavioral practice; and communicating is process-oriented and requires learning and interrelating the key steps in the process. Because these three competencies require different knowledge and skills, how do we continue the process that we started with this book?

The key to starting the process of changing behavior is sharing what you have learned with other people in your own organization. Two things occur when people who work together all have a common language. First, they are able to give each other feedback and help in a very rational, unemotional way that affects behavior. For example, we once worked with an autocratic manager, "Bill," who was noted for his Theory X memos, such as, "It has come to my attention . . . and, therefore, as of Monday all personnel will be required to . . ." Shortly after this manager and his staff from two levels below him were trained in Situational Leadership, the manager sent out one of his famous Theory X memos. Several days later, he told us that he had received several written (unsigned) comments on the memo. The comments included such remarks as "A little Theory X today, don't you think?" "Do you have anything else in your repertoire besides S1 style?" "Are we really that unwilling?" This feedback had a real impact on the manager as he reexamined his memo and his approach. It was difficult for him to rationalize away the feedback, because like R. D. Laing's *Knots*, "he knew that they knew that he knew the theory" and "they knew that he knew that they knew the theory."[13] As some of the managers suggested, this was one of the first times he had really "heard" feedback. As a result of this incident and use of the language in meetings, everyone started helping each other (not just the manager) make changes in their behavior so they could become a more effective working team. This is the essence of contemporary leadership

Second, when followers start to realize that if their manager is using Situational Leadership, it is not the manager, but their behavior, that determines the leadership style to be used with them. For example, if everyone knows Situational Leadership in a family, the children (especially teenagers) realize how they can keep their parents off their backs. All they have to do is behave in solid, responsible ways, which everyone has agreed are appropriate, and their parents will be supportive (S3) or leave them alone (S4). But if they want to get hassled and closely supervised by their parents, all they have to do is misbehave and be irresponsible. Thus, theory is a vehicle to help people understand and share expectations in their environment so that they can gradually learn to supervise their own behavior and become responsible, self-motivated individuals. An observation on leadership by the Chinese philosopher Lao-tsu sums it up well: "Of the best leaders, when their task is accomplished, the people will remark, 'We have done it ourselves.'"[14]

We have provided many examples and illustrations throughout this book showing how the behavioral sciences can make a positive difference in the performance of both individuals and organizations. But perhaps our primary objective in writing this book is to make a contribution to world peace. We believe that significant contributions to human well-being will not come primarily through economic, social, military, political, or technological decisions. If we are going to achieve our long-sought goal of world peace, it must come through more effective leading of our human resources—toward helping people become more productive and to have a greater share of the benefits that human productivity can achieve. Our outlook is a world outlook for practical, applied behavioral science—an outlook that sees all peoples sharing in the benefits that informed leadership can bring, a world of people living and working in a way that contributes to their personal well-being, a world of peace.

We invite you to join us in working toward this goal.

ENDNOTES

1. Abraham Maslow, *Motivation and Personality* (New York: Harper & Row, 1954).
2. Frederick Herzberg, *Work and the Nature of Man* (New York: World Publishing, 1966).
3. Douglas McGregor, *The Human Side of Enterprise* (New York: McGraw-Hill, 1960); Rensis Likert, *The Human Organization* (New York: McGraw-Hill, 1967); Chris Argyris, *Personality and Organization* (New York: Harper & Row, 1957). See also Chris Argyris, Robert Putnam, and Diana M. Smith, *Action Science* (San Francisco: Jossey-Bass, 1985).
4. Chris Argyris, *Management and Organizational Development: The Path from XA to YB* (New York: McGraw-Hill, 1971); see also Argyris

and Donald A. Schon, *Organizational Learning: A Theory of Action Perspective* (Reading, MA: Addison-Wesley, 1978); Argyris, *Reasoning, Learning, and Action: Individual and Organization* (San Francisco: Jossey-Bass, 1982).
5. Edgar H. Schein, *Organizational Psychology*, 2nd ed. (Upper Saddle River, NJ: Prentice Hall, 1970), pp. 50–72; see also Schein, *Organizational Culture and Leadership* (San Francisco: Jossey-Bass, 1985); Schein, *Career Dynamics: Matching Individual and Organizational Needs* (Reading, MA: Addison-Wesley, 1978).
6. David C. McClelland, John W. Atkinson, R. A. Clark, and E. L. Lowell, *The Achievement Motive* (New York: Appleton-Century-Crofts,

1953); and McClelland, Atkinson, Clark, and Lowell, *The Achieving Society* (Princeton, NJ: D. Van Nostrand, 1961). See also McClelland, *Motivation and Society* (San Francisco: Jossey-Bass, 1982); McClelland, *Motives, Personality, and Society: Selected Papers* (New York: Praeger, 1984).

7. Paul Hersey, Kenneth H. Blanchard, and Walter E. Natemeyer, "Situational Leadership, Perception, and the Impact of Power," *Group and Organizational Studies,* 4, no. 4 (December 1979), pp. 418–428.

8. Thomas Gordon, *P.E.T. (Parent Effectiveness Training)* (New York: Peter H. Wyden, 1970). See also Gordon, *T.E.T. (Teacher Effectiveness Training)* (New York: Peter H. Wyden, 1974).

9. Kurt Lewin, "Frontiers in Group Dynamics: Concept Methods, and Reality in Social Science; Social Equilibria and Social Change," *Human Relations,* 1, no. 1 (June 1947), pp. 5–41.

10. B. F. Skinner, *Science and Human Behavior* (New York: Macmillan, 1953).

11. Paul Hersey and Kenneth H. Blanchard, "Change and the Use of Power," *Training and Development Journal,* January 1972.

12. Lewin, "Frontiers in Group Dynamics."

13. R. D. Laing, *Knots* (New York: Pantheon Books, 1970).

14. Lao-tsu, *The Way of the Ways: Lao-tsu,* translated and with a commentary by Herrymon Maurer (New York: Schocken Books, 1985), p. 52.

Appendix

Life Cycle Theory of Leadership Revisited[1]

Paul Hersey
Founder, Center for Leadership Studies
Author, *The Situational Leader*

Ken Blanchard
Cofounder, Blanchard Training
and Development, Inc.
Coauthor, *The One Minute Manager*

EDITOR'S NOTE

My original thought was to ask Paul and Ken to comment separately about their 1969 article because, in the last decade, they had taken somewhat different stands on Situational Leadership. I was delighted, though, when they decided to work on a response together that captured their united front as well as their separate voices.

Some Personal Reflections of Paul and Ken

After writing an earlier edition of *Management of Organizational Behavior,* we went our separate ways and crystallized our different approaches to the field of applied behavioral sciences. We are excited about once again working together to produce this latest edition of *Management of Organizational Behavior.* We considered several ways

470

of sharing the commonalities and differences in our views and have decided, with the permission of *Training and Development Magazine,* to share these thoughts adapted from our recent article, "Life Cycle Theory of Leadership Revisited," published in their special 50th Anniversary Issue. We think the informal point and counterpoint style of the following paragraphs captures our united front as well as our separate voices.

PERSONAL REFLECTIONS/PAUL HERSEY

The world refers to our behavioral model of how best to influence and lead people as Situational Leadership, and it has truly taken on a life of its own. The different ways people describe their experience and sense of the model continue to instill feelings of pride in us—"A touchstone, a cornerstone, a map, a compass, a sextant and a powerful lens." Ken and I often hear from clients that their introduction to Situational Leadership has been their most important and valuable training experience ever.

It is also a pleasure to pick up a pen/computer once again with Ken Blanchard. Collaborative efforts with Ken have been the most richly rewarding of my professional life.

PERSONAL REFLECTIONS/ KEN BLANCHARD

When I was asked to write a commentary to accompany the reprinting of our 1969 article "Life Cycle Theory of Leadership," I had two reactions. First of all, I was thrilled that Paul's and my "Life Cycle Theory of Leadership" article would be reprinted in the 50th Anniversary Issue of *Training and Development.* That acknowledges the fact that Situational Leadership is still alive and well today and more widely used around the world than ever before, even though the first thinking on the concept was done almost 30 years ago.

Secondly, I began to reminisce. The article was written when Paul and I were both at Ohio University. I had come to Athens in the fall of 1966 as administrative assistant to the dean of the College of Business. Paul had arrived shortly before to serve as chairman of the Management Department. Dean Harry Everts put me in the Management Department and asked that I teach a course. He wanted all his deans to teach. Initially, Paul was not excited about having me dropped into his department, but that fall he assigned me a course and I began teaching.

During that fall, I heard from students and faculty what a fabulous organizational behavior course Paul Hersey taught. When I saw Paul in the hallway one day that December, I asked him if I could sit in on his class the next semester. He was quick to reply, "No one audits my course. If you want to take it for credit, you're welcome." Because I already had my doctorate, I was surprised by his initial reaction. However, my wife, Margie, helped me get my ego out of the way, and I signed up for the course. It turned out to be as fabulous a course as I had heard. Paul was a great teacher.

In June 1967, after the course ended, Paul came to me and asked if I would be interested in writing an organizational behavior book with him. Paul had been teaching in the management field for 10 years but had shied away from much formal writing. I had always been told by my faculty members in graduate school that my writing wasn't academic enough. I later learned that meant you could understand it, but at the time I had never thought about writing a book. I didn't think I had the writing skills. It was with that unlikely alliance that Paul and I began to write our textbook, *Management of Organizational Behavior: Utilizing Human Resources.*[2] We turned out to be quite a writing team, as that text, published by Prentice Hall in the fall of 1969, has been a best-seller in the field for all these years.

Paul's course ended with a presentation of William Reddin's 3-D model.[3] His work was an outgrowth of the Managerial Grid[4] but suggested there was no best leadership style. Though Reddin made a significant contribution to the field, Paul and I felt his approach still had some major limitations. That's when we began to develop the "Life Cycle Theory of Leadership" for *Training and Development* and our text.

PERSONAL REFLECTIONS/PAUL HERSEY

Sometimes you just have to accept the blessings of some seemingly unrelated events. Such is the case with Situational Leadership. As a young man working my way through college, I made myself several important promises. I made an early decision that I would teach, and the subject I would teach was about working with people. I was excited by the whole academic exercise but felt that if I was going to be truly effective as a teacher, I really needed to work in the real world before standing in front of the classroom. After college, I kept that commitment and filled several challenging positions. For over a decade, I put my education to the ultimate test—improving performance and impacting the ability of managers to improve the performance of others. When I had had a good dose of practical experience, I felt prepared to walk back into the classroom and talk with the leaders of tomorrow.

Ken has relayed the story of our initial meeting at Ohio University pretty much as I remember. In his usual modest way, he has left out a few important points. I was working on a book for Prentice Hall. In some ways, the phrase "wrestling with" might be a better phrase than "working on." I had the content for the book and knew the relevant research. What I needed was a partner who could get things down on paper and organize and think things through. Ken had those talents and more. His genuine interest in this field and in helping people made him the perfect partner. Look at the long list of Ken's collaborative efforts—Spencer Johnson, Norman Vincent Peale, Sheldon Bowles, William Oncken, Jr., and Don Shula.[5] I was impressed with that special talent on our very first project—and still am!

INITIAL CHANGES IN THE MODEL/ HERSEY AND BLANCHARD

In the 1972 edition of *Management of Organizational Behavior*, we not only began to use the term "Situational Leadership" rather than "Life Cycle Theory of Leadership" to describe our approach to leadership, but also made other important changes.

Leader Behavior Dimensions

With the development of Situational Leadership, we emphasized that the dimensions of leadership were "task behavior" and "relationship behavior." Earlier models such as Blake and Mouton's Managerial Grid[6] and Reddin's 3-D Management Style Theory[7] used attitudinal dimensions like "*Concern* for Production" and "*Concern* for People" and "Task *Orientation*" and "Relationship *Orientation*." With a behavioral emphasis, Paul and I argued that although there could be "best" attitudes for managers, there was no "best" leadership style. For example, every manager should be concerned about both production and people, but that attitude could be expressed in a variety of leadership styles depending on the situation.

Leadership Styles

In the "Life Cycle Theory of Leadership," we did not label the four leadership quadrants. With the development of Situational Leadership, we began to call quadrant 1 "Telling," quadrant 2 "Selling," quadrant 3 "Participating," and quadrant 4 "Delegating."

FURTHER EVOLUTION OF THE MODEL/HERSEY AND BLANCHARD

Situational Leadership has evolved and undergone a number of advancements in the last 3 decades. We continued to work closely together on the model until 1979, when Ken and his wife, Margie, founded Blanchard Training and Development, Inc. (BTD). Since then, our separate clients and colleagues have helped us to grow with the model, to relearn it, and to gain a new and deeper appreciation of the subtle dynamics of influence. Our own journeys have, at times, taken us down different paths, with diverse conclusions of what we see. In a way, it is not unlike raising a child. There is a uniqueness in the relationship the child has with each parent. One can argue over or celebrate the differences. We have chosen the latter. Respecting the other's opinion continues to provide volumes of common ground from which we continue to "grow" Situational Leadership and further its applications.

LEADERSHIP STYLE AND THE CHANGING ROLE OF THE MANAGER

When the "Life Cycle Theory of Leadership" article was published in 1969, the management hierarchy and the command and control approach to people management were alive and well. Even though managers and trainers got excited about Situational Leadership and the fact that there was "no best" leadership style, managers were still considered to be in charge. In fact, it was rare indeed to even involve the follower in discussions about their own readiness or development level. Thinking back to the terminology used then—superior/subordinate, department head/hired hand, supervisor/laborer/worker—such conversations would not have been very fruitful.

Today, managers speak of change as a constant process. Many managers can give a pretty detailed explanation of empowerment, total quality control, team development, and partnering for performance. In essence, a transformation has occurred since the original article. It is now accepted that *leadership is done with people, not to people.*

Although each of us uses different labels to conceptualize the leadership styles of Situational Leadership, we feel this is not a major difference in our approaches. The years have taught us that within the simple and useful model, artistry and sophisticated skills are needed in each of the four styles. No matter what the label—telling or directing, persuading or coaching, participating or supporting—it can limit the possibilities for any of the styles. To understand the choices available within each of the four quadrants, you need only to gather several leaders, provide them with a chart pad and marker, and then ask for various descriptors for each style. You'll see pages of leadership style choices.

The critical point here is that the leaders select the descriptor that best draws them into the appropriate style for the situation. For example, both coaching and persuading are types of style 2. Yet, when you think of someone coaching or persuading, distinctly different mental pictures are created. We need this type of variety to meet the moment-to-moment changes required of today's leaders.

In today's Situational Leadership application, there is a greater emphasis on the task or activity you are attempting to impact. The first step in using the model has always been to decide on the task. For a whole host of reasons, people tend to generalize or look at too large a piece. To effectively assess a person's needs, a leader may have to break a job into smaller elements. As a rule, if assessing a person's needs seems confusing, begin by breaking down the task.

Maturity Level

As times changed, so did our thinking about diagnosing a person's ability to perform a specific task, as well as the terminology used. (During the 1960s, the term *maturity* in reference to assessing people did not seem offensive; it does now.) It is in the area of assessing the needs to perform of the employee or follower—that we, the authors, have diverse conclusions of what we see.

First, the common ground. We would both state with conviction that Situational Leadership is not as much about leadership as it is about meeting follower needs. By getting people to focus on the follower, we can improve leadership skills more than by trying to teach a style. Leading without diagnosing is the same as a doctor prescribing without diagnosing—a clear case of malpractice.

In this case, the doctors have some disagreement. We draw different conclusions about the same studies and about the applicability of those conclusions. We frame our content from different life experiences and find support for our interpretations from family, friends, colleagues, and business clients around the world. We are both men of conviction, so we believe heart and soul in our own evolutions of the model. And such are the behavioral sciences—as long as we are dealing with understanding people, there will be considerable room for interpretation. We serve best by not becoming prisoners of our own doctrine or by not providing the appearance of unity for some commercial reason.

What follows is a brief presentation of where each of us is today in our thinking on development or readiness level. It's a long way from maturity being low, moderate, or high in the days of the Life Cycle Theory of Leadership. Keep in mind that you are about to read two broad overviews. Given the natural confines of an article, we can provide little more than a brief exposure to our current thinking. (For further elaboration, we invite you to call our respective organizations. You'll find our staffs eager to elaborate on key points of interest to you. We're both in Escondido, California.)

Development Level—Ken Blanchard

The work of BTD colleagues Drs. Don Carew and Eunice Parisi-Carew[8] with Group Development theory was the initial impetus to create Situational Leadership II[9]. In particular, the Carews cited the extensive research of Lacoursiere,[10] who found there is a sequence to the stages of development that groups and teams go through over time. The initial stage is *orientation* (stage 1), when group members first come together and are eager to participate but are unsure of how to work together. Next comes the seemingly inevitable occurrence of *dissatisfaction* (stage 2), as working together turns out to be more difficult than anticipated. If the group is able to work through this dissatisfaction, it moves into *resolution* (stage 3), where members learn how to work together. If interactions continue to improve, the group reaches the final stage of *production* (stage 4). The Carews were able to show that the leadership styles needed to move a group through these stages correspond to the flow of the four leadership styles of Situational Leadership II. Style 1 *Directing* is appropriate for *orientation* where goals have to be made clear and roles defined. Style 2 *Coaching* is necessary to move through the *dissatisfaction* stage because the group still needs direction but now also needs support, encouragement, and listening behaviors. Once a group gets to the *resolution* stage, the leader's role could change to style 3 *Supporting*, as a facilitator is needed. Now direction is provided by the group. Finally, in the *production* stage, an outside observer would not be able to determine the designated leader. Here, Style 4 *Delegating* is appropriate.

If groups go through these stages of development, the Carews argued, why would the development process for individuals be that different? In particular, they were concerned about the first two levels of maturity in the original model—(1) being "unwilling and unable" and (2) "unable but willing." If the old terms were used, they felt the first level of development/maturity should be willing but unable, to correspond with the initial orientation stage of group development. When I thought about it and talked with practicing managers, what the Carews said began to make sense. It became clear that most of us hire either winners—people who are experienced and already developed in a particular job and can operate effectively with an S3 or S4 style—or else potential winners who need to be trained. Potential winners are often low in ability (knowledge and skills) but are high on willingness because of their initial motivation and eagerness to learn this particular job and their confidence in their learning capacity.

The Carews felt the second level of development/maturity should be "unwilling and unable" to correspond with the dissatisfaction stage of group development. Again, consistent with the stages of group development, managers told us that when people take on a new task where they are inexperienced, after a while disillusionment often sets in because they need more time and energy to gain competence than they had anticipated.

The new thinking required reconstructing how we looked at people and how to represent their stages of development. We needed a way to depict individual growth that moved from an *enthusiastic beginner* to a *disillusioned learner*, on to a *capable but cautious performer*, and finally to a *self-directed achiever*. The result was a continuum from "developing" to "developed."

Readiness Levels—Paul Hersey

The term *maturity* became obsolete when the model evolved from a Life Cycle broad view of leadership into a Situational Leadership task-specific focus.[11] I must admit it took a couple of years to abandon trying to explain what we meant by the term *maturity*, but in the effort to explain it we came to a greater understanding of the follower. Perhaps the most profound learning for me was that managers willingly embrace complex learning if you provide a few solid touchstones. After creating some well-researched, sophisticated explanations such as Psychological Maturity and Job Maturity, we were humbled to find that time and time again managers would distill the elaborate explanations into the simple and timeless "Ready, Willing, and Able."

In the most general of terms, *readiness* is the amount of willingness and ability the follower demonstrates while performing a specific task. Previously understated was the degree to which willingness and ability interact to determine readiness. Discovering more about the interaction has provided significant refinements in our thinking.

The number-one error in diagnosing willingness is to view someone who is insecure or apprehensive as unmotivated. *Willingness* is a combination of the varying degrees of confidence, commitment, and motivation. Any one of these variables can be prepotent; that is, I may be completely committed to the job, quality, and the organization. I may be motivated with a strong desire to do well—and at the same time be insecure about my ability to do the job. Even though my commitment and motivation are strong, my insecurity will have to be addressed before I can move forward in my readiness. Someone or something will have to help me over this hurdle.

Ability is determined by the amount of knowledge, experience, and demonstrated skill the follower brings to the task. A diagnosis is based on actual display of ability. The warning here is not to select a leadership style based on beliefs of what the follower *should* know. A frequent error is to impact knowledge and hold the follower accountable for skills he or she has not had an opportunity to demonstrate.

Being task specific is critical to the success of correct diagnosis. This surpasses any implication that readiness is linear or accomplished in a highly predictive progression. For example, I would agree with Ken that most people enter a position or new task at readiness level two (not one). Realizing that improves their accuracy in diagnosing development and helps leaders be more responsive in dealing with performance regression. It also highlights that a leadership intervention can be made anywhere along the readiness continuum; everyone does not start at the same place in their ability or willingness.

In Unity/Hersey and Blanchard
Employee Development or Follower
Readiness/Follower Readiness
or Employee Development

To cut to the heart of the matter, if you gain a better understanding of the people you work with, if communications improve, you're using a great leadership model. We offer you one even better. Here is a guaranteed win. Should either version of our models get you to be more follower driven—celebrate! Responding to the needs of the follower is the surest way to achieve success and effectiveness.

TRIBUTE TO MY MENTOR AND FINAL COMMENTS—KEN BLANCHARD

When I developed Situational Leadership II, generating a debate with Paul Hersey was the furthest thought from my mind. Why? He is my mentor, teacher, and friend. I had never thought about being a teacher or writer until

Paul took me under his wing. He'd sit in the back of my classes at Ohio University and then give me honest and helpful feedback. When I'd finish a chapter for *Management of Organizational Behavior,* he'd not only critique my content presentation but my writing style. He wanted me to be good—"Someday better than I am," he would say. That's a gift that few are willing to give.

Paul, like Don Shula, former head coach of the Miami Dolphins with whom I coauthored *Everyone's a Coach,*[12] has always cared more about respect than popularity. He pushed me and others hard. And yet everyone who has worked closely with Paul has learned and gotten better. I certainly have. So, want to debate with Paul? I'd rather not. I'd probably lose anyway. I can't recall ever winning an argument with Paul. My bigger interest is beating him on the golf course, especially because the last time we played he eagled the first hole and cleaned my clock.

Gordon MacDonald wrote a wonderful book entitled *Ordering Your Private World*[13] in which he explains the difference between people who are "driven" and those who are "called." *Driven people* think they own everything—their relationships, possessions, ideas. They spend all their time trying to defend what they own. *Called people,* on the other hand, think everything is on loan. Their job is to shepherd and nurture what comes into their lives. Situational Leadership has been on loan to Paul and me for a long time. Even if we have shepherded it differently over the last decade or so, I hope we have nurtured it well. It certainly has seemed to make a real difference in the lives of many people.

As I approach my sixties, I hope I will always be viewed as an educational pioneer. Although Situational Leadership II is important to me, I never want to get stuck in one place. My image is that when the enemy swoops down to take over my camp, all they find are warm ashes because I've gone somewhere else. I'm working on a new concept. Thanks for letting me reminisce about Situational Leadership and its evolution—one of my favorite loans.

We hope that these thoughts will lead to your better understanding of the antecedents of Situational Leadership and the important role it has played in our personal and professional lives.

ENDNOTES

1. This article was prepared for submission to the *Training and Development* magazine for its 50th Anniversary Edition, January, 1996. A somewhat condensed version appeared on pages 42–47 of that issue.

2. Paul Hersey and Kenneth H. Blanchard, *Management of Organizational Behavior: Utilizing Human Resources,* 6th ed. (Upper Saddle River, NJ: Prentice Hall, 1993).

3. William J. Reddin, "The 3-D Management Style Theory," *Training and Development Journal,* April 1967, pp. 8–17. See also *Managerial Effectiveness* (New York: McGraw Hill, 1970).

4. Robert R. Blake and Jane S. Mouton, *The Managerial Grid,* 3rd ed. (Houston, TX: Gulf Publishing, 1984).

5. See Kenneth H. Blanchard and Spencer Johnson, *The One Minute Manager* (New York: William Morrow & Co., 1982) and Norman Vincent Peale, *The Power of Ethical Management* (New York: William Morrow & Co., 1988) and Sheldon Bowles, *Raving Fans* (New York: William Morrow and Co., 1993) and William Oncken, Jr., *The One Minute Manager Meets the Monkey* (New York: William Morrow and Co., 1989) and Don Shula and Ken Blanchard,

Everyone's a Coach (New York: Harper Business, 1995).

6. Reddin, "The 3-D Management Style Theory" and *Managerial Effectiveness.*

7. Blake and Mouton, *The Managerial Grid.*

8. For an example of the Carews' impact on Situational Leadership II see Kenneth H. Blanchard, Don Carew, and Eunice Parisi-Carew, *The One Minute Manager Builds High Performing Teams* (New York: William Morrow and Company, 1990). In addition to the Carews and Zigarmis, BTD colleagues Marjorie Blanchard, Fred Finch, and Laurie Hawkins were also helpful in the development of Situational Leadership II.

9. The best description of Situational Leadership II can be found in Kenneth Blanchard, Drea Zigarmi, and Patricia Zigarmi, *Leadership and the One Minute Manager* (New York: William Morrow and Co., 1985). See also Kenneth H. Blanchard, Drea Zigarmi, and Robert B. Nelson, "Situational Leadership after 25 Years: A Retrospective" (Escondido, CA: Blanchard Training and Development, Inc., November 1993).

10. R. B. Lacoursiere, *The Life Cycle of Groups: Group Developmental Stage Theory* (New York: Human Service Press, 1980).

11. For popular presentations on Situational Leadership, see Paul Hersey, *The Situational Leader,* (Escondido, CA: Center for Leadership Studies, 1984) and Paul Hersey, *Situational Selling* (Escondido, CA: Center for Leadership Studies, 1985).

12. Shula and Blanchard, *Everyone's a Coach.*

13. Gordon MacDonald, *Ordering Your Private World* (Nashville: Oliver-Nelson, 1985).

Recommended Supplementary Readings

Adler, Ralph, and Markus Milne. "Communication Skills and Attitude," *Chartered Accountants Journal of New Zealand*, December 1994, pp. 28–32.

Albrecht, Karl. *Service Within: Solving the Middle Management Leadership Crisis.* Homewood, IL: Dow Jones-Irwin, 1990.

Aldefer, Clayton P. *Existence, Relatedness, and Growth: Human Needs in Organizational Settings.* New York, NY: The Free Press, 1972.

Argyris, Chris. "Empowerment: The Emperor's New Clothes," *Harvard Business Review,* May/June 1998, pp. 98–105.

Argyris, Chris. "Good Communication That Blocks Learning," *Harvard Business Review,* July/August 1994, pp. 77–85.

Argyris, Chris. *Knowledge for Action: A Guide to Overcoming Barriers to Organizational Change.* San Francisco, CA: Jossey-Bass Publishers, 1993.

Argyris, Chris. "Teaching Smart People How to Learn," *Harvard Business Review,* May/June 1991, pp. 99–109.

Argyris, Chris. *Strategy, Change and Defensive Routines.* Belmont, CA: Pitman Pub., 1985.

Asch, S. E. *Social Psychology.* Upper Saddle River, NJ: Prentice-Hall, Inc., 1952.

Asch, S. E. "Effects of Group Pressure upon the Modification and Distortion of Judgments," in *Group Dynamics,* 2nd ed., pp. 189–200, eds. Dorwin Cartwright and Alvin Zander. Evanston, IL: Row, Peterson & Company, 1960.

Austin, Nancy, and Tom Peters. "A Passion for Excellence," *Fortune,* May 13, 1985, pp. 20–30.

Axley, Stephen R. "The Practical Qualities of Effective Leaders," *Industrial Management,* September/October 1990, pp. 29–31.

Axline, Larry L. "TQM: A Look in the Mirror," *Management Review,* July 1991, p. 64.

Ayman, Roya, Galen J. Baril, and David J. Palmiter Jr. "Measuring Leader Behavior: Moderates of Discrepant Self and Subordinate Descriptions," *Journal of Applied Social Psychology,* January 1, 1994, pp. 82–95.

Bachman, J. G., D. G. Bowers, and P. M. Marcus. "Bases of Supervisory Power: A Comparative Study in Five Organizational Settings," in *Control in Organizations,* ed. Arnold S. Tannenbaum. New York, NY: McGraw-Hill, 1968.

Baher, Connie. "How to Avoid Communication Clashes (Due to Different Communication Styles of Men and Women)," *Human Resource Focus*, April 1994, p. 3.

Bales, R. F. "Task Roles and Social Roles in Problem-Solving Groups," in *Readings in Social Psychology*, 3rd ed., N. Maccoby, et al. New York, NY: Holt, Rinehart & Winston, Inc., 1958.

Bandler, Richard, John Grinder, and Connirae Andreas. *Reframing: Neuro-Linguistic Programming and the Transformation of Meaning*. Moab, UT: Real People Press, 1989.

Bandler, Richard, and John Grinder. *Frogs into Princes: Neuro-Linguistic Programming*. Moab, UT: Real People Press, 1979.

Barnard, Chester I. *The Functions of the Executive*, 30th Anniversary ed. Cambridge: Harvard University Press, 1968.

Barnett, Timothy R., and Danny R. Arnold. "Justification and Application of Path-Goal Contingency Leadership Theory to Marketing Channel Leadership," *Journal of Business Research*, December 1989, pp. 283–292.

Barr, Steve H., and Edward J. Conlon. "Effects of Distribution of Feedback in Work Groups," *Academy of Management Journal*, June 1994, pp. 641–655.

Bartlett, Christopher A., and Sumantra Ghoshal. *Managing Across Borders: The Transnational Solution*, 2nd ed., Boston, MA: Harvard Business School Press, 1998.

Bartlett, Christopher A., and Sumantra Ghoshal. "Beyond Strategic Planing to Organization Learning: Lifeblood of the Individualized Corporation," *Strategy & Leadership*, Jan/Feb 1998, pp. 34–39.

Bartlett, Christopher A., and Sumantra Ghoshal. "Changing the Role of Top Management: Beyond Systems to People," *Harvard Business Review*, May/June 1995, pp. 132–142.

Bartlett, Christopher A., and Sumantra Ghoshal. "Changing the Role of Top Management: Beyond Strategy to Purpose," *Harvard Business Review*, November/December 1994, pp. 79–88.

Bass, Bernard M. *Transformational Leadership: Industrial, Military, and Educational Impact*. Mahwah, NJ: Lawrence Erlbaum Assoc., 1997.

Bass, Bernard M., and Bruce J. Avoloio. "Transformational Leadership and Organizational Culture," *Public Administration Quarterly*, Spring 1993, pp. 112–122.

Bass, Bernard M., and Ralph Mell Stogdill. *Bass and Stogdill's Handbook of Leadership*. New York, NY: The Free Press, 1990.

Bass, Bernard M. "From Transactional to Transformational Leadership: Learning to Share the Vision," *Organizational Dynamics*, Winter 1990, pp. 19–31.

Bass, Bernard M. *Leadership and Performance beyond Expectations*. New York, NY: The Free Press, 1985.

Batten, Joe D. *Tough-Minded Leadership*. New York, NY: American Management Association, 1991.

Batten, Joe D. *Beyond Management by Objectives*. New York, NY: American Management Association, 1966.

Bavelas, A., and G. Strauss. "Group Dynamics and Intergroup Relations," in K. Benne and R. Chin, eds. *The Planning of Change*. New York: Holt, Rinehart & Winston, Inc., 1962.

Beck, Don Edward and Christopher Cowan. *Spiral Dynamics: Managing Values, Leadership, and Change*. Blackwell Publishing, 1996.

Beck, Don Edward. *The Leader's Window: Mastering the Four Styles of Leadership to Build High-Performance Teams*. New York, NY: John Wiley & Sons, Inc., 1994.

Benjamin, Maynard H. "The Power of Information," *Association Management*, 47 (1995), pp. 30–32.

Bennis, Warren. "Old Dogs, New Tricks," *Executive Excellence,* 1999.

Bennis, Warren. "Five Competencies of New Leaders," *Executive Excellence,* July 1999, pp. 4–5.

Bennis, Warren. *On Becoming a Leader.* IL: Austin Press and Erwin, Inc., 1995.

Bennis, Warren. "Why Leaders Can't Lead," *The Manager's Bookshelf: A Mosaic of Contemporary Views,* 3rd ed. New York, NY: HarperCollins College Publishers, Inc., 1993.

Bennis, Warren. *Leaders on Leadership: Interviews with Top Executives.* Boston, MA: Harvard Business School Press, 1992.

Bennis, Warren. "Managing the Dream: Leadership in the 21st Century," *Training,* 27 (May 1990), pp. 43–46.

Bennis, Warren. "How to Be the Leader They'll Follow," *Working Woman,* 15 (March 1990), pp. 75–79.

Benziger, Katherine. "The Powerful Woman," *Hospital Forum,* May/June 1982, pp. 15–20.

Berne, Eric, and C. Stelner. *Beyond Games & Scripts.* New York, NY: Grove Press, 1978.

Berne, Eric. *Games People Play.* New York, NY: Grove Press, 1964.

Bernstein, Albert J., and Cindy Craft Rozen. "Why Don't They Just Get It?" *Industry Week,* November 21, 1994, p. 28.

Blair, John D., and Carlton J. Whitehead. "Can Quality Circles Survive in the United States?" *Business Horizons,* 24 (September/October 1984), pp. 17–23.

Blake, Robert R., and Anne Adams McCanse. *Leadership Dilemmas-Grid® Solutions.* Houston, TX: Gulf Publishing Company.

Blake, Robert R., and Jane S. Mouton. *The Managerial Grid III,* 3rd ed. Houston, TX: Gulf Publishing Company, 1984.

Blanchard, Kenneth, John Carlos, and Alan Randolph. *Empowerment Takes More Than a Minute.* San Francisco, CA: Berrett-Koehler Publishers, 1998.

Blanchard, Kenneth, Charles Schewe, Robert Nelson, and Alexander Hiam. *Exploring the World of Business.* New York, NY: Worth Publishers, 1998.

Blanchard, Kenneth, and Don Shula. *Everyone's a Coach.* New York, NY: HarperBusiness, 1995.

Blanchard, Kenneth, and Sheldon Bowles. *Raving Fans: A Revolutionary Approach to Customer Service.* New York, NY: William Morrow and Company, Inc., 1993.

Blanchard, Kenneth, Donald Carew, and Eunice Parisi-Carew. *The One Minute Manager Builds High Performing Teams.* New York, NY: William Morrow and Company, Inc., 1991.

Blanchard, Kenneth, and Robert Lorber. *Putting the One Minute Manager to Work.* New York, NY: Berkley Pub. Corp. , 1987.

Blanchard, Kenneth, D. W. Edington, and Marjorie Blanchard. *The One Minute Manager Gets Fit.* New York, NY: William Morrow and Company, Inc., 1986.

Blanchard, Kenneth, Patricia Zigarmi, and Drea Zigarmi. *Leadership and the One Minute Manager.* New York, NY: William Morrow and Company, Inc., 1985.

Blanchard, Kenneth, and Robert Lorber. *Putting the One Minute Manager to Work: How to Turn the Three Secrets into Skills.* Pat Gobilitz, ed. New York, NY: William Morrow and Company, Inc., 1984.

Blanchard, Kenneth, and Spencer Johnson. *The One Minute Manager.* New York, NY: William Morrow and Company, Inc., 1982.

Bottoms, David. "Facing Change or Changing Face?" *Industry Week,* May 1, 1995, pp. 17–19.

Bowen, David E., and Edward E. Lawler III. "Empowering Service Employees," *Sloan Management Review,* Summer 1995, pp. 73–84.

Bowers, David G., and Stanley E. Seashore. "Predicting Organizational Effectiveness with a Four-Factor Theory of Leadership," *Administrative Science Quarterly,* 11, no. 2 (1966), pp. 238–263.

Bradford, Leland P., Jack R. Gibb, and Kenneth D. Benne. *T-Group Theory and Laboratory Method.* New York, NY: John Wiley & Sons, Inc., 1964.

Bradford, L. P. *National Training Laboratories: Its History 1947–1970.* Bethel, ME: National Training Laboratories, 1974.

Bredin, James. "Short and Simple: Eschew Jargon and Wordiness (Such As This)," *Industry Week,* September 19, 1994, p. 18.

Brewer, Geoffrey. "Seven Secrets to Building Employee Loyalty," *Incentive,* December 1995, pp. 20–26.

Brewer, Geoffrey. "The New Managers," *Performance,* March 1995, pp. 31–35.

Brown, Andrew D. "Transformational Leadership in Tracking Technical Change," *Journal of General Management,* Summer 1994, pp. 1–12.

Brown, Jane Covey, and Rosabeth Moss Kanter. "Empowerment: Key to Effectiveness," *Hospital Forum,* May/June 1982, pp. 6–12.

Brown, Stephen W. "Managers Are Not Necessarily Leaders," *Marketing News,* October 23, 1989, p. 16.

Brown, Thomas L. "The Executive Gap: Are You Getting Out of Touch," *Industry Week,* November 5, 1990, p. 19.

Brown, Thomas L. "Leaders for the 90s: What Key Traits Are Called For?" *Industry Week,* March 5, 1990, p. 34.

Brown, Thomas L. "Putting Vision into Perspective," *Industry Week,* July 4, 1988, p. 11.

Calano, James, and Jeff Salzman. "Move from Management to Leadership," *Women in Business,* November/December 1990, pp. 11–12.

Cartwright, D., and A. Zander. eds. *Group Dynamics: Research and Theory,* 2nd ed. Evanston, IL: Row, Peterson & Company, 1960.

Cartwright, D., and R. Lippitt. "Group Dynamics and the Individual," *International Journal of Group Psychotherapy,* 7, no. 1 (1957), pp. 86–102.

Cartwright, D. "Achieving Change in People: Some Applications of Group Dynamics Theory," *Human Relations,* 1951, pp. 381–392.

Caudron, Shari. "The Top 20 Ways to Motivate Employees," *Industry Week,* April 3, 1995, pp. 12–14.

Certo, Sam. *Supervision: Building Quality and Diversity through Leadership.* Burr Ridge, IL: Irwin, 1993.

Champy, James, and Nitin Nohria. *The Arc of Ambition: Defining the Leadership Journey.* Cambridge, MA: Perseus Books, 2000.

Champy, James. *Reengineering Management.* New York, NY: HarperCollins Publishers, 1996.

Chris, Lee. "Can Leadership Be Taught?" *Training,* July 1989, pp. 19–26.

Christner, Charlotte A., and John K. Hemphill. "Leader Behavior of B-29 Commanders and Changes in Crew Members' Attitudes toward the Crew," *Sociometry,* 18 (1955), pp. 82–87.

Church, Murray. "Do Communication Professionals Need New Skills in Research and Measurement?" *Communication World,* March 1993, pp. 34–35.

Clemens, John K, and Steve Albrecht. *The Timeless Leader.* Holbrook, MA: Adams Publishing, 1995.

Clemmer, Jim. *Pathways to Performance.* Prima Publishing, 1995.

Coch, Lester, and John R. P. French, Jr. "Overcoming Resistance to Change," *Human Relations,* 1, no. 4 (1948), pp. 512–532.

Coffey, Robert, Curtis Cook, and Philip Hunsaker. *Management and Organizational Behavior.* Burr Ridge, IL: Irwin, 1994.

Cohen, William A. *The Stuff of HEROES: The Eight Universal Laws of Leadership.* Atlanta, GA: Longstreet, 1998.

Cohen, William A. *The Art of a Leader.* Upper Saddle River, NJ: Prentice Hall, 1994.

Collins, James C., and Jerry Porras. *Built to Last: Successful Habits of Visionary Companies.* New York, NY: HarperCollins, 1994.

Conger, Jay A. *Learning to Lead: The Art of Transforming Managers into Leaders.* San Francisco, CA: Jossey-Bass Publishers, 1994.

Conger, Jay A. "Inspiring Others: The Language of Leadership," *Academy of Management Executive,* February 1991, pp. 31–45.

Conger, Jay A. *The Charismatic Leader: Behind the Mystique of Exceptional Leadership.* San Francisco, CA: Jossey-Bass Publishers, 1989.

Conner, Daryl R. *Leading at the Edge of Chaos.* New York, NY: John Wiley & Sons, Inc., 1998.

Conner, Daryl R. *Managing at the Speed of Change.* New York, NY: Villard Books, 1993.

Conner, Patrick E., and Linda K. Lake. *Managing Organizational Change.* Westport, CN: Greenwood Publishing Group, 1987.

Covey, Stephen R. "Unifying Leadership," *Executive Excellence,* Oct. 1999, pp. 3-4.

Covey, Stephen R. *Principle Centered Leadership.* New York, NY: Simon & Schuster, 1990.

Covey, Stephen R. *7 Habits of Highly Effective People.* New York, NY: Simon & Schuster, 1989.

Cox, Taylor Jr., *Cultural Diversity in Organizations.* San Francisco, CA: Berrett-Koehler Publishers, 1993.

Crowe, Sandy. "Leadership Lore," *Executive Female,* January/February 1991, p. 10.

Culpan, Refik. "Leadership Styles and Human Resource Management: A Content Analysis of Popular Management Writings," *Management Decision,* 27 (1989), pp. 10–16.

Curphy, Gordon J., Joyce Hogan, and Robert Hogan. "What We Know about Leadership: Effective and Personality," *The American Psychology,* June 1994, pp. 493–505.

Curtis, Keith. *From Management Goal-Setting to Organizational Results.* Westport, CN: Greenwood Publishing Group, Inc., 1994.

Cyert, Richard M., and James G. March. *A Behavioral Theory of the Firm,* 2nd ed. Blackwell Publishing, 1992.

Cyert, Richard M., W. R. Dill, and James G. March. "The Role of Expectations in Business Decision Making," *Administrative Science Quarterly,* December 1958, pp. 307–340.

Dalziel, Murray M., and Stephen C. Schoonover. *Changing Ways: A Practical Tool for Implementing Change.* New York, NY: American Management Association, 1988.

DePree, Max. "Attributes of Leaders?" *Executive Excellence,* April 1997, p. 8.

DePree, Max. "A Sense of Quality?" *Executive Excellence,* September 1996, p. 12.

DePree, Max. "What Is Leadership?" *Planning Review,* July/August 1990, pp. 14–15.

DePree, Max. *Leadership Is an Art.* Dell Publishing, 1989.

Dilenschneider, Robert L. *Power and Influence.* Prentice Hall Press, 1990.

Doll, Bill. "Avoiding Culture Conflict: Dangers Threaten Long-Term Client-Firm Relationships," *Public Relations Journal,* May 1991, pp. 22–25.

Dreyer, R. S. "Do Good Bosses Make Lousy Leaders?" *Supervision,* March 1995, pp. 19–20.

Drucker, Peter F. "Dr. Peter Drucker Tells All About the Network Society," *Bottom Line Personal,* July 1, 1995, pp. 13–14.

Drucker, Peter F. *Managing in a Time of Great Change.* Duttin, NY: Truman Talley Books, 1995.

Drucker, Peter F. *Managing in Turbulent Times.* New York, NY: Harperbusiness, 1993.

Drucker, Peter F. *The Practice of Management.* New York, NY: Harperbusiness, 1993.

Drucker, Peter F. *The Effective Executive.* New York, NY: Harperbusiness, 1993.

Drucker, Peter F. *Age of Discontinuity: Guidelines to Our Changing Society.* New York, NY: Harper & Row Publishers, 1969.

Duck, Jeanie Daniel. "Managing Change: The Art of Balancing," *Harvard Business Review,* November/December 1993, pp. 109–120.

Dumaine, Brian. "What the Leaders of Tomorrow See," *Fortune,* July 3, 1989, pp. 40–51.

Edwards, Mark R., and S. Ruth Sproull. "Making Performance Appraisal Perform: The Use of Team Evaluations," *Personnel,* March 1985, pp. 28–32.

Elmes, Michael B., and Melinda Costello. "Mystification and Social Drama: The Hidden Side of Communication Skills Training," *Human Relations,* May 1992, pp. 427–445.

Etizioni, Amitai. *Complex Organizations.* New York, NY: Holt, Rinehart & Winston, 1961.

Euster, Joanne R. "The New Hierarchy: Where's the Boss?" *Library Journal,* May 1, 1990, pp. 40–44.

Fairholm, Gilbert W. *Leadership and the Culture of Trust.* Westport, CN: Greenwood Publishing Group, Inc., 1994.

Farrant, Don. "The Simple Math of Leadership," *Supervision,* March 1989, pp. 11–12.

Fayol, Henri. "Managing in the 21st Century," *The British Journal of Administrative Management,* Jan/Feb 2000, pp. 8–12.

Fayol, Henri. *Industrial and General Administration.* Paris: Dunod, 1925.

Ferster, C. B., and B. F. Skinner. *Schedules of Reinforcement.* Copley Pub. Group, 1997.

Festinger, Leon. *The Human Legacy.* New York, NY: Columbia University Press, 1983.

Festinger, Leon. *A Theory of Cognitive Dissonance.* Stanford, CA: Stanford University Press, 1957.

Fiedler, Fred E., and Martin M. Chemers. *Improving Leadership Match Concept,* 2nd ed. New York, NY: Wiley Press, 1984.

Fiedler, Fred E., M. M. Chemers, and L. Mahar. *Improving Leadership Effectiveness: The Leader Match Concept.* New York, NY: John Wiley & Sons, Inc., 1976.

Fiedler, Fred E. "Validation and Extension of the Contingency Model of Leadership Effectiveness: A Review of Empirical Findings," *Psychological Bulletin,* 1971, pp. 128–148.

Fiedler, Fred E. *A Theory of Leadership Effectiveness.* New York, NY: McGraw Hill, 1967.

Field, Anne. "Get the Most from Your Employees," *Money,* November 1994 pp. 104–113.

Field, Richard H. G. "Leaders As Stars, Pulsars, Quasars, and Black Holes," *Business Horizons,* May/June 1989, pp. 60–64.

Fisher, Kimball, and Maureen Ducan Fisher. *The Distributed Mind: Achieving High Performance through the Collective Intelligence of Knowledge Work Teams.* New York, NY: AMACOM, 1997.

Fisher, Kimball. *Leading Self-Directed Work Teams.* New York, NY: McGraw-Hill, Inc., 1993.

Flatow, Peter J. "Unappreciated Task: Managing Change; Yet It Should Be a Core Competency," *Advertising Age,* March 27, 1993, p. 14.

Fleishman, E. A. "Twenty Years of Consideration and Structure," in E. A. Fleishman and J. G. Hunt, eds. *Current Developments in the Study of Leadership.* Carbondale, IL: Southern Illinois University Press, 1973.

Fotheringham, Allan. "In Search of Leadership," *MacLean's,* May 1, 1995, p. 80.

French, J. R. P., Jr., Joachim Israel, and Ås Dagfinn. "An Experiment on Participation in a Norwegian Factory," *Human Relations,* February 1960, pp. 3–19.

French, J. R. P., and B. Raven. "The Bases of Social Power," in *Studies in Social Power,* ed. D. Cartwright. Ann Arbor: University of Michigan, Institute for Social Research, 1959.

French, J. R. P., Jr. "A Formal Theory of Social Power," *Psychological Review,* 63, no. 3 (1956), pp. 181–194.

Freund, Ray J. "Leadership Training for Long-Term Results," *Management Review,* July 1991, pp. 50–53.

Galbraith, John Kenneth. *The Anatomy of Power.* Boston, MA: Houghton Mifflin Co., 1985.

Gardner, John W. *On Leadership.* New York, NY: The Free Press, 1993.

Gardner, John W. "Leadership and the Future: Leaders Help People to Believe in Themselves and in the Possibilities of the Future," *The Futurist,* May/June 1990, pp. 8–12.

Gardner, John W. "Mastering the Fine Art of Leadership," *Business Month,* May 1989, pp. 77–78.

Gellerman, Saul W. *Management by Motivation.* New York, NY: American Management Association, 1968.

Gellerman, Saul W. *Motivation and Productivity.* New York, NY: American Management Association, 1963.

Ghiselli, Edwin E. *Measurement Theory for the Behavioral Sciences.* W. H. Freeman, 1981.

Ghoshal, Sumantra and Christopher Bartlett. *The Individual Corporation: A Fundamentally New Approach to Management.* New York, NY: Harperbusiness, 1999.

Gibb, Cecil A. "The Sociometry of Leadership in Temporary Groups," *Sociometry,* 13 (1950), pp. 226–243.

Gibbs, Barrie. "The Effects of Environment and Technology on Managerial Roles," *Journal of Management,* September 22, 1994, p. 581.

Gili, John, and Sue Whittle. "Management by Panacea: Accounting for Transcience," *Journal of Management Studies,* March 1993, pp. 281–295.

Gilmore, Thomas North. *Making a Leadership Change: How Organizations and Leaders Can Handle Leadership Transitions Successfully.* San Francisco, CA: Jossey-Bass Publishers, 1988.

Glassman, Myron, and Bruce R. McAfee. "Enthusiasm: The Missing Link in Leadership," *Advanced Management Journal,* Summer 1990, pp. 4–6.

Goodkin, Sanford R. "Can You Be Both a Leader and a Manager?" *Professional Builder and Remodeler,* March 1, 1991, p. 56.

Gordon, Thomas. *Leader Effectiveness Training.* Putnam Pub. Group, 1997.

Gordon, Thomas. *P.E.T. Parent Effectiveness Training.* New York, NY: Peter H. Wyden, Inc., 1970.

Gouillart, Francis J., and James N. Kelly. *Transforming the Organization.* New York, NY: McGraw Hill, Inc., 1995.

Greiner, Larry E. "Evolution and Revolution As Organizations Grow," *Harvard Business Review,* July/August 1972, pp. 37–46.

Grove, Andrew S. *High Output Management.* Vancouver, WA: Vintage Books, 1995.

Grove, Andrew S. "Taking the Hype Out of Leadership," *Fortune,* March 28, 1988, pp. 187–188.

Grover, Mary Beth. "Letting Both Sides Win," *Forbes,* September 30, 1991, p. 178.

Guest, Robert H. *Organizational Change: The Effect of Successful Leadership.* Homewood, IL: Dorsey Press and Richard D. Irwin, Inc., 1964.

Gulick, Luther, and L. Urwick, eds. *Papers on the Science of Administration.* New York, NY: Institute of Public Administration, 1937.

Gyllenpalm, Bo. *Ingmar Bergman and Creative Leadership.* Toro, Sweden: Stabin, 1995.

Hackman, J. R., and G. R. Oldham. "Development of the Job Diagnostic Survey," *Journal of Applied Psychology,* April 1975, pp. 159–70.

Haire, M. *Psychology in Management.* New York, NY: McGraw-Hill Book Company, 1956.

Hale, Guy. *The Leader's Edge.* Burr Ridge, IL: Irwin, 1995.

Halpin, Andrew W., and Ben J. Winer. *The Leadership Behavior of Airplane Commanders.* Columbus, OH: The Ohio State University Research Foundation, 1952.

Halpin, Andrew W. *The Leadership Behavior of School Superintendents.* Chicago, IL: Midwest Administration Center, The University of Chicago, 1959.

Handy, Charles. *Age of Unreason.* Boston, MA: Harvard Business School Press, 1998.

Harari, Oren. "Working Smart: The New Strategic Imperative," *Management Review,* May 1994, pp. 30–32.

Hargie, Owen, and Dennis Tourish. "Communication Skills Training: Management Manipulation or Personal Development?" *Human Relations,* November 1994, pp. 1377–1389.

Hargrove, Robert. *Masterful Coaching.* San Diego, CA: Pfeiffer, 1995.

Harmon, Shirley. "How to Become Changehardy, Part 2," *Medical Laboratory Observer,* August 1993, pp. 41–47.

Harris, Philip R., and Elashmawi Farid. *Multicultural Management 2000: Essential Cultural Insights for Global Business Success.* Houston, TX: Gulf Publishing Company, 1998.

Harris, Philip R., and Robert T. Moran. *Managing Cultural Differences.* 4th ed. Houston, TX: Gulf Publishing Company, 1996.

Harris, Thomas. *I'm OK—You're OK: A Practical Guide to Transactional Analysis.* Galahad Books, 1999.

Harvard Business Review. Harvard Business Review on Managing People. Harvard Business Review Press, 1999.

Harvard Business Review. Harvard Business Review on Leadership. Harvard Business Review Press, 1998.

Hass, Howard G., and Bob Tamarkin. *The Leader Within.* San Francisco, CA: HarperCollins Publishers, 1993.

Heifetz, Michael L. *Leading Change, Overcoming Chaos.* Berkeley, CA: Ten Speed Press, 1993.

Heifetz, Ronald H. *Leadership without Easy Answers.* Cambridge, MA: Harvard University Press, 1994.

Heill, Gary, Tom Parker, and Rick Tate. *Leadership and Customer Revolution.* New York, NY: Van Nostrand Reinhold, 1995.

Heller, Robert. *The Leadership Imperative.* Duttin, NY: Truman Talley Books, 1995.

Hemphill, John K. "Why People Attempt to Lead," in *Leadership and Interpersonal Behavior,* Luigi Petrullo and Bernard M. Bass, eds. New York: Holt, Rinehart & Winston, Inc., 1961.

Hemphill, John K. *Leader Behavior Description.* Columbus, OH: The Ohio State University, 1950.

Hemphill, John K. *Situational Factors in Leadership,* Monograph No. 32. Columbus, OH: Bureau of Educational Research, The Ohio State University, 1949.

Henderson, George. *Cultural Diversity in the Workplace: Issues and Strategies.* Greenwood Publishing Group Inc., 1994.

Hersey, Paul. "The Toll Road to Empowerment," *Executive Excellence,* April 1996, pp. 14–15.

Hersey, Paul. *Situational Selling: An Approach for Increasing Sales Effectiveness.* Escondido, CA: Center for Leadership Studies, 1985.

Hersey, Paul. *The Situational Leader.* Escondido, CA: Center for Leadership Studies, 1984.

Hersey, Paul, and John E. Stinson. *Perspectives in Leader Effectiveness.* Columbus, OH: Ohio University Press, 1980.

Hersey, Paul, Kenneth H. Blanchard, and W. E. Natemeyer. "Situational Leadership, Perception, and the Impact of Power," *Group and Organizational Studies,* December 1979, pp. 418–428.

Hersey, Paul, and Kenneth H. Blanchard. "What's Missing in MBO?" *Management Review,* October 1974.

Hersey, Paul, and Kenneth H. Blanchard. "So You Want to Know Your Leadership Style?" *Training and Development Journal,* February 1974.

Hersey, Paul, and Kenneth H. Blanchard. "Cultural Changes: Their Influence on Organizational Structure and Management Behavior," *Training and Development Journal,* October 1970.

Hersey, Paul, and Kenneth H. Blanchard. "Life Cycle Theory of Leadership," *Training and Development Journal,* May 1969.

Herzberg, Frederick. "One More Time: How Do You Motivate Employees?" *Harvard Business Review,* January/February 1968, pp. 53–62.

Herzberg, Frederick. *Work and the Nature of Man.* New York, NY: World Publishing Co., 1966.

Hesselbein, Frances, Marshall Goldsmith, and Richard Beckhard. *The Leader of the Future.* San Francisco, CA: Jossey-Bass Publishers, 1996.

Hickman, Craig R. *Mind of a Manager, Soul of a Leader.* New York, NY: John Wiley & Sons, Inc., 1992.

Hill, Norman C. "The Need for Positive Reinforcement in Corrective Counseling," *Supervisory Management,* December 1984, pp. 10–11.

Hoffman, Richard, and Gary B. Kleinman. "Individual and Group in Group Problem Solving: The Valence Model," *Human Communication Research,* September 1994, pp. 36–60.

Hogan, Robert, Dan Fazzini, and Robert Raskin. "How Charisma Cloaks Incompetence," *Personnel Journal,* May 1990, pp. 72–76.

Hollander, E. P. "Emergent Leadership and Social Influence," in *Leadership and Interpersonal Behavior,* eds. Luigi Petrullo and Bernard M. Bass. New York, NY: Holt, Rinehart & Winston, Inc., 1961.

Homans, George C. *The Human Group.* Somerset, NJ: Transaction Pub., 1992.

Hosking, Dian Marie. "Organizing, Leadership, and Skillful Process," *Journal of Management Studies,* March 1988, pp. 147–166.

Hosking, D. M., and C. Schriesheim. "Review of Fiedler et al.," *Improving Leadership Effectiveness: The Leader Match Concept.* New York: Wiley, 1976. *Administrative Science Quarterly,* 1978, pp. 496–504.

House, Robert J., and Terence R. Mitchell. "Path-Goal Theory of Leadership," *Journal of Contemporary Business,* Autumn 1974, pp. 81–98.

House, Robert J. "A Path-Goal Theory of Leader Effectiveness," *Administrative Science Quarterly,* September 1971, pp. 321–338.

Howell, John P., David E. Bowen, and Peter W. Dorfman. "Substitutes for Leadership: Effective Alternatives to Ineffective Leadership," *Organizational Dynamics,* Summer 1990, pp. 20–38.

Howell, Jane M., and Christopher A. Higgins. "Champions of Change: Identifying, Understanding, and Supporting Champions of Technological Innovations," *Organizational Dynamics,* Summer 1990, pp. 40–55.

Huey, John. "The Leadership Industry," *Fortune,* February 21, 1994, p. 54.

Hughes, Richard, Robert Ginnett, and Gordon Curphy. *Leadership: Enhancing the Lessons of Experience,* 3rd ed. Burr Ridge, IL: Irwin, 1998.

Hunt, J. G. "Personal Factors Associated with Leadership: A Survey of the Literature," *Journal of Psychology,* January 1982, pp. 35–71.

Hunt, J. G., and L. L. Larson, eds. *Contingency Approaches to Leadership.* Carbondale, IL: Southern Illinois University Press, 1974.

Hussein, Raef T. "Understanding and Managing Informal Groups," *Management Decision*, November 8, 1990, pp. 36–41.

Ingram, Larry C. *The Study of Organizations.* Praeger Publishing, 1995.

Ivancenvich, John M., and Michael Matteson. *Organizational Behavior and Management*, 3rd ed. Burr Ridge, IL: Irwin, 1992.

James, Art, and Dennis Kratz. *Effective Listening Skills.* Burr Ridge, IL: Irwin, 1994.

Jauch, Lawrence R., and Sally A. Caltrin. *The Managerial Experience: Cases and Exercises.* 6th ed. Fort Worth, TX: The Dryden Press, 1993.

Javidan, Mansour. "Leading a High-Commitment, High-Performance Organization," *Long Range Planning,* April 1991, pp. 28–36.

Jennings, Eugene E. "The Anatomy of Leadership," *Management of Personnel Quarterly,* Autumn, 1961.

Jessup, Harlan R. "New Roles in Team Leadership," *Training and Development Journal,* November 1990, pp. 79–83.

Johnson, Dewey E. *Concepts of Air Force Leadership.* Washington, DC: Air Force ROTC, 1970.

Jones, Stanley E. *The Right Touch: Understanding and Using the Language of Physical Contact.* Cresskill, NJ: Hampton Press, Inc., 1994.

Jongeward, Dorothy, and Muriel James. *Born to Win: Transactional Analysis with Gestalt Experiments,* 25th Anniversary ed. Cambridge, MA: Perseus Press, 1996.

Jongeward, Dorothy. *Everybody Wins: Transactional Analysis Applied to Organizations.* Reading, MA: Addison-Wesley Publishing Company, 1974.

Kahn, R. L. "Productivity and Job Satisfaction," *Personnel Psychology,* 13, no. 3 (1960), pp. 275–278.

Kahn, R. L., and D. Katz. "Leadership Practices in Relation to Productivity and Morale," *Group Dynamics: Research and Theory* 2nd ed., eds. D. Cartwright and A. Zander. Evanson, IL: Row, Peterson & Company, 1960.

Kaine, Jack W. "How to Be Negotiator-In-Chief," *Association Management,* January 1994, p. 63.

Kanter, Donald L., and Philip H. Mirvis. (David Jamieson and Julie O'Mara) *Managing Workforce 2000: Gaining the Diversity Advantage.* San Francisco, CA: Jossey-Bass Publishers, 1991.

Kanter, Rosabeth Moss, Barry A. Stein, and Todd D. Jick. *The Challenge of Organizational Change: How People Experience and Manage It.* New York, NY: The Free Press, 1992.

Kanter, Rosabeth Moss. "The New Managerial Work," *Harvard Business Review,* November/December 1989, p. 85.

Katz, R. "Job Longevity As a Situational Factor in Job Satisfaction," *Administrative Science Quarterly,* June 1978, pp. 204–223.

Katz, Daniel, and Robert L. Kahn. *The Social Psychology of Organization,* 2nd ed. New York, NY: John Wiley & Sons, Inc., 1978.

Katzenbach, Jon R. *Real Change Leaders.* Times Books, 1997.

Katzenbach, Jon R., and Douglas K. Smith. *The Wisdom of Teams: Creating the High-Performance Organization.* New York, NY: HarperCollins Publishers, 1994.

Kenney-Wallace, G. A. "Managing the Unexpected," *Canadian Business Review,* Autumn 1994, pp. 44–47.

Kepner, C. H., and B. B. Tregoe. *The Rational Manager.* New York, NY: McGraw-Hill Book Company, 1965.

Kerlins, Marvin, and Edyth Hargis. "Beyond Leadership: The Human Factor in Leadership," *Management Solutions,* August 1988, pp. 18–21.

Recommended Supplementary Readings

Keys, Bernard, and Thomas Case. "How to Become an Influential Manager," *Academy of Management Executive,* November 1990, pp. 38–51.

Kiechel, Walter. "A Hard Look at Executive Vision," *Fortune,* October 23, 1989, p. 207.

Kinni, Theodore B. "Leadership up Close: Effective Leaders Share Four Major Characteristics," *Industry Week,* June 20, 1994, pp. 20–25.

Kirkland, Richard I. "What Makes Business Leaders," *Fortune,* September 24, 1990, p. 215.

Kirkpatrick, Shelly A., and Edwin A. Locke. "Leadership: Do Traits Matter?" *Academy of Management Executive,* May 1991, pp. 48–60.

Kiser, Glenn A., Terry Humphries, and Chip Bell. "Breaking Through Rational Leadership," *Training and Development Journal,* January 1990, pp. 42–43.

Klein, Howard J., and Paul W. Mulvey. "Two Investigations of the Relationships among Group Goals, Goal Commitment, Cohesion, and Performance," *Organizational Behavior and Human Decision Process,* January 1995, pp. 44–53.

Klien, J., and W. Conrad. "The Right Approach to Participative Management," *Working Woman,* May 1985, pp. 28–29.

Knippen, Jay T., and Thad B. Green. "How the Manager Can Use Active Listening," *Public Personnel Management,* Summer 1994, pp. 357–359.

Koestenbaum, Peter. *The Heart of Business: Ethics, Power, and Philosophy.* San Francisco, CA: Saybrook Pub. Co., 1988.

Kolb, David A., Irwin M. Ruben, and James M. McIntyre. *Organizational Psychology.* Upper Saddle River, NJ: Prentice Hall, Inc., 1971.

Konieczka, Richard J. "Sharpen Your Communication Skills Using Quality Concepts," *Quality Progress,* December 1993, pp. 113–114.

Korman, A. K. "'Consideration,' 'Initiating Structure,' and Organizational Criteria— A Review," *Personnel Psychology,* Winter 1966, pp. 349–361.

Kotter, John P. *What Leaders Really Do.* Boston, MA: Harvard Business School Press, 1999.

Kotter, John P. *Leading Change.* Boston, MA: Harvard Business School Press, 1996.

Kotter, John P. *The New Rules.* New York, NY: The Free Press, 1995.

Kotter, John P. *A Force for Change: How Leadership Differs from Management.* New York, NY: The Free Press, 1990.

Kouzes, James M., and Barry Z. Posner. *The Leadership Challenge,* 2nd ed. San Francisco, CA: Jossey-Bass Publishers, 1996.

Kouzes, James M., and Barry Z. Posner. *Credibility: How Leaders Gain and Lose It, Why People Demand It.* San Francisco, CA: Jossey-Bass Publishers, 1995.

Kouzes, James M., and Barry Z. Posner. "The Credibility Factor: What Followers Expect from Their Leaders," *Management Review,* January 1990, pp. 29–33.

Kuczmarski, Susan Smith, and Thomas D. Kuczmarski. *Value-Based Leadership.* Prentice Hall, 1995.

Kuhnert, Karl W., and Philip Lewis. "Transactional and Transformational Leadership: A Constructive/Development Analysis," *The Academy of Management Review,* October 1987, pp. 648–657.

Kushel, Gerald. *Reaching the Peak Performance Zone: How to Motivate Yourself and Others to Excel.* New York, NY: AMACOM, 1994.

Langhlin, Patrick R., and Andrea B. Hollingshead. "A Theory of Collective Induction," *Organizational Behavior and Human Decision Processes,* January 1995, pp. 94–107.

Larkin, T. J., and Sandar Larkin. *Communicating Change.* New York, NY: McGraw-Hill, Inc., 1994.

Lawrie, John. "The Differences between Effective and Ineffective Change Managers," *Supervisory Management,* June 1991, pp. 9–10.

Lawrie, John. "The High Price of Being a 'Yes' Manager," *Supervisory Management*, October 1989, pp. 13–16.

Leads, Dorothy. "Eight Steps to Better Body Language," *Real Estate Today*, June 1994, pp. 35–38.

Leavitt, Harold J. *Managerial Psychology*, 5th ed. Chicago: University of Chicago Press, 1988.

Lee, Chris. "Followership: The Essence of Leadership," *Training*, January 1991, pp. 27–35.

Leon, Raymond O. *Superior Supervision*. New York, NY: Lexington Books, 1994.

Lewan, Lloyd S. "Diversity in the Workplace," *HR Magazine*, June 1990, pp. 42–45.

Lewin, K., R. Lippett, and R. White. "Leader Behavior and Member Reaction in Three 'Social Climates,'" *Group Dynamics: Research and Theory* 2nd ed., eds. D. Cartwright and A. Zander. Evanston, IL: Row, Peterson & Company, 1960.

Likert, Rensis. *The Human Organization*. New York, NY: McGraw-Hill Book Company, 1967.

Likert, Rensis. *New Patterns of Management*. New York, NY: McGraw-Hill Book Company, 1961.

Liley, William. "Leadership beyond the Obvious," *Fortune*, October 9, 1989, pp. 193–194.

Lindholm, C. E. "The Science of 'Muddling Through,'" *Public Administration Review*, Winter 1959, pp. 79–99.

Livingston, J. Sterling. "Pygmalion in Management," *Harvard Business Review*, July/August 1969, pp. 81–89.

Locke, Edwin A. *The Essence of Leadership: The Four Keys to Leading Effectively*. Lanham, MD: Lexington Books, 1999.

Loeb, Marshall. "Leadership Myths," *Executive Excellence*, September 1999, p. 12.

Loeb, Marshall. "Where Leaders Come From," *Fortune*, September 1994, p. 241.

Lord, Robert G., and Karen J. Maher. *Leadership and Information Processing: Linking Perception and Performance*. New York, NY: Routledge, 1994.

Maccoby, Michael. "Understanding the Difference between Management and Leadership," *Research Technology Management*, Jan/Feb 2000, pp. 57–59.

Maccoby, Michael. "From Analyzer to Humanizer—Raising the Level of Management Thinking," *Research Technology Management*, September/October 1994, pp. 57–59.

Maccoby, Michael. "How to Be a Quality Leader," *Research Technology Management*, September/October 1990, pp. 51–52.

Machiavelli, Niccolo. *The Prince*. New York, NY: Mentor Classic—New American Library, 1952.

Maier, Norman R. F. *Frustration*. Ann Arbor: The University of Michigan Press, 1961.

Maier, Norman R. F. *Psychology in Industry*, 2nd ed. Boston, MA: Houghton Mifflin Company, 1955.

Mainiero, Lisa A. "On Balancing the Glass Ceiling: The Political Seasoning of Powerful Women Executives," *American Management Association*, 1994, pp. 4–12.

Manz, Charles C., and Christopher P. Neck. "From GroupThink to TeamThink: Toward the Creation of Constructive Thought Patterns in Self-Managing Work Teams," *Human Relations*, August 1994, pp. 929–953.

Manz, Charles C., and Henry P. Sims. "Superleadership: Leading Others to Lead Themselves," *The Manager's Bookshelf: A Mosaic of Contemporary Views*, 3rd ed. New York: HarperCollins College Publishers, Inc., 1993.

March, J. G., and H. A. Simon. *Organizations*. New York, NY: John Wiley & Sons, Inc., 1958.

Marshall, Edward M. *Transforming the Way We Work*. New York, NY: American Management Association, 1995.

Mascari, Patricia A. "Leading with a Vision," *Association Management*, September 1990, pp. 34–36.

Maslow, Abraham H. *Motivation and Personality*, 3rd ed., Reading, MA: Addison-Wesley Publishing Company, 1987.

Maslow, Abraham H. *Eupsychian Management*. Homewood, IL: Richard D. Irwin, Inc., and The Dorsey Press, 1965.

Maslow, Abraham H. *New Knowledge in Human Values*, New York, NY: Harper & Row Publishers, 1959.

Maynard, Roberta. "It Can Pay to Show Employees the Big Picture," *Nation's Business*, December 1994, p. 10.

Mayo, Elton. *The Human Problems of an Industrial Civilization*. New York, NY: The Macmillan Company, 1933.

McAfee, R. Bruce, and Paul J. Champagne. *Effectively Managing Troublesome Employees*. Westport, CN: Greenwood Publishing Group, 1994.

McCall, Morgan. *High Flyers*. Boston, MA: Harvard Business School Press, 1997.

McClelland, David C. *Personality*. Irvington Publishing, 1980.

McClelland, D., and D. H. Burnham. "Power Is the Great Motivator," *Harvard Business Review*, March/April 1976, pp. 100–110.

McClelland, David C. *The Achieving Society*. Princeton, NJ: D. Van Nostrand Co., Inc., 1961.

McGregor, Douglas. *The Human Side of Enterprise: 25th Anniversary Printing*. New York, NY: McGraw-Hill Book Company, 1985.

McGregor, Douglas. *Professional Manager*. New York, NY: McGraw-Hill Book Company, 1967.

McNerney, Donald J. "Improve Your Communications Skills," *Human Resource Focus*, October 1994, p. 22.

Mealiea, Laird W. *Skills for Management Success*. Boston, MA: Irwin, 1996.

Menkus, Belden. "Leadership and Professional Performance," *Journal of Systems Management*, July 1991, p. 19.

Meyers, Scott M. "Who Are Your Motivated Workers," *Harvard Business Review* January/February 1964, pp. 73–88.

Milkovich, George, and Jerry M. Newman. *Compensation*, 6th ed. McGraw Hill College Div., 1999.

Miller, Sandra A. "Controlling How Others See You Is Good Business," *The CPA Journal*, October 1994, pp. 75–76.

Milliman, John F., Robert A. Zawacki, Carol Norman, Lynda Powell, and Jay Kirksey. "Companies Evaluate Employees from All Perspectives," *Personnel Journal*, November 1994, pp. 99–103.

Miner, John B. *Role Motivation Theories*. New York, NY: Routledge, 1993.

Moravec, Milan. "The Well-Managed SMT," *Management Review*, June 1998, pp. 56-58.

Moravec, Milan. "Leaders Must Love Change, Not Loathe It," *HR Focus*, February 1994, p. 14.

Morrison, Ann M. *The New Leaders: Guidelines on Leadership Diversity in America*. San Francisco, CA: Jossey-Bass Publishers, 1996.

Moskal, Brian S. "Tomorrow's Best Managers: Where Are They Now?" *Industry Week*, July 18, 1988, pp. 32–34.

Murnighan, J. Keith, and Stephen Ghee-Soon Lim. "Phases, Deadlines, and the Bargaining Process," *Organizational Behavior and Human Decision Processes*, May 1994, pp. 153–171.

Myers, Olga. "Supervisors Don't Have Job Conflicts?" *Supervision*, June 1991, pp. 14–16.

Nadler, David A., and Michael L. Tushman. "Beyond the Charismatic Leader: Leadership and Organizational Change," *California Management Review,* Winter 1990, pp. 77–97.

Nanus, Burt. *Visionary Leadership: Creating a Compelling Sense of Direction for Your Organization.* San Francisco, CA: Jossey-Bass Publishers, 1995.

Natemeyer, W. E. "An Empirical Investigation of the Relationships between Leader Behavior, Leader Power Bases, and Subordinate Performance and Satisfaction," an unpublished dissertation, University of Houston, August 1975.

Nelson, Robert B. *Empowering Employees through Delegation.* Burr Ridge, IL: Irwin, 1993.

Nelson, Bob. *1001 Ways to Energize Employees.* New York, NY: Workman Publishing, 1997.

Nelson, Bob. *1001 Ways to Reward Employees.* New York, NY: Workman Publishing, 1994.

Nicholls, John. "Nearly All There Is to Know about Leadership," *International Management,* April 1988, pp. 65–66.

Noble, Barbara Presley. "The Gender Wars: Talking Peace," *The New York Times,* August 14, 1994, p. 21.

Nordland, Linda, and Jacklyn Twining. *Principle-Centered Leadership.* Burr Ridge, IL: Austin Press and Irwin, Inc., 1995.

Nohria, Nitin, and Sumantra Ghoshal. *The Differentiated Network: Organizing Multinational Corporations for Value Creation.* San Francisco, CA: Jossey-Bass Publishers, 1997.

Nohria, Nitin, and James D. Berkeley. "Whatever Happened to the Take-Charge Manager?" *Harvard Business Review,* January/February 1994, pp. 128–137.

Odiorne, George S. *Management by Objectives.* New York, NY: Pitman Publishing Corp., 1965.

Olcott, William. "How to Survive in a World of Permanent White Water," *Fund Raising Management,* 24 (1993), p. 6.

Olesen, Eric. "Mastering Change: CEOs' Secrets for Exploiting Opportunity," *Success,* October 1993, pp. 44–45.

O'Leary-Kelley, Anne M., Joseph J. Martocchio, and Dwight D. Frink. "A Review of the Influence of Group Goals on Group Performance," *Academy of Management Journal,* October 1994, pp. 1285–1301.

O'Reilly, Brian. "360-Degree Feedback Can Change Your Life," *Fortune,* October 17, 1994, pp. 93–100.

O'Toole, James. *Leading Change: Overcoming the Ideology of Comfort and the Tyranny of Custom.* San Francisco, CA: Jossey-Bass Publishers, 1995.

Parker, Glenn M. *Cross-Functional Teams: Working with Allies, Enemies, and Other Strangers.* San Francisco, CA: Jossey-Bass Publishers, 1994.

Parkinson, C. Northcote. *Parkinson's Law.* Boston, MA: Houghton Mifflin, 1957.

Pascarella, Perry. "Winning Trust," *Executive Excellence,* June 1998, p. 19.

Pascarella, Perry. "Visionary Leadership Will Design the Future," *Industry Week,* August 21, 1989, pp. 48–49.

Passmore, William A. *Creating Strategic Change.* New York, NY: Wiley, 1994.

Payne, Tom. "MBWA—Management by Walking Away," *Supervision,* June 1999, pp. 8-10.

Payne, Tom. "Go Forth and Manage Wisely," *Supervision,* August 1994, pp. 10–12.

Pearce, John A., and Richard B. Robinson, Jr. *Strategic Management: Formulation, Implementation, and Control,* 7th ed. Burr Ridge, IL: Irwin, 1999.

Pedersen, Cynthia Ross. "Communication Skills in Need of Repair," *Computing,* January 18, 1995, p. 9.

Peter, Lawrence J., and Raymond Hull. *The Peter Principle.* New York, NY: William Morrow and Company, Inc., 1969.

Peters, Tom. "The New Builders," *Industry Week,* March 5, 1990, pp. 27–28.

Peters, Tom, and Robert Waterman. *In Search of Excellence.* Warner Books, 1988.

Peters, Tom, and Nancy Austin. *A Passion for Excellence—The Leadership Difference.* New York, NY: Random House, 1985.

Petrock, Frank. "Planning the Leadership Transition," *Journal of Business Strategy,* November/December 1990, pp. 14–16.

Pfeffer, Jeffrey. *The Human Equation: Building Profits by Putting People First.* Boston, MA: Harvard Business School Press, 1998.

Pfeffer, Jeffrey. *Power in Organizations.* Marshfield, MA: Pittman Publishing, Inc., 1981.

Phegan, Barry. *Developing Your Company Culture: The Joy of Leadership.* Berkeley, CA: Context Press, 1995.

Philips, Kevin John. "Six Keys to Basic Success," *Supervision,* May 1994, pp. 11–13.

Pitman, Ben. "How Do I Motivate and Lead My People?" *Journal of Systems Management,* March 1991, pp. 32–34.

Plunkett, Lorne, and Robert Fournier. *Participative Management: Implementing Empowerment.* New York, NY: John Wiley & Sons, Inc., 1991.

Podsakoff, P. M., et al. *Transformation Leader Behaviors and Their Effects on Followers' Trust in Leader, Satisfaction, and Organizational Citizenship Behaviors. Leaders & The Leadership Process: Readings, Self-Assessments, and Applications.* Burr Ridge, IL: Austin Press and Irwin, Inc., 1995.

Pollock, Ted. "What Makes a Leader?" *Automotive Manufacturing & Production,* October 1999, pp. 10–12.

Pollock, Ted. "Ten Ways to Put Change Across," *Supervision,* October 1993, pp. 25–26.

Quickel, Stephen W. "Forget Managers: What We Need Are Leaders," *Business Month,* January 1989, pp. 69–70.

Quinn, James Brian. "Managing Innovation: Controlled Chaos," *Harvard Business Review,* May/June 1985, pp. 73–84.

Reddin, William J. *Effective Management by Objectives: The 3-D Method of MBO.* New York, NY: McGraw-Hill Book Company, 1971.

Reddin, William J. *Managerial Effectiveness.* New York, NY: McGraw-Hill Book Company, 1970.

Reddin, William J. "The 3-D Management Style Theory," *Training and Development Journal,* April 1967, pp. 8–17.

Rehfeld, John E. *Alchemy of a Leader.* New York, NY: John Wiley & Sons, Inc., 1994.

Roebuck, Deborah Britt, Kevin W. Sightler, and Christina Christenson. "Organizational Size, Company Type, and Position Effects on the Perceived Importance of Oral and Written Communications Skills," *Journal of Mathematical Economics,* Spring 1995, pp. 99–115.

Roethlisberger, F. J., and W. J. Dickson. *Management and the Worker.* Cambridge: Harvard University Press, 1939.

Rogers, Carl. *On Becoming a Person.* Boston, MA: Houghton-Mifflin Company, 1995.

Rogus, Joseph F. "Developing a Vision Statement—Some Considerations for Principals," *NASSP Bulletin,* February 1990, pp. 1–4.

Rosenbaum, Bernard L. "Leading Today's Professional," *Research Technology Management,* March–April 1991, pp. 30–35.

Rosener, Judy B. *America's Competitive Secret: Utilizing Women As a Management Strategy.* Oxford University Press, 1995.

Rosener, Judy B. "The Valued Ways Men and Women Lead," *HR Magazine,* June 1991, p. 147.

Rue, Leslie W., and Lloyd L. Byars. *Supervision: Key Link to Productivity,* 6th ed. Burr Ridge, IL: Irwin, 1998.

Rusher, William A. "How to Win Any Argument," *Bottom Line Personnel,* June 15, 1995, pp. 11–12.

Sanford, Fillmore H. "Leadership Identification and Acceptance," *Groups, Leadership and Men,* ed. Harold Guentzkow. Pittsburgh, PA: Carnegie Press, 1951.

Schachter, Stanley. *The Psychology of Affiliation.* Stanford, CA: Stanford University Press, 1959.

Schein, Edgar. *The Corporate Culture: A Survival Guide,* San Francisco, CA: Jossey-Bass Publishers, 1999.

Schein, Edgar. *Organizational Culture and Leadership,* 2nd ed. San Francisco, CA: Jossey-Bass Publishers, 1997.

Schein, Edgar H. *Organizational Psychology,* 3rd ed. Upper Saddle River, NJ: Prentice Hall, Inc., 1980.

Schragenheim, Eli. *Management Dilemmas.* Kansas City, MO: CRC Press, 1998.

Schriesheim, Chester A., Bennett J. Tapper, and Linda Tetrault. "Least Preferred Co-workers Score Situational Control and Leadership Effectiveness," *Journal of Applied Psychology,* August 1994, pp. 561–574.

Schriesheim, Chester A. "The Great High Consideration—High Initiating Structure Myth," *Journal of Social Psychology,* April 1982.

Schroeder, Patricia K. "The Other Side of Leadership: Strengthening the Support Base," *Economic Development Review,* Summer 1990, pp. 16–18.

Schwarz, Roger M. *The Skilled Facilitator.* San Francisco, CA: Jossey-Bass Publishers, 1994.

Seashore, Stanley E. *Group Cohesiveness in the Industrial Work Group.* Ayer Co. Pub., 1977.

Selected Readings. "Compensation and Benefits," *Performance Management: What's Hot—What's Not,* 26 (1994), pp. 71–75.

Seltzer, Joseph, and Bernard M. Bass. "Transformational Leadership: Beyond Initiation and Consideration," *Journal of Management,* December 1990, pp. 693–703.

Senge, Peter M. *The Fifth Discipline: The Art and Practice of the Learning Organization.* Doubleday Books, 1994.

Senge, Peter M. "The Leader's New Work: Building Learning Organizations," *Sloan Management Review,* Fall 1990, pp. 7–19.

Sherman, Tiffany. *Visionary Leadership.* Burr Ridge, IL: Austin Press and Irwin, Inc., 1995.

Simon, H. A. *Administrative Behavior,* 4th ed. New York, NY: The Free Press, 1997.

Skinner, Burrhus F. *Science and Human Behavior.* New York, NY: The Free Press, 1965.

Slater, Stanley F. "The Influence of Managerial Style on Business Unit Performance," *Journal of Management,* September 1989, pp. 441–455.

Smeltzer, Larry R., and Donald L. Leonard. *Managerial Communication: Strategies and Application,* 2nd ed. Burr Ridge, IL: Irwin, 1997.

Smith, Douglas K. *Taking Charge of Change: 10 Principles for Managing People and Performance.* Cambridge, MA: Perseus Press, 1997.

Smith, Jonathan E., Kenneth P. Carson, and Ralph A. Alexander. "Leadership: It Can Make a Difference," *Academy of Management Journal,* December 1984, pp. 765–776.

Smith, Perry M. *Taking Charge: Making the Right Choices.* Garden City Park, NY: Avery Pub. Group, 1993.

Smith, Perry M. "Twenty Guidelines for Leadership," *Nation's Business,* September 1989, pp. 60–61.

South, Laurie. "What Business Needs: Core Skills and the 16 Plus Careership Compact," *Training Tomorrow,* December 1993, pp. 17–19.

Sparks, Bonnie J. "Make the Right Moves with Body Language," *Real Estate Today,* June 1994, pp. 35–38.

Speck, Bruce W. "The Manager As Writing Mentor," *Training and Development Journal,* April 1990, pp. 78–81.

Stern, Barbara B. "A Revised Communication Model for Advertising: Multiple Dimension of the Source, the Message, and the Recipient," *Journal of Advertising,* June 1994, pp. 5–15.

Stevenson, Howard H. and, David E. Gumpert. "The Heart of Entrepreneurship," *Harvard Business Review,* March/April 1985, pp. 85–94.

Stogdill, Ralph M. *Handbook of Leadership.* New York, NY: The Free Press, 1974.

Stogdill, Ralph M. "Personal Factors Associated with Leadership: A Survey of the Literature," *Journal of Psychology,* January 1948, pp. 35–71.

Stogdill, Ralph M., and Alvin E. Coons, eds. *Leader Behavior: Its Description and Measurement, Research Monograph No. 88.* Columbus, OH: Bureau of Business Research, The Ohio State University, 1957.

Stoner, Charles R., and Richard I. Hartman. "Team Building: Answering the Tough Questions," *Business Horizons,* September/October 1993, pp. 70–77.

Stumpf, Stephen A., and Thomas P. Mullen. "Strategic Leadership: Concepts, Skills, Style, and Process," *Journal of Management Development,* Winter 1991, pp. 42–53.

Sussland, Willy. "Turning Points: Managers Seeking a New Direction Should Bear Three Points in Mind," *International Management,* April 6, 1995, pp. 38–39.

Swinburne, Penny. "Management with a Personal Touch," *People Management,* April 6, 1995, pp. 38–39.

Tannenbaum, Robert, and Warren H. Schmidt. "How to Choose a Leadership Pattern," *Harvard Business Review,* March/April 1958, pp. 95–102.

Taylor, Susan L. "Devine Discontent," *Essence,* July 1994, p. 51.

Taylor, Frederick W. *The Principles of Scientific Management.* New York, NY: Harper & Brothers, 1911.

Thornton, Scott J. "Leadership Traits That Work Worldwide," *Association Management,* August 1990, p. 22.

Tichy, Noel, and Eli Cohen. "Teaching: The Heart of Leadership," *Health Forum Journal,* March/April 1998, pp. 20–24.

Tichy, Noel. The *Leadership Engine.* New York, NY: Harperbusiness, 1997.

Tichy, Noel. *Transformational Leader,* 2nd ed. New York, NY: John Wiley & Sons, Inc., 1997.

Townsend, Patrick I., Joan F. Gebhardt, and Nancy K. Austin. *Five-Star Leadership: The Art and Strategy of Creating Leaders at Every Level.* New York, NY: John Wiley & Sons, Inc., 1999.

Trice, Harrison M., and Janice M. Boyer. "Studying Organizational Cultures through Rites and Ceremonials," *Academy of Management Review,* 9, no. 4 (1984).

Umiker, William. "Powerful Communication Skills: The Key to Prevention and Resolution of Personnel Problems," *Health Care Supervisor,* March 1993, pp. 30–34.

Urwick, Lyndall F., *The Theory of Organization.* New York, NY: American Management Association, 1952.

Vake, Brett. *On Leadership.* Burr Ridge, IL: Austin Press and Irwin, Inc., 1995.

Valenzano, Joseph M. "New Leadership for a Changing Workforce," *Journal of Business Strategy,* March/April 1990, pp. 62–63.

Vicere, Albert A. "The Changing Paradigm for Executive Development," *Journal of Management Development,* Summer 1991, pp. 44–47.

Vroman, H. Wilson and Vincent Luchsinger. *Managing Organizational Quality.* Burr Ridge, IL: Irwin, 1994.

Vroom, Victor H., and Arthur G. Jago. *The New Leadership: Managing Participation in Organizations.* Upper Saddle River, NJ: Prentice Hall, 1988.

Vroom, Victor H. "Can Leaders Learn to Lead?" *Organizational Dynamics,* Winter 1976, pp. 17–28.

Vroom, Victor H., and Philip Yetton. *Leadership and Decision Making.* Pittsburgh, PA: University of Pittsburgh Press, 1973.

Wageman, Ruth. "Critical Success Factors for Creating Superb Self-Managing Teams at Xerox," *Plan Design,* September/October 1997, pp. 31–41.

Watson, Tony. *In Search of Management: Culture, Chaos, and Control in Managerial Work.* New York, NY: Routledge, 1994.

Weber, Max. *The Theory of Social and Economic Organization, Trans.* A. H. Henderson, and ed. Talcott Parsons. New York, NY: Oxford University Press, 1946.

Weisberg, Jacob. "Build Your Information Power Base," *Folio: The Magazine for Magazine Management,* 24 (1995), pp. 34–36.

Werther, William B. "Loyalty at Work," *Business Horizons,* March/April 1988, pp. 20–24.

White, Robert W., and R. Lippitt. *Autocracy and Democracy: An Experimental Inquiry.* New York, NY: Harper & Row Publishers, 1960.

Whyte, W. F. *Man and Organization.* Homewood, IL: Richard D. Irwin, Inc., 1959.

Whyte, W. F., ed. *Money and Motivation.* New York, NY: Harper & Row, Publishers, 1955.

Wilhite, Jim O. "A Point of View: Toughness and True Leadership in the 1990s," *National Productivity Review,* Summer 1989, pp. 219–222.

Wilke, Henke, and Roel W. Meertens. *Group Performance.* London: Routledge, 1994.

Wirth, Arthur G. *Education and Work for the Year 2000: Choices We Face.* San Francisco, CA: Jossey-Bass Publishers, 1992.

Zaleznik, Abraham. "Real Work," *Harvard Business Review,* Nov/Dec 1997, pp. 53–62.

Zaleznik, Abraham. "The Leadership Gap," *Academy of Management Executive,* February 1990, pp. 7–22.

Zander, A., E. J. Thomas, and T. Natsoulas. "Personal Goals and the Group's Goals for the Member," *Human Relations,* 1960, pp. 333–344.

Zigon, Jack. "Team Performance Measurement," *The Journal for Quality and Participation,* May/June 1998, pp. 48–54.

Zigon, Jack. "Making Performance Appraisals Work for Teams," *Training,* June 1994, pp. 58–63.

Index

Humble, John, 139
Hygiene factors, 67

I

Identification, defined, 381
Immaturity-maturity theory, 65–66, 453–455
Implementation process, 380
Impoverished management, 101–102
In Search of Excellence, 24, 440
Incentive, in ACHIEVE model, 352
Incrementalism, 388
Individual need satisfaction, defined, 318
Individual values, 441
Industry environment, 161
Ineffective cycle, 231
   breaking, 232–233
Informal work groups, 62–64
Information power, 212, 217, 433
Initiating structure, 92–93, 117, 141
Inspiring actions, 426
Institute for Social Research, 95
Institutional isomorphism, 389
Institutionalization, 151
Instrumentation, 120–121
Intel, 4
Interacting influence system, 177
Interaction model of communication, 299–300
Interactions, 62–64
Intermittent reinforcement, 245
Internal noise, 300–302
Internalization, defined, 381
Internally caused behaviors, 74
International business communication, 313–314
Interpersonal competence, increasing, 64–66
Intervening variables, 131, 133, 379, 458
ISO (International Organization for Standardization) 9000–2000, 400
Israel, Joachim, 138
Ivancevich, J. M., 214

J

Jago, Arthur, 117
James, William, 12

Jamieson, D. W., 214
Jennings, Eugene E., 89
Job demands, 152
Job enlargement, 71
Job enrichment, 71–72
Job expansion, 72
Job rotation, 71
Job-centered supervisors, 95
Johari Window, 269
   disclosure, 271, 272
   feedback, 270–271
   self-perception versus style, 271–273
   timing of management, 273–275
Johnson, Spencer, 473

K

Kane, Kimberley F., 296
Kanter, Rosabeth Moss, 3, 5, 402
Kaplan, Robert S., 132
Katzenback, Jon, 321–322
Keilty, Goldsmith, and Boone, 362, 363, 364
Keiser, Tom, 366
Kirkpatrick, Shelley, 91
Knots, 467
Knowledge, defined, 176
Knowledge age, 5–6
Koontz, Harold, 12, 78
Korman, Abraham K., 141
Kruglanski, W., 209
Kuzins, Rebecca, 153

L

Lacoursiere, R. B., 475
Laing, R. D., 467
Lao-Tsu, 468
Lawler, Edward E., III, 6, 72, 350
Lawrence, Paul, 350
Lazo, D., 154, 155
LEAD (Leader Effectiveness and Adaptability Description) instrumentation, 264–268
   flexibility, 266–267
   LEAD Other, 265
   LEAD Self, 265
   leadership style, 265
   one appropriate style?, 267–268
   style adaptability, 266

Technological values, 132
Technology, competition and, 3–4
Telling, defined, 182–183
Terry, George R., 78
Texas Instruments, 321
Theory X and Theory Y, 59–61, 108,
    122–123, 124, 147, 453–455
Thomas, K. W., 214
3-D Management Style theory, 118, 122,
    123, 472, 473
360-degree assessment process,
    348–349
Time, 152
Time and development cycle,
    241–242
Tolliver, James, 107
Toso, Robert, 51
Toyama, Eisuke, 367
Training, 17
Training and development, 229–230
    developmental cycle, 233–242
        areas of influence, 234
        benefits to managers, 233
        readiness, determining, 234–235
        readiness, increasing, 235–237
        readiness level of worker, 234
        successive approximations,
            237–241
        time and development cycle,
            241–242
    effectiveness, increasing, 230–233
    ineffective cycle, breaking, 232–233
    readiness, changing through behav-
        ior modification, 242
    consistency in reinforce-ment, 245
    individualizing reinforcement, 244
    positive reinforcement, 243–244
    schedule of reinforcement,
        244–245
Trait approaches to leadership, 89, 92
    negative, 91
    positive, 90–91
Transactional communication model
    external and internal noise,
        300–302
    semantic noise, 302–305
Transcendental values, 132
Transformational leadership, defined,
    420–421
    See also Organizational
        transformation

Tridimensional Leader Effectiveness
    model, 117–118, 119, 123

U

Ulrich, Dave, 2
Unfreezing, 380–381, 395
Unlimited substitution, 4
Upward communication, 309

V

Vaill, Peter B., 132
Validity, in ACHIEVE model, 350,
    352–353
Values, 441
    kinds of, 132
    manager's, 147
Variable task structure, 152
Variables, 458
    environmental, 144–146, 160–162,
        160–162
    kinds of, 131–132
    See also Generations
Verbal communication, defined, 297
Vertical job expansion, 72
Vinson, Mary, 349
Vision, 435–436
Vision creators, leaders as, 79–85
Vision to Results (VTR) model, 79,
    81–85
Vision triggers, 438
Visionary Leadership, 400, 417
Vroom, Victor, 33, 107, 112–117, 148
Vroom-Yetten Contingency model,
    113–117

W

Waterman, Robert, 24
Wayland, Robert, 366
Weiner, Edith, 162
Weiss, W. H., 322
Welch, Jack, 80, 438
Weschler, Irving R., 78
Wheatley, Margaret, 445–446
"Where Have All the Leaders Gone?", 110
White, Robert W., 47, 48
Whiting, Charles, 49
Whyte, William F., 51
Wilcox, D. S., 214